85 -96

KU-422-210

The Kingship of the Scots, 842–1292

Succession and Independence

A. A. M. Duncan

Edinburgh University Press

© A. A. M. Duncan, 2002
Edinburgh University Press Ltd
22 George Square, Edinburgh

Typeset in Ehrhardt
by Norman Tilley Graphics, Northampton
and printed and bound in Great Britain by
The Cromwell Press Ltd, Trowbridge, Wilts

A CIP record for this book is available
from the British Library

ISBN 0 7486 1626 8 (hardback)

The right of A. A. M. Duncan
to be identified as author of this work
has been asserted in accordance with
the Copyright, Designs and Patents Act 1988.

UNIVERSITY
GLASGOW
LIBRARY
WITHDRAWN

Contents

Genealogical tables

List of tables

List of plates

Between pages 150 and 151

Plate acknowledgements

The plates are reproduced by permission of: the Royal Commission on the Ancient and Historical Monuments of Scotland (Plates 1 and 8), the Keeper of the Records of Scotland (Plates 2A and B, 3, 4B and C, 5), from National Archives of Scotland, RH17/1, the Trustees of the National Museums of Scotland (Plate 2C), the Trustees of the British Library (Plate 6); Plate 7 is reproduced from Ordnance Survey mapping on behalf of The Controller of Her Majesty's Stationery Office © Crown Copyright MC 100037177.

Preface

This study takes its origins in an invitation to give a paper to the Thirteenth Century England conference in 1993; when I came to prepare the lecture on the Great Cause for publication, I found myself increasingly doubtful of the accuracy of any of the notarial records which Lionel Stones and Grant Simpson had edited so skilfully in their *Edward I and the Throne of Scotland*. As a result I wrote a monster paper which the conference editors rightly could not publish, so that only a small part of it appeared in the published volume, as 'The Process of Norham'. I had already received a great deal of help from Dr Paul Brand, who had commented upon several drafts, and who then urged me not to jettison but to amplify the rest of my script. In consequence I turned to the history of succession before 1291, which might have informed Edward I and his associates. When the early chapters look forward to 1291, the reader now knows the reason.

Despite this history, neither the editors of *Thirteenth Century England* nor Dr Brand bear any responsibility for the shape or content of the finished work. I have, I hope, acknowledged the particular points made to me by the latter where they occur, but the sum of them goes no distance in measuring the debt I owe to him for his long-suffering care over, and interest in, the later chapters. Similarly Professor Janet Nelson read an earlier version of Chapter 7 and offered most helpful comments. I have pestered Professor Geoffrey Barrow with numerous queries over the years and thank him now for his patient, prompt and usually decisive responses; he read a draft of the book, and in my revision I have not only found his comments helpful, but also his criticisms just. And my colleague at Glasgow, Dr Dauvit Broun has courteously met my requests for guidance in the literature, and not flinched when I tried out on him proposed solutions to some knotty problems of early Scottish kingship. I have had help or comment on specific points from Tom Clancy, Sean Duffy, John Gillespie, John Gillingham, Bill Gordon, Antonia Gransden, Arthur Kennedy, Elizabeth Kirkpatrick, J. A. Kossmann-Putto, Norman Reid, Mrs Elizabeth Roads, Peter Sawyer, David Sellar, Norman Shead, Grant Simpson, Lord Stewartby, Keith Stringer, Simon Taylor, Donald Watt and Alex Woolf. To all these my heartfelt thanks.

By page 315 it will be obvious to the reader that I have little faith in the work of John of Caen, notary public. But that conclusion was made possible only by the exemplary edition of Caen's work alongside the contemporary record of 1291–92 published by Lionel Stones and Grant Simpson and the University of Glasgow in 1978. It was and is a remarkable achievement, a model of painstaking scholarship preceded by a thorough exploration of the record's history and significance. As I read in their Preface 'If [our edition] leads others to study the subject, to seek to fill gaps revealed and to wrestle with problems exposed, we shall be content', I can only hope that my dissent from some of their argument would not or will not discontent them; my admiration for the inheritance they have left us is unqualified.

In searching manuscript material, I have spent more time at the Public Record Office, Kew, than at the National Archives of Scotland, Edinburgh, but thank the staffs of both places for their willing assistance, particularly since I seemed to spend so long with a document and an ultra-violet lamp. The staff of Edinburgh University Press have smoothed the path of my text to publication with exemplary thoroughness and speed. But my principal institutional thanks must go to the Library of the University of Glasgow, both for the freedom of its magnificent collections and for the courteous helpfulness of its staff over many years, which I enjoy by right of an honorary research fellowship generously conferred by the University Court. I am truly grateful also to the present members of my former department, now a 'field', for a generous grant to meet the cost of illustrations. They tolerate my visits, occasional or frequent depending on the point of view, but will be relieved to know that I do not anticipate using my reader's ticket up to its expiry date, Hogmanay 2035.

Archie Duncan

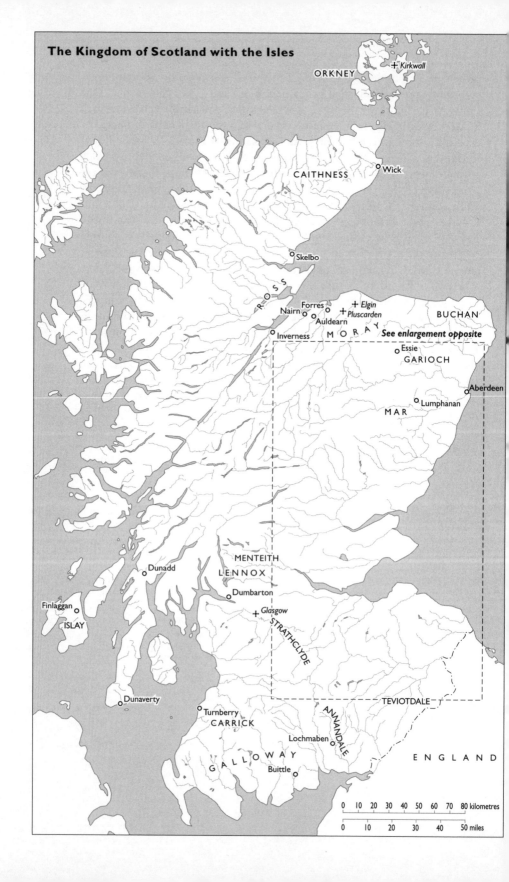

The Kingdom of Scotland with the Isles

ORKNEY

✝ *Kirkwall*

CAITHNESS

○ Wick

○ Skelbo

R O S S

Forres
○
Nairn ○   ✝ *Elgin*
○ ✝ *Pluscarden*   BUCHAN
○ Auldearn
○ Inverness   M O R A Y   *See enlargement opposite*

○ Essie
GARIOCH

○ Aberdeen
M A R
○ Lumphanan

MENTEITH

○ Dunadd   L E N N O X

○ Dumbarton

Finlaggan ○   ✝ *Glasgow*
ISLAY   S T R A T H C L Y D E

○ Dunaverty

○ Turnberry   TEVIOTDALE
CARRICK
A N N A N D A L E
○ Lochmaben   E N G L A N D
G A L L O W A Y
○ Buittle

| 0 | 10 | 20 | 30 | 40 | 50 | 60 | 70 | 80 kilometres |

| 0 | 10 | 20 | 30 | 40 | 50 miles |

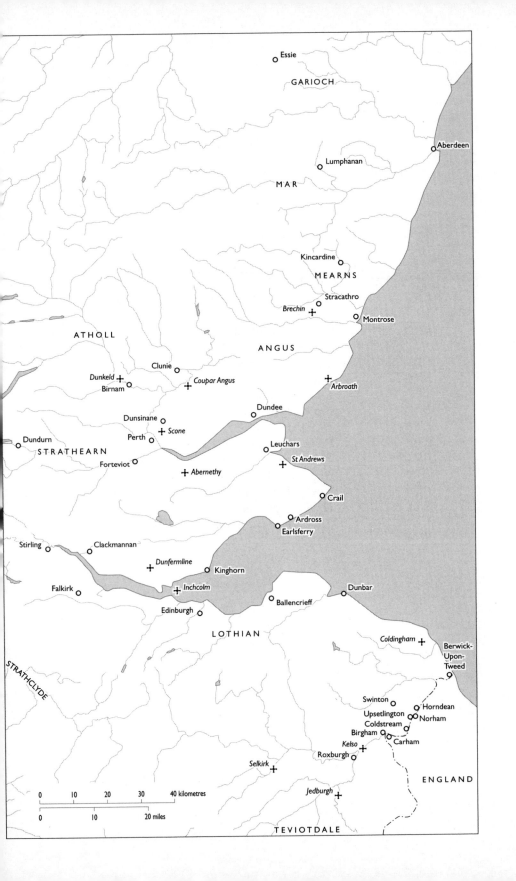

Essie

GARIOCH

Aberdeen

Lumphanan

MAR

Kincardine

MEARNS

Stracathro

Brechin

Montrose

ATHOLL

ANGUS

Clunie

Dunkeld
Birnam

Coupar Angus

Arbroath

Dundee

Dunsinane

Perth
Scone

Dundurn

STRATHEARN

Leuchars

St Andrews

Forteviot

Abernethy

Crail

Ardross
Earlsferry

Stirling

Clackmannan

Dunfermline

Falkirk

Inchcolm

Kinghorn

Dunbar

Edinburgh

Ballencrieff

LOTHIAN

STRATHCLYDE

Coldingham

Berwick-
Upon-
Tweed

Swinton

Horndean

Upsetlington
Coldstream

Norham

Birgham

Carham

Kelso
Roxburgh

Selkirk

ENGLAND

Jedburgh

0   10   20   30   40 kilometres

0   10   20 miles

TEVIOTDALE

Abbreviations

ASC	Anglo-Saxon Chronicle
APS	*Acts of the Parliaments of Scotland*
ATig, and ATig	Annals of Tigernach
AU, and AU	Annals of Ulster
CK	King list in *Chron. Picts-Scots* and Anderson, *Kings and Kingship*
CKA	Chronicle of the Kings of Alba, in the same two works and Hudson, 'The Scottish Chronicle'
CP	*The Complete Peerage*
ESSH	Anderson, *Early Sources of Scottish History*
LF	*Libri Feudorum*
NAS	National Archives of Scotland, Edinburgh
NEB	*New English Bible*
PRO	Public Record Office, Kew
PSAS	*Proceedings of the Society of Antiquaries of Scotland*
RMS	*Registrum Magni Sigilli Regum Scotorum*
RRAN	*Regesta Regum Anglo-Normannorum*
RRS	*Regesta Regum Scottorum*
SAEC	Anderson, *Scottish Annals from English Chroniclers*
SHR	*Scottish Historical Review*

CHAPTER I

Introduction

When may we date the emergence of a Scottish identity as something known to the inhabitants, or at least to large numbers of them, of what we call Scotland? Thirty years ago I gave a traditional view: that Scotland was put together first as a kingdom, then as a community. I would not now abandon that view, but I would make a different judgement taking the origins of the community into an earlier part of the kingdom's history.[1] It was no part of my intention to establish when that happened, and I doubt if the exiguous materials for our early history would permit a firm date. But an approach through the history of early medieval kingship can throw light upon the response of the kingdom's inhabitants, or its community, if that word is preferred.

The history of kings is not fashionable and kingship is not prominent in the articles governing a competent education. Yet kingship was almost ubiquitous in Christian Europe from the collapse of imperial Roman authority in the west until the late eighteenth century, so that any history which explores political structures within those parameters must give it a due, perhaps a prominent, place. That place will shift gradually as the societies within which kings exercised their rights and discharged their functions also changed. Moreover, recent scholarship has suggested a drastic reinterpretation of the 'peoples' and kingships of the age of migrations, a salutary warning that long-accepted scholarly accounts are not to be exempted from re-examination, if only because they may have taken too much upon trust the evidence of later, usually ecclesiastical, sources.[2]

The fluidity found in the creation and disappearance of migration-era kingships has been recognised by those who see their kings as war-leaders of 'barbarian' peoples as well as by those who recognise the peoples as Romano-'barbarian', their kings as lords of the Roman fisc as well as of the 'barbarian' host. But this fluidity persisted not only into the Carolingian age, with its divisions and subdivisions of the empire into kingdoms varying in number and bounds, but also later. The best-known examples in the

[1] Duncan, *Making of the Kingdom*, 13; Broun, 'Origin of Scottish Identity', is a thought-provoking challenge.
[2] A simple example is the supposed survival of the Visigothic kingship of Spain after 711 as the kingdom of the Asturias. Linehan, *Medieval Spain*, 80–81, 101–5.

English-speaking world are the Anglo-Saxon kingships, homologated into one kingdom in the tenth century, but in the Iberian peninsula the struggle against Muslim rulers produced the kingdom of Leon and the Asturias, conquered in the eleventh century by the first king of Castille, then divided and reunited; in the east a king of Navarre divided his kingship into Navarre and Aragon, both petty realms until in the twelfth century marriage united Aragon to the county of Barcelona; when Valencia was taken in 1238, it became another kingdom of the king of Aragon. In the west in the twelfth century an ambitious French count who recovered northern Portugal from the Arabs by 1128 styled himself king and belatedly won recognition from the papacy.

Beyond the bounds of the Roman and Carolingian worlds, early political structures are obscure. The evidence from Scandinavia, whence comes our word 'king', is late, but suggests provincial rulers falling under the hegemony of one of their number in the Viking era, and producing the known Scandinavian kingdoms by the eleventh century. Only the Irish annals, literature and law-books give us insight into a hierarchy of kingships, but the peoples (*tuatha*) whom the lesser kings ruled derived their identity from the king, while the greater kingships might have the name of a geographical province or the name of a kindred who shared kingship.

Some of these kingships owed their origins not to the needs of migrating peoples but to the example of neighbouring Carolingian and post-Carolingian kingdoms. In the same way there may have been example and influence upon Scotland from Irish and Anglo-Saxon kingship, from Ireland certainly in the kingship of the Scots in Dalriada, though whether upon the Cumbric and Pictish peoples of the lands south and north (respectively) of the Forth valley is less certain. I see no evidence of a king among the Gododdin of Lothian, but there certainly was a king of Britons at Dumbarton by the mid or late sixth century. In the genealogy of Dumbarton (or Strathclyde) kings, no ancestor earlier than c.500 is indicated, but there is a suggestion that the earliest ruler enjoyed a title or imitated an authority conveyed by Romans.[3]

The Romans knew of leaders, but not kings, among the peoples inhabiting later Pictland. By the third century they thought that two principal tribes inhabited this area, and it is likely that they sought to maintain stability there by treaty with Pictish leaders. But by the fourth century the Picts were raiding Roman Britain for its wealth in silver, and it may be that the leadership called for in these raids became an over-kingship of Picts. The truth is that while we have been left a list of Pictish kings which would stretch back into Roman times, the early names are clearly mythical, and a historical king can be identified only in Bridei son of Maelchon, the king visited by Columcille near the Ness in the late sixth century. We simply do not know

[3] Macquarrie, 'Kings of Strathclyde', 2–8.

how one line of rulers, those of Fortriu (Strathearn at least), came to dominate the Picts, whether there were many tributary kingdoms or few (for only Atholl is named, and that only once), and how succession through the female worked in practice. On these as on other aspects of early kingship in Scotland, I could only only tread in the authoritative footsteps of Dr Marjorie Anderson.[4]

Until the creation of the Anglo-Saxon Chronicle we are largely dependent for descriptions of peoples, kings and kingdoms in Scotland upon Irish annals. Certainly Bede knew of the Picts and had a mythical account of their arrival in Britain by way of Ireland; Ireland is both *Hibernia* and *Scottia*, but its inhabitants are *Scotti*, and those who migrated to Argyll are *Dalreudini* and '*Scotti* who inhabit Britain'; Adamnan, abbot of Iona, writes of the 'people of Picts and of Scots of Britain'.[5] Irish annals know of *Picti*, of various rulers called *rex Pictorum* and very occasionally *rex Fortrinn*; Fortriu was a province (like Atholl) for in 836 its host was called *fir Fortrenn*, 'men of Fortriu'.[6] They also know of a people, *Dalriada*, with kings of Dalriada and on one occasion *regiones Dail Riatai*, perhaps 'kingdoms of the Dalriada'.[7]

The Dalriada disappear from the annals in the 840s,[8] but although, in chapter 2, I have used *Alba* (for want of an alternative) for the kingdom from 842, this Gaelic name first occurs in 900, and was used consistently thereafter in Irish-language entries with a new meaning of the post-Pictish kingdom, no longer the whole island of Britain; in Latin it could be *Albania*. The diversity of peoples (who may sometimes have included Norse as well as Picts, Dalriada, Britons) in the following of kings in Gaelic Scotland was expressed by the territorial common denominator *Alba*.[9] Scarce indeed is any trace of the derivative which became the Gaelic for 'Scotsman', *Albanach*. In the eleventh-century Prophecy of Berchan there is much play about Britons and Saxons, but save for one mention of *Albanaich*, the Scots in his verses are uniformly *Goidil*, 'Gaels'.[10]

Also missing from Irish sources are references to *Scotti* as inhabitants of Scotland; that usage is found in the writings of our other neighbours, the

[4] Anderson, *Kings and Kingship*; see now D. Broun, 'The Seven Kingdoms ...', and Bruford, 'What happened to the Caledonians?', both in *Alba*, eds Cowan and McDonald, 24–42, 43–68. And see now, Charles-Edwards, *Early Christian Ireland*, 158–63.

[5] *Pictorum plebe et Scotorum Britanniae*. Bede, *Ecclesiastical History*, index under Pict, Scotti, Ireland; Adomnan, *Life of Columba*, 178, and index under Ireland, Picts.

[6] *AU*, i, 298 (839.9); also used p. 354 (904.4).

[7] *AU*, i, 188 (736.1); *ATig*, 199.

[8] The name is used of a people who fought off a Viking fleet about 840 in a late source which may represent an earlier lost annal; *Cogadh Gaedhel*, 226–28; *ESSH*, i, 277.

[9] Herbert, '*Rí Éirenn, Rí Alban*...'; David N Dumville, 'The Chronicle of the Kings of Alba'; articles 4 and 5 in *Kings, Clerics and Chronicles*, ed. Taylor; D. Broun, 'Origin of Scottish Identity', *Nations, Nationalism and Patriotism*, eds Bjørn and others, 35–55; AU, i, 368 (918.4).

[10] Hudson, *Prophecy of Berchan*, c.161.

English. In 920 a contemporary annal in the Anglo-Saxon Chronicle records a meeting in England with *Scotta cyning 7 eall Scotta þeod*, 'king of Scots and all the people of the Scots'; in a Latin poem in praise of King Athelstan (924–39) one stanza commends the faithful service given by *Constantinus rex Scottorum*.[11] There may be earlier uses of *Scotti*, for example in the battles between *Danarii* and *Scotti* recorded in the Chronicle of the Kings of Alba, but their date could equally well be considerably later. The name itself may have been borrowed in England from the Old Norse form, *Skottar* (there was direct Norse contact with Gaelic Scotland in the ninth century), but the word seems to be a learned name for the Irish, including the Dalriada, with no Gaelic vernacular form, and the manner of transmission into vernacular Norse or English remains a puzzle.

Yet the coincidence of phrases in Irish and English is striking: *fir Alban* and *eall Scotta þeod*. The last word can have many meanings (e.g. people, race, nation), but in the context of a meeting in central England it must surely denote a 'large (royal) following', and scarcely differs from the *fir Alban* who fought in the wars of their kings against the Vikings. The kings of Alba defined their kingship by the folk over whom they had leadership and command, and had this much in common with the migration-period rulers of Franks, Alemanni and so forth, for these folk were of diverse ethnic origin and (often) language. In *ri Alban*, the people(s) were perceived in territorial terms, which differs from the Latin titles given to migration-age kings of peoples and their medieval successors. But when the age of written record came to Scotland, the style adopted for its kings was usually *rex Scottorum*, king of Scots.

In fact there are exceptions, particularly the very earliest written act of a king, the charter of Duncan II to the monks of Durham, in which he is called *rex Scotie*, almost certainly the choice of a scribe of Norman extraction, for in Normandy the forms *comes/dux Normannie/Normannorum* were used indiscriminately. In the reign of Malcolm IV *regnum Scotie* is first found, evidence that *Scotia* could signify geographically Scotland, and in the thirteenth century a king who calls himself *rex Scottorum* could refer to a predecessor as *rex Scotie*. The attempt to read a constitutional significance into the *Scot(t)orum* form which lived on till the reign of James VI is to ignore its roots in the accepted royal styles of western Europe and particularly England in the post-migration centuries.[12] For it seems most likely that the *rex Scottorum* style of Scottish kings from about 1100 was borrowed from the style *rex Anglorum*.

The division of Scotland between Gaelic-speakers and Anglophones must mean that the two linguistic groups used different names for them-

[11] ASC, MS.A 920; M. Lapidge, 'Some Latin poems as evidence for the reign of Athelstan', *Anglo-Saxon England*, ix (1981), 90, 98.
[12] Reynolds, *Kingdoms and Communities*, 259.

selves; so far as the evidence goes the fomer were Gaels. Edgar addressed his charters to those 'in *Scotia* and Lothian, Scots and English', and David I's clerks addressed writs occasionally to French, Scots and English (adding Galwegians rarely); the address of royal writs to peoples died out by 1190.[13] There are other indications, (notably the Firth of Forth as 'Scottewatre' in the 1180s, the 'Scottish sea' in the thirteenth century) that *Scotia* was the land of Scots and lay north of the Forth;[14] to the south was Lothian, land of English. *Scotia* continued in that sense as a jurisdiction until the end of the thirteenth century, in parallel with its use then for the whole kingdom.

The last known use of 'Scots' for men north of Forth occurs in the Melrose Chronicle for 1216 when Alexander II besieged Carlisle 'with his whole army, excepting the Scots from whom he took aid in money'.[15] With this we may contrast the account of King William's invasion of Northumbria in 1173 with 'Highland Scots (*montanos Scotos*) whom they call brutes'.[16] The chronicler's source seems to be English, but his report is born out by the seal of the town of Stirling engraved in the thirteenth century, and depicting Stirling Bridge, with a central rood (the dedication of Stirling burgh kirk), dividing three men armed with bows and arrows on the north side from three on the south armed with spears, clearly two hostile groups, and a legend translatable variously: HIC ARMIS BRVTI SCOTI STANT HIC CRVCE TVTI; 'here brute Scots stand in arms, here safe in the cross', or 'here brutes with arms, here safe in the cross, stand Scots'.[17] The second contrasting *bruti* with *tuti* as a description of two kinds of Scots, Highlanders and townsfolk, suits the fierce enmity depicted, and gives the better sense . This was a society divided by linguistic and cultural prejudice, but still a society of 'Scots', with an assumption, even assertion, of ethnic unity.

Now ethnicity did not create peoples or kingdoms; rather in the evolution of a kingdom the point at which law became territorialised, enforced by a common royal authority, then the king's subjects would come to feel themselves a people and would search for a 'historical' origin in migration and conquest, partly or wholly mythical. In Scotland this process seems to have been slower than in, for example, England, recognising the people north of Forth as Scots, those south thereof as English and Galwegians, until the third quarter of the twelfth century. The persistence of these differences

---

[13] *David I Charters*, 13.

[14] Anderson, *Kings and Kingship*, 242 for Scottewatre in the *De Situ Albanie*, for whose geographical usages see Howlett, 'The Structure of *De Situ Albanie*' in *Kings, Clerics and Chronicles*, ed. Taylor, esp. 144–45. See the usages in King William's acts, *RRS*, ii, 76–77. The usual address was to men of his whole land, with only three examples of 'his whole kingdom'. In four 'all *Scotia*' is used, and the texts relate to north of Forth.

[15] *ESSH*, ii, 409

[16] *Chron. Fordun*, i, 262; *montanos Scotos quos brutos vocant*.

[17] Stevenson and Wood, *Scottish Heraldic Seals*, i, 80.

reflects the slow incorporation of Lothian and the Cumbric west under the authority of the 'king of Scots', 'king of Alba'; I shall argue that the Cumbric kingdom of Strathclyde survived rather longer than William of Malmesbury or later historians have allowed.

Scotland was not the only ethnically and linguistically diverse kingdom on the medieval map of Europe, but the myths with which its community identity was bolstered traced its origin in the migration of Gaels, in Dalriada and Alba, dismissing the Picts and Britons as conquered and 'destroyed' peoples. The English of Lothian featured not at all. These were myths of kings, for by the time of their creation the identity of people, territory and kingdom was accepted without question. But it was the command of kings, first in war, in the thirteenth century in law, which had created a sense of regnal community (what would be called 'nation' in modern times) in the kingdom no later than the thirteenth century.[18]

There was precious little theorising about kingship in Scotland before the wars of independence, almost no recorded give-and-take between monarch and prelates or magnates; we look in vain for inauguration charters, for treatises on law or custom, and while there was occasional civil strife, the opponents of the king never articulated in writing their wrongs or their objectives. Between 842 and 1005 there was strife between segments of the ruling kindred, with kingship oscillating from one segment to the other. The anthropologist would not find it unprecedented, though it was neither Pictish nor Irish kingship, and the evidence is too slight to tell us whether brothers and cousins were bought off by appanages.[19] It is, however, certain that partition of the kingdom did not occur, and this unity must have facilitated the shift, after 1097, to primogeniture within one segment, that of Maelcoluim III.

In the twelfth century the Mac William kindred did lay claim to the throne as descendants of Duncan II, oldest son of Maelcoluim III. But William fitz Duncan was passed over, probably because a child at his father's death, and became a loyal subject of David I; his claimant son was illegitimate and found his support in Gaelic areas where illegitimacy was not an insurmountable barrier. Male primogeniture was not the only custom to which appeal could be made in the twelfth century, but by the end of that century it ruled for succession to the kingdom as to other landed heritages within Lowland society. The Mac Williams apart, this was a peaceful transition, even when beset with crisis as in 1195 and, perhaps, 1163–65.

On the other hand there was a constant tension in relations with the kings of England, a story that has been told more than once in recent times. My original purpose was to give an account of the great crisis which arose in these relations after the king of Scots died in 1286, leaving no direct heir in

---

[18] Reynolds, *Kingdoms and Communities*, ch. 8.
[19] The descendants of Dubh were perhaps given Fife as appanage.

the male line, and Edward I determined to downgrade the Scottish kingship into a subject principality over which he had sovereignty. One of his arguments, which had the merit of truth, was that Scottish kings were neither crowned nor anointed, raising the questions 'why not, to what disadvantage and with what alternative?' Another was his citation of many historical precedents for dependence, where the evidence in some cases seemed worth re-examining. But above all, in deciding who had the best right to succeed to the throne, all were agreed that Scottish custom and precedent should be followed – that is, the Scots were a kingdom and a people – but few were agreed on the fall-back if there were no precedents. To follow the progress of the case (Cause) in 1291–92, as I planned to do, required an understanding of the developing custom of succession to the kingship, and, less well studied by earlier scholars, of the attempts to regulate or clarify it. So the study grew to its present shape.

CHAPTER 2

Kings of Alba, 842–1005

Scotland lacked the annalistic traditions of Ireland, England or the Frankish kingdoms as well as the sagas which illuminate early history as seen by the literary classes of Ireland and Scandinavia. The historiographical cupboard may be barer in eastern Europe, but in the west the prize for poverty of native sources before the twelfth century surely goes to Scotland. No time is darker than the century after 842 when the kingdom of Alba was formed, for, isolated by Scandinavian raids and settlements, it passes almost unnoticed in English sources, and the only fairly reliable dates vouchsafed to us, usually the obits of kings, come from Irish annals. These give us a control of sorts over two other sources, lists of the kings usually with patronymics, with reign lengths and places of death, in two main traditions, which I call CK-X and CK-Y; and a king list up to *c.*980 with a selection of events, some dated by reign year, none by AD, which I call CKA (for Chronicle of the kings of Alba).[1]

The genealogical tree (Table A, p. 345) is based upon these sources and shows how the succession shifted among the descendants of Alpin. It differs in some details from similar tables elsewhere, the consequence of judgements upon the sources, for example when it seems impossible to reconcile the reign lengths in the king lists (for these also vary in the several manuscripts of CK-X and CK-Y) with the interval between two royal obits in the annals. If, however, we count inclusively both the year of presumed accession and the year of death, as a clerk using annals would do, then a reign length may fit.

By the eleventh century Irish writers seem to have been sure about the end of Pictish kingship and the arrival of a new line, that of Cinaed mac Alpin king of Dalriada. He and his men slaughtered Picts at 'Scone of the high shields', a theme presumably reflected in the lost Irish literary work on the 'betrayal of Scone',[2] and in Giraldus Cambrensis' account of slaughter at a feast at an unnamed place. But one tradition of the Pictish king lists (Q) says of the last Pictish king, Drest son of Ferat, that 'he was killed at

---

[1] Cowan, 'The Scottish Chronicle', *Innes Review*, xxxii (1981), 3–21; Dumville, 'Chronicle of Kings of Alba', *Kings Clerics and Chronicles*, ed. Taylor.

[2] Anderson, *Kings and Kingship*, 198.

Forteviot, according to others at Scone, by Scots'. The 'at Scone' obit reflects the legend of the 'betrayal of Scone' but the Forteviot one is unique. This slaughter has several literary parallels elsewhere, and is discounted, but, once removed, there is little else to put in its place.[3]

Recent scholars, however, have offered an alternative view reducing the catastrophic nature of Cinaed's accession by emphasising the usage of annalists, presumably contemporary, wherein kings from 842 to 878 are 'king of Picts' and only in 900 is Domnall II at his death 'king of Alba'. This does not tell us how Cinaed became king, but it does suggest a continuity which is more believable than the slaughter legend, especially if Alba is indeed a Pictish name.[4]

The slaughter legend relied upon the assumption that *the* Pictish royal centre was Scone, and since Fordun's time it has been thought that Scone may have been the place of inauguration of Pictish kings. There is no good evidence for this assumption; even in the Pictish list Q, where Scone is mentioned, it is an added alternative to Forteviot. Since 1982 archaeological investigation of early historic sites has given us an appreciation of the importance of Forteviot in Strathearn as an early royal centre. An eleventh-century version of the St Andrews foundation legend describes St Regulus and his companions bringing relics of Andrew to Scotland, going via Kilrimont (St Andrews) to Forteviot where they met three named sons of King Oengus (the names suggest that the legend was known well before the eleventh century), he being absent fighting in Argyll. They gave a tenth of the *urbs* of Forteviot to God and St Andrew, and a cross was erected there, and a *basilica* by Oengus. Fragments of a cross survive at Forteviot, with which this legend may be associated. Oengus II (early ninth century) seems to have founded the church of St Andrew(s), and the association of Forteviot with it may have been little later.[5]

Our attention is drawn to this later account because there survives from Forteviot a remarkable carved and curved archstone, which was retrieved from the local burn in the early nineteenth century, probably tumbled there through erosion of the plateau on which medieval and (presumably) more ancient buildings had stood. The arc is about two metres long and depicts a major figure grasping a staff in both hands and two lesser figures each grasping a staff in one hand, with the likelihood of a third on a lost fragment. Dating from stylistic features must be broad, so 'ninth century' will take account of its Pictish features. Professor Alcock has made a strong case for it being either a doorway arch or more probably a chancel arch from a church serving the royal *urbs*, and has suggested that the figures upon it are

[3] Bruford, 'What happened to the Caledonians?', *Alba*, eds Cowan and McDonald, 66; Bannerman, 'The Scottish takeover of Pictland', *Spes Scotorum*, eds Broun and Clancy, 71–94.
[4] Bruford, 'What happened to the Caledonians?', *Alba*, eds Cowan and McDonald, 65.
[5] *Chron. Picts-Scots*, 138–40.

Oengus and his three sons.[6] No expert in the iconography of the period, I nonetheless venture the suggestion that they are travelling clerics (hence the staves) and represent Regulus and his companions. In either case they are evidence that the core of the legend existed when the arch was carved and that Forteviot was then an important ecclesiastical and royal centre. It is a royal centre in the legend because it attracted the relic-bearing pilgrims, and because the *urbs* in the legend clearly belonged to the king; it remained a royal thanage in the twelfth century when its unappropriated parsonage was given by Malcolm IV to his chaplain.[7]

The village is almost equidistant from the sites of two other early Christian monuments, one a cross (fragments survive), a kilometre south at Invermay,[8] the other a cross recently removed from Dupplin, about 1.5 km to the north of the village. Apart from interlace, the east face of this cross has a squarish panel with a mounted king or chief, moustachioed, riding with a spear, above a panel with four shield-carrying foot-soldiers, with two more on the narrow north side. On the west side the panel corresponding to the mounted figure is much weathered and was interpreted in several different ways. Recently, however, Dr Kathleen Forsyth has shown that it carries an inscription the first part of which is the name Causantin son of Forcus, a king found in both Dalriadic and Pictish king lists who died in 820, possibly the last Pictish 'kings of Picts'. This stone brings Forteviot very close indeed to a Pictish king of the early ninth century and his *militia*.

According to CKA, about 13 February (858) Cinaed I died 'in the palace of Forteviot';[9] CKA, moreover, places in the time of his brother Domnall I (858–62), 'the Gaels with their king, in Forteviot, made the rights and laws of the reign of Aed son of Ecdach',[10] most plausibly identified with Aed son of Eochaid, king of Dalriada (c.748–78), whose long reign would earn him a reputation as maintainer of peace.[11] However we interpret this law-making, Forteviot undoubtedly retained its significance into the reigns of the first two Scotic kings, its 'palace' perhaps a rath or cashel, and the most important royal centre in the kingdom.

[6] Alcock and Alcock, 'Reconnaissance Excavations on Early Historic Fortifications and Other Royal Sites ...', *PSAS*, vol. 122 (1992), 215–42; Driscoll, 'Political Discourse and the Growth of Christian Ceremonialism in Pictland', *The St Andrews Sarcophagus*, ed. Foster, 168–78.

[7] *RRS*, i, 271–72; ii, 228, 259. Forteviot was an unappropriated parsonage in the fifteenth century; see the indices to *Calendar of Scottish Supplications to Rome* (5 vols so far).

[8] Allen and Anderson, *Early Christian Monuments*, ii, 327–28.

[9] Anderson, *Kings and Kingship*, 250. See also her 'Creation', 120–21.

[10] Anderson, *Kings and Kingship*, 250; *Chron. Picts-Scots*, 8. The tone of this remark seems hostile, and suggests a source defensive of Pictish customs.

[11] Anderson, *Kings and Kingship*, 189–90 comments on this and adduces evidence that Aed had a reputation as a holder of assemblies. In 'Creation', 122, Dr Anderson suggests that under Aed the Dalriada regained independence from the Picts and may have reaffirmed their customary law. I have translated *regnum* as 'reign'.

Domnall I, according to CKA, died on 13 April (862) in a 'palace of Cind-Belachoir' (an unidentified place) but in a variety of other places in other sources,[12] but the royal centre which Cinaed inherited from Pictish kings was Forteviot, and it is nearby that we should locate, I suggest, the inauguration rite of ninth-century kings. The work of Dr Fitzpatrick has shown that in Ireland a significant number of inauguration sites were mounds, enclosed or unenclosed, and that some medieval inauguration sites were on land belonging to the inaugurator, but adjacent to the lands of the ruler. If this model be applied to Scotland, then the most likely place of inauguration is Dunning ('little *dun*'), close to Forteviot, which in the thirteenth century was a thanage of the earl of Strathearn, who then took second place after the earl of Fife in royal inaugurations.

Two kings 'of Picts' associated with Forteviot, Cinaed I and his successor Domnall I, were presumably sons of the same mother, so that the matriliny of the Picts (whose patronymics vary greatly) may have continued until 862. But after the death of Domnall I in 862, the succession reverted to the agnatic descendants of Cinaed I, Causantin I and Aed, when Viking incursions seriously afflicted the heartland of Alba. That of 866 which lasted from 1 January to 17 March 'went into Fortriu' (in which lies Strathearn) and 'plundered all the Picts'. In 875 a second invasion recorded by the Irish annals is probably that of CKA in Causantin I's fourteenth year, which led to a defeat of the Scots at Dollar, after which the Northmen passed a whole year in Pictland. Causantin himself was killed by Vikings at Inverdovat in Fife in 877.[13] These catastrophic events must also have been connected with the death of his brother and successor, Aed, in 878, at the hands of his *socii*, associates, according to the Irish annal,[14] in battle at the hands of his successor Giric son of Dungal (878–89), according to CK-X.

Giric presents several problems. He occurs on his own in all the king lists, but has no obit in the annals. Instead in CKA there is a conflation of two kings.

Echodius autem filius Run regis Britannorum nepos Cinadei ex filia regnauit annis xi set Ciricium filium alii dicunt hic regnasse eo quod alumpnus ordinatorque Eochodio fiebat. Cuius secundo anno Aed filius Neil moritur ac in ix eius anno in ipso die Cirici eclipsis solis facta est. Echodius cum alumpno suo expulsus est nunc de regno.[15]

---

[12] Conveniently collected together in *ESSH*, i, 351–55.

[13] *AU*, i, 330–31 (876.1); Anderson, *Kings and Kingship*, 250. The death of Causantin is also recorded in *Cogadh Gaedhel*, c.25 (*ESSH*, i, 351 and n. 5 on 352) in a part which is based upon earlier annals, placed after the death of Halfdan (877). I have preferred that year for the death of Causantin in a battle 'where the earth gave way under the men of Alba'; Smyth, *Scandinavian Kings*, 263–65.

[14] *AU*, i, 332; Anderson, *Kings and Kingship*, 283.

[15] Anderson, *Kings and Kingship*, 250–51.

Eochaid, however, son of Rhun king of Britons, grandson of Cinaed by a daughter, reigned for eleven years, but others say Giric son of reigned here, in that he was made foster-father and ordinator to Eochaid. In his second year Aed son of Neil dies and in his ninth year on the very day of Giric an eclipse was made of the sun. Eochaid with his foster-father was now expelled from kingship.

At least some of this comes from annals. The death of Aed s. Neil on 20 November 879 would indeed fall in Giric's second year by inclusive reckoning,[16] but the eclipse on St Ciric's day (16 June) occurred in 885, which, calculated inclusively was Giric's eighth year; there was either a slippage in the annals or *uiii* was misread as *uiiii*, whence the *ix* of CKA.[17] The identification of Eochaid's *alumpnus* as Giric is introduced in such a way, *eo quod*, as to mark it as an addition to explain why the clerk has found two kings. We should reject the suggestion that Eochaid was king of Alba and that Giric, a successful warrior king in the king lists, was but his Lord Protector. Eochaid, expelled from kingship, was surely a king, and the source of CKA may have called him *r' Brittanorum*, where *r'* was for *rex*, not *regis*. His grandfather died in 872, his father, who was king of Strathclyde Britons, in 878, so he succeeded as a youth.

The 'others say' does suggest two sources behind the entry in CKA, and we cannot be sure how many stages there were before his account; variants on the following account are possible, but the final point, the misattribution of 'grandson of Cinaed …' stands. There were annals with the death of Aed in 878, and that of Aed. s. Neil in 879; subsequently under 885 or 886 came the entry of an eclipse *in ipso die Cirici*, where *ipso* implies that Giric the king had already been mentioned, though the context is not reported. We also cannot tell exactly how this came to be associated with 'Eochaid son of Run king of Britons with his *alumpnus* was expelled now from kingship', but at some stage this expulsion followed the mention of Giric as we find him in CKA, as *Ciricium filium*. The lack of a patronymic explains the remaining puzzle in CKA's account, the words 'grandson of Cinaed by a daughter, he reigned eleven years', added in a margin to remedy the deficiency of Giric's patronymic, but wrongly applied by a copyist to Eochaid, whose apparent descent from Cinaed then made him a Scotic king for CKA.

Giric was not mayor of the palace, duke of the Scots (to borrow Frankish terms) nor *alumpnus* of Eochaid – indeed I suspect that word is a misread abbreviation for *auunculus*. He was a king, king-worthy by reason of matriliny, perhaps a final Pictish reaction to the Scotic succession.

[16] The present tense of *moritur* suggests an annal written soon after the event. But this word may represent an abbreviation (e.g. *m*) for another tense, in the annal.

[17] The figure *ix* is altered from *xi*. Dumville, 'Chronicle of Kings of Alba', *Kings, Clerics and Chronicles*, ed. Taylor, 78 suggests that 'in terms of narrative and structure' *xi* should be correct.

The king lists CK-X break their pattern by giving two achievements to Giric, the first being the subjugation of all Bernicia and almost (all) England.[18] The creation of the Danelaw after 866 left the ancient Northumbrian kingdom unable to resist an extensive Scandinavian settlement in Yorkshire, while north of the Tyne was terribly ravaged by Halfdan of York. But the Danes of Yorkshire seem to have desisted from harrying beyond Tyne after Halfdan's death in Ireland in 877, leaving a weak northern Anglian province, led, perhaps, by an ealdorman at Bamburgh, to face any enemy.[19] From this situation, it seems, Giric benefited; the wars in which he subdued 'Bernicia' must have required army service in no small amount, for 'subduing' would be more sustained than the raids of Cinaed I to Melrose and Dunbar. The provinces of his kingdom would have sent their leaders and men to serve under him, manifesting, even consolidating, his authority over the whole kingdom.

The king lists also claim that he freed the 'Scottish church', hitherto under servitude by appointment and custom of Picts, and, although *Scoticane ecclesie* belongs as a phrase to the twelfth century rather than the ninth, some uncertain substance is generally given to this claim.[20] The transaction is so vague that it can scarcely be the invention of a twelfth-century churchman, when the servitude feared was threatened from York, and these notes, even if added in the twelfth century, represent events perhaps updated by translation from Gaelic into Latin. If so, the word *Scoticane* is most likely to be a translation of a form of *Alba* or *Albanaig*, and the use of *Alba* for the kingdom might be taken back into Giric's reign.

In a careful study of all the sources for the second half of the ninth century, Dr Dauvit Broun has underlined the significance of the use of *rex Pictorum*, king of Picts, up to 878 in the annals. Cinaed I is also said to have brought relics of Columcille to a church that he had constructed, which must be Dunkeld, site of those relics throughout the Middle Ages.[21] Dunkeld had been founded not long after 800 by the Causantin commemorated on the Dupplin Cross, so that Cinaed's act was an identification of his line and its saint with Pictish kingship and its churches. One source, however, takes a different view: the list with most annalistic information, CKA, which begins with Cinaed I's 'destruction' of the Picts, and depicts him and his successors as kings of 'Scots'. This, Dr Broun suggests, was a tenth-century effort by the compiler of the CKA to place the terminology

[18] Anderson, *Kings and Kingship*, 267, 274, 283, 288; the best list, CK-I, gives Bernicia (283); other versions of CK-X have *Hibernia*.

[19] Stenton, *Anglo-Saxon England*, 251–55; Smyth, *Scandinavian Kings*, ch. xx; *Symeonis Opera*, ii, 110–11.

[20] Anderson, 'Creation', 127–28 rejects this claim: 'The note was very probably not in writing before 1105'. *Scotichronicon*, ii, 468–69 summarises discussion.

[21] CKA in Anderson, *Kings and Kingship*, 250; Broun, 'Dunkeld and the origin of Scottish identity', *Spes Scotorum*, eds Broun and Clancy, 95–114.

and sense of identity of his own day in the time of the man now seen as 'founding father' of the kingdom. The Irish annals are a better guide to contemporary ninth-century views where the name Alba, appearing *c.*900, represents a new political identity, 'an increasing concentration of political power and the rise of a more extensive territorial kingship'.[22]

But Giric is not mentioned in the annals where the first king to be called *ri Alban* was his successor, Domnall II (889–900). Dr Maire Herbert has shown that this change reflects one in contemporary Ireland, where Mael Sechnaill (846–62, married to a daughter of Cinaed I) and his son, Flann Sinna (880–916), who established kingship over northern and southern Ui Neill and took hostages from all Ireland, were called *ri Erenn* in poetry and inscriptions, to express leadership of the men of Ireland (*fir Erenn*). Although *fir Alban*, men of Alba, first occurs in an annal for 918 of resistance to the Vikings,[23] that resistance had been the preoccupation of Domnall II, and the argument that his title represents his leadership of an 'aggregation of people', proposing a common identity for Gaels and Picts in the present and future, is a compelling strengthening of the suggestion of Dr Broun.[24] But if this new expression of kingship took place a little earlier, in the reign of Giric, it would be more nearly contemporaneous with the Irish precedent, and it would express his successes, in the way that *ri Erenn* expressed the success of the Ui Neill.

Moreover, it would be mirrored by another break with the Pictish past which occurred about this time: the abandonment of Forteviot as *the* royal centre. The recorded stays of Viking forces in the region of the Tay in the tumultuous years before 878 would explain the destruction of Forteviot in Strathearn suggested by the fragment of its church found there, and its abandonment as a royal centre. It is possible that Giric shifted these functions to the hill-fortress, Dundurn, in the remoter west of Strathearn, where he is known to have died, apparently in peace. It was besieged in the late seventh century, and archaeological investigation by Professor Alcock identified an early palisade of 460 x 645, a citadel of 600 x 910 (phase 2B), and rebuilding at some later date (phase 3). Which of the two latter phases belong to Giric's occupation is uncertain.[25]

If the role of Forteviot suggested here is correct, Giric or his successors, Domnall II or Causantin II, chose Scone, first reliably mentioned as a royal centre in CKA after a great Viking raid to Dunkeld in Causantin's third year (*c.*903) and the slaughter of the raiders in Strathearn in the following year.

---

[22] Dauvit Broun, 'The Origin of Scottish Identity', *Nations, Nationalism and Patriotism in the European Past*, eds Bjørn, Grant and Stringer, 35–55.

[23] *AU*, i, 368 (918.4).

[24] Herbert, '*Rí Éirenn, Rí Alban* ...', *Kings, Clerics and Chronicles*, ed. Taylor, 62–72.

[25] Alcock, 'Excavations at Dundurn', *PSAS*, vol. 119 (1989), 198 draws attention to a ledge carved in the rock of the fort, traditionally known as St Fillan's chair, perhaps 'an inauguration seat for the rulers of Strathearn'.

In his sixth year (*c*.906), he and Bishop Cellach (I of St Andrews) 'upon the hill of credulity near the royal city of Scone, undertook to preserve the *leges et disciplinas* of faith and the rights of churches and gospels, equally with Scots (*pariter cum Scottis*); from that day the hill has deserved this name, that is, Hill of Credulity'.[26]

I doubt if we can ever be certain what this (and particularly the rights of gospels) meant. To Dr Anderson it concerned 'autonomy in matters of religious practice', but not 'freedom from secular dues, military service and the rest'.[27] Dr Tom Clancy has identified the occasion as an acceptance of Culdee discipline of the Irish (*Scotti*) into the church, involving a rejection of lay control and presumably exactions like military service, for in the Viking age the royal right to army service from tenants troubled churches in many lands, including Ireland. Such generosity fits with Causantin's ultimate entry into the Culdee church at St Andrews to become its abbot.[28] Thirdly it might also have been a peace-making in which the status and rights of churches as places of sanctuary respected by feuding kindreds were restored, and churches in accepting a restriction to 'the laws and disciplines of faith' disavowed the interests of secular lords.[29]

But finally, the whole passage may be a translation from Irish, the phrase *pariter cum Scottis* referring not to Irish but to *fir Alban*, reflecting the emerging concept of *Alba*, a homologating kingship of Picts and Scots. *Scotti* seems to mean 'men of Alba' in its three further occurences in CKA, in a raid into England (*c*.950), the acquisition of Edinburgh (*c*.960) and a raid into Cumbria (980s–990s). And if the 906 promises are expressed in religious terms but concern king, bishop[30] and people, their import may have been as much secular as ecclesiastical, an undertaking to maintain the laws for churches and for people under divine or ecclesiastical sanction, equally for Scots and Picts. Causantin had fought his way out of one Viking incursion and here his kingship was reaffirmed for all the men of Alba, with episcopal validation.

Whichever gloss we give to CKA's words, the role which Scone played in

---

[26] Anderson, *Kings and Kingship*, 251; *Chron. Picts-Scots*, 9. *ESSH*, i, 445, translates that they 'pledged themselves that the laws ... should be kept in conformity with [the customs of] the Scots.' I do not find this at all convincing, for it significantly changes the sense by turning the verb from active to passive. Nor am I persuaded by Dr Anderson's translation, that king, bishop 'and the Scots likewise ... swore to preserve the laws' ('Creation', 127). King and bishop swore to preserve the laws along with the Scots – that is they swore for the Scots.

[27] Anderson, 'Creation', 127.

[28] Hughes, *Church in Early Irish Society*, ch. 20 for lay control in the post-Viking church in Ireland; Clancy, 'Columba, Adomnan and the Cult of Saints in Scotland', *Innes Review*, xlviii (1997), 1–26.

[29] Compare the Irish assemblies of 851 and 859, attended by kings and clerics; Byrne, *Irish Kings and High Kings*, 263–65; Ó Corráin, *Ireland before the Normans*, 99–100.

[30] The title *episcopus Scottorum* borne by twelfth-century bishops of St Andrews would have been inherited from an earlier age.

906 was, as it were, inherited from Forteviot, where there had been a royal rath and where there was law-giving, a generation earlier. The implication of 'palace' or 'city' and law-giving at each place is that law-giving followed from the presence of the king at his *ciuitas*. The appositeness of 'hill of credulity' is not obvious, and it may have been a 'learned' interpretation of a lost Gaelic name.[31]

With Domnall II, son of Causantin I, the kingship of Alba had been restored to the descendants of Cinaed mac Alpin; there is no further trace of Pictish succession, nor is *rex Pictorum* found. Yet the succession did not pass directly from father to son (or grandson) in any instance in the ninth or tenth century, for in each generation the kingship passed to a collateral, brother or cousin, before passing to the next generation. Recent scholarship has suggested that eligibility for kingship in Ireland was limited to descendants to the second generation of a king from a kindred which normally held that office, but that there were exceptions when kingship left that kindred. In the choice of a man from those eligible to be king, *damnae ríg*, 'the decisive criterion is *febas*, personal ability and standing'.[32] What went to make up *febas* varied widely: a father and/or grandfather as kings, with kingly qualities of wealth, wisdom, generosity, multiplicity of noble clients, success in combat. These qualities mattered more than dealing for a share of power among the different lineages (segments) descended from a king, and neither seniority nor a principle that segments should enjoy kingship in turn outweighed outstanding *febas* in the choice of a king, though they could be influential where other claims were equal. The very varying qualities which the sources demand of a king-worthy candidate suggest 'that succession was not decided by rules, but rather by a variety of considerations and rival principles, leaving great room for argument'.[33]

Kingship in Ireland did sometimes pass from one branch or segment of a dynasty to another in a 'circuit upon the branches', with seniority, wealth and ability playing a role in the choice of a successor; but examples of this 'circuit', which depended upon a balance of power among the branches, are limited. There are many cases where it collapsed after one generation and it virtually disappeared in the early eleventh century. Those eligible to succeed a ruling king, and particularly the man who is expected to succeed, were known as *rígdamna* in the sources; the *rígdamna* who is accepted by the

---

[31] Professor Barrow has suggested to me that *meruit* means that from 906 it 'deserved' the name which it had long had, rather than that it newly 'gained' that name.

[32] Charles-Edwards, *Early Irish and Welsh Kinship*, 89–111. The quotation is on p. 100. Subsequently Jaski, *Early Irish Kingship and Succession* has taken the discussion further. He comments on Charles-Edwards, pp. 29–30.

[33] Charles-Edwards, *Early ... Kinship*, 98; for the argument that where segments remained evenly balanced, kingship alternated between them, since none was powerful enough to exclude the others, see D. Ó Corráin, *Ireland before the Normans*, 37–39.

whole people as the next king may be described as *tánaise ríg* and given some royal lands.[34]

That the Irish terms just described do not occur in Scottish sources does not signify, for those sources are exiguous to the point of vanishing. But neither do they occur in any Irish annal relating to Scotland, and we can assess persisting Irish influence in succession in Scotland only from the succession itself. However, there is really evidence of only one succession apparently by a *rígdamna* or *tánaise ríg* in Alba. On other occasions, would-be kings from a different segment may have secured recognition as *tánaise ríg* by the weight of noble support, and have succeeded in due course; but if so, the sources are silent.

The succession in Alba between 842 and 878 could be accommodated readily within the Irish analysis. There were as yet only two generations of kings, and the descendants of Domnall I, if any, did not show qualities which might secure them kingship, while Causantin I recovered kingship for the segment of Cinaed I. After the reign of Giric, there is clear evidence of the circuit upon the branches, not always achieved without strife. Two segments, descended from sons of Cinaed I, Causantin I the senior, and Aed the junior,[35] alternated the kingship from 889 until the death of Maelcoluim II in 1034.[36] From 889 until 971 a king of the junior segment succeeded one of the same generation from the senior segment, and was succeeded by one of the next generation from the senior. In 971 succession returned to the senior segment, but in the same generation as one who had already reigned. So long as the succession alternated thus, no mighty provincial ruler was able to seize the throne. Thus kings were increasingly remote cousins in each generation; was this succession of alternate segments a peaceful arrangement or the chance result of power struggles?

That question is answerable only from the circumstances of royal succession as they are reported to us – and the reports in CKA, king lists and Irish annals are brief and contradictory. The view that kings were killed by their successors or in the interests of their successors is supported unambiguously only by the death of Aed at the hands of Giric in 878, and is likely of the death of Dubh and of Cinaed III in the interests of Maelcoluim II in 1005.

Domnall II was son of Causantin I, and hence took kingship in 889 for the senior line; he was probably a young man, leaving only children at his death in 900, either at the hands of the Vikings at Dunottar or at Forres in unknown circumstances.[37] It seems likely that the Scots then looked for a

---

[34] Jaski, *Early Irish Kingship*, 229–75.

[35] Their ages are assumed from the order of their succession.

[36] It is assumed that Constantine I was older brother of Aed.

[37] CKA says *Opidum Fother occisum est a gentibus*, where *Opidum Fother* is Dunottar, which can hardly have been 'killed'. Read *[Ad] opidum Fother occisus est ...*, referring to Donald. *Fother* could have been misunderstood as *Fores*, the readings of the lists.

Table 1 The reign lengths in king lists, and years of obits in the Irish annals

1.	2.	3.	4.	5.	6.	7.	8.	9.	10.	11.	12.	13.	14.	15.	16.
2–14 MS siglum	A	B	D	F	G	I	K	L*	N	E	H	L	M		
2–14 k-list group	A	B	X	X	X	X	X	X	X	Y	Y	Y	Y		
Name														ann. obit	list length
Cinaed I s. Alpin	16	16	16	16	16	16	16	16	16	16	16	16	16	858	*16*
Domnall I s. Alpin	4	4	4	4	4	4	4	–	4	4	3	4	4	862	*4*
Causantin I s. Cinaed I	16	20	15	16	16	16	16	6	20	20	19	20	16	876	*16*
Aed s. Cinaed I	1	1	1	1	1	1	1	18	–	1	1	1	1	878	*1*
Giric s. Dungall	11	11/3	12	12	12	12	12	11	15	12	12	10	10	–	*12*
Domnall II s. Causantin I	11	11	11	11	11	11	2	30	11	11	11	–	2	900	*11*
Causantin II s. Aed	40	45	40	40	40	40	40	9	40	25	45	45	45	952*	*45*
Maelcoluim I s.Domnall II	8	4	9	9	9	9	21	–	–	9	9	20	20	954	*11*
Ildulb s. Causantin II	5	7	9	9	9	9	9	4.6	9	4.6	9	9	9	962	*9*
Dubh s. Maelcoluim I	5	4	4.6	4.6	4.6	4.6	4.6	4.6	4	4.6	3.6	10	4.6	967	*9 to-*
Cuilen s. Ildulb	–	1½	4.6	4.6	4.6	4.6	4.6	4.6	4	4.6	4.6	10	4.6	971	*gether*
Cinaed II s. Maelcoluim I	–	24	24.2	24.2	24.2	24.2	24.2	24	24	22.2	22.2	–	–	995	*24.2*
Causantin III s.Cuilen	–	1½	1.6	1.6	1.6	1.6	1.6	1½	2	1½	1½	–	–	997	*1.6*
Cinaed III s. Dubh	–	8	–	8	8	8	8	8	–	1.4	1.3	1.3	1.3	1005	*8*
Maelcoluim II s. Cinaed II	–	30	30	30	30	30	30	30	30	30	30	30	30	1034	*30*
Donnchad I gds. Maelcoluim II	–	6	6	6	6	6	6	6	5	–	5.9	5.9	5.9	1040	*5.9*
Column no.	*2.*	*3.*	*4.*	*5.*	*6.*	*7.*	*8.*	*9.*	*10.*	*11.*	*12.*	*13.*	*14.*	*15.*	*16.*

In column 2, A is CKA; the other lists are grouped in their agreed filiations, B, X and Y. The list L of the Y group (column 13) contains alternative lengths from the X group, here L* (column 9). The form 1.6 means 1 year 6 months. The italicised column 16 gives suggested reign lengths for a common ancestor-list.

*The death of Causantin II occurred some years after he had given up kingship (CKA).

king of warrior age and capabilities, one of the same generation as Domnall, and found him in the segment of Aed, whose son, Causantin II, took kingship. Causantin, since he lived till *c.*952, cannot have been born long before his father's death in 878, and would be too young to qualify at the death of Giric in 889. He held kingship for forty-four years, resigned voluntarily to enter religion, and according to CKA gave kingship[38] to Maelcoluim I son of Domnall II (944). This suggests that nomination of a *tánaise rig* occurred only when the king abdicated; nonetheless the fact that the nomination was to the alternate segment, when Causantin must have had an adult son, points to a clear and general expectation of alternation.

In these alternations between the two segments, the clients of the deceased king seem to have accepted the superior king-worthiness (*febas*) of the other segment in 900, 954 and 962. In 954 Maelcoluim I was killed in a battle with domestic foes and was succeeded by Ildulb son of Causantin II, who acquired Edinburgh, and who died at the hands of the Norse in 962, to be succeeded by Dubh son of Maelcoluim I; but the sources give no hint of nomination, and agreement by provincial lords is likely to have followed a demonstration of power by the king-to-be. Nonetheless on the death of a king, custom may have sent the lords flocking to the senior member of the alternate segment – the custom of circuit upon the branches.

Where a king's brothers had to sit out the reign of the alternate segment, his son was given time to mature and hence increase his standing and qualities as king-worthy; we have no evidence of formal recognition of a cousin as *tánaise* except in 944. Any tree of succession to an Irish kingship will show a rapid turnover among a large number of kings, most with reigns of short duration; Scotland displays a quite different pattern, a turnover certainly, but with a much smaller number of kings and from only two or three segments. Hence kingship in Alba, where no king was succeeded by his son, diverges strikingly from that in Francia, where son succeeded father, and from England, where succession passed from father to his sons in succession.[39] Even in Ireland, where competition among segments was fierce, a detailed study of the Ui Chennsalaig kings has shown that the number of segments far exceeded the two (after 971, three) found in Alba, and that only thirty-eight kings out of seventy were sons of kings, with direct succession in six cases.[40] In Scotland son first succeeded father in 1214.

---

[38] Anderson, *Kings and Kingship*, 251: *regnum mandauit*.

[39] Æthelwulf (839–58) was succeeded by four sons, the last Alfred (871–99); he by one son, Edward (899–924), whose four sons acceded successively (924–55); the third of these was father of two kings (955–75), and the second of these father of the next two (975–1016). It may be that some older sons avoided matrimony in order not to challenge sibling succession.

[40] Ó Corráin, 'Irish Regnal Succession, a Reappraisal', *Studia Hibernica*, xi (1971), 7–39; Sharpe, 'The thriving of Dalriada', *Kings, Clerics and Chronicles*, ed. Taylor, 47–61 shows that Dalriada differed from Ireland, making it likely that succession practices were carried over

If we can see something of a pattern in royal succession, the detail is less secure. By inclusive reckoning Causantin's forty-five years were 900–44, allowing Maelcoluim eleven years, 944–54 and Ildulb nine years, 954–62.[41] The two last certainly died violently, one at the hands of provincial Scots, the other killed by Vikings, but the latter death (962) is the last occasion noted by Irish or Scottish sources of a Viking incursion into Alba. The Norse kingdom of York ended in 954, and that of Dublin had ceased raiding overseas by the same period; Viking raiders (e.g. Olaf Trygvasson) had not wholly disappeared, if sagas are to be trusted, but Alba seems to have escaped the incursions which engulfed the Anglo-Saxon monarchy between 980 and 1016. After 962 the kings of Alba were left to their own internal disputes over resources and authority, and though it seems to be safe to see the succession of Dubh s. Causantin II in that year as a peaceable alternation of segment, thereafter this form of 'circuit' deteriorated into internecine strife.

Between them Dubh and Cuilen seem to have reigned for nine, or inclusively ten, years (962–71), with Dubh expelled from kingship (CKA) and killed (CK-X); it is only implied, not said, that Cuilen s. Ildulb was responsible. Two hands at work were at work in CKA with Dubh (*Niger*) and his successor Cuilen (*Caniculus*):

> *Niger*[42] son of Maelcoluim reigned for five years. Bishop Fothach died. [A battle] between *Niger* and *Caniculus* ... *Niger* had the victory ... *Niger* was driven from the kingship and *Caniculus* held it for a short time. Domnall s. Cairill died. *Culenring* reigned for five years ... [three obits, a pilgrimage and an episcopal succession] ... Cuilen and his brother Eochaid were slain by Britons.[43]

Here the latinised personal names of the kings, Dubh (the black, hence *Niger*) and Cuilen (the pup, hence *Caniculus*), were not carried over into the latter's reign; one hand wrote soon after the succession of *Caniculus* and death of Domnall s. Carill but well before the death of *Caniculus*. The very full record of Cuilen's reign was added by a compiler, who did not realise that *Caniculus* was Cuilen, and who added *breui tempore*, 'for a short time', to provide *Caniculus* with a reign length. According to printed texts he wrote *Culenring v annis regnauit*. It has been suggested that *ring* is a Norse epithet, *hringr*, but a textual misreading is much more likely. CKA's manuscript has

---

[41] This prefers CKA's 11 for Maelcoluim to the list's 9, and for Ildulb the list's 9 to CKA's 8.

[42] Dr Hudson claims that the MS reads *inger*, but the reading is clearly *Niger*; *SHR*, lxxvii, 151.

[43] Anderson, *Kings and Kingship*, 252. Niger, Caniculus and Cuilen are not given patronymics.

Culenrig. v. a. rg, with bars over the *i, a, r, g*; this text uses *tenuit regnum annis*, or *regnauit annis*, except in two instances, Maelcoluim I and Cuilen, where *annis regnauit* is found. *Culenring* represents a stage in the transmission of this text reading either *Culen rg v. a. rg*, a careless dittography with the first *rg* marked for deletion in a way which was subsequently misread as *rig* or *ring*; or alternatively *Culen rig v. a.* with *rig* marked for deletion as an error for *reg*, and *rg* added. In the king lists he is Cuilen s. Ildulb.

The X king lists claim that Dubh was killed at Forres and that his body, hidden under the bridge of Kinloss, lay undiscovered during an eclipse of the sun, which has been identified as that of 20 July 966; on the other hand the annals of Ulster place his death as the first entry under 967, which fits the given reign lengths better. Neither source names his killer, but Cuilen can scarcely have been innocent. The depiction on Sueno's stone by the side of the Kinloss road at Forres of a mighty battle, with one panel showing an arch under which lie corpses, one with a framed head, fits the list account of Dubh's death, save in not suggesting the eclipse, whose association with the death, if it occurred in 967, is a later synchronism to improve the tale. If the framed head is truly Dubh, then the stone would probably have been erected by his brother Cinaed II (Plate 1).

A number of other details in CK-X suggest the existence of a feud-saga about these kings: Cuilen was certainly killed by Britons, but the list names Rhydderch of Strathclyde and adds 'on account of his daughter'; Cinaed II was killed by his own men in Fettercairn through the treachery of Finella, daughter of Cunchar earl of Angus, because Cinaed had killed Finella's only son. The events of Cuilen's reign in CKA have convincingly been shown to derive from annals,[44] but those of Cinaed II, in whose time CKA was apparently compiled, are punctuated by unrecognisable place names and may be fictitious. Efforts to make them fit with evidence from elsewhere have not been noticeably successful.

Cinaed's succession was an alternation from the line of Aed to that of Causantin I, but with a difference, for he was the brother of Dubh, and a brother had not succeeded since the generation of their great-grandfathers in the 870s. Whether that or his visits to England aroused opposition we do not know; all we can say is that Amlaib (Olaf) s. Ildulb and brother of Cuilen seems to have made a bid for the throne, in which he was temporarilly successful, for his death as *ri Alban* at the hands of Cinaed (without title) s. Maelcoluim is recorded by annals under 977. That Amlaib was king is confirmed by an Irish genealogy of kings showing the two brothers as sons of Ildulb.[45]

Only these Irish sources know of this interruption (for such it must have been) of Cinaed's kingship about 976–77, suggesting that it was indeed

---

[44] Dumville, 'Chronicle of the Kings of Alba', *Kings, Clerics and Chronicles*, ed. Taylor, 82.
[45] *AU*, i, 413 (977.4), *ATig*, ii, 231 where the name of the slayer is correct. *Corpus Genealogiarum Hiberniae*, 426.

short; Cinaed's recovery meant that, from the viewpoint of record-makers in Scotland, there was no hiatus, for Amlaib is found in no king list. Nonetheless his bid was that of a brother, on behalf of the segment of Causantin I, or perhaps of Ildulb, seeking to exclude the segment of Aed and Maelcoluim I s. Domnall, feuding which continued for perhaps forty years. Cinaed II died 'by treachery at the hands of his own men' in 995 and the succession passed to Causantin III s. Cuilen, the last of his lineage to reign, and that briefly. In 997 he was killed by Cinaed III s. Dubh,[46] from whose time kingship remained among the descendants of Causantin I and Maelcoluim I.

CK-X consistently names Cinaed III as Giric s. Cinaed s. Dubh, where, it has been suggested, Giric was a by-name or the name of a sub-king under his father Cinaed. Yet it is very rare for the king lists for Alba to give three generations, even rarer for the lists to name anyone by patronymic with no personal name. In CK-X 'Giric s. Cinaed s. Dubh' (i.e. Cinaed III) was killed 'by Cinaed's son', *a filio Kinet*. The most likely explanation of this double oddity is that the name in common, Cinaed, has caused transfer of 'Giric s.' from killer to the slain king, Cinaed III. If Giric s. Cinaed II delivered the fatal blow, it was evidently in the interests of the next king, his brother Maelcoluim II s. Cinaed, whom one annal names as the slayer, a not unnatural assumption.[47]

The circuit upon the branches had become a bloody struggle for kingship but the monopolising segment now became a monopolising line, that of Maelcoluim II, generating its own feuds, which punctuated the eleventh century. They are recorded by brief obits in the Irish annals, which are particularly informative about Scotland in the 1020s and 1030s; the relative silence of these annals in the tenth century means that we know almost nothing of the deaths of non-royal laymen, the brothers and cousins of kings, in that century. That there were such relatives is beyond doubt, and they may well have fallen to inter-lineage rivalries which passed unrecorded. The obscurity of the career of Amlaib king of Alba should warn us that even the jejune lists of kings are not complete.

It is also difficult to make their tale of frequent raids in search of booty accord with that transmitted in English sources, especially the Anglo-Saxon Chronicle, which tell a rather different story. CKA tells that Cinaed I invaded English territory six times, burning Dunbar and attacking Melrose, while Giric is said to have 'subjugated all Bernicia' which may mean only Lothian; even so, we should probably envisage looting, not occupation. These were the booty-expeditions expected of a successful king by his following. Not until the tenth century did the kings of Scots became parties

---

[46] CK-X erroneously names the slayer 'Cinaed s. Maelcoluim', i.e. apparently Cinaed II, an error for Cinaed (III) s. Dubh.

[47] *Chronicon Scotorum*, 242. No slayer is mentioned in *AU*, i, 435 (1005.5).

in the unstable politics of the island of Britain, entering into relationships with the kings of an emerging England. At the end of the thirteenth century, the assiduity of Edward I's clerks followed up the mythical early history of the island with a dossier of instances in which Scottish kings accepted the overlordship of the king of the English.[48]

The earliest item in Edward I's chronicle (after the 'Brutus' myth) claimed that Edward the Elder subjected to his authority the kings of the Scots, Cumbrians and men of Strathclyde;[49] this was to massage slightly the statement of the sources, John of Worcester (under 901) and William of Malmesbury, that Edward received the submission of these kings,[50] a later version of the statement in the Anglo-Saxon Chronicle A that these kings and Ragnald, king at York, chose Edward as 'father and lord' in 920 or 921.[51] A few years later, in Chronicle D under 926, King Athelstan 'brought under subjugation all the kings in this island', including Causantin II, the king of Strathclyde and the ruler of Bamburgh; but John of Worcester claims that he defeated them, and that they made peace with him at Eamont on 12 July, when oaths were given and a treaty made.[52] In 934 Athelstan attacked and 'subdued' Scotland, taking hostages from Causantin according to John of Worcester, but Causantin and his Norse ally launched a sea-attack by the Humber in 937, only to go down to crushing defeat by Athelstan at Brunanburh – acknowledged by CKA. There is no word of peace between Athelstan and Causantin, but the latter had lost his son in the battle and probably made a settlement of some kind with the English king.

Athelstan's successor, Edmund (939–46), having secured Northumbria only in 944, in the following year 'harried all Cumberland and let it all to Maelcoluim (I) king of Scots, on the condition that he be his together-worker (*midwyrhta*) on sea and on land'. As more fully retailed to us by Roger Wendover, who used a lost version of the annal, Edmund despoiled Cumbria, blinded the two sons of its king, Dunmail, and gave the kingdom to Maelcoluim, to hold of him for the defence of northern England.[53] The

---

[48] Stones and Simpson, ii, 301–6.

[49] Stones and Simpson, ii, 301.

[50] *Chron. John of Worcester*, ii, 354–55; William of Malmesbury, *GRA*, i, 135.

[51] ASC, chronicle A, under 923, erroneously for 920. This is discussed by Davidson, 'The (Non)submission of the northern kings in 920', *Edward the Elder*, eds Higham and Hill, 200–11, who argues against literal acceptance of the chronicle's submission, and suggests that it may have been a general peace-making. *Chron. John of Worcester*, ii, 382–83, where it is added that Edward 'made a firm treaty with' them. The date in John of Worcester is 921.

[52] ASC, MS D; *Chron. John of Worcester*, ii, 386–87.

[53] The succession of kings in Cumbria in the tenth century is ill-attested. Owen king of Cumbrians was among those defeated at Brunanburh in 937, Malcolm king of Cumbrians was among those who rowed Edgar in 973–74, but another king there was Dyfnwal. Was he the Donald son of Eogan (?= Owen) king of Britons who died on pilgrimage in 975, and the Dunguallon, king of Strathclyde, who went to Rome in that year? Macquarrie, 'Kings of Strathclyde', *Medieval Scotland*, eds Grant and Stringer, 15–16, which does not mention the Dunmail of 945.

Anglo-Saxon verb *let*, meaning 'released' or 'let', is not the same as 'gave' and implies leaving under the control or lordship of Maelcoluim a province which had not been Edmund's. If 'Cumberland' here means (as it should do) the territory around Carlisle, then Maelcoluim may already have dominated the more northerly British kingdom, Strathclyde; I think it more likely that Edmund harried what became English Cumbria and 'let' Strathclyde to Maelcoluim.[54]

Maelcoluim I at least began by honouring his promise for the Chronicle records that Eadred (946–55) lost Northumbria to Eric Bloodaxe in 947 but recovered it in 948, the probable date of the Scots renewing their promise 'that they would all that [Eadred] would'. In 949–50, however, Olaf Cuaran again established himself in York for a couple of years; Maelcoluim 'plundered the English as far as the Tees, seizing many people and cattle', an event recorded only by CKA, and placed in his seventh year, probably 950. This, then, would not be directed against the English king, but the depth of penetration does suggest that the authority of Maelcoluim did not cease at the Forth. Under his successor, Ildulb, CKA records that *opidum Eden* passed under the authority of the Scots.[55] The place may be identified with some confidence as Edinburgh, but it would probably be a mistake to draw a frontier line by the Water of Leith, for the fortress may have been bypassed by the Scots years or even decades earlier.

There can be no doubt that the kings of Alba in the tenth century on occasion promised to be the helpers of the English kings, and that this relationship became more regular from mid-century. Both in opposition and in submission the kings of Strathclyde were associated with those of Alba, most notably when, after an imperial coronation ceremony at Bath in 973, King Edgar took his army to Chester, where the other kings of Britain, including Cinaed II and the king of Cumbrians, gave him pledges and, according to the Anglo-Saxon Chronicle, promised to be his helpers (*efenwyrhtan*, even-workers) on sea and land. A recent historian has commented 'no submission is implied', but I find that more confident than the source.[56] A northern English source describes Edgar as dividing the Northumbrian ealdormanry into a southern part and a northern from Tees to 'Myreforth', 'mud ford', a description which fits ill with the Tweed but might be the flats between the mouth of the River Esk and the opening of the Solway Firth.[57] If that identification is correct, modern Cumberland was

---

[54] A revised chronology of the kingship at York is proposed by Sawyer, 'The last Scandinavian kings of York', *Northern History*, xxxi (1995), 39–44.

[55] Anderson, *Kings and Kingship*, 252.

[56] ASC, MSS DE; Davidson, 'Non-submission', in *Edward the Elder*, eds Higham and Hill, 208.

[57] *Symeonis Opera*, ii, 382. The name Solway is 'pillar ford', *sul* referring to the Clochmabenstone near Gretna, a meaning which Cameron, *English Place Names* (London, 1996), 177 finds 'probable'.

already English, Northumbrian, and no part of the kingdom of Strathclyde. The same source states that Edgar gave Lothian to Cinaed and sent him home 'with great honour', an episode placed by Roger Wendover in 975 and described by him more elaborately: for Lothian the Scottish king was to come to the English king's crown-wearing feasts each year, to which end he was given residences on his route.[58]

There is much uncertainty about this grant of Lothian because it is found only in later sources, is not mentioned in the Chronicle and seems to be contradicted by the evidence that Lothian was given in 1018, evidence which is also northern and later. The Chronicle may fail to mention the grant because it was a recognition by Edgar that the province was now tributary to Cinaed, while the manors, held later by the Scottish king, must have been granted before 1066 – and it is difficult to name a period between 980 and 1066 when this is likely to have happened. No source mentions Cinaed II being Edgar's helper, perhaps, because the Viking menace which had required collaboration seemed to have passed. In short, the evidence for an attempt by Edgar to regulate the relationship between himself and the king of Alba, involving recognition that the Scottish king had become subordinate ruler of Lothian, is likely to be correct. Knowledge that Lothian had passed from Anglian lordship to the control of kings of Alba was preserved at least by the clergy of St Cuthbert, now at Durham; but nothing would certify that the transfer was intended to be permanent.

For the reign of Cinaed II, CKA (which is thought to be contemporary here) claims a ravaging of Britain (Strathclyde, presumably), three raids on England, once to Stainmoor in Cumbria (which was thus not in British Strathclyde), to *Cluiam*, for *Duiam*, the (Chester) Dee and 'the pools of Derann', all early in the reign and fitting ill with the visits to Edgar in 973–75. There may be echoes of later activities in the Anglo-Saxon Chronicle, for in 980 Cheshire is said to have been ravaged by a northern naval force, and in 1000 Æthelred II employed his first respite from Danish attacks in ravaging Cumberland, of which he had presumably lost control.[59]

There is no hint that Cinaed II renewed to Æthelred the promises which he had made to Edgar, and save for 1000, no hint that the English king had the capacity to safeguard his northern province and frontier. If the short-lived Causantin III (995–97) and Cinaed III (997–1005) led their followings on booty-gathering raids southward, in the manner of their predecessors, the Chronicle, devoid of northern information, took no notice.[60] Northern England up to the Tees was in the hands of earls appointed by Æthelred, but the men of Yorkshire were reluctant to challenge the Danes when they invaded, as in 993, and the Danes, perhaps sensing this sympathy, did not

---

[58] Paris, *Chronica Majora*, i, 467–68, repeating the text of Wendover's *Flores Historiarum*.
[59] ASC, MSS CDE.
[60] Except for Æthelred's ravaging of Cumberland in 1000.

invade there again until 1013, when the north submitted. Beyond the Tees, until Cnut's reign, rule was exercised by earls of the house of Bamburgh perhaps to the Haddington Tyne, the Tweed or somewhere in between. The kings of Alba pursued their own feud until a more ruthless ruler took the throne in 1005. So far as we can tell the promises made to Edgar died with him, but about the same time, it seems, CKA also died, and English sources became wholly south-Humbrian. The lacuna is in our sources.

It may seem ungracious, therefore, to ignore one source which purports to give an account of kings of Alba, the Prophecy of Berchan. I find it a work of fiction. But its superabundance of unnamed kings has recently been used to validate a supposedly named one, a Causantin mac Dungaill, brother and immediate successor of Giric.[61] He occurs only in the CK-Y list L, where he is obviously the result of careless copying. Following this list's usual formula, 'to A succeeded B', Aed's successor (in 878) is given as *Grig filius Douenaldi*, where Domnall is an error for Dungall. The next entry is *Gryg filio Douenaldi successit frater eius Constantinus qui regnauit ij annis*, followed by CK-X list L*'s correct alternative, that Giric was succeeded by Domnall II, who reigned for eleven years. Here *Gryg f. Douenald. successit Douenald f. Constantini* suffered haplography by the omission of the second *Douenald*, and the second *f* for *filius*, was read as *frater eius*. Misreading of 11 as *ij* may be later.

Finally it is worth noticing how these kings fared in the search for a custom of succession in 1291, when the circuit upon the branches would have been met with horrified disbelief. Nonetheless Bruce in 1291–92 was able to cite the succession in 858–78 as demonstrating the superior claims of a younger brother over a son. None of the kings of 878–1005 is mentioned by Bruce nor by Balliol, and their succession 'custom' pass unremarked in the arguments, for their lawyers could make nothing of the rights of these men to succeed one another, or at least nothing which would support the claim of their principals. It could, however, have been argued from the successions of Cinaed II and Maelcoluim II that the nearest by degree to a previous king succeeded; but when the throne went to a distant line (citing the kings from 889 to 971), it went to the heir of line, not to the nearest by degree. Such arguments would have required a wider range of sources than was available in 1291, and would have thrown little light on the situation then; nonetheless in a precedent-driven debate, it is striking that Bruce had more recourse to Anglo-Saxon England than to Gaelic Alba.[62]

[61] Hudson, *Prophecy of Berchan*, 86 vv. 141–42, 207–8. Hudson, *Kings of Celtic Scotland*, 57, 132–33.

[62] Only Bruce could cite non-Scottish cases, since he relied on a 'law by which kings reign'.

CHAPTER 3

The eleventh century

For this period there is a marked improvement in the quantity and quality of the sources by which the king lists may be controlled. The relics of St Cuthbert found a new home at Durham in 995, attracting plundering raids by the Scots; but the clergy of Durham also stimulated tracts and annals about their tribulations. The Anglo-Saxon Chronicle in one version took an interest in northern affairs, and in another, lost, version informed twelfth-century writers, William of Malmesbury and John of Worcester. The Irish cleric, Marianus Scotus, a monk at Cologne, in the 1070s wrote a world-chronicle surviving in eleventh-century manuscripts, one with precisely dated notes about Scottish kings.

Important too is the fourteenth-century chronicle by John of Fordun, using a king list but with added details, including a supposed law made by the princes of the Empire in the time of Otto III, whereby no one could succeed as emperor unless elected by the seven electors. Influenced by this, Cinaed II with consent of the nobles decreed a new rule of succession for Scotland: that each king should be succeeded by his son, daughter, grand-son, granddaughter, or, in collateral line, brother or sister – in short by the nearest in blood to the king surviving, even if an infant.[1] Rejected on Cinaed's death, his decree was ratified when his son, Maelcoluim II, succeeded in 1005.

The (much later) rule of imperial election (here derived from Vincent of Beauvais) would have undermined the hereditary succession which Cinaed II supposedly introduced. Cinaed's decree, analagous to an imperial law, anticipates one Bruce argument in 1291; another such anticipation is 'the nearest by blood to the king surviving'. Fordun's fictions were written for a fourteenth-century readership, aware of the problems which had beset the Scots after 1290, and they sought to justify as imperial a law which fitted succession from the time of Maelcoluim II to that of David II, validating the title of Donnchad I and Robert I alike.

In fact contemporary sources tell us little of Maelcoluim II. He sought to consolidate his kingship by a massive attack upon the north of England, in

---

[1] *Chron. Fordun*, i, 172; at ii, 165, *nepos aut neptis* are mistranslated 'nephew or niece', hence missing the point that this 'statute' was meant to explain the succession of Duncan I.

1006, besieging Durham unsuccessfully; but England was suffering from further devastating Danish attacks, culminating in Cnut's attempt to conquer England and his partition of it with Edmund Ironside, after whose death on 30 November 1016 Cnut was accepted as king of all England. As the heritable claims of the West Saxon royal house went down before this Danish *conquistador*, another royal house, Strathclyde, is said to have died out in the north. But the evidence is difficult.

The victory of Maelcoluim II over the Northumbrians in 1018 is recorded in the *Historia Regum* formerly attributed to Symeon of Durham, as the great battle at Carham 'between Scots and English, between Uhtred son of Waltheof, earl of Northumbrians, and Maelcoluim son of Cinaed, king of Scots, with whom was in battle Eugenius the bald, king of the men of Clyde'.[2] Earl Uhtred's death is mentioned in the Anglo-Saxon Chronicle annal for 1016, words written in 1019 which I have suggested really mean 'who died soon after', i.e. in 1018; others suggest that naming Uhtred at Carham was a mistaken addition in the *Historia Regum*. But the name can scarcely be an addition without the others being so too, and it cannot have been transferred by mistake from a memory of the siege of Durham in 1006, for Uhtred was not then earl of Northumbria.[3]

The tract about the siege of Durham in 1006 describes Uhtred's consequent promotion as earl and his death at Cnut's hands, yet makes no mention of a further battle (Carham) against the Scots. Instead it claims that Uhtred was succeeded as earl by his brother Eadulf, a cowardly man who, fearing the vengeance of the Scots for the slaughter of 1006, 'granted them the whole of Lothian for amends and firm peace. In this way Lothian was added to the kingdom of the Scots'.[4] The final sentence looks like the gloss of the compiler of this treatise, writing about 1100, and the only safe part of the narrative is Eadulf's concession to buy security.

The arguments about events and their chronology are complex and may be read in the pages of Dr M. O. Anderson and Professor Kapelle.[5] Whoever has the truth of it, resolution is unlikely without the discovery of new evidence. Here we should note that this 'cession' of Lothian was made by an

---

[2] *inter Huctredum ... et Malcolmum filium Cyneth regem Scottorum cum quo fuit in bello Eugenius calvus rex Clutinensium*; *Symeonis Opera*, ii, 156; *SAEC*, 82.

[3] Duncan, 'Battle of Carham', *SHR*, l (1976), 20–28; Kapelle, *Norman Conquest of the North*, 21–22, 242–43 (an excellent summary of the arguments); Morris, *Marriage and Murder in eleventh-century Northumbria: a study of the 'De Obsessione Dunelmi'*, Borthwick Paper no. 82 (1992), 11, where it is claimed that 'the passage in which the statement [that Uhtred was at Carham in 1018] is made, under 1072, comprises an interpolation on the earls of Northumbria ...'. The statement about Carham is made under 1018, and the interpolation under 1072 says nothing of Carham; *Symeonis Opera*, ii, 155–56, 197. Fletcher, *Blood feud: Murder and Revenge in Anglo-Saxon England* (2002) appeared while this book was in press.

[4] The tract *De obsessione Dunelmi*, printed in *Symeonis Opera*, i, 215–20, at 215–16; *SAEC*, 80–81.

[5] Kapelle, *Norman Conquest of the North*, 16–26; Anderson, 'Lothian and the Early Scottish Kings', *SHR*, xxxix (1960), 104–11.

earl about whom little is otherwise known, that the date usually given for it, 1018, is without early authority, and that no English king was said to be party to the act. The alternative date sometimes given, 1016, is found in early authority for Uhtred's death, but not for the battle. At most the cession was recognition by a northern magnate that the Scottish kingdom extended to the Tweed, and does not annul the evidence for a grant of Lothian by King Edgar to Cinaed II in the early 970s.

There is another difficulty – the *Historia*'s Eugenius (death not mentioned) is identified with Owen son of Dumnagual, the latter identified with Dunguallon, king of Strathclyde who became a cleric at Rome in 975, having two sons, Maelcoluim (d.997) and Owen, both kings.[6] Owen son of Dumnagual's violent death occurs in identical words twice, in one manuscript of the Welsh annals, in a year about 991, and again in a year which must be 1015; he is not called king nor associated with any kingdom (which, however, does not rule out Strathclyde).[7] Both dates mean that, whoever he was, his identification with Eugenius/Owen the bald in 1018 is chronologically impossible. The battle of Carham, fought in 1018 involved a Northumbrian earl (probably Uhtred), Maelcoluim II and Owen king of Strathclyde who may have been son of the King Maelcoluim who died in 997.

Owen, who could have long survived 1018, is the last king of Strathclyde to be so named; we do not know if he had sons, though the absence of a named king of Strathclyde at Maelcoluim II's submission to Cnut in '1031' suggests that Strathclyde was then part of the Scottish kingdom. A rhetorical history of the possessions of the see of Glasgow of the early twelfth century claims that this 'Cumbrian' region had been laid waste and its inhabitants exiled so that pagan immigrant peoples took over, living irrationally till God sent a corrector, David [I].[8] Like the clerics of Glasgow, we do not know how Strathclyde became part of the Scottish kingdom.

Under Maelcoluim 'King' Macbeth enters history. In 1031, according to the Anglo-Saxon Chronicle, versions DEF, Cnut king of England went to Rome and, as soon as he came home, to Scotland,[9] where according to version E, 'Maelcoluim [II] king of Scots, and two other kings, Mælbætha and Iehmarc' submitted to him. Dr Hudson has shown that Mælbætha was beyond a peradventure Macbeth son of Finnlaech, and less convincingly has placed Iehmarc in Man and the Rhinns of Galloway at least in his last years, 1061–64; Macbeth was the more significant participant. In a Scandinavian version of this event 'two kings came south to [Cnut] from Scotland, from Fife, and he laid aside from them his anger and gave them all the lands they

---

[6] Macquarrie, 'Kings of Strathclyde', *Medieval Scotland,* eds Grant and Stringer, 1–19.

[7] *Annales Cambriae*, 21–22.

[8] *Glasgow Registrum*, no. 1.

[9] Cnut's letter about the visit is preserved by John of Worcester and William of Malmesbury under 1031. For a discussion of the date see Lawson, *Cnut*, 102–5. I follow Hudson, 'Cnut and the Scottish Kings', *English Historical Review*, cvii (1992), 350–60.

had previously had ...'.[10] Although this is late (twelfth century) and imaginative ('Fife'), it confirms Macbeth's kingship, and that Cnut claimed no lands from Maelcoluim, though later writers sometimes regarded him as lord of Scotland.[11]

The date of the expedition is much debated, for Cnut certainly went from Denmark to the coronation of Conrad II as emperor at Rome at Easter 1027, and on his way home wrote to England that he was going to Denmark to make peace with his enemies but would be in England 'this summer'. It has been suggested that the annalist copied by Chronicle DE knew that Cnut went to Rome and Scotland after a great Scandinavian battle, and wrongly identified this as Stiklestad (July 1030) rather than 'Holy River' battle (1026 or 1025); hence the 1031 annal should have been placed under 1027. That requires that in 1027 Cnut travelled Denmark–Rome–Denmark–England–Scotland, a fairly tall order but not impossible if the visit to Denmark was very brief. Given the very specific words of the '1031' annal, we cannot really have a Rome visit in 1027 separate from a Scottish expedition in 1031, and a case for a second visit to Rome in 1030–31 is admitted to be improbable.

That the events of '1031' should be dated to 1027 is, I believe, confirmed by the confused version given in the history written by the Burgundian Ralph Glaber, according to whom, Æthelred II having died in Denmark, Cnut, 'king of west Angles' attacked his kingdom. After terrible wars (1014–16) he made peace with Richard duke of 'Rouen' (Normandy), marrying Richard's sister, Æthelred's widow (Emma, in 1017).

> After this ... Cnut set out with a very great army to subdue the people of Scots whose king was called *Melcolus*, strong in forces and arms and ... very Christian in faith and works ... [Maelcoluim resisted Cnut's invasion; Cnut persisted vigorously] for a long time, but at last he ended his barbarous behaviour for the love of God on the urgings of Duke Richard ... and his sister ... and lived in peace. Moreover also for friendship's sake, having affection for the king of Scots, he received his son at the font of baptism.[12]

The passage links two quite different relationships: those of Cnut with Duke Richard II and with Maelcoluim II, a linkage which had occurred in Ralph's source. He knew of Cnut's hostile expedition against Maelcoluim, and we either assume that he wrongly associated it with the the battle of Carham (1018), of which he is unlikely to have heard, or that he wrongly associated it with the marriage to Emma in 1017. The second alternative, that the source was Norman or Norman-derived, is much more likely. There is no other evidence that Maelcoluim had a son to whom Cnut stood

[10] *ESSH*, i, 547.
[11] *ESSH*, i, 549.
[12] *Glaber Opera*, xlv, 54–57.

godfather, and the gesture seems inappropriate to Cnut's relationships with his enemies. The son would be mentioned because he followed from the marriage described, that of Cnut to Emma; perhaps the source intended to say that Duke Richard was godfather.

But why Ralph's excursus on Cnut? Because recently he had attacked the noble Maelcoluim king of Scots and made peace with him. The 'long' wars, used also of Cnut's war of 1014–16 with Æthelred, is rhetoric only. This book two of Ralph's history, a 'short, clumsy ... crude piece of writing',[13] written by him after the Scottish expedition and peace, was compiled before he went to Cluny, that is before the death of St William of Dijon in 1031, and probably in 1030. This is certainly too early to reflect knowledge at Dijon of an expedition in 1031. Ralph, therefore, supports the dating of the Scottish expedition to 1027, even though he does not mention Cnut's pilgrimage to Rome for the coronation of Conrad II, to whom Ralph was very hostile.[14]

Ralph is full of praise for men of piety, including Duke Richard II, generous to the church, and Robert II, king of France, described as 'most learned and most Christian', words echoing the description of Maelcoluim II as not only powerful but also 'most Christian in faith and works'.[15] This unexpected and exaggerated testimonial suggests that Ralph had picked up a general opinion of Maelcoluim of which we have hints in king lists, written perhaps fifty years later, where he was *victoriosissimus*, most victorious,[16] and in ATig's annal recording his death in 1034, as 'the honour of all the west of Europe'.[17] The most probable Christian and European act which prompted these remarks was a pilgrimage to Rome, during which he left Macbeth as ruler, 'king', in his absence.

Cnut himself said that in 1027 'a great crowd of nobles gathered for the Easter celebration there ... namely all the leading men (*principes*) of the peoples from Mount Garganus to the nearest sea',[18] and it is recorded that he and Rudolph king of the Burgundians escorted the emperor on the day of coronation. Whether Maelcoluim qualified for such an honour or not, if he were present and refused to acknowledge Cnut as lord we would have an explanation of the latter's hurry to obtain his subjection on return from Rome. There is much hypothesis here; but the alternative, that Cnut was concerned about support in Orkney and Moray for King Olaf of Norway, is no better evidenced.[19] Whatever the reason for Cnut's invasion, and Ralph

---

[13] *Glaber Opera*, xxxix–xli.
[14] Conrad was crowned with the devil's help; *Glaber Opera*, 178–79.
[15] *Glaber Opera*, 140.
[16] Duncan, 'Laws of Malcolm MacKenneth', *Medieval Scotland*, eds Grant and Stringer, 241–44.
[17] *ATig*, 266.
[18] *Chron. John of Worcester*, ii, 514–15, c.5.
[19] This is the suggestion of Dr Hudson, 'Cnut and Scottish Kings', *EHR*, cvii, 358–60.

Glaber says that he sought 'to subdue to himself the nation of Scots', the two versions of the Chronicle use different verbs for the submission, which may have been poorly reported in England. There is no mention of help by land and sea, and we can only conclude that Maelcoluim promised fidelity, good behaviour, peace. To Edward I's researchers, this was a grant of homage, and in spirit they were probably not far from the truth.

To the north of his kingdom Maelcoluim II certainly faced trouble.[20] Finnlaech 'king of Alba' son of Ruaidri and father of Macbeth, was killed in 1020 by his own people according to AU;[21] in annals of Tigernach (ATig) he is 'mormaer of Moray', and his killers are named as the sons of his brother Maelbrigte – suggesting a more accurate record.[22] The death in 1029 of Maelcoluim son of Maelbrigte, called 'king of Alba' in ATig but with no title in other annals, may have been peaceful, but that of his brother Gillacomgain, 'mormaer of Moray' (showing that Macbeth was not then ruler of Moray), burned with fifty of his men in 1032, surely arose from a feud. The following year according to AU 'the son of the son of Boite son of Cinaed (*M. m. Boete m. Cinaedha*) was killed by' Maelcoluim II.[23] Since a four-generation name is most unusual, the first *M* perhaps represents a lost personal name, that of a brother to Gruoch, widow of the slain Gillacomgain, by whom she had a son Lulach. Were Maelcoluim II and Macbeth parties to the feud? The latter probably was, actively avenging the death of his father, but marrying Gruoch, daughter of Boite and widow of Gillacomgain, to recruit Gillacomgain's following and staunch the feud – an act very reminiscent of Cnut's hurried marriage to Emma, widow of Æthelred II, for the same purpose. When in 1033 Maelcoluim II killed *m. m. Boite*, that is Gruoch's kin, he furthered the same business, leaving Macbeth without rivals in Moray.[24]

The occasional title of king may be evidence that a northern kingdom, based on Moray, existed from the mid-ninth century. Irish genealogies show Finnlaech as descended from cenel Loairn, one of the ruling kindreds of Dalriada, which held kingship there in the eighth century. Eleven generations, at least 200 years after Muiredach of that kindred raided Atholl in 736, the genealogy names Morggan who was the great-grandfather of Macbeth. We have to believe that this kin had moved up the Great Glen

[20] 'Dunkeld was totally burned' in 1027, perhaps an accidental fire, though a hoard of some sixteen Hiberno-Norse coins was found in 1989 at Dull (the lands of the abbacy of Dunkeld); alternatively this hoard was buried in 1045, when Crin abbot of Dunkeld, married to Bethoc daughter of Maelcoluim II, was slain in a battle. Graham-Campbell, *Viking Age Gold and Silver in Scotland*, 152, no. 34.

[21] *AU*, i, 456 (1020.6); *ESSH*, i, 551. He is also called king of Scotland in the version of the annal in the Book of Leinster.

[22] *ATig*, 251.

[23] *AU*, i, 466 (1029.7), 472 (1933.7); *ATig*, 261; *ESSH*, i, 571.

[24] *AU*, i, 470, (1032.2); *ESSH*, i, 571, 580. For a different version, Hudson, *Kings of Celtic Scotland*, 136–38, and his *Prophecy of Berchan*, 218–23.

(? *c*.850) and that around 950 Morggan was established in Moray – though there is no trace of his kin being called kings or indeed of a link as yet with Moray. This comes only with the annal for 1020, where the diverging titles in AU and ATig, king of Alba and mormaer of Moray, would be explained if the common source called Finnlaech *satraps* of Moray, *satraps* being used for king of a *tuath* in Ireland and for mormaer in Scotland; the Ulster annalist translated it as *ri*, and, knowing that Moray had no king, substituted *Alba* for Moray.

Relevant also to the supposed existence of a kingdom of Moray is the Orkneyinga saga narrative for the early (and perhaps the whole) tenth century, probably a careful concoction of pseudo-history in which the fictional Earl Sigurd the mighty (early tenth century) anticipates the historical Earl Sigurd the stout, killed in 1014. Their enemies from the northern mainland of Scotland are called Maelbrigte ('earl of the Scots', late ninth century), Macbeth ('the Scottish king and Earl Macbeth', late tenth century) , Finnlaech ('earl of the Scots', *c*.1000), and Melsnati (a form of Malsnechtai; 'earl', *c*.1000). These names found in the Moray family of the eleventh century but not earlier in their genealogy were borrowed by the twelfth-century saga-compiler from historical persons of eleventh-century Moray to which they related. They show the 'earl' there as agent of the Scottish king and give no hint of a Moray kingdom. Finally, if there is substance to the saga's claim that Earl Sigurd the stout married a daughter of Maelcoluim (II) king of Scots[25] who gave their son Thorfinn the title of earl and authority over Caithness, then the nominal authority of the kings of Alba stretched to the Pentland Firth. The rulers of Moray were mormaers, great stewards, for the Scottish king.[26]

Maelcoluim II died at Glamis on 25 November 1034, the first month-dated royal obit since 862, and the first eastern Scottish event for three hundred years for which we have an exact date;[27] it is attested by Marianus who recorded the deaths of Maelcoluim's successors as violent, and his silence here implies a peaceful death.[28] That would help to explain what no source remarks upon: the succession of his daughter's son, Donnchad, son of Crin abbot of Dunkeld, a succession carried through in the absence of strife. Donnchad may have been recognised as *tánaise*, but his youth in 1040 was commented upon, and it is likely that senior figures carried out

[25] Dr Hudson identifies him as Maelcoluim son of Maelbrigte, *ri Alban* of Moray (died 1029).

[26] The recent discussion of 'The Moray Question and Kingship of Alba in the Tenth and Eleventh Centuries', by Woolf; *SHR*, lxxix (2000), 145–64 also rejects a second Scottish kingdom in Moray.

[27] The king lists give a month-date for the death of Kenneth macAlpin, but the year is given by Irish annals; *ESSH*, i, 287.

[28] Berchan, of course, implies that he, if it is he, died in battle. Fordun and Wyntoun describe his death at the hands of local robbers or rebels, but this has the marks of literary invention.

Maelcoluim's will, in particular Macbeth, described as 'his *dux*' (i.e. of Donnchad) in 1040, a description recalling the Capetian *dux Francorum* before the end of the Carolingian line and the use of *dux* for 'ealdorman' in Anglo-Saxon diplomas. Macbeth was very close to the throne of Alba before 1040.

But the provincial leaders who accepted and backed a new king looked for his patronage, gifts and success in war, for the promise of which they might overlook a defect in his lineage. Thus Donnchad's parentage may have had less to do with his fall than the failure of his assault upon northern England in 1039, when he and his huge force were driven from a siege of Durham with heavy losses, a connection noted by a Durham source.[29] It was his own people led by Macbeth who killed him near Elgin,[30] yet the place implies that Donnchad had gone in search of Macbeth, not the reverse, so we should beware of the influence of the Macbeth legend, casting him as the ambitious rebel general. It is possible that the king sought to deprive him of Moray (though he is is nowhere called either king or mormaer of Moray) as a means of restoring diminished royal fortunes.

The argument against the existence of a kingdom of Moray is not to deny for a moment the importance of mormaers, and the particular importance of the mormaer of remote Moray, in the kingdom of Scotland,[31] where the annals are fragmentary and charters with names of office-holders do not exist. Even though other functions of mormaers are a matter of conjecture, when Maelcoluim II killed *m. m. Boite* and Donnchad I took on Macbeth near Elgin, they surely did not fight alone but called upon the armies of other northern provinces, under the leadership of their mormaers.

A later generation, for example in 1291, would be quite clear that Macbeth was an usurper, and that is Fordun's position, Latinising 'Macbeth' as *Machabeus*, a hero's name of the Biblical Maccabees.[32] As early as 1291 the chronicle of the canons of Huntingdon as supplied to Edward I, in passages which seem to owe something to John of Worcester or William of Malmesbury, adds to its account of Earl Siward's defeat of Macbeth in 1054 the claim that the latter was *nepos* (grandson) of Maelcoluim II, whereas to Wyntoun he was 'sister's son' to Donnchad I, that is, great-grandson of Maelcoluim II.[33] These claims, of which there is no trace in the Irish genealogies, illustrate the desire of a legally-minded age to provide Macbeth with a 'hereditary' title and are pretty certainly false. In truth, it is far more difficult to identify the attitude of Scottish nobles to Macbeth's

[29] Symeon of Durham, *Libellvs de Exordio*, 168 = *Symeonis Opera*, i, 91; *SAEC*, 83.

[30] 'Bothngouane' and variants = Pitgaveny; *ESSH*, i, 581. Alexander II's endowment of a chaplainry at Elgin Cathedral for Donnchad's soul implies death near the church.

[31] On all this see Hudson, 'Cnut and Scottish Kings', *EHR*, cvii, 350–60.

[32] *Chron. Fordun*, i, 188–89.

[33] *Chron. Picts-Scots*, 210; *Chron Wyntoun*, iv, 258–59, 272–73. The difference arises from the ambiguity of *nepos*.

'right' than to discern the response of Englishmen to Cnut's kingship. Both Scots and English eventually resumed kings from the old royal lines, but that does not mean that they rejected Macbeth and Cnut as 'usurpers', that, given successful progeny, the lines of these two men could not have ruled for generations in their place.[34] It is not rhetorical to ask 'what was the alternative to Macbeth?' for Donnchad's sons would be small children.

There is scant evidence of contemporary adherence to a notion of heritable right. Of the Irish genealogies of Scottish kings[35] the first establishes the line from Maelcoluim II and III (in two versions) through Erc back to Duach Ladrach, whose descent from Adam is given earlier in the collection, the second the line of Malsnechtai through Gillacomgain and Morggan to Erc, and the third of Macbeth to Morggan; thus each genealogy hooks on to another. The genealogists' concern was not with kingship among the generations, but rather with descent from distinguished or heroic ancestors in remote antiquity,[36] and it is possible, indeed likely, that such pedigrees were fabricated to join a successful 'new' king to an ancient line of ancestors. The ancestry of Macbeth and Lulach may be the result of such pedigree-making, linking them to Loarn son of Erc, while Maelcoluim II descended from Fergus son of Erc.

Fordun is our only source for Donnchad I's supposed marriage to an unnamed cousin of Siward earl of Northumbria (d. 1055), who, before the death of Maelcoluim II, bore him two sons, Maelcoluim III and Domnall III bán.[37] The world knows of these from the history made popular for modern generations by Shakespeare's *Macbeth*, but an earlier version is to be found in the vernacular metrical chronicle of Andrew Wyntoun, written *c.*1400. Its narrative is in summary this, revealing plainly the history which reached Wyntoun in Fife *c.*1400:

Donnchad (I) had two sons by his lawful wife, but when hunting as a youth became separated from his companions, wandered by the mill of Forteviot and took the miller's daughter as his mistress; she bore him a son, Maelcoluim (III), and was married off to a ferryman. Donnchad was murdered at Elgin by his sister's son, Macbeth, who had dreamed that when hunting with the king he had seen three women who had acclaimed him successively as thane of Cromarty, thane of Moray, and king; since he then achieved the thanedoms, he was moved to slay Donnchad and become king. Macbeth had been born of an encounter between his mother and the devil, who promised that no man

---

[34] For a stimulating account of Macbeth, with an excellent bibliography, Cowan, 'The Historical MacBeth', *Moray: Province and People*, ed. Sellar, 117–42. Aitchison, *Macbeth, Man and Myth* (Stroud, 1999) describes the evolution of the myth.

[35] *Corpus Genealogiarum Hiberniae*, i, 328–30; the genealogy of the house of Alpin begins with Maelcoluim II in Rawl. B 502, and with Maelcoluim III in the Book of Leinster.

[36] A Scottish version of the genealogy to Adam is in Anderson, *Kings and Kingship*, 256–58.

[37] *Chron. Fordun*, i, 187.

born of woman could slay their son. Maelcoluim Canmore fled to England, while Macbeth built a new fortress at Dunsinane; in this work some oxen failed in their task, and Macbeth vowed quietly that he would replace them in the yoke by their owner, Macduff, thane of Fife, who, when forewarned, fled to the court of Edward the Confessor. He went by his house at Kennoway to warn his wife to delay Macbeth till he got away by the Earl's ferry. In England he found Donnchad's three sons; the two lawful sons were too fearful to take up the challenge of recovering their heritage, and the illegitimate Maelcoluim, fearful that Macduff was dissimulating, tried Macduff's faith by admitting to three grievous faults. When Macduff's loyalty passed these tests, Maelcoluim promised to lead the attack on Macbeth. King Edward commanded Siward earl of Northumberland to help him, and together they marched into Scotland, to Brynnane.[38] Since Macbeth was known to believe that he would never be discomfitted till the wood of Brynnane was brought to Dunsinane, they cut branches and advanced; Macbeth fled across the Mounth to Lumphanan wood, where a knight of Macduff, born by Caesarian section, caught up with and slew him; his head was taken to King Maelcoluim at Kincardine. Macduff was rewarded with three rights: to lead a new king from the altar to seat him in his throne, to lead the van in the royal army, and to a fixed tariff for the slaying of Macduff kin.[39]

Some of this tale is familiar from Shakespeare, though it was much elaborated by Hector Boece on its way to becoming the play.[40] It is in touch with fact, in the king lists, by placing Donnchad's death near Elgin and Macbeth's death at Lumphanan. The geography is correct, but otherwise this is a work of fiction, containing elements from folk tales (the miller's daughter, the devil), to which Mrs Chadwick has found parallels; she draws attention in particular to places in Norse sagas where 'motifs' found in this tale also occur, and prefers Norse to Irish sources for it.[41] Whatever the more remote origins of these tales, the ensemble, with its supernatural elements, is quite unlike a Norse saga. The repetition of threesomes – three sons, three faults, three rights – points to a later literary composition, a romance whose subject was as much Macduff as Macbeth. The designation of Maelcoluim as 'Canmore' is not found in any source earlier than the 1290s, and takes its

[38] Presumably Birnam, as in the popular version.

[39] *Chron. Wyntoun*, iv, 256–58, 272–300.

[40] There is a good short introduction to this in *Scotichronicon*, iii, 179–81. See too for the later evolution Farrow, 'The Historiographical Evolution of the Macbeth Narrative', *Scottish Literary Journal*, vol. 21, no. 1 (May 1994), 5–23. This properly takes account of the fantasies of Hector Boece (1527), but they are of no relevance here, for they were his invention or borrowed from other places in Fordun.

[41] Chadwick, 'The Story of Macbeth', *Scottish Gaelic Studies*, vi, 189–211; vii, 1–25; Mrs Chadwick seems to be the only modern writer to consider the sources of Fordun and Wyntoun here.

origin as soubriquet for Maelcoluim III (I shall argue) from the romance which was Wyntoun's source.

The taking of Macbeth's head to the king at Kincardine suggests the betrayal, in 1212, of Guthred mac William who was presented to the king's son at Kincardine and there beheaded and his body hung up, and with another episode three years later when the heads of other rebels were presented to the same Alexander II, now king, by a noble at an unknown place.[42] The attribution of Kennoway to the Macduff family does not fit with its later lords, Merleswain and his son Colban, also lords of Ardross, and the castle at Dunsinane must be conjectured from the remains of an earler dun. But the thanages of Cromarty and Moray also fit with the years after 1211, when royal authority was extended around the Moray Firth. The slender evidence is that this romance was most probably of the thirteenth century, perhaps of the reign of Alexander II, in French, Scots or English, in prose or verse. The historical setting was authenticated by the use of archaisms such as 'thane', and the author was clearly familiar with the geography of *Scocia*. But what this narrative is very definitely not is an orally transmitted history of Macbeth and his contemporaries on which we can build a view of the eleventh century.

That is what John of Fordun did. He wrote some forty years before Wyntoun, using the same romance but less of it, rejecting the visions, the supernatural and much else, but he also included some detail omitted by Wyntoun, such as Donnchad I's wife as a cousin of Earl Siward, a widely accepted historical 'fact', given in the romance to explain why Siward helped Maelcoluim in Scotland. It is contradicted by one king list, which names Maelcoluim III's mother (and therefore Donnchad I's wife), as Suthen, a Gaelic name.[43] Otherwise Fordun starts his borrowing with Macbeth's threat to place Macduff's neck in a yoke 'I know not on what pretext' (thus presumably avoiding the story of Dunsinane). Macduff fled by sea to Ravenscar or Ravenspur (in Yorkshire), the name probably coming from the romance. At the court of Edward the Confessor, Maelcoluim subjected him to the three trials, and Macduff returned to Scotland on his behalf. Maelcoluim followed with Siward, but pressed ahead to confront and kill Macbeth (who had been deserted by most of his men) at Lumphanan on 5 December 1056, a date unique to Fordun.[44]

Though he used the romance Fordun also used a source of the romance, William of Malmesbury's *Gesta Regum Anglorum*, written *c.*1125,[45] not a

[42] *Chron. Fordun*, i, 278–79. On 15 June 1215 the heads of the rebels Donald mac William and Kenneth mac Heth were presented by Fearchar mac an t-saccairt to Alexander II, presumably in *Scocia; Chron. Melrose*, under 1215; *ESSH*, ii, 404.

[43] Anderson, *Kings and Kingship*, 284; Hudson, *Kings of Celtic Scotland*, 123. Her name is given in CK-I.

[44] *Chron. Fordun*, i, 188–205; the date is on 204, in the form *mense Decembri, die quinto*.

[45] On William see Gransden, *Historical Writing in England, c.500 to c.1307*, ch. 9.

set of annals but a highly literary work in which we first find, without any specific date, that Siward (who died in 1055) killed Macbeth and made Maelcoluim, son of the king of the Cumbrians, king in Macbeth's place, as King Edward commanded, a version largely repeated by Fordun.[46] Both William's and Fordun's versions of events are impossible, for Macbeth reigned for seventeen years from 1040 and was killed in 1057, but they have had an effect on later historiography out of all proportion to the terms of the annal which lies behind their versions.

The source of William's information was a corpus of materials now lost but represented by the chronicle of John of Worcester, William's contemporary but writing perhaps a decade later, who, unlike William, stuck to an annalistic format and also used these materials.[47] There, under 1054, Siward, at Edward's command, entered Scotland with a mounted force and ships, fought with Macbeth, killing many thousands of Scots and some Normans (who had taken refuge from Edward's court in 1052), putting the enemy to flight and making king Maelcoluim, son of the king of Cumbrians, as King Edward had commanded.[48] Here Macbeth is not killed (that must have been William of Malmesbury's misunderstanding), and there is no claim that Maelcoluim was made king in Macbeth's place.

The main element in this corpus of materials was a lost version of the Anglo-Saxon Chronicle, related to MSS C and D thereof.[49] D under 1054 has Earl Siward go to Scotland, with naval and land forces, where he 'fought with the Scots and routed the king Macbeth and killed all the best in the land'; his son and brother-in-law and some of his and the king's housecarls were killed there on the day of the Seven Sleepers (27 July). C is briefer, lacks the day-date, but tells us that Macbeth escaped, implying that his kingship continued. The contemporary fame of this battle as a mighty

---

[46] *Chron. Fordun*, i, 203–4.

[47] For the relationship between William of Malmesbury, John of Worcester and Symeon of Durham: Howarth, 'The Chronicle of John of Worcester previously assigned to Florence of Worcester', *Archaeological Journal*, lxxiii (1916), 1–170, esp. 115–35; Körner, *The Battle of Hastings, England, and Europe, 1035–1066* (Lund, 1964), ch. 1; Brett, 'John of Worcester and his contemporaries', *The Writing of History in the Middle Ages*, eds Davis and Wallace-Hadrill, 101–126; Darlington and McGurk, 'The *Chronicon ex Chronicis* of Florence ...', *Anglo-Norman Studies*, v (1982), 185–96; William of Malmesbury, *GRA*, ii, 13

[48] William of Malmesbury, *GRA*, i, 348; *Chron. John of Worcester*, ii, 574–75: *Malcolmum regis Cumbrorum filium, ut rex iusserat, regem constituit.* In the Durham Easter tables with annals from 532 to 1199 (Glasgow University Library, MS Hunter T. 4. 2.), in which the 1054 campaign appears twice, in 1046 and 1054, the former represents a miscalculation from Marianus' idiosyncratic year system. *Monumenta Germaniae Historica, Scriptores*, xix (1866), 502–8; *SAEC*, 84; Levison, 'Die "Annales Lindisfarnenses ac Dunelmenses",' *Deutsches Archiv*, xvii (1961), 447–506; *Symeon of Durham*, ed. Rollason, 354, and plates 39–41.

[49] William of Malmesbury is said (*GRA*, ii, 12–13) to have used 'a version resembling E ... [which] was not E itself ... [but] very probably E's direct ancestor or a MS closely related to it'. But the 1054 campaign is not in E.

slaughter is borne out by its description in the annals of Ulster, correctly under 1054, and counting the heavy losses.[50]

The striking thing about these contemporary sources is surely what they do not say: there is no 'and Maelcoluim son of Donnchad took kingship' in the annals of Ulster; neither Chronicle C nor D suggests that it was intended to make Maelcoluim king of Scots, nor that Siward did so – neither even mentions Maelcoluim, present or not. Yet, if it happened, this installing of a new king was surely reportable as the triumphant justification of a costly expedition. Sensitive material on contemporary English politics was perhaps omitted or excluded from C and D, but this victory in Scotland needed no partial censorship. So did King Edward and Siward really make Maelcoluim III king?

On a number of other matters in the 1050s John of Worcester has information, presumably from the same source, which is not in any version of the Chronicle, and his account of the 1054 campaign twice mentions King Edward's command, where the Chronicle claims no such authority. This is part of a pattern whereby John mentions royal participation ('the king forfeited X') and command, where the Chronicle is impersonal ('X was forfeited') or has no account, a pattern which seems to begin in 1049, and is very marked in 1054, 1055, 1057 and 1063.[51] Since John is 'thin' in the same years as the Chronicle (1059–61), these royal participations are likely to have come from the version he used, which either had, or pretended, knowledge of King Edward's commands in these years; it is too frequent, and on most occasions too probable, to be the result of haphazard additions by John. Maelcoluim's appointment as king in 1054 stands or falls as one of these commands of King Edward, one of many such phrases which command respect as sober chronicling, not guesswork.

One other source may help us to resolve the puzzle of John's statement, and certainly throws valuable light upon events after 1054, the *Vita Ædwardi Regis*, a life of Edward the Confessor written between 1065 and 1067. The author claims that 'about the same time' Gruffydd of Wales and a king of Scots with a barbarous name rebelled against Edward; the Scottish king was first defeated and put to flight by Earl Siward, and then, when Earl Tostig controlled the earldom of Northumbria, the Scots harassed him frequently with booty-raids rather than war; the earl wore them down 'so that they, with their king chose to serve him and King Edward rather than rebel, and to ratify this also by giving hostages'.[52]

This text is preserved in only one manuscript, and there is no evidence that it was known to John of Worcester, or influenced him. It does, however,

[50] *AU*, i, 490 (1054.6).
[51] Of such citations of royal will, not found in the Chronicle, I have counted, 1049–2; 1050–1; 1051–2; 1053–1; 1054–3; 1055–4; 1056–?1; 1057–2; 1058–1; 1063–2.
[52] *Vita Ædwardi Regis*, ed. Barlow, 66–67.

make clear a contrast between the heavy defeat inflicted by Siward, that of 1054, upon the king with a barbarous name, Macbeth, from which flowed no political consequences, and the 'containment' strategy of Tostig (earl 1055–65), leading to submission by a Scottish king. This is surely early evidence that the 1054 expedition did not lead to the appointment of Maelcoluim as king of Scots on Edward's orders, even though William of Malmesbury thought that it did. The reproach of the Durham chronicle under 1061, that Maelcoluim 'harried the earldom of his sworn brother ... Tostig',[53] shows that Maelcoluim, not Macbeth, had become Tostig's 'brother', probably when he became client of King Edward at his visit to Edward's court in 1059, escorted by archbishop, bishop and Tostig.

Maelcoluim II with no surviving son was said (for example by Fordun) to have conferred a subordinate kingship of the Cumbrians upon his grandson Donnchad to ensure his succession in Scotland, where his father, Crin abbot of Dunkeld, led his supporters.[54] That is based, and only based, upon John of Worcester's and William of Malmesbury's very curious description of the Maelcoluim made king in 1054 as 'son of the king of Cumbrians', where, if Siward made him king of Scots (as William *and only William* claimed),[55] we should surely expect 'son of Donnchad' or 'son of a king of Scots'. And, since Macbeth was king of Scots until 1057 and was succeeded not by Maelcoluim but by his stepson, Lulach, William's account is impossible.

He erred in identifying this Maelcoluim son of the king of Cumbrians with Maelcoluim III, an error which has bedevilled our understanding of the century ever since. In the hands of Fordun it became a much larger myth, for he took the idea back to 945, when King Edmund harried Cumbria and 'let' it to Maelcoluim I.[56] Maelcoluim passed Cumbria as a subordinate kingship to his heir, Ildulb, and future kings of Scots did the same thing, so that the king of Cumbria was tanist, Dauphin, next-in-line to the Scottish throne. Save for the lease of 945, this tale is fiction, totally without historical foundation.[57] John of Worcester's statement reproduces his and William's source accurately and means something entirely different: that Siward, having defeated Macbeth, following King Edward's command, made king of the Cumbrians Maelcoluim son of a previous king; Maelcoluim was a puppet king akin to those who were to be installed in Wales.[58] There is no good evidence that in 1054 Maelcoluim son of Donnchad I was in Scotland,

[53] *Symeonis Opera*, ii, 174–75.

[54] Crin abbot of Dunkeld was killed in a battle among Scots in 1045 according to Irish annals; *AU*, i, 482 (1045.6); *ATig*, 277; *ESSH*, i, 583.

[55] William of Malmesbury, *GRA*, i, 348–49; *Chron. John of Worcester*, ii, 422–25.

[56] ASC, MSS ABCD under 945; *SAEC*, 74.

[57] Cf. Smyth, *Warlords and Holy Men*, ch. 7.

[58] In 1063 Edward sent Earl Harold and Tostig to destroy King Gruffydd of North Wales; after this was accomplished two brothers were installed as puppet rulers, tied to Edward by giving hostages, and promising fealty, military service and tribute. Barlow, *Edward the Confessor*, 211–12; Davies, *Age of Conquest*, 24.

Northumbria or England, or that he had anything whatever to do with the defeat of Macbeth by Siward.[59]

Maelcoluim of Cumbria was presumably a son of Owen the bald or an unrecorded successor, excluded from his father's kingship in Strathclyde by a Scottish king after 1018, and restored by Siward in 1054 after the defeat of Macbeth.[60] His name had been borne by a tenth-century Strathclyde king, and might have been repeated as a compliment to Maelcoluim II, who surely dominated that kingdom. It is true that this leaves us ignorant not only of what happened after 1018 in Strathclyde, though it was clearly part of Macbeth's kingdom by 1054, but also of what became of Maelcoluim king of Cumbrians after 1054. In fact the Scottish king seems to have intervened in the Strathclyde succession more than once in the tenth century, but the record is fragmentary and obscure, and its absence after 1018 and 1054 should not surprise us. Maelcoluim III could well have swallowed the kingdom of Strathclyde again after 1058, for he certainly controlled it in 1070, when he invaded England from the west.[61]

The striking event of Macbeth's reign was surely his visit to Rome in 1050, when, according to Marianus, he gave money to the poor like seed.[62] Some twenty years earlier Cnut, too, had visited Rome, and other rulers (including Iehmarc) can be shown to have done so. The ability of Macbeth to leave his kingdom for such a long period makes nonsense of the later view of him as merely a 'usurper' with an uncertain hold on the throne. Like Cnut he must have relied upon powerful earls or mormaers to maintain his position; but he may also have had an understanding then with Edward king of England, for he cannot have feared English intervention on behalf of the lineage of Alpin. In other words, his kingship was as secure as Cnut's because it had been accepted; he had been inaugurated, had killed a powerful dissident, Crin, and had exiled rivals. As with Cnut, if he had left an able and uncontested heir, his might have become the new royal lineage.

In the tangled tale of Kings Macbeth, Lulach and Maelcoluim, the misleading dates given by Marianus Scotus have not helped. In what follows I adopt the dating argued for in the Note at the end of this chapter, derived in part from Fordun. Let us start in 1040, and Maelcoluim's 'I'll to England' (Macbeth, Act II, scene 3), when he was probably a small boy (he lived till

---

[59] In 1975, influenced by the supposed victory of Siward in 1046, I gave a misleading account of Maelcoluim's journey to the throne; Duncan, *Making of Kingdom*, 100.

[60] Given its place at the end of the annal, the latter seems more likely.

[61] The best discussion of the region is Phythian-Adams, *Land of the Cumbrians*, who accepts Maecoluim III as 'son of the king of Cumbrians' (p. 113) and the identification of Crin abbot of Dunkeld with Crinan the thegn, father of Maldred, who thus becomes a brother of Donnchad I (p. 134); this was discounted by Barrow, 'Some Problems ...', *Scottish Genealogist*, xxv (1978), 97–112.

[62] For eleventh-century Rome, Cowdrey, *Pope Gregory VII*, 1–21. In 1050 the pope was the German reformer, Leo IX (1048–54).

1093); his father had recently retired from Northumbria with a bloody nose. His mother would flee with her sons in any direction in which Macbeth was not, and from Donnchad's death near Elgin the most likely protection was to be found north, into the land of jarls. And that is exactly where we find Maelcoluim, evidently before his recovery of the kingdom, in his marriage to Ingebiorg.

Ingebiorg, a lady unknown to Irish and Scottish sources, is named as Maelcoluim's wife only in saga, written at least a century after her marriage to him; it greatly exaggerates the lifespan of her first husband, Earl Thorfinn of Orkney, to whom she bore two sons;[63] after his death she married King Maelcoluim, and bore him Duncan, later king and father of William the nobleman, whose son, 'called William the ætheling [i.e. "the boy of Egremont"] all the Scots wished to take as their king'.[64] William of Malmesbury calls Duncan 'bastard' so modern comment has suggested that she was related to Maelcoluim in some way which made their marriage canonically invalid. Alternatively if Thorfinn really died about 1060, then she was not Thorfinn's widow but his daughter, and could have married Maelcoluim in the 1050s; there is neither evidence for, nor likelihood in, these suggestions.

It is, however, striking that the Orkneyinga saga gives Thorfinn (said to have been a grandson of King Maelcoluim (II)) two famous victories over a king of Scotland whom it calls Karl Hundison; Thorfinn ended as the ruler of nine earldoms. Such fantasies warn us against putting faith in the saga's specious detail, and I shall not join the debate on the identity of Karl Hundison – Donnchad I or Macbeth? But the tradition of warfare between Thorfinn and a Scottish king, would fit with Orkney as a refuge for the children of Donnchad I and ultimately the marriage of Ingebiorg and Maelcoluim III.[65]

Ingebiorg's marriages were real enough, but she seems to have been forgotten as the repute of her fecund successor, Margaret, grew. In 1040 Maelcoluim was at least two, possibly as much as ten, years old, and by 1058 he was likely to be married and a father. The appearance among obits to be commemorated at Durham in the twelfth century of an *Ingeborg comitissa*, for whom no other identity is really possible, in company with monks whose

[63] The saga claims that Thorfinn was five when Maelcoluim II his grandfather gave him the earldom of Caithness and was earl for seventy years, dying towards the end of the reign of King Harald Hardrada of Norway (killed 1066); and that 'some time after' Thorfinn's sons succeeded him, King Harald came west to invade England (1066) – irreconcileable figures. Thorfinn, who went to Denmark, met King Swegn (1047–74), then in Saxony the Emperor Henry, went to Rome where he saw the Pope, and returned home to rule peaceably; this is likely to be later than 1049 (Pope Leo IX), and Thorfinn probably died in the early 1050s.

[64] *ESSH*, ii, 4–5; *Orkneyinga Saga*, c. 33.

[65] On Thorfinn and Karl Hundison, see Crawford, *Scandinavian Scotland*, 70–79. Dr Crawford does not give a date for Thorfinn's death.

names are of *c.*1085,[66] would fit Thorfinn's wife or widow but not his supposed daughter, and suggests that Thorfinn's widow married Maelcoluim, became mother and died before 1058 when she would have become queen. Duncan II may have been their only son. Maelcoluim set out to recover Scotland in 1057–58 from the territories of the earls of Orkney, and with their help.

The events of 1057–58 seem straightforward. Accepting Fordun's dates, Macbeth reigned for seventeen years, that is 1040–5 December 1057, and was killed at Lumphanan by Maelcoluim (III). Lulach succeeded on 8 December and four and a half months later, on 23 April 1058, was killed at Essie in Strathbogie either with treachery (ATig) or in battle (AU), by Maelcoluim III, who took the throne on 25 April 1058; the king list does not name Lulach's killer. Both AU and ATig, misplacing the death of Macbeth *after* that of Lulach, name his killer as Maelcoluim (III).[67] The misplacement is curious, as is Maelcoluim's need to kill two kings from the house of Moray, but we have no evidence to explain Lulach's succession after the defeat of his stepfather. It is possible that Maelcoluim, having come from Orkney to defeat Macbeth, secured Tostig's help to overthrow Lulach.

Maelcoluim III had a tempestuous relationship with the kings of England, recorded wholly from the English side. Two years after his visit to King Edward's court in 1059, when Earl Tostig and the archbishop of York were in Rome, Maelcoluim ravaged Northumbria, but the northern sources for these events have no knowledge of what had happened at Edward's court. The English monk Orderic Vitalis, writing sixty or more years later in Normandy, has Maelcoluim 'assert that King Edward, when he gave me Margaret, his great-niece, in wedlock, gave to me the county of Lothian'. Margaret and her brother came to England with their father (who promptly died) in 1057; it is not unlikely that in 1059 she was affianced to Maelcoluim in this way, and that failure to send her north (and hence to guarantee Lothian) explains the ravaging of 1061.[68] There was no retribution for this and when Tostig was expelled from his earldom and from England in 1065 he went to Scotland with twelve small ships and received Maelcoluim's help. If Maelcoluim was privy to Tostig's alliance with Harald king of Norway, he played no part in their invasion by the Humber, and hence avoided the slaughter at Stamford Bridge on 25 September 1066. Nor did he invade northern England to help William duke of Normandy.

The Norman Conquest of England created a situation in northern

[66] *Liber Vitae Ecclesiae Dunelmensis*, 141. One of the monks is named Duncan who occurs in the Liber Vitae also, but cannot be Duncan II.

[67] *AU*, i, 495 (1058.6) where Maelcoluim is Mael Sechlainn son of Donnchad; *ATig*, 290–91.

[68] *Orderic Vitalis*, iv, 270–71. Orderic visited Worcester and knew the chronicle of John of Worcester; he may have seen the version of ASC known to John. But ASC and John of Worcester have nothing on the visit of 1059, this proposed marriage or the 1061 invasion.

England not dissimilar to that of the early tenth century. Whereas the tenurial revolution in the south and midlands was rapid, the north was left to native landowners and governed through native earls, the first, Copsig, murdered in 1067, then Cospatrick (grandson of Earl Uhtred of 1018), who joined Northumbrians seeking to resist William, but entered his peace by the summer of 1068. But the leading Northumbrians and the Ætheling Edgar, with his sisters Margaret and Christina, fled to Scotland, for Maelcoluim had been prepared to help an insurrection. He accepted peace terms brought to him by the bishop of Durham, and according to our only source, Orderic Vitalis, 'by his messengers he swore obedience (*obsequium*)' to William.[69] Given that king and kingdom of Scotland were intact, it is more likely that he swore to a peace, and that Orderic has here antedated the outcome of later troubles.

For in 1069 the north rose in a serious revolt, when a new, French, earl, Robert de Comines, was murdered at Durham. Cospatrick and the ætheling returned south, and were joined by Waltheof, Earl Siward's son, and even by King Swegn; there is some evidence that they had Scottish as well as Danish ships, but otherwise King Maelcoluim held back from active involvement. Together they enjoyed some success, but in October the Danes were forced to agree to withdraw, and over the winter King William harried northern England mercilessly. Nonetheless he did not feel strong enough to reject the submission of Cospatrick and Waltheof, and even appointed the former as earl again. This was the background to Maelcoluim's decision, in the spring of 1070, to invade northern England from the west. From Cumberland he turned east, ravaged Teesdale and Cleveland, and then northwards towards Durham. Meanwhile Earl Cospatrick launched a counter-attack into Cumberland, recovering Maelcoluim's booty, before retreating to Bamburgh, from where he often emerged to weaken the enemy's strength, 'for at that time Cumberland was under King Malcolm's dominion, not possessed by right but subdued by force'.[70]

The purpose of this expedition remains obscure. Our knowledge of it comes from the Durham *Historia Regum*, which yet makes no mention of Maelcoluim approaching or attacking that city, where he later showed singular devotion to St Cuthbert. On the other hand he is said to have met the ætheling and his sisters on ships at Wearmouth, whither they had come after the Danish withdrawal, and the *Historia* tells of their taking refuge in Scotland as though it had not happened before. Dr Kapelle argues that this was surely more than a raid for booty and slaves, and suggests that it was intended to detach Northumbria from England. Certainly we should not confuse method with aim; war was conducted by ravaging the enemy's

[69] *Orderic Vitalis*, ii, 218–19.
[70] *Symeonis Opera*, ii, 191; *SAEC*, 92.

territory, killing, looting and enslaving, and in this Maelcoluim acted conventionally.

But his purpose was surely more than this, and may have been part of a larger intention to support the ætheling and Swegn of Denmark, who again sailed up the Humber to York, where the local people made a truce with Swegn, fearing that he meant to conquer England. Although he and Maelcoluim made no recorded contact, it is possible that with the ætheling they planned to expel William and the Normans from England, something which Maelcoluim had hoped for vicariously in 1068 but now supported openly. Certainly his chancing upon the ætheling in Wearmouth seems a remarkable coincidence.

Much has been built upon the *Historia*'s comment that Cumberland was under Maelcoluim's dominion in 1070, for it has been supposed that in 1061 or 1070 he conquered this province, holding it until 1092; the basis for this view, however, is the false belief that he was 'son of the king of Cumbrians' intent upon recovery of this territory. His 'dominion' seems to have been a consequence of his unusual step in invading by the west march, while Swegn attacked in the east, and was temporary. For there is no mention of English loss or recovery of Cumberland when in the early autumn of 1072 King William launched a delayed response to the assault of 1070; it would seem that Maelcoluim's dominion lasted as long as his men ravaged the English march and no longer.

With fleet and army William entered Scotland, which he blockaded, crossed the Forth and marched to the Tay, finding 'nothing that he was any the better for'. Harrying had proved unrewarding, not because Scotland was so poor – its pastoral economy was easier to loot than an agrarian one – but because the Scots had prepared by withdrawal from the invaded lands, just as they were to do in 1322. William's strategy was judged by the chronicler to be of limited success, but at Abernethy the two kings met and made peace; Maelcoluim became William's man and gave him hostages, probably including the king's son by Ingebiorg, Duncan. It is possible that estates for the journey to attend the English king's crown-wearing were now restored, for they are attested shortly after this.

In 1031 and 1072 the same word was used in Chronicle D of the king of Scots' position: he was the 'man' of the English king. The word is not in E's account of 1031 and may reflect the preferred vocabulary of a scribe of D writing after *c*.1050; certainly it does not tell us the words used or actions performed on these two occasions. If 'homage' is an acceptable description of the act, we should avoid 'vassal' for the man; it is not found till later, and then rarely and not for the king.

In 1074 Maelcoluim supported the ætheling in an expedition against the Conqueror which went wrong, and thereafter persuaded him to make terms, which the English king generously granted. There is no known reason for this ambiguous behaviour, nor for the great raid which Maelcoluim led into

Northumberland in 1079. According to the *Historia Regum* it prompted William I to send his oldest son, Robert, in 1080, with a force which reached Falkirk but achieved nothing. The Abingdon chronicle makes more of the event: Robert offered peace or war, Maelcoluim gathered the army of Lothian but accepted peace, gave hostages and promised subjection to the English king.[71] If this is correct it was apparently a renewal of the terms of 1072. They seem to have held for a decade, during which William I was succeeded by his son, William II, Rufus, in England, while Robert ruled as duke of Normandy, releasing Duncan son of Maelcoluim.

The occasion of renewed war in 1091 seems to have been Rufus's violation of the terms given to the ætheling, now stripped of his Norman possessions and fleeing to the Scottish court. When Maelcoluim raided Northumbria, but not Durham, Rufus was provoked into a rapid response, bringing Duke Robert, an army and a fleet (which was wrecked), while Maelcoluim brought an army 'out of Scotland into Lothian in England'. The ætheling and Duke Robert negotiated a peace between the kings, whereby Maelcoluim became Rufus's man 'for all such subjection as he had made before to his father', confirmed by an oath, and Rufus 'promised him in land and in everything all that he had had before under' the Conqueror. That is the account of ASC E, but John of Worcester is more specific: Rufus was to restore twelve vills which Maelcoluim had had in England under the Conqueror and to give him twelve marks of gold annually.

This last version is the key to subsequent events, not the acts of Rufus in 1092 when he 'went with a great army north to Carlisle', restored the town, built the castle and drove out the previous ruler, Dolfin; after his return south he sent peasant colonists to that land. It is thought that Dolfin was son of Cospatrick, the former earl of Northumbria who had fled to Scotland to be given the earldom of Lothian, and Dolfin may well have fled to Scotland. But the wording of the Chronicle is far from suggesting that this was a reconquest by the English king of a territory which the Scots had taken earlier in the century; the 'great army' certainly suggests an expectation of resistance from Dolfin and a recalcitrant peasantry, whose loyalty the king did not trust. All the earlier evidence suggests that Cumberland had been an appendage of the English earldom of Northumbria for a century or longer; as John of Worcester says, in 1092 Rufus 'went to Northumbria' and restored Carlisle.[72]

Nor does the account of 1093 even hint that Maelcoluim was reacting to the takeover of Carlisle. It is quite specific that he sent to Rufus 'and asked for the fulfilment of the terms that had been promised him', that is the terms agreed in 1091, which themselves harked back to the agreements of the Conqueror's time. Whether his complaint was over the twelve vills,

[71] *Chron. Abingdon*, ii, 9–10
[72] *Chron. John of Worcester*, iii, 62.

intended to house him on his way to the English court, or over the twelve marks of gold, is not known, but when Rufus summoned him to Gloucester, giving hostages, presumably for his safe return, Malcolm obeyed, visiting Durham, where he joined with the bishop and prior in laying the foundation stones for rebuilding the cathedral. It is to this occasion that we can also attribute the agreement of the Durham convent with Maelcoluim, Margaret and their family, for spiritual services during their lives and after, and I have suggested that in return Maelcoluim promised to restore some of the lost lands of St Cuthbert in Lothian. These activities are consistent with a visit, intent upon peace, to secure justice at Rufus's court, but not with a demand for the return of territory annexed by him.[73]

The outcome as recorded by the Chronicle shows Rufus, recovered from illness, refusing to see Maelcoluim and denying him what had been promised. John of Worcester, dating a 'meeting' to 24 August, seems likely to have more of the truth: that, despite the wish of his chief men for peace, William refused to meet or to discuss matters, but offered judgement of his barons in his court, while Maelcoluim demanded judgement upon the Border 'where the kings of Scots were wont to do right by the kings of the English, and by judgement of the chief men of both kingdoms'.[74] We may discern an initial encounter where Maelcoluim was bluntly independent, and subsequent to-ing and fro-ing by, among others, Bishop William of Durham, in which each king accepted a need for judgement but would not compromise on the forum. Finally Maelcoluim rushed home to raise an army and ravage Northumberland. He met death, along with his son Edward, at Northumbrian hands, on 12 or 13 November 1093, near the River Aln.[75]

That he took to war has, I am sure, been largely responsible for the assumption that he had sought the 'restoration' of Cumberland from Rufus; but the alternative, and I believe the correct, view is that Maelcoluim saw the peace, for which he had become Rufus's man, broken by Rufus's unfulfilled promises. We do not know why Rufus refused his part of the 1091 peace, but it is possible that what was brokered by Duke Robert and the ætheling had not been fully reported to William, or that its terms were simply that Maelcoluim would become Rufus's man as he had been the Conqueror's and that Rufus would restore to Maelcoluim what he had from the Conqueror. That this could mean restoring twelve vills and paying twelve marks of gold may have emerged only later.[76] Rejection of adjudication upon the Border

---

[73] For the traditional view, Kapelle, *Norman Conquest of the North,* 150–53; Phythian-Adams, *Land of Cumbrians,* 24–28; cf. Summerson, *Medieval Carlisle,* i, 47–49.

[74] *Chron. John of Worcester,* iii, 64–65.

[75] John of Worcester says St Brice's day (13 November) but Durham observed the obit on 12 November. The *Historia Regum* (*Symeonis Opera,* ii, 221–22) says near the Aln; Alnwick is named by Gaimar, *Estoire,* line 6111.

[76] John of Worcester reports the twelve vills and twelve marks under 1091 (pp. 60–61), but he may have read them back from an account of the dispute in 1093.

by a joint tribunal, for which there were precedents elsewhere, and probably in Border law for rustling disputes, left Maelcoluim with no option but to ravage the enemy's land.

Our knowledge of the terms on which Scottish and English kings reached agreement is better in quality than that of Edward I, but in quantity differs only in our having the Anglo-Saxon Chronicle. Edward I found what he wanted in John of Worcester, William of Malmesbury and other Latin writers who found no difficulty in translating Old English words for 'agreement' and 'subordination'. John of Worcester's 'oath to be faithful' under 946, became in Edward I's Great Roll 'swore a due oath of fealty to a lord',[77] but in general the compilers of the 1290s found surprisingly little evidence in the tenth century to present as the overlordship which Edward I sought to justify. From the eleventh century, the submission of Maelcoluim II in 1031 was noted, and the 1054 annal emerged as: 'Siward ... constituted Maelcoluim son of the king of the Cumbrians as king of Scots by order of King Edward, and it is found thus in [certain] chronicles: "King Edward gave the *regnum* of Scotland to Maelcoluim ... to hold of him".' Thus not only had Maelcoluim become unequivocally king of Scots, but his *regnum*, kingship, had evidently become the kingdom held (though fief and lord are not mentioned), of the English king.

Such anachronisms are to be expected, and, in different fields, are not unknown in our own day. But they tell us nothing about the relationship as it was in Maelcoluim's time, for which his version does not survive, save in the claim that a dispute be settled on the Border by men from both sides. That the English sources for 1080 are so discrepant, with no mention of Duke Robert's campaign in the Chronicle, should warn us against treating surviving accounts of the relationship as a full or official record of it. Thus in the key event, the submission of Abernethy in 1072, Maelcoluim made peace with William, gave hostages and was his man, according to the Chronicle; these words suggest that the peace and the hostages (and not any act of homage) made Maelcoluim William's man. But when John of Worcester came to make his Latin version, he saw William as setting out to bring Scotland under his control; without any mention of peace or hostages, Maelcoluim 'became [William's] man'.[78] This does imply an act of homage, possibly more usual in the 1130s when John wrote, especially for making clear the king's control, subjection (*ditio*) of the kingdom – an anchronism of which the Chronicle has no knowledge.[79] Likewise the author of

[77] Stones and Simpson, ii, 302, under 947. By a wonderfully funny misreading of John of Worcester for 949, the Great Roll adds that 'a certain Eric [Bloodaxe] was placed as king over Scots'.

[78] *Chron. John of Worcester*, iii, 21; *homo suus deuenit*.

[79] Reynolds, *Fiefs and Vassals*, 340, 370–73. But Miss Reynolds does not suggest any marked change between 1072 and the 1120s.

Chronicle E in 1072 makes no mention of *manrædene*, homage, though it was certainly given in the 1090s.

In 1091 the bonds were tightened: Maelcoluim came to William and 'became his man for all such subjection as he had made before to [William I] and he confirmed that with an oath' (Chronicle E). At least one act is described here, but more probably two – an act of homage and an oath. These were qualified, that is limited to what had been agreed in 1072, and the oath should not be seen as the later oath of fealty, but there is no doubting that in some sense Maelcoluim accepted Rufus's lordship – not over a territory, but over Maelcoluim. Why? What was there in it for Maelcoluim? The avoidance of ravaging of Scotland, certainly, and the vills and money recorded by John of Worcester in 1091. But it is possible that there was a third element, that William agreed that Lothian should continue to be ruled by Maelcoluim. After 1018 we hear of that province only when Edward the Confessor gave it to Maelcoluim, presumably in 1059, an act which shows persistent knowledge that it had been part of English Northumbria, as in the military stand-off in 1091 Maelcoluim went out of Scotland into Lothian in England to await his enemy. It was as though he sought peace while showing a determination to retain this province – which is exactly what he achieved.

Two Notes

1. The dates of eleventh-century kings

William of Malmesbury, ignorant of any other outcome, thought that Macbeth was succeeded by Maelcoluim III.[80] Fordun knew from his king list that Macbeth was killed in Lumphanan by Maelcoluim (III) and that his successor was Lulach *fatuus*, the fool, with no patronymic, slain at Essie in Strathbogie, by whom is not said, after a four and a half month reign. He therefore placed the 1054 battle in 1056 and invented a desertion of Maelcoluim by Siward, allowing Lulach, whom he made Macbeth's cousin (*consobrinum*), to be brought by his kinsfolk to Scone, placed on the royal seat and so constituted king there. He was killed by Maelcoluim or his men – Fordun is uncertain which – after four months, at Essie on Thursday, 3 April 1057, in Easter week. This date, like 5 December 1056 for the death of Macbeth, is unique to Fordun, as is the 'crowning' of Maelcoluim III at Scone on St Mark's day, 25 April, of 1057.[81]

The dates found only in Fordun are directly contradicted by marginal entries added by an amanuensis, perhaps under the eye of the author, to one manuscript of the chronicle of Marianus Scotus, written on the continent

---

[80] *Chron. Wyntoun*, iv, 304–5 gives no explanation of how Lulach came to reign, but gives him three months before being slain at Essie.

[81] *Chron. Fordun*, i, 206.

between *c.*1070 and 1083; this version of Marianus was not known to John of Worcester, but it sometimes gives us two dates for the same event.[82] In its version, Donnchad I reigned from St Andrew's day [30 November] 1034, for five years nine months, and was killed in the autumn 1040 (text), on 19 kal. Sept. [14 August](margin) and on the Nativity of St Mary [8 September] (margin under 1057); Macbeth reigned for seventeen years to the same feast-day and was killed in August (margin) 1057; Lulach succeeded him reigning from the Nativity of St Mary [8 September] (margin), presumably of 1057, to St Patrick's day [17 March], i.e. of 1057/58.

Modern historians have on the whole used Marianus up to Lulach's death, but then Fordun's date for Maelcoluim III's accession – despite the inconsistency in this selectivity, and the impossibility of following Marianus literally.[83] Let us start with A. O. Anderson's suggestion, surely correct, that, for the death of Donnchad I in August, the Nativity (8 September) must be an error for the Assumption of Mary (15 August), making the reign length of five years nine months pretty correct. More importantly, this implies a source which noted these events as taking place on an undifferentiated feast of Mary.[84] Marianus' glossator, most improbably, places the death of Macbeth and the inauguration of Lulach on the same day, the Nativity of Mary, probably because he knew, or was told of, an annal in words like: '1057, the death of Macbeth and Lulach took kingship on the feast of Mary'. Macbeth died, according to Fordun, on 5 December; Lulach was inaugurated on a St Mary, misguessed in Marianus as the Nativity for which we should read the Conception, 8 December.

Of the two forms of Fordun's date for Lulach's death, 3 April and Thursday in Easter week, which are in agreement for 1057, one would be calculated from the other; the more probable original form is Thursday in Easter week, which Fordun or an intermediate source identified from a calendar for 1057 as being 3 April, after four months' reign. But according to the Irish annals and Marianus, Lulach died in 1058, when Thursday in Easter week fell on 23 April, an appropriate two days before Fordun's inauguration of Maelcoluim III on 25 April. That extension of Lulach's reign gives the extra half month required by the king lists. But the *Duan Albanach* king list of the late eleventh century gives Lulach a seven month reign, thus apparently but wrongly confirming Marianus' date of Mary's

---

[82] For Marianus see Kenney, *Sources for the Early History of Ireland, Ecclesiastical*, no. 443. The relevant text is in *Chron. Picts-Scots*, 65. In late Anglo-Saxon England months would pass between the secular ceremony of accession and unction-coronation. Harold II and subsequent kings until 1216 were crowned and anointed immediately after accession; Garnett, 'Coronation and Propaganda', *Transactions of Royal Historical Soc.*, series 5, xxxvi (1985), 91–116.

[83] Dunbar, *Scottish Kings*, 13–23; *Handbook of British Chronology*, 56–57.

[84] *ESSH*, i, 602.

Nativity (8 September) for his accession; behind this is a misreading of *iiii* as *uii*.[85] Marianus says Lulach was killed in March and that he reigned till St Patrick's mass, in March, a curious repetition, explained by the final addition, 'Maelcoluim has reigned twenty years from then up to the mass of St Patrick'. This comment from Marianus' source would date that source to March 1078, near enough twenty years since 23 April 1058, and led Marianus to deduce, incorrectly, that Lulach had been killed on St Patrick's day.[86]

In brief, Fordun's feast-dates for the succession in the 1050s are more likely to be correct than those of Marianus, though his years 1056 and 1057 are errors for 1057 and 1058. Fordun's only source in common for all four kings from 1034 to 1093 was a king list of the X family, and the most likely explanation of these month dates is that they had been entered on this king list.

2. Malcolm III, Canmore?

Fordun's *Chronica* cites Turgot as using 'Canmore' but it is not found in earlier texts of Turgot.[87] The *Chronica* has it in two earlier places describing the flight of Donnchad I's sons at his death, and in two chapter headings, but not in the many other references to Maelcoluim as king. In Wyntoun it occurs in two rubrics and three lines of the earliest (Wemyss) version, but was edited out of the Cottonian version. 'Wemyss' has it twice to describe how Donnchad I bedded the daughter of the miller of Forteviot one night, 'and gat a sone on hir or day / That callit wes Malcome Canmore'.[88] The context in which both Fordun and Wyntoun found 'Canmore' was the romance which lies behind their narrative. Its use from the fifteenth century to the twentieth does not validate it.

The earliest example of its use seems to be in the poem with which Bower claimed to summarise his *Scotichronicon*, where, listed among Scottish kings, is *Malcolm Kenremor*, seven lines later called simply *Kenremor*. Dr Broun, in editing this section, the 'Scottish poem', has shown that it varies in several places from Bower's chronicle; to these instances he could have added the odd spelling, *Kenremor*, presumably including a misunderstood *n*-abbreviation in *Kennmor*, while the *Scotichronicon*, following Fordun, always has *Canmore*. The editor concludes that this 'Scottish poem' is, apart

[85] *Chron. Picts-Scots*, 63; Jackson, 'Duan Albannach', *SHR*, xxxvi (1957), 133.

[86] It is unlikely that Patrick was an error or misreading of Marianus' source for Ibar of Bec-Eire, a supposed contemporary of Patrick, whose feast (with that of St George) falls on 23 April; *Martyrology of Oengus*, 108, 119; Clayton, *Cult of the Virgin Mary*, ch. 2.

[87] *Chron. Fordun*, i, 206. See the argument in *Scotichronicon*, iii, 193, attributing this passage to Aelred's *Genealogia*, where also 'Canmore' is not found; *Patrologia Latina*, vol. 195, col. 735.

[88] *Chron. Fordun*, i, 188, 190, rubrics: 143, 192. *Chron. Wyntoun*, iv, p. 258 lines 1669, 1685, p. 318 line 2542, rubrics p. 254, 272.

from a few lines, 'a verse history of the Scots from their origins to the conquest of 1296, which Bower has copied'.[89] This conclusion places the attribution of 'Canmore' to Maelcoluim III, and the Macbeth–Macduff romance, in the thirteenth century. If, as seems possible, it explains the appearance of the name Macduff as a personal name for the younger son of Earl Malcolm of Fife (earl 1228–66), born after *c.* 1252,[90] that would suggest an attribution of the romance to the reign of Alexander II. In thirteenth-century sagas Maelcoluim III is 'Long-neck'.

  [89] *Scotichronicon*, ix, 54–127; the references to Maelcoluim are on 72, lines 141 and 148; the discussion by Dr Broun on 54–59, the quotation on 57. It is noteworthy that the poem gives Duncan II a six-month reign (line 144) but the chronicle one year six months (*Scotichronicon*, iii, 84–85); the poem is correct.
  [90] *Scots Peerage*, iv, 9–10. Macduff was the key appellant to Edward I in 1293; he was killed at Falkirk in 1298.

CHAPTER 4

Maelcoluim's sons and grandson, 1093–1165

We move into a time when king lists are no longer a useful source of information, when charters and writs give us significant insight into ecclesiastical and lay society, and when the 'deeds' of Scotland's kings were more fully chronicled by a variety of English hands, one at least, Orderic Vitalis, writing in Normandy. But there was precious little chronicling of domestic affairs in Scotland until the very end of the twelfth century; the gaps in our knowledge are not trivial.

But the final tussle over the throne, between 1093 and 1097, in which victory went to the son of Maelcoluim, Edgar, who bought firm English support by an act of homage to the English king, is comparatively well documented. Less certain are the circumstances in which his yougest brother, David, was provided with an appanage under Alexander I, and the precise nature of Alexander's undoubted obligations to Henry I. But it was commented that Alexander designated David his heir, despite which his illegitimate son tried to seize the throne from an absent David. David secured from King Stephen what a historian might call a *damnosa hereditas*, the earldom of Northumbria, for his son Henry, who was clearly his recognised heir, and which passed to Henry's sons to be surrendered to Henry II of England by the oldest, Malcolm IV.

That sums up the narrative covered in this chapter, but the sources present not a few problems along the way. One thing they do not give us is a generic name for these kings and their successors, and I ignore 'House of Canmore', 'Canmore dynasty', 'Mac Malcolms' and 'Margaretsons', unknown in the twelfth century or later. Thus Domnall ban's succession in 1093 was possible because he and his supporters held all the sons of a king (his father, Donnchad I) as king-worthy, but the Scots 'chose' Domnall in 1093 and 'took [him] to themselves as king' again in 1094,[1] the best evidence that in uncertain times leading subjects had a voice in the succession, and that exclusive 'right' for either collateral or heir of line was not yet firm; the rights of the royal *stirps* and of the king's eldest son were still in uneasy tension. Yet Domnall was at least fifty-three years old, had no known son to

---

[1] These phrases come from ASC E, which is the only version of ASC to go beyond the year 1080.

lead an army in his place, and may have been chosen because the heir of line, Duncan, was not available, having long abandoned Scotland for the life of a French knight.[2] If so, Domnall was preferred as a stop-gap king to the children of Margaret and Maelcoluim.

Thus, according to the Durham *Historia Regum*, Edward, eldest son of Maelcoluim III and Margaret, mortally wounded at the battle of Alnwick, had been named by his father 'heir of the kingship (*regnum*) after him',[3] a nomination mentioned by no other source (Table B, p. 346). But William I of England in his last illness, torn between the claims of his oldest son Robert with whom he had quarrelled bitterly and who was not with him, and his own predilection for William his second son who was,[4] reluctantly allowed Robert to succeed to the patrimony (Normandy) but gave the conquest (England) to William. Such a division was not available to Maelcoluim III, but his oldest son, Duncan, long a hostage till released by Duke Robert in 1087, stayed south until 1093 or 1094;[5] he had 'gone over' to the Anglo-Norman monarchy and to Rufus with whom Maelcoluim had a bitter personal quarrel. It is not surprising that Maelcoluim, to avoid the strife which the attempted succession of such an absentee would certainly provoke, should designate Edward as successor, acknowledging that among the sons of Margaret, the eldest had the best right, but, by the fact of designating, acknowledging that his oldest son (Duncan) also had a right. Thus succession by male primogeniture was a familiar concept, even though in 1093 many leading Scots rejected both it and the English at Maecoluim's court.

In 1094, after the succession of Domnall III, Duncan came to Rufus, offered military service, asked for his father's kingship (*regnum*), was given it, did such homage (*manrædene*) to Rufus as the king wished to have of him, then went with his consent to Scotland with a force of English and French.[6] Duncan moved only after serving Rufus, becoming his man and with his leave, but with an army scratched together, his success was lucky and short-lived. William of Malmesbury was the first writer to suggest that Duncan was *nothus*, a bastard.[7] There is no hint in the Anglo-Saxon Chronicle nor in John of Worcester's chronicle of this slur on Duncan, which was surely intended to highlight the virtues of Malcolm's second marriage and children, especially Maud (wife of Henry I) and David I. In the letter to David prefacing his *Gesta Regum Anglorum*, William praises the 'line of ancestors famed for sanctity, praised for royal valour, and adorned with

---

[2] It is not known exactly when he was knighted, possibly not till after his release in 1087.

[3] *Symeonis Opera*, ii, 222.

[4] Barlow, *William Rufus*, 40–50.

[5] ASC states under 1093 that Duncan had remained at the English king's court.

[6] *Chron. John of Worcester*, iii, 66–67; this and the ASC place Duncan's defeat of Domnall in 1093, but Duncan's death in November 1094 after a six-month reign makes May 1094 certain, despite the argument of Kapelle, *Norman Conquest of North*, 154, 274, n. 130.

[7] William of Malmesbury, *GRA*, i, 724–25.

every virtue; ... You are held [to be] sole heir of such kings and princes'.[8] Duncan II's reputation stood little chance against this sycophancy, and (apparently) widespread ignorance of Ingebiorg the Orcadian. He was her only surviving son by Maelcoluim, a possible brother, Domnall son of Maelcoluim king of Alba, having been killed in 1085.[9] In his 1094 charter to St Cuthbert, Duncan is called 'son of King Maelcoluim, heritably certain king of Scotland', a statement aimed against Domnall ban, who was king as Duncan went north to win his heritage, and remained at large after he had succeeded in doing so.[10]

The charter itself was produced by a clerk familiar with Norman forms, whence the use of the patronymic, and in Norman fashion asserted the concurrence of Duncan's brothers; its anathema on anyone seeking to undo it was a warning particularly to the family. The gift is made for himself, his father's soul, his brothers, wife and children; the absence of his mother is curious, but since Duncan clearly regarded himself as legitimate, it is not evidence that her marriage was invalid. She had died perhaps thirty-six years before 1094, when she would be little remembered. But the drafter of the charter was in no doubt that lawful succession to a king came to his eldest son.

'My brothers', i.e. Margaret's sons, included Edgar, one of the signatories. They must have supported his taking of the kingship and recognised him as Maelcoluim's eldest lawful son, as Edgar's charter of 1095, considered below, undoubtedly shows. It is possible that Duncan promised an appanage in the south to his oldest half-brother, Edmund, and that he had to renegue on this when the Scots forced him to get rid of his followers and promise never again to introduce English or French into the land. For when Duncan was betrayed and killed by Scots in 1094 at the instigation of Domnall III,[11] according to William of Malmesbury, Edmund was involved in the killing (an Irish annal confirms this),[12] helping to restore Domnall, and 'bargaining for half the kingdom'.[13] It is not unlikely that Edmund was

[8] William of Malmesbury, *GRA*, i, 2–3; *Cum uero solus habeamini tantorum regum et principum heres* ...

[9] *ESSH*, ii, 47, n. 1, 160, n. 2, and corrigenda thereto in the reissue.

[10] *filius regis Malcolumb, constans hereditarie rex Scotie*. This charter was most recently discussed in my 'Yes, the Earliest Scottish Charters', *SHR*, lxxviii (1999), 1–35, where there is a photograph of it. Photo, text and translation in *Nat. MSS. Scot.* i, no. II. Its date must lie in the year between Maelcoluim III's death on 13 November 1093 and Duncan's on 12 November 1094, and is most plausibly placed in May 1094 when Duncan was on his way north to expel Domnall ban.

[11] The king lists attribute his death to the mormaer of Mearns and place it at 'Monacheden', Mondynes in the Mearns; *Chron. Picts-Scots*, 175, 181; Dunbar, *Scottish Kings*, 39.

[12] *AU*, i, 528 (1094.7). The names of Domnall and Edmund are added by interlineation.

[13] William of Malmesbury, *GRA*, i, 726–27; ii, 364. This alliance is not mentioned by the Anglo-Saxon chronicle (E), an edition made about 1120, when it would be convenient to remove Edmund's lapse.

given an appanage, with the expectation that he would succeed the elderly Domnall. Edmund was later imprisoned for life, and the third brother, Ethelred, who inherited the abbacy of Dunkeld, probably died young.[14]

Probably within weeks of Duncan II's death on 12 November 1094, his half-brother Edgar followed in his footsteps and sought the kingship from Rufus. At Norham on the Tweed, on 29 August 1095, Edgar granted a charter to St Cuthbert, based on Norman forms, in the presence of the bishop and prior of Durham, by advice of King William and of Edgar's *fideles*, for the souls of his parents and of his brothers Duncan and Edward. He was the man of Rufus:

> I Edgar, son of Maelcoluim king of Scots, possessing the whole land of Lothian and kingship (*regnum*) of Scotland by gift of King William my lord and by paternal heritage ...[15]

This maintains the Norman contrast between something inherited and something given: kingship came from his father, Lothian by Rufus' gift. In 1095 Edgar did not possess the kingdom; indeed there is a contrast between the use of *totam* for the land of Lothian, and the absence of *totum* before *regnum*, which is therefore not a territory. In his title Edgar, in Norman fashion, names his father, as did Duncan II, but also gives his father's style of *rex Scottorum*; we expect that he would call himself *rex*, but Norman practice allowed the clerk to express 'king' flexibly, 'possessing kingship' (*regnum possidens*), to balance the land of Lothian. When it came to the signatories this meaning was made clear: *Signum Edgari regis*.

Moreover Rufus was his lord, that is had received his homage, a personal relationship not confined to Lothian. But neither man had possessed Lothian, so Rufus's gift would be based on the ancient history of that province as part of the Anglian kingdom and English earldom of Northumbria; he had invited Edgar to acquire it. Edgar, having been recognised as king and 'given' Lothian by Rufus, had left him at Bamburgh to invade and conquer that province; now, 'possessing' it, he recrossed the Tweed on 29 August, to be met by the clergy of Durham and persuaded to restore in his new territory their lost lands, the shires (i.e. estates) of Berwick and Coldingham. Doubtless this was in thanks for his success, but also in exchange for Duncan II's gift of Tyninghame to St Cuthbert, and to fulfil the promise of a gift probably made by their father in 1093. Rufus's new authority in Lothian was affirmed by his issuing of a charter of confirmation of Edgar's endowment.

---

[14] The *notitia* of his grant to the clergy of Loch Leven, Lawrie, *Early Scottish Charters*, no. 14, implies this.

[15] *Ego Edgarus filius Malcolmi Regis Scottorum totam terram de Lodeneio et regnum Scotie dono domini mei Willelmi Anglorum Regis et paterna hereditate possidens* ...This charter is also discussed in my article, 'Yes, the Earliest Scottish Charters', *SHR*, lxxviii, 1–35. Lawrie, *Early Scottish Charters*, no. 15. It survives only in fifteenth-century copies.

But how had Edgar become king? It is very unlikely that he just assumed the style on news of Duncan II's death and he certainly did not then go to Scone for inauguration. He became king in England, through recognition by William II of England, with the gift of Lothian, by a symbolic investiture, as part of that recognition. No source tells of this act, whether it was of 1094 or of 1095, but investiture by a powerful ruler in recognising a neighbour as king is well documented. In the year 1000 the Emperor Otto III visiting Gniezno in Poland recognised Duke Boleslas as king, placed a crown on his head and presented him with a lance-relic. In 1086 Duke Vratislav of Bohemia was made king, as a personal dignity, by the Emperor Henry IV, who gave him a crown. And there are examples subsequent to 1095, e.g. Danish kings in 1134 and 1152. Edgar's was not a new kingship, and Rufus' recognition of his succession to Duncan II was not an imperial pretension. But he may have aped the emperor by giving Edgar a crown, and even by placing it on his head.

For already in 1095 Edgar was using his royal seal,[16] single-faced as most seals were but showing a crowned king, seated in an X chair with claw feet, with sceptre and sword (Plate 2A). The legend, [I] or [Y]MAGO EDGARI SCOTTORVM BASI[LEI] recalls the seal of Edward the Confessor, and the charters of Anglo-Saxon kings, with *basileus* for 'king', while holding a sword occurs first in the west on Edward's seal.[17] From the sides of Edgar's crown hang cataseistae (such as still hang from the Holy Crown of Hungary), found not on the Confessor's seal, but on that (and on the coins) of William I, showing that the design of Edgar's is eclectic, based on English models. Surviving western crowns of the twelfth century do not suggest that cataseistae were a usual feature,[18] and their appearance here and on English royal seals may be a result of copying Byzantine models. The depiction of Edgar wearing a crown when he was still a pretender and client of William II suggests that he did have one, and that he had it by courtesy of the English king.

A century later William, the son of Duncan II, would have stood in the way of Edgar's succession; in 1094 he was too young and was perhaps a captive. Rufus was importuned by 'King' Edgar to make a reality of his gift of kingship and agreed to spend some of his war-chest on the project. The mistake of Duncan's ill-prepared and unsupported expedition was not repeated, for in October 1097 Rufus sent Edgar Ætheling to Scotland with an army which gained Scotland in a 'hard-fought battle', while Domnall ban was expelled (the Anglo-Saxon Chronicle), killed by David (Malmesbury),

---

[16] This seal is described as attached to the 1095 charter.

[17] Perhaps copied from the seal of Isaac I Comnenus (1057–59), the first Byzantine emperor shown carrying a sword. B. Bedos-Rezak, 'The King enthroned, a new theme in Anglo-Saxon royal iconography', *Kings and Kingship*, ed. Rosenthal, 53–88, and no. IV in B. Bedos-Rezak, *Form and Order in Medieval France.*

[18] Twining, *European Regalia*, 8–9, 88 (Ottonian imperial crown), 97 (Hungarian crown).

taken by Edgar, imprisoned, blinded and died at Rescobie (the king-lists), or blinded by 'his brother' (Irish annals).[19] His fate is less important than the contradictions of the sources which confirm the 'improving' tendencies of Malmesbury. Edgar is not said to have accompanied his uncle the ætheling, nor is he said to have been made king (though he presumably went to Scone for inauguration), but to have been 'set up as king ... in fealty (*heldan*) to King William'.[20] The ætheling may have remained in Scotland for some time to consolidate his nephew's rule which was also a deliberate extension of the English king's lordship.

In his history Gaimar remarks on Rufus's generosity in not demanding service or payment for Scotland, but he also remarks that Rufus promised Edgar a payment of 40s or 60s every day when he visited the English court.[21] This remarkable concession assuaged the dispute over reception in England which had destroyed Rufus's relations with Maelcoluim III in 1093; the amount may have been less than Maelcoluim claimed, but it was nonetheless acceptance that a king must be received with special honour, even if he was bound in fealty. The payment effectively required Edgar to respond to a summons from the English king, and that in itself questions Gaimar's claim that Edgar owed no service. When William returned from Normandy at Easter 1099 one of his first acts must have been to send for Edgar, for when he wore his crown at Westminster abbey and held a great feast in the newly completed hall there on 29 May 1099, Edgar was present to carry the sword in presence of the English king.[22] It was a position of great honour, but also the duty of a great *fidelis*.

For the remainder of Edgar's life there is no evidence of similar calls. He was not present at the hurried coronation of Henry I in 1100, nor did he help in the war between Henry and his brother, Robert duke of Normandy. On the other hand, so far as we can tell, he was not consulted when Henry I married one of his sisters and gave the other as wife to the count of Boulogne,[23] just as William II and Henry were not consulted when Edgar altered the terms of his gift to St Cuthbert of Durham to recover the shire of Berwick.[24]

---

[19] William of Malmesbury, *GRA*, i, 724–25; ii, 363; *Chron. Picts-Scots*, 175, 181; *ATig.*, 324 (1099); *Ann. Clonmacnoise*, 187 (1098). The dates of the Irish sources are probably simple errors; there seems no reason why Edgar should delay the blinding of Domnall from which he died.

[20] *ASC* under 1097.

[21] Gaimar, *Estoire*, ed. Bell, lines 6176–83, which make the army besieging Bamburgh (1095) go to Scotland to restore Edgar. The amount is xl and lx in different MSS.

[22] *Annales Monastici*, ii, 40 (annals of Winchester); *SAEC*, 120; but cf. the story told by Gaimar, *Estoire des Engles*, ed. Bell, lines 5975–6020; Barlow, *William Rufus*, 400–1.

[23] It seems that the daughters of Maelcoluim and Margaret were in Henry's custody. Did Henry fear that Edgar might marry one of them to, for example, William Clito? The more likely suggestion is that Henry could find them better husbands than could Edgar.

[24] *Chron. Fordun*, i, 225.

Duncan II and Edgar both stressed their heritage from Maelcoluim III; yet Edgar would not have been his father's heir in the eyes of a later generation, for Duncan II left at least one son, William. If William of Malmesbury is correct in saying that Edmund was later 'captured and kept in fetters for life', he too had a prior right, though this he presumably forfeited by his support of Domnall ban. It is nonetheless striking that there is no hint in any chronicle that any of the first four sons of Maelcoluim III and Margaret were married or had issue, and we can be sure that Edgar did not. This abstention, if such it was, has been remarked among Anglo-Saxon kings, and might have been a means of ensuring peace among siblings by guaranteeing their succession. There may also have been pressure to endow the next oldest brother with an appanage, to ensure his loyalty, as Edmund sought half the kingdom from Domnall. The only evidence that Edgar endowed Alexander comes from John of Worcester, who calls the latter *comes*, earl, when describing his presence and gifts at the translation of St Cuthbert in 1104. His earldom, if any, was north of Forth, for, despite this devotion, he is not found dealing with Durham's Scottish possessions in Lothian until he became king.[25]

But the first signatory to Alexander I's diploma to Scone priory, after the bishops and before the earls, is 'Alexander nephew of King Alexander'.[26] In this ranking he must surely have been a legitimate descendant of Maelcoluim III, perhaps a son of Duncan II older than William, as Sir James Dalrymple suggested in 1705. But his name, Alexander, seems a recognition of the ruling king of Scots, implying that he was born in or after 1107, which would rule out Duncan II, Edward and Edmund as his father. David had married late in 1113, which really rules him out as father of this Alexander. It is true that two daughters are ascribed to him by Orderic, along with a son murdered by a cleric, and that the latter story was repeated and embroidered by later writers.[27] But while David in his charters was solicitous for the souls of his parents, brothers, sisters and son Henry, he apparently cared naught for daughters or deceased son, for they do not rate a mention. In short, wherever Orderic found them, it was not in David's family.[28] The elimination of these possibilities, leaves only the possibility that the fifteenth-century Scone cartulary scribe, in *Alexander nepos regis Alexandri*, fell into

---

[25] *Symeonis Opera*, ii, 236. There is no evidence that Alexander was earl of Gowrie; *cf. Making of the Kingdom*, 126.

[26] *Ego Alexander nepos regis Alexandri de his testimonio perhibeo*; Lawrie, *ESC*, 30. *Nepos* could mean grandson, but that is really impossible of Alexander I.

[27] *Orderic Vitalis*, iv, 274–77; *Chronicles of Stephen*, iv, 111 (Torigni listing the children. He does not have the murdered child); Skene, *Chron. Picts-Scots*, 181, lines beginning *Istius in regno*; *Chron. Wyntoun*, iv, 412–17; *SAEC*, 156–57; *ESSH*, ii, 119.

[28] They are found in Dunbar, *Scottish Kings*, 64; also in *Handbook of British Chronology*, 57, whence they should be removed in a fourth edition.

dittography, and that the miscopied name of the *nepos* was *Willelmus* (son of Duncan II).[29]

This suggestion is uncertain foundation for a further one, but we should at least entertain the possibility that William's prominence (if it is indeed he) in this diploma occurs because he was then the intended, and perhaps designated, successor to Alexander I. The illegitimate descendants of William fitz Duncan, as we shall see, thought that they had a claim to the throne. And the appanage bequeathed to David by Edgar, often assumed to be provision for the heir in waiting, surely looks more like provision made for one who was not expected to become king; Ailred of Rievaulx says Alexander's illegitimate son inherited his father's hatred and persecution of David. Against all of which we have to set contemporary statements that Alexander left the kingdom to David, and the loyal service given by William fitz Duncan to the latter. Without further evidence the case must rest there.

When Edgar died at Edinburgh on 8 January 1107 his brother Alexander succeeded 'as King Henry granted him' according to the Anglo-Saxon Chronicle. The phrase is not found in John of Worcester, and it seems very unlikely that there would be a delay for consultation in January 1107. But we know that Edgar bequeathed an appanage to his youngest brother David, a move which implies some acknowledgment also of the king's successor – that is, that he designated Alexander as his heir. When these arrangements were made is not known, but it is entirely possible that they were put to, and approved by, Henry I some time before 1107, whence the Chronicle's 'granted'.[30]

David's appanage stretched from Lennox to the Solway but included also Teviotdale, as we know from his foundation of a monastery at Selkirk and restoration of the see of Glasgow. A clerk of that church called him *princeps et dux* of the inhabitants of the diocese, an echo of Frankish usage for 'the sub-royal rulers of places like Aquitaine, Bavaria and Brittany'.[31] He is also *Cumbrensis regionis princeps*, and *princeps Cumbrensis*, adding 'but he did not control all the Cumbrian *regio*'.[32] This last word, for 'kingdom', shows that

---

[29] The possibility that he was William son of Henry I, who is not known to have been in Scotland, is remote. On the other hand the *Willelmo nepote comitis* who witnesses Earl David's charter founding Selkirk, and whom Professor Barrow tentatively identifies with the English William, was, in my view, more probably William fitz Duncan, who occurs as *Willelmus nepos ... principis* [David]; *David I Charters*, nos 14, 15 and p. 180, col. 3. He is the king's *nepos*, in *ibid.*, nos 23, 52, 70, 83, 120, 121, 126, 130, 196. These descriptions as *nepos* (and not *filius Dunecani*) make more likely the identificantion of *Alexander nepos regis* as William.

[30] In his letter of congratulation to the new king (?1107), Archbishop Anselm thanked God 'who raised you into the paternal kingship by hereditary right after your brother'; *Councils and Ecclesiastical Documents*, ii, 169. A blunter letter from Henry I acknowledging Alexander's accession is quite likely and may underlie the Chronicle's comment.

[31] Crouch, *Image of Aristocracy*, 92.

[32] Lawrie, *Early Scottish Charters*, no. 50, partly re-edited in *David I Charters*, no. 15, where

the memory of the kingship of the Cumbrians, which Edward the Confessor had sought to restore in 1054, was still alive, even though it had no king but only a *princeps*, ruler, the word which came to be used in Welsh kingdoms after 1150.[33]

How David came by his appanage is revealed mainly by the rhetoric of Ailred of Rievaulx, who makes Robert Bruce the elder in 1138 claim that English and Normans restored Edgar (in 1097), and that 'you yourself, oh king, when you demanded from your brother Alexander the part of the kingdom which [Edgar] bequeathed to you at his death, obtained without bloodshed all that you wanted through fear of us'.[34] Such a bequest to David implies recognition that Alexander would inherit the kingship. It is possible that this division was one of heritage and conquest, that is that Edgar had acquired Strathclyde and was free to bequeath it to a younger brother, but this is unlikely because Maelcoluim III was lord of the south-west, and there is no hint of Strathclyde being outside Scottish control so late as *c.* 1100.

Rather this seems to have been a partition of the kingdom like that demanded by Edmund of Domnall III. David got much more than villages or even royal shires, but it is noticeable that Ailred says also that David obtained all that he wanted – which could be something different from the bequest. Edgar probably left him the Cumbrian *regio* (the former kingdom of Strathclyde), which was the diocese of Glasgow. In this 'kingdom' David acted without a hint of deference to the authority of Alexander I (for example in his general charter to Selkirk abbey), a *princeps* indeed; when king he was to refer to the four districts 'which I had when King Alexander was alive', anodyne hindsight.[35]

But this was not the whole of David's lordship before 1124, for charters show that it extended beyond Cumbria to include Lower Tweeddale, the land between Lammermuir and the Tweed, the later sheriffdom of Berwick. Here David was not *princeps* for both he and Alexander I took responsibility for protecting the monks of Durham. Each gave a writ confirming 'for my part' Edgar's grant of Swinton to St Cuthbert; Alexander's forbids the monks to answer any claim to this land unless the king orders it himself, 'because I and my brother David will acquit [it] to the monks'. David's writ makes no reference to Alexander's but forbids his men to trouble the monks over Swinton which they are to hold perpetually. But each also had to issue

there is a comprehensive modern bibliography and discussion. The facsimile in *Glasgow Registrum*, i, is helpful for the text.

[33] Crouch, *Image of Aristocracy*, 85–96; Jenkins, 'Kings, Lords and Princes'.

[34] *Chronicles of Stephen*, iii, 193.

[35] In his general charter to Selkirk abbey, David is called *David comes filius Malcolmi regis Scottorum*, the patronymic used by his brothers as kings in 1094–95; this document is dated in the reigns of Henry in England and Alexander in *Scocia* – in that order. *David I Charters*, no. 14. For Cumbria and the four districts (*cadrez*) of 'Galloway', identifiable with Strathgryfe (Renfrewshire), Cunningham, Kyle and Carrick (Ayrshire), *ibid.*, nos 14, 183 (p. 144), and nos 57, 58.

another writ on this toun, David granting it free 'to do your will on it ...; from now for sure I will not suffer anyone to trouble you over it', while Alexander wrote to the prior of Durham forbidding him to enter into any plea over Swinton 'before it comes before me'. Dispute over these lands was to continue, but here we can identify the troublemakers as tenants of the absentee Earl David, whose court was evidently unable to protect the monks; they appealed over his head to the king, who obligingly insisted that he should hear any case.

King Edgar had given Fishwick and some of adjacent Horndean, to St Cuthbert. Later the tenants (drengs) of Horndean resisted the monks' possession there, and David heard the plea between them, deciding that if the monks had witnesses or Edgar's writ, they should keep the land; subsequently they produced Edgar's writ, which David read and sent to his agents in Scotland so that the monks should have what it evidenced.[36] Alexander I was not called upon to intervene, for David's tenants here were not men of substance. The agents (as with Swinton) were men of Teviotdale but evidently with authority also in Lower Tweeddale, where David and his agents were the immediate authority. But it was held, perhaps as a fief, under Alexander I, a relationship which did not exist in the Cumbrian *regio*. The difference arose in the circumstances of David's acquisition, which was surely resisted by that devotee of St Cuthbert, Alexander I. Lower Tweed-dale, it seems, was no part of Edgar's legacy but was yielded under pressure.

Earl David confirmed Swinton as held 'on the day [Edgar] was alive and dead and as I granted it after the death of that brother of mine', words which imply a lapse of time between the death and David's grant. The only evidence that David acquired his southern Scottish lands soon after Edgar's death in 1107 is the designation of him as 'David my brother' (without 'earl') in Alexander I's Swinton charter,[37] whose partner is a charter of Earl David, so that the omission was probably an oversight – or perhaps delib-erately ignored an English honour.[38] David cannot be shown to have acted in any capacity in Scotland after Edgar's charter to Durham of 1095 until his own charters, in all of which (before 1124) he is *Earl* David, acting after his marriage to Maud de Senlis and Henry I's conferment of an earldom. That marriage took place around Christmas 1113,[39] the grant of the earldom then or shortly thereafter.

[36] Lawrie, *Early Scottish Charters*, nos 20, 22, 26, 27, 29–32; *David I Charters*, nos 9–11. The Horndean letter of David (no. 11) was written up at Durham (*ibid.*, plate 1), and contains the memorable Latin *Et ideo uolo sciatis quod. Ut* is presumably omitted after *uolo*; see *ibid.*, p. 15.

[37] Lawrie, *Early Scottish Charters*, no. 26.

[38] Dr Judith Green, however, has taken this reference as evidence that David possessed his Scottish lands 1109 x 14; 'David I and Henry I', *SHR*, lxxv (1996), 5. After Henry became earl in 1139 he could still be described as David's son, without title.

[39] *David I Charters*, 53, comment to no. 1; Green, 'David I and Henry I', *SHR*, lxxv, 6.

He had acquired his Scottish lands by then, for Selkirk abbey was founded from Tiron in 1113. From the rather confused account in the life of St Bernard of Tiron, David, in possession of Lothian and Northampton (that is already earl), requested monks from Tiron who established their monastery by the Tweed close to Northumbria (that is Kelso); later he went to see St Bernard, arriving to find him dead (1116 or 1117), but after he became king, he visited Tiron again and brought back an abbot and twelve monks. The monastery David established was at Selkirk, not close to Northumbria; and if he brought back Abbot William, as is most likely, the date was the earlier visit, of 1116–17, for William returned to Tiron when elected abbot thereof in 1118. Earl David visited Tiron in 1116–17, but the foundation of a Tironensian house, which must be Selkirk, had already taken place, but, despite the life of St Bernard, before he was earl: the later-written annal which claims that in 1113 'monks of Tiron came to ... Selkirk' is correct and David was in possession of Teviotdale by that date.[40]

Yet that does not tell us how long he had been in possession, for the truth is that while 'David brother of the queen' was active in England as late as 1108, there is no trace of his whereabouts from then until the (1113) foundation of Selkirk, marriage and grant of an earldom. The silent assumption has been that, having recovered his inheritance, he was in Scotland, though there is no trace of him there, either, in these years. He must have formed an opinion of Tiron and its monks at some time, must have become acquainted with John 'a certain religious man who educated him', his chaplain whom he made bishop of Glasgow c.1116. John later (1138) exiled himself to Tiron, suggesting that as 'a religious man' he had been there before entering David's service. In short, we need a French period in David's career, which, given his enthusiasm for the monastic order, would have ended in or not long before 1113. To this period his lordship in the Cotentin peninsula can also belong; he was still exercising that lordship c.1114, but no more is heard of it thereafter.[41]

While Orderic's account of David being brought up at Henry I's court among the household young bloods (*domestici pueri*) and being knighted by the king is doubtless correct, 'inseparable from [Henry's] court' is probably not to be taken literally.[42] Nonetheless the passage does hint that the English force which helped David to obtain his land 'without bloodshed' (in Ailred's words) would have at least the blessing of Henry I and perhaps his over-sight.[43] Now the later (c.1400) account of Nostell priory has King Henry on his way to Scotland with an army to repress rebels, leaving at Pontefract a clerk Ralph who had fallen ill and who joined the hermits at Nostell; Henry,

[40] The evidence is discussed in Barrow, *Kingdom of the Scots*, 174–76, 199–204.

[41] Lawrie, *Early Scottish Charters*, no. 50; *David I Charters*, nos 2, 1.

[42] *Orderic Vitalis*, iv, 274–75.

[43] Dr Green calls it 'armed forces provided by King Henry', but (sadly) Ailred does not say that; *SHR*, lxxv, 3; *Chronicles of Stephen*, iii, 193; *SAEC*, 193.

'the business for which he had gone having been despatched in peace, entered England with his army [and] came to Pontefract' where he introduced the Augustinian rule in '1120'.[44]

The visit of Henry to Pontefract and the Ralph episode are attributable to 1105,[45] when a peaceful invasion of Scotland is unlikely – as is the date 1120 in the Nostell account. Different episodes have here been combined (as in the life of St Bernard of Tiron), and while there is no other evidence that Henry himself went to, or across, the Border, the implication of a royally-sponsored expedition into a recalcitrant Scotland which achieved its aim *without warfare*, is unambiguous and may be associated with Ailred's version of David's recovery of his appanage *without bloodshed*, which must have occurred between 1107 and 1113.

Of Henry's three known visits to the north of England only that between 1108 and 1114 is a possible date for these events. It is shown by charters dated at York, and the editors of Henry's *Regesta* suggest that its most probable year, between 1108 and 1114, is 1109; but the evidence is not strong.[46] Henry was in France in 1108 – June 1109 and again August 1111 – July 1113; if David was as close to him as Orderic would have us believe, he could well have been justifying his knighthood in French fields in the same years, and possibly continuously from 1108 to 1113, for this would explain his acquaintance with Tiron and his lands in the Cotentin. The invitation to monks of Tiron to come to Scotland would have been extended while David was still in France in anticipation of recovery of his appanage, and would be activated on that recovery.

Henry I could have gone to York soon after his return to England in July 1113 to arrange the expedition to Scotland. David's acquisition of his appanage plus Lower Tweeddale, followed by the honours of his marriage to a wealthy widow and heiress at Christmas and of his earldom, become a fitting recognition of his French service to the English king. Moreover the unique appearance of Alexander I when king, in England, leading a contingent in the war against the Welsh in 1114, is more readily understood as a personal submission to, or reconciliation with, the English king, after Alexander's unsuccessful defiance of David, whom, Ailred would have us believe, he hated and persecuted.[47] The addition of Berwickshire to David's

[44] *Negociis pro quibus rex ierat expeditis in pace cum exercitu suo Angliam ingressus Pontefractum deuenit.* The full text is printed in *SHR*, vii (1910), 157–58.

[45] *RRAN*, ii, no. 653 (25 September, probably of 1103) shows Ralph the chaplain as addressee of a writ; he seems to have had custody of Bury St Edmunds abbey; *ibid.*, p. x. Henry I was apparently at York in the autumn of 1105; *ibid.*, nos 713–15.

[46] *RRAN*, ii, p. xxx, nos 710, 925–27, dated at York. In 1109, Henry I dated charters at Westminster in June and at Christmas, and at a council at Nottingham on 17 October. Robert Bruce witnessed one charter at the Nottingham council and the York charters which is the reason for placing the latter in 1109. On the other hand, there is no firm evidence as to Henry's whereabouts in 1113, between July and Christmas at Westminster.

[47] *Chronicles of Stephen*, iii, 193; Orderic makes no such suggestion.

Cumbrensis regio was a bonus extracted by the English expedition, and is to be seen in the context of the 'Norman conquest' of northern England carried out largely under Henry I;[48] David's holdings placed a reliable client along the whole northern border of the English kingdom.

But there is more, for version B of the foundation legend of St Andrews, written by Robert, a canon of Nostell who became prior of St Andrews, is explicit that when Alexander restored the Boar's Rake to St Andrews, with the purpose of establishing religious life there, there were many witnesses and 'his brother Earl David also granted [it], whom the king had named (*destinauerat*) his heir and successor in the kingdom'.[49] Written by a man who knew St Andrews and David I well, this is invaluable testimony that the designation of an heir by Maelcoluim III was practised also by at least one of his sons, testimony confirmed by Orderic: Alexander 'bequeathed the kingship' (*regnum dimisit*) to David.[50] This makes it the more probable that Edgar too had recognised Alexander as his successor, but it shows that if Alexander had intended William fitz Duncan as his successor, he must have changed his mind by 1124.

The date at which David was recognised as heir is likely to have been latish in Alexander's reign, possibly after the death of Queen Sibilla on 12 July 1122. The only possible rivals to him were William fitz Duncan, and Alexander's illegitimate son, Malcolm. The *Historia Regum* comments that in 1124 David succeeded without opposition to the kingship (*regnum*) which his brother had held with great effort (*laboriosissime*), so no claim was made by or on behalf of William fitz Duncan, who fought to obtain for himself the honour of Skipton in the civil war of Stephen's reign.[51] Had Alexander I had a lawful son, mature at the time of his death, to become king, the Cumbrian *regio* would presumably have remained with David and his heirs, its status a running sore within the kingdom of Alexander's descendants.[52] Perhaps we should note that William of Malmesbury, who hailed David as 'sole heir of such kings and princes', his ancestors, and who damned Duncan II as a bastard, admitted that Sibilla bore Alexander no issue 'that I know of', suggesting an imperfect acquaintance with David's accession.[53]

There is no hint that Henry I was asked, or spoke up, when David became king, but this succession was not without event, for Ailred of Rievaulx, in

---

[48] Kapelle, *Norman Conquest of the North*, ch. 7; Dalton, *Conquest, Anarchy and Lordship*, chs 2, 3 and pp. 196–203.

[49] *Chron. Picts-Scots*, 190.

[50] *Orderic Vitalis*, iv, 274–75.

[51] Dalton, *Conquest, Anarchy and Lordship*, 211–17.

[52] A more interesting question is, what would have happened if Alexander had remarried and died leaving a child-son?

[53] William of Malmesbury, *GRA*, i, 724–26; *de qua ille uiua nec sobolem, quod sciam, tulit …* William goes on to decry Sibilla's charms and Alexander's affection for her. The slight documentary evidence suggests that they were a devoted couple.

his obituary of the king, remarks among David's virtues that he accepted kingship reluctantly, 'and hence so abhorred those *obsequia* which are offered by the race of Scots in the manner of their fathers upon the recent promotion of their kings, that he was with difficulty compelled by the bishops to receive them'.[54] This is valuable evidence that already the bishops played a part in the inauguration, though from 1115 until 1126 there was no bishop of St Andrews to do so; bishops of other sees, notably Dunkeld, would doubtless fill any gap. For the *obsequia*, gestures of subordination or allegiance, we can import ancient Roman acclamation by raising on shields, but must acknowledge that a century later, apart from the enthronement itself, which was surely unexceptionable, the only known trace of the *obsequia* was throwing cloaks on the ground before the new king. Whatever David objected to unsuccessfully was evidently modified under his successors.

Yet his rejection of some ancestral custom was a sign of his upbringing in the culture of the court and army of Henry I of England. His earliest acts were the grant of Annandale to his familiar Robert de Brus, and the recording of that grant in a charter dated at Scone, and perhaps therefore at his inauguration in 1124, the earliest known to a layman.[55] Within a few years, too, he began the establishment of religious houses south of Forth (in addition to Selkirk) and generosity to others in Fife, houses which were to transform the religious map of Scotland. While the migration of knights from England to Scotland undoubtedly received a boost from the English civil war after 1138, it had already begun in the 1120s, encouraged by David's continuing contact with the realm of England and his earldom there. In 1126–27 he spent the best part of a year in England and in 1130 was at Henry I's court when rebellion broke out in Scotland.

Orderic Vitalis, in an otherwise highly-coloured passage on Scotland, seems to be on factual ground in identifying the rebel, Malcolm, 'the bastard son of Alexander [I]' – the only explicit statement of his origins, for he was not Malcolm mac Heth – as seeking to seize the kingdom from David in two fierce battles. Orderic alone associates Malcolm with the rising by Angus earl of Moray in 1130 which was known to the Anglo-Saxon Chronicle and to Irish annals and ended in Angus' defeat and death and the king's annexation of his earldom. Ailred of Rievaulx claims that Malcolm surrendered to an English contingent which had met David at Carlisle, and was handed over in fetters to him. The year was 1134, when Malcolm was imprisoned at Roxburgh, and we can date the two battles to 1130 and 1134.[56]

---

[54] *SAEC*, 232; *Chron. Fordun*, i, 237.

[55] *David I Charters*, no. 16. Professor Barrow suggests that the reference in this charter to Ranulph le Meschin (who lost Carlisle in 1120) means that Brus had been given Annandale before 1124.

[56] The last entry in ASC MS D, which ended in 1079, is this rebellion of Angus (without mention of Malcolm), added under mlxxx instead of mcxxx. It is not found in MS E which

He had apparently married a sister of Somerled, lord of Argyll who rebelled in 1153; in 1156 Donald son of Malcolm was taken prisoner and joined his father in captivity in Roxburgh.[57] Thus both languished in Roxburgh, owing escape from a rebel's fate of death and even the blinding to which Domnall III seems to have been subject, to their royal filiation.[58]

Orderic, who was writing c.1135, ignorant of the imprisonment, gives us a comprehensible motive for the rising of 1130, that Malcolm sought the kingdom. That there was significant northern support for such a claim suggests that the discrimination between lawful and illegitimate sons, widely accepted in lowland society by this date, had not penetrated the Gaidhealtachd; but support for this cause in David's reign was evidently limited. Orderic's placing Angus's name first may suggest that Malcolm was a tool of this earl, leader of the rising. Doubtless both men sought to exploit the occasion of the king's absence in England, but the absence may also have been sufficient cause of a feeling among magnates that rebellion might succeed. Resentment at subservience to the English king was certainly a feature among magnates thirty and fifty years later.

In fact there is no hint that David I had renewed his homage to Henry I in 1124 when he became king of Scots. It sufficed that he had already become Henry's *fidelis* when given the midland earldom and that he continued to act as such by attending Henry's court and acting as his justice on occasion. From 1124 there was no Welsh war to require his service, and though Henry was much in Normandy, an uneasy peace with Louis VI held. The problems which Henry faced in holding together his Anglo-Norman domain, were compounded by his need to secure the succession for his daughter, the Empress Matilda, whom he married to the heir, later count, of Anjou, thereby adding to her unpopularity, yet giving her no territorial base within his domains.[59]

From 1127 Henry I saw David's support after his own death as essential to securing Matilda's succession; he had more incentive, more need, to honour the Scottish king than to exploit him. From 1130 till 1136 David seems to have remained in Scotland, perhaps warned of the dangers of absence by the rising of Malcolm. He was not king of Scots by gift of King Henry, and King Henry was not his lord in Scotland. Nor did David I become the *fidelis* of Stephen king of England; his son Henry, inheriting a claim to the midland earldom and to the earldom of Northumbria from his

---

ends in 1154. *AU*, i, 578 (1130.4). *Orderic Vitalis*, iv, 276–77; *Chronicles of Stephen*, iii, 193; *Chron. Melrose*, under 1130; *ESSH*, ii, 173–74.

[57] *Chron. Holyrood*, 128, saying that Donald was imprisoned with his father – but there is no entry for Malcolm's imprisonment in 1130; both events are in the Melrose chronicle.

[58] I leave aside the claim and rebellions of Wimund, for whom we have, in effect, only the tale told by William of Newburgh; he was blinded and emasculated.

[59] Stringer, *Reign of Stephen*; but see now Crouch, *Reign of King Stephen, 1135–54*, ch. 1.

mother, did do homage to Stephen and retained Northumbria from 1138 (as earl from 1139) until his death in 1152, but David did homage neither for the Midland earldom nor for anything else.

In 1141 he openly joined the Empress in her war against King Stephen, but after their defeat at Winchester, David fled north and played no further part in the desultory war of the 1140s. His son Earl Henry retained the earldom of Northumbria, but the western part of it, including Carlisle, remained in David's hands, perhaps as security against the claims of Ranulph earl of Chester; in law David's only title was in right of his deceased wife. Both David and Earl Henry are found there; coins were struck there in the names of King Stephen and of David and Henry. Only in 1149 was the Angevin cause revived by Henry son of the Empress, who came to England, then north to David I at Carlisle at Whitsun (22 May). In the festivities which followed the sixteen-year old Henry was knighted by King David, assisted by Earl Henry and the earl of Chester, who now abandoned his claim to Cumbria and in return was recognised as lord of northern Lancashire.

This earl did homage to King David, but there is no sign in contemporary sources of a new relationship – such as fealty – between David or his son on the one hand and Henry fitz Empress on the other. Two later chroniclers claimed independently that before being knighted Henry promised that he would never deprive David's heirs of the lands they held in northern England, and that Northumbria was to be held by David and his heirs of Henry fitz Empress when he succeeded to the English throne; but this claim is unknown to contemporary sources and was possibly invented in reaction to the deprival in 1157.[60]

With only one son, two, later three, grandsons, and no surviving brothers, David had little to fear about the succession to his throne. In England Henry I, perhaps anxious about the claims of the son of his brother and prisoner, Duke Robert, tried to associate his own son William in the kingship in 1114–15, by securing homage and fealty to him in both Normandy and England, and from 1127 tried to ensure the Empress's succession.[61] The *locus classicus* for such anticipatory succession is Capetian France, where every king before Philip II (1180–1223) save one secured the consecration of his heir as king during his own lifetime. Only Philip I (1060–1108) had Louis VI recognised as, and entitled, *rex designatus*, but did not secure his

---

[60] *Chron. Howden*, i, 211; *Symeonis Opera*, ii, 322–23; *Chronicles of Stephen*, i, 70. I have greatly benefited from the discussion by Dr David Crouch in his *Reign of King Stephen*, 242–43, 322–24. The later chroniclers are William of Newburgh and Roger Howden, both writing in the 1190s. Howden does not seem to have used Newburgh, and has no account of the 1157 episode. My account of 1149 in *Making of the Kingdom*, 222–23 needs revision.

[61] William of Malmesbury, *GRA*, i, 758–59; *ASC*, under 1115; Green, *Government of England under Henry I*, 11.

consecration, and Louis' accession (1108) was accompanied by baronial turbulence.

Nonetheless *c.*1120 Louis himself designated as king his heir, Philip, a child, securing a promise that the prelates and magnates would crown him after Louis' death. This move away from a consecrated associate king to a nominated *rex designatus* was reversed when, in 1129, Philip was crowned. At the latter's death in 1131, Louis swiftly had consecrated his second son (Louis VII) who, on the death of the father in 1137, hastened to Paris 'to forestall the pillagings, scandals and commotions which customarilly break out when kings die'.[62] The last such association, that of Philip II to Louis VII, was to share the burden of rule in old age. The interpretation of a royal line in danger from alternative claimants has been effectively dismissed for France, where the Capetians were the only royal race and where by the eleventh century, anticipatory association was becoming 'not the cause but the result of the hereditary character of the holding', and of the kingship.[63]

In two charters for St Andrews priory (1140 x 41), Henry son of David I was styled *rex designatus*;[64] and the same phrase recurs in the later version (B) of the legend of St Andrews, all probably the work of Prior Robert of that house.[65] It indicates familiarity with France under Louis VI on the part of the author, and may mislead us if we deduce from it that there was a formal designation of, or a magnates' oath to, Henry as the next king, for the title is found nowhere else. Any designation would have to be placed at the beginning of the reign, for from 1126 at least, when Henry was probably little more than ten years old, the king sometimes made special mention of him.[66] Some royal charters are paired by acts running in Henry's name, and in others his consent to David's act is specifically indicated.[67] There is even one act by David and Henry jointly, but it concerns Swinton and is perhaps to be explained by Henry acting as justice in an action over that troublesome toun.[68]

Professor Barrow, analysing these occurrences, has pointed out that they are found only with perpetuities, and that there are no such joint

---

[62] This paragraph is based upon Lewis, *Royal Succession in Capetian France*, ch. 2, and upon his paper, 'Anticipatory Association of the Heir in Early Capetian France', *American Historical Review*, 83 (1978), 906–27. The quotation is from Suger's life of Louis VI. The matter has been discussed recently in *David I Charters*, 5–6.

[63] Lewis, 'Anticipatory Association', 921.

[64] Lawrie, *Early Scottish Charters*, no. 162; nos 163, 164 = *David I Charters*, nos 126, 129. The latter two call Henry *heres ... et rex designatus*. I hope to justify the revised date for these charters in a separate paper.

[65] *Chron. Picts-Scots*, 193.

[66] *David I Charters*, nos 31–32. where the date is followed by *testimonio et concessu Henrici filii mei. Et isti alii sunt inde testes ...* For examples of similar formulae, *ibid.*, nos 39, 47, 96, and for Earl Henry as witness, *ibid.*, p. 7, list 5a, reading 14, 31, 32, 34 ...

[67] *David I Charters*, 6–7, where the documents in the various categories are listed.

[68] *David I Charters*, no. 53, cf. 54.

or duplicate brieves, suggesting that the two did not act administratively together. The general bias of David's charters is towards churches and lands south of Forth, and so parallel acts by Henry for the north will also be less likely; nonetheless he did consent in David's two diplomas to Dunfermline abbey and in another grant to that abbey, and participated in the moves to found the priory in St Andrews, in the two *rex designatus* charters.[69] While Henry's activity in government was less north of Forth, this was probably because involvement with English lands kept him in southern Scotland from 1139 rather than a formal limitation of authority.

But the mentions of Henry in perpetuities fulfilled a positive function. In 146 charters of David I there are over fifty references to 'my son', or '(Earl) Henry my son', of which only two also call him 'heir'.[70] 'Son and heir' was tautologous: all sons were potential heirs, but a single son – and from 1130 it was clear that Henry would have no sibling unless David remarried – would inevitably inherit if he survived. The point of associating Henry in David's grants, therefore, was to assure the beneficiary of the grant that he would have title for two generations, an early form of royal warrandice. That is why in some cases the beneficiary drafted the acts to mention Henry, or sought a pair from Henry – for it is inherently unlikely that the king and his son urged, or insisted on, these forms.

David I was able to assume that on his death Henry, an experienced adult and the only possible heir, would succeed rapidly and without disturbance. He was the anticipated king, succeeding by an indefeasible heritable right. The only hint that William fitz Duncan, or, after his death about 1151, his son William the ætheling, was seen as having a claim to the succession, is found in the Orkneyinga saga's claim that all Scots wished to have William the ætheling as king, a claim which probably reflects the Mac William risings after 1179.[71] On the death of Earl Henry in June 1152, the lineal descent of the succession was not endangered, but there was a much increased likelihood of turbulence at the king's death. Following the death of Earl Henry, John of Hexham has David take (Malcolm) 'his son's eldest son, and, giving him Earl Duncan [of Fife] as *rector* with a numerous army, ordered that this boy should be taken round the provinces of Scotland and be proclaimed heir to the kingship'.[72]

---

[69] *David I Charters*, 7–8; nos 33, 172, 171, 126, 129. Henry was also involved in no. 159, the general charter to Cambuskenneth abbey, which is north of Forth, though most of its endowments were to the south thereof.

[70] *David I Charters*, nos 120, 126. In 51 charters of Henry, he calls himself heir once, in *rex designatus* no. 129 (corresponding to no. 126); but not in no. 121 (corresponding to no. 120). In no. 200 he is neither son nor heir. This underlines how uncharacteristic the *rex designatus* charters are.

[71] *Orkneyinga Saga*, c. 33.

[72] The title of *rector* was later given to William Marshall as leading regent for the young

Either Earl Duncan was merely tutor for the lad during the tour of Scotland, or something more long term was intended, including securing the peaceful accession of Malcolm. The earl's leading role in the king's inauguration (attested much later), supports the longer-term purpose. The large army, which must have taken several weeks to travel between Galloway and Buchan, even if a troop of twenty or so knights and some infantry is all that was meant, was a costly display, far greater than the provision of a fitting retinue; it was designed to overawe and prevent serious turbulence at David's death. For that purpose, an authority which could command the king's knights to maintain peace before and after the young Malcolm's accession was surely Earl Duncan's intended function.

He was evidently successful. John of Hexham, writing between 1153 and 1165, described how 'the whole people of the land, bearing (*tollens*) Malcolm ... constituted him, still a boy of twelve years, as king at Scone, as is the custom of that nation',[73] implying a form of recognition by elevation and/or acclamation. The date of that inauguration, accepting a reign length of twelve years, six months and fourteen days,[74] by inclusive reckoning would be Wednesday, 27 May 1153,[75] three days after the death of his grandfather at Carlisle, too short a time to have brought David to burial at Dunfermline abbey. The attacks on Malcolm's authority by those described vaguely by William of Newburgh as 'who either thought fit to attack him or refused him his dues',[76] did not begin till November 1153, when the revolt of Somerled of Argyll broke out; associated with him were the 'sons of Malcolm', that is of Alexander I's bastard.

However, they are usually taken as the sons of Malcolm mac Heth, who, in 1157 was reconciled with King Malcolm. The earl called Aed or (h)Eth who witnessed two charters early in David I's reign disappears without leaving an identifiable successor and may have lost his earldom in 1130;[77] he was probably the father of this Malcolm who subsequently became earl of Ross and died in 1168. He was not replaced and his descendants resurfaced as rebels in the early thirteenth century. He is often compounded with the bastard Malcolm because one is mentioned in 1156 as a prisoner, the other in 1157 as reconciled.[78] But the patronymic given to the 1157 Malcolm was

Henry III of England in 1216. *Chronicles of Stephen*, i, 70; *Symeonis Opera*, ii, 327; *SAEC*, 228–29.

[73] *Symeonis Opera*, ii, 331; *SAEC*, 232. The correct reading, *apud Sconam*, is established by Professor Barrow, *RRS*, i, 7n.

[74] The alternative, twenty days, is impossible. *Chron. Picts-Scots*, 133, 175, 181, 207, 212, etc. Dunbar, *Scottish Kings*, 74, n. 22 reports only the Chronicle of Huntingdon, and errs in giving thirteen days: Palgrave, *Docs. Hist. Scot.*, 103.

[75] The following day was the feast of the Ascension.

[76] *Chronicles of Stephen*, i, 76; *SAEC*, 236–37.

[77] *David I Charters*, nos 33, 44; he also signed Alexander I's diploma and witnessed one writ for Scone priory as *Beth comes*. (Lawrie, *Early Scottish Charters*, 30, 44, nos 36, 49.)

[78] *Chron. Holyrood*, 129–31, 150–51; *RRS*, i, nos 157, 179. For the compounding, found from *Gest. Ann.* to Anderson, cf. the text and translation of *Orderic Vitalis*, iv, 277.

surely to distinguish him from the 1156 one; they were separate individuals, and the 1157 Malcolm may not have been a rebel, but a son to whom his heritage was restored.[79]

Malcolm IV was heir to Scotland but also to Northumbria, of which he kept Cumberland in his own hands; he and his brother, William earl of Northumberland, were briefly left in peace by their cousin, Henry II, crowned in 1154. Yet the right of Henry to homage could not be denied, and in 1157 Malcolm met him at Chester for that purpose. If there had been a promise in 1149 that David's heirs should keep Northumbria, Henry now renegued upon it, refusing to tolerate the usurpation of the earldom under Stephen; it was surrendered. Huntingdon was given, not in exchange, but as another part of Henry II's firm aim, the restoration of title in England to that of Henry I's time.

Malcolm IV, the new earl, became Henry's man 'as his grandfather had been the man of the elder Henry, saving all his dignities', terms appropriate to the occasion but leaving specific obligations unclear to us. It is tempting, but almost certainly wrong, to see 'dignities' as Malcolm's royal dignity in Scotland; these were his rights as king of Scotland, not in Scotland, but in England when he came to the English court: dignified reception and escort and probably a daily allowance when there.[80] In 1158 when the two kings met again at Carlisle, they parted on bad terms, Malcolm denied the knighthood which he craved; the following year he took a contingent to France to help his lord, King Henry, in the siege of Toulouse, and was rewarded with knighthood by Henry. Whether this help was the act of a king of Scots or of an earl of Huntingdon we are not told; it was certainly the act of a man desperate for knightly arms, but that did not make it any more acceptable in Scotland.[81]

Malcolm returned in 1160 to face a major rebellion by Ferteth earl of Strathearn and five other 'earls' because he had gone to Toulouse.[82] They besieged the king in Perth, seeking to make him prisoner, but failed, suggesting that he had significant support, including probably Duncan IV earl of Fife, who would have taken priority in the annal if among the king's enemies. But even if we recognise Fergus lord of Galloway as one 'earl' (Malcolm campaigned thrice in Galloway to subdue his enemies), a rising by five others showed a very significant resentment at his absence in Henry's service. This may explain the events of 1163 when Henry II procured the

---

[79] Anderson, 'Wimund', *SHR*, vii, 29–36 accepts the 'one-Malcolm' assumption. His survey of the evidence on p. 32 is useful.

[80] See the discussion in *RRS*, i, 9–10, where Professor Barrow suggests that the homage phrase was 'deliberately vague and undefined'.

[81] *RRS*, i, 10–11.

[82] *Chron. Melrose*, under 1160; *ESSH*, ii, 244–45. There is an account of this rising in *Chron. Wyntoun*, iv, 422–23, which calls the rebels 'master men' (not earls), and names Ferteth and 'Gillandris Erdanagh' or 'Ergemauche'; he is not otherwise known.

submission of two Welsh princes, then went to Carlisle where Malcolm seems to have joined him. Certainly he was put to the test subsequently at Woodstock by Henry, when, with the Welsh princes, he was required to do homage to the Young Henry, and perhaps to the king himself also.[83] Henry also demanded castles, unspecified but clearly in Scotland, as surety for keeping the peace, but Malcolm averted what would have been a plain acknowledgment of Henry's authority over him as king of Scots by handing over his youngest brother, David, and sons of his barons, as hostages for keeping the peace.

Malcolm's severe illness at Doncaster in this year may have occurred on his way south, but I am more inclined to place it on his return journey and to dissociate it from Henry's demand, which was surely not an arbitrary whim. Its stringency anticipates the submission of King William a decade later after a major rebellion and suggests that Henry felt he had a serious grievance against Malcolm. That impression is strengthened by the word used by the chroniclers of the outcome, 'peace', meaning that a war-threatening disagreement had been settled. Henry's grievance may have been a failure or refusal by Malcolm to serve in the Welsh campaign, because of the hostile Scottish reaction in 1160 to his Toulouse expedition.[84]

This interpretation of the peace must remain speculative; if my suggestion is correct it brought a benefit to the kings of Scots, for not until 1294 was military service demanded of them, even in Henry II's frequent French campaigns in the years after 1174. Nothing suggests that it involved homage explicitly for Scotland, and the treaty of 1174 shows that if Henry was to have rights in Scotland, such explicitness was now necessary. The hostages given in 1163 were released, probably by 1170, when Henry II knighted one of them, David brother of the Scottish king.

Since the twelfth century historians have disagreed in their evaluations of Malcolm's rule, and of the weight to be given to his reputation as a virgin, attested soon after his death, apparently so at odds with his desire for knighthood and his military activity.[85] But his lack of interest in women may itself have been a consequence of the progressive illness which afflicted him from at least 1163 till his death in December 1165. A writ of 1162 x 64 is addressed to the justice of *Scotia*, the first mention of so wide a justice-ship, and a charter of 1162 x 65 speaks of pleas of the king only in the presence of the king or his 'supreme justice', an office recalling that by which England was ruled under kings absent for long periods in France – a form of regency in effect.[86]

---

[83] Ralph of Diss notes homage to the king and his son (*Diceto*, i, 311), Robert of Torigni homage to the son only (*Chronicles of Stephen*, iv, 218). For these years, *RRS*, i, 18–20.

[84] *Chron. Howden*, i, 219 is alone in mentioning the illness and does place it before the peace with Henry II; *Diceto*, i, 311; *Chronicles of Stephen*, iv, 218; *SAEC*, 242.

[85] A masterly survey in *RRS*, i, 22–26, with a balanced conclusion.

[86] *RRS*, i, nos 223, 220.

Now the author of *Gesta Annalia*, after a warm encomium of the king, concludes that out of piety he neglected government, so that the people (*plebs*) appointed his brother William as guardian (*custos*) of the kingdom. Later, on Malcolm's death, the prelates and magnates met at Scone at the command of William, 'then guardian', and set him up as king.[87] We may discount the pious neglect as a later 'improvement', and the title '*custos*' was familiar to the fourteenth-century compiler of *Gest. Ann.*, but is unlikely for 1165. Nonetheless the source used here, possibly a Coupar Angus abbey chronicle, knew of a delegation by Malcolm of some royal authority to William, perhaps as *suprema justicia*, and acceptance of his special position as king-in-waiting after Malcolm died.

His ecclesiastical activity, the establishment of Coupar Angus abbey (planned by David I) in 1164, and intervention with Henry II and Thomas Becket to promote peace between them, both suggest a concern with his spiritual welfare reflected by that clerk who in 1164–65 altered the usual addresses of royal charters, the king's 'good men', to 'all sons of catholic mother church'. In the king's final charter, issued in 1165 at Jedburgh, he sought 'remission and absolution from the church of Glasgow for all trespasses' done by him and his ancestors 'namely for lands which I gave to my barons and knights up to the day when I took the staff of pilgrim to Compostella'. First witness to the charter is William, the king's brother, 'granting the same', a phrase already used once by Malcolm in a charter to Glasgow cathedral, but here recognising William's special authority.[88] This is a king aged twenty-five desperately making his peace with the church, hoping to seek healing from the apostle James,[89] a king who was mortally ill.

For soon after his death, Richard, a clerk, composed verses consisting of one-line questions to the king's spirit and his one-line answers; these tell us unmistakeably that Malcolm had died in prolonged pain:

> Do you suffer torment or not?
>> I suffer no torment, indeed I am at rest
> What was your penance?
>> My harsh lot before death ...
> Formerly you were ill
>> Now I have recovered well ...[90]

William of Newburgh adds invaluable detail of the symptoms, severe head and foot pains for several years before death,[91] a description which fits with

---

[87] *Chron. Fordun*, i, 257, 259. Professor Watt tells me that the MSS clearly justify *custodis*, not Hearne's nonsensical reading *custodes* accepted by Skene.

[88] *RRS*, i, nos 257, 261, 263, 265, 114; cf. *David I Charters*, no. 200. William witnessed thirteen of Malcolm's 161 acts.

[89] Ten years later he would probably have gone to St Thomas at Canterbury, as Louis VII did.

[90] *Scotichronicon*, iv, 378–79, 496–97; *Chron. Fordun*, i, 452; *Chron. Wyntoun*, iv, 432–35.

[91] *Chronicles of Stephen*, i, 147–48; *SAEC*, 243–44.

the one-word description of the king in his obit in the Annals of Ulster: Maelcoluim *Cennmor* son of Henry, high king of Alba, died.[92] That the soubriquet 'big-head'[93] was applied to Malcolm IV in Scotland is attested only in the fifteenth century when Bower comments that he was called Malcolm 'Keanworth', to distinguish him from his great-grandfather, Malcolm 'Kenremor'; both are garbled versions of *Cennmor*. Although the Ulster annals are preserved only in a fifteenth-century manuscript, *Cennmor* is integral to the text[94] and it is most unlikely that *Cennmor* was added later to an obit written probably soon after 1165.

For all the evidence points in one direction. Malcolm IV suffered from Paget's disease, *osteatis deformans*,[95] now commoner in patients aged over forty, but 'not unknown in younger people', whose hallmark is 'excessive and disorganised resorption and formation of bone', particularly observable in the tibia and the skull. In the skull there is 'a characteristic enlargement of the vault, which is said to look like a soft beret or "tam-o'-shanter", which appears to descend over the ears'. William of Newburgh's 'feet' could well have been misreported legs. Those with such pronounced symptoms experience pain, even severe pain, in the affected bones, but, even before modern treatments, the disorder itself was not rapidly fatal unless bone sarcoma, signalled by rapidly worsening pain, set in.[96] Whether Malcolm suffered this latter or some other secondary ailment we cannot tell, but the descriptions we have point unmistakeably to Paget's disease as the reason for his soubriquet, and at least a contributory cause of his early death. His reputation as *Cennmor* must have reached Ireland from Scotland. Why he was not *Grosseteste*, nor *Gretheued* we cannot know, but *Cennmor* would seem to have persisted in a native written source until it was borrowed for the Macbeth–Macduff fiction, to be applied to Maelcoluim III. Such transfers can be parallelled elsewhere, for example in the legend of Kyffhäuser which arose after the death of Emperor Frederick II in 1250 and was later applied to his grandfather, Frederick I.[97]

That the Scotland which William inherited was a very different land from that of Maelcoluim III is shown by the peaceful – an earlier generation would have said 'constitutional' – transition which, in very exceptional

[92] *Maelcoluim cennmor mac Eanric ardri Alban. AU*, ii, 148–49.

[93] Without the modern pejorative meaning. Dunbar, *Scottish Kings*, 25 prefers 'great chief'.

[94] That is not interlined nor marginal. This was kindly checked for me by the Department of Manuscripts, Trinity College, Dublin.

[95] See another case: Byock and Skia, 'Disease and Archaeology in *Egil's Saga*: A First Look', *Haskins Society Journal*, iv (1992), 11–22. I owe this reference to Dr Alex Woolf.

[96] I asked a medical colleague to consider what illness could lead to the soubriquet 'big head'; we later met and I cited William of Newburgh. My colleague had had three possibilities, but with no hesitation discarded the alternatives in favour of Paget's disease. The quotations are from *Oxford Textbook of Medicine* (1996 edn), iii, 3075–77.

[97] Munz, *Frederick Barbarossa*, ch. 1. I owe this reference to Mr N. Shead.

circumstances, brought him to the throne. It was a land of immigrant lords and of monastic houses founded for the most part by David I, and of an ecclesiastical organisation whose elements were familiar throughout the western church. The process has been called Normanisation, the time an Anglo-Norman era. Yet some things had clearly not changed even by 1153. Lords and abbeys were given lands, but what they derived from these is revealed by the revenues from his estates which the king shared with his new monasteries, revenues in grain, fish, cheese and meat.

The long-developed economy of southern England, rich in silver coin, busy with commerce and manufactures, taxed relentlessly, acre by acre, to finance the king's needs, is a different world from the subsistence practices persisting in David I's Scotland. Coinage there was minted in England with the name of Henry I or Stephen until, in the late 1130s, mints were opened using dies with David's name upon them, centuries after kings in other European realms displayed their authority upon coins.

The Scottish king did have some ready cash, which came initially from his English 'fief' (as he called it) and from the rents paid by Scottish towns, and from customs paid on the cargos of merchant ships. Towns were centres of exchange, made possible by the use of money, some of which must have gone into the pockets of landowners selling wool, hides, even grain, to be shipped overseas. But if it was used by them to buy imported or urban manufactures, it did not yet trickle down into the economy of the countryside, for there is no trace of rents paid, or even assessed, in money until the middle of the twelfth century.

The king, however, was in a privileged position, for the towns were his, the custom of ships was his and the right to mint was his. As the money economy expanded, it enriched him more than other landowners, and gave him the means to enforce his peace, the precondition of a stable polity and developing economy. It is apparent that economic development, sometimes slower, sometimes rapid, was the determining characteristic of the twelfth and thirteenth centuries. This age of commerce, rural and urban, offered exploitation to kings, magnates and even peasants, whence the development of administration to increase revenues from land, of infeftment to secure title on transfer of land, and of written instruments, charters, to facilitate commerce in land. Commercialisation faces us wherever we look in twelfth- and thirteenth-century society, a progressive transformation of institutions and relationships which derides static concepts such as 'feudalism'.

Yet we do read for the first time under David I of knights, and of knight service as a condition for the owning of land – though the evidence is much more plentiful for the later twelfth century. There can be no doubt that noble immigrants had to produce knights for the king, and would retain 'men', also immigrants, for that purpose.[98] When that maintenance was

---

[98] Barrow, *Kingdom of the Scots*, 279–314.

arms, mount, bed and board it passed unnoticed in our sources. For under-standable reasons – expense, riotous behaviour, irregular calls for service, ageing and the wish to settle with a family – maintenance became grants of land, feus, of which we do hear. Knights reflect the danger of internal disturbance as in 1130 and 1160, and the need to match the military capacity of an English enemy, as in 1138–41 or 1173–74. The recorded feus held for knight service tell of a possession made secure by charter, and reflect the stable polity of a more peaceful society; but the king's army, when sum-moned, included knights serving under their lord because of the land they had, and native freemen serving as their ancestors had done, on foot (and perhaps on horseback) under the lord to whom they paid a farm, because of the land they had.

The rapid improvement in the knight's social standing during the twelfth century suggests that the military skill which secured him the lordship of king or great man under David I was soon limited to what might be required for the land with which he had been endowed. The penetration of the class of large and middling landowners in Scotland by migrants from the south was a striking feature of twelfth century social development and certainly brought with it Anglo-French names for persons, institutions and relation-ships. A good deal of evidence suggests that townsmen and lesser land-owners (knights and lairds) spoke English and extended the use of English from Anglian Lothian to other lowland areas in the east and north of the Tay, though the upper rank of the nobility (including earls of native origin) perhaps spoke Anglo-Norman in the reign of King William. Thus around 1200 free society in lowland Scotland was a reasonable simulacrum of that in England, poorer, less numerous, more primitively housed, but expressing the same ideas and ideals in related languages.

The division of the kingdom between this lowland agrarian society and the pastoral 'brute Scots' of the Gaelic north and west was no novelty; it is implied by the dominance of Fortriu among the Picts, and by the evidence that royal estates were scattered on the eastern side of the kingdom in the twelfth century and presumably for centuries before. What was new, however, perhaps from the 1070s, was the intercommuning between the lowland-based kingdom of the Scots and the neighbouring kingdom of England.

Two illustrations: the kingdom of Alba is a distant wraith to the compilers of the Anglo-Saxon Chronicle until the mid-eleventh century, when the Chronicle becomes a major source of our knowledge of Scotland; the Irish annals are a vital guide to tenth-century Alba, confirm what is told else-where of the eleventh century, but cease their interest from the 1130s; for the rest of the twelfth century, narrative comes, with little exception, from English writers. From the 1130s too Scotland had native coins, but their weight and fineness was generally that of the English penny, and the coins used here continued to be overwhelmingly English pennies; the Scottish kingdom, that is, belonged commercially to the English sterling area.

To reflect this change I have made another here, which the reader may have noticed, ceasing from 1094 to use the Gaelic forms of names of rulers and adopting the more familiar English forms. Alexander I is not Alasdair, and Malcolm IV, so anxious for knighthood and opposed by Somerled and many earls, does not seem comfortable as Maelcoluim. This is not lack of appreciation of the Gaelic element in Scottish society of the time, but is a compromise with tradition in the interests of intelligibility, and also to mark a real change in the culture of aristocratic society, nourished by closer intercommuning with England.

There was no Norman Conquest of Scotland, in the modern sense used of England in 1066, a devastation of the aristocracy and ultimately of the whole social structure of a colony whose king treated it as *tabula rasa* on which to write the names of his followers, and in which new rules of possession – tenure – were grafted onto the old law of English communities. The Norman who received land from William I or from a magnate held it as his acquisition – conquest – which he might give to a member of his family other than the oldest son who was, by Norman custom, the undisputable heir to his heritage (in effect his fief in the duchy of Normandy). Not until the next generation had succeeded did the English land become heritage whose descent the tenant could not lawfully divert from his eldest son. Acquisition and redistributed forfeiture endowed younger sons in the first generation after 1066, but by the reign of Henry I (1100–35), when northern England was given in fiefs, these resources were much rarer, and younger sons must take a fief from a father of limited generosity, or look elsewhere with an offer of service.[99]

Elsewhere included Scotland, where immigration begins as demand outstripped supply of new fiefs in England. Early in his reign or perhaps before his accession, David I gave Annandale to Robert de Brus, lord of Cleveland, whom he had probably known for some twenty years; the charter grants the castle also and the customs of the land, but there is no mention of fief. This was Robert's conquest, which, following the accepted custom of his generation, he destined for his younger son and namesake, a fief confirmed by David 'in fee and heritage to [the younger Robert] and his heir in forest'.[100] The witnesses to David's charters concerning Scotland show that his court was dominated by immigrants, some known to him in Normandy, some in his English honour, some younger sons, some refugees from the civil war in England after 1138; their number (excluding clerics) is

---

[99] On inheritance of land in England after 1066, the articles by Holt in his *Colonial England* and Hudson, *Land, Law, and Lordships*, chs 3, 4 and 6 are essential modern expositions.

[100] *David I Charters*, nos 16, 210. The use of the singular 'heir' in the later charter is not to be taken as a limitation to one generation; if it does imply a limitation, and that is not sure, then it would be to one son in each generation. See Hudson, *Land, Law and Lordship*, 97 n.4.

about seventy, but only twenty-three attested more than twice, i.e. put down roots in Scotland as significant landowners.

At the same time the number of native laymen witnessing is smaller, of the order of sixty, but twenty attested more than twice.[101] The earls may represent the aristocratic families of the eleventh century – a claim which is at best probable, for we know the name of not one of Maelcoluim III's earls, nor do we know by what custom lands or earldoms descended. A few non-earls were significant landowners,[102] but do not occur with the frequency of leading immigrants, to whom they often yield precedence, and others present were relatively humble *ministeriales*. Nonetheless they show that David had no *tabula rasa* in Scotland, and what we know of their endowments shows that the immigrants were confined to Scotland south of Tay, and mainly south of Forth.[103]

In the second half of the twelfth century immigrant influence greatly increased; native names, other than those of earls, disappeared from the court of King William, the names of those dependants of the great who followed them to Scotland become known to us, and families, great and less great, sent sprigs to settle north of the Tay and as far north as Moray and eventually Ross. The engine which moved them was no different from that which sent Normans to England, Spain or Sicily, French to the Holy Land, or Germans to the service of Slav princes beyond the Elbe: the demand for land created by population increase, and by the opportunity of more intensive and extensive cultivation.

By this time the distinction between heritage and conquest was disappearing. The landowner sought assurance that his endowment, land, belonged to him as *feodum* or feu, so that it would descend to his heir as 'feu and heritage', two words now with a single meaning. This acceptance of primogeniture as the custom of inheritance was not limited to land held in return for service of knights or serjeants, but whether it spread into lowland peasant tenures or into the highland zone where a 'kin-based' society is reputed to have existed, the lack of evidence forbids us to say. What we can say is that as the younger son lost prospect of his father's conquest, younger sons were increasingly likely to be endowed by their father with fiefs of their own, and by warrandice of record in a charter.

This is not the place to evaluate the relationship between the introduction of knight service and the clerkly terminology of the fief. But the endowments of monasteries speak eloquently of the concern of heads of noble families for the welfare of their descendants and imply the continuing

---

[101] I owe these figures to the lists in McDonald's thesis 'Kings and Princes in Scotland' (Guelph, 1993), 452–56.

[102] For example, Fergus of Galloway and his son Uhtred, Uviet the White, Leod of Brechin, Thor of Tranent.

[103] David granted one known charter at Aberdeen, witnessed by three earls and five others who were certainly not immigrants, and are not found elsewhere; *David I Charters*, no. 136.

responsibility of the noble for the status of the family, a responsibility identified with the heir in each generation. He might have the title of earl or office of steward; he would have the chief place or places of the lordship, and the right to services and to some judicial authority within that lordship. Primogeniture in heritage became part of the mind-set of noble society in the twelfth century.

And not just male primogeniture, for property passed from son-less noble to eldest daughter and her husband even before 1100 in England; 'she was the only means of continuing the lineage, the only legitimate route whereby her father's blood could be transmitted'. At some point after 1130 and probably before 1135 a new rule was made: that in these circumstances all daughters had equal rights, and the property was divided equally among their husbands as parceners (portioners), the eldest daughter having right to the chief place.[104] When Henry I sought to establish a right for his only daughter to the English throne in 1127, he was not making public law of private custom, for he would deny the kingship to her husband, Geoffrey of Anjou.

In Scotland primogeniture in the male line became the rule for heritage in the time of David I, if not earlier; succession by the husband of an heiress and then by portioners may have been contemporaneous or nearly so. The transformation from whatever customs (including perhaps freedom of bequest) which had theretofore applied is unremarked in our sources, but we can see it in the succession of the earldom of Fife, which probably passed to a brother in the 1130s, then to Earl Duncan, relationship unknown, who received a charter of the earldom from David I, specifying the service due.[105] The charter is lost, but this detail tells us that the tenure was as a feu, that is it was heritable; thereafter the earldom did descend by male primogeniture.

For the kingship, the eleventh century marked a shift from collateral succession among descendants of Cinaed mac Alpin to an uncertain inheritance by line, punctuated by conquest by Macbeth and perhaps his stepson. It may be that designation of an heir, as by Maelcoluim III, Edgar and David I, was designed to prevent usurpation from Maelcoluim's lineage – that is that there was already an acceptance of inheritance by line, even though the senior line (Duncan II's issue) might be excluded. The lack of children of Edgar and Alexander I may mean that collateral succession was seen by some in 1107 and 1124 while others discerned primogeniture; but since 1005 there had been only one instance of succession by a collateral (Domnall ban in 1093) where there were sons, and the royal house itself

---

[104] Holt, *Colonial England*, 245–69; the quotation is on 247. But the first statement is true only of the father's lineage, not of a lineage seen in the longer terms of, for example, a great-grandfather.

[105] *Nat. MSS. Scot.*, i, no. L; *David I Charters*, no. 267. It seems that Gillemichael, earl c.1130–36, was probably brother of his predecessor, Earl Constantine, since his tenure was so short. Constantine was not earl when in the company of 'King' Edgar in 1095.

was probably committed to lineal descent, as became apparent in 1153. Male primogeniture had become the preferred custom of succession to the throne.

There were still many differences between Scottish society and government on the one hand, and those of England on the other, but in a way not true in the time of Maelcoluim II. In the twelfth century Scotland shared the culture of catholic Europe in its English guise. The ceremonies for the making of a king in France and England varied yet had borrowed from one another and, sharing the use of Latin, contained many of the same symbolisms. Scotland, however, did not share in this ecclesiastical heritage, but practised an inauguration which, while admitting some ecclesiastical participation, was more overtly secular. It was, if not the Achilles heel, then at least a weakness, in the claim of Scottish kings to parity of esteem and authority with the English king. Parity of resources they could never have.

Note

Malcolm IV's bequests

Malcolm IV is recorded as having left 100 s. annually to Dunfermline abbey, where he was buried, but it seems that King William decided on the day of Malcolm's burial that it was to come from the burgh farm of Edinburgh 'until I assign the said payment to come from elsewhere' – though it was still coming from Edinburgh in the mid-fifteenth century.[106] That Malcolm did not specify a source points to a will made on his death-bed, which was not unusual. One of his charters giving the church of Forteviot to Richard of Stirling his chaplain, with witnesses datable to 1164 and the 'catholic mother church' address, survives only in a cartulary copy with the king's initial not 'M' but 'W'; it may have been reissued (or even issued for the first time) by King William to make it effective as part of Malcolm's will.[107] I suggest that the beneficiary was the clerk Richard who wrote the poem of dialogue with Malcolm's soul and was surely close to him.

[106] RRS, ii, 144, 142; Exchequer Rolls, vi, 25, 134, 313, 398.
[104] RRS, i, 22, 272; ii, 228.

CHAPTER 5

Scone and St Andrews

Much is made of the piety of Margaret and her husband, Maelcoluim III, on the evidence of the life of Margaret written by Turgot, prior of Durham. What little fact that it has shows the lady as patron of, for example, the shrine of St Andrew, but while she was responsible for the foundation of a Benedictine priory at Dunfermline, her husband took no known interest in the churches of his kingdom. He is completely absent from the correspondence of Gregory VII, a pope (1073–85) who took not a little interest, pastoral and political, in other peripheral lands. He wrote to the kings of Norway, Sweden and Denmark, and to Toirdhealbhach king of Ireland; he took an immediate interest in the province of Hamburg which included Scandinavia, and in a proposal to make Lund an archbishopric for Denmark, a situation not unlike York and St Andrews. Perhaps most interestingly, he encouraged the Scandinavian kings to remedy the 'divisiveness of ancient succession rights ... by their limitation to a single son who followed his father'.[1]

There is no papal letter to Scotland earlier than 1100, no sign that before then the clergy or king of Scotland sought guidance or authority from the papacy, and little evidence that they looked to England or northern Europe to learn about monastic life or canon law. But isolation ended, partly because the sons of Maelcoluim visited the new monastic houses in England, and partly because the claims of York, stated in terms of canon law, had to be repelled in the same terms. This chapter looks at one facet of royal involvement, at the establishment of canons of the Augustinian order at the royal inauguration place, Scone, by Alexander I, and the uncertain steps to secure the recognition of St Andrews, where they were also introduced, as a metropolitan see, and hence its archbishop as fit to give the church's rites of king-making.

John of Fordun claimed that a priory was 'founded and erected in Scone, superior seat of *regnum*' by Alexander I, 'in the place where kings, both Scottish and Pictish, anciently appointed the first seat of *regnum*'.[2] These

[1] Cowdrey, 'The Gregorian Reform in Anglo-Norman Lands and in Scandinavia', no. IX in his *Popes and Church Reform in the Eleventh Century*. The quotation is on p. 330.

[2] *Chron. Fordun*, i, 227; but *Gest. Ann.* describes it as 'where ancient kings had appointed the seat of the *regnum* of Alba, Cruthne [being] first king of Picts'; *ibid.*, i, 430.

antiquarian statements echo Malcolm IV's charter of confirmation to the abbey, which he said been founded 'in the principal seat of our *regnum*'.[3] Alexander I was perhaps following English precedent where Edward the Confessor (crowned at Winchester) refounded Westminster abbey, consecrated just before his death; his solemn crown-wearing there at Christmas 1065 has suggested that he intended it as the place for coronation, which it certainly was for Harold II and William I in 1066, and for all their crowned successors.[4]

Was Scone priory a place of similar kind, modelled by Alexander I upon Westminster? Scone had certainly been an important royal centre, where Causantin II and Bishop Cellach made a promise in 906 at the *ciuitas regalis*, royal rath, of Scone. The same chronicle, CKA, described Cinaed II (971–95) as giving 'the great *ciuitas* of Brechin to the Lord' – i.e. giving a great royal enclosure as a minster. From this sense of 'enclosure', *ciuitas* was used of monastic sites in Ireland, but it does not necessarilly mean 'monastery'.[5] Brechin, St Andrews where there was a Culdee monastery from the ninth century, Dunkeld, whither Cinaed I brought relics of Columba, and Abernethy, all left traces of their minster status in an abbot or 'abbacy' lands described as such in the twelfth century. There is no hint of such a survival from the church of Scone; on the contrary, Alexander I's endowment of the priory does not include Scone itself, which was one of four royal manors of Gowrie in the time of David I and Malcolm IV.[6] It was a royal thanage in 1234 and had its own sheriff from the 1130s until at least 1228,[7] presumably collecting royal dues from Gowrie. Alexander II certainly, and his son presumably, was lord of the toun or settlement of Scone, doubtless part of the thanage which was granted to the abbey by Robert I as late as 1312.[8] *Ciuitas* did not mean that there were Culdees in Scone before the Augustinians,[9] but that it was the centre of a royal estate, and so remained after the foundation of the priory. As Westminster was close to the great commercial centre of London, so was Scone to Perth, already important in the commerce of Scotland under Alexander I. The major difference between the two lies in the *re*foundation of West*minster*; Scone was a new foundation.

---

[3] *RRS*, i, no. 243 (1163 x 4): *in principali sede regni nostri fundate.*
[4] Henry III was crowned at Gloucester in 1216 but later crowned again at Westminster. Edward V was not crowned.
[5] See the discussion of *cathir*, possibly the word translated *ciuitas*, and in Scotland perhaps implying a shire or thanage (estate), in Barrow, *Kingdom of the Scots*, 65–66.
[6] *RRS*, i, no. 243.
[7] *Scone Liber*, no. 66 (thanage). For the sheriffs: Malotheni (1136) *Charters David I*, nos 44, 56 (x 1136); Ewen (1163–64) *RRS*, i, nos 243, 252; Macbeth (1190s) *Arbroath Lib.*, no. 35, *Inchaffray Lib.*, no 2; Malcolm (1203 x 10) *Coupar Angus Rental*, i, no. 71; Randolph (1216 x 19) *Scone Lib.*, no. 68; William Blund (12 April 1228), *St Andrews Lib.*, 237.
[8] *Scone Liber*, nos 74, 77, 94, 122; *RRS*, v, no. 17, and see the discussion there.
[9] Cowan and Easson, *Medieval Religious Houses, Scotland*, 236.

On 30 August 1104, when Henry I was busy in Normandy, the monks of Durham took from the raised coffin of St Cuthbert relics of him and of many other saints, including the head of St Oswald, the martyred Northumbrian king regarded as one of the founders of the church of Lindisfarne and hence of Durham. They replaced St Cuthbert but with Oswald's head alone, and by inspection vindicated the incorruption of Cuthbert's body; the translation proceeded with Oswald's head enshrined beside Cuthbert, to receive the prayers of the faithful.[10] Only one layman was present at the critical inspection: Earl Alexander, brother of Edgar king of Scots. Probably he came because of the family's devotion to the cult of Cuthbert, and persuaded by Prior Turgot who had known his mother. But his presence honoured his social distinction and strengthened his link with the saints at Durham and their community.

When he became king, Alexander at once asked Henry I for Turgot to become bishop of St Andrews, 'in which church is the see of the primate of the whole race of Scots' as its clergy claimed.[11] Turgot's consecration was delayed by controversy over the consecration of the new archbishop of York, Thomas, from whom the archbishop of Canterbury as 'primate' wanted a profession of obedience, and whom he forbade to commission other bishops to consecrate Turgot – though not denying that York should do so when himself consecrated. Behind this lay the acceptance into canon law of a rule that a bishop should be consecrated by his metropolitan and two other bishops, an archbishop by another archbishop and two bishops, and the claim of Canterbury to be not only a metropolitan archbishop (as York was) but also to be 'primate of all Britain', and as such entitled to profession of obedience from York, Scottish, Welsh and Irish bishops, as well as the bishops in Canterbury province. This claim had chimed with the view of his authority in Britain held by King William I of England, but the quarrel of Archbishop Anselm with Henry I meant that that king was less favourably disposed to the claims of Canterbury. When Anselm died in April 1109, there was no alternative (in Britain) to the consecration of Turgot by York in August 1109, without profession, but after a compromise brokered by Henry I whereby bishop and archbishop each reserved his rights.[12] Alexander I thus got his bishop from the church of Cuthbert and Oswald.

The first papal letters to Scotland, datable 1110 x 1114, reflect concerns raised by Turgot with Alexander I,[13] concerns essentially pastoral, with no

[10] *Symeonis Opera*, i, 248–61; *Chron. John of Worcester*, iii, 106–7.

[11] I quote from the Durham *Historia Regum* (*Symeonis Opera*, ii, 204) but have slightly changed its sense, for it claims that 'at the request of Alexander, Turgot was chosen by Henry I'. Eadmer, at Canterbury, has Alexander and his clergy and people appoint Turgot. The *Historia*'s remark about primacy was aimed, of course, at Canterbury's pretensions.

[12] *SAEC*, 130–32. The best discussion of the Canterbury–York difference in the context of the British Isles is in Flanagan, *Irish Society, Anglo-Norman Settlers*, chapter 1.

[13] *Cf.* Turgot's Life of Margaret, c. 8, e.g. in *ESSH*, ii, 70–74. For the bulls, Somerville,

hint urging foundations or endowment of the monastic order. Yet Turgot probably agreed with the establishment of Augustinian canons at Scone, for according to an addition to the Melrose chronicle made about a century later, in 1115 'the church of Scone was given over to canons',[14] a church presumably close to the royal centre, *ciuitas regalis*. Fordun, without date, records that Alexander I had a church built at Scone of stone and dedicated in the presence of a large company, and gave it over to canons regular from St Oswald of Nostell. This was copied by Walter Bower, abbot of Augustinian Inchcolm, in his *Scotichronicon*, adding 1114 as the date of foundation of the monastery; he then came upon an old leaflet (*libellus*) from which he was able to add that the dedication was by Turgot, bishop of St Andrews and monk of Durham, and that six canons were summoned from the church of St Oswald 'which is in Nostell' by agreement of Æthelwold, then its prior; one of the six, Robert was immediately elected prior of Scone.[15] The stylistic quirk of the church not 'of', but 'which is in', Nostell/Scone was found in the leaflet and in Alexander's diploma for the new priory, a link which suggests a common author, perhaps Prior Robert.

If the Melrose chronicle began the year '1115' at Christmas 1114 (as seems to be usual), while Bower's source began it on Lady Day, then the institution of canons may be datable to Christmas 1114 x 24 March 1115. The twentieth century rejected the 1114–15 date for the foundation of Scone priory on the fairly straightforward ground that the priory of Nostell in Yorkshire, whence the canons came, was not founded by this date, but only by *c.*1120. But the detail of the Nostell evidence suggests that secular clergy of Nostell, some or all, had accepted the Augustinian rule before February 1114, and influenced Alexander I to build a new church at Scone and secure its dedication before the spring of 1115, when Turgot departed Scotland. It is tempting to link these events with Alexander's service in Wales in the summer of 1114, a visit which could well have taken him by way of Pontefract and piously to St Oswald's church at Nostell. Such a contact would explain the call for canons thence, rather than from, say, the rather older (and nearer) convent of St Andrew, Hexham. Nostell canons arrived in 1115.

The failure of Alexander's diploma to name Turgot places its date in 1115 or later, but the two bishops subscribing it are 'bishop by authority of the holy apostles Peter and Paul and of the holy apostle Andrew', invoking the churches of York (dedicated to St Peter, often conjoined with St Paul)[16] and St Andrews. They have been consecrated by Turgot, perhaps also by York –

Scotia Pontificia, no. 2, 3 prints them as does Bethell, 'Two letters of Paschal II to Scotland', *SHR*, xlix (1970), 33–45 (misdating them), with discussion of the canonical issues.

[14] *Canonicis tradita est ecclesia de Scon.*

[15] *Chron. Fordun*, i, 227–28; ii, 217–18; *Scotichronicon*, iii, 106–11. *Ibid.*, 239 shows that the dedication by Turgot was added by Bower, presumably when he found the old leaflet.

[16] Aylmer and Cant, *History of York Minster*, 113.

or the reference may be to Turgot's consecration by York. In either case the Nostell-Scone canons who drew up the diploma had regard for the mother church of York and for Turgot's role at Scone.

The earlier church at Scone seems to have been parochial, in the western part of the Carse of Gowrie, where it was later revealed to have three dependent chapels.[17] But the choice of this place for royal kirk-building must surely be attributed to a more lively appreciation of the numinous significance of Scone itself, the place where kings of Scots received their dignity. The absence of coronation and unction from the Scottish in-auguration rite makes a shift of inauguration to a new monastic church quite improbable, unless the secular rites were put within the church and inte-grated within a catholic liturgy – which, as we shall see, they were not. The rededication of Scone by Turgot when the new monastic church was built implies that the purpose of bringing regular canons to it was a new one, a church-based inauguration rite. That should be seen in the wider context of Alexander I's generosity to the Augustinian order.

St Andrews, perhaps because it held a relic of the apostle, had established a leading role within the kingdom by 906; the title used by its bishop, *episcopus Scottorum*, though not attested until the twelfth century, was certainly older, and the form given in the annals of Ulster for Bishop Fothad in 1093, *ardepscop Alban*, 'chief bishop of Scotland', described his position.[18] To use 'primacy' or 'metropolitan' of Scotland is to introduce words which had acquired other implications in canon law, notably that of 'archbishop' recognised by receipt of a *pallium* from the pope, and enjoying the right to profession of obedience from other bishops. The earlier of two foundation legends of St Andrews stridently assserts that 'from this city, where the see is apostolic, ought to be the archiepiscopacy of all *Scotia*', that all bishops of *Scotia* should be ordained only by advice of its clergy (*seniores*), 'for this is a second Rome from the first [Rome], this is a pre-eminent city of refuge, this is the city of cities of *Scotia*', and it names leading figures of the church of St Andrews, of whom the first is 'Archbishop Giric', perhaps holding the see about 1100.[19]

Such was the claim, but no such recognition had been given canonically to the bishop of St Andrews, and, since the western church was organised into archiepiscopal provinces made up of episcopal dioceses, the bishops of Scotland, including St Andrews, lacking an archbishop, were either an

[17] The church of Scone is first explicitly named among the canons' possessions in a charter by Bishop Richard of St Andrews (1162–78), when the dependent chapels of Kinfauns, Craig and Rait are listed.

[18] *AU*, i, 527 (1093.2). The twelfth-century bishops of St Andrews called themselves *Episcopus Scottorum* on their seals. Professor Barrow has pointed out to me that similarly Irish *ri Alban* (= of Scotland) becomes Latin *rex Scottorum* (= of Scots).

[19] Broun, 'The Church of St Andrews and its foundation legend in the early twelfth century', *Kings, Clerics and Chronicles in Scotland*, ed. Taylor, 111–12.

anomaly or were part of the province of York. York claimed the latter, a claim rejected by the bishops and king of Scotland, whose dilemma was to justify the anomaly. It would disappear if St Andrews might receive archiepiscopal standing, for which Alexander I and David I certainly made bids.

In 1115 Alexander sought help from Ralph, formerly abbot of Séez who had been at the tomb-opening of 1104 and who was now archbishop of Canterbury, over the succession to Turgot, implying that the new bishop would be consecrated by him[20] – inevitable since Archbishop Thurstan of York, elected in 1114, was not consecrated until 1119. Alexander's letter suggested wholly mythical precedents for Canterbury's right to do this, probably because the letter was drafted by Peter, prior of Dunfermline, a former Canterbury monk and one of Alexander's messengers to Kent in 1120.[21] No reply from Ralph in 1115 is recorded and nothing is known of the next five years, save that the episcopal revenues of St Andrews were plundered by a monk of Bury St Edmunds. After the return of Archbishop Ralph to England in January 1120, Alexander asked him specifically for the Canterbury monk Eadmer to become bishop, a request passed to Henry I who gave curt approval.[22]

Eadmer came to Scotland, but insisted upon seeking consecration from Canterbury, which the king would not permit, though his letter of 1115 had envisaged it. In fact Canterbury's primatial claims were effectively destroyed by the pope in 1119–20, when he consecrated and gave definitive bulls to Archbishop Thurstan of York. Henry I wrote forbidding consecration of Eadmer by Ralph, and early in 1121, Eadmer, refused permission by the king to go to Canterbury 'for counsel', was permitted to resign his see and return south to his literary labours.[23] This withdrawal marked the collapse of Dunfermline-Canterbury influence on Alexander's ecclesiastical policy.

I have tried to set this foundation in the context of the struggle over the claims of York to be metropolitan of Scotland, and of Canterbury to be primate of all Britain, because I believe that Alexander's concern over these claims was not born, or not born merely, of a dislike of English ecclesiastical authority. His initiatives suggest that he had a more positive programme for St Andrews: to free it from all such authority, that is to procure recognised metropolitan and archiepiscopal status for it within his kingdom, so that his

---

[20] Lawrie, *Early Scottish Charters*, no. 28; *SAEC*, 138. For Bishop Turgot, Eadmer, bishop elect, and Bishop Robert, see Watt, *Series Episcoporum*, VI, 1, 81–84.

[21] *Councils and Ecclesiastical Documents*, ii, 197 quoting Eadmer's *Historia Novorum*; *SAEC*, 138.

[22] *Councils and Ecclesiastical Documents*, ii, 196–98; *SAEC*, 138–41.

[23] *SAEC*, 136–47. Compare the refusal to allow Turgot to go to Rome. But Alexander must have known that once in Canterbury, willy nilly Eadmer might accept consecration and profess obedience.

successors, and perhaps he himself, might receive the rites of Christian kingship, as was customary, from an archbishop. His position would then be that of other kings, and not dependent upon the gift or assent of the English king.

He did not seek to abandon traditional elements, but to admit new ones to his coronation and anointing on the model of which he must have heard from England, not because he understood or accepted the ecclesiology of those acts, but because they would represent a political gain. Now there is no direct evidence for this argument, for Alexander is not known to have asked the papacy for an archbishopric. Nonetheless there are circumstances which suggest his aims: his quarrel with Turgot, which was not over investiture but over the latter's wish to visit Rome – where he might accept the claims of the newly elected Thurstan, and Alexander's seeking a successor from Canterbury, whose help he expected – in what, if not in getting the pallium for St Andrews?

In 1124 Alexander nominated Robert, prior of Scone, to the see of St Andrew, a sign that he wished to reform the clergy of that see. The narrative of the foundation of the Augustinian priory there shows David I, about 1139, lecturing Bishop Robert 'since he had not hastened on the worship and service of God, as he had said he intended to do and as King Alexander had ordered that he should institute a religious life (*religionem*) in the church of the blessed Andrew'. The bishop offered an excuse, 'no resources', to which the king replied that King Alexander's statement that the Boar's Rake had been given to institute a religious order, would suffice. The Boar's Rake, a group of settlements in East Fife, supposedly given by a Pictish king, was not a new endowment, but the king was evidently determined to use this for the Augustinian version of the religious life.

He had the repute of founding the Augustinian house of Inchcolm in Dunkeld diocese (Bower's abbey),[24] but neither this nor St Andrews had Augustinian canons till fifteen or more years after Alexander's death, probably through resistance by the incumbent Culdees. Inchcolm, where, according to the foundation story, there was a hermit,[25] would have been intended as a similar anticipation from which the regular life might be introduced to the cathedral of Dunkeld, for St Andrews and Dunkeld were the two great reliquary churches and pilgrimage centres of *Scotia*. But Inchcolm priory became a reality only in the reign of Malcolm IV.[26]

Alexander emerges as a determined ecclesiastical reformer, successful at Scone which was free of earlier monastic settlement, but frustrated at St Andrews and Inchcolm. His concern with St Andrews was to avoid sub-

[24] Barrow, *Kingdom of Scots*, 172.

[25] The legend claimed that Alexander I was driven by a storm, promising that if he attained the island he would establish a shelter there. Hence, somewhat inconsequentially, he founded the priory.

[26] *Inchcolm Charters*, no. I.

ordination to York or Canterbury, which in effect was to seek metropolitan status for it, with the possibility of coronation and anointing of the king himself. The creation of the religious house at Scone, the place where kings were made, a small replica of the great abbey of Westminster, like it outside a busy town, like it with a royal palace or hall, and like it at a moderate distance from the metropolitan see, was evidently part of the king's aspiration, providing an ecclesiastical setting and community at the inauguration site. It was the only part of that aspiration which was achieved.[27]

When lord of the Cumbrian *regio*, David had promoted his chaplain, John, who seems to have been a monk of Tiron, to the see of Glasgow, with consecration by the pope in 1119. Twice John went to Rome to contest the claims of the archbishop of York, in 1122 to defend his own see, when he also visited Jerusalem, and in 1125 on behalf of the metropolitan rights of St Andrews. Ignoring a summons to all the Scottish bishops to attend at the curia in 1127, Robert, elect of St Andrews, was consecrated by Archbishop Thurstan, both men reserving the rights of their sees. In 1128 John and in November 1131 the Scottish bishops ignored orders by Innocent II to obey York. By then John was familiar with the papal court, with the York controversy and with the project to promote St Andrews, and judging by the frequency of his appearance as witness to David I charters, he was in close attendance upon that king, a court chaplain-bishop who also looked after his see.[28]

On 22 April 1136 Pope Innocent II, on information clearly laid by York, accused John of having rebelled against the churches of Rome and York and 'having brought some into the error of schism', i.e. having accepted the authority of the schismatic Anacletus II (1130–38); correction was entrusted to the archbishop of Canterbury as legate, indicating that John was then in Scotland, which is likely, since Glasgow cathedral was dedicated in that year. The 'some' misled by John into schism probably included King David, whom the pope, seeking universal acceptance, would not indict publicly. On the same day Innocent claimed that he had ordained a see at Carlisle, which Henry I had been prevented by death from carrying out, King Stephen was adjured to complete the task, though at this time, unknown to the curia, David was seeking to control the region. The common date of these bulls suggests that John had opposed the institution of the see of Carlisle, of which Bishop Æthelwold could not obtain possession from 1136 until, in 1138, a papal legate, at Carlisle with David I and his prelates who had 'favoured too greatly' Anacletus II, secured the restoration to his see of

[27] My text was completed before the publication of Veitch, '"Replanting Paradise": Alexander I and the reform of religious life in Scotland', *Innes Review*, lii (2001), 136–66, and I have not taken account of it here.

[28] Watt, *Series Episcoporum*, VI, i, 55–58; for his presence at court, see the Index to *David I Charters*.

Bishop Æthelwold and the recall from Tiron of Bishop John of Glasgow,[29] the latter a quid pro quo for the former.

In a confused account attributed to the reign of Malcolm IV, Bower claimed that John had acted as bishop in Cumberland (which is most improbable), but was excluded when his diocese was diminished by the consecration of Æthelwold for the new see of Carlisle (in August 1133); John then retired to Tiron.[30] If this were correct, John went to Tiron both before and after the dedication of his cathedral in 1136, which seems improbable. He pretty certainly would object to the see of Carlisle, and if Innocent II would not offend Henry I by revoking its creation, his only recourse was to Anacletus. Before 1136, I suggest, he was not at Tiron but in Italy, visiting the two papal courts.

For Anacletus had made a significant move in an effort to win adherents after his election in February 1130. In the summer of that year the magnates of Roger (II) duke of Sicily and now master of southern Italy suggested that he was worthy to be promoted to kingship. On 27 September 1130 a bull of Anacletus II recognised his only significant lay supporter, Roger, as king of Sicily and granted that he and his successors might be crowned by an archbishop from their lands and chosen by them – for Palermo was not a metropolitan see. Roger summoned his subjects to gather at Palermo, where on Christmas Day he was anointed by a (schismatic) cardinal and crowned by the prince of Capua in the cathedral.[31] Anacletus, who remained in possession of Rome, died in January 1138 and the schism ended in May. From 1139, when Roger made peace with Innocent II, he persuaded the popes to concede most of what he needed, including, in 1150, metropolitan status for Palermo.[32]

In the light of this, it is not surprising that David was at least inclined to adhere to Anacletus, from whom there was some hope of obtaining the grant of a right to coronation and anointing, and perhaps the pallium for a Scottish bishop. He may have failed to recognise either pope, whence the lack of papal letters to Scotland in these years, or may even have recognised Anacletus. In 1133–35 John could have travelled to Anacletus in Rome, to

[29] *Councils and Ecclesiastical Documents*, ii, 28–32; *SAEC*, 210–11.

[30] *Scotichronicon*, iv, 254–57.

[31] Ménager, 'L'institution monarchique dans les États normands d'Italie', *Cahiers de civilisation médiévale*, ii (1959), 445–68, at 445–49; he dates Anacletus' bull 27 December; Kehr, *Italia Pontificia*, viii, no. 137 shows that it was dated 27 September, as in Jaffé, *Regesta Pontificum Romanorum*, i, no. 8411. (In an article in *Le Moyen Âge*, xxv, 39–40, it is dated 27 November, with a reference which has no relevance.) The kings of Sicily had their heirs crowned during their own lifetime, but *rex designatus* was not used. In 1130 Roger was called *Rex Siciliae, ducatus Apuliae et principatus Capuae*, which brought his kingdom to the outskirts of Rome. In 1139 Innocent conceded merely *Rex Siciliae*, and the two men settled upon a myth that an ancient kingdom had been restored; Hollister, 'Anglo-Norman *Regnum*', *Speculum*, li, (1976), 221; Kehr, *Italia Pontificia*, viii, no. 159; Matthew, *Norman Kingdom of Sicily*, ch. 2.

[32] John of Salisbury, *Historia Pontificalis*, ed. Chibnall, 66–69.

seek inclusion of Cumbria in his see and coronation for his master.[33] Tainted with schism, and threatened with legatine correction by Innocent II in 1136, David had Bishop John depart then for Tiron.[34]

Bishop Robert of St Andrews, formerly prior of Scone, promoted to the see of of St Andrews early in 1124,[35] but his consecration delayed until 1127, built a church, generally identified as the nave of St Rule's church,[36] at his see, just as a church had been built at Scone. Otherwise he did nothing to bring Augustinians to St Andrews until, after 1133, he asked Æthelwold, now bishop of Carlisle as well as prior of Nostell, for Robert, a canon of Nostell, who could be prior of the canons whom he intended to institute in the church of St Andrew[37] – the limit of his efforts to bring the Augustinian rule to his see.

Prior Robert of St Andrews was very probably author of a narrative of his own times, which describes the Augustinian foundation there. He tells us that he laboured at St Andrews '*aliquamdiu* without canons, not however without clerics', and that Bishop Robert provided necessities for him 'and his [folk]' (*sui*). Professing to seek no authority in the church until the Lord should give him what he sought – a community (*societas*) for the service of God – he prayed that God would provide sufficient for a religious foundation which was firm and strong. He deliberately did not seek to recruit elsewhere lest brethren from other churches might spoil unity by differing opinions, but he received kindly those whom God sent who were ready to live 'in the way in which he was minded [to live]'.[38] In this obscure passage the clerics, *sui* and those whom he received kindly are not the Culdees, discussed elsewhere by Prior Robert, but a group, perhaps no more than three or four, who hoped to be canons of a priory when a sufficient endowment replaced episcopal handouts. In these circumstances *aliquamdiu* must surely be translated 'for some considerable time' and imply a number of years, say from 1135, during which the bishop moved 'very slowly' (*segnius*).

---

[33] During the schism Innocent drifted around Europe, with two brief visits to Rome, when he was excluded from St Peter's by Anacletus; Mann, *Lives of the Popes in the Middle Ages*, 1–55.

[34] If John did not attend the dedication of 1136, which I find very unlikely, he could have returned from Italy to Tiron.

[35] Eadmer and his archbishop wrote to King Alexander, claiming that Eadmer's resignation was invalid and that he should be restored; he would now be willing to agree to what he had previously rejected. These letters must be dated before Archbishop Ralph's death in October 1122, so would not have been prompted by the nomination of Robert as bishop. *SAEC*, 151–54.

[36] Though this is controversial, I am warned by Dr Simon Taylor.

[37] *Chron. Picts-Scots*, 192.

[38] *Chron. Picts-Scots*, 192, second paragraph (*Memoratus autem*), but the printed text is manifestly corrupt: in line 10 *sibi* for *si*; in the second last line *paratos* for *paratis*. Perhaps read *modo quod ipse disponebat*, 'in the way he laid down'. I am most grateful to Dr Simon Taylor, who let me see his text and translation of this work, known only from an eighteenth-century transcript.

It was surely complaints from Prior Robert which brought about royal action. David I visited the church with his son and magnates, and in the incomplete cloister lectured the company on 'many unimportant things' before upbraging the bishop for having failed to institute a religious life (*religionem*) in the church. The bishop replied that he could not deprive his successors of episcopal endowments, to which the answer that the Boar's Rake had been given for the purpose was enough.[39] The king and his son made a grant towards stocking the land (implying that the Boar's Rake was released) and 'compelled certain others by oath to help'. The bishop, under some compulsion, gave to the prior as interim sustenance for brethren, revenues from the lands of some absent 'persons' which were in his hands and the bishop's half-brother, a third Robert, became a canon of the new priory, surrendering to the canons his church or fifty shillings annually.[40]

Upon no other monastic foundation by David I is so much light thrown, yet we are still left in ignorance of the origins of the first canons (other than the third Robert) of St Andrews priory. Bower claims that in 1140 Robert prior of Scone (an error) became prior of St Andrews, while Wyntoun claims that canons came from Scone to St Andrews.[41] Some such move is possible, but it is unlikely that it wholly staffed the new priory, for Prior Robert's clerics would surely now profess the rule and enter the convent. The key change was the decision, imposed by the king, that an Augustinian priory be endowed, and to this endowment David I himself contributed. That process is recorded in the priory's charters, which bear out Bower's date, 1140, for the institution of the priory. It was followed quite soon, then or in 1141, by a fuller royal endowment brought together by the king in a compendium charter.[42]

These moves coincided with the visit of Malachy, bishop of Down, formerly bishop of Armagh, to the papal curia whither he was sent to press the claim of the Irish church for the recognition of Armagh and Cashel as

---

[39] This passage is cited above, p. 65.

[40] *Chron. Picts and Scots*, 191–93. On p. 193, line 27 for *ut Dei servitium* read *ad Dei servitium*. The tense of *debuissent* suggests a translation 'whence [i.e. from this revenue] the brethren coming to serve God there ought to *have been* sustained in the meantime.' If this is correct, it refers to Prior Robert's clerics, not to possible new recruits. But there may have been a mistranscription. Taylor, 'The coming of the Augustinians to St Andrews ...', *Kings, Clerics and Chronicles*, ed. Taylor, 115–23.

The church of Tyninghame or 50s. annually does not appear in the early charters or bulls of the priory, and the church continued to belong to the episcopal mensa. But Bishop Robert did give the 'abbacy' of Lochleven to St Andrews priory, perhaps an alternative. The third Robert is not called the first canon of the new priory, which modern comment has assumed he was.

[41] *Scotichronicon*, iii, 417; *Chron. Wyntoun*, iv, 390–91.*Chron. Picts-Scots*, 192.

[42] *David I Charters*, no. 126; the bishop's charter with the misleading date 1144, is Lawrie, *Early Scottish Charters*, no. 162. I hope to publish elsewhere an examination of the early charters of the priory and my reasons for rejecting the hitherto accepted date for its foundation, 1144.

metropolitan sees. On the outward journey (1139) he went 'from Scotland' via York;[43] his request for *pallia* was rejected by Innocent II, who sent him back to Ireland as a legate to seek from a church council a united request, on receipt of which Innocent would reconsider the matter. On this return journey[44] he stayed briefly at the Scottish court, when he restored health to the king's son.[45] The struggle in England between King Stephen and supporters of the Angevin claim, David among them, and the results of Malachy's Irish mission with the implications for Scotland of papal actions must surely have been discussed. It would seem likely that David's interest in the state of the church of St Andrew and his wish to provide it with a reforming order as chapter would be invigorated.

Bernard, bishop of St David's, who had taken up the cause of his see to be recognised as metropolitan of a Welsh province, provided another chance to raise the issue. Bernard had been chaplain to David's sister, Queen Maud, before he became bishop in 1115, had been with David and the Empress at London in the summer of 1141, and was firmly committed to the Angevin cause.[46] In 1143 he was in contact with David, and presumably told him that on behalf of the claims of his see he intended to approach the pope, probably the very Innocent II who had fobbed off St Malachy in 1140. This we know only from the outcome. Innocent II died in September 1143, his successor on 8 March 1144, and it was Lucius II who on 14 May 1144 responded to letters from Bishop Bernard; in his bull he accepted that the dignity of St Davids had been long alienated, but prevaricated about a decision.[47]

On the same day, in another bull, Lucius, 'moved by the prayers of Bishop Bernard', gave a privilege, addressed to Prior Robert and the Augustinian brethren of St Andrews, taking their church, and its possessions 'by gift of the bishop or of others … by generosity of kings or princes', into papal protection.[48] The document is in no way exceptional[49] – similar ones must

---

[43] When Malachy was at York early in 1140, David's stepson, Waltheof [de Senlis], prior of Kirkham, a daughter house, probably, of Nostell, was Angevin candidate for the vacant archbishopric of York.

[44] The date of this seems to be uncertain; it should have been before the summer of 1141, when David I was at London, then at the siege of Winchester; he would not be back in Scotland till the end of September.

[45] *Life of Malachy*, 50–54, where the constitution of a new metropolitan see (Cashel added to Armagh) was approved, p. 52; *ESSH*, ii, 184–85.

[46] For Earl Henry as steward to Bishop Bernard, see *David I Charters*, 108a.

[47] *Giraldi Cambrensis Opera* (Rolls Series, 1861–91), iii, 52–53; *Councils and Ecclesiastical Documents*, i, 348.

[48] Lawrie, *Early Scottish Charters*, no. 165; *Scotia Pontifiicia*, no. 25. Dr Flanagan, in one sentence, misdates these bulls to 1140, makes the Scottish one 'in favour of St Andrew's, Glasgow', and claims that 'both were granted "at the request of the bishop of St Davids" [*sic*, *cf*. St Andrew's]' whereas the St Davids bull says no such thing and was a denial of Bernard's request; *Irish Society*, 35. On p. 36, line 11 the pope's name should be Eugenius III.

[49] Eugenius' bull of 1146 for Holyrood abbey, given at the request of Abbot Alwin, is very similar and includes the phrases quoted; *Holyrood Liber*, 167–68; Somerville, *Scotia Pontificia*, no. 26. This was not reprinted by Lawrie.

have been issued annually in numbers by each pope of that era – but it does place the new priory in the context of a Welsh request for archiepiscopal status. Dr Flanagan has suggested that about 1140 David I was central to moves to end the claims of Canterbury to authority over the Scottish, Welsh and Irish churches,[50] moves which would elevate the see of St Andrews, if successful. It is a truly astonishing comment on Bishop Robert that the new priory was petitioned for not by letters from him, but through a Welsh bishop.

The death of Lucius II in February 1145 would further delay any action, and though the new pope, Eugenius III, was favourable to the Angevin cause, he took no action for some years. On 29 June 1147 at Meaux he presided over an argument between the archbishop of Canterbury and Bishop Bernard on the latter's claim to the *pallium*;[51] at Auxerre on 30 August in the same year Prior Robert of St Andrews obtained two privileges from him, one for Cambuskenneth abbey, the other for his own priory, which, if effective, would have eliminated the Culdee community.[52] If Prior Robert was present at the papal court at this time, he is more likely to have come with Bishop Bernard than in order to attend the church council held at Reims in March 1148.

In the same year, 1147, St Malachy set out from Ireland for this council, and to obtain the *pallium* for Ireland's two archbishops; again he visited the Scottish court en route, but, denied passage through England by King Stephen, missed the council and failed to achieve his goal, dying at Clairvaux in November 1148.[53] Nonetheless the Irish pressed and at last achieved movement in 1150, when Eugenius III appointed Cardinal John Paparone as legate to the Irish church. Refused transit by King Stephen, in 1151 he sailed from Flanders to Tynemouth, in the earldom of Henry son of David I. From there he wrote to David who was in Cumbria, 'announcing himself, *telling the reason for his coming* and asking for escort'.

They met at Carlisle at the end of September 1151, where hospitality was generous, and the cardinal sailed on to distribute the *pallia* to four Irish archbishoprics at the synod of Kells in 1152. In April 1152 he returned to King David 'to whom he was bound by a strong disposition of love because of a most devout sense of reverence', and then by invitation visited King Stephen.[54] He died in 1156, profoundly disliked by all in the province of Canterbury, whose apologist, John of Salisbury, tells us that when with David (at Carlisle) Paparone 'promised to persuade the lord pope and the

---

[50] *Irish Society*, 71; 'co-ordinated ... under the leadership of King David'.

[51] *Councils and Ecclesiastical Documents*, i, 354.

[52] Somerville, *Scotia Pontificia*, nos 27, 28; Lawrie, *ESC*, nos 180, 181. It is possible that the lost privilege for (Augustinian) Jedburgh abbey was given at the same time; Somerville, *Scotia Pontificia*, no. 31.

[53] *Life of Malachy*, 85–88; *ESSH*, ii, 208–9.

[54] *Symeonis Opera*, ii, 326–27; *SAEC*, 227.

Roman church to give a *pallium* to the bishop of St Andrews and that his see should be made metropolitan of the Scots and of the Orkneys and adjacent islands'. John comments that since Calixtus II York had this right over Scotland, but that the Scots had rejected it, instead offering obedience to Canterbury, to which the papacy would not agree.[55]

This legation took place at a time when Stephen's influence at the curia was slight or nil, when the Angevin cause was ascendent, the young Henry Plantagenet on the way to the English throne, but it also followed a visit by Henry Murdac, archbishop of York to the curia, whence he took two bulls, dated 16 June 1151, one ordering his bishops (including those of Scotland) to obey him, which said nothing new. The other 'commanded' David I to 'compel' his bishops to obey, under threat of the rigour of papal justice against them if they were obdurate,[56] a new and bold device recognising the king's authority over his bishops. But it represented Murdac's information, and its delivery would depend on him. While its terms might have provoked David I's discussion with the cardinal,[57] the timing would be tight and the king had no need of such prompting to press his wishes. The Carlisle episode is important because it shows the Scottish king seizing an opportunity, remote from the see of St Andrews and its bishop, to press its claim for metropolitan status; it gives probability that the episodes of 1137–38, 1140, 1144 and 1147 were directed to the same end.

In straying somewhat from Scone, I have postulated a connection between that foundation and the development at St Andrews of an Augustinian house contemporaneously with efforts to win a papal grant of metropolitan status for its bishop. In passing I cited what may be the strongest evidence of that link, the reported aversion of David I from the traditional *obsequia* of the Scots at 'the recent promotion of their kings' which the bishops imposed upon their reluctant king. The David who extended his patronage to one and then to another of the new religious orders may have made his protest and left it at that, but a positive reaction would seem more in character, a determination to bring to Scotland the rites used by the other contemporary kingships known to him – England, France and (through his niece) the Empire, where anointing and crowning were performed by an archbishop, whence the attempts to raise the status of the church and see of St Andrew.

Despite the success of the Irish church in acquiring four metropolitans, the longevity of Bishop Robert inhibited any further moves on behalf of the see of St Andrews. On his death in 1159, Waltheof, stepson of David I, formerly

[55] John of Salisbury, *Historia Pontificalis*, ed. Chibnall, 6, 72; John of Salisbury was writing this before the bull of 1176 which ended the claims of York.

[56] Somerville, *Scotia Pontificia*, nos 29, 30.

[57] Watt, *Medieval Church Councils*, 18–19 thinks this probable.

a canon of Nostell and then abbot of Melrose, was elected and refused the see. At the papal curia for important business, a royal clerk, Nicholas, dreamed of the Waltheof's death which took place the next day, 3 August 1159. This narrative comes from the *Vita* of Waltheof written fifty years later, errs in calling Nicholas 'chancellor', and omits the king's role in nominating Waltheof, chosen no doubt as the king's uncle, but also, perhaps, as a Cistercian like Malachy. Nicholas must have quit Scotland before the king left for France in mid or late May 1159, and it seems very unlikely that he went without a royal request to consecrate a named elect to St Andrews – Waltheof, whose refusal could have been expressed when he was *in extremis*.

But the Melrose chronicle claims that the king also sent Bishop William of Moray to the curia, and that he and Nicholas went to Pope Alexander III at Anagni.[58] This suggests that William arrived after the death of Adrian IV on 1 September, and probably not long before 27 November when Alexander responded with a bull which is an enigmatic guide to their missions. Both have transmitted the king's requests about St Andrews, which would have been granted if possible; indeed to that end the pope had corrected these petitions and 'redacted them in a better state'. Let us pause there to suggest that William had hastened to King Malcolm in France with news of Waltheof's death, and been sent on to the curia with amended requests from the king, which apparently anticipated a new election to St Andrews.

Alexander's bull went on: in justice the requests could not be granted because St Andrews currently lacked a pastor so 'it was not at all appropriate to give a confirmation to the church on those things which were asked'.[59] The pope then made Bishop William legate to all the kingdom and allowed his translation to St Andrews, if agreeable to the king and the church there; he would be both bishop and legate there.

It is clear that the king's request through both messengers was for archiepiscopal status for St Andrews, claimed as one of the ancient customs and dignities of St Andrews, for Pope Alexander promised that, as soon as William was translated, he would then confirm the 'ancient and reasonable customs and dignities' of that church. The requests would also bewail the delays and absence of a pastor in other sees through lack of an archbishop in the realm. If the Englishman, Adrian IV, was reluctant to respond positively to Nicholas, after the double papal elections of 7 September the Scots were in a stronger position, and William's decision to approach the lawful pope would earn a more favourable hearing.

Alexander nonetheless, as he says, consulted the cardinals, and was presumably warned of the claims of York, so made the one-off concession that William might be translated, avoiding the need for his consecration.

---

[58] *ESSH*, ii, 243–44.

But finally an alternative was offered: if William was not translated to St Andrews, another should be elected, 'and if you wish to present the elect to us we will treat him honestly and will take care to honour him in whatever ways we see expedient. From then, the legatine office [of William] ceasing, he who has been confirmed and consecrated will obtain ... and exercise [it]'. The intimation seems to be that a new elect might go to the curia where his claims to the *pallium* would be considered, or he might accept consecration from the legate and become legate himself.[60] William was not translated but consecrated the newly elected Arnold, abbot of Kelso, to St Andrews on 20 November 1160 in King Malcolm's presence, foregoing the opportunity to further press the pope.

The Melrose chronicle under 1161 states that Alexander then made Arnold legate, that as such he consecrated a new bishop of Ross, but 'afterwards by [papal] command ... he ceased to hold the office of legate'.[61] It seems probable that the chronicler, unfamiliar with the terms of the 1159 bull, assumed wrongly that Alexander named Arnold as legate, whereas in fact he seems to have rescinded the office pretty swiftly. Named once 'Arnold legate of Scotland', as witness to Malcolm IV's endowment of Coupar abbey, without his see, and before the bishops, he was seen to give a corporate existence to a church coterminous with the realm.[62] His successors refer to charters of his now lost, but of the eleven or so of which texts survive, none mentions his legatine office, but in three he adopts the style *episcopus Scottorum*, used on the seals of twelfth-century bishops of St Andrews, but rarely on parchment, a claim to some pre-eminence within the Scottish church. But there was no known attempt to secure another legate and neither king nor prelates seem to have faced up to the need for a sustained campaign for a metropolitan, carried out by a weighty and persistent delegation at the curia supplied with ample funds to oil the wheels of bureaucracy.

The claims of York continued to trouble the Scottish bishops and king who were indeed fortunate that Pope Alexander III excluded York in 1176. And the issue of coronation and anointing had no interest for Malcolm IV's brother and successor.

---

[59] *Confirmationem ecclesie super his que postulabantur fieri nullatenus congruebat.*

[60] *Scotia Pontificia*, no. 43; *Councils and Ecclesiastical Documents*, ii, 233–34; Lawrie, *Annals*, 52–54.

[61] *ESSH*, ii, 247.

[62] *RRS*, i, no. 226. Between consecration in November 1160 and his death less than two years later, Arnold witnessed fifteen more royal acts, simply as bishop, indicating that he held the legateship very briefly. As *episcopus Scottorum*, *St Andrews Liber*, 126–28. One of these is witnessed by Robert, his chancellor, who may have taken the style from the bishop's seal; but he also witnesses a charter of Arnold, *ecclesie Sancti Andree apostoli humilis minister*, Arnold's more usual style. *Ibid.*, 127–28.

CHAPTER 6

The lion of justice and the red fox, 1165–1249

> After King Malcolm's death, [at Jedburgh on 9 December] the prelates and all the nobles of Scotland met at Scone at the command of his brother William, then guardian of the kingdom, whom they unanimously raise up to be king. Therefore on Christmas eve, fifteen days after the king's death, this William, friend of God, lion of justice, prince of peace, is blessed by Richard, bishop of St Andrews and by other assisting bishops, as king, and is raised in the royal seat.[1]

The tenses of this passage from *Gest. Ann.* suggest that, though the epithets for William would have been added later, this is otherwise a contemporary account, probably made at the newly-founded abbey of Coupar. The Melrose chronicler is briefer: William was 'elevated to the kingship in royal manner, on Christmas eve',[2] but obscures what *Gest. Ann.* implies: that a day or more elapsed between the 'unanimous raising-up' and Christmas Eve.

Why the delay? Because the Advent season lasted from 28 November in 1165, so that the first day available for a festive occasion was 24 December. Before this Malcolm would be buried at Dunfermline – the date is unknown but perhaps about 16 December. William, we have seen, had taken over some reins of government from Malcolm and his heritable right to succeed his brother was recognised by the political establishment – but had to be briefly delayed out of respect for the coming of a higher King.

In the three-stage process in 1165, 'raising up', ecclesiastical blessing as king and elevation in the royal seat, the 'unanimous raising-up' was a form of recognition, similar to the acceptance of Malcolm after his father's death in 1152, recognition that each had a better right to succeed than his brother(s). It would complement, not contradict, that right, and while 'unanimous' scarcely suggests a debate, may have been more formal than

---

[1] *Chron. Fordun*, i, 259; ii, 254–55. The bishops bless William to become king (*in regem*, accusative case), but he is raised in (not into) the royal seat (ablative case); but this may be error from omission or addition of a superscript line for *m*. This quotation comes from the annals formerly attributed to John of Fordun. But since Dr Broun has called that attribution into question, they are here called *Gesta Annalia*, usually abbreviated as *Gest. Ann.* Broun, 'A new look at *Gesta Annalia*', *Church, Chronicle and Learning*, ed. Crawford, 9–30.

[2] *successit Willelmus frater eius in uigilia natalis Domini more regio eleuatus in regnum;* Chron. *Melrose*, under 1165.

acclamation, with speeches lauding the king-to-be. It may explain Count Florence's claim in 1292 that Earl David's supposed right had yielded to William's. Finally, *Gest. Ann.* placed the ecclesiastical blessing before secular enthronement in 1165, perhaps wrongly; his source may have wanted to stress the role of churchmen in the inauguration rites, and to ascribe the constitutive act to them.

King William reigned for forty-nine years, during which one issue dominated his policies:[3] the earldom of 'Northumbria' of which he had been deprived by Malcolm IV and Henry II in 1157, when Malcolm was given the earldom of Huntingdon and became Henry's *fidelis*. William was compensated with a derisory fief in Tynedale for which he too would do homage. In 1166, when he visited Henry II in Normandy and the latter burst into a furious rage at hearing words favourable to him, he was now earl of Huntingdon and must surely have renewed his homage and fealty, though no source mentions the act.[4] Henry would be enraged either because the wording of the homage had been contested, or because William asked for restoration to Northumbria.

If at first he asked, in 1173 he joined the rebellion of the young King Henry who promised it to him. In 1174 he was taken prisoner at Alnwick and at the end of the year, to secure his release, by the treaty (*conuencio et finis*) of Falaise he became Henry's liege man for Scotland and all his other lands, promising that his earls and barons would do homage and fealty, the prelates swear fealty, to the English king as their liege lord. In August of the following year, at York, these promises were confirmed. King William and his brother David did homage and fealty to Henry II 'for all their holdings, namely for *Scotia* and Galloway', followed by prelates (fealty only) and earls and barons.[5]

The due subjection of the Scottish church to the English church was the second promise in the treaty, made both by the king and by four prelates who were present at the conclusion of the treaty, the negative equivalent of freedom promised to the church at the beginning of an English coronation charter. Despite the space which it took up in the treaty, it is difficult to believe that this matter was of great importance to Henry II, and indeed when it came to fulfilment at Northampton in 1176, the Scots, on good grounds, escaped, probably with the connivance of the archbishop of Canterbury. The issue was allowed to drop, the pope, with whom Henry did

---

[3] There is a most helpful overview by Barrow of 'The Reign of William the Lion, King of Scotland', in *Historical Studies*, vii (1969), 21–44, and in his *Scotland and its Neighbours*, 67–90. Owen, *William the Lion* for the cultural background. The issue of Northumbria is well summarised in Hudson, *Land, Law, and Lordship*, 116–17.

[4] *Materials for ... Becket*, vi, 72; *Correspondence of Thomas Becket*, ed. Duggan, i, no. 112, pp. 542–43. *ESSH*, ii, 264. Anderson suggested John of Salisbury as the writer but the editors of John's letters do not include it, and Dr Duggan suggests Master Walter de Insula.

[5] *Anglo-Scottish Relations*, no. 1; *Benedict. Peterb.*, i, 94–99.

not wish another tussle, reacted against the English claim and forbade York to exercise any metropolitan authority in Scotland. Effectively this clause of the treaty secured exactly the opposite of its provision.

In the brief provision for a territorial settlement, the men of the Scottish king were to have the lands which they had or ought to have of King Henry, while King Henry's men were to have the lands which they had or ought to have of King Henry or King William. There was an important practical consequence: Henry gave the earldom of Huntingdon-Northampton to Simon de Senlis while leaving to William his Tynedale fief; and, of course, Henry could disregard the issue of Northumbria.

There was also provision for extradition of felons fleeing to the other country, almost equally balanced, save that an English felon would be extradited to England, but a Scottish felon might not be extradited to Scotland. If this distinction, which made plain the lordship of Henry II over King William's subjects, was of little practical importance, its terms bear on a problem to which the treaty does not refer explicitly: Galloway.

The two lords of Galloway had risen in rebellion on news of William's capture, expelling his baillies and destroying the castles of the king and any immigrant lairds. What happened next occurs in two versions in the works of Roger of Howden. Writing in the late 1170s he recorded that the brothers fell out, that Gilbert had Uhtred slain, and that Henry sent Howden himself and a knight to meet the two brothers to bring them over to his service; Gilbert offered a large tribute to be received as Henry's subject, but the messengers refused until speaking to the king, who rejected the deal offered by the killer of his cousin, Uhtred.[6]

It is usual to add the 1190s version in which Howden claimed that, after William's capture, the brothers urgently approached Henry with offers of gifts to become his subjects, and subsequently quarrelled, Gilbert procuring the death of Uhtred.[7] This later account ignores Henry's move to break the Galwegians' allegiance to their king, clearly taken in ignorance of the murder; perhaps its early approach by the brothers was in fact Gilbert's later offer. If we can never know the whole truth, it is fairly certain that the protagonists in Normandy would long be in ignorance of events in Galloway, and vice versa.

The treaty speaks of the clergy and of the magnates 'of the land of the king of Scots',[8] yet declares that William has become Henry's liegeman 'for *Scotia* and all his other lands', vagueness where clarity was called for. The usual meaning suggested, 'for Scotland and Tynedale', is unconvincing, since 'other land' recurs in the proviso that a fugitive felon from 'the land of

---

[6] *Benedict Peterb.*, i, 67–68, 79–80; *SAEC*, 256–58.
[7] *Chron. Howden*, ii, 63, 69.
[8] In *Anglo-Scottish Relations*, Stones translated *terra regis* ... as 'the realm of the king ...'.

the king' [Henry II] will not be received by the king of Scots or his men 'in *Scotia* or in other land of his'.[9] Despite the wide continental possessions of Henry II, 'other lands' do not figure in the provision that a fugitive 'in England' from 'the land of the king of Scots' will not be received in 'the land of the [English] king'. 'Other land' seems to have been for the king of Scots only, a phrase designed to cover uncertainty about Galloway, offered by its lords to Henry II at the time the treaty was made, for at York in August 1175, according to Howden, William and his brother did homage 'for all their holdings and specifically for *Scotia* and Galloway'. *Scotia*, at least in contemporary English eyes, did not include Galloway which might be William's 'other lands'.[10] After the ceremony Henry gave William permission to subdue Gilbert, who had abandoned his fealty. With discovery of Gilbert's crime, the ambiguity had gone and Galloway was to remain in the kingdom of William.

As guarantee for observance of the treaty, five castles were placed at Henry's disposal and four, Roxburgh, Berwick, Edinburgh and probably Jedburgh, were occupied, all at William's expense, as the treaty provided; Stirling probably was not. In fact Henry gradually withdrew so that only two castles were still occupied in 1189.[11] Nonetheless this occupation was a sign to all the Scots at York that the treaty was not a making of 'peace and friendship' between two kings but a surrender, humiliating, permanent but inescapable, of one kingdom to the king of another.[12] It spelled out the consequences of homage such as had been undreamt of in 1072, 1094 or 1097: that the political community owed a greater allegiance to its overlord than the one owed to its lord, and that the overlord had a presence whereby he could oversee that allegiance.

Yet it is noteworthy that nowhere in the treaty, not infrequently seen as the 'feudal subjection' of Scotland, does the word 'fief' occur, nor is the kingdom or land of Scotland said to be 'held' or 'had' by its king 'of' the English king or in any other way; indeed the word *regnum* (kingdom) also does not occur in the treaty. Subjection there certainly was, fealty 'for' (*de*) Scotland, not merely personal to William and Henry but to be inherited by their heirs. The treaty gravely restricted the rights of the Scottish king, even in relation to his own subjects, but it did not provide that the king of Scots must provide men or money for the wars of the king of England, nor

---

[9] A possible translation is 'land of theirs', which I find unlikely.

[10] The word 'specifically' translates *nominatim*; *Benedict Peterb.*, i, 95. I do not think that *Scocia* in the treaty has the sense of 'Scotland north of Forth'; between 1174 and 1189 King William's charters show him making grants both north and south of Forth, despite the English garrisons in Lothian.

[11] Edinburgh was handed over as a wedding present to William in 1186.

[12] Van Eickels, '"Homagium" and "Amicitia", Rituals of Peace', *Francia*, xxiv, part 1, (1997), 133–40.

(looking to 1293) that the king of England would provide justice to a Scot complaining of denial of it in the court of the Scottish king.[13]

King William was not a free agent after 1174; he played his cards fairly well, but he had to secure King Henry's permission, for example, to reduce the rebellious Gilbert of Galloway, whom he brought, as ten years later he brought his successor Roland, to submit to Henry in England. After 1178 William was also involved in a bitter controversy with the church, in which Henry tried to act as mediator, also requiring William's presence at his court. William was in England or Normandy in 1175, twice in 1176, in 1177, 1179, twice in 1181, in 1184, 1185, and thrice in 1186.[14] His behaviour paid off in the restoration of the earldom of Huntingdon, immediately passed to his brother David (1185), though the wife Henry found for the Scottish king (1186) was considerably less distinguished than the wife he wanted and than the wife subsequently married by Earl David.[15]

Moreover it is clear that there was considerable discontent within the Scottish political community at their king's, and their own, humiliating position. Unfortunately William's opponents were reluctant to reveal themselves by open dissent, and while the chronicles hint, they point the finger at no named individual. A crucial figure was Donald MacWilliam, son of William fitz Duncan. The latter's lawful son, William (of Egremont), about 1151 inherited his father's lands in England and died, while still a minor, in or soon after 1163, leaving his inheritance to his three sisters and their husbands – any half-brother must have been illegitimate. The sagas which tell of Maelcoluim III's marriage to Ingebiorg and trace their male descendants, claim that 'the Scots wished to have as king' this boy, 'whom they call *ødlingr*', the ætheling.[16] Of his possible right there can be no doubt, but there is no other evidence to support the saga's view that it was articulated by some Scots; nor was there occasion, for the boy was too young in 1153 and dead by 1165. The families of two of his sisters had died out by *c.*1275, but the middle sister was represented by two de Lucy co-heiresses who made no claim to Scotland in 1291.[17]

The saga's statement probably belonged not to William of Egremont but to the rebel Donald Mac William, whose paternity is noted, somewhat sceptically, by *Gest. Ann.*[18] His mother is unknown, but, it has been suggested, was of the house of Moray, since William fitz Duncan was called 'earl

---

[13] Though possibly a plaintiff might have alleged to Henry that William had broken his fealty.

[14] See the itinerary in *RRS*, ii, 97–105.

[15] For her parentage, Dunbar, *Scottish Kings*, 79; on the marriage, *RRS*, ii, 14; Stringer, *Earl David*, 38–39.

[16] *Orkneyinga saga*, c. 33.

[17] *Early Yorks. Charters*, iii, 468–70; vi, 10–14 and index under 'Duncan' and 'Egremont'. The heiress of the oldest Lucy sister married Edmund, second son of Henry III, but died without an heir.

[18] *Chron. Fordun*, i, 268.

of Moray' in a genealogy of the lordships of Coupland and Allerdale; this source was drawn up after 1272 and describes Dolfin (expelled from Carlisle in 1092) as 'earl of Northumberland' and Ranulph Meschin (lord of Carlisle thereafter) as 'earl of Carlisle'.[19]

Its title of earl for William derives from a foggy historical memory of the northern Scottish support in the 1180s for his illegitimate son Donald, who might have held land in Moray. The history of that province after 1130 is obscure, documents are scarce and none can be sure of the meaning of the annal for 1163: *Et rex Malcolmus Murevienses transtulit*, 'And King Malcolm transferred Moray-men'.[20] There was no fixed see for the bishop, but a daughter house of Melrose abbey was established at Kinloss in 1150, and towns, Inverness, Auldearn, Elgin and probably Forres, were recognised as burghs, evidently with a significant Low Countries element in their population. Two landowners are known to have had the same origin. Moray was a frontier province to be held by settlers, but they were probably few in number outside the king's burghs and castles.

The annal for 1163 had no ambiguities for *Gest. Ann.*: Malcolm IV cleared the rebellious Moray-men from their homes, dispersing them throughout Scotland. This was guesswork but *Gest. Ann.* is very close to the Melrose chronicle for northern events in 1179 and 1187. In 1179 Melrose records that King William, his brother David, earls, barons and a large army went to Ross and built two (named) castles there; *Gest. Ann.*, omitting earls and barons, claims that the expedition was 'against Mac William'.[21] Neither source records the attacks upon the kingdom by Donald Mac William in 1181 (when William and David were in Normandy), and 'many times' before, reported by Howden; in his later version the attack was 'upon the sea-coast', piratical landings.[22]

The same account of Mac William's attack of 1187 was also mediated to Howden, who alone tells that it was a force of the Galwegians, under Roland fitz Uhtred, which killed Donald. Howden did not realise that his 'Donald son of William fitz Duncan' of 1181 was the same man as his 'Mach Willam' or 'William' of 1187, so that he must have had independent evidence of two claims: first that in 1181 Donald had 'very often claimed the kingdom of Scotland and many times made incursions into [it] by command of certain powerful men of [it]', and secondly that in 1187 Mac William claimed to be of royal stock 'and by right of his kindred (*parentum*) claimed the kingdom ... and often did ... harm to King William through consent and counsel of

---

[19] *RRS*, ii, 12–13; *Cal. Docs. Scot.*, ii, no. 64. William occurs in David I's charters and in chronicles, never as earl.

[20] *Chron. Holyrood*, 142.

[21] Duncan, 'Roger Howden and Scotland', *Church, Chronicle and Learning*, ed. Crawford, 135–60; and 'Sources and uses of the Chronicle of Melrose', *Kings, Clerics and Chronicles*, ed. Taylor, 146–85.

[22] *Benedict Peterb.*, i, 277–78, 281; *Chron. Howden*, ii, 263–64; *SAEC*, 278–79.

earls and barons of the kingdom of Scotland'. The king sent against the enemy earls and barons, who squabbled about proceeding further because some 'loved the king not at all'.[23]

The Melrose chronicle says nothing of these differences, and has the earls send the army out, and to plunder, but *Gest. Ann.* claims that Donald had taken Ross, Moray and (exaggerating) the greater part of the kingdom and that he 'relied on the treachery of some disloyal men'.[24] Treachery was often enjoyed by medieval annalists, when they could describe its failure and punishment; the strong taint of it recorded in these sources is the more striking because it is anonymous – no one is pursued, no one punished. Yet we have documentary evidence that there was indeed treachery, and by the man who would have been a commander of the contingent from Strathearn, the marshall of the earl, Gillecolm, who forfeited his land 'for the felony which he did to me [the king], as one who in felony handed over my castle of Auldearn and afterwards went to my mortal enemies and stood with them against me' – yet seems to have escaped.[25]

Taken together these sources do not suggest in any way that Donald sought to become earl of Moray; he claimed the throne, had some local support in Ross and caused trouble there perhaps from 1168 when local control by Earl Malcolm mac Heth ended. But in the 1180s he was given support, perhaps covert, by a discontented element among the Scottish magnates, for reasons which must surely have been the king's willingness to leave the kingdom and to pay court to Henry II. It may be doubted that these two reasons were clearly distinguished, and it is possible that there were other factors, such as the king's patronage of a number of non-Scottish clerics. But dislike of Henry's rights over Scotland there surely was.

In 1188 William offered Henry II 4,000 marks for the return of his two Scottish castles, which was in effect accepted if William would secure for Henry the Saladin tithe (to fund recovery of Jerusalem, lost to Saladin in 1187) from Scotland. William wanted to agree but when he brought a very large assembly of his men to meet Henry's ambassadors at Birgham on the Tweed, presumably to consent to the tax, he had to confess that they refused. To Henry's ambassadors they said that even if William had given an oath to give the tithe, they would never do so. The best William could offer was 5,000 marks for castles and tithe.[26]

The picture is a vivid one, from Roger Howden who was certainly there on the English side. Striking is the difference between Henry's authority in securing this new tax in England and William's failure to do so in Scotland, his need to subject prelates and barons to pressure from the emissaries of his

[23] *Benedict Peterb.*, ii, 7–9; *SAEC*, 294–95.

[24] *Chron. Melrose* under 1187, *ESSH*, ii, 312; *Chron. Fordun*, i, 268.

[25] *RRS*, ii, no. 258 and p. 12. I would date to the 1187 expedition *RRS*, ii, no. 281, dated at Elgin and witnessed by Patrick earl of Dunbar and Gilbert earl of Strathearn.

[26] *Benedict Peterb.*, ii, 44–45; *Chron. Howden*, ii, 338–39; *SAEC*, 300–1.

and their English overlord, on the border between his and their kingdoms, because his authority was not sufficient. The episode surely justifies the view that tension over the subordination of Scotland within the political community had increased between 1175 and 1189, despite the relative gentleness of Henry II's lordship. The prelates and magnates doubtless stood firm on the three customary reasons for an aid, clutching their purses ever closer, but there is no denying their success as a community, where, a century later, their successors compromised with a more wily and determined English ruler. The difference? In 1188 their lord was the king of Scots; in denying him they asserted the pre-eminence of his lordship.

The oath taken by William and his younger brother together in 1175 points unambiguously at David as the accepted heir to the Scottish throne at this time. Of William's charters (some 520 in number), some sixty-five were witnessed by David, of which two or three only (all before 1185) use the form 'witnessing and granting'.[27] It had clearly come to the end of its useful life, implying that turbulence on the death of a king, if it happened, would not upset the title of those who held his charters, for it went without saying that his successor would respect them. A full decade later William was married to Ermengarde de Beaumont, probably a child-bride. By the quittance of Canterbury in 1189, he was freed of the burden of English lordship since 1174, and owed Richard I only what Malcolm IV 'did to [Richard's] predecessors of right and ought to have done'.[28] He could now press his claim to the earldom of Northumbria, and came close to buying it from Richard in 1194, but refused to pay 15,000 marks for it without its (crucial) castles.[29]

In 1195, claims the *Scotichronicon* of Walter Bower, the king suffered a long illness at Clackmannan, 'where all the gathered magnates swore fealty to his daughter Margaret as his true heir, unless he should have a son by Queen Ermengarde'. William had 'fathered this Margaret by the daughter of Adam de Whitsome', a statement which clearly made her illegitimate. Worried by this, Bower added to the notice of William's marriage to Ermengarde the claim that he had previously married Adam's daughter who bore him Margaret.[30] This attempt to bowdlerise shows that Bower found the illegitimacy of Margaret in his source for 1195; his account is with a group of notices which are found in the Melrose chronicle, though this one

[27] *RRS*, ii, nos 192 (Glasgow cathedral), 204 (William de Haya). The doubtful case is no. 190 which really has to be of the 1170s and is witnessed by 'Earl' David, a title which he bears nowhere else in that decade, even though he was given the earldom of Lennox then. The Glasgow cartulary reads *Test' . Com' . DD . fre'. meo*, which was, I suggest, a miscopying of *Test' et conc' DD*, 'witnessing and granting David my brother'.

[28] *Anglo-Scottish Relations*, no. 2.

[29] *Chron. Howden*, iii, 249–50; *SAEC*, 313–14; Duncan, *Making of the Kingdom*, 235–38.

[30] *Scotichronicon*, iv, 410–13, 368, 548.

is not there and may have come from the chronicle draft used in Coupar abbey. We must conclude that whoever wrote the annal *c.*1200 thought that the 1195 oath was to this illegitimate Margaret – a remarkable error which, however difficult to explain, is not a reason for discarding acceptance of the king's daughter as heir if he had no lawful son. For William had a lawful daughter called Margaret born between 1187 and 1193; despite her youth – perhaps infancy – it must have been she who was the object of the oath.

For the king's illness at Clackmannan in 1195, probably in April–May,[31] is confirmed by Roger Howden, who visited Scotland late in that year. In his account, the ill king decided that Otto of Brunswick, son of the exiled Duke Henry the Lion of Saxony and nephew of Richard I, was to succeed him as king, taking William's first daughter (Margaret) as wife. Thereafter the king recovered but persisted in the plan, to which many consented, but others, led by Patrick earl of Dunbar, opposed it. They would not accept William's daughter as queen because it was not the custom of the kingdom for a woman to have *regnum* (the kingdom or kingship?) when there was a brother or nephew in the family who could have it by right.[32]

Bower's source appears not to have known of Dunbar's opposition, but is not in serious contradiction of Howden, whose 'many consented' represents Bower's oath, played down by Howden who knew of the collapse of the scheme. But there is a contradiction within these accounts. Bower's oath was to have Margaret as the heir, yet subsequently Dunbar objected to this on principle, suggesting, if Howden is correct, that she (and not her proposed husband) would succed William, which is also what Bower's oath suggests. In these accounts we meet on the one hand an attempt to replicate in Scotland the proposed (1127) succession of Matilda in England by a law of kingship that, failing a son, the king's daughter would succeed to the kingdom; on the other hand King William proposed to apply the law of fiefs, whereby the heritage would pass to the husband of his daughter.

In truth, our sources are too reticent; it seems likely that from the first King William intended that the succession would pass to a son-in-law in right of his daughter and heiress. And although Howden may well report Dunbar's argument accurately, the timing of his objections, after Otto was proposed as Margaret's husband, suggests that the real objection was to Otto, a foreigner, probably nominated by Richard I. Earl Patrick was evidently defending Earl David's rights, but he was also proposing a 'custom' of kingship different from that of fiefs and one for which there was, in fact, no precedent.

It may be doubted that the theoretical limits of Dunbar's position were tested – if the king had a married daughter and a male cousin, who had the

---

[31] *RRS*, ii, nos 375–78.
[32] *Chron. Howden*, iii, 298–99; *SAEC*, 315. The use of 'first-born' here shows that a second daughter had been born, so Margaret must have been born in 1193 at the latest, and probably several years earlier.

better right? – and doubted too that the precedent of Donnchad I's succession in 1034 in right of his mother was invoked, but there must have been some who pointed out that, failing a son, succession through the female of a son-in-law was now well established custom for all or most free tenures. Yet 120 years later, in 1315, Earl Patrick's 1195 view still prevailed, when the rights of the king's married daughter were set aside in favour of the king's brother and his heirs male. A kingdom was not as other holdings. As yet all this was hypothesis – *if* the king had no son. All were now agreed, both in the oath required by the king and in the arguments of Earl Patrick, that right to the throne descended to the king's son before all other claims.

Unfortunately we do not know whether William's second daughter had been born by 1194–95; if she had, then the recognition of Margaret as heir presumptive rejected the partition among daughters which was the law of baronies and may have intended a new law whereby the throne went to the elder daughter. In fact this issue was to arise for earldoms, for the first time it seems, later in William's reign, and judgement was given against partition and for the right of the oldest daughter – a different rule from that in England. Subtly argued this might have given Balliol a powerful case for the throne in 1291–92. In both Scotland and England settlement of the throne upon a woman could not be left to the deathbed and the last will but required a special sanction. But it was not inconceivable.

When he recovered, William persisted, probably seeing the proposed marriage as a way of gaining Northumbria as a dowry to the couple from Richard I. In an agreement, perhaps negotiated by Howden in the late autumn 1195, Otto was to be given Lothian, Northumbria and Cumberland, but the English king was to have *in custodia* Lothian and its castles, the Scottish king Northumbria, Cumberland and their castles.[33] The *custodia* intended was probably the garrisoning of castles, as in the English occupation of Lothian in 1175–89, and the castles in Lothian were the price squeezed from William for the castles of northern England. In time 'King Otto' would have had both Northumbria, Cumberland and their keeping, presumably within the English kingdom, but he would not have had the keeping of Lothian within his own kingdom.

This proposal was so attractive to Richard I that he sent his justiciar to York at Christmas to formalise the marriage contract with William, but the latter resiled because his wife was now pregnant, and he hoped for a son. That, at least, is Howden's explanation; we may wonder if opposition to the succession and to the price to be paid did not have something to do with the king's change of mind. Richard took the whole proposal so seriously that he felt impelled to grant Poitou and his own title of duke of Aquitaine to the disappointed Otto, who went on to a turbulent reign as king of the Romans and ruler of Germany.

[33] *Chron. Howden*, iii, 308; *SAEC*, 315–16.

The 1195 episode is the final occurrence of Lothian as an annexe to the kingdom of Scotland. It remained administratively distinct, so that there were justiciars of Lothian (as there were of *Scotia*, i.e. north of Forth) throughout the thirteenth century, but from 1095 there is no mention of separate treatment of the province until the proposed marriage treaty exactly a century later. Nonetheless the arrangements imposed in 1174 reflected political reality, that the English king could be master of Lothian through its castles, but scarcely of more northerly territory.[34] We do not know if these arrangements were inspired only by knowledge of political reality, or also recalled the Scottish kings' acquisition of Lothian with English recognition in the tenth century. In the thirteenth century English claims to lordship were revived, but were not linked to the status of Lothian;[35] they recalled lordship over the king acknowledged from the tenth century to 1174, but they redefined it. Homage was claimed by Henry III and his son *for the kingdom*, that is, it was required as a condition whereby the Scottish king ruled. Of this condition there was no hint until 1174, and even then it was secured not only by King William's oath, but also by the oaths of his prelates and magnates.

The child of William expected in 1195 (if it survived) must have been a daughter, for he did not have a son until 24 August 1198, when, thanks to the intervention of St Kentigern, the boy Alexander was born at Haddington. He was baptised by the bishop of Glasgow and the whole kingdom, we are told, rejoiced, then and on anniversaries.[36] Less than a year later Richard I died of wounds in France (6 April 1199), and his younger brother John moved at once to secure the succession. But John was doubtfully Richard's heir; the brother born between them, Geoffrey, duke of Brittany by marriage to King William's niece, had indeed died, but leaving a son, Arthur, whom Richard I, at Messina in 1191, had recognised as his heir should he die childless. On his death-bed, however, he designated John as heir to all his dominions, and first Normandy then England accepted the brother rather than the twelve-year-old nephew. Arthur was accepted by Anjou, Maine and Touraine, and by the French king. There was the rub – Philip II of France, a dangerous enemy and faithless ally.

From April 1199 William tried hard to extort the northern earldom from John as the price of homage for his English lands, and was wooed by Philip II, who offered marriage of his daughter to Alexander. By November

---

[34] I base this judgement on the history of attempts by Edward I–Edward III to annexe Scotland. Edward III's division of the kingdom with Edward Balliol showed that he recognised some reality.

[35] The exception is Mathew Paris's claim that in 1251 Alexander III did homage 'by reason of the possessions which he holds of [Henry III] ... namely in the kingdom of England, that is for Lothian and other lands'. I discuss this below on p. 154.

[36] *Chron. Melrose*, under 1198; *ESSH*, ii, 349; *Chron. Howden*, iv, 54 (for baptism); *SAEC*, 318–19; *Chron. Fordun*, i, 275 (for Haddington).

1200, when William, who had contemplated invasion of England but lost courage, caved in and did homage to John at Lincoln, Philip had deserted Arthur. As yet the boy was safe with his mother in their duchy of Brittany, but his chance of inheritance of any of the Plantagenet domains diminished steadily as the months passed. In the summer of 1201 John visited Philip's court and was sumptuously entertained, leaving an impression (wholly false as it turned out) that John had not only succeeded to his brother's domains but had won the peace with Philip II which had so eluded Richard I. In these circumstances 'the magnates of [Scotland] swore fealty to Alexander, the king's son, at Musselburgh' in October 1201.[37]

As with the young Malcolm in 1152, the vulnerability to internal disturbance of an heir so young, should he succeed, was undoubtedly behind this move, for which there was English precedent in 1155 and 1162, when Henry II was already envisaging the coronation of his heir, Henry (accomplished in 1170),[38] to whom Malcolm IV as earl of Huntingdon added his fealty in 1163, King William in 1170, and, of course, in 1175. The oath was perhaps designed to protect the English king's heir from an ambitious brother should the king himself die, but it was not repeated for Henry II's other sons after the death of the young Henry. The sons of Henry II showed how the rivalries of siblings swept aside filial duty; it was perhaps as well that the Young Henry and Richard I died without issue.

These rivalries may just have been William's concern in 1201,[39] for his brother Earl David had acted as John's emissary in the negotiations of 1199–1200 and was clearly not prepared to place his earldom in jeopardy. It would not be surprising if King William felt that his heir was vulnerable to King John, riding the crest of a wave of success in England and in his continental possessions, and quite capable of exploiting the accession of a child king in Scotland by claiming the fealty of Scottish magnates. The 1201 oath of fealty was a reversal of that 1175 oath which had humiliated William, when his magnates promised fealty to the English king, even against their own king. But William may have feared something even more drastic, that John would intervene to instal Earl David on the Scottish throne, and thus seek to validate the *casus regis*, his own title to the English throne as a younger brother against that of the young son of his older brother.[40]

For years William pressed his claim to Northumbria until a crisis in 1209

---

[37] Duncan, 'John King of England …', *King John; New Interpretations*, ed. Church, 262. The Melrose chronicle gives the date of the Musselburgh oath as iv. Id. Oct. = 12 October. *Gest.Ann.* gives 'about the feast of Sts. Simon and Jude' = about 28 October; iv. Kal. Nov. would be 29 October.

[38] Robert de Torigni in *Chronicles of Stephen*, iv, 184. The circumstances are described in Barlow, *Thomas Becket*, 67–70. It is not known who was present on either occasion

[39] For what follows on the relations of King William with John, a fuller discussion in Duncan 'John King of England …', *King John; New Interpretations*, ed. Church, 247–71.

[40] Holt, 'The *Casus Regis*', in his *Colonial England*, chapter 16.

in which he was so humiliated that he sought to conceal the terms of the settlement from his own subjects. Early in 1209 he seems to have entered negotiations with Philip II, who offered to marry William's daughter, probably Margaret, despite the fact that he had a repudiated second wife. John reacted strongly to news of these dealings with his bitter foe by hurrying north with a force; William capitulated at Norham, and again there was a peace, though there had been no war. Among other provisions, William handed over his two daughters to be married to John's son or sons and promised to pay 15,000 marks over two years. He was again put off with a promise that the lands of the Scottish king in England (undefined), which he would resign, would be held by the heir to the Scottish throne, and there was also a verbal agreement that the young Alexander would marry a daughter of John. Alexander did homage to John immediately thereafter, presumably in anticipation of receiving Northumbria, which eluded him as it had his father. William, humiliated, returned home, his juridical position unchanged.

The hold over the Scottish king taken by John in 1209, possession of his daughters, hostages and an obligation to pay £10,000, was presented as evidence of John's lordship over Scotland from the time of Edward I, and, as the easiest interpretation, is sometimes so presented still. There could be only one valid piece of evidence for such lordship – that William did homage for Scotland – and that happened neither in 1200 nor in 1209. In fact the steps taken in 1209, when there was no homage on either old or new terms, were necessary because John did *not* have such lordship; if he had, a marriage-alliance between William and Philip II would have been un-thinkable. To avoid this threat, John needed another hold over the Scottish king, and this William gave him, perhaps to avert the alternative of war and the subordination of his kingship. But John too had given a promise, that William's daughter would marry his son, and it was later admitted[41] that in return for this William had abandoned his own claim to English lands in favour of his heir.

The kings met again in 1212, when John, although his sons were a decade younger than William's, was a vigorous forty-four, had campaigned success-fully in Ireland in 1210, subdued the Welsh in 1211, and had no idea of the scale of trouble which was then impending in England. William, aged sixty-eight and intermittently an invalid, was faced with a resurgence of the Mac William family, perhaps expelled from Ireland by John's 1210 campaign there. Guthred, son of Donald mac William, landed in Ross with local support in January 1211, and a royal army failed to corner him. William came north and established two castles in Ross, but, after he went south again, one surrendered and was burned by Guthred.[42] With this failure on

---

[41] In the charges against Hubert de Burgh in 1232; Paris, *Chronica Majora*, iii, 222.

[42] William was probably at Aberdeen on 28 June, Nairn on 18 August, Forres on 2 October

his record, on 2 February 1212 William met John at Durham or Norham and, through the good offices of his queen, negotiated a marriage treaty for Alexander with the daughter, Joan, born to King John in 1210.[43]

Unfortunately the 'original' of the treaty survives only in a text written thirty or more years later, whereby William granted to John the marriage of Alexander within six years of Ash Wednesday (1212) (which is acceptable),[44] but goes on to promise that 'whatever may happen about (*de*)' John (words surely written after 1215–16), William and Alexander will maintain faith to Henry, John's son, as their liege lord, and will help him to maintain himself in his kingdom (written after Henry III survived to become king in 1216), saving their faith to their lord King John (surely meaningless if Henry is king). This text is based on a genuine original, for the names of those purporting to have sealed must be dated 1211–12, but it has been significantly altered to meet the circumstances of Henry III's reign, probably in 1244 when Henry was granted the marriage of Alexander (III).

An accurate account of 1212 is to be found in Bower's *Scotichronicon*, here using a narrative written probably by William Malveisin, bishop of St Andrews, himself involved in these affairs: in addition to the marriage agreement, each king swore to maintain the other in his just quarrels, and that the survivor would protect, help and cause to be invested in his kingdom the heir of whoever died first.[45] The detail is so circumstantial that it must command respect; it fits a situation in which William had failed to cope with the Mac William rising, and though framed as a mutual obligation, it was surely designed to protect the impending succession of Alexander in Scotland.

It invited positive action by King John within Scotland – 'cause to be invested' means more than messages of goodwill. It is possible that we should see this agreement as another serious defeat for King William, a concession that John might actively participate in the king-making of Alexander; if so it was the most dangerous concession made to an English monarch in the century before November 1289. But the words 'cause to be' suggest that this view is overly sinister, and that military help, not king-making, was what William sought. The important phrase is probably 'support the other in any just quarrels', for this is exactly what John did forthwith. Alexander went with him to London and was there knighted with appropriate splendour. He was then given a contingent of mercenaries

and Fyvie on 9 October; *RRS*, ii, nos 499–502. All were probably given in 1211. No. 500 (18 August) refers to castles built in Ross and is datable 1211 x 1213, but William was not in the north in 1212 or 1213 (*ibid.*, no. 522 for 1214).

[43] The youth of Joan in 1212 shows that William could well have affianced his Margaret to Otto when she was a child in 1195.

[44] In 1212 Ash Wednesday fell on 8 February, but the six years would end on Ash Wednesday, 28 February 1218.

[45] *Scotichronicon*, iv, 469. For the purported original of part of the agreement, *Anglo-Scottish Relations*, no. 4; *RRS*, ii, no. 505.

with which he returned to Scotland, where Guthred was betrayed to him, beheaded and hanged by his feet at Kincardine castle.[46]

As with the rebellion of Donald in 1187, the denouement suggests that this was a little local difficulty, but the contemporary view by an ailing king might be quite different. The Mac Williams were a serious threat to the stability of the kingdom, for the good fortune which delivered them to the king could as easily have run against him and in their favour. William's well-attested infeftment of Anglo-French followers should be seen as an attempted remedy for a serious deficit in his power, a lack of knights; but the infeftment was too small in scale to have a significant effect. By 1212 the collapse of the system of obtaining adequate service from enfeoffed knights was apparent in England, and the alternative of mercenaries paid from scutage and other levies was well developed. If scutage was not used in Scotland, it was probably because the total of knight-service due was so small; but the need for active well-horsed and equipped men-at-arms remained, to be met from mercenaries, as had happened in 1174 and now again in 1212.

In 1212 King John did help the Scottish king to maintain his authority, which reached to the Pentland Firth after a final royal expedition in 1214 to make peace with John, earl of Caithness and Orkney. Yet William's magnates remained suspicious of the English king; in 1213, when William was too ill to meet John, he was persuaded by the more powerful group among his advisers to refuse the attendance of Alexander in his place, on the grounds that John might detain him until the rebel Eustace de Vescy was handed over. Eustace had married Margaret, illegitimate daughter of King William, and his presence in Scotland did not sit well with the agreement that John would be helped by William in his just quarrels; but William perhaps restrained Eustace, whom John had to restore in 1213. The real breach of the treaty of 1212 came in 1215, at the hands of a young and vigorous Alexander II, who entered upon his kingship untrammelled by the fetters accepted by his father at Falaise in 1174.

Gest. Ann. is our only source for William's expedition to Moray in August 1214, return to Lothian and illness and death at Stirling on 4 December: 'lingering there for some time with strength failing day by day, *his son having been received as future king by bishops, earls and barons*, he departed from human concerns full of good days and in good old age', with further

---

[46] The Barnwell chronicler says William fled to John, to whose provision he committed himself, his kingdom and his son. *At ille cingulo militari commendatum sibi donans, in partes illas cum exercitu proficiscens ... Guthredum ... cepit* (*Memoriale Fratris Walteri de Coventria*, ii, 206). The translation of this defeats me. *Ille* refers back to John, but it was Alexander, a belted knight, who took Guthred. Did the annalist think that King John (*ille*) bestowed something (*donans commendatum*) with the belt of knighthood? The translation in *SAEC*, 330 ignores the difficulties, treating the text as John, *donans cingulum militare commendato sibi*, took Guthred, where Alexander is the *commendato*. The evidence that Saer de Quincy was involved in this campaign relates to 1210–11 and probably to the campaign in Ireland.

comment on his pious death.[47] We simply cannot know whether the italicised words referred to the oath to Alexander sworn in 1201 (as I was at first persuaded) or to another act of recognition as heir near the dying king in 1214. The argument for the latter is that it falls into place with the designation of Earl Henry, the recognition of Malcolm in 1152, the 'raising-up' of William in 1165 and the debates about inaugurating Alexander III in 1249; it was the recognition by prelates and magnates that Alexander was to be their next king. An old king, once shriven, had nothing to trouble his mind as life slipped away save fear of a Mac William resurgence on his death.

King William earned an obituary of remarkable generosity from both the Melrose chronicle and *Gest. Ann.* In the former he was 'of pious memory, his kingdom being in the greatest peace', while the latter dilates upon his goodly death; a similar eulogy comes from Gerald the Welshman.[48] The first hint of this pious reputation comes in Roger Howden's account, written in 1200, of how William planned to invade England in 1199, but, when sleeping at the tomb of Queen Margaret in Dunfermline abbey, was warned by her not to do so.

More remarkable is the obituary in *Gest. Ann.*, claiming that at York in 1206, 'in the presence of many nobles of England and Scotland, a boy was miraculously cured of a serious malady (*infirmitate*) which was upon him, by [William's] touch and blessing'.[49] This miracle falls in the period when royal thaumaturgy was in abeyance,[50] but the report of it seems to be nearly contemporary,[51] and the source may well have been a curial sycophant reporting to a chronicler after return to Scotland. A few years later the reputation had reached Canterbury where according to the monk Gervase, writing before William's death, the soldiers whom John led against William in 1209 were reluctant, exclaiming 'How can we attack the holy man, that king of Scotland? Certainly God, for whom he has done several miracles, will fight against us for him'.[52] *Gest. Ann.* was not quite so sure: 'may God be gracious unto his soul!'[53]

Some three years after his death came another testimony to his virtues, from another curialist, Walter bishop of Glasgow, at Cîteaux, on his way back from the fourth Lateran Council. Without detail, the king at mass saw

[47] *Chron. Fordun*, i. 279; ii. 275: *filio suo ab episcopis, comitibus et baronibus in futurum regem recepto.*

[48] *Giraldi Cambrensis Opera*, viii, 138–41; *ESSH*, ii, 400–2.

[49] *Chron. Fordun*, i. 279; ii. 275, where *miraculose* is omitted from the translation.

[50] Barlow, 'The King's Evil', *English Historical Review*, xcv (1980) 3–27; Barlow, *Edward the Confessor*, 270–71.

[51] The annalist says William was then at York to meet King John. There is no other evidence of this meeting but it fits with John's itinerary, *Rotuli Litterarum Patentium*, ed. Hardy, vol. i.

[52] *SAEC*, 328; *Historical Works of Gervase of Canterbury*, ii, 102–3.

[53] *cuius anime propitietur Deus*; *Chron. Fordun*, i, 280.

Christ arise from the host and received a blessing from him.[54] This tale was certainly influenced by the definitive assertion of the doctrine of transsubtantiation by Innocent III at the Lateran Council, and belongs with the second episode as testimony to the king's reputation for holiness, and not to the efficacy of sacral kingship, against which the papacy had set its face.

William's miracles were credited because in his own lifetime he had an established reputation for devoutness. Its roots probably lay in his devotion to the cult of St Thomas the martyr, who had apparently interceded for Henry II at the time of William's capture at Alnwick, and whose support he sought to win by the generous foundation (in 1178) of the wealthy abbey of St Thomas at Arbroath. Despite his prolonged quarrel with Pope Alexander III after 1178, he received from Alexander's successor in 1182 absolution from excommunication and a gift of signal honour, the Golden Rose which the pope carried on Laetare Sunday (7 March), usually given to the prefect of Rome, and now sent to a king for the very first time. It was still in the royal treasury in 1296 and may have been used by William and his successors as a sceptre.

In one domestic respect, William's reign differed from that of his predecessors. His writs attributed to David I an 'assize' whereby the payment of ecclesiastical teinds was enforced by the king's agents; what form that law-making took we do not know. But legislation by William does survive, indicating that he was influenced by contemporaries, especially the English kings, to institute new procedures for the repression of crime and the discovery of criminals. In 1197 an assize was issued to enforce incorrupt justice in baronial courts, clearly inspired by Richard I's *edictum regium* of 1194. But the royal assizes whose authenticity is probable are few and lack the thoroughness of contemporary English royal assizes. With the disappearance of the ordeal and battle in the early thirteenth century, the need for legislation about judicial procedures also seems to have disappeared, for apart from an inquest ordered in 1244, there was very little royal law-making under the Alexanders.[55]

The lack of a rite of anointing and coronation, which, in some realms, but not in all, had come to be attached to more ancient and essentially secular rites of inauguration, figures larger in our estimation than it did in that of twelfth-century writers, because Edward I, whose word is sufficient evidence for some schoolmen, saw it as a *preuve* that the Scottish kings were subordinate to those of England. Gerald the Welshman, who alone thought that King John had subordinated Scotland in William's old age, made no connection between this view and the fact that 'the chief men (*principes*) of the Scots however, who are also called kings, as are the chief men of Spain,

---

[54] Linehan, 'The posthumous reputation of King William', *SHR*, lvii (1978), 182–86. Much the same story is told of King William's uncle, Waltheof of Melrose in Jocelyn of Furness's Life of him.

[55] Duncan, *Making of the Kingdom*, 200–6, 539–41.

who yet were accustomed to be neither crowned nor anointed ...';[56] these rites were not essential to kingship.

Contemporary Europe saw other kings adopt them, in Scandinavia and Sicily, for example, but rarely in Iberia. Recent scholarship has asked us to look at the pressure for these ecclesiastical rites in Carolingian Europe as coming not from secular society, nor even from kings, but from churchmen themselves, anxious to extend their own role and authority by, in effect, hijacking king-making.[57] I doubt if this was true of David I and Malcolm IV, but as they did not advance beyond the first step of seeking an archbishopric, their attitude to the second step, seeking coronation, remains hypothetical. But to achieve it, a price had to be paid: acknowledgment of pope or emperor who gave the rite as overlord. There is no evidence that the Scots made that offer to the pope, nor was Henry II of England in a position (after 1170) or a need (after 1174) to act as emperor by giving a crown to his northern neighbour.

King William and his bishops made no approaches to Rome for the archiepiscopal *pallium* before 1174; the blatant infringement of ecclesiastical freedom and papal authority in the treaty of Falaise was perhaps a missed opportunity, for Pope Alexander III certainly put York in its place. His quarrel with William over the intrusion of a royal clerk into St Andrews in 1178–79 ended any such prospect, and William's obduracy cost the Scottish church dearly, for the bull *Cum universi*, whereby the Scottish church became the special daughter of the Roman see in 1192, stifled the hopes of St Andrews and made the achievement of coronation the more difficult.

The papacy was in any case reluctant to permit these rites free of cost. King William may have known of the visit by Pedro II of Aragon to Rome in 1204, when in return for an oath of fealty and an annual tribute, he was crowned by Innocent III himself, while the pope directed that his successors be crowned at Zaragoza by the archbishop of Tarragona. (His son refused to be crowned or anointed, though later kings of Aragon accepted the rite while seeking to be rid of fealty to the papacy.) Alfonso VI, king of Castille and Leon, responded to Gregorian claims of papal suzerainty over the peninsula by use of the title 'emperor' in 1077, as did his successor Alfonso VII, who in 1135 underwent an imperial coronation, it has been suggested to compensate for his failure in war against Aragon.[58] Gerald's statement about Spanish kings, if not exactly correct, was near enough the truth in his day to pass as a generalisation.

But what the Spanish experience brings home is the papacy's exploitation

---

[56] *Giraldi Cambrensis Opera*, viii, 139–40, 138 for comment on Spain; see also 156–57.

[57] Nelson has explored this issue in her papers, collected in *Politics and Ritual in Early Medieval Europe*.

[58] Ruiz, 'Unsacred Monarchy: The Kings of Castille', *Rites of Power*, ed. Wilentz, 109–44; Linehan, *Medieval Spain*, 393, 430, 440–47, 571, 592–601; and for Aragon, 506–7; Folz, *Concept of Empire in Western Europe*, chapter 5 for the Spanish 'empire'.

of its control of coronation to secure acknowledgment of subordination of a kingdom to the Holy See, a subordination acknowledged by King John of England in 1213 as a way out of his political difficulties, and by the king of the Isles in 1216. King William took no advantage of John's excommunication nor of the interdict imposed on England by Innocent III from 1206 to 1213, to curry favour at Rome and secure coronation as Pedro II had done. It may be that the cost would have been too high, but there is no evidence that William tried to find out; instead he bent his energy to securing 'his' earldom of Northumbria, putting himself in John's hands save for a brief dalliance with Philip II of France (no favourite of the pope) in 1209. The conclusion must be that to William the earldom mattered a great deal and coronation and anointing very little – not surprising, perhaps, for a king who had already reigned for forty years. And from 1213 the Scottish king played in a whole new ball-game, for the papacy was committed to its *fidelis*, the English king, and dismissive of any Scottish claim to which the English government took objection. Hence the frustration of Alexander II, a young man with ambitions for what his father had neglected.

Preparations for William's death had clearly been made. On the next morning, Friday, 5 December 1214, seven earls – Fife, Strathearn, Athol, Angus, Menteith, Buchan and Lothian[59] – along with William Malveisin bishop of St Andrews, took Alexander to Scone where he was made king.[60] His inauguration must have taken shape following oral tradition, including that of canons of Scone, for it was forty-nine years since the last inauguration, which few, if any, of those present could have seen – not one of the witnesses to King William's early charters survived to witness in 1210 and later. An *ordo* for the liturgical elements is possible, but the secular acts are unlikely to have been put in writing, and it is quite possible that there was improvisation and change in what was done in 1214. The Melrose chronicle, written soon after, notes that 'Lord Alexander, son of King William, having proceeded to Scone with no small train of magnates, there, both peaceably and honourably, in royal manner and with fitting solemnity, took up the governance of the kingdom (*regni*) of Scots'.[61]

---

[59] *Chron. Fordun*, i, 280. 'Lothian' was Dunbar. Orkney-Caithness and Sutherland were not present, presumably by reason of distance. The other earldoms not represented are Mar (Earl Gilchrist was either dead or disabled by 1211; his son does not appear as earl till 1228 and was not earl in 1222; *Scots Peerage*, v, 571–73) and Carrick (where it is likely but not certain that Duncan had received an earldom by 1214).

[60] I hope to show elsewhere that the document published by Sayles, 'A reputed royal charter of 1218', *SHR*, xxxi (1952) 137–39, relating to the inauguration church of the Scottish kings, is a work of imagination.

[61] *Dominus Alexander filius predicti Willelmi regis, cum non modico agmine mangnatum (sic) ad Sconam profectus, ibidem tam honorifice quam pacifice, more regio et digna celebritate, regni Scott' gubernacula suscepit; Chron. Melrose*, under 1214. *Regnum* here has to mean 'kingdom'; *celebritas* can mean a gathering or assembly.

Gest. Ann. describes the earls as taking (*assumpserunt*) the king and *adducentes* him to Scone (in 1249 it is said that they *adduxerunt* him to the cross in the cemetery there); for the 1214 ceremony itself the passive voice (*sublimatus est*), presumably to include all the rites of that day, obscures the role of the earls. However, the Lanercost chronicle, which also derives from earlier materials, is brief and unambiguous about Alexander's inauguration: he was 'enthroned at once at Scone'.[62] Put together, these sources suggest that the magnates dominated the occasion, that the king was made by enthronement at the hands of the earls, but that other ceremonies, probably ecclesiastical, followed, whence the presence of the bishop of St Andrews.[63] The rites of king-making completed, on Monday, 8 December 1214, the company moved to Perth Bridge to meet the funeral cortege of the old king, led by his widow, two bishops, the chancellor and others of the household. Earl David and the earls carried the coffin for a space on the way to Arbroath abbey, where William was buried on Wednesday, 10 December.[64] He must have made a will requiring this abandonment of Dunfermline abbey as the royal necropolis.

For all of 4 December, the day King William was alive and dead, his peace still prevailed; on 5 December a new king was made and with him a new peace. There was no interval without royal authority, no time for disaffection or rebellion, which may explain why in 1214, in contrast to 1165, the season of Advent was disregarded by the participants; but the young Alexander may also have been of a less pious cast of mind than his father. Very soon Moray was again troubled by a descendant of Duncan II: Domnall ban mac William and Kenneth mac Heth landed with a force from Ireland in the spring of 1215. They were soon dealt with by Fearchar, a Ross-shire magnate, who presented their heads to his king on 15 June,[65] and in time Fearchar was rewarded with the former Mac Heth earldom of Ross.

But trouble in the north persisted. In 1221 the king was with his army at Inverness 'against Donald mac Neil', while in 1228 the lord of Abertarff, by Loch Ness, was killed in his castle by a Gillescop who went on to burn part of Inverness; Mac Neil is otherwise unknown, but Gillescop is probably the man of the same name, 'of the race of Mac William', who with his sons and a Roderic, troubled the furthest parts of Scotland – an episode which the Lanercost chronicle places under 1230, commenting that they wished to obtain the kingdom by force, seeking alliance with many 'wicked men' of the

---

[62] *inthronizatus est apud Sconam statim*; the death of William is misdated to 1213 in this source. *Chron. Lanercost*, 11.

[63] The see of Dunkeld was vacant. The bishop of Brechin was consecrated shortly before; he may have been at Arbroath abbey.

[64] On the reliability of *Gest. Ann.* for 1214 see Scott, 'Inauguration of Alexander II', *SHR*, I (1971), 198–200.

[65] *Chron. Melrose*, under 1215. Fearchar was knighted as a reward; his earldom did not come until 1225 × 35.

kingdom, but were betrayed.[66] This is the last we hear of the MacWilliams, significantly and consistently still claiming the whole kingdom. Such successes as they had were doubtless won because the province of Moray resented the loss of its earl and the king's introduction of planted towns and southern knights. The Mac Heth with whom Mac William allied in 1215 probably sought the earldom of Ross, but an earldom was never the aim of the Mac Williams, and the evidence, consistently hostile to them, nonetheless suggests that there had been first a stream, then a trickle, of support for them, within *Scotia*.

Rejecting the treaty of 1212 with King John, to whom as king he never did homage, Alexander II engaged with the rebellious English barons against him, supporting Louis of France against John and Henry III. He was awarded the Northumbrian earldom (including Cumberland) by the rebels, and managed to seize some thereof. In 1216 he crossed England to do homage for it to Louis at Dover – a move which establishes conclusively that he made no claim to it as part of the Scottish kingdom. When abandoned by his allies in 1217, Alexander went to Northampton and 'came to the faith and service' of Henry III to 'do what he ought to do' to him. These phrases were used for other rebels on submission and presumably meant homage and fealty. While we have no hint of the wording used at Northampton, the English government was in no position to impose new terms.

In 1221, as agreed in 1212 and 1220, he married Joan, Henry's sister. In the early 1220s he led an expedition to Argyll and another to Caithness to punish the earl and *bondr* who had killed their bishop. At the end of the decade came the Mac William troubles already referred to, and in 1235 a serious rebellion in Galloway, whose chiefs rejected partition among the co-heiresses of Alan of Galloway, seeking his illegitimate son as lord. In none of these is there evidence of support among the magnates for the king's enemies, save where, as in the Isles, there was the competing claim of allegiance due to the king of Norway, the claim which took Alexander II to Argyll in an expedition against Ewen of Argyll, on which died on 8 July 1249 on the island of Kerrera.

His relations with Henry III after 1217 were for a time amicable, although, ignoring his own questionable behaviour in 1215–17, Alexander pressed his grievance: that none of his sisters had married King Henry, despite payment of 15,000 marks and resigning claims to English lands under the treaty of 1209. The interim settlement reached in 1220 provided for Alexander's marriage, but also, it seems, for a papal legate to Scotland to advise Alexander, doubtless included under pressure from the legate Pandulph who would seek to extend to Scotland the papal overlordship of England. A

---

[66] *APS*, i, 398, c. II; *Scotichronicon*, v, 117, 143; *Chron. Lanercost*, 40; *ESSH*, ii, 471. Discussion of these episodes and of the disturbances in Caithness in *Making of the Kingdom*, 528–29.

legate who came in 1220–21 was met by a request from Alexander that he crown and anoint the king. Reference to Rome produced a stern papal rebuke not to meddle in the matter 'since that king is said to be subject to the king of England', yet allowing the legate to act with consent of the English king and his counsellors and advice of the prelates of England – revealing whose proctors at the curia had leaned on the pope.[67] It must have been particularly galling to discover that the legate was to seek advice from prelates of England, but not from those of Scotland, whose church was the special daughter of the Roman see.

In asking for the rite from a legate, Alexander was reviving a long-forgotten issue, and seizing a chance to overcome the lack of an archbishop in his realm.[68] He did not leave the matter there, for, through his bishops, he pressed for an archbishopric for his church as a step towards negating these English claims. The evidence is the bull *Quidam vestrum* issued by Honorius III to all the Scottish bishops in 1225, on the urging of certain of them that 'since you did not have an archbishop by whose authority you could hold a provincial council ... [and] since provincial councils ought not to be foregone ... we command ... that you hold a provincial council by our authority'.[69] Professor Watt has recently shown that this was no privilege but a command, a letter of justice, drafted in the light of a canon of the Fourth Lateran providing for annual provincial councils, and he has rejected the idea that it was intended to authorise only a single provincial council meeting.[70] It was certainly used to permit the holding of later Scottish provincial councils, but that does not remove the strength of the contrary argument – that having dilated on the virtues of *councils*, it summarily orders *a council*, with no guidance on how it was to be called, an unlikely omission by the papal chancery if regular councils were here provided for.

This relatively cursory document is, I suggest, to be explained as an interim measure responding to one of the arguments put forward at the curia by Scottish bishops in favour of the grant of an archbishopric, i.e. so that the Lateran decree could be observed, an argument whose over-whelming force even English prelates could not entirely gainsay. The case for an archbishop was *sub judice* (if jostling at the curia could be so dignified), and was apparently allowed to drift into oblivion, probably because the Scottish church and king had no permanent proctors, no fee'd cardinals and no clout in Rome.

We do not know what persuaded Alexander to try his luck again, but it

---

[67] *Concilia Scotiae*, p. xlv, a text of the papal letter; *Cal. Pap. Letters*, i, 83; the date of the letter is July 1220 x July 1221, but probably in 1221. Cf. *ESSH*, ii, 443 and Watt, *Medieval Church Councils*, 42.

[68] Strictly there was one – York in Whithorn diocese.

[69] *Concilia Scotiae*, 3; translated in Watt, *Medieval Church Councils*, 44.

[70] The discussion by Professor Watt in his *Medieval Church Councils*, 43–47 is essential, for it puts the letter in its canonical context.

may have been the bishops in provincial council who led him to think that he might be crowned without an archbishop. All we know is that in the first half of 1233 the archbishop of York appealed to the pope on behalf of himself and the English king that the Scottish king should not have himself crowned to the prejudice of English royal dignity and the archbishop's liberty.[71] Since King Henry did not approach the pope directly, it seems that the Scottish move had again come from the Scottish church, which could only have infringed the 'archbishop's liberty' by a Scottish bishop exercising metropolitan standing. Doubtless there was quiet royal support, and though there was no papal response to the English, none was needed if the Scottish request was ignored.

That may be the reason why in 1234 Alexander apparently pressed for his undischarged rights under the treaty of 1209. The English government, when pressed for its debts, as by Alexander II, found the claim to over-lordship a useful stopper. If put forward by Henry III to Alexander this claim would have implied enforcement, war; propounded through the Roman curia it was a threat, but no more, which might reduce the Scottish king to more circumspect behaviour. Hence the pope was given a tendentious version of Anglo-Scottish relations since Henry II's time and on 4 January 1235 duly reprimanded Alexander, commanding him to observe his (unspecified) duties as *fidelis* under the treaty of Falaise; a year later on 26 April 1236 the pope chided him for ignoring this command and plotting against Henry's honour.[72]

In 1234–35 Henry was unmarried, though not for want of trying by his advisers to find him a bride, which shortly before April 1235 had reached the point of commitment to Joan of Ponthieu; that fell through. But on 1 August 1235 Alexander's youngest sister, Margaret, married Gilbert, earl of Pembroke and marshall of England at Berwick, in the presence of her brother and with King Henry's blessing.[73] Both kings must have known that the treaty of 1209 could not now be fulfilled, and the English aim may have been to free Henry from that obligation, for he married Eleanor of Provence by proxy in December 1235.[74] Alexander was not to be put off and his insistent demands were not softened by the papal admonitions. In September 1236 Henry felt compelled to meet Alexander at Newcastle and offered an inadequate settlement of the claim to the northern earldom: lands worth eighty marks annually. At the papal court Alexander made his case more effectively, and in March 1237 the legate Otto, appointed to England, was

[71] *Foedera*, i, 209, Henry III's approval of this appeal, dated 6 May 1233.

[72] *Anglo-Scottish Relations*, no. 6 (and misdated in *Foedera*, i, 215); *Cal. Docs. Scot.*, i, no. 1277; *Registres de Gregoire IX*, ed. Auvray, nos 2337–38, 3137.

[73] *Chron. Melrose*, under 1235; *Cal. Patent Rolls, 1232–47*, 126; *CP*, x, 371–74; *ESSH*, ii, 498–99; *SAEC*, 340.

[74] Howell, *Eleanor of Provence*, 10–13.

charged to make peace between the two kings, who were complaining of each other.[75]

By his mediation, they reached a compromise settlement at York, whereby Alexander gave up all claims to the earldom and money arising from the 1209 treaty in return for lands worth £200 annually in the northern counties, for which he did homage and fealty, though they were not assigned on the ground for another five years. Each king had a proxy swear on the royal soul to keep the agreement, but in addition fifteen barons, most but not all Scottish, swore to the keeping of 'this peace' and joined with Alexander in submitting themselves to papal jurisdiction over it.[76] This is the first certain occasion on which the Scottish king swore his oath (not the oath of fealty) vicariously. The peace, however, was between equals as the method of swearing showed. An issue which had bedevilled relations between the two kingdoms, arising from a weak English response to a dubious claim by the king of Scots, followed by a century of mishandling in which neither side was without blame, was at last laid to rest. But the settlement left the Scottish king as *fidelis* of the English king, required to do homage and fealty for the honour of Penrith.

In 1244 relations had deteriorated again, with Henry III suspicious that Alexander was supporting his enemies, domestic and foreign. According to Matthew Paris the Scottish king wrote to Henry denying that he held, or ought to hold, a fragment of the Scottish kingdom, from the English king. Such a letter is not impossible, but, if it existed, must have been a riposte to claims by King Henry, perhaps in terms such as: 'as our liege man, you must not give refuge to our enemies in your kingdom'. No such letters exist, and Paris may mislead or have been misled. But the diplomacy of the English at the papal curia shows that a claim to lordship over the Scottish king had been fostered there, and when Anglo-Scottish relations became strained, as they were in 1244, it could well have been brought into play within Britain.

To add to other English complaints there was an unjustified suspicion that Alexander was seeking alliance with Louis IX of France, whence the crisis in Anglo-Scottish relations in August 1244, with a threat of invasion of Scotland. Peace was made at Newcastle through the mediation of Henry's brother; Alexander promised to preserve good faith to Henry and his heirs as his lord, and never to treat with his enemies to stir up war or other harm, unless the English king should 'unjustly oppress us'. This obligation was sworn to on the king's behalf and on his soul by four barons, then sealed by him, but in addition four bishops, seven earls and seventeen barons swore that if the Scottish king should break this promise, they would give him no aid, but would seek to have the obligation upheld.[77]

---

[75] *Chron. Melrose*, under 1236; *Cal. Docs. Scot.*, i, nos 1291–95; *ESSH*, ii, 501.

[76] *Anglo-Scottish Relations*, no. 7.

[77] Paris, *Chronica Majora*, iv, 379–380; *Chron. Lanercost*, 51; *SAEC*, 353–54; *ESSH*, ii, 538. Duncan, *Making of the Kingdom*, 535–36 is wrong in identifying the Bisset affair as a cause of

It may be that the English negotiators had consulted the treaty of Falaise when they demanded this oath, for it is reminiscent of the fealties given at York in 1175. Yet it was markedly less than those fealties, for it contained no promise to support the English king, nor to constrain the Scottish king, but only to give the latter no help should he make a treaty for war against England. And Alexander's promise was likewise carefully restricted, preserving his freedom of action if he felt 'oppressed' by the English king. In sum the treaty amounts to a promise of good behaviour, an acceptance of the realities of politics, that Scotland could cause trouble if allied with France, but that isolation and the balance of power would, as in 1174 and 1209, make the alliance much too costly; it was better to accept the logic of inferior Scottish power and give a promise of good behaviour. The Scottish king retained his independence, dealt as equal with the king of Norway, and gave neither castles nor renewed homage to Henry III.

There was, however, more to the treaty, for Margaret, daughter of Henry III, was promised in marriage to Alexander, three-year-old son of the Scottish king. It was probably for this betrothal that the treaty of 1212 was produced in an 'improved' text,[78] but Alexander II nonetheless secured from Henry a recognition that the marriage agreement should not prejudice his right to make marriages freely – a careful protection of his juridical position while accepting good sense and political reality, the defensive posture of the Scots.[79]

There was another political reality of which the leading Scots must have been very aware in 1244: that the boy Alexander was now, after his father, the only representative of David I in the direct male line. From 1165 to 1198 David's only male descendants had been King William and his brother David, earl of Huntingdon, whence the attempt by William to secure the throne for his oldest daughter and Otto of Brunswick. Earl David, too, married late, in 1190, and his only surviving son was not born until 1206.[80] On the earl's death in 1219, this son John, a ward of Alexander II, would be heir presumptive to the throne of Scotland, and, because the marriage of Alexander and Joan of England was childless, he remained heir until his death, without issue, in June 1237 (for what follows see Table B, p. 346).

We do not know where the next heir to the Scottish throne would have been found had Alexander II then died. His three sisters were all married to English earls, the oldest to Hubert de Burgh, earl of Kent, by whom she had a daughter, Megotta, secretly married to Richard de Clare, earl of Gloucester. Megotta died childless in November 1237,[81] but Hubert

---

the trouble; I discuss this in 'Sources and uses of the Chronicle of Melrose', *Kings, Clerics and Chronicles*, ed. Taylor, at 171–72.

[78] That is, *Anglo-Scottish Relations*, no. 4.
[79] *APS*, i, 108.
[80] Two sons died young.
[81] *CP*, v, 700.

survived until 1243 and his wife until 1259.[82] The second sister, married to Roger Bigod, earl of Norfolk, was childless but survived until the 1260s, her husband until 1270.[83] The third sister, married to Gilbert, earl of Pembroke (died 1241), died childless in 1244.[84] In 1238 Queen Joan died, and a year later Alexander married Marie de Coucy, who bore him only one child, Alexander, in 1241. Between 1237 and that birth, all three sisters and their husbands were alive, yet we have no sign that any was recognised as heir presumptive, nor was royal favour shown to the husband of any one of them. It is the merest guesswork that if Alexander II, rather than Queen Joan, had died in 1238, the Scots would have enthroned King Hubert – but what alternative would there have been?[85]

With the death of John earl of Huntingdon and Chester (the latter earldom in right of his mother) in 1237, Henry III decided to exclude his co-heirs and take the earldoms into his own hands. He bought off John's sisters, including Isabel, who thereby became a richer widow than she had been the wife of Robert Bruce IV (who had died in the 1220s);[86] in particular she acquired the manor of Writtle in Essex, which thus passed to her son. Robert Bruce V was also to claim that he had inherited through his mother a right to the Scottish throne which was recognised in the time of Alexander II. In the winter of 1290, in a document sent to Edward I, the Guardians were attacked for usurping the functions of the Seven Earls in making a king when the throne fell vacant, and in particular for favouring John Balliol against the interests of 'us Robert Bruce, lord of Annandale'. The authorship of the document is thus not in doubt, and accords with an attached memorandum which gives the first surviving account of the recognition of Bruce as heir to the throne in the time of Alexander II.[87] The second, much shorter, version of the story is contained in the petition by which Bruce formally claimed the throne, dated 3 August 1291,[88] and a third is included in arguments submitted by him to the court in June 1292.[89]

Comparison of these three versions reveals considerable changes in the facts averred. The first account places events when Alexander II (born 1198) had almost reached very old age (*senilis*), despaired of procreating an heir of his body and feared dissension after his death. The second version is placed when he despaired of having an heir and the third when he went to make war in the Isles. All three are agreed, therefore, in pointing to the end of

[82] *CP*, vii, 141–42.

[83] *CP*, ix, 593.

[84] *CP*, x, 373–74.

[85] Roger Wendover claims that in 1232 Hubert was charged with having raped Margaret and with the ambition of becoming king of Scotland through her. *CP*, vii, 141 n. *d*.

[86] Duncan, 'Bruces of Annandale', *Transactions of Dumfriesshire and Galloway Natural History and Antiquarian Society*, lxix (1994), 95–96.

[87] Stones and Simpson, ii, 185–86.

[88] Stones and Simpson, ii, 145.

[89] Stones and Simpson, ii, 170.

Alexander's reign, for he made war on the western seaboard in 1221–22 and in 1249; the latter date (when he died there) was clearly meant. Yet his son was born in 1241, and he cannot have despaired of an heir after that year. All three are agreed that Sir Robert Bruce was declared to be heir to the kingdom, the second and third implying, the first stating, that this was Robert Bruce V.

The first version, with much circumstantial detail about how this decision arose, is not wholly legible, but does claim that the king put an issue of principle, who has the better right in the kingdom of Scotland, the son of a second daughter or the daughter of an eldest daughter [of Earl David], to a meeting of the nobles and prelates[90] of Scotland, that they declared for the son of the second daughter, whereupon the king took Bruce by the hand and presented him to them as his lawful heir (the source does not say 'if he had no heir of his body'), and they all swore fealty to Bruce on the king's command. All this was inscribed in the rolls of the king's treasury, 'but we do not know into whose hands it has come'.[91] The second and third accounts are broadly agreed: Alexander ajudged Bruce as his heir, if he had no heir of the body, by the assent of the good men (second account), or of the bishops, earls and baronage (third account); no oath is suggested. The second account mentions no documentary record, but asserts that some who participated then were still alive and could bear witness to the truth; the third puts first and second together: a record was in the treasury which should be searched for, but if it is not found, then surviving barons remember the events.

The most damning feature of these accounts is the variations in the tale they tell, variations which show that they were tailored to meet the circumstances for which each was prepared. The shift from an assize of sorts delivering a verdict to the king deciding by the assent of his magnates was called for by the change in circumstances from late 1290, when Bruce wanted Edward I to enforce Bruce's right (i.e. the claimed verdict), to 1291–92 when his claim was being examined by a new court, to which the supposed decision of Alexander II was more likely to be authoritative. The disappearance of what was surely a telling, even conclusive, point in favour of Bruce's right, the oath of fealty to him alleged in the first account, suggests that it would not stand up to a moment's scrutiny. The reported record in the treasury – the correct place to deposit it, though the inventories of that treasury contain no hint of its existence[92] – was alleged to be missing because it had never existed, and when Bruce fell back upon the

[90] *nobiles et magnates regni Scotie episcopos et alios clericos et laicos*; from *episcopos* has been added; Stones and Simpson, ii, 185.

[91] Stones and Simpson, ii, D.76 (J), pp. 185–86; A.65 = D.65(i), pp. 144, 145; D.76(B)vii, p. 170.

[92] *APS*, i, 107–18.

testimony of his friends in the second account, he had to drop the fealty as too serious a perjury to ask of them.

These are harsh words, but the alternative to them is to excuse the erroneous date as poor recollection and to look for another time before 1241 when Alexander might have nominated Bruce. At her death in 1238 Queen Joan was only twenty-eight years old, and such action in her lifetime, a substantial insult to her reputation, is unlikely. The only possible year for a recognition of Bruce as heir is 1238–39, when he was aged eighteen or less, was probably still in wardship and when the king was forty and intent upon remarriage (1239) to father an heir. Modern historians have gone for 1238, despite the objection that the king's sisters[93] and any sons they might still have were then much closer to the throne.

There remains the possibility that about 1249 Alexander II recognised Robert Bruce as heir presumptive to his young son, and I have suggested that a charter issued by Bruce, at Edinburgh on 9 August 1248, might have been given on the occasion of such a recognition; alternatively a royal court, either that held at Stirling on 19 May 1248 which issued an assize or that at Edinburgh in December 1248, with the king, Bruce, his mother, the earl of Mar, Steward and John Comyn of Badenoch present.[94] But the suggested purpose implies a degree of royal favour to Bruce which the circumstances of Alexander's last years do not confirm. The prominence of Alan Durward as justiciar brought him a dominant role after the king's death (when he was already married to Alexander's illegitimate daughter); that role should have fallen to the heir of Alexander III, if one had indeed been recognised. Or, at least, the heir should have played a part of some significance until the birth of a royal child in 1261.

Yet Robert Bruce is mentioned only once in the tense years after 1249, when, in 1255, with the help of Henry III, he was one of the eight prelates and seventeen magnates (including four earls) 'with many others' who ousted the monopolising Comyn family and took over the royal council.[95] In 1257 the Comyns seized the king, yielding power to a compromise council of ten in 1258, a council from which the name of Bruce is absent.[96] I conclude that the recognition of Bruce as heir to Alexander II was, at best, a hope entertained by the family which may have been built upon hints around 1238 that he had a possible right. Any such hints would be overtaken

---

[93] Only the youngest, Margaret countess of Pembroke, married in 1235, was of child-bearing age.

[94] Duncan, *Making of the Kingdom*, 239 n. 67. (For *Lindores Cartulary*, LXI, read XLI.) The king made a law at Stirling on 19 May 1248, limiting those who might take judicial oaths. No earl but eleven barons were present with Bruce second, after Alan Durward, justiciar of *Scotia*; *APS*, i, 404. For the Edinburgh court in December, the most likely occasion of a decision to proceed against Ewen of Argyll, *Historical Manuscripts Commission, Fourth Report* (1873), 493 = *Aberdeen-Banff Collections*, 548.

[95] *Foedera*, i, 329 (*cf.* 326, where Bruce precedes the Steward); *ESSH*, ii, 581–84.

[96] *Chron. Melrose*, under 1257, 1258; *ESSH*, ii, 589–93; *Anglo-Scottish Relations*, no. 11.

by the birth of another possible heir, a son to the lady Dervorguilla, married to John Balliol. The claim in Bruce's petition for the throne in August 1291, that Alexander III, failing his own issue, also held him as heir 'and gave many closest to him (*de specialibus suis*) to understand this', was not mentioned in Bruce's other imaginative claims and is not worth the parchment it was written on.[97] The recognition of Robert Bruce V as heir or heir presumptive to the Scottish throne by Alexander II and III was fiction.

[97] Stones and Simpson, ii, 144; unfortunately the original version in French is defective here.

CHAPTER 7

Creacio regis: making a king

It is not seriously in doubt that all kings from the eleventh century at least, until James I in 1424, were inaugurated at Scone. But within that period two changes in the inauguration are documented: first the looting in 1296 from Scone and Edinburgh of the Stone, crown, sceptre and other regalia, given to Westminster abbey; second the grant of coronation and unction by John XXII to Robert I and his successors, exercised for David II in 1331 and subsequently till 1633. Both Edward I and Robert I referred to the inauguration as *creacio*, king-making.[1] We have no inauguration *ordo* from the pre-Reformation church, no directory of proceedings, little comment on what went on, and that little from the final period of the Stone's residence at Scone, the thirteenth century.

Something can be said of that period which may throw light on earlier origins, but little that is certain. The *Scotti*, coming from Ireland to Dalriada, might well have brought royal inauguration rites with them, rites with origins in Indo-European tradition.[2] For the ordination of Aedan as king by Columcille consisted in a laying of the cleric's right hand upon the king's head.[3] A survey of all the evidence from Irish literature and medieval record reveals great variation both in space and time, with presence of tributary chiefs, conferment of a rod by an *ollamh* (praise poet) or, from the thirteenth century, *coarb* (an ecclesiastic) and acclamation not uncommon; also found is the use of a rock or flagstone sometimes with the carved impression of a footprint. Some footprints are found, however, with no known association with inauguration.

In Scotland there are examples from Argyll to Shetland, but most notably at Dunadd, attested as a fortress in the seventh and eighth centuries. The combination of footprint with other rock carvings there has won for the place the repute of inauguration-place of the kings of Dalriada though there is no written evidence to this effect. The footprint beside the church at Southend could presumably be attached to a kingship of Kintyre, whose king is named in 721, and whose fortress might have been Dunaverty. A

---

[1] *Rot. Scot.*, i, 12a; *RRS*, v, 129, 488, 510.
[2] Simms, *Kings to Warlords*, 21–32, 39.
[3] *Adomnán's Life of Columba*, ed. Anderson, 188–89 (107a–b); *cf.* 66–67 (36b). See now Charles-Edwards, *Early Christian Ireland*, 360–61.

description of inauguration of a Lord of the Isles at Finlaggan in Islay, written a century and a half after the supression of that lordship,[4] reflects either the persistance of Irish custom in late medieval Scotland or the familiarity of the author with an account of an Irish inauguration; it shows: use of a flagstone with footprint (and one turned up at Finlaggan in the 1960s) into which the Lord placed his foot; vesting in a white habit, the discarded clothes given to the *ollamh*; and conferment of a rod (probably by the *ollamh*, though that is not explicit).[5]

Early medieval Irish literature associates chairs with kings, *ollamhna* and saints, and some stone chairs survive, but the only positive identification of an open-air stone inauguration chair is that of sixteenth-century Ui Neill chiefs of Tir Eoghain at Tulach Óg depicted on a map of about 1600.[6] Its crude base may have been the Flagstone of the Kings recorded in 1432, to which the back and sides were added, perhaps to exalt the prestige of the Ui Neill.[7] That is the nearest we get in Irish sources to the central act of inauguration in Scotland, enthronement upon the Stone of Scone. Irish sources place much more emphasis upon the inauguration hill or mound (and the Tulach Óg stone was on the slope of a hill).[8]

There are other uses of a stone, or other examples of enthronement: in Sweden election of a king 'at Mora stone' in 1275 and 1319, and until the fifteenth century, but sceptical modern scholarship has argued that this was an innovation adopted in exceptional circumstances.[9] There is one fragment of twelfth-century evidence of a myth that Dan was made first king of Denmark upon a stone, which does not reappear in Denmark, and in Norway saga literature, including the 'sagas' of twelfth- and thirteenth-century kings, makes no mention of a stone in the many 'takings' of kings.

The Frankish kingdoms provide many statements associating royal accession with a throne, and it is likely that this was the more sedate formality used on all or most occasions for the descendants of Clovis, possibly after elevation upon a shield in some cases.[10] With the validation of the Carolingians as a new royal lineage, by ecclesiastical anointing in the mid-eighth century, and by coronation from the ninth, enthronement lost its significance for these kings by the high Middle Ages. But the royal church at Aachen had not merely the splendid marble *sedes* in the gallery, but another throne erected in the atrium, to which the king, after *universalis*

[4] *Highland Papers*, ed. Macphail, i, 24.

[5] Gruamach, 'Finlaggan "footprint stone" found', *Clan Donald Magazine*, 3 (1965), 5–9; RCAHMS, *Inventory of Argyll, vol. 5, Islay Jura*, 275–81, although published in 1984, makes no mention of this find.

[6] Depicted on the cover of the paperback edition of Simms, *Kings to Warlords*.

[7] This paragraph is wholly indebted to the work of Dr E. Fitzpatrick.

[8] Simms, *Kings to Warlords*, 35.

[9] I owe knowledge of this to Professor Peter Sawyer. Magnus, *Historia de Gentibus Septentrionalibus*, ii , 350–51, 398.

[10] Schneider, *Königswahl und Königserhebung im Frühmittelalter*, esp. pp. 213–17.

electio, was led by counts and other magnates to receive 'after their custom' their proferred hand, oaths of loyalty and help against enemies; ecclesiastical ceremonies followed in the church. This passage in the description of Otto I's coronation in 936 by Widukind of Corvey has been much debated, for similar proceedings are not recorded for later coronations, but weighty opinion is in favour of its authenticity.[11]

Enthronement and the use of a stone come together in the inauguration of dukes of Carinthia, attested from 1286 until 1414, but thought to go back to the Carolingian creation of the duchy. The ceremony took place *alfresco*, upon a throne made of a column and other fragments of Roman masonry, was entirely secular and the peasant who played the role of an Irish *ollamh* received the duke's clothes and the animals he brought to it. From this the duke went to another (even stranger) stone throne to dispense justice. Some of this would have been familiar in Ireland.[12]

Enthronement was a normal feature of royal inauguration in England and has persisted there, taking place in modern times in Westminster Abbey. But probably from William II's building of Westminster Hall, a king-to-be was enthroned there before entering the abbey for unction and coronation, a ceremony which continued at least until the fifteenth century. The Yorkist kings entered the Hall and were enthroned, robed and carrying a sceptre, upon the throne there, described as a marble chair, and surrounded by lords. They were hailed as king in an entirely secular ceremony which gave them the usurped kingship; coronation had to be delayed in order that a court might sort out claims to functions at that ceremony.[13]

Enthronement of a ruler is found in, for example, ancient India, but the most likely origin for use of a stone throne is ecclesiastical, in the seating of a newly-consecrated bishop upon a *cathedra* in his church as a sign of his possession of church and diocese. Such thrones in stone survive in a number of cathedrals, most notably at Hexham, a seventh-century example with a low back.[14] The borrowing of a secular rite of possession came early in the church's history, which may have extended its use for the rite of Christian king-making in some kingdoms. But nowhere is there anything quite the same as the use of a stone such as the Stone of Scone as an inaugural chair.

The closest link of the Scottish inauguration, as it is described in the thirteenth century, is with the secular enthronement found in England; both may go back to a non-Christian king-making in which the essential elements

[11] Widukind von Corvey, *Sachsengeschichte*, 63–67; *Krönungen*, i, 38, 265–73.
[12] Huber, *Der Kärntner Fürstenstein im Europäischen Vergleich*. The article by R. Palme, 15–33 is a good short summary on inauguration stones, but the whole symposium gives a 'European comparison'. Curiously the marble throne in Westminster Hall seems not to be mentioned.
[13] Armstrong, 'Inauguration Ceremonies of the Yorkist Kings', *Transactions of the Royal Historical Society*, 4th series, xxx (1948), 51–73.
[14] The fullest account I have found is the article 'Chaire épiscopale' in *Dictionnaire d'archéologie chrétienne et de liturgie*, iii, 19–75, with numerous illustrations.

were enthronement and taking a rod or sceptre. But the English ceremony, and possibly that at tenth-century Aachen, had become only a preliminary to the king-making within the minster which was dominated by ecclesiastics and by Christian imagery in word and deed. Scottish ceremony would not escape the claims of the church and churchmen in the high Middle Ages, but it was nonetheless preserved – not fossilised – by the hostility of English prelates and their kings to any Scottish use of ecclesiastical rites which might confirm the independence of the king. By the twelfth century the right to crowning and anointing came from the pope, who, while he was unsuccessfully pressing these rites upon Iberian monarchs to urge and bless their slaughter of Muslim Spaniards, and was granting them willingly to Balkan kings to win them over from the Patriarchate of Constantinople[15] and grudgingly to kings of Scandinavia, nonetheless turned a stony eye on, and deaf ear to, the pleas of Scottish kings.

By this time inauguration rites, which previously had shifted (e.g. from Kingston to London and thence to Westminster) had become associated with traditional places – Aachen, Reims, Westminster. Scone seems to share antiquity with Aachen, but, I have argued, probably replaced Forteviot and Dunning in this function late in the ninth century. That enigmatic survey of anonymous kings, the Prophecy of Berchan, speaks of Scone 'of the high shields' and 'of melodious shields', reflecting eleventh-century practice there.[16] It would be particularly valuable to have clearer evidence pointing to elevation on a shield, which is known as part of the inauguration ceremony of Byzantine emperors in the fifth and sixth centuries. Early references, including Tacitus' description of the elevation of a German chief[17] suggest that it was a usage among 'barbarians', perhaps fairly widespread, for it is attested among the Khazars in the tenth century. It had been adopted by the Romans as the elevation by an army of their general to be ruler, but probably went out of use in the seventh century, and its revival after the fall of Constantinople in 1261 may have been conscious antiquarianism.

In Navarre, whose kingship dates back to the ninth century, it remained the manner of inaugurating kings as late as 1238 when a *fuero* described it

---

[15] In 986 x 89 the Byzantine emperor gave the king of Croatia a golden crown and recognised his title to secure support against the Bulgars; a century later Pope Gregory VII had a claimant to the throne crowned by a papal legate and the new king swore fealty to the pope; Eterovich and Spalatin, *Croatia, Land, People, Culture*, i, 95, 100. But when Geza I of Hungary asked Gregory for a new crown, the pope at first supported his rival, the exiled king Solomon, then demanded papal overlordship in exchange for recognising Geza; the latter turned to Byzantium whence the emperor sent him a crown; Engel, *The Realm of St Stephen*, 32; Szovák, 'Image of the Ideal King in ... Hungary', *Kings and Kingship*, ed. Duggan, 242–43. In 1204 Innocent III allowed his legate to crown the ruler of Bulgaria, but the claims of Serbia were rejected; in 1217 the ruler of Serbia, having failed to get a crown from the patriarch, secured coronation by a papal legate and is known as 'Stephen the first-crowned'; Temperley, *History of Serbia*, 45.

[16] *ESSH*, i, 273, 519.

[17] Tacitus, *Histories*, IV, c. 15.

as ancient custom, following upon an oath by the king-elect that he would defend the laws, and it was retained in 1257, when coronation and anointing were sought additionally. Its roots may well lie in the recognition of ninth-century war-leaders in the struggle against Islam,[18] for it was a military gesture for the chief of a war-band or retinue, and particularly appropriate to one whose claim to inherit was small, a preliminary to kingship for, say, Macbeth or even Maelcoluim III. If practised or retained in Scottish king-making, it ceased to be a distinct ceremony and perhaps became a clash of acclamation.

With this survey of royal inaugurations not involving unction and coronation, let us turn to what we know and what we must conjecture for the ceremonies used in thirteenth-century Scotland. There is a depiction of inauguration on the seal of Scone abbey (Plate 3), depictions of the king in majesty on seals (Plate 2BC), and one important account of the inauguration of Alexander III in 1249 in *Gesta Annalia*, a related one in *Scotichronicon*. That in *Gest. Ann.* is clearly an edited version of a contemporary account into which references to the Stone (probably fourteenth-century) have been introduced. If these are removed, the contemporary account would read as follows:

> Bishops, abbot and magnates, all the clergy and people, when they had heard the same Earl Walter Comyn, with one voice gave their consent and assent to [Alexander] being set up as king. Earls, namely ... Fife and Strathearn, and many other nobles led Alexander, soon to be king, to a cross standing in the cemetery on the east side of the church. [Alexander having been] placed there in the royal chair adorned with silken cloths woven with gold, [David] bishop of St Andrews, and the rest assisting, consecrated him fittingly to be king, the king himself sitting on the royal chair, under whose feet the earls and other nobles, on bended knees, cast their clothes. And lo, when these things had happened, a certain highland Scot, suddenly genuflecting before the throne, with bowed head, saluted the king in [his] mother tongue 'God bless Alexander king of Scots ...' and speaking thus he read the genealogy of the kings of Scots up to the end ... until he came to the first Scot, namely Iber Scot.[19]

There are acts revealed by other sources upon which this does not touch, but, with the Scone seal, it must remain our main guide to what went on. In the following discussion I shall try to follow the steps of inauguration as we know, or as we conjecture, they happened

[18] Nelson, 'Symbols in Context, Rulers' Inauguration Rituals in Byzantium and the West ...', *Studies in Church History*, xiii (1976), ed. Baker, 97–119; Walter, 'Raising on a Shield in Byzantine Iconography', *Revue des Études Byzantines*, xxxiii (1975), esp. 157–66; Schramm, 'Der König von Navarra, 1035–1512', *Zeitschrift der Savigny-Stiftung für Rechtsgeschichte, Germanistische Abteilung*, lxxxi (1951), 110–210, esp. 149–67.

[19] *Chron. Fordun*, i, 294–95. I have altered the beginning to eliminate the chapter-transition, and have omitted the text of the genealogy.

At the unexpected death of Alexander II on Kerrera in Argyll on 8 July 1249, his only son, Alexander III, was approaching eight years of age; who should govern till he came of age?[20] A meeting at Scone on 13 July, convoked by we do not know who but responsible for a decision to 'raise up' (the word used in 1214) the new king, was asked to postpone inauguration on that day in favour of the conferment of knighthood, which might now be seen in relation to kingship as priesthood was to episcopal orders,[21] but was rebuffed when Walter Comyn, earl of Menteith, 'a man of foresight and shrewdness in counsel', claimed that he had seen a consecrated king who was not a knight and had heard of others. The kingdom (*regio*) without a king (*rege*), he said, is like a ship without rudder (*remige*) or steersman (*rectore*). He loved the boy for his father's sake, and therefore urged his immediate elevation as king, for delay is always hurtful. All agreed.[22]

The case for postponement had been made by Alan Durward, justiciar of Scotia, married to an illegitimate daughter of Alexander II, continuing in his office after the inauguration and seen by *Gesta Annalia* as justiciar of 'all *Scotia*' and as Chief Justiciar,[23] probably a misunderstanding of his contemporary title, justiciar of *Scocia*, that is north of Forth. It must be admitted, however, that there may not have been a justiciar of Lothian in 1249–51. There is no doubt that Alan dominated the government until Christmas 1251 in such a way as to arouse jealousy among the magnates.

The bishops, abbot, magnates, all the clergy and people, in one voice,

---

[20] On the period 1249–60 see Watt, 'The Minority of Alexander III of Scotland', *Transactions of the Royal Historical Society*, fifth series, xxi (1971), 1–23. Alexander III was born on 4 September 1241.

[21] Henry III of England, at the age of nine, was knighted by William the Marshall just before his coronation, at which he was belted with a sword by the archbishop. The boy Louis IX was knighted at Soissons on his way to coronation at Reims in 1226, and the coronation order probably drawn up in his reign included a ceremonial presentation of sandals, spurs and sword which had been placed upon the altar; spiritually blessed, they were to be used for the church. By contrast, in the Iberian kingdoms, kings eschewed conferment of arms by ecclesiastic or a lay magnate: Fernando III succeeded to Castille in 1217, and in 1219 knighted himself with the assistance of his mother; his cousin, Alfonso IX of Leon had been knighted by his father in 1188, but seems to have reknighted himself in 1197. Jaime (Catalan Jaume) I of Aragon, who succeeded at the age of three in 1213, signalled his inauguration as king when, at his marriage in 1221, he girded himself with a sword taken from the altar; Alfonso IV of Aragon knighted himself, assisted by his brothers, in 1328. In his second *Partida*, of *c.*1280, Alfonso X of Castille claimed that only when he had been knighted could an emperor or king be crowned. His descendant, Alfonso XI, therefore, in 1332 went to Compostella, where the archbishop blessed the king's arms, after which the king put on his sword and took his arms from Santiago's altar; he then approached an articulated effigy, an automaton, of the saint (it still exists), and received from it the blow to the face which constituted the accolade of knighthood. Linehan, *Medieval Spain*, 393–94, 571, 592–601 and plate III.

[22] *Chron. Fordun*, i. 293; *regio* was used rather than *regnum* presumably because it gives better alliteration with *rege, remige* and *rectore*. The words attributed to Walter Comyn were translated by Skene as 'he had seen a king consecrated who was not yet a knight...' (*Chron. Fordun*, ii. 289), but this misleads in implying Comyn's presence at a foreign inauguration.

[23] *Chron. Fordun*, i, 293, 297 (c. LI).

agreed to inaugurate Alexander[24] just as in the English coronation *ordo* a bishop asks the people if they wish to subject themselves to such a prince and ruler, and the 'clergy and people' present answer *volumus et concedimus*, the 'acclamation' of modern discussions.[25] Where this Scone agreement took place we are not told, but *Gest. Ann.* then takes the company into the churchyard for the enthronement, implying acclamation in the abbey church. Thus we have a move from debate over knighting to agreement or acclamation and then enthronement. But *Scotichronicon*, repeating the debate, claims that to end controversy the earl persuaded the company that a king, with crown and sceptre, 'should be considered a knight' and that he should be marked as knight by the bishop of St Andrews, 'who should fill the office of king ... This was done'. As Bishop David de Bernham 'girded the king with a knightly belt in the presence of the magnates and set out the rights and promises which pertain to a king, first in Latin, then in French, the king, accepting all of this, readily underwent blessing and ordination by the bishop'.[26]

The passage takes a very ecclesiastical view of inauguration: the bishop fills the kingly office.[27] The earl's argument is that a king is by his office a knight, his insignia are knightly and the conferment of them by the bishop recognises this knightly dignity. Bower then goes on to present investiture with sword as, in effect, conferment of knighthood, but the intention (evidently muddied by Bower), was to single out the element of investiture which particularly recognised the responsibility of a king to defend the church. Elsewhere the sword would be upon the altar, dedicated and then girded, and it seems likely that this happened at Scone also, within the abbey church. In the final clause of this passage, the word 'ordination' has probably been chosen to include knighthood, but despite the secular audience (magnates are mentioned but no clergy) Alexander was not a knight before Christmas 1251.

That Bower is correct in making a sword part of the royal insignia conferred upon Alexander is confirmed by his small seal, made in 1249 x 50,[28] showing the crowned king with sceptre in his left hand and holding with the right the pommel of the sword laid across his knees (Plate 4A),[29] a

---

[24] *Una voce ipsum in regem erigere consensum prebuerunt et assensum*; *Chron. Fordun*, i, 293.

[25] *Claudius Pontificals*, 115; Nelson, 'The Rites of the Conqueror', *Politics and Ritual*, 385–87.

[26] *Scotichronicon*, v, 292–93. Most MSS seem to have *ut rex ab episcopo ... qui officium regis impleret, ipsum eciam in militem consignaretur*. The word *ipsum* is impossible; read ? *ab ipso [episcopo] ... consignaretur*. The Corpus MS has *consignaret*, implying that *ipsum* is the king, and the bishop is the subject of the sentence, but it also has *rex* as the subject.

[27] Nelson, 'The Problem of King Alfred's Royal Anointing', *Politics and Ritual*, 313–14.

[28] The only remaining impression is so fragile that it could not be photographed. In 1252 the matrix was engraved with additional words *DEI GRA REX SCOTT*, and returned to use. For the 1250 and 1252 versions see Plate 4.

[29] *Cf.* the contemporary royal seal of Aragon. Bautier, *Chartes, Sceaux et Chancelleries*, ii,

seal whose legend was intended to recall Adomnan's Life of Columba with its account of Columcille's ordination of Aedan, and so make a case for unction and coronation of Alexander III. Depiction of an enthroned king wearing a belted sword is virtually impossible, which explains why English royal seals from 1066 to 1259 and Scottish ones from 1107 to c. 1260 (and the young Malcolm IV in the initial M to his Kelso abbey charter) are shown in majesty holding the sword erect.[30] This position was deliberately avoided in Alexander's small seal, for reasons we can only conjecture: he had not yet been knighted; or he had a sword to defend the church but it was in no immediate need of defence. There are other possibilities.

The sword cannot have been worn throughout the rites of inauguration, but must have been taken off (as it was in England) and either placed on the altar or given to another to carry. An illustration of the scene, made c. 1440, shows it held upright by a lay magnate behind the enthroned king, just as swords were carried by nobles at English coronations.[31]

Bower goes on to claim (we are still before the enthonement) that the bishop 'expounded to [the king-to-be] the rights and promises (iura et vota) which pertain to a king first in Latin, afterwards in French, [and] the king, graciously granted and accepted everything'. The use of French is most unlikely to be later than the thirteenth century. The content of promises, not a command to subjects (mandatum), and in question form ('Do you promise ...?', 'I promise', 'Will you ...', 'I will'), seems to have been adopted in England late in the twelfth century, where the earliest description of a coronation, that of Richard I in 1189, shows him going to the altar and there swearing upon the Gospels and relics (1) to show peace, honour and reverence to God, the church and its hierarchy (ordinati), (2) to maintain right and justice, and (3) to annul evil laws and perverse customs if any have been introduced, and to found and keep good laws. The format reiterating 'he swore', and the final ceremony in which the archbishop asked him if he would keep these promises and he answered that he would, suggest that question and answer had been used throughout.[32]

206, no. 15, the seal in use from 1207, showing the king in majesty, crowned, holding sceptre and orb, with sword across his knees, not held. Burns, *Society and Documentation in Crusader Valencia*, 87, illustration no. 7, the seal in use after 1241, showing the king in majesty, crowned, still holding the orb in his left hand, but the right hand now grasping the hilt of the sword across his knees; the sceptre has gone. At 88 n. 7 Burns comments that 'The sword amid the insignia on Jaime's seal of majesty was far more important than crown or sceptre and was his "preferred symbol of sovereignty"'. This latter seal was in use 1241–76 and in the display of the sword bears a remarkable resemblance to Alexander III's small seal. *Cf.* also the Agilulf (king of Lombards) panel of 590x, frequently illustrated and discussed in McCormick, *Eternal Victory*, 289–98.

[30] Crouch, *Image of Aristocracy*, 189–98, especially Figure 3.

[31] *Scotichronicon*, v, opposite p. 288.

[32] *Benedict Peterb.*, ii, 79–82; *Chron. Howden*, iii, 9–12. Richardson, 'The Coronation in Medieval England', *Traditio*, xvi (1960), 111–202. This form of the oath seems to go back to Anglo-Saxon times for it is recorded in one version of the 973 coronation; the Ramsay account

The substance of the Scottish king's promises is given only in Walter of Guisborough's account (written *c*.1300–5) of John's inauguration in 1292

> when the king swore [*A*] that he would defend holy mother church and the people subject to him by ruling justly, [*B*] would establish good laws and [*C*] would continue those used and found until [his] death.

> *facto tamen iuramento* [*A*] *quod sanctam matrem ecclesiam populumque sibi subiectum iuste regendo defenderet,* [*B*] *leges bonas conderet* [*C*] *usitatasque et inventas usque ad mortem continuaret.*[33]

A is pretty certainly abbreviation of fuller wording, since *iuste regendo* can scarcely apply to defending the church, which a king did not rule. In 1250 the Scottish bishops reminded their boy-king that in a recent council, with magnates present and not a church council, it had been decided 'that churches and their prelates should enjoy the peaceful possession of all those rights and liberties which they enjoyed in the time of [Alexander II]';[34] the magnates had accepted this practical application of 'defend the church' as a royal obligation also binding upon them.[35] It was part of the oath in 1249 as well as 1292, and included also the church's prelates, who in an oath would be *ordinati* or *rectores*.

In 1296 John justified defying Edward I as 'our own defence and that of our kingdom, to whose defence and protection we are bound by the bond of oath',[36] an oath perhaps to defend and protect both church and people. But that would leave unexplained the phrase *iuste regendo*, and a more satisfactory reconstruction of *A* would seem to be two promises by the king expanding Guisborough's words in line with the prayer found in the English *ordo*, third recension, firstly to defend the church and its hierarchy, then to protect (*or* defend and protect) the people subject to him by ruling justly.[37]

---

of the *mandatum regis* at Edgar's coronation of 973 claims that it was sworn 'with the archbishop questioning', *interrogante archiepiscopo. Historians of … York*, i, 437 = Schramm, *Kaiser, Könige und Päpste*, ii, 242, § 6. In John of Worcester's account of the coronation of William I in 1066 the king swore his promises 'as the archbishop required of him', *Chron. John of Worcester*, ii, 606–7 = Stubbs, *Select Charters*, 94. Lack of space precludes a fuller discussion of the English coronation oath in the twelfth and thirteenth centuries, but we may note that 'customs introduced' is first found in the oath of Henry II at his reconciliation with the church in 1172.

[33] *Chron. Guisborough*, 239. It must be said that there is much in common between this version of the Scottish oath and the version given by John of Worcester of the Conqueror's oath in 1066: *se velle sanctas Dei ecclesias ac rectores illarum defendere … cunctum populum sibi subiectum iuste et regali providentia regere, rectam legem statuere et tenere, rapinas iniustaque iudicia penitus interdicere* (*Chron. John of Worcester*, ii, 606–7).

[34] *APS*, i, 425; *Concilia Scotiae*, ii, 241–42.

[35] For a discussion of this episode in its ecclesiastical context, Watt, *Medieval Church Councils*, 70–74.

[36] *Anglo-Scottish Relations*, 142.

[37] 'may he defend and raise up your holy church and rule justly the people committed to him by you'; Legg, *English Coronation Records*, 33, 259.

Some of the words, and more of the spirit, of the English 1189 oaths (1) and (2) are in this reconstruction of *A*.

B is found verbatim in (3) of the 1189 oaths; the laws to be continued in *C* are 'existing good laws', also part of (3) in 1189. Is it too bold to emend here Guisborough's rhetoric of death to the Biblical one of life, also found in 1189 (1): *bonas leges conderet, usitatasque et inventas omnibus diebus vite sue continuaret?*[38] Much of this was ecclesiastical platitude on good kingship in a legally-minded age; the phrases found in common may be less significant than the differences between the English oaths and this reconstruction of the Scottish ones. But English influence must surely be seen in the two languages used, the interrogatory format and the content as oaths, rather than the earlier English *mandatum*. The content (at least) was an innovation of 1189, and in Scotland, therefore, of 1214, when the presiding prelate was William Malveisin, bishop of St Andrews, who, about the time of John's coronation in 1199, had known both Roger Howden and Philip, bishop of Durham, a key figure at John's coronation;[39] he may have brought to Scotland the 1199 equivalent of Howden's account (a directory) of the 1189 coronation.

Guisborough's account mentions the oath after enthronement by the earl of Fife, but cumbrously places it before the act (*facto iuramento*); Bower describes belting with the sword and the oath-taking which 'the king graciously conceding and accepting all [the oaths] readily underwent and permitted ordination by the said bishop', followed by enthronement of the king, seated crowned, with sceptre and purple robe. The royal small seal confirms sceptre and crown, as does the seal of Scone abbey which on one side depicts a royal inauguration.

This seal was in use by 1296, but the king depicted upon it is very young, beardless, and can scarcely be other than Alexander III, of whom we have another depiction on the 1250 small seal, where the detail of the royal figure bears such a striking resemblance to the Scone seal's (much coarser) depiction that the latter may well have used the small seal as model (Plates 3 and 4). On the Scone seal the field is sewn with small dots and dashes, grass – we are on open ground. In the centre the crowned king is enthroned on a cushioned bench seat, a simple trefoiled (or lily) long sceptre in his right hand, his left pulling down over his chest the cord fastening his mantle, which is grasped at the sides by two ecclesiastics holding the royal mantle.

Behind these two prelates are figures with sword and shield whose identity is given by shields of arms on either side of the royal arms shown beneath the king's feet. On the king's right are the arms of the thirteenth-

---

[38] *Cf.* Deuteronomy 17: 18–19, 'the king, *when he sitteth upon the throne of his kingdom,* ... shall write a copy of this law ... out of that which is before the priests, the Levites, and it shall be with him and he shall read therein *all the days of his life* ... to keep all the words of this law'. The Latin *omnibus diebus vitae suae*, is the same as that of the 1189 oath.

[39] Duncan, 'Howden and Scotland', *Church, Chronicle and Learning*, ed. Crawford, 147.

century earls of Fife,[40] on his left those of the earls of Strathearn. Floating above these figures are three others: above the bishop another ecclesiastic carrying a square object bisected horizontally which might be a Gospel book used for the royal oaths; above the abbot is a figure whose legs are not seen, holding vertically a narrow object, half a man's height, shown only in outline; behind him a small figure appears to perch on the head of the earl of Strathearn.

The depiction is theatrical, but the maker of the matrix has not been able to display all that went on. He depicted the ceremonies at a particular point, that at which the clergy took their part in the investiture of the king with a mantle. Before this he had certainly been enthroned, and, since he holds a sceptre and wears a crown, he had been given these. The anonymous 'Appeal of Seven Earls', intended for Edward I and therefore likely to be accurate in matters indifferent, asserted that seven earls and the community of the kingdom, made a king, set him on the throne, and 'gave to him (*eidem attribuere*) honours pertaining to rule of the kingdom'.[41] Enthronement seems to come before investiture with regalia. But in 1328–29 the pope was informed that 'kings of Scotland, from ancient former times, have been accustomed to receive insignia of royal dignity from bishops of St Andrews'.[42] Both were tendentious but neither claimed that *all* honours or insignia were given by the favoured group or person.

Since the clerics on the Scone seal touch neither sceptre nor crown, it seems that they did not invest the king with them, though the sceptre was an ancient symbol of royal authority whose assumption and use required no papal approval.[43] The elaborately floriated sceptre shown on Alexander III's small seal (1249 x 50), on his second great seal (*c.* 1260), on King John's seal (1292) (Plates 4BC and 2C) and on the second seal of Robert I (*c.* 1316) was not copied from English models and may be seen as a depiction of the Scottish royal sceptre.[44] In 1297 Edward I presented Scottish regalia, looted in 1296, to the shrine of St Edward in Westminster abbey, among them a gold sceptre of King John and with the crown a silver-gilt apple and golden rose. The apple, I suggest, was the base screwed on to the rod-stem of the golden rose, for this item is invaluable evidence that the Scottish treasury had retained the one sent to King William by the pope in 1182.[45] That it would be carried by succesive kings is very likely, and it may be that the head of the elaborately foliated sceptre depicted on royal seals was modelled upon

[40] Specifically of Earl Colban, 1266–*c.*1270 on his seal. No other representations of the arms of thirteenth-century earls of Fife seem to be known.

[41] *Anglo-Scottish Relations*, no. 14, 88–89.

[42] *National Manuscripts of Scotland*, ii, no. XXX.

[43] Jaski, *Early Irish Kingship*, 59 and the literature cited there.

[44] The seals are depicted in *National Manuscripts of Scotland*, i and ii, and in Birch, *History of Scottish Seals*, i, Royal Seals.

[45] Stevenson, *Documents*, ii, 142–44. For a depiction of a thirteenth-century Golden Rose, *Innes Review*, xx (1969), opposite p. 156.

it when it had become worn, or when a crown was made; the sceptres depicted recall the rods laid up by the princes of Israel in the tabernacle, one of which, Aaron's, 'budded and brought forth buds and bloomed blossoms and yielded almonds ... to be kept for a token against rebels' (Numbers 17: 8–10) – and in 1291 the Scottish treasury contained *virga Aaron*, perhaps one of these sceptres.[46]

If the clergy did not invest with sceptre, by default it seems most likely that a secular lord, presumably an earl, handed the sceptre to the king. The verb *attribuere*, used in 1290 and translated as 'confer upon', has the simpler, if ambiguous, sense of 'give', 'hand over'; in the case of the sceptre, however, 'giving' would mean 'conferring'. At John's inauguration in 1292, the deputy for the earl of Fife was to exercise 'certain definite offices in the new making of a king of Scotland in placing him in his royal seat'.[47] The plural *officia* hints that in addition to enthronement he was involved in the *attributio* whose nature was not known to the clerk drawing up these letters.

Save for the crown worn by Edgar (1097–1107) on his seal, Scottish kings are shown without crown from then until 1249,[48] a period when (William excepted) they showed themselves anxious for the right to be crowned. The sudden appearance of a crown worn by Alexander III, including the depiction of his inauguration, is unlikely to have been an innovation of 1249, and we may reasonably conjecture that his father had owned a crown which he wore upon festive occasions; the 1249 novelty would be to wear this at the inauguration.[49] In addition to the crown looted in 1296, King John still possessed another when he was sent to France in 1300, and which was then forfeited.[50] In England and France the coronation regalia were kept by Westminster and St Denis abbeys, and the king, if he wished to wear a crown elsewhere, must needs possess one of his own. If this were the practice in Scotland it would follow that inauguration insignia were kept at Scone abbey, perhaps since 1249. The source of the gold *coronella* worn in 1306 by Robert I at his inauguration is unknown.[51]

The clergy certainly did not crown Alexander III, and unless magnates crowned the king which is unlikely, they gave this honour to the king or he took it from, say, the altar; he put it upon his own brow. For this he would need two hands, so the crown would have to come before investiture with

[46] *APS*, i, 112, line 27.

[47] *Foedera*, i, 785 = *Rot. Scot.*, i, 12; *quedam certa officia in nova creacione regis Scotie de ponendo ipsum in regiam sedem suam*

[48] Except on the illuminated initial M of Malcolm IV's charter to Kelso abbey.

[49] If Alexander III wore his father's crown, it must have been reduced in size in some haste.

[50] Stevenson, *Documents*, ii, 142–44 for the 1297 list; *Chron. Rishanger*, 390–91 for the 1300 crown.

[51] *Foedera*, i, 1012 = *Cal. Docs. Scot.*, ii, no. 1914; this letter of Edward I says Robert 'had himself crowned' with it, a widespread English misapprehension. There is no proof that John Balliol wore a crown at his inauguration, but it is entirely possible.

the sceptre. These are conjectures with some, but not overwhelming, probability; we are on firm ground only with the king wearing a crown, but without coronation. And despite the order enthronement – investiture with insignia suggested in 1290, it is likely that the insignia were kept in the abbey and assumed by the king there after he had sworn his oath. He wore them as he was led to the enthronement outside.

That ceremony is described in *Gest. Ann.* and by Bower. In the former earls led the king to a cross in the cemetery where he was seated in a royal chair (*cathedra*), a version confimed by the 1290 Appeal and by Guisborough. Bower has bishops with earls lead the king to the cross where 'they' placed him in the chair; in this he may be following *Gest. Ann.* or another source. The clergy were excluded from enthronement, a customary rite probably with remote origins. In 1249 the two earls of Fife and Strathearn are are named as participants, representing the whole cohort of earls, the 'other nobles' who accompanied them as they held the king (presumably each by an arm) and placed him on the royal seat.[52] Three earls were present in 1249, Fife, Strathearn and Menteith, but not Angus, a child in wardship, Lennox, probably so, Atholl an heiress in wardship, nor, possibly, any of the more distant, Carrick, Dunbar, Mar, Buchan. That this was not felt to be a lack is significant – there was no custom or convention that seven earls (as were present in 1214) were needed for the inauguration, despite the 1290 claim by Robert Bruce on behalf of seven (unnamed) earls.[53] The earls may have represented the provinces of the kingdom of Alba, but uncertainty as to who would appear argues against that interpretation.

The earl of Fife was, however, thought to act as head of clan Macduff.[54] The leading role which he played is attested in 1249, 1292 and 1306 (in the latter two cases unavoidably by depute),[55] and is strikingly confirmed by the terms of restoration of Earl Duncan IX[56] by Robert I in 1315, when it was agreed that this earldom must remain separate and distinct – i.e. could not escheat or forfeit to the crown – because 'kings of Scotland must be made by

---

[52] The mention of the same two earls in *Gest. Ann.* and on the Scone seal strengthens the case for identifying the latter with the 1249 ceremony.

[53] *Anglo-Scottish Relations*, no. 14. At this point, late in 1290, possibly early in 1291, Bruce had the support of a majority of earls in his claim to the throne. I believe that Bruce borrowed the seven from the electors of the Empire.

[54] Bannerman, 'Macduff of Fife', *Medieval Scotland*, eds Grant and Stringer, 20–38. The lineage may have descended from King Dubh (d. 966) and been given this leading role when excluded from the kingship. It became one of three privileges accorded to the kindred by Maelcoluim III according to Wyntoun *c.*1400; *Chron. Wyntoun*, iv, 302–3. But his Macduff of that time is not a historical figure.

[55] In 1292 it fell to the earl of Fife to exercise an office 'in the new creation of the king of Scotland, of placing him in his royal seat at Scone, according to the custom of that kingdom'. And an official inventory of Scottish records was made a month after John was 'seated in his royal seat (*sedes*) of Scone by the folk of the king of England and the magnates of Scotland and held and publicly proclaimed as king'. *Rot. Scot.*, i, 12a; *APS*, i, 113.

[56] The *Peerage* shows him as no. X, but Ethelred (no. I) was probably not earl.

a definite earl of Fife',[57] a leading kindred supportive of the king. The dignity of earl was a novelty of the twelfth century, generally thought to have replaced that of mormaer, provincial steward or governor for the king. But the men who would receive such a position would be chosen from local lords of wealth who supported the king; they too would be the heads of kindreds, and their place and role at the inauguration would derive from that, strengthened by their identification with a province. We can only speculate whether this role at Scone had earlier origins in heads of kindreds who brought an Irish king to his installation in Pictish times, or was a recognition of interdependence found also in the secular king-making outside the cathedral at Aachen and in the nobles grouped around the English king enthroned in Westminster Hall.[58] Once, it would seem, this had been the choice of the man to be king.

The new ruler was placed upon a throne, for the best accounts speak of *cathedra* or *sedes*; they do not mention the Stone. If laid upon the ground, our Stone would have entailed an undignified royal squat, for, as surviving, it has been carved from a larger rock of stone local to Scone.[59] Royal seals between 1107 and 1260 show the king in majesty upon a bench-type throne with a cushion (as on English royal seals). There was no effort to show the Stone contained within the throne, even on the Scone abbey seal and the small seal of Alexander III (which do show the bench divided horizontally, perhaps by a shelf for the Stone). Nonetheless, unless Edward I was deluded in 1296–97, impossible in the light of later Scottish complaints, the Stone must have been part of, contained within, a bench throne.

As we have it today the Stone is a puzzling object.[60] It is rectangular, 670 mm wide, 420 mm from front to back and 265 mm deep; it weighs 152 kg or three hundredweight. Two surfaces have been dressed fairly flat, the top (it is presumed) and one long side (i.e. the front); the rest was much more roughly shaped. For unknown reasons a beginning was made to cut a rectangular recess in the top, but this was not placed at equal distance from each side, so was extended leftward by a cut on the left short side some 4 cm

---

[57] *Foedera*, i, 785 = *Rot. Scot.*, i, 12 (1292): *quedam certa officia in nova creacione regis Scotie de ponendo ipsum in regiam sedem suam apud Scone secundem consuetudinem dicti regni Scotie. RRS*, v, no. 72, of August 1315: *les royis d'Escoce deusent estre feste par certan conte de Fyfe.*

[58] Bouman discusses ecclesiastical enthronement of the king, with the prayer *Sta et retine*, as part of the coronation rites and cites Widukind for the 936 secular *sublimatio* outside the church. Bouman, *Sacring and Crowning*, 136–40, esp. 138–39.

[59] Fortey, Phillips and others, 'A geological perspective on the Stone of Destiny', *Scottish Journal of Geology*, vol. 34 (2) (1998), 145–52; and a letter on the same subject from Phillips and others in the same *Journal*, vol. 35 (2) (1999), 187–88.

[60] The following account is based upon information in Breeze and Munro, *The Stone of Destiny*, 44–45. The name 'Stone of Destiny' presumably refers to the supposed prophecy that where it was, Scots would rule. The official publication uses this name, but the royal warrant for its partial return, with proper dignity, calls it the Stone of Scone. A volume of papers on the Stone is promised by the Society of Antiquaries of Scotland and Historic Scotland.

nearer the edge. This work may have been abandoned from fear that the stone would split – as it has done in the twentieth century. Iron staples are sunk in the two short sides, with a hole through which passes a flattened iron loop, at the other end of which is a ring. The Stone was then cut with recesses in the side and top (impinging on the rectangular recess incisions) into which this metalwork could fit when not in use; subsequently two surfaces of the Stone were smoothed and (probably last of all) the staples were cut back because they had protruded from the Stone. This last is probably to be associated with the making of the Westminster throne, but the metalwork was not added for the transportation to London, for which carts must have been used, but belongs to the life of the Stone at Scone.

Ignoring the metalwork and its housing, we have a roughly rectangular stone intended to receive an inset rectangular object some 45 cm wide and 22 cm from front to back, a cushion or a holy relic, it has been suggested. But the first scarcely fits with upstanding stone edges. It is much more likely that the Stone was to receive a reliquary or a portable altar, which would be a consecrated stone of about the size of the inset. If it was to be an altar carrying relics, it would have Greek crosses at the four corners and centrally at the front, and there are traces on the Stone of two or three lightly incised crosses on the long side of the top, between the back edge and the intended rectangular recess. If these were indicators for a set of five crosses, then the Stone was to be an altar with relics in the recess. If it was to be a table with an inset portable altar, that intention must have been given up when the recess had been merely outlined.

Either purpose would give this artefact a numinous significance for those who sought a stone suitable for royal inaugurations, at the end of the ninth century if my earlier suggestion of a move to Scone then be accepted. Either then or later it would be smoothed off and raised into a bench-chair. The metal rings reflect the need to carry it, apart from its bench, from the church into the cemetery and back, and the recesses carved to hold that metalwork show that (as later at Westminster) the containing bench was little wider than the Stone. But it is also noteworthy that the staples are inserted below the middle of the short faces, closer to the Stone's 'bottom'. If lifted by a pole through the rings, gravity might turn the Stone so that the smooth 'top' would seek to become the bottom. This was surely the intention, a smooth face to slide on the wooden base of the king's bench, while the rings tucked away beneath the Stone, with a wooden seat of the king's bench and cushion above the Stone. In short, the Stone today is displayed upside-down – though we thus see its more interesting face.[61]

The Stone of Scone is not mentioned in any source which, as we have it,

[61] In a letter Dr David Breeze tells me that the centre of gravity does seem to be above the iron staples, but a photograph of 1974 shows that it did not then turn upside down when lifted by the metalwork – an operation too risky to try today because the staples are thin and might break.

was written before the looting of 1296, and only Guisborough's description of it is of that period. Its prominence in modern times is due largely to its survival, alone among the regalia, and its use in later coronations. In the Scottish 'pleadings', developed for Boniface VIII in 1301, Edward I was said to have removed 'the very ancient royal seat of the same kingdom',[62] but this was soon reformulated in the mythical story of Scota's migrations from Egypt when she took the 'royal seat, which [Edward] carried off by violence'.[63] This is the earliest appearance of an origin myth for what is *not* called the Stone, presumably because Boniface was unlikely to be impressed by theft of a rock. The identification of the Stone as Jacob's pillow (which would have impressed Boniface) came later, in England.

This is slight evidence that the Scots valued the Stone at all highly. In 1306, determined to become king, Robert Bruce took steps to secure the presence at Scone on his chosen day, Lady Day, of the sister of the earl of Fife who had died in 1289 (the male heir, Duncan IX, was an adolescent in England).[64] Robert had to make do without the Stone, but he was set 'in the kingis stole',[65] an enthronement by earls, which was never impugned as invalid. The place, Scone, and the inaugurator, a representative of the earl of Fife, were important, but the Stone was quietly forgotten. In 1324 it was said that among Scottish demands for a peace treaty was the return of the Stone, but when, after the peace of 1328, which made no mention of it, the English government proposed to secure further concessions from Robert by returning it, he showed no interest,[66] perhaps because his proctors were busy at the curia securing the right to coronation and unction.

Guisborough described it as a 'very large stone made to the manner of a round chair (*cathedra*)'.[67] Unless the whole account is imaginary, foisted upon Guisborough or us, these words represent his attempt to make sense of a source, perhaps a newsletter of 1292 or 1296, which must have been misunderstood. The critical word is *rotunde*, 'round', which, I suggest, had been written *rote* with a line above *ote* to mark abbreviation, not of *rotunde* but of *robuste*. *Lapis pergrandis ... ad modum robuste cathedre confectus*, 'made to the manner [that is, shape] of an oaken chair', does not merely save Guisborough's account from rejection as impossible.[68] It also gives a precedent.

[62] *Scotichronicon*, vi, 162–63.

[63] *Scotichronicon*, vi, 182–83.

[64] *Anglo-Scottish Relations*, no. 35; *Flores Historiarum*, iii, 324.

[65] Barbour, *Brus*, book 2, lines 150–51, 178–81, 185–86.

[66] *Vita Edwardi Secundi*, ed. Denhold-Young, 132–33 for 1324; 'famous because upon it the kings used to receive *gubernacula* of the kingdom with the sceptre'. I owe this reference to Professor Barrow. But Bruce is also said to have demanded return of his Essex barony (Writtle), which I find very unlikely. Were these English offers? For 1329, Breeze and Munro, *Stone of Destiny*, 29.

[67] *Chron. Guisborough*, 239.

[68] The text may also have been influenced by the description of Solomon's throne made of ivory with a round back: *et summitas throni rotunda erat in parte posteriori*; I Kings 10: 19.

In Joshua 24: 25–27, where the prophet Joshua, in Shechem, 'made a covenant with the people that day; he drew up a statute … for them, and wrote its terms in the book of the law of God, he *took a great stone and set it up there under an oak, that was by the sanctuary of the Lord*. And Joshua said … "This stone shall be a witness against us for it has heard all the words of of the Lord which he has spoken to us"'.[69] The Vulgate, *tulit lapidem pergrandem posuitque eum subter quercum que erat in sanctuario Domini*, actually places the oak in the sanctuary, hence making the biblical phrase more apposite to the Stone in Scone kirkyard. But this place acquired a further significance in Judges 9: 6, in the Vulgate, 'All the men of Shechem and all Beth-millo came together and made Abimelech king, beside the oak which stood in Shechem'.[70] King-making next to the oak was king-making upon Joshua's stone, the biblical precedent for the ceremonies at Scone. Although no claim was made that Judah's stone was later in Scone, the cladding of the stone for royal inauguration in an oaken chair would be suggested by these biblical precedents.[71] The Scone stone, it might be said now, was a witness to God's covenant with the people of Scotland, a covenant made when He gave them a king.

For the book of the law would be the Mosaic law of Deuteronomy, whereby 'It shall be, when [the king] sitteth upon the throne of his kingdom, that he shall write him a copy of this law … and it shall be with him and he shall read therein all the days of his life … to keep all the words of this law and these statutes' (Deuteronomy 17: 18–19). In the Christian dispensation the church was keeper of the Mosaic book, but King John's promise when enthroned 'that he would defend holy mother church and the people subject to him by ruling justly, would establish good laws and would continue those used and found until [his] death', was a covenant that he would rule according to God's law.[72]

This is all a Christian gloss, and does not explain the roots of enthronement upon a stone. Nonetheless the biblical precedent may have been seen long before 1292, for we are told by both *Gest. Ann.* and Guisborough that the stone was kept in the abbey church, and by Guisborough that the chair was kept there beside the altar. Joshua's stone stood in an open-air sanctuary of the Lord, such as was the cemetery of Scone abbey. The Christianising of

[69] This is largely the *NEB* translation, but I have followed the Vulgate, *quercum*, oak, rather than 'terebinth' or 'pole' as in *NEB*.

[70] *constituerunt regem Abimelech iuxta quercum quae stabat in Sichem.* I am much indebted to Professor Janet Nelson for this further Biblical reference.

[71] *Gest. Ann.*'s cloth over the chair, *pannis sericis auro textis ornata*, is so close to that over the throne in Westminster Hall, *pannis sericis et inauratis decenter ornata* as to support the suggestion that an English coronation *ordo* was known in Scotland. The English description is from the fourth recension of the *ordo*.

[72] One wonders if another Mosaic precept was considered in 1292: 'Thou shalt … set him king over thee whom … God shall choose, one from among thy brethren … thou mayest not set a stranger over thee which is not thy brother' (Deuteronomy 17: 15).

the Scone ceremony was marked by the high cross at which the throne was placed,[73] a cross which, it is tempting to suggest, replaced a tree sacred to an earlier generation. For that there is no evidence, but the *alfresco* character of the rites presumably antedates the foundation of the priory in 1115 and perhaps of the church of Scone. Although the clergy played no part in enthronement, it could be seen as a version of the inauguration of Old Testament kings, a valid alternative to anointing as recorded for David and Solomon.

So far the role of the clergy has been limited to girding with a sword and probably administering an oath; but the claim that they gave the king his royal insignia is borne out by the scene on the Scone seal. In *Gest. Ann.*'s description, 'the bishop of St Andrews and the others helping [who] consecrated him as king' would be, on the seal, the bishop of St Andrews, the mitred figure on the left, while the unmitred cleric on the right is surely the abbot of Scone, whose participation is not mentioned until 1306. With both hands each holds one edge of the mantle which is furred on the inside,[74] but which is already fastened on the king by a cord, pulled down from his throat across his chest by a finger of his left hand, which grasps it.[75] Lower down it is drawn over the king's knees, the tunicle underneath being shown on the upper half of his body and just above his feet. The unmistakeable message is that the mantle was a symbol of his kingship with which the clergy invested him after enthronement – even though this may seem to be contradicted by seating the king already upon the mantle!

This act, like the depiction of Alexander III on seals, gives credence to Bower's enthroned king sitting with crown, sceptre and 'clothed in royal purple'.[76] That mantling was an important rite is shown in 1306 when, after the murder of Comyn, the bishop of Glasgow caused to be made in his wardrobe 'the robes and the attire with which [Bruce] had himself vested and attired on the day' of his inauguration. The bishop sent these 'and a banner of the royal arms which he had long hidden in his treasury' to Bruce at Scone abbey before his inauguration.[77] 'Had himself vested' points to a robing by others than the king.[78]

---

[73] *Chron. Fordun*, i, 294, *ad crucem in cimiterio*.

[74] The *pallium* put on at English coronations was lined with ermines; Legg, *English Coronation Records*, xlii n. 4, and frontispiece.

[75] For the early history of royal and priestly robing, Moore, 'The King's New Clothes: royal and episcopal regalia in the Frankish empire', in *Robes and Honor*, ed. Gordon, 95-136. For long I was inclined to attribute significance to grasping the fastening, but the gesture is shown in many depictions of enthroned kings. I noted it most recently in the Solomon window, north transept of Chartres cathedral.

[76] *Scotichronicon*, v, 292–95.

[77] Palgrave, *Docs. Hist. Scot.*, i, 346; see also 336 where Bruce *se fist coroner et apeler roi d'Escoce*.

[78] The abbot of Scone would be present, but I must disagree with Professor Barrow and numerous English narrative sources which place the bishops of St Andrews and Glasgow

In twelfth-century England and probably earlier, after girding with the sword the king was vested in armill (stole) and mantle (*pallium*) before being crowned.[79] The mantle was delivered with the words 'Receive the mantle, formed with four corners, by which you shall understand that the four corners of the world are subject to divine power, and no one can reign successfully on earth except he to whom the power of ruling was conferred from heaven', words derived from *Wisdom of Solomon*, 18: 24.[80] Now, more than gold and silver was looted by Edward I in 1296; he also took 'one *pallium* to hang in a church, offered by [him] to the altar of St Edward in ... Westminster to hang beyond (*ultra*) that altar'.[81] It may be have been among the copes listed in the Scottish Treasury in 1291, two of which were purple,[82] but 'to hang in a church' suggests otherwise. For in the 1297 inventory this *pallium* is listed immediately before the Stone of Scone, which, despite the inventory heading, cannot have been 'found' in Edinburgh castle, for it was kept in Scone abbey church. That, surely, was where the mantle had hung before being taken to hang beyond St Edward's altar in Westminster.[83]

That it was kept hanging in a church, probably near the high altar at Scone, suggests that it too was not fan-shaped, but rectangular; the hanging meant here may have been a vertical display, a retable, or a horizontal covering, a baldachin suspended above the altar, and brought down for use as the king's mantle at his inauguration. The ceremony of robing him in it was part of that liturgification which the church had imposed upon coronation rites throughout the West, and its origins may lie in coronation *ordines* of other countries. There is, to my knowledge, no biblical precedent for putting on a robe at the making of a king, though linking of robe-wearing and kingship is found there, not least in the mockery of Christ after his condemnation.[84]

there (Barrow, *Bruce*, 151). I do so because when Edward I drew up his charges against these bishops to be sent to the pope, he alleged their adherence to Robert, but not any presence at the inauguration. *Anglo-Scottish Relations*, no. 35; Palgrave, *Docs. Hist. Scot.*, 336, 347; see also 330 for the bishop of Moray.

[79] The regalia of Hungary include a chasuble presented by the Hungarian king to a monastery in 1030 and subsequently used as the coronation mantle; even more striking is the superb fan-shaped mantle made in Sicily in 1133 for King Roger and subsequently taken to Germany and used at royal coronations (now at Vienna). Tronzo, in *Robes and Honor*, ed. Gordon, 241–53; *Krönungen*, i, 446.

[80] Legg, *Eng. Coron. Recs.*, 34. Wisdom of Solomon, 18: 24, *In veste totius erat orbis terrarum*.

[81] Stevenson, *Documents*, ii, 144.

[82] *APS*, i, 112.

[83] The back of the high altar at Westminster carried a wooden retable. The choir of the abbey had hangings with rhyming Latin inscriptions, bequeathed in the 1240s and depicting the story of St Edward on the north and the life of Christ on the south. Binski, *Westminster Abbey*, 56, 123; for the retable, *ibid.*, 152–67. The existing reredos with which the coronation chair is back to back, was not erected till the 1440s; it is possible that the Scottish mantle was hung where the reredos was built, between altar and chair.

[84] I Kings 22: 10; I Chron. 15: 27; Job 29: 14; Matthew 27: 28; 27: 31; John 19: 2, 19: 5.

It must be a possibility that the ceremonial degradation of King John at Montrose castle on 10 July 1296 sought to undo his mantling. Descriptions of the event are not unambiguous: 'his cape is clipped, his tabard is empty'; and 'they took the fur out of his tabard' so that he was called Toom (empty) Tabard.[85] We do not know if heraldic markings or fur trimmings were torn off, or perhaps the tabard was stripped from his shoulders. But with any of these, it is also possible that the tabard at Montrose was used to represent the furred royal mantle recently looted at Scone, so that the king was both un-knighted and un-kinged.

The rectangular *pallium* was a sign that the king ruled here under the protection of a Heavenly King. The *Dei Gratia* used increasingly in the twelfth century is found on the seals of William II and his successors in England. But when Alexander I was provided with a seal based upon Rufus' design, he was shown without a crown, and with a legend proclaiming him *Deo rectore rex Scottorum*, 'king of Scots, God [being] ruler', and this followed the king's name from 1107 until 1286 and under Robert I.[86] David II, the first king to be anointed, had *Dei gratia* on his seal, his advisers probably seeing unction as the giving of God's grace.[87] But the adoption two hundred years earlier of *Deo rectore* need not have been avoidance of *Dei gratia* from lack of unction, but a positive statement, king under God and righteous king by God's will – the same statement as was made by vesting in a mantle.

Our written sources do not mention mantling but follow enthronement by two quite different acts. The first is found in *Gest. Ann.*: the earls and other nobles stretched out their clothes under his feet on bended knees.[88] This re-enacts a biblical scene in which Elisha's messenger anointed Jehu, captain of the host, in private, and saluted him as king of Israel. When Jehu told his following of this, according to the Vulgate (4 *Regum*, 9: 13). *Festinaverunt itaque et unusquisque tollens pallium suum posuerunt sub pedibus eius in similitudinem tribunalis et cecinerunt tuba atque dixerunt 'regnauit Jehu'*; 'They hastened and each man, lifting his cloak, placed [it] under his [Jehu's] feet in the likeness of a dais, and they sounded the trumpet and said "Jehu reigned"' or perhaps, 'Jehu is king'.[89]

---

[85] The quotations are from Pierre Langtoft (*c*.1300) and Wyntoun (*c*.1400). See the discussion by Simpson, 'Why was John Balliol called Toom Tabard?', *SHR*, xlvii (1968), 196–99.

[86] King John, otherwise much influenced by English example, had *Dei gratia*. When the small seal of Alexander III was altered in 1252, it was by the addition of *Dei gratia rex Scottorum* – without his name.

[87] But the seal was in existence and use before the king's coronation in November 1331; *RRS*, vi, nos 2, 5, 6.

[88] *Ipso quoque rege super cathedral regalem, scilicet lapidem, sedente, sub cuius pedibus comites ceterique nobiles sua vestimenta coram lapide curvatis genibus sternebant* (*Chron. Fordun*, i, 294). Presumably under the king's feet, not the feet of the chair. Bower is equally ambiguous.

[89] This biblical reference was spotted by Dr Broun, who kindly drew it to my attention. 2 Kings 9: 13 in the Authorised Version. *NEB* translation is: 'they snatched up their cloaks

This text is echoed only by the words *sub ... pedibus* in *Gest. Ann.* and the borrowing cannot be direct. But the debt is undeniable, perhaps unrecognised by *Gest. Ann.* or its source, so this was scarcely the survival of an archaic ceremony, but a piece of ecclesiology to recall the preceding anointing of Jehu as king, a rite which some Scottish kings had sought, and which Alexander III was soon to seek. This was an obvious attempt at liturgification but using the dominant laymen to suggest that the priests had played their Old Testament role in king-making. It also led to, and was surely suggested by, the next element recorded by *Gest. Ann.* and in 2 Kings, a salutation.

At Scone the highlander's royal genealogy, '*Benach De, re Albanne, Alexander ...*', 'Blessing of God, king of Scots, Alexander son of ...', seems quite different from the recognition shouted by the captains of Judah, '*regnavit Jehu*'. The genealogy was not a claim to the kingship, nor perhaps an acclamation of acceptance, but a triumphant proclamation that the new king was descended from the founding kin. In 1292 John was seated 'and held and publicly proclaimed as king'; in 1306 the bishop of St Andrews spoke of Bruce being crowned (or so the English clerk wrote) and proclaimed king, and the bishop of Glasgow spoke of the day on which he wished to have himself called king. The proclamation that a new king had acceded came in the reading of the genealogy showing that he was of the seed of ancient kings.[90]

The *Gest. Ann.* account explains that the Highlander knelt to *read* the genealogy back to Iber Scot, the first Scot, son of Gathalos and Scota. Bower had additional evidence which said that he was old and grey-haired, yet duly dressed *honeste* and wore a scarlet cloak (*pallium*). He is there on the Scone seal, above the bishop of St Andrews, a figure from the thighs up only, so kneeling, with a long beard, carrying in both hands the outline of an object about one metre long and ten centimetres wide. It is depicted as virtually two-dimensional and can only be a long scroll on which was written the king's genealogy, the figure being the Highlander.[91] Certainly he was no wild man of the woods, though his beard fits with Bower's claim that he was old and claims credibility for Bower's description of decent attire covered by a scarlet mantle. The Scone abbey seal shows him with bare, or tightly covered, outstretched arms, but there could be a mantle over his shoulder, and if scarlet it would be a mark of both wealth and distinction.

and spread them under him on the stones of the steps, and sounded the trumpet and shouted "Jehu is king"', with a note at 'stones' that the Hebrew is obscure.

[90] Dumville, 'Kingship, Genealogies and Regnal Lists', *Early Medieval Kingship*, eds Sawyer and Wood, ch. 4. I have accepted *Gesta*'s *Albanne* as representing *Albannach*, 'of Scots', rather than *Alban*, 'of Scotland'.

[91] See the discussion in Bannerman, 'The King's Poet', *SHR*, lxviii (1989), 120–49. However, the *ollamh* is not found reciting the royal genealogy in Ireland, and if at Scone this figure made the king by conferring the sceptre, why is he not shown touching it as the prelates touch the mantle?

His function certainly descended from pre-twelfth-century rites, for he spoke in Gaelic; the genealogy which he recited reached back to the the dynastic founder in Alba, Cinaed mac Alpin, then to the founder in Dal Riata, Fergus son of Erc, and finally to the Irish ancestors who gave the kingship of Alba a place among the kingships descended from the supposed kingdom of Ireland. This pseudo-history was the work of Irish historians in the mid-eleventh century, and in the form reported by *Gest. Ann.* can scarcely be older than that time. There is at least a case for seeing the old Highlander in his red cloak as the Scottish successor of these historians, his share in the rites, and the text which he read, being no older than the accession of Maelcoluim III.[92] Later commentators described him as *sennchaidh*, and while Dr Bannerman is right to reject the later sense of 'storyteller' attached to that word, in the sense of 'historian' it may be the correct one.

The alternative account is given by Bower, who, having placed the king's blessing and ordination, a 'coronation', before enthronement, rejected *Gest. Ann.*'s consecration by the bishop and also the casting of cloaks. Instead he suggests a hill by having the nobles set down their seats under the king's feet to hear a (*or* the) *sermo*,[93] when, lo!, suddenly the Highlander appeared. These few words are the most puzzling in all the sources for these rites. The *sermo* might have been the king's oath, had not Bower placed that before enthronement, where English precedent would lead us to expect it. It might have been an episcopal sermon, for which the church was suited, and for which there was no English precedent. Then where did twenty or thirty seats come from? Was the ground so hard that the feet did not sink unevenly into the turf? What did the nobles do with shields and swords which the Scone seal shows them carrying? In truth, the incongruous element in this narrative is less the *sermo* than the *sedilia* which the nobles put in place.

It is, however, clear that Bower is following closely the narrative in *Gest. Ann.*, including the words 'under whose feet the earls and other nobles', and that after six more Latin words about placing seats for a *sermo*, he resumes that narrative with 'and lo! suddenly ...' *Gest. Ann.* has the nobles 'with bended knees' (*curvatis genibus*) 'cast' (*sternebant*) clothes. Despite the 'lo! suddenly', the Highlander's appearance cannot have been an impromptu surprise; I suggest that Bower meant that the nobles were to hear his genealogical *sermo*. This may have been in the source which told of the beard and red cloak, but I am still sceptical about the seating. If Bower could make no sense of the casting of clothes, then sitting down may have come from 'bended knees' – a fairly desperate explanation, and we may have to rest content with the casting of clothes.

---

[92] For the evolution of the genealogy, the origin legend, and their significance, Broun, *Irish Identity of the Kings of Scots*, especially 183–93.

[93] *sub cuius pedibus comites ceterique nobiles sedilia sua pro sermone audiendo collocantes, et ecce subito* ... The first six words are in *Gest. Ann.*

If the Highlander was historian not poet, Irish literature does provide an 'abundance of inaugural odes', which, it has been suggested, may have been recited at royal inauguration ceremonies.[94] Now behind the pedigree-reader on the seal is another small figure, shown from the waist up. Dr Bannerman identified the triangular object at his shoulder and in front of him as a harp.[95] He would scarcely be accompanist to the pedigree-reader but might himself be the *ollamh* who would sing and not merely recite the praises of the new king. If this be correct, he belongs, one would expect, to the feast following the inauguration, well attested for 1214, when it went on for two days, surely inside the abbey for the date was mid-December. An inauguration feast was a widespread custom, important to secular society as a symbol of the bonding of king with what was to be called 'community'. Its origins were, doubtless, as a rite of the mutual assurance of ruler and war-band in loyalty, support, sustenance. But it was of little interest to the liturgifiers of the church and did not enter into their written accounts. The inclusion of our harpist upon this seal tells us that it did not set out to present only the ecclesiastical presence and acts at the inauguration; he belongs to ancient tradition with the pedigree, two miniaturised earls and the almost invisible royal throne.

The evidence of these several sources gives no complete account of the inauguration describing the sequence of rites. If the Scone seal depicts the mantling and what followed, but shows the earls who had previously enthroned the king, then written sources place the oath before moving to the churchyard for enthronement (Guisborough and Bower), and girding with the sword before the oaths (Bower). If I have correctly seen the cleric holding a rectangle as proffering a Gospel book for the oath, then either the written sources' chronology is wrong, which I think unlikely here, or the seal alludes to the oath as another rite, although it preceded enthronement, just as it may allude to the feast after inauguration by the presence of a harpist.

In 1292 King John heard mass after his inauguration; in 1306 Robert I, who was inaugurated on Lady Day, a Friday, but without the dithering bishop of St Andrews, persuaded him to come to Scone for Sunday, Palm Sunday, when the bishop celebrated mass for the new king.[96] It is likely that earlier kings too went to mass in the abbey kirk, and indeed that the priory was founded by Alexander I at Scone so that they might do so in greater solemnity; but our sources for 1214 and 1249 make no mention of this act. That fealties and homages were sworn outside, after mass, is suggested by Barbour's account of 1306 placing them at the end of king-making, and by a

---

[94] Dr Fitzpatrick remarks that there is no direct evidence of the recital of genealogies or inauguration odes in Ireland. See also Dillon, 'The consecration of Irish kings', *Celtica*, x (1973), 5–8; Simms, *Kings to Warlords*, 24–25, 43.

[95] I discerned a harp in the detail, but Professor Barrow thinks the image too indistinct for this identification; there must be doubt.

[96] *Anglo-Scottish Relations*, no. 35.

record that they were given outside at Scone in 1371, after coronation in the abbey church.[97]

There remains one riddle: the moot hill at Scone. No written source before 1300 mentions it, or places inauguration upon a hill, and the Scone seal does not suggest a mound. Hills were inauguration sites and places of law-giving in Ireland. In Scotland law was made at the 'hill of credulity' at Scone in 906; Fordun claims that Maelcoluim II, impoverished, gave away all except 'the little hill of the royal seat of Scone, in which kings, royally clad, sitting on a throne, issue judgements and laws ...', but of the assizes made between 1165 and 1280, almost none was issued at Scone. After 1280 it was frequently a place of parliaments and judgements, and in the later fourteenth century the first Stewart kings acted as Fordun described, on a hillock, though it was to the north of the abbey, outside the cemetery. Fordun has given this law-making a bogus antiquity, but it is significant that he does not place, and did not know of, king-making there.[98] It may be that inauguration had taken place there, and before 1249 had been moved by the liturgifiers within the cemetery.

If this survey leaves some large question marks, some alternative answers could certainly be given, but uncertainty about the origins, symbolism and contemporary significance of the various ceremonies will remain. In 1249, I believe, the church and king had advanced as far along the road to unction and coronation as was possible without papal approval; the insignia of a Christian king were used but the critical one, the crown, was not conferred by the church and of unction there was no trace. But even at that time plans were afoot to end this defect in the royal dignity.

[97] Barbour, *Brus*, book 2, line 186; *APS*, i, 545.
[98] *Chron. Fordun*, i, 186; *APS*, i, 545 (1371), 578b (1390).

Plate 1   A: Sueno's Stone, Forres (background eliminated from photo).
B: Detail enlarged ×2 from A.

Plate 2 A: Cast of single-faced seal of Edgar (1097–1107). B: Cast of obverse of seal of Alexander II (1214–49). C: Cast of obverse of seal of John (1292–96).

Plate 3 Cast of reverse of large seal of Scone abbey (slightly enlarged).

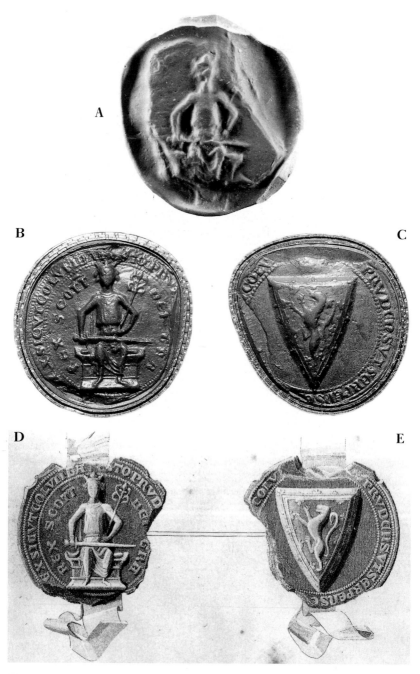

Plate 4 A: Cast of obverse of small seal (1250) of Alexander III. The reverse is unchanged in C. B & C: Casts of obverse and reverse of the seal with added inscription on the obverse (1252). D & E: Engraving of the seal (B & C) published in 1837.

Plate 5 Casts of the obverse (upper) and reverse (lower) of the seal appointed for government of the kingdom in 1286: the Seal of Guardianship, 1286–92.

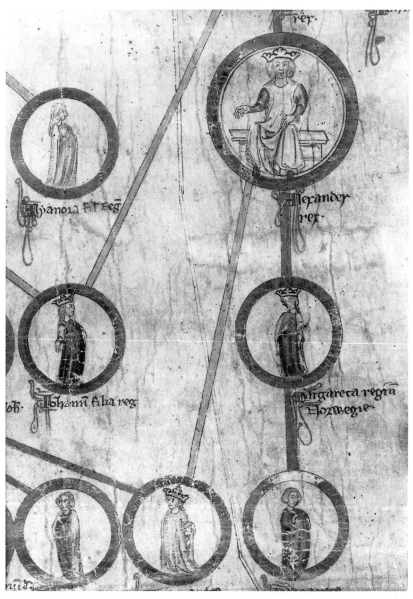

Plate 6 British Library, Cotton Charter XIV, 4, intermarriages of the Scottish and English royal houses: left row, centre, Joan, dau. of K. John, wife of Alexander II; centre at bottom, Margaret, dau of Henry III wife of Alexander III; right row (from top), Alexander III, his daughter and granddaughter, the Maid of Norway (slightly reduced).

Plate 7 Norham from the air: A: the castle – on the other side of the Tweed, beyond the island is the meadow of Upsetlington where the Scots waited; B: the parish church, site of the submission of John Balliol and John Comyn to Edward I.

A

B

Plate 8 Berwick castle (now the site of Berwick-upon-Tweed railway station):
A: about 1700; B: in 1790.

CHAPTER 8

The last years of peace and friendship, 1249–86

Like the Scandinavian kings, Alexander III could claim a saint among his ancestors, for in 1248 Queen Margaret, wife of Maelcoluim III, had been canonised and on 19 June 1250 her body was solemny translated, in presence of the king and a distinguished company in Dunfermline abbey, to a new and splendid shrine before the high altar. This remarkable recognition of sanctity[1] may have been the catalyst which about this time added to the royal arms of a lion rampant, a double tressure, flory counter flory, the lilies celebrating the sanctity of Margaret.[2]

The new arms were first displayed in any surviving form upon the reverse of the small seal appended to one of first acts issued by Alexander III on 3 June 1250, some two weeks before the translation at Dunfermline; the obverse of this seal shows the king enthroned, a mantle at his neck, behind his back and over his knees, crowned (the first depiction thus on a seal since 1107), with sceptre and, across the knees, a sword grasped by the pommel, the honours which he wore or carried at his inauguration (Plate 4).[3] The seal went out of use by December 1250 when a new great seal is found, so falls at that time about which, as the canon lawyer Hostiensis, writing 1250 x 53, tells us, a request of the king of Scotland for anointing 'is daily' before the pope.[4]

Now, on 6 April 1251 Innocent IV refused a request from Henry III who had asked 'that the illustrious king of Scotland may not be anointed or crowned without your [Henry's] consent, since he is your liege man and has done homage to you'. In the same letter he also refused Henry's request for a tenth of ecclesiastical revenues from Scotland, justifiable by a papal grant to Henry on 11 April 1250 of a tenth from his kingdom and 'other lands

[1] For if female saints were rare, married female saints were considerably rarer.
[2] There is no proof of this and Professor Barrow has suggested to me that they may represent the Capetion blood inherited through Marie de Coucy, mother of Alexander III.
[3] Simpson, 'Kingship in Miniature', *Medieval Scotland*, eds Grant and Stringer, 131–39 discusses the seal in its emended (1252–57) form.
[4] '*Si quis de novo ungi velit, consuetudo obtinuit quod a papa petatur sicut fecit rex Aragonum et quotidie instat rex Scotiae*', Bloch, 'An unknown testimony on the history of coronation in Scotland', *SHR*, xxiii (1926), 105–6, where the date 1250 x 61 is given. For other dates see *Dictionnaire de droit canonique*, v, 1215. The king of Aragon must be Pedro II, anointed in Rome by Innocent III on 11 November 1204.

subject to your jurisdiction'.[5] The request may be dated to the second half of 1250. This démarche by the English king would be prompted by a danger that the pope would grant unction and coronation to a Scottish king, and therefore by a Scottish petition for them. This may have come from Alexander II or his bishops, but a more likely occasion would be the accession of a new king, who could claim descent from the new saint, and was a boy with a reign still ahead of him – Alexander III.

Look again at that remarkable small seal (Plate 4) with its legend, ESTO PRVDENS VT SERPENS ET SIMPLEX SICVT COLVMBA, which appears on each side with the king's image or arms, but without his name and title, and which must have been intended to have a particular resonance for the recipient. The repeated legend was integral to the purport of the document for which the seal was intended. The words are part of Christ's charge to the disciples in Matthew 10: 16: 'Behold I send you forth as sheep in the midst of wolves. *Be ye* therefore *wise as serpents and simple as doves*',[6] but on the seal in the singular. The charge had been referred to in a significant place, the second preface by Adomnán to his Life of Columba: 'the Saviour himself bade his disciples to have implanted in a pure heart the simplicity of doves, for indeed *the dove is a simple and innocent bird*, therefore a simple and innocent man also [Columcille] was rightly called by this name, since he, with dove-like disposition offered to the Holy Spirit a dwelling in himself'.[7]

The linking here of *columba*, *simplex* and *innocens* (for 'innocent' is close to the sense of *simplex*), is the key to the small seal, created, I suggest, for the king's approach to *Innocent* IV asking for coronation rites. The approach does not survive but it would make full use of one passage in the Life of Columba, in which he dreamed of a visitation by an angel bearing a glass book of the ordination of kings, given to Columcille to read. After suffering visitations on three successive nights the reluctant saint submitted and travelled to Iona where 'among the words of ordination, he prophesied future [events] concerning [Aedan's descendants] … and laying a hand on his [Aedan's] head, ordaining he blessed [him]'.[8] The man in whom the Holy Spirit dwelt conferred it upon his earthly king, by a laying on of hand, but to a later age 'ordination' would suggest the panoply of unction with oil or chrism, the very thing which the Scots were seeking from Innocent IV for Aedan's descendant. That in 1249–50 they would exploit this precedent of the ordaining of a king by Columcille, with his prophecy pointing to future

[5] *Anglo-Scottish Relations*, no. 9. On the tenth see Lunt, *Financial Relations of the Papacy with England*, i (Cambridge, MA, 1939), 255–56.

[6] *Estote ergo prudentes sicut serpentes et simplices sicut columbe.*

[7] *Saluator … praecepit discipulis ut columbarum in corde puro insertam simplicitatem contenerent. Columba etenim semplex et innocens est auis. Hoc itaque uocamine et homo semplex innocensque nuncupari debuit, qui in se columbinis moribus spiritui sancto hospitium praebuit.* Dr Tom Clancy kindly drew my attention to this passage.

[8] *inponensque manum super caput eius ordinans benedixit.* Adomnán's *Life of Columba*, ed. Anderson, 188–89 (bk iii, c.5).

ordainings, is likely; what puts it beyond that are the emphatic references to 'Columba' in the small seal engraved for the new king, with its display of his kingly honours and quotation of the Gospel emended to the singular and invoking the quality of an 'Innocent'.

The reverse of the seal, with the shield of royal arms, recalls the banner with the arms of a late king of Scotland, presumably Alexander III, which Robert Wishart bishop of Glasgow had concealed for a long time and which he sent to Scone for the inauguration of 1306,[9] as well as the shields displayed under the feet of the secular participants on the abbey seal. A thirteenth-century inauguration would be ablaze with the heraldic emblems on coats of the magnates, but the royal arms, it would seem, were displayed above all on a banner; the secreting of this particular banner at Glasgow suggests that it may have had some numinous significance, like the French *Oriflamme*. The small seal, then, without showing another participant, represents the king as inaugurated, displaying his kingship to convince the pope that it justified the Christian sacral character which St Columcille gave to King Aedan.

The remains of Columcille were held at Dunkeld cathedral in a glorious *châsse*, his staff in a separate reliquary; under the feretory, *sub patre Columba*, was buried Bishop Geoffrey, who must have shown unusual devotion to the saint, and who is singled out for an encomium in the *Gest. Ann.* account of the 1249 inauguration. He is the most likely initiator, before his death on 22 November 1249, of an approach to Innocent IV to abandon papal reluctance and concede to the successors of Columcille, the clergy of Scotland, what a vision from God had commanded the saint to do.[10] The approach failed but the seal survived with its particular message, in its legend, but also in its depiction of the nominal sender enthroned with the insignia of a king and therefore entitled to the rite of ordination. The lack of unction and coronation became one anchor of English claims to the subordination of the king of Scots.

When Alexander III succeeded five days after his father's death, on 13 July 1249, the leading figure in the kingdom was a middle-ranking baron, Alan Durward, who was continued in the office of justiciar of *Scotia*. The widowed queen, Marie de Coucy, probably protected her son's interests for a time, but at the end of September, a year after it must have been plain that she was not pregnant, Marie de Coucy returned to her family in France.[11]

[9] Palgrave, *Docs. Hist. Scot.*, 346–47.

[10] It is possible that after Bishop Geoffrey's death, the recently appointed dean of Dunkeld, Robert de Stuteville, brought the Life to the attention of the clergy and that the seal was made between December 1249 and June 1250.

[11] This is placed by Matthew Paris (*Chronica Majora*, v, 265; *SAEC*, 362–63) in September 1251, a date accepted in Dunbar, *Scottish Kings*, 92. But the correct period was certainly September 1250 (*Cal. Docs. Scot.*, i, nos 1785, 1791); she came back from France to England in 1251.

Before the end of 1250 Durward had seized his opportunity, commissioning a great seal for Alexander III, which could be used for permanent grants as though the king were of age; it was frequently employed in the following year,[12] and would lend verisimilitude to claims that Durward was exploiting his authority with the king.

In December 1251 the Scottish court moved to York to meet that of the English king and also Queen Marie de Coucy, so that Alexander III might be married to Margaret, eldest daughter of King Henry. An English royal marriage had been promised in 1244, but the decision on Margaret and on the date must have been finalised in 1251 with the agreement, perhaps at the instance, of Durward, upon whose head much obloquy was soon to be heaped. The young Alexander was knighted by Henry on Christmas Day, and married the following day. Immediately thereafter he did homage to Henry III, the first such occasion since a settlement of Scottish royal claims in England in 1237.

For this act we have only the account of Matthew Paris, claiming that Alexander did homage in 1251 'by reason of the holding which he holds of the king of the English, namely of the kingdom of England, that is for Lothian and other lands'.[13] He was then asked (Paris does not say who did the asking) 'to do homage and fealty with allegiance by reason of his kingdom of Scotland', as his predecessors had done according to many chronicles.[14] To this he returned a dignified refusal, that he had come to be married and not to answer upon so difficult a matter which required full deliberation with his counsellors, and Henry accepted this, refusing to turn this time of rejoicing into one of controversy.[15]

The wording of Alexander's homage as given by Paris can scarcely be accurate, for the novelty, mention of Lothian, would certainly not have been introduced by the Scots, since by 1251 it was an integral part of the kingdom, not an adjunct thereto. The Latin shows pretty clearly that to homage done for lands 'which he holds of the king of the English' there have been added clumsily two glosses, 'namely of the kingdom of England', and 'that is Lothian and other lands'. The first was accurate but unnecessary, the second perhaps an attempt by Paris or his source to justify the claim for homage for Scotland, based on the report in the *Chronica Majora* that King Edgar gave Lothian to the king of Scots, about 975, along with gold and precious stones, but without a hint of homage for the province.[16] Paris rather than Henry III is likely to be the author of the claim that homage for

[12] Simpson, *Handlist of the Acts of Alexander III* ..., nos 3–13, all in one year.

[13] *homagium ratione tenementi quod tenet de domino rege Anglorum de regno scilicet Anglie Laudiano videlicet et terris reliquis.*

[14] *conveniretur rex Scotie ut ratione regni Scotie faceret homagium et fidelitatem cum ligantia domino suo regi Anglorum prout evidenter in cronicis multis scribitur.*

[15] Paris, *Chron. Majora*, v, 268.

[16] Paris, *Chron. Majora*, i, 467, his only account of how Lothian came to be Scottish.

Scotland was justified by chronicles. In 1278 Alexander's homage and fealty was attended by two reporters who evidently heard quite different words; so also, perhaps, in 1251.

After the knighting of King Alexander, in a dispute he rebuffed the English earl marshal, stating that he could receive knighthood from any Catholic prince or any of his nobles. Henry III then appointed the queen of Scots' household and promised to send a 'prudent counsellor' to the young couple. Paris was clearly well informed about all these proceedings, but is wholly silent about the background to this last promise, that, after Christmas, Durward was accused before Henry III by leading Scottish magnates of betrayal (*proditio*), and he and his supporters were forced to resign their offices. The English king agreed that these resignations in England would not prejudice the rights of the Scottish king, who would appoint new officials, but the 'prudent counsellor' (Robert de Ros, lord of Wark on Tweed)[17] was pretty certainly the price of Henry's interest. It was his one success, sending a meddler with uncertain authority, to set against the determination and courage of a ten-year-old boy-king.

Two chronicles report the specific charge against Durward, one that he intended to use the great seal to legitimise his wife, the king's illegitimate sister, the other that he had sent an embassy with gifts to the pope, to secure legitimation of the daughters of that marriage, so that if anything happened to the king, they (*sic*) should succeed to the kingdom as lawful heirs.[18] It must have been apparent to the second chronicler that it was not the daughters but their mother who was in need of legitimation, but presumably she was now dead, for otherwise she would have had a claim, not her daughters. Legitimacy was a matter for the church courts, and, if anything was planned, it would be an approach to the pope, though the grounds are unknown.[19] Contemporaries in Scotland accepted the enormity of Durward's plans or actions, as though he planned to usurp the throne; this was unfair. Had he succeeded, his daughter would have been only heir presumptive, i.e. as long as the king had no child. So far as we can tell there was no agreement on who, otherwise, was heir presumptive, and the king's death would have launched a power struggle such as occurred in 1290–91, and, almost inevitably, English intervention. Durward probably acted without significant consent, in an underhand way, but the strong reaction suggests that had he succeeded, his daughter would indeed have been heir presumptive to the kingdom – legitimation would make a difference. Already, it seems, in the absence of a male heir, succession could pass to a woman, though probably in the person of her husband.

[17] A descendant of an illegitimate daughter of King William.

[18] *Chron. Fordun*, i, 296; *Chron. Melrose*, under 1251, *ESSH*, ii, 571.

[19] Compare the succession in Sicily after 1189 when the taint of illegitimacy was overcome; Matthew, *Norman Kingdom of Sicily*, 285–303. As this showed, the real danger was disease, of which the Scots of 1249 would be well aware, and as they encountered in 1290.

The homage at York and sacking of Durward were preamble to eight troubled years, 1251–59, of Scottish factionalism in which Henry III played a role sometimes calming, sometimes meddlesome. It all began well enough early in 1252 with the appointment of a new, predominantly Comyn, government. By 1255 complaints by the royal couple and other magnates persuaded Henry to intervene. His supporters secured the persons of the king and queen, and met with Henry at the Border, where a settlement was drafted and accepted by some magnates but rejected by the Comyns. Thus in an exasperated settlement dated 20 September 1255, Alexander III, on Henry's advice, excluded the Comyns and their supporters from office for seven years, and appointed new councillors from a wide range of families. This was in effect an undertaking to Henry III, to whom it was sent, and who in his confirmatory letters called the Comyns 'rebels', claiming to have appointed the new government. That was his gloss, and not the formal position, but Henry had undoubtedly won a temporary veto over the composition of the Scottish government for the seven years up to Alexander III's twenty-first birthday.

On 5 September, Henry had promised that Alexander and his wife would stay in England only with the will of all magnates of Scotland and that he would do nothing to cause prejudice to the rights of the king, to the kingdom or to his royal liberties. Henry's letter (of 20 September) acknowledging receipt of Alexander's settlement, promised that when the term of seven years expired, the document would be invalid, would be returned and would cause no prejudice, repeating the phrases of 5 September.[20] These were not the first documents to speak of the king's right(s) but were the first to link them to 'the kingdom' and to 'royal liberties', while leaving us to guess at what these might be. Protection against interference from the English king, they surely anticipate those 'rights, laws, liberties and customs' guaranteed in 1290 to a kingdom 'separate and divided from the kingdom of England, free in itself, without subjection'.

A surprising feature of Henry's 1255 undertaking is the absence of any reservation, *salvo iure nostro*, to protect that vestigial right over the Scottish kingdom which Henry had been prepared to air in 1251. This omission is perhaps understandable when the English king was acquiring a significant right to interfere for seven years, a right which was respected by the Scots when they sought Henry's agreement to a formula for peace with the Comyns in 1257. A palace revolution brought the latter to power in October 1257, and they sought alliance with Llewelyn, prince of Wales in March 1258, a treaty which shows them uncertain of Alexander III's position, but fearful of Henry III. In fact he lost control of the English government to

---

[20] *Foedera*, i, 327, 329; after it was drawn up the 20 September undertaking was seen and approved by the English council at Carlisle. *Cf.* the summary in *ESSH*, ii, 584 *n*, 'the rights of the king or the liberties of the kingdom'.

baronial reformers in May 1258, and the Scots worked out a compromise in government later in that year without interference.

We do not know that the document of settlement of 1255 was returned as it should have been in 1262, but by then Alexander was in full control of his kingdom and had visited his father-in-law in amicable circumstances, in 1260. Nonetheless guarantees were demanded and given: during his visit Alexander was not to be addressed on any matters concerning his kingdom without his consent, nor would the English king make any change in the *status* of the Scottish king or his councillors, plain references to 1251–55. Amicability showed, however, in provisions to leave the queen, who was pregnant, with her mother and father until the birth of the child. But the chance that Alexander might die while the baby was in England was also foreseen, for then a named group of Scottish magnates would be able to take it back to Scotland, 'the status of neither kingdom, that is England and Scotland, being taken into account as far as concerns the matter'. Oaths to this were sworn by Henry III and his brother Richard, king of the Romans (both by proxy) and by five English councillors.[21]

These words and solemn acts show an acute recollection of Henry's request for a wider homage from the boy Alexander ten years before, with a determination to avoid repetition and to preserve the status of the kingdom. But the provisions for the unborn baby are equally striking, for they show that, whatever its gender, it would be heir to the kingdom, and they firmly place upon the magnates a responsibility to bring it to its heritage. The situation which was to arise with Alexander's second queen (Yolanda) in 1286 was thus not entirely novel, for the role which the magnates then assumed, as guardians for the unborn child, had already been ascribed to them a quarter of a century earlier.

In 1259, Henry III had at last reached a settlement with the French king over his rights to the family's French inheritance. In return for some territorial concessions, Henry gave up his claim to the duchy of Normandy and county of Anjou, lost by his father in 1204, and agreed to do liege homage for Acquitaine, always due, and for Gascony, a novelty. After a breach since 1202, the English king at last did homage in person to Louis IX for his possessions in France; the oath of fealty which made this homage 'liege' was sworn by his proxy, to avoid the derogation from his majesty which swearing in person would have implied. There were those at Paris who felt that too much had been conceded, but, more important, Henry's heir Edward also opposed the settlement by 1260, and for the rest of his life was to scrutinise the French non-fulfilment of its terms in order to qualify the words in which he did homage to successive French kings, and from the 1290s to contemplate arguing for his own sovereignty in Gascony. The

---

[21] *statu neutrius regni, scilicet Anglie et Scotie, quantum in hoc considerato*; *Foedera*, i, 402–3. The child was a daughter, Margaret, the Maid of Scotland, queen of Norway.

obligations of the treaty of Paris of 1259 made Henry III's successor far more aware than his father had been of the rights of the royal overlord to whom he must do homage as duke, and of whose court he was now a 'peer'.[22]

Limits imposed by Simon de Montfort and his supporters on Henry III in 1263–65 prevented him from exercising the English protectorate over the Isle of Man which had existed for fifty years.[23] In 1264 Alexander III set about the conquest of the Isles, frightening their king, Magnus, into doing homage in 1264 and suppressing the kingship on Magnus' death in 1265. By then England had fallen into civil war and Henry III, presumably before the battle of Lewes, had sought help from his son-in-law, with an assurance that this help would be received as an act of grace, not of right. After Lewes he was a prisoner but Edward, when he escaped captivity, wrote to Alexander III, begging his help against Simon de Montfort.[24] Scots certainly fought at the battle of Evesham (1265), though no royal contingent had been sent. Royal authority was re-established in England, but in effect the reign of Edward had begun in tandem with his father, engaged in a complex territorial and legal settlement. Edward is known to have visited the Scottish court once or possibly twice in 1268,[25] apparently to bring about a visit of Alexander and his wife to Henry III, but without known consequences for the two kingdoms; in 1270 Edward set out for Palestine, while Henry lapsed into invalidity.

A judgement of the two decades 1251–72 might blame the boy Alexander for his complaints to King Henry against his own advisers. The Scots were careful to protect the liberty of their king by written undertakings from Henry, but their factionalism was the root of the 1250s crises, and each faction was led to invoke the power of England against its enemies. It was a lesson which some in the English court probably noticed, a poor augury for the future. But after his démarche at Christmas 1251 Henry III took no steps to impose his authority on Scotland, contenting himself with parchment undertakings and unhelpful representatives; he meddled, with good intentions, but, apart from listing the homage and the appointment of Henry's representatives in 1251,[26] his meddling found no place in the alleged *preuves*

---

[22] This paragraph is based upon chapter 3 of Vale, *Origins of the Hundred Years War*.

[23] The king of the Isles, who owed allegiance to the king of Norway, had done homage to King John and had accepted Innocent III as his lord; in 1256 King Magnus of the Isles went to Henry III's Easter court to be knighted; he was given letters of protection to last as long as he was faithful to King Henry (*Foedera*, i, 338).

[24] Henry III's letter is attested only in the bull *Scimus fili*, on information supplied from Scotland, which the Scots must have been able to document (*Anglo-Scottish Relations*, 165); but it does not appear in the 1282 inventory of Scottish records which notices *littera Edwardi de succursu petendo a rege Scocie et est dupplicata* (*APS*, i, 108).

[25] *Scotichronicon*, v, 371, 480.

[26] *commissa est regina Scocie tutele Roberti de Ros et Johanni de Balliolo et regnum Scocie cum rege de consilio magnatum utriusque regni*; Stones and Simpson, ii, 306 from Paris, *Historia Anglorum*, iii, 118. In the *Chron. Majora*, v, 272 Paris made no mention of the kingdom, king or magnates, which are embellishments.

of English overlordship collected by Edward I in 1291; it cannot have offered grist to that mill. The will of Henry III left to his wife guardianship of his heir and other children until they came of age, and of 'my kingdom of England and all my other lands of Wales, Ireland and Gascony'.[27] There can be no better evidence of the status of Scotland in relation to Henry III.

His successor, Edward I, was a man of different mettle. He returned to England from crusade and a period in Gascony only on 2 August 1274, though his reign had formally begun four days after his father's death in November 1272. He was crowned on 19 August 1274, but the date had been fixed by 27 June, and a summons must have gone to Alexander III, along with Edward's letters allowing that 'the attendance of the king of Scotland at his coronation, and service asked of him there, should not be prejudicial to the same king'; another summary of this letter says 'shall not prejudice the kingdom of Scotland', and it is possible that both king and kingdom were mentioned, though only 'king' is reliable.[28] The mention of service must relate to the various coronation duties, of which the king's brother had unsuccessfully claimed the right to carry one of the three swords borne at the ceremony. The suggestion that this sword was carried by Alexander has been rejected on the grounds that Edward did not cite this later as a proof of overlordship. But Edward clearly intended to ask a coronation duty of Alexander making it more likely that he did carry one of the swords.[29]

The sumptuous celebrations which followed were protracted, with the queen of Scots, Edward's sister, also present; but the king and queen probably did not stay for long.[30] It is nonetheless surprising that Alexander is not known to have been asked to do homage, and certainly did not do it on this occasion; the reason is hinted at in a letter of the English king listed in the Scottish archives: 'it shall not prejudice the Scottish king that he came once to England without conduct'.[31] The conduct which was lacking would be that of bishops and sheriffs in the shires through which the king passed, whose escort he was entitled to under the settlement of 1194;[32] presumably

[27] *Foedera*, i, 496.

[28] *APS*, i, 112 line 4; 109 line 10. Since the king was summoned, he would not be prejudiced.

[29] Prestwich, *Edward I*, 89–90; Richardson, 'Coronation of Edward I', *Bulletin of the Institute of Historical Research*, xv (1937–38), 94–99.

[30] Alexander was paid £175 for his expenses in coming to the coronation, at £5 per day; *Foedera*, i, 520. But the £5 allowance was for days spent travelling; 30s. per diem was the allowance for time at court, and there is no trace of this payment; *Anglo-Scottish Relations*, no. 3. Alexander was at 'Lochcumberey' (in or by Great Cumbrae?) on 23 September 1274; *National Manuscripts of Scotland*, i, no. LXIII.

[31] *APS*, i, 108, 111. The second summary reads: *vna carta quod adventus regis Scocie non trahatur ad consequenciam de veniendo ad coronacionem regis Anglie.* In 1299 the pope was told that Edward had given letters patent declaring that Edward procured Alexander's presence 'not of right but of grace'; *Anglo-Scottish Relations*, 164–65. There was fact behind these assertions, but it was twisted to suit the party's case.

[32] *Anglo-Scottish Relations*, no. 3.

they would be in London for the coronation, and the lack of what was due may have been an obstacle to Alexander's performance of homage and fealty. But Edward may have been glad of time in which to consider his rights thereto.

There was evidently no attempt to ask for homage over the following two years, when it was certainly demanded from Llewelyn of Wales, whose refusal led to a brief war and Llewelyn's capitulation in 1277. In 1277 and early 1278, however, a number of embassies travelled between the two kings, and on 21 March 1278, Edward told his chancellor that Alexander's messengers had conveyed his unconditional offer to do homage, for which London on 13 October had been fixed. A whole series of letters were drafted about 20 March, including a royal safeconduct to come in October and undated safeconducts from the archbishop of York and two earls. A much altered draft reveals that Edward had ordered 'so and so' to escort Alexander, who, however, had asked for the customary escort of other prelates and magnates or at least a letter testifying that if he came under the first terms it would not be to his prejudice. Then a draft of Edward's letters dated 5 June attested that the conduct to Alexander should not be to his future prejudice or that of his heirs, letters evidently not transmitted. Finally on 12 June the king's safeconduct was issued and three earls told to issue theirs.[33]

It is clear that the most elaborate steps were taken to ensure that Alexander's attendance was secured and that it could not be faulted for want of courtesies, both those due and those demanded. As lord of Penrith Alexander was surely bound to do homage when summoned, and the letters of no prejudice would be otiose, unless the summons required his attendance at parliament – but since the summons is not preserved, we cannot know its content.[34] The multiple letters show the importance attached to the occasion, but also reflect the flaws in the summons and reception of August 1274.

Parliament had been summoned for 29 September 1278, but it assembled at least two weeks later.[35] The Scottish king was at Roxburgh on 2 October with his chancellor, chamberlain, two bishops, three earls and other prominent men, among them probably Ralph de Greenlaw, abbot of

---

[33] *Cal. Docs. Scot.*, ii, nos 107–24 from PRO C47/22/12 (8–15); the letter of 5 June and much-altered draft are no. (15). In the *Calendar* the word *conductus* is translated as 'safeconduct', which is misleading, since it often means 'escort'; also the fact that these documents are clearly drafts, with incomplete address or date, is ignored. For the letters of 12 June, *Foedera*, i, 558.

[34] The inventories of Scottish archives show no trace of the no-prejudice letter of 5 June. Nor were the letters of March and 5 June enrolled by the English chancery; the safeconduct and letters of 12–14 June were.

[35] Mid-October according to the Waverley annalist; *Annales Monastici*, ii, 390; iv, 474. But Edward did not go to London till about 24 October.

Dunfermline.[36] All this large company is unlikely to have accompanied the king, and the discussion of the homage which surely took place would, I think, include the precise formula to be used by the king. This is hinted at by the choice of Robert Bruce earl of Carrick, to swear fealty as the king's proxy. Unlike the others known to have been present, he was a rare witness of the king's charters, but the indications are that, like his father, he had competence in Anglo-Norman, and he was chosen, I suggest, to ensure that the script agreed at Roxburgh was adhered to.

If Alexander went to London for 13 October, the king was not there. His safeconduct was to Edward's presence wherever he was in England, and at Tewksbury on 16 October Alexander offered his homage to Edward. Asked to defer it to London, since Edward's council was not present, Alexander agreed and was given a letter that this prorogation should not be to his prejudice or that of his heirs.[37] Accompanied by the earl of Carrick, he eventually appeared before his lord at Westminster on Friday, 28 October to do homage and swear fealty; there was a company of over thirty but no other Scots are known to have been present. The transaction would be conducted in Anglo-Norman, but our two records, English and Scottish, are in Latin, and therefore quoted words were not actually spoken.

When was the official English account written? The matter of a dispute between the Scottish king and the bishop of Durham, over the shifting course of the lower Tweed, was evidently raised during Alexander's visit of 1278 when an agreement was reached, probably to secure a finding from an assize drawn from both kingdoms.[38] The new bishop of Norwich, William Middleton, was to head a commission charged to go to the Border on Edward's behalf, and on 29 January 1279, wrote to the king reminding him that he had asked Middleton to send a man to bring back the king's will on matters discussed between Edward and Alexander, if any had occurred to the king's memory on which the bishop had not been informed.[39] When the commissions to the bishop and others were issued on 4 February, they were accompanied by a letter close which looks like just such a belated royal thought: the bishop is to enquire diligently about the homage and all circumstances touching it in the most cautious and secret way possible, but do nothing in the matter without a specific royal mandate.[40] The context makes clear that Alexander's homage was meant and implies that no adequate record of it then (early 1279) existed.

[36] *Dunfermline Registrum*, no. 87.

[37] This was seen as an important concession by the Osney chronicler Thomas Wykes, who records the homage as for English lands; *Annales Monastici*, iv, 277–78. Another annalist notes the English saving clause; *ibid.*, iv, 474. *Foedera*, i, 554; *APS*, i, 109 line 5.

[38] *Chron. Fordun*, i, 306; *Scotichronicon*, v, 408–9. See also *Cal. Docs. Scot.*, ii, no. 144, undated but November 1277 x November 1278.

[39] *Cal. Docs. Scot.*, v, no. 40.

[40] *Cal. Patent Rolls, 1272–81*, 339. The second letter and the memorandum are printed in full in *Foedera*, i, 565; these letters are not in *Cal. Docs. Scot.*

Bishop Middleton evidently now produced the version of events at the homage which was entered belatedly upon the Close Roll for the previous regnal year (1278), in the miscellany of private documents placed on the dorse to be of much the same date as those on the front of the membrane. His memorandum was dated only 'in the Michaelmas [29 September, a month before the homage] parliament' and was entered well out of place after texts of late August, where there was a gap sufficiently long to take the belated text.[41] The English record, then, was a later ad hoc production by one who was there (though the text does not say so), for a king troubled by the independence of the Scottish realm, in a dispute over the Border.

This record puts homage in simple terms: 'I, Alexander king of Scotland, become the liege man of lord Edward king of England against all men'; Edward then reserved his and his heirs' right and claim to homage for the kingdom of Scotland when they wished to discuss this. Alexander's words are profoundly unconvincing in naming both kings; to be expected are simply 'I ... of you'. 'Liege man' was used in the treaty of Falaise (1174) and would certainly be expected by Edward, as would 'against all men'.

The Scottish account dates the event precisely; Alexander said: 'I become your man for the lands I hold of you in the kingdom of England for which I owe you homage, saving my kingdom', and the bishop of Norwich interjected 'and let it be saved to the king of England if he has right to your homage for the kingdom'. The king's words are clumsily repetitive, in that 'for which I owe you homage' seems otiose, and if the bishop said 'and let it be saved to the king of England' (which shows that Alexander had saved something), would he admit to the doubt in the longwinded '*if* he has right ...' phrase?

For the reasons given in the last sentence I was initially sceptical of the Scottish version as a record. But Alexander must have chosen, and possibly learned by heart at Roxburgh, the words he would say, and even if there was an English script represented by Middleton's version, he could simply ignore it. The very fact that Middleton spoke out – and the Scottish version is surely correct that he did so – suggests that the English may have been caught unawares by what Alexander said.[42] But if Alexander's words surprised the English, the bishop's words would equally surprise the king and Carrick, whose recollection of them may have been faulty.[43] If the bishop really admitted that Edward *might* have a claim to homage for the kingdom, he slipped up badly. There is a verbal shift in 1278 from 'saving my right', the phrase used as late as 1200 by King William, to 'saving

[41] *Cal. Close Rolls, 1272–79*, 505, from PRO C54/95, m.5d. The subsequent documents on m. 4d are dated 29, 30 August, 5, 11, 12 September, 15, 27 October.

[42] English and Scottish texts have the solecism *devenire/devenio hominem vestrum...*, *Anglo-Scottish Relations*, no. 12.

[43] Thus I think it likely that the bishop said not what the Scots reported but *et salvum sit regi Anglie homagium vestrum de regno*, in Anglo-Norman.

my kingdom', which is carried through the rest of the Scottish account especially in Alexander III's spirited response to the bishop: 'to homage of my kingdom of Scotland, no one has a right except God alone, nor do I hold it except of God alone'.[44]

After homage, the English record claims, Alexander asked to swear fealty by proxy, and this was allowed by Edward, of grace, for this occasion; the Scottish version makes no mention of the request, but agrees that fealty was sworn by a proxy, Carrick. 'Of grace, for this occasion' was perhaps a later improvement on what was said. The wording in the English record, 'I ... will bear true faith ... in life, limb and earthly honour ... I will do the services due from the lands and tenements which I hold from the king of England' is unexceptional, and, having been spoken by Carrick was (it is claimed) confirmed by Alexander. Again we may conjecture that Carrick came with a wording prepared by Alexander's clerks, but if the English account is correct he must have abandoned it for one given him by, for example, the bishop of Norwich. Carrick's career was not that of a man of courage. In the Scottish version the king interrupted Carrick after he had sworn that 'Alexander ... will be faithful in life, limb and earthly honour and will keep your counsels secret',[45] with words from the homage formula attributed to him, 'for the lands which I hold of you in ... England.' Then, in a descriptive passage, he agreed (Carrick is not mentioned) to do the services due from the lands for which he had done homage, 'saving his kingdom'.

The only serious discrepancies between the two versions are Alexander's interjection and the final limitation of services, which would occur if the words used by Carrick were not to Alexander's liking.

In his 1301 response to the 1299 bull, *Scimus fili*, Edward I mentioned the homages of 1251 and 1278 as 'for the kingdom of Scotland';[46] even if we accept only the English record, that 1301 claim was false. The Scottish version, as recorded in the bull, had claimed that Alexander had offered fealty only for Tynedale and Penrith, not as king of Scotland, and had protested that he did not owe fealty for the kingdom which was not subject to Edward, and that Edward accepted the fealty offered,[47] a slightly distorted version of the Scottish account, but it does not go so far for a simple reason: the 1278 riposte claimed that the kingdom was held from God alone, but by 1299 the Scots were desperately urging the pope that the kingdom was held of the Holy See.

---

[44] The Latin *homagium regni mei* presumably represents *homage de mon reaume*.

[45] This phrase is odd; Alexander owed counsel to Edward, not vice versa. *Consilia* here must mean 'what is said in your councils'.

[46] *Anglo-Scottish Relations*, 208–9.

[47] *Anglo-Scottish Relations*, 164–65. The account in *Gest. Ann.* also specifies 'homage for his lands in England, saving all his dignities', and has no knowledge of a protest by either side; *Chron. Fordun*, i, 305; *Scotichronicon*, v, 406–7.

Exactly how much we may believe of the Scottish account must remain debatable, but an interjection by the bishop of Norwich was surely fact, and would follow the homage, since it was important to state Edward's reservation at the earliest possible moment. I would accept the Scottish account of the homage, followed by an interjection by the bishop saving the English king's right to homage for Scotland, with Alexander's spirited response, but then, from the English report, Edward I's answer that he might raise the matter again later. Alexander then indicated that Carrick would swear fealty as his proxy and Edward accepted this. The wording of fealty probably followed the English version but Alexander, in confirming it, may have added the rider that it was for his English lands, as the Scottish version says.

Other reconstructions, more friendly to the English version, are possible, because some of the proceedings were extempore. The Scottish version is not closely datable, and might have been produced to answer the claims of the English version.[48] But on reflection I have come to the view that, rather, it was defensive by anticipation, that before going to Westminster the Scots had reflected on earlier English claims to subordination (e.g. 1251) and had produced the wordings used by their king. The English version reflects this, by recording Edward's reaction, a reservation of his claim to homage for Scotland, which had probably not been part of the English plan for the ceremony; otherwise the homage and fealty recorded in the English version, and probably taken from an English script, are neutral. The Scots, and especially their king, seized the higher ground that day. Alexander went home and resumed aimiable correspondence with Edward I over Border disputes and family news. But his wife, Edward's sister, had died in 1275 and he never again visited the English court or England.

On a leaf inserted into the chronicle of Melrose between 1198 and 1214 is a king list and genealogy with reign lengths and some explanatory matter.[49] The text, compiled soon after 1198, but with additions to 1263, is in effect a short treatise on heritable right and on God's favour among the kings of Scotland, reflecting particularly the cult of Queen Margaret, who had not yet been canonised. Although two doubtful kings, Domnall III and Duncan II (a 'bastard') 'reigned' and Duncan became 'king', all the others, the right male heirs of line, received or took up *regnum* – kingship. In the eyes of this compiler, about 1200, the succession was not a matter of doubt, wherein a king might practice anticipatory designation to avert rival claims and civil war; anticipatory designation was, at least by then, a means of hastening the transition of power and averting local disorder. After 1093–94, when the

---

[48] Professor Barrow has suggested to me that if Abbot Ralph of Dunfermline accompanied the king, he may have been the author, for the text is preserved in the Dunfermline cartulary between deeds of 1276 and 1282; *Dunfermline Registrum*, nos. 320–22.

[49] *Chron. Melrose*, xl, 25–26 for this folio. The oath of fealty of 1201 is not mentioned at the end of the original account, which, I suspect, was written 1198 x 1201.

Scots 'chose' Domnall III as king, election was a recognition of, and offer of support to, the man who was heir because he was not only of the royal *stirps*, but also the senior in line as son, grandson or brother of the deceased ruler. Election and anticipatory designation do not show a weakness in the hereditary principle.

That principle had become the norm throughout landholding society in lowland Britain by the late twelfth century, but the status of women remained ambiguous; they had an expectation of provision in the form of a husband of equal standing, and therefore of a significant tocher. A woman had right of inheritance after the male descendants of her father, but, perhaps by the middle of the twelfth century she shared that right with her sisters, without benefit of seniority,[50] except, it seems, in the case of earldoms, where, in the thirteenth century, the oldest sister had a better right than her juniors. A woman would succeed to her father's heritage in preference to her uncle, and in 1195 the king willed it to be so for the throne and then dropped the proposal. The further dilemmas which might have arisen from it were not faced,[51] and were to recur.

If it be asked why these uncertainties were left, one answer might be found in the contrast between the lord of a fief and the king. Both were subject to customary expectations, such as primogeniture among males, but the lord of a fief had an overlord, the king, who would ensure that right was done in the lord's court; out of this emerged, uncertainly at first, the parage rights of co-heiresses. But the king had no earthly overlord, and, unless the kingdom was treated as a fief and subject to partition, no custom could be found for female succession. The king must make his own custom in such matters, by the advice of his magnates, among whom there must be a reasonable consensus.

Alexander III and his wife, Margaret, had three children who survived infancy. The oldest, Margaret, was born in England in 1261, the second, Alexander, in 1264 and the third, David, in 1273, so the succession seemed assured in 1275 when Queen Margaret died. But David died either in 1280 or at the end of June 1281.[52] The treaty concluded at Roxburgh on 25 July 1281, an agreement for the marriage of Margaret, the Maid of Scotland, to Eric II, the new king of Norway, was the result of embassies sent at, or possibly before, Eric's accession in May 1280, and may have owed something to Edward I's good offices.[53] Negotiated by a Scottish council of twelve earls and magnates, it contains lengthy and elaborate provisions for Margaret's

---

[50] But the oldest co-heiress secured the caput of the fief in Scotland as in England, suggesting that in the twelfth century the younger sisters' husbands had done homage to that of the oldest sister.

[51] For example, if an uncle had a better right than an only daughter and succeeded but left only daughters, who should succeed?

[52] *Chron. Fordun*, i, 307 (not Lindores as *ESSH*, ii, 669); *Scotichronicon*, v, 409, 501.

[53] Helle, 'Norwegian Foreign Policy', *SHR*, lxix, (1990), 148.

dowry and her tocher, showing the familiarity of the parties with mortality even among kings and queens. It then plunges without warning into a provision that

> If it happens that the king of Scotland dies without a lawful son, and any of his sons does not leave lawful issue (*prolem*) and Margaret has children (*liberos*) by the king of Norway, she and her children shall succeed to the king of Scotland and his children, both in the kingdom (*regnum*) and in other goods, or she, even if she is without children, according to Scottish law and custom; and the king of Scotland agrees generally that his daughter and all her descendants shall be freely admitted to all successions and all other rights which can belong to them according to Scottish law or the custom of the said *regio*.[54]

The *mélange* of sons, issue, children, daughter and descendants in this passage is presumably deliberate; when it was drafted the use of 'sons' (plural) shows that David was then alive. Since the word *proles*, like *liberi*, is gender-neutral, it follows that if the king's son predeceased his father leaving a daughter, by representation she would have a better right to the throne than Margaret; the male line, if there was one, had preference. But if the male line had no issue, the right of Margaret to succeed was unqualified, and though there is no suggestion that her husband would be king of Scots, that would surely be assumed. Apart from the succession of Donnchad I in 1034, there was no precedent for succession by or through a woman, and when the treaty cites Scottish custom it must mean the custom of succession in Scottish society at large or in the noble class, succession to heritage by the daughter-heiress of a magnate, rather than by his brother.

Margaret sailed to Norway and married Eric in late August 1281. Less than two years later she died on 9 April 1283, leaving a daughter, Margaret, the Maid of Norway.[55] Since Eric had reached the marriageable age of fourteen some time after the treaty was made, and probably in 1282, it seems likely that the Maid of Scotland died in, or soon after, childbirth, that is, that the Maid of Norway was born March x 9 April 1283. By this time the king's son Alexander had been married to Marguerite of Flanders for perhaps four months (15 November 1282) as a result of an agreement with Guy de Dampierre count of Flanders, sealed by the king, sixteen bishops, earls and barons in December 1281. This date of completion suggests that Alexander III, prompted by the death of David, had sought a wife for his son about the same time as he sought a husband for Margaret. The agreement is recorded in three separate documents, two of which concern the financial settlement.

---

[54] *APS*, i, 422b. The word *regio* here probably means 'kingdom'.

[55] *Chron. Fordun*, i, 307–8. According to the Lanercost chronicle (p. 111) she died in February, thirty days after the death of her brother Alexander in January '1283', i.e. on 27 February 1283/84. There seems little doubt that Margaret died in 1283, in February or more probably April.

All were published in Belgium in 1844 but passed unnoticed by historians of Scotland until after 1945.[56]

The third was printed accessibly in 1978 and is a remarkable statement in Picard French, running in King Alexander's name, beginning with a general principle (P) that 'the customs and usages have been such in the kingdom of Scotland for so long a time of which there is no memory, and are still, that if the son of a king of Scots and [= who is] his heir male has an heir [gender unspecified] and predeceases the king, the heir of this son remains and must remain heir to the kingdom'. The emphasis in this last verb, 'remains' is a striking reassurance that for the succession the grandchild represents its father. This principle is then applied to the forthcoming marriage of Alexander (A) and Marguerite (M) by *Dont ...*, 'So ...'

(1) If A and M have an heir male, he remains heir to the kingdom, even if A predeceases his father, nor can an heir of the king claim anything in the kingdom by reason of heritage. *Oirs*, 'heir', of the king, without qualification in (1) is a child who is not A nor his son, and (from the absence of 'male') is a child of either sex; it will have that sense also in P, which therefore gives to a daughter of the king's son a right to the kingdom. (2) If M predeceases A without heir male, and A takes another wife who bears an heir male [B], no prejudice is intended to this B whereby he would not have his inheritance of the kingdom of Scotland, according to the aforesaid custom. This convoluted statement, with its double negative, must assume, but does not mention, that A and M have had a daughter [F], and protects the right of A's son against that daughter; it discloses the purpose of the whole text: to reassure the Flemings about the rights of M's children, as in the next provision. (3) If B, the heir male of A by his second marriage, dies without heir [gender unspecified], the kingdom reverts to F the eldest surviving female heir of A and M, provided that the king does not have an heir male [C]. (4) And if this C, heir male of a second marriage by the king, has no heir [gender unspecified], the kingdom reverts to F the female heir of A and M.[57]

If this is a challenge to sanity, it nonetheless conveys the importance of heritage to the society which agreed to it, but also provokes questions and doubts. In each clause the right of the child of A and M is compared with that of another descendant of the king, a procedure which leaves some possibilities unexplored, even though P seems broad enough to cover all eventualities. That within each generation of a line, a male has a better right than a female was so obvious that it occurs only in the unstated possibility in (2); it does not say that right descends in the line of the senior male, to the senior male, whom failing female, i.e. male primogeniture, which failing,

---

[56] Stones and Simpson, ii, 188–90.

[57] In the printed text the provisos are numbered in roman numerals, here arabic, but I place the words *sensi nestoit ke nous eussions oire male de no char* at the beginning of (4), not at the end of (3).

Table 2   The succession: possibilities arising in 1281*

Margaret of England		= Alexander III	=	second wife
Margaret = Eric II of Norway	Marguerite of Flanders M =	Alexander A =	second wife	Son C
Margaret, Maid of Norway	daughter F	son B		daughter G

*Hypothetical issue are indicated by a dotted line. In the text the possibility that F died leaving a younger sister and a daughter is also discussed.

female primogeniture. If this had been accepted, stated and remembered, the history of 1290–92 might have been very different.

Instead the issue of female *v* male right is explored in clauses *ad hominem et ad feminam*. This presents no problems in (1) and (2), and in (3) it means that F, the daughter of A and M, who has no right against B, the son of A and his second wife, also has no right against B's issue, male or female. F's right revives only by reversion, if there is no such issue. So far, apparently so good: representation of the line is consistent. But there is an elision from (1) where A has predeceased the king, to (2) and (3) where it may be that A has actually succeeded as king; the point is simply not mentioned, but it would become important with the qualification of (3), that, B being childless, Alexander III's younger son C had a better right than F, A's daughter. King A's daughter should have a better claim than C, Alexander III's second son, both by nearness of degree to the last king and by representation; here the reverse is asserted without clarifying whether A had been king or not. As in the *casus regis* of John king of England, representation is abandoned.

In (4), it is implied, but not said, that C has become king, for his heiress-daughter [G] has a better right to the kingdom than her cousin, F; the daughter of the younger son succeeds because she is nearer to the last king, C, and of his line. But if A and C both predeceased Alexander III, leaving daughters, surely F, not G, should succeed? Not if the letter of (4) be followed. In (3) it seems that, failing other lines, the succession goes to the oldest *surviving* daughter of A and M; that is the children of a *deceased* oldest daughter are ruled out; the only rational explanation is that the surviving daughter is a degree nearer to the common ancestor-king. There is a sense throughout, though not at all well articulated, that where the choice is between women, nearness by degree to the king is a factor which should outweigh seniority of line.

The reader must by now sympathise with the Scots, called upon to reassure Count Guy about the prospects of his daughter's issue, peering at hypothetical instances, without a doubt anxious to provide Scotland with a king if at all possible, but allowing inheritance by a woman if all males failed. But the document does not reconcile these aims by any recourse to a legal principle and even avoids recourse to the rule of succession cited in the treaty with Norway which was already customary for an earldom in Scotland, surely a deliberate avoidance, arising from a sense that succession to the throne must look to more than the heir of line in order to achieve male succession.

At the same time these two marriage alliances forced the Scots to think about the possibility of female succession. The 1281 treaty provided that if Eric and Margaret had a daughter or daughters, they should succeed to everything they are entitled to according to Norwegian law and custom, 'even to the kingdom if it is the custom'. Were the Norwegians deceiving the Scots? For because its kings were 'great womanisers', they procreated many children, who sometimes shared a divided kingdom, but from 1130 struggled for a single kingship – without regard to legitimacy in the eyes of the church. From 1130 to 1240, forty-six males sought the kingship, all of royal descent, about a quarter legitimate; twenty-four became kings, but only one of these was the legitimate son of a king. Only after the the long-lived Haakon IV had designated his second son (the elder had died leaving a son) as heir in 1257 was legitimacy built in as precondition to succession in order to avoid the struggles which had marred Norwegian kingship.[58]

In 1273 a council at Bergen agreed a law of succession to the throne which named twelve male relatives of a king in order of the right of each to succeed, whom failing the general law of inheritance was to be followed, but always a man not a woman; this was included in the codification of 1280.[59] The daughter of Eric and Margaret could not, in this law, succeed to the kingdom; when Eric II died in 1299, leaving a year-old daughter by his second wife, he was succeeded by his brother. On the brother's death in 1319, also leaving only a daughter, the Norwegians, lacking alternatives, chose her three-year old son as king.[60] The Norwegian example is particularly interesting in that a law was born of chaos in the succession – chaos which Scotland manifestly lacked – and in that the church won the struggle for legitimacy, but not that for primogeniture and representation.

The young Alexander married his Marguerite on 15 November 1282; in the following year his sister died in Norway, and on 28 January 1284 Alexander himself died. The king did not wait to discover if Marguerite

[58] Jochens, 'The Politics of Reproduction: Medieval Norwegian Kingship', *American Historical Review*, xcii (1987), 327–49.

[59] Gjerset, *History of the Norwegian People*, i, 459. I have consulted the text in *Regis Magni Legum Reformatoris Leges Gula-Thingenses*, 48–59, which has Norse text with Latin translation. The twelve qualified are named in c. IV of Kristindóms-Bólkr and include, for example, cousins. The seventh in line is the king's illegitimate son, and the eighth and ninth the son of a king's daughter and sister. In 1319 the eighth succeeded. There is also provision in c. V laying down the manner of choice of a king if the royal line died out.

[60] He was also chosen king of Sweden, to which he had a claim through his father.

were pregnant; eight days later, on 5 February 1284, a gathering of the secular magnates at Scone put their seals to an obligation to the king to cover the situation should he die. All thirteen earls are named, with twenty-four barons,[61] including John Balliol (unusually), and (again unusually) the chiefs of three Gaelic kindreds, the Macdonalds, Macdougalls and Macruaraidhs.[62] These considerations suggest that the document was drawn up for sealing by officials intent upon committing all men of importance, but particularly all earls, and perhaps men of all regions of the kingdom. Comparison with the witnesses to royal charters of the 1280s shows only two absent names which might be expected on 5 February 1284: Andrew Moray and Patrick Barclay. The clergy were not included because the bishops, all eleven or twelve,[63] were to use ecclesiastical sanctions to hold the laymen to their promise. Balliol's name suggests that he was already identified as having an interest in the succession.

The king had no expectation of an adult succession, and knew that royal authority would be weak, dependent upon the determination of lay magnates, for the second part provided that on the death of the king, any officials or other debtors who refused to pay what they owed to the executors of the king's will (i.e. to pay in royal revenues) would be constrained to do so and to pay amends under ecclesiastical sanction. The document opens with an undertaking – an *obligatorium* – to the king and the heirs immediately or mediately proceeding from his body who rightly ought to be admitted to succession to him, that if the king died leaving no son or daughter, or if his son Alexander left none, then the thirty-seven would receive the Maid of Norway and her lawful issue as 'our lady and right heir' of the king in the whole kingdom of Scotland, Isle of Man and other islands and in Tynedale and Penrith, and would support her in this with all their strength.

The 'mediate' heirs of the king's body must refer to his grandchildren, presumably to the possibility that Marguerite might yet produce a child, as well as to the Maid of Norway. The intention of the king to remarry is evident in the place given to his son or daughter, but not only does his son oust the Maid's right, as male primogeniture would provide, but so too does his daughter. That a younger daughter of the king has a better right than the daughter of his older daughter can only be based upon her nearness of degree to the king himself, as had been implied in the Flemish settlement of December 1281. The right of a possible daughter of Alexander III is

---

[61] It is possible that one name is wholly illegible, making twenty-five in all.

[62] *APS*, i, 424. After the name *Willelmus de Moravia filius Walteri de Moravia* the word *milites* means that the preceding seven barons (and thirteen earls?) were knights and the following seventeen barons were not. I suggest that the word be read as *militis*, applying to Walter de Moravia.

[63] Ross and the Isles are not named but the parchment is defective at this point. The sees of Dunkeld and Dunblane, which are named, may well have been vacant at this date.

the only thing here which was not said or implied in the 1281 treaty with Norway.

The Maid received as 'our lady and right heir of the king' would become queen by due process,[64] either as soon as she arrived in Scotland, or after marriage, when her husband might become king. That is uncertain, but when Edward I sent a friar with a message of condolence for the death of the young Alexander, the Scottish king did not send back an oral message of thanks. Instead his letter dated 20 April 1284,[65] thanking Edward recalled that 'through your kinswoman, the daughter of your niece ... who is now our heir apparent[66] many good things may come to pass yet which ...' and here the text is worn away, but perhaps 'we [Alexander] seek', or 'we [the two kings] should seek'. Hence Edward should listen to what Alexander's envoy has to say. The passage is not merely unsolicited, it is forward, proposing to Edward discussion of a suitable husband for the Maid, but her position and her marriage were suddenly crucial matters, the first concerns of her grandfather and his magnates. They were already contemplating a marriage in England, probably to the English royal house, where, after all, Alexander II and Alexander III had found their spouses. The form of the undertaking of February 1284, 'we oblige ourselves very strictly to the king and his heirs ...,' might imply unwilling acceptance of a female right by many who really preferred a male – especially Balliol or Bruce. Presumably there were some of that persuasion among the forty (almost certainly Bruce of Annandale), but the success of the regency after 1286 suggests that they were very few.

But matters were not left thus. Ten years after the death of his wife and a year after the death of his son, the king, eschewing another English marriage, chose a new wife, Yolanda, daughter of the count of Dreux. They were married at Jedburgh on 14 October 1285, with every hope that the union would produce an heir to the Scottish throne. On 18 March 1286 the king and his counsellors sat in Edinburgh castle to discuss a knotty issue. The party dined and the king set out for Fife, where his new wife awaited him at Kinghorn. He crossed the Forth by the Queen's ferry, became separated from his companions, and was found, probably on the next day, dead with a broken neck, near to Kinghorn. He was forty-five years old, had no brothers or sisters and was predeceased by all three of his children who survived infancy. It is not known whether he died on 18 or 19 March.[67]

The king's death was recorded in a number of English chronicles but it

---

[64] In the inventory drawn up by Edward I's orders in 1291 this document is listed as an obligation to receive the Maid 'as lady and queen'; *APS*, i, 111.

[65] *Anglo-Scottish Relations*, no. 13. By this date it would presumably be clear that Marguerite was not pregnant.

[66] That is, heir presumptive.

[67] Nor whether his horse stumbled, a suggestion frequently made as fact.

passed unnoticed beyond these islands, for Scotland was remote from the busy trading centres of Europe and her king and nobles had shown little concern with the politics which engrossed men of their class in other realms. King Alexander was uninterested in the struggle for the kingdom of Sicily, and a passive observer of the fate of the last fragments of the kingdom of Jerusalem, thereby sharing his predecessors' inaction. The clamour of his subjects is said to have dissuaded David I from serving in the Holy Land and no king of Scots went on crusade or even took the cross. Nor were they greatly familiar with Capetian France or Hohenstaufen Germany, though twelfth-century kings did visit France until the 1180s, and King William married a French wife.

Yet in the twelfth century 'Scotland' enjoyed some recognition in courtly literature in French, which showed no familiarity with either the history or the geography of the country. Presumably Scotland was chosen as a site in these romances because its kings had established their credentials as patrons of nobles of French origin and (probably) speech; here chivalry was known to flourish. But beyond that, an author had no need to labour after accuracy, for readers knew little wherewith to denounce the romance as unhistorical or topographically impossible. Nor could the head of any noble or royal lineage take offence, claiming to have found his ancestor in a false knight, for these were tales of Lothian or Galloway – never-never land.

But from the early thirteenth century different heroes and villains peopled different fictional landscapes, partly because after 1187 the Muslim, the paynim, was the dangerous enemy of Christian chivalry. The slight cosmopolitan record of the Scottish kings ended in 1174, and while Alexander II reached Dover and his son Westminster, neither set foot in Continental Europe. In 1239 Alexander II chose his second wife from France, and his contacts with Louis IX in 1242 sent Henry III into a war fever by 1244 which fortunately abated when wiser English counsels prevailed. Alexander III also chose his second wife from the French nobility. But the first wife of each was the daughter of an English king, and these marriages were entered into as part of wider bargains to preserve Anglo-Scottish peace.

This independence of Continental Europe was not maintained absolutely by the upper reaches of clerical and aristocratic society. Embassies (which would have included laymen) to, for example, the count of Flanders or the king of France, were rare, and in the latter case could provoke a reaction by the English king which seems excessive but undoubtedly confirmed the restricted European role of the Scottish kings. A few earls, barons and even lairds participated in the crusades, but the impact of such Scots upon the societies and governing eites of mainland Europe was insignificant.[68]

[68] Macquarrie, *Scotland and the Crusades*, shows that the Crusading movement did affect Scotland in various ways.

However, ecclesiastical preferment through merit or education took the sons of lairds (and even burgesses) up a career ladder which might include stays on the Continent. Many of the graduates in the entourages of bishops who might rise to a canonry, archdeaconry or even to episcopal office were educated in England and/or France, some at Bologna. Because of the lack of a metropolitan in the Scottish church, there was a steady stream of clerical visits to the papal curia for confirmation and consecration, and thrice in the thirteenth century visits from Scotland to general councils of the church. Some became familiar with the papal court, which was equally familiar with the unique position of the Scottish province. In this respect did Scotland impinge upon the consciousness of the main Continental players in the politics of the thirteenth century.

With England it was a different story. If the junior branch of a migrant family – the fitz Alans, for example – had not retained close links with elder brothers and cousins of the senior branch in the twelfth century, nonetheless intermarriage between Scottish and English baronial families probably became more frequent as the twelfth and thirteenth centuries progressed, so that by the reign of Alexander III a number of magnates were in possession of marriage portions in England, while important lordships in Scotland, including the earldom of Angus and a moiety of the lordship of Galloway, were held by English nobles. The Scottish baronage was not, however, divided in its allegiance by the claims of baronies held in two realms, as events were to show after 1296, when, for example, the earl of Angus, ignoring his matrilinear inheritance of Angus, was loyal to the English king of whom he held the barony of Prudhoe; his distant cousin, Ingram de Umfraville, with Ayrshire and Northumbrian lands, was not only loyal to John king of Scotland, but took a leading part in forcing John to defy Edward.

In one important respect the two groups, English and Scottish nobles, had come to differ by the later thirteenth century – language. Whereas Anglo-Norman was the language of aristocracy in England under Edward I, there is little trace that it was then used in Scotland, where the language of record and correspondence was Latin, and of speech Scots or Gaelic.[69] After 1304, the letters to Edward I from his English servants in Scotland were in French; those from his Scottish supporters were in Latin. The cultural effect of this difference must have been substantial, for it distanced the Scots from the literature of chivalry and the Arthurian 'history' found there. Some must have turned to other, native, history, so that some Celtic personal names were revived after c.1250; there was also renewed scholarly interest in the lists of ancient kings and the origin legends of the Scots. To the extent that speech marked a social divide, the nobility of Scotland were set apart from

[69] Barrow, 'French after the Style of Petithachengon', *Church, Chronicle and Learning*, ed. Crawford, 187–94. Professor Barrow would regard French as more widely used than I do, but we are agreed that usage was much less than in England.

their English cousins; whether history set them apart, or they used history to validate recent changes in their own attitudes, is a complex, and perhaps unanswerable, question. Secular literature from the time does not exist.

In brief, in Alexander III's reign free society in lowland Scotland was a reasonable simulacrum of that in England, poorer, less numerous, more primitively housed, but expressing the same ideas and ideals in related forms of the English language. There was no iron curtain at the Tweed, and Scotland was not in any sense isolated in the twelfth and thirteenth centuries. Its kings and nobility had close relationships with English society, but did not widely share Anglo-Norman speech.

By their actions after the death of the king in 1286, and especially by the oath which they took then to secure the heritage of the rightful heir, the prelates and magnates showed their acceptance of the kingdom as the framework for their political actions, and of the king as their only political allegiance. It was not a xenophobic loyalty; there is little trace in any Scottish source of the distaste for foreigners and demand for native ('natural') advisors of the king which are evident in some quarters of Henry III's England.[70] Nor had the peace of the kingdom been shattered by revolt against royal exactions, or by civil war over the scope of administrative reform, as in England in 1215–17 and 1264–65, when those opposed to the king had to articulate their place in the kingdom and the proper relationship between Ruler and ruled. Any consciousness of Scottish nationality was correspondingly subdued, and included a sense of what, for want of a better word, I call 'cousinhood' with the kingdom of England. Scotland, the motto might have said, was 'separate but similar'.

Separate because it was an ancient kingdom. The curious cleric in 1286 would have found little in his sources about the early kings, still less about kingship, and it behoves us, in studying the dilemmas of the thirteenth century, to remember that our understanding, immediate and comparative, of early Scottish kingship was not available to the men of that time. Our sources for early times, mostly of the fourteenth century, were probably copied from manuscripts written in the twelfth and thirteenth, but, save for the mythical history of Macbeth and Macduff preserved by Wyntoun, there is no treatise or history from those centuries to tell us how men thought Scotland had evolved. They believed in a succession of peoples who had conquered the land: Britons, followed by Picts, whose kings were known and who succumbed to, and were obliterated by, Scots. That the first Scottish ruler over Alba, Scotland north of Forth, was Cinaed mac Alpin, may have been picked up from the jejune annals in the X tradition of the king list, but in historiography the 'destruction of the Picts' was not a turning point such as was the Norman Conquest in England.

[70] But there was considerable hostility to John de Cheam, bishop of Glasgow, 1259–68, an Englishman appointed by papal provision against opposition from Alexander III; his chapter made his life a misery.

CHAPTER 9

The Maid of Norway

In the earliest fragment written in Scots, the kingdom is forlorn by the death of King Alexander:

> Crist born in virginyte
> Succoure Scotland and ramede
> That stade is in perplexite.[1]

Yet much thought had recently been given to the royal succession, and there was only one immediate perplexity: was Queen Yolanda pregnant? For this predicament, awaiting an answer and then the child, the magnates swore to preserve the kingdom for the right heir and chose Guardians for an undefined interim. A second phase, from late 1286, when the child was still-born, until 1289, began with civil strife but settled into peace, perhaps uneasy, attendant upon the return of Edward I to England. Yet even before his return Eric II, king of Norway, a debtor of Edward, besought his help over the rights of the Maid of Norway whom they resolutely called 'lady and queen' of Scotland. The third phase began with tripartite agreement to bring the girl to Britain, but developed into a war of nerves between Edward I, seeking possession of Scottish castles, and the Scots refusing to yield them, with an agreement at Northampton on 28 August 1290 which probably pleased neither side. The Maid sailed from Norway and died in Orkney in September. The poem, I think, reflects despair at the extinction of the line of King Alexander, after, perhaps soon after, her death.

From the burial of the king at Dunfermline on 29 March 1286, the bishops of St Andrews and Glasgow sent two Dominicans to tell Edward I of events. A second meeting in parliament at Scone, according to *Gest. Ann.*, was only four days later, on 2 April when six Guardians were elected, two earls, two bishops and two barons. Bower, omitting this passage, gives a wholly new account of a parliament on Sunday, 28 April, and Wyntoun in effect agrees. All three claim that the Guardians were elected at their assembly, but Bower and Wyntoun had a version which offered the name of an additional Guardian, the bishop of Dunkeld.

---

[1] *Chron. Wyntoun*, v, 145. Some witnesses read 'in to virginite'.

Bower also seems to place there a fierce debate over the succession between Balliol and Bruce supporters, leading to the despatch of an embassy to Edward I and to his claim to overlordship.[2] The new edition of *Scotichronicon* suggests that we translate not as 'where there was a fierce debate', i.e. in that parliament, but as 'When there was a fierce debate' [the following arguments were deployed]. Bower clearly took the former meaning, but the latter, introducing a later argument, makes better sense, and was, I think, that intended by his source.[3]

Thus the parliament at Scone pretty certainly met on 28–29 April, forty days after the king's death;[4] its first business (though no source places the event) would be the oath to the nearest by blood to the late king who by right should inherit, to keep the peace of the land. It was later claimed by John Balliol that this oath had explicitly named the Maid, while a Bruce document suggests that it included 'by right, according to ancient customs ... used in the kingdom', but these were interpretations added to suit the two Claimants;[5] other accounts show that such words were not used,[6] and they are to be preferred. To the men who took it, its authority was absolute, and it overrode all political considerations for individuals and for the magnates as a whole for the next six years. It was not their first act of constructive statesmanship – others can be suggested in the years 1251–58 – but it was certainly the boldest and most far-reaching.

It was articulation of a shared duty to the kingdom when there was no king, and was expressed by a corporate name for those responsible: community of the kingdom. This phrase had been used in varying circumstances in England, for example in 1258 when the community is tax-paying landholders; or the 1264 peace between the 'king, prelates, magnates and whole community of the kingdom commonly approved', where again the phrase comprehends supporters who had no direct political voice.[7] But in the Scotland of 1286 it stated a greater claim: the Guardians were 'appointed by common counsel' in domestic letters, but to Edward I they were 'chosen by the community of the kingdom'. These descriptions were chosen for their familiarity to the recipients or their clerks, but there is a claim to universality and to unity in the word 'community' which is not there in 'prelates and magnates', an alternative and factually correct

---

[2] Stevenson, *Documents*, i, no. 3; *Chron. Fordun*, i, 319, 310; *Scotichronicon*, vi, 2–3, 8–11; *Chron. Wyntoun*, v, 154–57.

[3] *Scotichronicon*, vi, 8–9; *Chron. Lanercost*, 125. Correcting my argument in 'Community of the realm of Scotland and Robert Bruce', *SHR*, xlv (1966), 185–86.

[4] The date of 2 April in *Gest. Ann.* may be that of a dispersal of those gathered for the funeral.

[5] Stones and Simpson, ii, 144 (Bruce); 179 (Balliol); it was also cited by Galightly (137).

[6] The letter of Bishop Fraser in 1290 and the response of the Scots to Edward I on 2 June 1291; Stones and Simpson, ii, 4, 31.

[7] Stubbs, *Charters*, 371, 400.

description. That claim would be founded in the oath which prelates and magnates had sworn at Scone.[8]

If this was their first act, the community next appointed those who would maintain the royal heritage, the six Guardians, perhaps chosen as three from north of Forth, three from south thereof – that is certainly the interpretation of *Gest. Ann.*[9] The two bishops, St Andrews and Glasgow, and the barons, John Comyn of Badenoch and James Stewart, call for no comment. The earl of Fife, however, was a very young and inexperienced man, quite unlike his companion earl, Buchan, who had been a justiciar since the 1250s; Fife was a landowner in Lothian as well as *Scotia*. Perhaps his leading function at a royal inauguration, his formal position as premier earl, won him his Guardianship, or it may be that he stood neutral or undecided among those who favoured Bruce or Balliol, should the issue of Alexander III fail – a possibility which must have been in the minds of many magnates. Bishop William Fraser of St Andrews went to London at once to tell Edward I of these acts in parliament; he was at Berwick on 11 May but failed to catch Edward (who crossed to France on 13 May) at London. Bower's and Wyntoun's guardianship of the bishop of Dunkeld makes sense as an interim replacement for Bishop Fraser.

A second embassy led by William Comyn bishop of Brechin, departed in early August and reached Edward at Saintes (where he was on 13–16 September); it was probably sent to tell the English king that Queen Yolande was certainly pregnant, with the prospect of a long royal minority recalling the 1250s. It asked for his counsel and protection (*patrocinium*) over the state of the kingdom, says Bower,[10] which would fit with Edward's suspension of proceedings at the Border, at the request of the Guardians.[11] But the Scots also looked elsewhere for protection. At an uncertain date, but no later than September 1286, the Guardians were using a seal, large like a royal great seal, bearing on the obverse a shield of the royal arms and a legend meaning 'seal of Scotland appointed for the rule of the kingdom'; the reverse showed St Andrew on his cross with the legend 'Andrew, be a leader to Scottish fellow-countrymen'.[12] Tutelary saints have but a nominal following in our day, but to the men of 1286 they were real, powerful, trustworthy, and

---

[8] These phrases are known in Latin from documents, but not their vernacular equivalent; the word 'community' had been adopted into Scots by the 1370s, quite possibly as a result of the Latin use in the 1280s, but by then it was used of 'the commons'.

[9] *Chron. Fordun*, i, 310.

[10] *Scotichronicon*, vi, 8, *ad implorandum suum consilium et patrocinium super statu regni Scocie et terrarum de Penreth.*

[11] *Scotichronicon*, vi, 8–11; Stevenson, *Documents*, i, no. 11; Watt, *Biographical. Dictionary*, 108 (for the bishop of Brechin).

[12] ANDREA SCOTIS DVX ESTO COMPATRIOTIS. The word *esto* (be!) and the vocative of *Andreas* make this a forceful injunction – even though addressed to a saint. Without them, the words would mean only '[This is a depiction of] Andrew, leader of Scottish fellow-countrymen'.

Andrew was present in the kingdom not as a spirit but corporeally, by the sea in Fife. We must take seriously this petition from the community of Scotland to him whom they held as their leader (Plate 5).[13]

The queen's pregnancy is attested by two chronicles, and though the chronology of one is mistaken, there is every reason to believe, with Bower, that the envoys from Saintes returned to meet the Guardians at Clack-mannan on St Catherine's day (25 November 1286), where they had gathered to witness the birth of the child. Bower's conclusion, that 'this event failed to take place or else there was a still-birth' shows that when hopes came to nothing with a still-birth, official silence encouraged pro-liferating rumour and scandal. But the events of 1286, and notably the absence of any reference to the Maid, fit well with the queen's pregnancy, as does the subsequent outbreak of violence, the reaction to a drastically changed situation.[14]

In September Robert Bruce had gathered his main supporters, including the Guardian James Stewart, with their heirs, at his son's castle of Turn-berry where they engaged themselves by solemn oath to adhere to and stand by the earl of Ulster and Sir Thomas Clare in all their affairs. The point of this undertaking for Irish nobles is obscure but it shows the formation or consolidation of a Bruce faction at the approach of the queen's term. In the ensuing winter Bruce and his son, the earl of Carrick, raised rebellion by seizing royal and Balliol castles in the south-west, to which area it was limited, apart from the posting of a few additional guards at Edinburgh castle 'because of the danger of war'. It was readily and swiftly suppressed in early 1287.[15] In the same winter, it seems, a prominent Norwegian coun-cillor was in Scotland, vainly seeking recognition of the Maid's right to the kingdom.[16]

The change which provoked these acts was the definitive failure of children born to Alexander III. Bruce showed that he rejected the right of the Maid and was prepared to assert his own, which he must have thought was better. Like the Maid, his claim was by descent through a female; nor was his the senior line of Earl David's descendants – his cousin Dervorguilla of Galloway represented that. The only case he could have had was that he was the male nearest in degree to Earl David and to the common ancestor of

---

[13] For the fourteenth-century transition from Denis to Michael as patron saint of French kings, and so of France, Beaune, *Birth of an Ideology*, chapters 1 and 5.

[14] *Chron. Lanercost*, 117–18 (s.a. 1287); *Scotichronicon*, vi, 10–11; for the date, my comment in *SHR*, xlv, (1966), 187–88. In 1289 the lady Ela of Fife, relict of Sir Andrew Garviach, travelled from Aberdeenshire to Stirling castle and back *in seruisio domine regine* for which the Guardians allowed her £10 in expenses. NAS, RH5/226 (4 and 5). Evidently Yolanda, of whom little is known until her remarriage in May 1294 to the duke of Brittany, had remained at Stirling castle enjoying her terce, on which see *Exch. Rolls*, i, 39, 40, 46.

[15] Stevenson, *Documents*, i, no. 12; *Exch. Rolls*, i, 35, 39, 42; Palgrave, *Docs. Hist. Scot.*, 42; *Barrow*, Bruce, 17 and 330, nn 42–44.

[16] Helle, 'Norwegian Foreign Policy', 149.

himself and the Maid, Earl Henry son of David I, which gave him a better right than the female Dervorguilla, but also than the Maid, who was nearer in degree to a king, but was female. The shakiness of this last claim, which rejected both the undertaking of 1284 and the oath of 1286 to the nearest by blood to Alexander III, is obvious, but that does not seem to have deterred Bruce, while the government evidently felt that it could not punish him for rebellion, for he was again an active member of the community at least by 1289.[17]

The Guardians ruled circumspectly until 1289, when Earl Alexander died and Earl Duncan was killed in a quarrel with distant kinsmen;[18] they were not replaced. The fragments of royal accounts reveal that several *colloquia* were held, the Guardians seeking shared responsibility for whatever matters were discussed. It is likely that these years saw an increased awareness of common weal, an expectation by the great men of involvement and participation in, and responsibility for, public affairs. This they were soon called upon to acknowledge in relations with the king of England.

At some point before February 1289, perhaps in 1288, Bishop Fraser had vainly set out for Edward I in Gascony;[19] on 1 April 1289 Eric appointed proctors to go to Edward for the 'business' of the Maid, the first mention thereof and calling her 'lady and queen', and on 1 May they were to go to him in France.[20] This cannot have been the first overture on this 'business', though earlier contact was perhaps by lower-level messengers.[21] Presumably having met the Norwegian envoys, Edward returned to England on 12 August, where he may have met Bishop Fraser, absent from Scotland at least in early August. A further English safeconduct for Eric's envoys was issued on 17 September.[22] So far as the record goes, these preliminaries were a dance for two kings, with the Scots little more than spectators.

Thus in the subsequent treaty, it is said that Eric and his daughter, 'queen and heir of the kingdom', asked Edward to give help and advice so that his

---

[17] For what follows there are important articles in *SHR*, lxix (1990), 117–84, a number of the periodical commemorating the death of the Maid of Norway. All are valuable, but I cite three in particular: Barrow, 'A Kingdom in crisis', 120–41; Helle, 'Norwegian Foreign Policy', 142–56; Prestwich, 'Edward I and the Maid of Norway', 157–73.

[18] Earl Alexander died after 29 April; an unprinted writ of five Guardians implies that he had died by 5 June, NAS, RH5/226 (4). Duncan was killed on 10 September 1289; *RRS*, v, 356.

[19] Stevenson, *Documents*, no. 53, which shows that he had been waylaid at Doncaster on his way to Edward I in Gascony some weeks or months before mid-February 1289. He is not attested in Scotland 12 September – 19 November 1288, nor 19 November 1288 – 10 March 1289. But his messenger reached the regent in London by 1 December 1288, possibly sent on if the bishop turned back from Doncaster in late October (*ibid.*, no. 46).

[20] *Foedera*, i, 706; Stevenson, *Documents*, i, no. 62

[21] See, for example, Stevenson, *Documents*, i, no. 59.

[22] Stevenson, *Documents*, i, nos 62, 74. Fraser was in Scotland on 10 July and 12 September 1289, but absent on 2 and 5 August, possibly for weeks; *ibid.*, nos 69, 32 (correctly of 1289), 69, 73.

[great] niece should be obeyed as lady, queen and heir, 'and that she could ordain and enjoy therein as other kings do in their kingdoms'. Edward it was who asked the Guardians to send envoys with power to treat about 'amendment' of the kingdom and 'reformation of the estate of the queen'. Three surviving Guardians and Bruce (not James Stewart) came to Salisbury in October, where they met the envoys of Eric and of Edward.[23]

The level of interest generated in England may be judged by the strip-cartoon history of the kings of Britain and England from Greek and Trojan antiquity to Edward I, compiled or copied on a roll four metres long at St Mary's abbey, York; to this was appended a further lesson in England's British mission, a depiction of the royal lines of England and Scotland and their intermarriages. Unfortunately Edward I's issue has been cut away, but Alexander III's marriage to Margaret of England is there, with issue Margaret, queen of Norway, and her daughter, the Maid of Norway (Plate 6). The absence of Alexander's sons and the presence of the Maid, unmarried but on offer, place this work after 1283 and before September 1290, and probably in 1289–90. Its message – a costly one – was not, I think, to further Edward I's claim to overlordship, but to proclaim the close relationship of the two kingships and the likely benefits of one last intermarriage.[24]

The Scots, then, had been fairly passive about the heiress to their throne, rightly, since aged seven years she could scarcely rule; the Norwegians were indeed active, to put it plainly, in offering her. The 1281 treaty with Norway had provided as part of her mother's tocher an annual payment of 700 merks secured on Scottish lands.[25] Ten days after the death of Alexander III, and just possibly in knowledge of it, the Norwegians sent an envoy to Edward I with power to borrow 2,000 marks, paid on 21 September 1286 by two London-based Cahorsin merchants on behalf of Edward I.[26] They later had a loan of 2,800 merks from two Cahorsins, one of them also involved in 1286, 'to expedite our [Eric's] business and that of Margaret our daughter', on the security of the 700 merks due annually for the dowry of the Maid of Scotland. Eric claimed in a letter to the English king, undated but possibly brought by his ambassadors to Salisbury, that at the forthcoming Whitsun, (21 May) 1290, he would have been deprived by the Scots of four years' payment and Edward was now asked to press the Guardians to repay the

[23] For the role of the Norwegians, always impecunious, see the excellent survey in Helle, 'Norwegian Foreign Policy', 142–56.

[24] British Library, Cotton Charter, XIV, 4. Another version is Bodleian Library, Ashmole Rolls, 50. Discussion with illustrations in Monroe, 'Two Medieval Genealogical Roll-Chronicles …', *Bodleian Library Record*, x (1981), 215–21. See also Sandler, *Gothic Manuscripts, 1285–1385*, ii, no. 16a, and Davies, *First English Empire*, 42.

[25] *APS*, i, 422a, 423b (lines 8–12).

[26] *Foedera*, i, 673; Stevenson, *Documents*, i, nos 2, 43, 98. The money should have been repaid in 1287–88, but clearly was not.

Cahorsins, who carried Eric's dunning letter to the Guardians.[27] Edward's financial accommodation would buy him Norwegian collaboration; he would see what he might gain by brokering the Maid's return, by regarding her as already queen, and by her marriage to his son. If the Maid was 'lady and queen' of Scotland for the first recorded time in Eric's credentials of 1 April 1289, that aspiration was certainly encouraged by his creditor, Edward I.

The making of the Treaty of Salisbury was the point of departure for all that followed in Anglo-Scottish relations, since it first involved the Scots with Edward I in designing the future of the kingdom. In 1289 the Maid, a mere child, could well have remained in Norway for four or five years, for the government of Scotland was in competent hands, blessed by a friendly neighbour, and would gain nothing by her immediate presence. Eric's discussions of her marriage with Edward therefore presented an unpleasant dilemma for the Guardians. Do nothing and a marriage treaty could deliver the Maid for a price to Edward, who could then exact a further price from the Scots for her release, married, into Scotland; participate in negotiations and Edward would have a powerful role and say over her future, with other possible marriages closed off. Do nothing and the Scots had no cards in their hand, participate and they had few. There can have been little joy in the choice made.

Save in a couple of letters to Edward,[28] the Scots showed no inclination to recognise the Maid as queen either before or after 1289; even in their part of the Northampton treaty, on 28 August 1290, the Scots, spoke only of their 'lady'. In all the claims and pleadings of the Great Cause she is 'lady' and/or 'heir' of the kingdom, 'queen' only in the belated claim of Eric II; she reappears as 'lady and queen' in King John's quittance (2 January 1293) of Edward's promises at Northampton, but the title is taken from that document.[29] Modern works without exception[30] call her 'queen', including reference books which give the date of her accession as 19 March 1286 (Alexander III's death); they are victims of Edward I's determined hustling.[31]

A list of Scottish rulers must surely be based upon the law and custom of

---

[27] *Foedera*, i, 732; Helle, 'Norwegian Foreign Policy', *SHR*, lxix (1990) 149, 151. I would place this letter of Eric not long after Whitsun (29 May) 1289, well before the visit of the Cahorsin merchants to Norway for which they had a safe-conduct on 20 April 1290 (*Cal. Docs. Scot.*, ii., no. 425).

[28] Discussed below, p. 000.

[29] Stones and Simpson, ii, 154, 272.

[30] So far as I can tell.

[31] For example, *Handbook of British Chronology*, 58; Dunbar, *Scottish Kings*, 103–9 (which gives a table of her 'regnal' years!). I am not suggesting that the Maid be excluded from such works (cf. the treatment of Matilda *domina Anglorum* in *Handbook*, 36), but the printing of letters from the Guardians as 'acts of Queen Margaret's parliament' (*APS*, i, 441–42) is a triumph of expectation over evidence.

Scotland, which called her 'lady and heir' in 1284 and still in 1290 when she was about to cross to Scotland. In the three years following Alexander III's death she is not mentioned in any record, and the Guardians never describe themselves as holding office for her, though on 17 March 1289 in letters to be discussed shortly, they did describe the common seal as that 'used in name of our aforesaid lady'; the phrase does not recur.[32] Her titles appear in 1289 for the first time, when Eric II's and Edward I's clerks called her 'queen', but after her death this was abandoned as quickly as it had been adopted. Never inaugurated, she was never queen of Scots.

To the treaty concluded at Salisbury on 6 November 1289, all three kingdoms were party. The Maid was to come to England or Scotland by 1 November 1290, free of all contract of marriage, a promise by Norway not to sell her off to another bidder. The naming of both British kingdoms was probably a realistic appreciation that when she sailed from Norway she might well come first to a Scottish port, for the treaty itself and subsequent documents assume that she would go to England. The Scots would provide assurances that the kingdom was secure and peaceful, when Edward would send the Maid north free of marriage contract, so long as the good folk (*bona gens*) of Scotland promised that they would not marry her off save with Edward's ordinance, will and advice, and with Eric's assent, a provision which in effect gave Edward the right ('ordinance') to choose her husband, and Eric a weak veto. There are provisions to remove from the Scottish government those disliked by Norway and for Edward to mediate if this was disputed, and also if they could not agree on matters touching the betterment (*adrescement, reformatio*) of the kingdom, a point not to be forgotten.[33] The folk (*gens*) of Scotland were to meet with Edward's envoys in mid-March 1290 to confirm this treaty and to give the assurances promised in it; it is possible that *gens* was used deliberately to describe a larger assembly than 'community' would have done.[34]

Ten days after the treaty was concluded, Nicholas IV issued a bull at Rome permitting the marriage of the Maid to Edward I's only son, Edward (II).[35] The view that this was deceitful and a breach of the Salisbury promise to send the Maid to Scotland free of marriage contract is unsustainable. Edward I sought the bull long before he knew of the treaty's promise; the bull permits a marriage, but in no way contracts one, and the prospect of the Maid's marriage had been dangled before Edward I by Alexander III as early as 1284. When they accepted the treaty of Salisbury the Scots must have

---

[32] *Foedera*, i, 730–31 = *APS*, i, 441–42.

[33] There is a difference between the French text, *ladrescement del estat du reaume*, and the Latin *regni statum et reformationem*.

[34] In November 1290 William de Bliburgh was reimbursed in 10 mks for his expenses in going to a parliament of Scotland in February on the king's business; PRO C47/4/5, fo. 26r. There may have been a *colloquium* at Haddington in the second week of February 1290.

[35] Stevenson, *Documents*, i, no. 86, dated at Rome, 16 November 1289.

known that a marriage treaty with Edward I was in prospect. The bull, based upon Edward's petition, claims that trouble might arise should Margaret marry *so that the kingdom came to the hand of another* (than Edward); thus if Margaret were queen her husband would rule as king. Edward I was determined that the kingdom should come to his son and calling Margaret queen was not a trivial anticipation but a means of speeding his grip upon the Scottish kingdom, as the sequel shows.

The treaty of Salisbury was a compromise and concession which the Guardians must have felt worth making; but they must also have had good reason to believe that it was acceptable to the 'good folk' representing the public weal. No fewer than 106 persons are named as confirming it at Birgham on 14 March 1290, twelve bishops, ten earls, thirty-four heads of religious houses (some very small) and fifty barons.[36] Such a high total suggests that this was partly a sederunt supplemented by seals from absentees. The list of barons comes further down the scale of importance than, for example, the 1284 undertaking with twenty-four barons; it is nonetheless the case that the Guardians who summoned barons or their seals took a broad view of the *gent de Escoce*, whom they had undertaken in November to summon.

Three days later, on 17 March 1290, from Birgham the four Guardians and the 102 others named in the confirmation wrote to Edward I asking to be told if it were true, as many said, that the pope had granted a dispensation for the marriage of 'the lady Margaret queen of Scotland, our lady', for, if it were, they favoured the marriage;[37] they proposed to send envoys to the forthcoming (Easter) parliament to discuss this and obtain assurances. The letter is sealed in the name of prelates and magnates and the whole community of the kingdom by the common seal used 'in Scotland in the name of our aforesaid lady'. 'Queen' and 'community' as used here show an English input to the drafting of this letter.

In a parallel letter to Eric II the Guardians write with 'the whole community' of the kingdom. Eric will seek the honour of his daughter, lady of Scotland; the pope has granted a dispensation for her marriage to the son of the English king, as is commonly said in various parts of the world, and the senders are agreed on the desirability of this union. Would Eric please send her to England as soon as possible and certainly before 1 November as has been agreed. If he does not do this the Guardians and community will take counsel for the estate of the kingdom and (of) the *bone gent* of the land; the Guardians and community append the seal used in the name of their aforesaid lady;[38] she is only 'lady', and the prelates and magnates *are* the

---

[36] Stevenson, *Documents*, i, no. 92.

[37] Otto de Grandison, the envoy to the curia, returned to the king's court on 8 March 1290, but the bulls were brought later by Richard le Alemaunt, who took fifty-one days on the journey to England.

[38] *APS*, i, 441–42 = *Foedera*, i, 730–31.

community, Scottish usage. There is no reason to doubt what they tell: that the existence of a papal dispensation was well known but that it had not been shown to the Scots, who had been waiting for it before proceeding to the contract of marriage. They accepted that the Maid would go to England and were firmly in favour of the marriage.[39]

Robert Bruce, seeing that his chances of succeeding to the throne had diminished to vanishing point, with characteristic deviousness set about finding compensation in the Garioch. On 19 April 1290 he made an agreement with Sir Nicholas Biggar, whereby the latter resigned his rights to the lands of Bruce, Balliol and Hastings in Garioch but was to 'recover' for himself at law, by a royal brieve of right, all the lands of Balliol and Hastings in the Garioch, which he, in this agreement, surrendered to Bruce for forty merks worth of lands in southern Scotland.[40] Biggar's unspecified right must have been a claim to all Earl David's lands in the Garioch because Biggar might be called to warrant a holding there, of which warrandice Bruce promised to acquit him. Apparently one of Nicholas's forebears acquired a brief title to the Garioch, which we know was held after Earl David's death by his son Earl John (d. 1237). Perhaps a forebear had married an illegitimate daughter of David, was given some right in Garioch but lost it at death, but other speculations are possible. Nicholas's action against Balliol and Hastings was probably never brought.[41]

The agreement was made at Bruce's castle of Lochmaben a month after Scottish confirmation of the the treaty of Salisbury ensured that the Maid of Norway would come to Britain. Bruce's chances of succeeding to the throne had almost vanished, wherefore he now cast eyes upon the Garioch. Part of that scheme was the deal with Sir Nicholas Biggar, but there was another part, a useful forgery, concocted at this time for Bruce: Earl David's supposed resignation to his brother King William and his heirs 'whomsoever', of all his right in the kingdom of Scotland, in return for the Garioch, 'so that neither I nor my heirs, nor any man or woman for or through me' can have any right or claim in the kingdom at any time. King William did indeed give the Garioch to David,[42] from whom it descended

---

[39] On 5 May 1290 two esquires were reimbursed by Edward I for hurrying with the bulls to his ambassadors in Scotland; the whole journey took only twelve days, and the messengers' horses were replaced because exhausted (*recruti,* translated 'recruited' by Bain). The journey may have been made some weeks before the end of April. PRO C47/4/5, fo. 6v = *CDS*, ii, 464 under May [4]. The bull was engrossed in quadruplicate; PRO C47/4/5, fo. 8v. The PRO has three originals of it; Stevenson, *Documents,* 111. Perhaps one was given to the Scots.

[40] Stones and Simpson, ii, C.106A, 342–43; Barrow, *Bruce,* 43–44, citing it as PRO DL 36/111/152. The forty-merk land would presumably have been in Annandale.

[41] For the descent of the Biggar family from Baldwin of Biggar, a Fleming, sheriff of Lanark, to his great-grandson, Hugh, in 1228, and the appearance of Sir Nicholas, sheriff of Lanark in 1273, presumably Hugh's son, see Black, *Surnames of Scotland,* 74. Nicholas probably died in 1292; *Rot. Scot.,* i, 14a.

[42] *RRS*, ii, no. 205. See also the discussion in Stringer, *Earl David,* 42 and ch. 4.

to Balliol, Bruce and Hastings. The resignation, which is undated but is a forgery of the later thirteenth century, does not say that David was the older brother, and since William is thrice called 'king', does not imply that.[43] On the contrary it validated the right of William's line to the Scottish throne, and took no interest in who might succeed if that line failed, save that it would not be Balliol, Bruce or Hastings (whence the use of *aliqua*, any female).

This resignation was a clumsy attempt to say what had been denied in 1195, that a female descendant of King William as sole issue had a better right to the throne than his brother, not because the magnates said so (as William wanted them to say in 1195) but because David had resigned his right. The condition for that was the grant of the Garioch, and should that grant be dishonoured, then Earl David's heirs recovered their right to the throne against a female descendant of William. Bruce was hoping to force the Scottish government into warranting Earl David's title to Garioch as the price of Bruce accepting the Maid as heir to Scotland. Sir Nicholas Biggar having 'recovered' David's rights in Garioch, they would be turned over to Bruce. The forged resignation belongs to the spring of 1290, became obsolete with the death of the Maid, and was presumably filed away by Bruce; we should have found it in his archive had it not been brought to light later for the benefit of Florence, count of Holland. It did him little good since the forger had failed to include a presumptive right of Ada, sister of King William; it was not forged for Florence, who had no interest in – or probably knowledge of – the Garioch.

From March 1290 the negotiations, which Edward entrusted largely to Anthony Bek bishop of Durham, progressed steadily. On 10 April 1290 Bek was appointed to deal with Eric's envoys, and on 17 April Edward wrote in Latin asking Eric to send the Maid, 'queen of Scotland', to England, in a letter which otherwise echoes that from the Scots on 17 March; on 24 April Bek and his brother made official summaries of five letters recording King Eric's 1286 borrowing of 2,000 marks from Edward I, a useful hold over the king because not yet repaid.[44] Scottish envoys certainly attended the parliament held in late April 1290 and undertook to pay £2,000 to Edward I, for on 15 May[45] he promised to refund it on 11 November if the Maid had neither come nor sent a legitimate excuse by 1 November. The money, or more probably the obligation to pay it, was somehow connected with fulfilment of the Salisbury treaty.

[43] Stones and Simpson, ii. D.69 and p. 312; Barrow, *Bruce*, 46. There are many peculiarities about this text, not least *pro terra de Garwiach mihi et heredibus meis data et concessa a predicto domino Willelmo rege Scocie a se et heredibus suis*. What is the function of the last five words? If *tenenda* has been omitted, the use of *a*, not *de*, is very unusual.

[44] *Foedera*, i, 731.

[45] Probably they undertook in April, since Edward's promise followed one already given to the Scots by Bek; *Foedera*, i, 734.

The 1281 treaty with Norway provided that if Margaret refused to complete the marriage when Eric became fourteen, he would recover Man, lost in 1264–66, upon which the Norwegians still had an eye.[46] In 1290 Edward moved to take custody of the isle, sending 'two Blackfriars ... to Ireland with letters ... for the land of Man', and on 6 February 1290 he issued letters to the keepers and others of Man of safeconduct to merchants (including the two Cahorsin creditors of Eric II[47]) going there.[48] Man was now vicariously in Edward's hands, probably through the earl of Ulster, who had bailiffs there when he surrendered it to Edward by 4 June 1290. On that day the king appointed Walter de Huntercombe as its keeper, and issued letters of protection to the inhabitants.[49] This protection either had been, or was to be, earned by the submission of the men of this island 'recently desolate and filled with many miseries from want of protection and defence', as their 1290 letter said – the lack of a day suggests that some time was spent collecting their submissions and seals. They promised subjection, and to obey the king's orders, under pain of £2,000 should they rise in revolt, commit an offence or maliciously harm any of his men – clearly Edward had little trust in their good behaviour.[50] The fact that the sum of money is identical with that given or promised by the Scots suggests a connection between events occurring about the same month. Since Edward's sasine was temporary, it is best understood as surety for the money promised by the Scots; if Man rebelled he would lose that surety so the Manx should be liable.

It seems likely that at Salisbury in November 1289 Eric's envoys pressed for payment of the tocher owed since 1286, and that the Scots refused, for their creditor was the Maid (as her mother's heir, and according to the 1281 treaty). Thus Eric still owed 2,800 marks; the Scots undertook to pay Edward (for the Maid?) the slightly larger sum of £2,000 if the Maid arrived timeously, yielding Man as surety, and Edward gave a discharge of that sum if she did not arrive. How the Cahorsin merchants were to be paid off is not clear, but in 1292 Eric claimed the tocher for three years only (1290–92), and it is possible that the Scots or Edward I had paid up.[51] If all this is too hypothetical, one fact is certain: Edward I took custody of the Isle of Man, but he did not try to annexe it. There is no hint of disquiet about Man

---

[46] *APS*, i, 423a.

[47] On the more important, William Servat, see *Cal. Pat. Rolls, 1281–1292*, 341, 352, 383.

[48] *Exch. Rolls*, i, 47 (for date see 46); *Cal. Pat. Rolls, 1281–1292*, 341.

[49] *Cal. Pat. Rolls, 1281–1292*, 359. Only one of the letters calendared there is printed by Stevenson, *Documents*, i, no. 103. Huntercombe and his clerk, William de Stynton, were given £25 on 20 June for their expenses in taking custody of Man; PRO C47/4/5, fo. 23v. For the earl of Ulster *Cal. Close Rolls, 1288–1296*, 137 where 'St Bartholomew' must be an error for St Barnabas and the date in line 1 is 13 June 1290, when the earl was at court.

[50] *Foedera*, i, 739. Man had rebelled against Scottish lordship in 1275.

[51] Stevenson, *Documents*, i, no. 252.

by the Guardians, and Edward I surrendered it to King John on 5 January 1293.[52]

Scottish envoys had come to Edward I's April 1290 parliament at London to discuss the prospect of a marriage of the Maid to the young Edward, on which they would submit 'matters', as well as 'for other matters touching the status of the kingdom'.[53] Edward's expensively provisioned ship sailed from Yarmouth on 9 May to fetch her, perhaps when the Scots were still at his parliament, and when Eric was campaigning against the Danes. It arrived back in the Humber on 17 June with neither the Maid nor, apparently, any assurances about her arrival. Edward turned at once to renewed negotiations with the Scots.

On 20 June two letters appointed Bek and five others as the king's proctors to treat with them. One stated the business: the state of the 'queen', the jurisdiction of the kingdom, keeping and garrisoning castles, forests, lands and possessions, and also the rights and customs touching 'the queen and kingdom, you and us and Edward our son'. It granted power to reach, and swear to, an agreement with the Scots in Edward's name.[54] The alternative commission narrated that Scottish envoys to parliament (in April) had come with insufficient powers so that the king had not answered articles expounded to him (evidently by the Scots). He now sent proctors to answer, and gave them power to treat; power to reach an agreement, however, is lacking from this procuratory, which was that used and left with the Scots.[55]

The difference between these two commissions is surely significant. Edward's agenda amounted to the constitution of Scotland, that he might secure authority for his son which the English king would exercise *pro tempore*. This authority would extend to the possession of the royal castles – the first sign on the horizon of this delicate and ultimately contentious matter. In April the Scots, bearing their own articles, had come face to face with Edward's agenda, and pled powers inadequate to deal with it; Edward riposted by ignoring their articles. Now in June he sent Bek north to deal with both his agenda and their articles, but the commission raising the former was returned unused by Bek to chancery. The Scots, we may presume, refused to accept it; instead, writing from Sprouston on 12 July, they acknowledged receipt of the commission which referred to their articles.[56]

Bek had with him Edward's reply to these articles, draft royal letters also dated 20 June (1290) on a cancelled parchment (A), now decayed, which was returned to chancery and partly copied on the patent roll.[57] It is possible to

---

[52] *Rot. Scot.*, i, 16b.

[53] *Foedera*, i, 730.

[54] Stevenson, *Documents*, i, no. 105.

[55] *Foedera*, i, 734; *Cal. Docs. Scot.*, ii, no. 441.

[56] *Foedera*, i, 736.

[57] Appendix A; PRO C 47/22/13 (12); *Cal. Docs. Scot.*, v, 144, no. 83; Stevenson, *Documents*, i, no. 106.

reconstruct almost all this text from A and from the concessions promised
by Bek's embassy at Birgham on the Tweed on 18 July 1290, which are
usually called the treaty of Birgham and 'a marriage treaty'. But these
concessions were formally an 'obligation' by the English envoys, though to
whom is not said,[58] and treat the marriage contract as a future event, so that,
unlike the treaties with Norway and Flanders in 1281–82, they mention no
promise, no date and no dowry; this 18 July document issued at Birgham,
which I call B, was not a marriage treaty. Indeed it was not a treaty.

Canon law was quite clear that espousal, the first stage towards marriage,
could not be made until both parties were at least seven years old; the Maid
was about that age, but the young Edward, born in 1284, was not, and
strictly espousal and the marriage contract should wait for a further year,
though this might be anticipated. Marriage itself should wait until the bride
was twelve, the groom fourteen, and if this was ignored, as it had been for
the marriage of Alexander III in 1251 and for that of Eric II in 1281, marital
relations must wait until that age. When Bek gave annuities amounting to
£400 to some Norwegians, presumably Eric's envoys, payable until the Maid
reached the age of fifteen[59] (when the young Edward would be fourteen) this
sweetener recognised the time when the marriage would be complete.

In the following discussion I refer to A by the letter given to each
provision in the text printed in Appendix A, for example (Af). The principal
difference from B is one of form: A is a letter of Edward I, 'we', while B is a
letter of his envoys and refers to him in the third person. While some
provisions in A overtly respond to Scottish articles (Aa–c, j) all clauses
therein protect Scottish custom in some measure. Ad, granting the laws,
customs and liberties of the kingdom and marches used in burghs, represents an article pressed by the mercantile interest, and Ae one pressed by
the church. Since Edward I was no friend of (for example) clerical liberties
(Ae), or limitations upon taxation (At), and an article rejected by him is
included (Ac), it is most likely that A gives a complete register of the
Scottish articles.

The two protections of sectional interests, mercantile and clerical, do not
appear in B, where they are replaced by a general concession of the 'rights,
franchises and customs of the kingdom in and by all things, throughout the
kingdom and its marches, entirely and without impairment', a much wider
concession. But it was not felt to be enough to protect the Scots from
financial demands other than for the common business of the kingdom,
conceded in At and expanded in B, which adds 'armies or maltoltes' to At's
'tallages or aids'. These changes from A to B result from careful examination
and redrafting.

---

[58] Stevenson, *Documents*, i, no. 108; Professor Barrow's translation in *SHR*, lxix (1990),
137–41.
[59] Stevenson, *Documents*, i, no. 111.

There is also a reordering of provisions, so that while A opens with brief words on the Maid's dower (Aa), goes into considerable detail on contingencies in the proposed marriage, death and restoration of the kingdom to the right heir (An-q), and places the independence of the kingdom and the liberties of various groups between these two (Ab-m), B opens with the kingdom's independence then brings together dower and simplified contingencies in the marriage. Either A or B could be justified as logical order, but the rearrangement can scarcely have been gratuitous, and suggests that the Scottish articles and Edward's responses were negotiated with some care.

In some of the details we can discern the anticipated future of the Scottish realm. The Maid would come to England and would be affianced to the king's son with a suitable English dower which would content the 'queen' and her friends – a message that the dower was no business of the Scots. The Guardians' seal is valid until the queen comes into her realm and does to God, church and community in 'a place specially appointed for the purpose' what is to be done according to the laws and customs of the kingdom (Ak). The most natural meaning, that she would swear an oath, is confirmed by the undertaking given by the Scots on 28 August that when Edward and Margaret came to Scotland they would make an oath according to the laws and customs of the kingdom.[60] We should not be far from the truth if we assume that it promised to maintain these laws and customs.

Al remits to the advice of the Scots and Edward's procurators to make any new regulation about the keeping of the seal, which they do in B, providing for a chancellor and certain other officials who are to be Scots, and for unchanged chancery routine. The new seal is another matter. Al's provision was made more detailed in B, requiring the 'usual' arms of a king and with 'circumscription of the name of king of Scotland only', that is to say without dimidiation or quartering of the arms of England and without any English title. It is just possible that a seal for Margaret was intended here, which, since she could not be depicted in armour on horseback, was to carry on the reverse a shield of arms (as on the obverse of the Guardianship seal) alone; she is the 'queen' who is to come to 'her realm' (Ak).

But the references to 'king' are found not only here but also in fealty and homage to the king of Scotland, homage by a tenant in chief of the king of Scotland, due in the personal presence of a (or the) king, of being in the wardship and marriage of the king of Scotland but not being disparaged by the said king, of chancery (*capella*) of the lord king, all in B's promises for the future. As Nicholas IV's bull had implied, when he espoused the Maid, Edward would become king of Scots; the great seal would carry his image and name, but not until the Maid came to Scotland.[61]

[60] *Foedera*, i, 737–38.
[61] Stevenson, *Documents*, i, no. 108. There are occasional variants between the French text

The proposals in Am would have sequestered the royal archives and prevented alienation of royal property also until the Maid came, but this was considerably strengthened in the interests of the Scots in B by adding the requirement that she must have surviving issue, which could not happen before 1299. For those barons who are allowed to do homage, fealty and make a fine, prelates seeking a *congé d'élire*, widows seeking their terces, or poor people justice, without leaving Scotland, B adds something not mentioned in A: that a person would be deputed by the English king to receive these and act thereupon in the names of Margaret and Edward.[62] This was not an attempt to place Edward's nominee in a powerful position, for it met a concern of the Scots – that if they were not to leave the realm, there must be a way whereby they could perform their duties and so gain their rights. It was another concession to secure their customs.

To the article which sought recognition that Scotland be separate, free and without subjection by its right boundaries, Edward I's response was a qualified acceptance that the kingdoms be separate and divided by their right bounds as from times past (Ab); there was no mention of freedom here. But in B his ambassadors had to go the full distance, granting the Scottish wording, by including 'free in itself, and without subjection, from the king-dom of England, as has been observed heretofore'. This was a significant, even dramatic, acceptance of the independence of the kingdom, a huge shift from what the king at first offered, indicating how far the English would go in reversing the claims and settled policy of a century in order to secure the prize of the royal marriage. Like the rest of the document it was nowhere said to be contingent upon conclusion of the marriage, and the Scots later regarded it as an unqualified promise which Edward tore up.[63]

But in B both here and in the promise to observe the liberties of the kingdom, there is reserved the right which the king or anyone else may have on the borders (Ab), which B extends 'or elsewhere'. This has been seen as a sinister loophole through which overlordship of the kingdom could be claimed; but overlordship would be unnecessary in a personal union, and the phrase, which can be found elsewhere, was intended to assure anyone with a valid claim in the other kingdom that he or she could still pursue it. The final clause of B, for which A had no equivalent, that 'by reason of this present deed (*facti*) nothing is in any way added to or taken away from the

---

and the Latin one confirmed by Edward I on 28 August. On p. 169, 7 lines up, read *capellae domini regis, justiciariis.*

[62] This is the only hint of a 'William and Mary' dyarchy.

[63] In Ao-q and B the provision for returning the kingdom to the rightful heir failing the Maid and Edward, also uses the phrase 'free and without subjection', but with a purpose: 'so that by reason of this present act (*facti*) nothing accrues or is lost to the king or his heirs or another'. Without *salvo* this is not a clause saving Edward's rights. It is explained by A where these provisions are said to be 'according to the ordinance made (*factum*) at Salisbury' (An-p), and the 'so that' phrase is designed to maintain the force of the Salisbury agreement.

right of one kingdom or the other, nor from any of the kings of these kingdoms, but that they shall freely have their standing', must have seemed a
protection of independence to the Scots – and in the circumstances of July
1290 it was. When it came to the point that the Birgham promises stood in
Edward I's way, he did not cite the saving clauses; on 2 January 1293, King
John annulled the promises.[64]

If there was a charter of liberties for the Scots, limiting royal rights as
did Henry I's charter of 1100 or Magna Carta in 1215–25, it is to be found
in the provisions of A and B covering homage, fealty, *congé d'élire*, litigation,
marriage, parliament and taxation, all in the interests of middling and
wealthy folk.[65] Scottish prelates and tenants in chief were protected from
having to take the high road to England, from social and financial exploitation, and in their hold on ministerial office, and secured a promise that
each kingdom retained its free status. In only one matter was a Scottish
article rejected: that no new strongholds be built in the marches. The
specious excuse, that this was a servitude not borne by the king's predecessors and was greater than that borne by the Scots, ignored the proposal
that the embargo should apply on both sides of the Border. The rejection
was a forewarning that at the heart of Edward's policy was his intention to
secure the castles of Scotland; that was his agenda, and because the Scots
rejected it stiffly, there was no treaty at Birgham.

The gaps in the concessions in both A and B are striking. There is no
word of accession to the kingship. The nationality of sheriffs and (a key
omission) constables of castles is not specified. There is nothing on, for
example, ecclesiastical patronage for Scots, on the nomination of royal
councillors, on military service in Scotland or – doubtless unthinkable –
furth of it, nothing on accountability for revenues or judgements since 1286.
King Edward's nominee, mentioned in B, has no relationship with the
Guardians, and there is no clarification as to whether the latter would
continue in office, or who would name their successors; continuation may be
implied by the keeping of the 1286 seal, but it is not beyond doubt. It would
be anachronistic to expect the powers of Edward I acting in the couple's
name, or of the young couple, to be spelled out; that was not an indignity to
which kings could be subjected. But some mention of the balance between
Edward I and the Guardians before the young couple came of age was
not impossible. Even in what they treat of, the concessions are sometimes
perfunctory, ill-expressed and no obstacle to a king with competent legists
at his beck.

On 18 July 1290 the Scots accepted B, these Birgham *obligationes et
instrumenta* by procurators based on articles and petitions, promising that

---

[64] Stones and Simpson, ii, 271–72, A127.
[65] *Cf.* Ae with MC 1225 c.1; Ad with MC 1225 c.31; Ar with MC 1225 c.6; At with MC 1215
c.12.

they would have force if Edward I confirmed them by 8 September; if not, they would be handed back [to the English] and become invalid.[66] A one-sided treaty was in the making, to be followed by a marriage contract; at Kelso on 31 July the Scots appointed two Guardians, Bishop Wishart and John Comyn, and the chancellor, the bishop of Caithness, as their proctors to negotiate the status of the Maid – which elsewhere means her dower.[67] But when they reached Edward I, they discovered that he was not willing to confirm the terms of Birgham, where his envoys, because of certain dangers and suspicions of which they had heard, had demanded surrender of the keeping of Scotland's castles, and would not drop this without advising their king – that is, the Scots had rejected the demand.

This was surely the matter on which the Scots had pled 'inadequate powers' at the preceding April parliament and for which they had rejected one set of English credentials at Birgham in July. The concessions nego-tiated at Birgham had been acceptable, but not the countervailing demand of the English king. Now at Northampton the three Scottish envoys were brought face to face with the king to hear the same demand. They surely anticipated this, for they consulted three keepers of Scottish castles, their companions, and the deadline of 8 September laid down in their under-taking of 18 July would have been meant to face down the English king.

On 28 August Edward confirmed the Birgham concessions (B), and the six Scots promised that when their lady (never 'queen') came to England or Scotland before 1 November, free of marriage contract, they would surrender the castles to her and to the young Edward, and from then on would obey them as lord and lady from the time when they came to Scotland and made an oath, at whatever age, according to the laws and customs of the kingdom; if they did not come by the due date, the keepers of the castles would swear to keep these for the lady and Edward. Any suspect officals would be removed by common advice of the Scots and the English king and (briefly) the Scots promised to agree to no other marriage than theirs, nor obey any other lord as long as they lived, unless by consent of King Edward and his son.[68]

The importance of possession of the castles cannot be underestimated. It gave possession of the kingdom, and must have been Edward I's aim from the beginning of the negotiations; it explains the generous confirmation in B of the kingdom's laws and liberties and of its freedom, as well as some hypothetical language and haphazard promises in B;[69] all this was but incidental to what the king really sought, fearing, he claimed, that without it the peace of the Scottish kingdom would not hold. The Scots would know

[66] *Foedera*, i, 736.

[67] *Foedera*, i, 737.

[68] *Foedera*, i, 737–38.

[69] Chapter elections, homage and fealty, dowers, legal actions, the seal, the chancellor and other officials, marriage, parliaments, taxes.

how important this issue was to him – it would be a very unperceptive community which did not do so – and they stuck firmly to their refusal, even on 28 August. It would in any case have been outside the powers of the envoys, and surely against the oath of 1286, to concede to any other than their lord and lady. Yet what their concession meant in practice is wonderfully obscure. New constables might be appointed in the names of the child queen and king, but who would really name them? The Scots seem to have thought that the Guardians would do so.

This concession of 28 August, therefore, was less than Edward I had sought, and it was obtained not from the Scottish community but only from their envoys at Northampton; as the obligation of the English envoys at Birgham required the king's confirmation, so this Scottish concession needed – but never obtained – more than the seals of three envoys. Yet with it the English king had to be content, issuing his unqualified validation of the Birgham concessions on the same day.[70] Proctors were appointed by the young Edward to contract marriage with the Maid, and his father involved the Scots by naming Bishop Wishart and John Comyn among his proctors for this; discussion would mostly be about endowment of the Maid in England.[71]

Also on 28 August, the English king issued letters to the Guardians and community: since he was now sworn to observe the liberties and customs of Scotland, he had appointed Bek as lieutenant for the 'queen' and the young Edward, to act with the other Guardians for the peace and tranquillity of the kingdom and for support of [? its] burden, to justify (*justificandum*) and to rectify (*rectificandum*) the kingdom, by advice of prelates and magnates, according to the kingdom's laws and customs. The Guardians are asked to be obedient to Bek in everything relating to the government and status of the kingdom.[72] The clear implication is that Edward has appointed a Guardian for the young couple who is in charge of the other Guardians; his functions recall the provision at Salisbury that if the Scots and Norwegians could not agree on *reformatio* of the kingdom, Edward would arbitrate, but Bek is more than arbiter, he is in charge of what amounts to *reformatio*.

These functions, far exceeding the provision in B for 'someone' to be appointed to allow clerical elections, receive homages and fealties and so forth, have no place in the Birgham concessions made by either side. Such a momentous step cannot have been anticipated by the Scots. But we know of no Scottish reaction, not even to the effrontery of its opening self-justification. Bek was certainly expected to go to Scotland,[73] and did so later

---

[70] Stevenson, *Documents*, i, no. 108. Prestwich, *Edward I*, 362 misdates this 28 July.

[71] *Foedera*, i, 737.

[72] *Foedera*, i, 737 (not 787 as in *CDS*, ii, 446); from a Treaty roll, where it is misdated 8 August and should read *ceteris* custodibus *ipsius regni incumbentis*. The patent roll copy has the correct text and date, 28 August; *Cal. Pat. Rolls, 1281–92*, 386.

[73] Stevenson, *Documents*, i, 176n. *Cal. Pat. Rolls, 1281–92*, 383.

in September, when the commission might have been produced, soon nullified by the Maid's death. Or it may have become valid only when the Maid expressed consent to espousal, and been confidential until then. I doubt that it was ever shown to the Scots, who had not ratified the Northampton terms upon which espousal depended.

Suddenly long-drawn negotiations had come to a resolution, described by the Scots in June 1291 as 'your deed and theirs which was made and affirmed at Northampton', evidently in their view a binding treaty.[74] But the abrupt activity at Northampton on 28 August was not the result of statesmanlike discussions with the Scottish envoys leading to the ratification of the concessions of Birgham. On the contrary the latter were an offer on the table, in some respects inadequately drafted, to secure the surrender of Scottish castles; the Northampton meeting was further pressure to the same end, which the Scots resisted. Something happened, perhaps on 27 August when the king underwrote promises of annuities of £400 made by Bek to the Norwegians. The Wardrobe book for 18 Edward I, which has few details between May and October, records that on 27 August the king gave 100s. to the king of Norway's cook, bearing a gerfalcon from Eric; slim but nonetheless evidence that a Norwegian came to court about that day.

Edward must have heard from Bergen or from Scotland that the Maid was at sea or about to sail, perhaps in letters from the bishop of St Andrews and John Comyn 'with rumours of the arrival (*adventus*) of the Maid at Orkney' received by 8 September.[75] Such news changed the situation radically, forcing Edward I to settle with the Scots on the basis of the Birgham concessions. There was now a reluctant agreement of sorts between two parties, the English king and the Scottish envoys. By 1 September further information seems to have clarified that Eric himself was not coming.[76] Bek was empowered to borrow £5,000 in the king's name, as were the Norwegian envoys, a further greasing of palms which showed the king's deter-

---

[74] *Anglo-Scottish Relations*, no. 16. Curiously *vostre fait et le lour* has a singular verb, *qe fust fet*.

[75] 8 September is the date of rewards paid to the bishop's and Comyn's messengers; PRO C47/4/5, fo.51r; *cf.* Stevenson, *Documents*, i, 175. The bishop's letter was about 'rumours' of the coming, and his messenger was given 20s. *in necessariis de curia*, evidently staying briefly at court. Comyn's letters were brought by the messenger of the earl of Orkney, were about 'the said coming' and earned him 13s. 4d. 'on his departure'. Clearly they did not come together.

[76] Edward I's procuratory to five envoys on 28 August was to King Eric or his envoys; on 1 September the credentials for three envoys to the king of Norway or his envoys were addressed only to the envoys; Stevenson, *Documents*, i, no. 113. In the Wardrobe book Elias de Hauville was going with Bek to meet the king of Norway bringing his daughter, an undated entry on fo. 17v (= *CDS*, ii, 464, fo. 16b), but later in the same book on 1 September he was given £5 because, in going to meet the envoys of the king of Norway and the Maid, he had had to return early with rumours; PRO C47/4/5, fo. 25r. These entries were copied from notes, as the extraordinary error on fo. 25r shows: 1 Sept. £9 to the abbot of Welbeck, going as envoy with Bek *in insultando Orkeney ... contra domicellam Scocie* [for *in insulam de Orkeney ... contra aduentum domicelle ? in Scociam* or *? Norwagie*].

mination.[77] Bek set out forthwith from court, but in the north did not immediately enter Scotland.

On 11 September 'jewels' were sent to Bek in Scotland, presumably as a gift either for the Maid or for her companions.[78] Bek's movements there are uncertain, but he seems to have been at Perth on 1 October to meet 'some' Scottish magnates and tell them the king's answer on the matters 'asked for and dealt with' by Scottish ambassadors before the king, an account which suggests that the terms offered at Northampton were now brought for confirmation by the Scottish community. Our informant, Bishop Fraser, remarks ambiguously that when this had been heard 'faithful magnates and a certain part of the community' returned thanks to the king.[79] But he mentions no Scottish confirmation of the Northampton terms.

Elias de Hauville, a household knight of Edward I, had also entered Scotland but spent only eighteen days there; probably he left Newcastle with the jewels on 21 September and, about 1 October, turned back from Scotland to report to the king 'rumours of the arrival of the Maid and of events of those parts'.[80] His turning point is not recorded, but it would seem likely that he had gone to the meeting at Perth on 1 October and hurried back to report its outcome.

On 15 September two envoys left Bek's party in Northumberland and travelled to Scotland. At Skelbo near Dornoch on Sunday 1 October they heard the first news of the Maid's illness or even a rumour of her death. They spent 4–5 October at Wick, then began the long journey home, obviously informed that the Maid had died; from Nairn (on 10 October) they did not hurry, presumably having sent letters ahead.[81] The Maid had died at Kirkwall about 26–29 September 1290 – the date is guessed from the envoys' itinerary – having been taken ill on the voyage.[82] How long she had lain ill on land is unknown but it could have been for as much as a week, and certainly from about 23 September; the ship was her father's, whose suppliers may have poisoned her with decaying food.[83] With her died the line of King William and Alexander III.

---

[77] Stevenson, *Documents*, i, no. 114.

[78] Stevenson, *Documents*, i, no. 115. Stevenson twice claims that these were 'for the use of Queen Margaret', but the text nowhere says this; it is quite probable. The jewels were taken to Newcastle and from there to Scotland and back; PRO C47/4/5 fos 16r, 17v = *CDS*, ii, 109.

[79] Stones and Simpson, ii, 3, the letter of Bishop William Fraser.

[80] PRO C47/4/5 fo. 17v = *CDS*, ii, 464, fo. 16b.

[81] Stevenson, *Documents*, i, no. 116.

[82] Joseph Anderson, 'Entries in the Icelandic Annals regarding the Death of the Princess Margaret', *PSAS*, xi (1873–74), 403–18; the evidence for her being taken ill at sea is *Chron. Rishanger*, 119 and *Chron. Trivet*, 316. See also Dunbar, *Scottish Kings*, 106–7, who comments that the exact date of her death is not known; this remains true.

[83] That she died of sea-sickness (as is sometimes suggested) is unlikely, for it is rarely mortal, though I am told that it is not impossible. She would be fit and well when she left Bergen, which makes a pulmonary affliction unlikely.

Throughout the 1289–90 negotiations a recurring theme was the danger of dispeace in Scotland; this was the matter on which Edward I demanded reassurance and for which he would hold up the arrival of the Maid in Scotland. In the treaty of Salisbury this 'explained' the need for reform of the kingdom, and in Bek's commission of 28 August 1290 for justifying and rectifying it. Was there in fact such a danger in Scotland, caused by some who did not wish the marriage because of their own claims, or fear for Scottish independence, or was dispeace Edward I's excuse to justify his demands of the Scots? We cannot know for sure, for we see these events entirely through archives preserved by English bureaucracy.

The debates among the Scots are hidden from us, but Bishop Robert Wishart of Glasgow was sent to the concluding negotiations at North-ampton, evidently prepared to stand by the ultimatum date of 8 September, but to accept the Birgham terms provided that the Scots kept their castles; he was to be the most outspoken defender of Scotland's freedom against Edward I, but at this time he showed no fear of dispeace at home. No Scottish magnate can be identified as opposed to the negotiations or to the marriage, which is perhaps not surprising, for there was no reasonable alternative to the Maid as heir to the throne, and little hope of extracting her from Norway save with English help.

In a cogent study of the background to this 'treaty', Professor Barrow has shown that while we may discern under Alexander III a group of magnates who were Comyns or related to that powerful family, and another group which was not, the king pursued an 'even-handed approach', 'rising suc-cessfully above faction and inspiring a genuine loyalty to king and crown which lasted long after [his] death'.[84] The disturbances of 1286–87 may seem to run against this judgement, but their failure from lack of support, and the reconciliation of Bruce thereafter, surely show that it has the essentials of the situation both before and after 1286. Nonetheless, if the Scots showed unity in their position, Edward, never forgetful of the rule by magnates in England in 1258–63 and the civil war of 1264–65, may still have been genuinely, if wrongly, fearful that that unity would turn against him once the Maid was in Britain, and that the Guardians would deny a position to his son and his son's advisers. As soon as the Maid was in Britain she was to be treated as married to his son for political purposes, pointing to a concern of that kind. If there is evidence to take us beyond this conjecture, I have not noticed it; Edward I may have exaggerated his groundless fears simply in order to get his own way.

---

[84] Barrow, 'Kingdom in Crisis', *SHR*, xlix (1990), 125.

CHAPTER 10

The road to Norham

Urgent news from the Scots at Skelbo, or from Orkney, would take at least a week to reach the Tay.[1] That such news was despatched about 23 September is suggested by the bishop of St Andrews' newsletter to Edward I from Leuchars on 7 October 1290.[2] First he reported on the Perth assembly of 1 October, then that he and the English envoys had prepared to set out for Orkney to treat with the Norwegian ambassadors and to receive 'our lady queen' – the only voluntary Scottish ascription of that title to her known to me. But a rumour arose among people that 'our lady must be dead', as a result of which the kingdom is in turmoil and the community *disperata*, 'in despair' or 'scattered'.[3] When this rumour was heard and published, Robert Bruce, who had been absent, came with a large following to hinder certain persons,[4] and the earls of Mar and Atholl (both Bruce supporters) gathered their armies. There is fear of civil war unless God provides a swift remedy through Edward's industry and service. This worried part of the letter was probably drafted not long after 1 October, but the next passage shows that it was not sent immediately.

Subsequently Bek, Warenne and the writer heard that 'our lady' had recovered but was still weak, and so they have agreed to remain near Perth until they hear definite news from the knights sent to Orkney – the two messengers even then travelling south from Wick. As soon as they hear good news, which is expected daily, they will set out for the north for the business committed to them. Here, I suggest, was a break in composition, somewhere near Perth. The bishop's comments on Bruce are unfriendly, and his hopes for peace from Edward evident.

[1] Based upon the envoys' journey north; Stevenson, *Documents*, i, 184. I have not counted the days they spent in St Andrews (*propter tempestatem*) and Duffus. They also seem to have taken a day to pass from Montrose to 'Aberbervie', Inverbervie, and a day from there to Aberdeen, probably because of bad weather.

[2] Stones and Simpson, ii, 3–4; *Foedera*, i, 741; *Nat. MSS. Scotland*, i, no. LXX, where there is a primitive photograph.

[3] Usually this has been taken as 'in despair', *desperata*. But I think it more likely that it represents a wrongly extended *disper[sa]*. The scribe had an unsure grasp of Latin.

[4] *Ad interpellacionem quorumdam*, translated 'at the request of' or 'to confer with' some people (Stones and Simpson, ii, 3 n. 4 and other published translations). But *interpellatio* means 'interruption', 'hindrance', hence 'for obstruction of certain persons'.

The remainder of the letter seems a hasty postscript on a new tack, a comment on the future. If Balliol comes to the king, 'we advise that in every outcome you take care to deal [or treat] with him so that your honour and advantage are preserved'. In the context of 'every outcome', that is whether the Maid be alive or dead, the wording 'we advise that you take care' is extraordinarilly forthright, and suggests that Fraser feared that Balliol would entrap King Edward into something dishonourable; whatever they foresee, these are not the words of a politician pushing the claims of Balliol.[5] They are a warning *against* promising support to Balliol in the disturbed state of Scotland, for that would be dishonorable to Edward.

Finally Fraser looks at the 'worst case' scenario: 'if [the Maid of Norway] has in truth died – God forbid – let your excellency deign, please, to approach the Border to the consolation of the Scottish people and to staunch effusion of blood, so that the true men of the kingdom can maintain their oath unbroken and set up (*preficere*) as king him (*illum*) who by law should inherit, if so be that he (*ille*) is willing to abide by your advice'.[6] Following upon the sentence about Balliol, these last words have been taken as referring to him, a hint that he will be Edward's surrogate. This is hindsight not available to the bishop, and ignores the bold assertion that it is the true men of the kingdom who are sworn to set up as king the rightful heir. Thus this extraordinary sentence qualifies what was absolute, the 1286 oath of the Scots and Bishop Fraser's duty to constrain them thereto; giving Edward a veto over, or the right to a promise of obedience from, the rightful heir, it contradicts itself. There is no doubt of its wording, which Edward would read as making him tutor of the future king, but the bishop, a man of political principle till the time of his death in France as a refugee (1297), simply cannot have intended this meaning.

Leuchars, from where the letter was despatched, is not near, but some forty km east of, Perth, five km north-east of the bishop's manor of Dairsie (where he probably had waited), nine north-west of St Andrews, so when he wrote from there the bishop was on his way north. By this time he was pessemistic about the Maid's survival, perhaps because he had had no news and had set out for a ferry over the Tay, to intercept word from Orkney. The partly-drafted letter was dispatched before going further, whence the final hurried admonition to Edward.

The text was composed not in one sitting but in at least two, though the original, a fair copy, shows no sign of this. It has errors in its Latin[7] despite

[5] Balliol assumed the style of 'heir of the kingdom of Scotland' by 16 November 1290; Stevenson, *Documents*, i, no. 125.

[6] *dum tamen ille vestro consilio voluerit adherere.*

[7] *Aripere; disperata; dignetur, si placet, vestre excellencie; valeat vestra excellencia ... prosperum et felicem.* Also *insonuit... rumor quod domina ... debuit esse mortua* for 'must be dead'; would not *debet* be correct if equally inelegant? There are other very clumsy phrases, e.g. *per milites qui sunt in Orchadiam missi* for *per milites in Orchadiam missos.*

its neat writing, so that the scribe made blunders in reading a draft with many abbreviations; specifically, towards the end he was seduced by one *ille* into writing another. It would make sense, as the present text does not, if the final clause quoted had been drafted *dum tamen ill' vestro consilio voluerît adherere* with a tick over the *i* of *voluerit* for *n*. The reading intended was *illi ... voluerint*, and not, as in the version sent, *ille ... voluerit*. This clause did not refer to Balliol and qualified not what Edward should do, approach the Border, but the *fideles*, true men of the kingdom, subject of the nearer verbs, *possunt conservare ... et preficere*. They will be able to keep their oath and set up the rightful king 'provided that they are willing to abide by your advice'. The supposedly craven attitude of Scotland's leading prelate was in fact a brief deference to the reputation of the English king as peace-maker and arbiter, in a sentence whose main or sole purpose was to *assert* the right of the Scottish community to find their rightful king. Respect for Edward and hope that he will act as friend of a neighbouring country and of its peace shine forth in the letter, but, as drafted, it did not reveal a committed adherent of Balliol selling the weakness of his candidate to the English king; nor indeed is the letter, even as sent, clearly doing so.[8]

By 7 October 1290 the Maid had indeed died. A writ of the Guardians dated at Edinburgh on 15 October, where they were perhaps protecting the royal treasury, is the last such document to survive before April 1291,[9] and we have no documentary evidence of activities by the Scottish government between those dates, or really until early May 1291. About the end of October 1290, a petition in the English parliament on a Border dispute was answered 'let it wait until there is a king in Scotland',[10] a phrase which reveals nothing of Edward's intentions at this point. But on the death of the Maid he did write a letter of condolence to the Scots, asking them that, to avoid dissensions and because of the danger of contending parties, they should take no steps on the succession until he could come 'to those parts', to give his advice as 'friend and neighbour'. This was clearly a response to the bishop's letter of 7 October, though cited as evidence of Edward's bad faith in a hostile Scottish source, the Bamburgh memorandum of 1321 (discussed later in this chapter). Such a letter, perhaps without 'as friend and neighbour', is exactly what we should expect King Edward to send, and the Scots to file away.

Its influence at the time is shown when Bruce turned from force at Perth in late September to invoking the 'presence' of Edward I in the undated

---

[8] The difficulties posed by the last phrase of this letter troubled me for decades, for I could not see how it suggested that Edward accept Balliol as the right heir 'in any event'.

[9] Stevenson, *Documents*, i, no. 123; *CDS*, ii, no. 472n. = NAS, RH 5/94.

[10] *Rot. Parl.*, i, 47, petition 26, misunderstood in Stones and Simpson, i, 6, as the endorsement of the original petition, drawn to my attention by Dr Paul Brand, makes clear: *Declaret quis potest consentire in inquisicionem pro rege Scocie*; PRO, C 47/22/9 (16).

document known as the Appeal of Seven Earls of Scotland – though each of its three sections states the case of a different group. All appeal from 'you', two men, Bishop William Fraser and John Comyn of Badenoch, purported Guardians, and their adherents, and give[11] authority over the two, who, it is asserted, have abused their positions, to Edward. Although addressed to the defenders, it appeals to the presence of Edward, king of England and to his crown of England, and having detailed the tort, the appellants place themselves, their adherents and their goods, under the 'special peace, protection and defence' of the English king and his crown. This phrase is an expectation that Scotland will know the presence of the English king upon, and perhaps within, its borders, where its ambiguity reflects the ambiguity of 'those parts' or 'your parts' in Edward I's letter.

Two of the sections, the first and third, are actually appeals against an intention, not an act, something for which no remedy could be given, so all three sections end with a complaint of the defenders' failure to make amends for losses and injuries done to the appellants since 1286, a material cause for which a remedy could be given. The first appeal, on behalf of seven earls (unnamed) and the community of the kingdom, whose right it is to make the king, protests against the two Guardians, with their party in the community, seeking to put forward someone as king to the prejudice of the appellants; it associates 'you John Balliol' with the defenders. The second, an appeal on behalf of Donald earl of Mar, one of the seven earls, and of the king's men of Moray, alleges that the two Guardians appointed under-Guardians without authority from the community, and that these have devastated Moray. In the third, the two defenders, sworn to preserve the laws and customs of the kingdom, propose to make Balliol king, though 'we Robert Bruce lord of Annandale as lawful heir and true assignee' have put forward a claim and are pursuing 'our' right. The actions of the two are contrary to the immemorial rights of seven earls and community to make a king and set him on the throne, whenever it is vacant in fact and law. Lest they make anyone king before 'we' receive full judgement of 'our' right in presence of the English king, this appeal is made, and places not only the appellant Bruce but also (again) seven earls under Edward's protection.[12]

The purpose has always been recognised as an attempt by Bruce to frustrate the pro-Balliol element in the community, but while the Appeals invoke Edward I, only the third suggests that he be involved in finding the new king, and that only to the extent that judgement be given in his presence. The Appeal is on behalf of the king-making role of seven earls and community, an elision from the undoubted comital role in the inauguration

---

[11] Strictly the document should go to them and is a protest and notice of appeal; but the name Appeal is well established and not misleading, since the document did go to Edward I.

[12] *Anglo-Scottish Relations*, no. 14. In the fifth-last line (p. 100) the word *patiencam* must mean 'delay', or, if it means 'forbearance', *vestram* must be a scribal error for *nostram*.

of a new king to a role in establishing who is rightful king. At this stage, then, Bruce is seeking to have Edward I by his presence protect these earls and the community in their task, without giving any indication of how this would be done, unless by implication before seven earls. There were of course thirteen earldoms in Scotland,[13] and the figure 'seven' may have been chosen because of its magical or ritual significance, or, as I suspect, it may have been borrowed from the electors of the king of the Romans, since 1257 seven in number.[14]

Bruce would certainly have in his scrip a list of those earls who supported him, including Atholl, Mar and Bruce's own son, Robert earl of Carrick. He could also count upon Patrick earl of Dunbar (or March), Walter Stewart earl of Menteith and Malcolm earl of Lennox, all of whom were later named by him as assessors in the Great Cause. Donald earl of Mar, knighted in 1270, was aged about thirty-five to forty, and it may be that his son and daughter were already married to Bruce's granddaughter and grandson (later Robert I, born in 1274). Moreover Donald had married the young widow of Malcolm, earl of Fife (died 1266); she was the mother and grand-mother of earls of Fife and since 1289 great-grandmother of the one-year old heir, Duncan, of whose person Earl Donald may have been guardian in right of his wife. Duncan and Donald were named as among the seven in the Appeal.

William earl of Sutherland, whose appearances in record are few, also committed himself:

> by this agreement and by oath taken we are obligated to ... Bruce ... in counsel and aid to maintain and succour him with all our power to pursue, seek and attain all his right and honour which he has in the rule of the kingdom of Scotland. And we faithfully promise this to ... Bruce ... by lawful agreement and faithful promise.[15]

There is no date, but one phrase in this, *ius suum et honorem ... in regimine regni Scocie*, is close to the Appeal's reference to Balliol's claim to *iura et honores regiminis regni*, while the refence to *potencia*, military power, fits with, indeed gives substance to, Bishop Fraser's fear of civil war. Sutherland's obligation belongs with the Appeal to late 1290.[16]

Balliol in 1291 listed four earls among his auditors, Buchan, Angus,

[13] Carrick, Dunbar, Menteith, Lennox, Fife, Strathearn, Atholl, Angus, Mar, Buchan, Ross, Sutherland, Caithness (from south to north). In 1290 Fife was in wardship. Angus was held by an English baron, Caithness by the earl of Orkney, though that did not make them ineligible politically.

[14] See the articles in *Krönungen*, i, esp. 87–119.

[15] Text in Appendix B.

[16] William earl of Sutherland did little if anything to fulfil his undertaking. He served Edward I in the collection of fealties at Inverness in the summer of 1291 and remained aloof from the war in 1296.

Strathearn and Ross; Bruce, with eight, had a majority in his camp, and at this juncture, late in 1290, was invoking a tribunal of seven earls, backed by the presence and authority of Edward I, to award him the throne.

Meanwhile that king was discovering how he might recover from the wreck of his Scottish hopes brought about by the death of the Maid. He was with his dying queen for a week till her death on 28 November, arranged her funeral, completed on 17 December, and spent his mourning till the end of January at the small religious house of Ashridge, where parliament opened on 6 January 1291.[17] We do not know who attended, but the Annals of Waverley have a unique account of a meeting with magnates where the king 'said that it was in his mind to reduce the king and kingdom of Scotland to his rule, as he had recently subjected Wales to his authority. He moved his army to those parts, where he shortly obtained the said king [*regem*] of Scotland', an error for 'kingdom', *regnum*.[18] The annalist, whose year normally begins on 25 March,[19] places this account as first event in 1291, probably using a source whose year began on 25 December, for there is no better – no other – candidate for this meeting than the January parliament. The moves which followed it are intelligible only on the assumption that Edward had reached the decision described by the annalist, which he would certainly share with his closest advisers.

It was prompted by new information. Florence V, count of Holland, had made a marriage treaty with Edward I in October 1285 so that Florence's son John (born 1281) should marry Edward's daughter Elizabeth, born in 1282. The count would receive £50,000 Tours (about £12,500 sterling), of which the first £2,500 sterling would be due when John came to England.[20] In the second half of 1290 Florence wrote promising that he would soon come over to England,[21] and on 1 November 1290 John and a group of nobles had crossed the sea on his father's business to join Edward I on 20 November at Harby (Notts.).[22] This was the first day of a new regnal year, for which we lack a wardrobe book and its detail, but it is not coincidence that when the queen had died, the Hollanders produced the first signs of revived royal interest in Scotland, a letter of protection on 28 November to Elias de Hauville going to Scotland on the king's service. On 28 December 1290 he and Antony Bek appointed attorneys for the same reason, and Hauville probably left in January and was apparently back by 10 March 1291. Bek was present at the Ashridge parliament and since the appointment of his

---

[17] Stones and Simpson, i, 7. There are no writs of summons.

[18] *Annales Monastici*, ii, 409.

[19] A death on 24 March 1291 is placed under 1290.

[20] *Foedera*, i, 658–59, 661; £10,000 Tur. was payable when John came.

[21] *Oorkondenboek van Holland en Zeeland tot 1299*, iv, p. 988, no. 2572. I am indebted to Dr J. A. Kossmann-Putto for sending me the text of this letter. The original is PRO SC1/18/113.

[22] PRO C47/4/5, fo. 16r–v; *de missione patris sui*.

attorneys was repeated on 20 January 1291,[23] he would go to Scotland about that date.

A sadly defective text coming from the Bruce camp reveals Bek's concerns.[24] Written in Anglo-Norman, without any salutation or farewell, it launches into an account of Anglo-Scottish relations: 'I heard from my father and old (*aunciens*) folk about the time of King David'[25] that in a war between the English and Scottish kings, Northumberland was lost. In the peace it was provided that if the Scottish king made any *desobeisaunce* against England, the seven earls were sworn to [support] the English king and his crown ... [*8–10 words illegible*]. Richard [I] sold the homage of the king of Scotland, but 'we' think that this sale must be invalid, 'for the English king and his council are so wise that they will soon advise themselves whether one can dismember the crown of such a limb, and then that one must keep the crown whole'. Let him [King Edward] know by Elias de Hauville that 'whenever he wishes to make his *demaunde droitureaument*, I will obey him and will help him by myself and by all my friends, and by my lineage whatever my friends want to do.[26] And I beg you [for] grace for my right and for my truth which I wish to show before you and I earnestly [? intend] to speak with the old folk (*aunciens*) of the land to seek out the truth of your affairs as ...' [*two or three words lost*, ? you have requested].

The garbling of the events of 1174 and of the York oaths of 1175 (though the quittance of 1189 is correctly attributed) reveals much about a layman's grasp of Scotland's past; invoking the seven earls[27] links it firmly to the Appeal and to Robert Bruce as sender.[28] It is also not in doubt that its substance was meant for Edward I, for the sender, Bruce, lays a foundation for a claim, *demaunde*, by the English king to homage from the Scottish king, to be made *droitureaument*, rightfully, or by way of law. And the recipient is told to let the king know Bruce's support for this by the messenger Hauville – which he did by sending Edward the extant copy of the letter. He was, of course, Antony Bek, who returned from Scotland to his diocese, but not to the royal court, by 9 March 1291.[29]

---

[23] *Cal. Pat. Rolls, 1281–1292*, 409, 412, 414, 424. Prestwich, *Edward I*, 363; Stones and Simpson, i, 6n; Fraser, *History of Anthony Bek*, 239 shows Bek at Gateshead on 15 November, Ashridge 8–16 January and in Co. Durham on 9 March.

[24] Stones and Simpson, ii, 187; I have examined the original and could read no more of it, but would take line 9 as ... *dun tiel menbre, e pus qe len doit tenir la corone entiere. Bien li faz a savoir* ..., where *faz* is imperative.

[25] An alternative meaning is 'old men of the time of King David', an error for King William.

[26] The last part should perhaps be translated 'I will help him by myself ... friends and ... lineage, to do what my friends wish'.

[27] This French text has *the* seven earls.

[28] He received the only Scottish royal document of the period in Anglo-Norman, a 1270 charter of Alexander III pardoning misdeeds; *National Manuscripts of Scotland*, i, no. LXI.

[29] Fraser, *History of Anthony Bek*, 239.

At the end, Bruce's right and its factual basis (*verité*) are mentioned, but this is quickly balanced by a promise to ask the old folk about the factual basis of the recipient's (Bek's) business. The result of these approaches survives in a membrane sewn to, and written by the same hand as, the Appeal of seven earls and containing three 'historical' memoranda.[30] The first and longest narrates the daughters and grandchildren of Earl David and the supposed recognition by an aged Alexander II of Bruce as heir to the throne, confirmed by a judgement and recorded in a lost document; this first memorandum justifies the claim in the third Appeal that Bruce was 'lawful heir and true assignee' of the kingdom, but it is also the *droit e verité* for which, in his letter, he asks grace and which he wishes to show to Bek.

As for 'your' (Bek's) business, the second memorandum deals with the right of the count of Holland, descended from Ada, the sister of King William, a right according to old men (*anticos* in the memorandum, *aunciens* in Bruce's letter) first to the earldom of Ross of which he was unjustly deprived, and second to be just and nearer heir to the kingdom if the case of the heirs of Earl David is deficient so that they cannot succeed to Scotland. This relates to the Appeal in that it deals with an earldom and might serve to oust Ross, a Balliol supporter, from a place among the seven. But it also reveals what Bek had come north to investigate, the right of Florence V count of Holland to succeed to the Scottish throne. Whether Florence had an inkling of this when sending his son John to England is unknown, though his lawyers' arguments later were so varied that at this point he probably knew only of his descent from Ada, daughter of Earl Henry, and of the loss of some Scottish lands, which in fact had been alienated by Count William in 1249.[31]

To the advisers of Edward I, despondent at the collapse of their earlier hopes to win Scotland by marriage, this descent had been surely a gleam of hope, for if Count Florence had a claim to the kingdom, and it could be found valid, this would allow an alternative to the lost personal union of the kingships if Edward could also establish his lordship over kingdom and king. Holding John of Holland at his court (as he did until 1297) for marriage to Elizabeth, and dangling financial rewards under the 1285 treaty, Edward was unlikely to meet dissent from Florence. In November 1290 when John and his entourage came to court, discovering the possibilities of a Holland succession made more seductive a claim to overlordship of Scotland; Bek had been sent to find out what the grounds might be, as Bruce evidently knew.

[30] Stones and Simpson, ii, D.76 (J) for all three memoranda. The first is discussed above, ch. 6, pp. 123–25.

[31] He granted to his sister and her husband the 'fief and land which our progenitors, counts of Holland, hitherto held from the illustrious king of Scots and his progenitors'. No word of an earldom. Kossmann-Putto, 'Florence V', *Scotland and the Low Countries*, ed. Simpson, 17 n. 2.

The third memorandum details the right of Earl Donald of Mar to land promised but not given by King William to Earl Morgund of Mar, for which Donald asks right and reason. This supports the second Appeal in which Earl Donald claims to have been deprived of land in Moray, and was presumably raised to tie Donald firmly to Bruce's interest.[32]

Out of all this a chronology emerges, in which the Appeals proper were put together in Bruce's interest, probably in late 1290, to be presented by 'so and so' – name to be added later – to the two Guardians at some political occasion, with the aim of frightening them away from Balliol's cause. Never (it seems) presented, another use was suggested by the visit of Bek and Hauville, of whose business Bruce learned. He wrote his letter to Bek, about early February 1291, enthusing about Edward I's 'right' and promising action on the Holland business. When he had found out what the count wanted (his ancestor's Scottish lands) and what Edward wanted (the count's right to the Scottish throne), latish in February he sent the Appeal and the three memoranda to Bek, from whom Hauville took to Edward I a dossier of copies; if there was no covering letter to the king – and none has survived – Hauville could expound the context.

The earliest post-1286 evidence that Edward I might now claim to be overlord of Scotland comes from this letter of Bruce. Whether Bruce put the notion in his head must be doubted, for Edward had already claimed it in 1278 and it must have come to his mind with the possibility of succession by the count of Holland. But Bruce gave it unambiguous political backing, which, with the bishop's call in his letter of 7 October, would suggest to Edward a temper of support, even a party of Scottish champions, of whose existence there is scant evidence. Perhaps he was also misled by reports from Antony Bek, from whom Hauville had probably returned by 8 March when Edward first showed that he intended to act on the Scottish succession.[33] He then issued a safe-conduct for Count Florence to come to England and he ordered research in chronicles for evidence on Anglo-Scottish relations; Edward had decided simultaneously to demand overlordship of Scotland and to use Count Florence as a Claimant.

What happened between 8 March and 10 May 1291 is, conventionally, a mystery, not least because the question 'how did the Scots come to meet Edward by the Tweed – did he invite them, or they him?' has no single answer. There are moves of two parties to establish, converging, no doubt, but at the time independent save for such messages or envoys as may have passed between them, leaving us no trace. But we have seen that individual Scots invited Edward's presence, while it is clear that he named Norham as

[32] It is just possible that there was some intention to claim that Donald should be recognised as earl of Moray, an earldom suppressed in 1130 but not forgotten.

[33] Hauville was certainly back by 10 March when the king made a grant to him. *Cal. Pat. Rolls, 1281–1292*, 424; Stones and Simpson, i, 139–40.

the place the Scots should meet him. To anticipate, I shall suggest that they expected him to arbitrate between the claims of Balliol and Bruce, to which end they executed an *obligatorium*, a promissory deed, that they would take as king which of the two he chose. From 6 May Edward put the evidence for his overlordship to a learned group from his parliament at Norham, and then, reassured by their approval, devastated the Scots by asking on 10 May for their acceptance also, while revealing that there were other claimants to their kingship. The evidence for these events is scattered but vital to understanding of the critical month of June 1291.

Only two of Edward's requests for chronicle extracts, plus a reminder, are known. The initial enquiry on 8 March 1291 to a limited number of houses asked for evidence on '[the right] which belongs to us in homage of the kingdom of Scotland', and 'our kingdom and the rule of Scotland in any way'. It produced disappointing material, and probably little of that. After a fortnight, reminders and a further trawl of houses changed the emphasis, dropping mention of homage for Scotland, for which there would be nothing after 1174, and searching for evidence which might bear on magnates taking up the government (*presidentes*).[34] This was certainly a major investigation, and it is at least possible that in the later trawl the royal advisers were interested in the possibility that a kingless kingdom escheated to its over-lord. Some responses survive; all were edited, probably in April, into a chronological survey of English royal rights, preserved to be trotted out in several 'vindications' of those rights.

By the end of March Edward I was in Nottinghamshire, where about 21–27 March he probably issued writs summoning parliament to Norham on the quinzaine of Easter, 6 May 1291. In County Durham on 16 April he summoned north-country magnates and sheriffs to muster with arms at Norham on 3 June. The purpose of that summons I shall discuss later.[35] He spent Easter (22 April) at Newcastle, then went slowly north to reach Norham on or about 3 May. There, according to the chronicler Walter of Guisborough, writing in north Yorkshire, he began parliament on Sunday, 6 May, a date confirmed by a later version of Brabazon's speech of 10 May which adds that Edward had 'requested you [the Scots] by his letters to come to this place' then,[36] agreeing, in effect, that it was the first day of the parliament.

For Scottish activity before 10 May, Guisborough, writing about 1300, tells of the Guardians after the Maid's death being fearful of civil war between supporters of Bruce and Balliol. By advice of the community they

[34] The evidence is marshalled in Stones and Simpson, i, 138–54, 222–24; ii, 6.

[35] *Foedera*, i, 753; among the 54 individuals summoned were John Balliol, Alexander Balliol, John Comyn earl of Buchan and Robert Bruce.

[36] Stones and Simpson, ii, A.3, C.3. The statement in p. 16, n. 1 that 6 May was 'four days before the actual opening of the Great Cause' misrepresents what the Scots got when they came to Norham. The Great Cause began only on 3 August.

sent to Edward asking that he would counsel them. He sent the bishops of Durham and Carlisle and John de Vescy who urged the Scots to submit the question of the succession to his ordinance, and after a parliament almost all the Scottish magnates submitted themselves in letters (*litteratorie*) to his advice and ordinance.[37] Two of Guisborough's three were not in Scotland after the Maid's death, and John de Vascy, who died in February 1289, must be an error for 'William';[38] Guisborough has confused the embassy to Birgham in July 1290 with Bek's visit in September–October 1290 or that in early 1291.

Yet the whole story should not be dismissed, for when civil war seemed possible in early October 1290, Bek, then in Scotland, would prod the Scots to act just as Guisborough claims; and his influence, urging that the Scots seek Edward's counsel, may be seen in the last phrases of Bishop Fraser's letter as I have emended them. There is then a gap in Guisborough's account, a period of some six months, October 1290 – March 1291, during which (in February 1291) Bek again visited Scotland; the rest of Guisborough's account, the parliament and the Scottish letter, belongs to the eve of the Norham meeting, according to the weight of other evidence. Although the Scottish case of Baldred Bisset produced for the papal curia in 1300–2 throws little light on the aftermath of the Maid's death, there are other, later, accounts of which the earliest, that in *Gest. Ann.*, presents Edward I in a surprisingly favourable light.

He is *princeps magnificus*, and the establishment of overlordship is ignored. Upon the death of the Maid there was contention between Balliol and Bruce, the nobles and Guardians frequently discussed the succession but to no effect, because it was a difficult matter, opinions changed, the interested parties were very powerful and they had no superior to put their judgement (*sentencia*) into effect, to force the parties to obey it. They sent Bishop Fraser and others to Edward I, then *in remotis*, to ask him to become supreme judge (*superior iudex*), to declare the right of each party, and to enforce his decision. Edward fixed a day for the Scots to meet before him at Berwick, and ordered the Claimants to be summoned there, without prejudice to the kingdom and without any overlordship accruing to him, to act 'not as overlord or as judge, but as friendly arbiter and a distinguished neighbour ...'; this he promised in letters patent. When the Scots met the king at Berwick, they gave him an oath that they would accept his decision, and the prelates, Guardians, magnates and community sealed an instrument that they would obey as king *de iure et de facto* and as superior lord, that one of the two contenders whom he declared ruler. Finally Edward appointed an

---

[37] *Chron. Guisborough*, 233; Stones and Simpson, ii, 4.

[38] William de Vescy was appointed justiciar of Ireland in September and certainly did not go to Scotland then. Bek obtained a commission of oyer and terminer on 20 October 1290 against thieves active during his absence on the king's service in Scotland (in July 1290); *Cal. Pat. Rolls, 1281–1292*, 407.

assize to establish the right heir, and (briefly) the Great Cause follows, with Bruce defeated because he refused homage to Edward I, as he later did to Balliol.[39]

Much of this is manifestly wrong, but, while emollient about Edward, it favours Bruce and must have been used at some point in his favour; the likeliest period was 1309–10 or possibly a little later, when Robert I was concerned to impugn John Balliol's kingship as much as Edward's over-lordship, with Philip IV, Clement V and possibly the Council of Vienne. This conclusion is based upon the English response to it which opens the memorandum submitted by the Scots to a peace-conference at Bamburgh in 1321, in the presence of papal and French mediators. This clearly picks up on points made in the *Gest. Ann.* text, accepting some, such as the embassy to Gascony which is an error, correcting others, for example by pointing out that the Scots appointed most auditors, and that Bruce did do homage to Balliol; overlordship is stressed, but no light is thrown on the Norham episode which is ignored. The detail makes it quite clear that this text rebuts a version of the *Gest. Ann.* account which was in English hands.

The Bamburgh memorandum then gives a Scottish rebuttal of the English version of events after 1289, claiming that Edward in his letter of condolence after the Maid's death promised to come to those parts as 'friend and neighbour' (*tamquam amicus et vicinus*) with advice on the contested throne, but came on the appointed day with armed forces to Norham and asked the Scots at Berwick to meet him there. They asked for letters of 'no prejudice' which were granted, and were 'stupefied' to be asked to recognise Edward's overlordship. There was an angry exchange with the bishop of Glasgow, a three-week adjournment after which by fear and fraud Edward imposed his will. This version is far more accurate than the *Gest. Ann.* account, which the Scots seem not to have had before them. But questions remain.[40]

Both agree that Edward offered his advice as friend and neighbour, in circumstances on which the Bamburgh source is convincing; such words contradict overlordship, and without Edward's letter we cannot be absolutely certain that they were used. But in October 1290 overlordship had been removed from the agenda by the Northampton treaty, and, given two separate Scottish allegations of this phrase, there is a strong probability that

---

[39] *Chron. Fordun*, i, 311–13; translation in Stones and Simpson, i, 74–75, but the translation professedly omits *eorum* (p. 74 n. 4), which would give a meaning of 'the Scots had no superior who could put *their* sentence into effect'. The writer is arguing that the Scots could reach a judgement but had no one to enforce it. The insertion (p. 75, line 13) of [notarial] in 'authentic instrument' is unjustified and misleading; a sealed instrument, as with all other such communications, was surely meant.

[40] The modern editor of the memorandum discovered in its account of Robert I's accession a small textual echo of the 1309–10 declarations of the Scottish clergy against the royal title of John Balliol, showing that materials of that date were in the Scottish file; Linehan, 'Spanish Manuscript', 121 n. bg.

it had been used in the letter of condolence. The elaborations of the *Gest. Ann.* version represent what the Scots would have liked it to say. Secondly, Edward cannot have summoned the Scots to Berwick, as *Gest. Ann.* would have us believe, but the Bamburgh version is curiously silent about how they came to be there. And thirdly, the sealed undertaking by Scots to accept Edward's judgement is not found in the Bamburgh account.

The Scottish Guardians were at Edinburgh on 15 April 1291, a week before Easter.[41] Whether they then knew of Edward I's summons (on or about 21 March) of parliament to Norham is uncertain but not unlikely; in any case Edward must about this time have notified the Scots of his coming, and it is possible that he said that he expected to find them at Berwick. Although Guisborough and versions of Brabazon's speech of 10 May say that Edward convoked the Scots to Norham, there is no reason to doubt that he sent to Berwick for them, as the Bamburgh text says. That summons would come in May. Berwick had plentiful lodgings as well as a royal castle, the obvious place for the Scots to muster but the fishermen's cots of Tweedmouth would scarcely serve for a parliament, and Norham was the nearest prestigious castle, for Edward presumably told the Scots of his intention to be there on 6 May. His words would be anodyne (he may even have used phrases about coming as a friendly neighbour), 'to treat of the business of the kingdom of Scotland and succession thereto', without mention of overlordship.

He could have asked the Scots at Berwick to come to Norham on 5 May for the sixth, but the evidence points rather to 9 May for the tenth, the days 6–9 May being given over in parliament to consideration of Edward's right to overlordship. Meanwhile, I suggest, at Berwick the Scots were engaged in a debate and decision to go to Edward, not seeking his advice nor Bruce's more robust 'judgement', but with a written undertaking to accept his ordinance on the succession; this was Guisborough's parliament at which most Scottish magnates submitted themselves in letters to Edward's advice and ordinance.[42] The same document is described by *Gest. Ann.*, with 'improvements' of 1309–10, that the communities of burgesses and freeholders participated and that the Scots would have the successful Claimant as 'king and superior lord', a swipe at Edward I's pretension. This instrument, claims *Gest. Ann.*, was executed before Edward at Berwick – though Edward's presence must be an error.[43]

In addition to these two sources, a sealed promise of the Scots was known to others, but in very confused contexts. According to the Bury annalist, writing no later than 1301, Edward I at Norham recited his right before the

<hr />

[41] NAS, RH 5/94, a warrant for the fee of the clerk of rolls, paid on 24 May 1291 at Dunfermline; Stevenson, *Documents*, i, no. 191, a very poor transcript; the original is dated Thursday after the feast of St Dunstan (NAS, RH 5/95).

[42] *Chron. Guisborough*, 233; Stones and Simpson, ii, 4.

[43] *Chron. Fordun*, i, 312–13.

notables of Scotland, who, having nothing to say, accepted his overlordship and gave him the castles of Scotland. They then 'gave security by letters patent and declared that those who had claimed a right in the kingdom of Scotland would abide by the judgement of the king of England's court'. There follows a relatively informed version of events in June 1291, with some errors.[44] To this can be added the testimony of three monastic chroniclers of the later fourteenth century, at Leicester (Henry Knighton), Meaux and Malmesbury. Knighton (who made much use of Guisborough, but not here), claims that in parliament at Northampton [i.e. Norham] the three claimants for the kingdom asked for Edward's judgement. This he would not give until they had sworn to abide by it; twenty-four senior Scots (four bishops, seven earls, ten barons and some others) also bound themselves in a sealed document to accept this judgement, and that he would be superior lord of their king.

The chronicler of Meaux, relying on Higden's *Polychronicon*, adds to it that after the Claimants had recognised Edward's overlordship, the king deferred acting until he could see the reaction of the communities of Scotland, lest they should revoke his finding in the future. The Claimants, on behalf of the other magnates and communities, brought to the king an *obligatorium* under the seals of four bishops, six earls and twelve barons, that they would accept as king whomever Edward chose from the claimants. He was then given sasine of the kingdom.

And thirdly the chronicler of Malmesbury abbey, another follower of Higden, writing *c.*1350–65, also departs from that author: 'when the kingdom was desolate without a prince and the magnates squabbling among themselves, even over which of them should be lord, eventually, spontaneously, without asking the English king, they agreed to send letters to this remarkable prince, sealed with their seals, saying that the Scots themselves would hold as king of Scotland (and his heirs after him) whomever of Scottish nation he, or his council in his presence, should choose as king.' The English king spent three days considering this and the descendants of Earl David, whence the Award of Norham, copied at length.[45]

The illogicality and ignorance of this narrative needs no exposition, yet at its heart is the same undertaking as we find in five other chroniclers, four of them English. The differences between these show that they are independent, yet not one of them gives a text of the *obligatorium*, some are very late, and the differences might suggest that they are all fiction. I do not think that six or seven witnesses can be so dismissed, even though some understood the *obligatorium* to have been linked to Edward's overlordship; if it had been, we should have known about it from Edward's notary. In seeking a context for such an instrument after October 1290, we must admit the

[44] *Chron. Bury*, 98–99
[45] *Chron. Knighton*, i, 285; *Chron. Melsa*, ii, 255; *Eulogium Historiarum*, iii, 149–50.

possibility that it was sealed not long thereafter. Such an early date is, however, very improbable, since it would have made the visit of Bek and Hauville otiose; it is far more likely that Bek encouraged the Scots to think of executing such a deed, to encourage Edward to come to the Border, but that its date was early May 1291.

It was not, after all, an innovation for the Scots, for as they had sworn to accept the Maid of Norway as heir presumptive in 1284 and sealed their undertaking, so now in 1290–91 they swore to accept as true heir the person so declared by Edward I. Perhaps many of the same phrases were used, and the advance in political initiative probably seemed small – indeed it is likely that the act of 1284 suggested that of 1290–91. But the *obligatorium* bore no more than twenty-four seals (Knighton and the Meaux chronicle agree on a small number like this) including those of four bishops, whereas thirty-seven lay magnates had sealed in 1284. Perhaps few of those present agreed with the decision and many withheld their consent, the document being the work of a faction. The number of earls, six or seven, points to Bruce's camp, and he had shown himself eager to support Edward's 'right' to overlordship; but he had the support of only two bishops, not four, and the *obligatorium* would not refer to overlordship.

A small gathering may have been imposed by the shortness of time since a summons to Berwick went out from the Guardians, or by a wish to limit the scope for quarrelling, with a compromise outcome, an acceptance and empowerment of arbitration by Edward I. This was a Scottish attempt to define the terms on which he dealt with the kingdom's business, and perhaps to ensure that he had no grounds for an exercise of overlordship. But when the Scots offered to Edward I *their* authority for his arbitration, a generous proposition which would remove any anxiety that his finding would be contested, they should have recalled that in 1263–64 Edward had seen his baronial opponents accept Louis IX as arbiter and then reject his finding. Nor was the notion of baronial authority for his decision at all in tune with Edward's view of his *maiestas*.

Meanwhile the English gathered at Norham (Plate 7) since parliament began on 6 May had also been busy. Guisborough relates (after the meeting on that day) that clerks expert in civil and canon law,[46] many religious with their chronicles, several bishops with the archbishop of York, met to deal with the overlordship of Scotland, in that the king claimed that he and his predecessors were chief lord of the king and kingdom. The implication is that chronicle evidence was adduced, and that is explicitly said by the chronicler of Bury, while that of Meaux claims that the king summoned representatives from each cathedral and monastery and examined the

---

[46] This would cover representatives of Oxford University who came, and possibly of Cambridge University.

chronicles which they brought, together with those found in Scottish royal archives at Scone.[47] The editors of the Great Cause records think that 'it is hardly possible to doubt that there is some substance in all these statements'.[48] Doubt might have arisen if the record of Norham said nothing; but the Great Roll has a short passage mentioning chronicle and documentary evidence for English overlordship before narrating events of 10 May – a way of eliding proceedings on which the notary wished to be unspecific.[49] No source mentions the form in which the chronicle evidence was examined, but I shall suggest later that it was already summarised in the form found in the notary's Great Roll.[50]

Guisborough's narrative shows that those clerics whom the king gathered, 'diligently examined past times, were asked one by one and separately, and all said on their consciences that the supreme lordship of the kingdom of Scotland should pertain to the king of the English unless anything to the contrary should exist (*haberetur*) through which extracts from chronicles should be excluded'.[51] The final qualification is a remarkable hesitation which can scarcely have been to the liking of the king's advisers; it suggests that opinion was not unanimous so that the question put to each individual had to include this escape for conscience. It also seems to admit the possibility of a record which would overturn the chronicles – and there was really only one such record, the 1189 quittance of Canterbury, which Edward I steadfastly ignored. The Bury chronicle noted no such hesitation: chronicles were inspected, investigated and discussed before all the king's council who all accepted that the king's overlordship was proved.[52]

Because of elision in the records of this consideration of the king's overlordship noted by chroniclers, it has had little significance in modern accounts of 1291. Yet on Elias de Hauville's return in early March 1291, research in chronicles was Edward's priority, and was followed up with a persistence which shows its importance in the whole Scottish enterprise. He prepared with great care for his seminar on overlordship, which was in his plans if not from the first, then by the date of summons to Norham, about 21 March. Edward wanted to be able to show that his claim had been

[47] Stones and Simpson, i, 147–48, citing *Chron. Guisborough*, 238; *Chron. Bury*, 98; *Chron. Melsa*, ii, 252. A letter of King William of Scotland 'touching his homage to King John' was sent north in haste to Edward I in early May, perhaps thought to have come from the Scottish archives; Stones and Simpson, i, 140, 152; Stevenson, *Documents*, i, 225.

[48] Stones and Simpson, i, 148. Stones discussed this evidence and subsequent events discussed here, in 'The Appeal to History ...', Part 1', *Archives*, ix (1969–70), 11–21. A very valuable analysis of the chronicle sources is made by Guenée, 'L'enquête historique ordonnée par Édouard Ier ...', *Comptes rendus de l'Académie des Inscriptions et Belle-Lettres, 1975*, 572–84.

[49] Stones and Simpson, ii, A.2.i.

[50] Stones and Simpson, ii, Appendix A, A.38.

[51] *Chron. Guisborough*, 234.

[52] *Chron. Bury*, 98.

examined and approved by learned clergy, perhaps already having in mind the Scots but also that authority about whom he made dismissive remarks, but on whom he nonetheless depended for the untroubled collection of large sums of money from the church: the pope. Eventually the recognition of his overlordship was indeed nullified by a pope, Celestine V, on the grounds that it was extracted by fear.

Against Edward's dossier, the Scots, represented by their 'good men', would remember what the notary John of Caen so conveniently omitted from his record, that for a century the king of Scots had held his kingdom of no earthly power, that in 1286 Scots had sworn an oath to preserve the kingdom for the rightful heir of King Alexander by blood, and that in 1290 Edward I had sworn to respect the Scottish realm as heretofore, distinct and separate, free in itself, without subjection. That oath was between Edward and his God, and few, if any, in his realm would harass him with it. The oath of the Scots weighed upon them as heavily as excommunication from the body of the faithful and more heavily than any other earthly allegiance; they told Edward on 1 June 1291 'they can give you no other answer, saving the oath which they took after the death of the king and the general sentence [of excommunication] ... For if they do otherwise, against their oath, they would be perjurers and to be disinherited by their liege lord'.[53] Penalties in the hereafter the Scots too could doubtless shrug off like the next man, but a defector from this oath must also risk the condign retribution of his society, here and now; this oath gave a special meaning to 'community of the kingdom'.

By 9 May Edward was ready to confront the Scots with his 'right', and they would now be invited to Norham. When they went there on 9–10 May, they did so in a very cautious frame of mind. First the group which came was a small one, two bishops and some magnates, a 'part of the community' which in the outcome insisted on taking Edward's demand for sovereignty to a wider community. Secondly, the Berwick assembly must have told the king that their members would come to Norham only if he would give them reassurances.[54] Royal letters were issued to them dated 9 and 10 May, similar in purpose, but varying significantly in their terms.[55]

On 9 May an uncontroversial letter of safeconduct to two named bishops, unnamed magnates and those with them, to come to Norham and treat of business of *terra Scotie*, was valid till 11 May;[56] of the same date was a letter that the coming of certain bishops and magnates of the kingdom who now

---

[53] *Anglo-Scottish Relations*, no. 16.

[54] The Bamburgh memorandum says that Edward came to Norham with horse and arms; Linehan, 'Spanish Manuscript', 120. Edward would certainly have a following, but the Scots seem to have antedated the force summoned for 3 June.

[55] Stones and Simpson, ii. D.6(i).

[56] The Latin text of the safeconduct from the patent roll is in Stevenson, *Documents*, i, 227–28, misdated 4 May for 9 May, and calendared in *Cal. Pat. Rolls, 1281–1292*, 428.

come to the king, to Norham, to treat on its business, is not to be made custom or consequence, nor to prejudice the *status regni* in future.[57] These two were probably offered by Edward, even sent by him unasked. But the second was rejected for on 10 May it was replaced by a letter (I italicise differences), claiming that the magnates (*hauts hommes*) *and a part of the community of the kingdom* came *at the king's request*, to Norham to treat on business of the kingdom, and that *this coming across the Tweed to treat* is not to *prejudice them or anyone of the kingdom, crossing to treat at another time while this treating lasts.*[58]

The replacement of 'to us' by 'at our request' made it clear that the Scots had not sought a meeting at Norham (i.e. in England) and had not been summoned. The emphasis on crossing the Tweed made more explicit the act whose prejudicial consequences the Scots feared. And the cumbrous wording of 10 May seems to indicate that while some Scots were to cross the river, others would not, at least at this time, though they might cross later. This explains the opening reference to a part of the community, with its implication that another part, perhaps the larger part, had not come to Norham – they were still at Berwick. The most striking change, however, was the replacement of custom, consequence and prejudice to the standing of the kingdom by prejudice to the magnates and community. The point about becoming 'custom' was met by the cumbrous wording about others crossing later. The 'consequence' of their crossing the Tweed, that the English king might again require this, was explicitly given up. In crossing at his request, they could have compromised their own position, but not that of the kingdom, for the 'status of the kingdom' was the concern of the Scottish king, whose position they had sworn in 1286 to uphold; it vanished from the letters of 10 May.[59] The Scots were already taking the ground on which they were to base their response to Edward I in early June – that only their king could answer for the standing of his kingdom.

The *bone gent*, leading folk, of Scotland approached Norham with caution, then, but reassured by the Northampton oath of 28 August 1290, and by Edward's stated wish that peace should be kept. Their intention was to elucidate the circumstances in which he would arbitrate on the succession; they probably kept their *obligatorium* in their own hands until an arbitration procedure had been agreed, but its existence, though not its text, would become known to the English. Guisborough writes of *arbitracio* and calls the auditors in the Great Cause *arbitri*; the Bury chronicle says that the auditors would give their *arbitrium*; *Gest. Ann.* calls Edward I *amicabilis arbiter et vicinus*; Knighton speaks of a finding by *arbitratores*; and the modern editors of the record of the Great Cause sought reasons 'why the

[57] Stevenson, *Documents*, i, 228; Stones and Simpson, ii. 25.
[58] Stones and Simpson, ii, 24.
[59] For earlier letters of 'no prejudice' to Alexander III, *APS*, i, 109.

majority of chroniclers thought that the Great Cause was an arbitration'.[60] Their first answer was that while monks were present at first at Norham, they did not stay long, and that the monks' great confusion over the number of auditors shows their ignorance of what happened. And their second answer, suggested by George Neilson, was that conflicting methods may have been discussed before the final proposal was adopted. Both answers contain something of the truth but by discounting the *obligatorium* miss the simple point that the Scots wanted and expected arbitration between Bruce and Balliol by a neutral friend.

After crossing from Upsetlington to Norham they were met by quite another proposal. According to Guisborough a speech had been prepared in Latin by William de Hotham, prior provincial of the Dominicans in England, and was delivered in French by Roger Brabazon. The first third of Hotham's Latin text is Biblical rhetoric on the beauties of justice and peace and is found only here, but gives weight to the claim that the whole speech was drawn up by Hotham. It represents the conclusions (and therefore the importance) of Edward's ecclesiastical seminar. When it came to the moment, a more secular spirit deleted the Biblical rhetoric; the rest was retained, for it is in most respects the same as the speech given in French by Brabazon to the Scots, as recorded in the Glasgow manuscript.[61]

This speech sought to massage the Scots into accepting Edward's over-lordship.[62] The dangers to peace after the deaths of Alexander III and his granddaughter were emphasised; Edward had come to do right to all claimants and to keep the peace, and promised justice, peace and security of possessions to all men; for this he asked the *debonere assent* of the Scots – just what the Scots sought and perhaps expected to hear. But within this message was another: he would do these things by virtue of overlordship, and he asked first for *assent*, then for recognition of this overlordship. The editors' suggestion that Edward may have revealed this claim in his letter of invitation[63] is utterly improbable, for it would have kept the Scots far from Norham, and it is contradicted by the words of Brabazon, who was clearly revealing something new.[64] On the other hand the tone of the Hotham-Brabazon speech is almost wheedling, not that of a man sure of both his right and his might. In one further respect it is remarkable. The king has come with 'a desire to do right to all who can make any claim to the

---

[60] Stones and Simpson, i, 206–7. Langtoft, and probably Lanercost, knew of a judgement.

[61] The French text speaks of *soveraine seignurie*, where the Latin has *superior dominacio*, but once *soverain* equates with *dominus supremus*. The Guisborough text is Stones and Simpson, ii, D.3 (ii, 17, 18, 19).

[62] Stones and Simpson, ii, D.3.i. Discussed, Stones and Simpson, i, 103, where the unreliability of the notarial record is hinted at by the editors, but not pursued; they are wrong to interpret 'you' as the parliament – it is clearly the Scots who are addressed.

[63] Stones and Simpson, i, 103.

[64] Stones, *Anglo-Scottish Relations*, no. 15.

inheritance of the kingdom of Scotland', the first hint that there would be more than two claimants to the throne.

The Scots were profoundly shocked by this 'request', as Guisborough calls it. The notarial records and English chroniclers say nothing of the stand-up row on 10–11 May revealed by the Bamburgh memorandum, where the 'stupefied' Scots said that they had never heard of such a novelty, and begged the king, among other things, for the sake of his reputation not to try to lord it over a headless people. Edward now spoke characteristically with a threefold promise: the Scots must concede his lordship or convince him that it was not owed to him or defend themselves by arms as his enemies. To this Bishop Robert Wishart of Glasgow gave the cogent answer of a patriotic schoolman: a headless people might concede the first but this would give him no right to the kingdom; secondly, they were not bound to prove a negative, of which the laws forbid proof, but he must prove the subjection which he claimed; and thirdly it would not be to the honour of such a king to invade a people thus divided and destitute of a defender, whereby, too, the Crusade which he had undertaken could be delayed. Wishart's bold words struck home for the angry king retorted that he would keep the cross he had assumed and would direct his crusading army against the Scots.[65]

The fifteenth-century chroniclers Andrew Wyntoun and Walter Bower ascribe to Bishop Wishart a brief rebuttal of the claim to homage made by Edward with solemn *evidencias*,[66] so the tradition of the bishop's courage was well established. But Edward I wanted acceptance from the Scots, not war against them, and what he said in the heat of the moment was soon replaced by a different approach, taking up Wishart's second challenge – that it was for Edward to prove his claim. This is surely what Bower's *evidencias* refers to, and it is confirmed by our two most reliable chroniclers, the Bury monk and Guisborough. Both go on from Edward I's rehearsal of his claim before his own council or leading clerics to say that this was also rehearsed before the Scots. True, neither explains whether a summary or full recital of texts had been prepared, nor who read out the evidences, but these points do not invalidate the testimony. It is in effect confirmed by grudging words in the Great Roll, where Burnell said that at Norham on 6 May (*sic*) the Scots had 'fully understood and heard' Edward's request for recognition of his overlordship 'which is suficiently evident by several manifest and very plain accounts and other reliable documents'. Within a notarial instrument this means that the accounts had played a part in events which the notary chose not to explain; he had no wish to record discussion

[65] Linehan, 'Spanish Manuscript', 120. The matter is dealt with as a tradition in a footnote in Stones & Simpson, ii, 20–21, where, cautiously, 'we suspect that Wishart did say something here'.

[66] *Chron. Wyntoun*, v, 212–15; *Scotichronicon*, vi, 28–29.

of their validity, but only to claim that the Scots, having had the chance to controvert them, produced nothing which did so.[67]

To controvert what? The chronologically arranged historical extracts given in Caen's Great Roll? That has been doubted because Caen attributes no date to this text. But the same text is found in the Glasgow MS and was in Liber A, first item in a compilation of documents of 1291 – 2 January 1293, telling us much about May–June 1291 which Caen did not wish us to know and which was put together during or just after the end of the Great Cause.[68] This is the latest likely date of the Liber A copy, which placed the text before events of 10 May 1291, showing that it was thought to have existed that early; in fact there was no point to editing the monastic submissions into the chronological text after 13 June 1291, when Edward became overlord. The overwhelming likelihood is that this text had been prepared before 6 May, was discussed then by Edward's English seminar and put to the Scots on 10 May, though whether written or read out we do not know.[69]

At point after point, from the *obligatorium* to this reading of evidences, there is independent evidence to confirm the narratives of Guisborough, whose probable source of information about Norham was the Dominican William de Hotham, and of the Bury chronicler, whose evidence 'may well rest on the testimony of a Bury monk present at Norham',[70] probably John de Shottesham, a Bury monk with 'service in Scotland'.[71] The response given by the Scots, I shall suggest, on 1 June tells us a little more of what was said on 10–11 May, when, evidently, the Scots were assured that Edward would maintain peace in Scotland according to its laws and customs, a conventional enough phrase, but not found in Brabazon's speech. More importantly, the Scots said that Edward had wished the Claimants to show the right of each before the king (as Brabazon had said), and wished to show

---

[67] Stones and Simpson, ii, A.12, A.13. The editors' comment is n. 3 on p. 35 and they discuss the whole question in Stones and Simpson, i, 146–48. Whereas Caen in the Great Roll placed the chronicle extracts after 13 June (A.38), Tang gave their production a definite date, 10 May 1291, (D.6. ii) though it has been written over an erasure. That may mean that Tang changed his guess or that he found the date belatedly; his evidence is not to be relied on.

[68] Stones and Simpson, i, 36. The date of Liber A is discussed in Cuttino, *English Diplomatic Administration*, 113–15, who suggests September 1282 x 'about 1292'. The editors of *Foedera* printed 49 texts from it from 1282, the last on 13 November 1290 (1290 texts in *Foedera*, i, 730–42). Apart from the Scottish section, the book seems to have been complete about the end of that year, when it included texts relating to the Birgham negotiations (*ibid.*). The lost Scottish section, then, was 'the latest in date in Liber A' (Stones and Simpson, i, 72) specifically devoted to overlordship in 1291–93, and not to Anglo-Scottish relations since 1282.

[69] The modern writers are cited in Stones and Simpson, i, 146.

[70] Stones and Simpson, i, 147.

[71] *Cal. Pat. Rolls, 1281–1292*, 488; I am indebted to Dr Antonia Gransden for drawing this to my attention. See her paper on 'John de Northwold, Abbot of Bury', *Thirteenth Century England*, iii (1991), 91–112.

his own right, something entirely new and a matter to which we must return.

Both sides, then, spoke at some length on 10 May. The Great Roll records adjournment to 11 May when there was a further adjournment of three weeks from 10 May, i.e. to 31 May or 1 June.[72] The instruments are un-ambiguous that the three-week delay was to enable the Scots to answer Edward's claim of overlordship and show anything they had to repel or weaken it.[73] A reasonable man would assume that they had been given the evidence on which it was based, but the instruments do not say so; that the chronicle-extracts text had only been read out to them is much more likely, given that they made no attempt to answer it and showed no real knowledge of its contents. One might ask whether three weeks was a reasonable interval in which Scottish monastic chronicles (e.g. at St Andrews) and records (at Edinburgh) could be consulted.

Was this adjournment decided upon overnight 10–11 May, or had it always been allowed for in Edward's plans, as the April summons of military service for 3 June suggests? This date was exactly four weeks after the quinzaine of Easter, 6 May, to which parliament had been summoned, when a muster to overawe the Scots might be expected. The force might have been too large as an escort into Scotland, and was certainly too small to mount a 'crusade' against the Scots. The Scots were to allege force as a reason for their submission, but this seems to have been a belated and weak excuse, not a present threat.[74] Moreover, while Edward had some 650 paid arbelasters and archers with him from 2 June to 6 August 1291, there is no evidence that the northern tenants summoned on 16 April did in fact muster, and their summons may have been cancelled by letters which were not enrolled, perhaps about 10 May, because a display of power after the adjournment, both of which he planned, turned out to be unnecessary.[75] I believe that the muster was cancelled, but not for that reason.

In April Edward had every reason to anticipate a pliant Scottish community, a reluctant acceptance of his claim, perhaps, but not a tussle; the game would be his on or soon after 11 May when the safe-conduct to Norham expired. In fact he became overlord a month later and then spent two weeks of business at Norham and Berwick, including the taking of Scottish fealties; on 28 June he set out on a July progress in Scotland,

---

[72] Stones and Simpson, ii, A.4, A7. By inclusive reckoning to 31 May, otherwise to 1 June. The Norham instrument abbreviates by ignoring the adjournment to 11 May, *ibid.*, C4.

[73] Stones and Simpson, ii, A.7, A.13.

[74] Linehan, 'Spanish manuscript', 120–21; *Scotichronicon*, vi, 158–59, 186–87. The prose is more purple in 186–87, where it is asserted that Edward brought with him all the armed might of England, Wales and Ireland, with strong support from the count of Savoy who was there, and with part of the armed might of Gascony. The count of Savoy was present in June 1292, but not in 1291.

[75] The size of the paid force is explained in the discussion in Stones and Simpson, i, 175–76.

returning to Berwick about 2 August; his contingent of archers was paid from 2 June to 6 August, and had evidently accompanied him. But the adjournment, an ad hoc decision of 10–11 May, and the reluctance of the Scots in early June had delayed everything by a month, so Edward, cancelling the April summons of northern knights to escort his progress, had replaced them by paid archers, perhaps a more reliable force. That reconstruction explains best the military forces involved and the absence of all warlike action.

We start, then, with a misunderstanding at Norham: the Scots went to meet a friend and neighbour who would arbitrate between two claimants to their kingship; Edward came convinced of his overlordship, expecting its acceptance by the Scots, some of whom had seemed willing to abet him in this. Within twenty-four hours both sides had learned of their mistake, and both must seek another way out of the impasse.

CHAPTER 11

The records and the loss
of independence

I intend to show that the notarial efforts of John of Caen in 1291–92 were limited to a couple of short texts, and that his daily instruments for 10 May – 13 June 1291, whose texts do survive, his Great Roll and his short or Norham instrument, were all compiled after September 1296, when 'direct lord' was retrospectively added to Edward I's title used in Scotland in 1291 to April 1296. The Great Roll alone deals with the Great Cause, but it includes also, at greater length, the establishment of Edward's overslord-ship, which is the sole concern of the daily and Norham instruments. The purpose of these highly inaccurate records was to defend Edward I's treatment of Scotland against papal interest. They all suppress the text and purport of the principal contemporary source for the Scottish position, the response, discussed here, to Edward's demand, and his subsequent concessions based on the treaty of Northampton, whereby the Scots, on 12 June 1291, were persuaded to recognise him as Claimant and chief lord on behalf of all the Claimants until there was a king.

In their 1978 edition, with critical commentary, of 'the record sources for the Great Cause',[1] Lionel Stones and Grant Simpson, whom I call 'the editors', did students an immense service by providing scholarly and accessible texts of what was hitherto scattered and poorly edited or, in some cases, unprinted. No one who has looked at the manuscript of the pleadings can fail to be impressed by their labours in clarifying these texts, while their introductory volume provides an invaluable guide and commentary based upon a deep knowledge of records. But, as they say, the events of 1291–92 had been little studied in detail, perhaps because the records are so plentiful, yet so riddled with contradictions.[2] Much is to be learned from their austere pages, without which this study would have been impossible, but while

---

[1] *Edward I and the Throne of Scotland, 1290–1296: an edition of the record sources for the Great Cause* (Oxford, 1978), eds Stones and Simpson, hereafter Stones and Simpson. Texts in vol. ii are usually cited by text number, e.g. C.37 or C.106.II (vi, 5), but where there is no initial letter, by page number.

[2] The most important discussions in books to appear since 1978 are in Barrow, *Bruce*, 3rd edn, ch. 2, and in Prestwich, *Edward I*, ch. 14.

benefiting from their work, I have reached conclusions on the significance of the records more radical than theirs.

The editors took the view that up to completion of Caen's Great Roll (probably mid-1297) 'the record had been prepared in order to set out the facts for general future reference, with a strong bias, indeed, towards the needs of future kings of England, but with no specific, and certainly no immediate, needs in mind.' I have concluded that the notarial records were prompted by the danger that Edward's conduct of Scottish affairs from May 1291 onwards would be scrutinised and condemned at the instance of the Scots. He had been unable to treat Scotland as Wales, could not march in his crusading army claiming that due homage had been refused. Instead he had somehow to dress up the process whereby he became overlord and John became king as peacable acceptance by the whole kingdom. Contrary evidence simply disappeared from Caen's narrative.

We should distinguish between two distinct processes: the establishment of Edward I's overlordship, a political process, and the judicial establishment of the right heir to the Scottish throne; both arose out of a vacancy in the kingship of Scotland but only the second of these may reasonably be called 'the Great Cause'. Overlordship took up the meetings from 10 May 1291 and included the chronicle evidence produced probably on 10 May and the taking of fealties until 7 August; it resurfaced on 3 July 1292 and at Balliol's fealty, homage and renunciation of Edward's promises, 20 November 1292 – 2 January 1293. The Great Cause, on the other hand, took place between 3 August 1291 and the giving of judgement on 17 November 1292.

The distinction between contemporary and later record is also crucial. Glasgow University Library MS General 1053 is a copy of a copy (a lost part of Liber A compiled no later than 1293) of documents from May–June 1291, with nothing on the Great Cause.[3] On the other hand the Norham instrument by John of Caen, a narrative of the same period written considerably later, ignores almost completely the documents in the Glasgow MS. For the Great Cause contemporary records survive in some written pleadings, and almost-contemporary records in minutes for 12 August 1291, and for the last phase, from 14 October 1292, written up in the style of plea rolls presumably from notes.[4]

The Glasgow MS was unknown until the 1920s, unstudied until 1978, its documents also ignored in the story from 10 May 1291 to 2 January 1293, covering both overlordship and the Great Cause, told by the notary John of Caen in his Great Roll. That Roll was begun after April 1296 and completed by May 1297.[5] In *Foedera*, where we may read an unbroken text, the Roll fills

[3] Stones and Simpson, i, 67–72.

[4] Stones and Simpson, i, 85–86.

[5] Stones and Simpson, i, 49. The whole of chapters III and IV in this volume are an indispensible preliminary to any use of these records.

some twenty-two folio pages, only seven of which are devoted to the Cause, the other two-thirds to the establishment and exercise of Edward's overlord-ship.[6] Not only is the balance misleading, but the narrative demonstrably has serious errors of chronology, of factual omission and of verbose com-mission. It should for the most part be set aside as wilfully false.[7]

Caen's 'Norham instrument' (the editors' 'long instrument' is an in-appropriate name since it is much shorter than the Great Roll) deals only with the Norham proceedings, whose events are undated until a final 'diary' which says that they took place on 10, 11 May, 2, 3, 5, 6, 11, 12, 13 June at named places. Events on these days, it says, were recorded 'more fully' in instruments by Caen.[8] These 'short instruments', the source for the Norham instrument, were thought by the editors to be part of a lost archive of daily instruments which Caen wrote as the case proceeded. They also suggest that there may have been instruments like the Norham instrument for later sections of the Cause.[9]

These short instruments are not lost, were not early in date and were not followed by others dealing with events after 13 June 1291 (though there are two short instruments contemporary with 1291–92); nor was the Norham instrument one of a similar series. The Great Roll is divided into sections by passages which are shortened versions of those prefacing or at the end (docquet) of an instrument. These divisions and the dates of proceedings which they contain are shown in Table 3.

The correspondence of the sections A.2–A.37 with the diary of the Norham instrument shows that the Great Roll has used the short instruments for 10 May – 13 June, including two for 3 June, which the diary wording certainly allows.[10] I have been able to identify only one obvious insertion (discussed in relation to 11 June)[11] which would not be in them. On the other hand the Norham instrument represents a severe editing of the short instruments, even omitting proceedings on days which its diary lists and which are in the Great Roll. The reverse is not true – almost everything in the Norham instrument is found in the Great Roll. That texts of the short instruments for May–June do survive is indicated by the notarial prefaces and docquets for each day in the Great Roll. For that time the short instruments, copied in series, make up the text of the Great Roll. This ceases with 13 June, A.37

It is followed by extracts (with a text of Falaise, 1174) arranged chrono-

---

[6] *Foedera*, i, 762–84, with 773–80 on the sessions of August 1291 – November 1292.
[7] I have ignored the existence and problems of Tang's instruments, which the editors show convincingly belong to 1315–18. These texts may vary the fictions told in Caen's instruments but are even less authentic.
[8] Stones and Simpson, ii, C.37.
[9] Stones and Simpson, i, 86–87.
[10] It says that there were instruments for these days, but not that there was one for each.
[11] Stones and Simpson, ii, A.30, p. 90; below p. 251.

Table 3. Make-up of the Great Roll, with notarial prefaces and docquets, in the sequence of the Roll (dates for which there were short instruments are italicised).

1291	
10 May 1291	A.2.ii; A.5
11 May	A.7
2 June	A.11; A.16
3 June	A.17
3 June	A.18; A.22
5 June	A.24; A.25
6 June	A.26; A.27
11 June	A.30; A.31
12 June	A.31; A.34
13 June	A.35; A.37
Chronicle etc. extracts (no preface or docquet)	A.38
12 June – 7 August 1291, fealties (no docquet)	A.39; A.51
[*12 July 1291*]	A.51* = A.48
3 July 1292	A.79
3 August 1291 – 2 January 1293	A.53; A.129
(including *27 December 1292*	A.123)

logically, from chronicles, Scottish royal charters, papal bulls, miracles of St John of Beverley and homages for Galloway. These were not a contemporary transaction and therefore not to be validated by a notary; but everything else in the Table is the work of John of Caen, and it is therefore likely that this edition of the chronicle and other materials collected in 1291 was also his.[12]

The fealties open with a notarial preface to cover all the days and acts following, in chronological order save for one misplacement, a fealty of 29 July placed under 29 June and before July entries.[13] The Glasgow MS contains a list of those who swore fealty up to 3 August 1291 classified according to social standing, but lacking names given in the Great Roll for 29 July and 4–7 August. The likeliest explanation is a series of loose sheets, one for each occasion, from which the classified list was made before the last sheets were received. The same sheets were written up as a chronological instrument with witnesses at each occasion but with no final notarial docquet; instead Caen appended an ephemeral memorandum of 12 July 1291 about arrangements for collecting more fealties, notably from Inverness and Galloway; those who excused themselves on this occasion should be dealt with at the 'next' parliament. This was a promise of 'more to come', which may explain why it took the place of the final notarial docquet to what is otherwise an instrument; but there is another possibility,

---

[12] Stones and Simpson, ii, 297–309, Appendix A for a full text.
[13] Stones and Simpson, ii, 126; but *Foedera*, i, 773 places this fealty correctly.

that the entries in this 'instrument' were drawn directly from the loose
sheets and did not exist as an instrument apart from and before the Great
Roll.

Leaving aside the next document, A.79, for later discussion, the final
section of the Great Roll is an instrument recording the Great Cause and
its aftermath (the homage and fealty of King John, with his annulment of
promises made by Edward) – an aftermath which relates not to the Great
Cause but to overlordship. Thus the Scottish business was recorded in four
major sections: an account of the establishment of overlordship, copied from
short instruments; an edited version of chronicles and other authorities;
an instrument of fealties sworn, lacking final notarial authentication; and
an instrument of the Great Cause and its aftermath. The second section
(chronicles etc.) was drawn up in 1291; it is reasonable to conclude that
of the notarial records the short instruments were drawn up first, the final
instrument thereafter, the fealty instrument possibly between them; only
thereafter were all four section put together in one instrument-roll.

When were these instruments compiled? The royal style determines
their date, and particularly that of the short instruments. During the first
period of Edward's lordship of the kingless kingdom, from 13 June 1291 to
19 November 1292, contemporary records style him 'superior lord of the
kingdom of Scotland', *superior dominus* in Latin, *soverein seignur* in French,
with parallel forms for 'superior lordship'.[14] This style was used in crucial
documents, of whose authenticity there can be no question: in the Claimants'
awards of Edward's authority, in his title to the castles of Scotland, in the
oath taken by magnates and freeholders, all in June–July 1291. The minute
for 12 August 1291 has the Claimants compear before Edward 'superior
lord', and this style alone recurs in the minutes from 14 October to
20 November 1292.[15] It is unbelievable that Edward I would accept Balliol's
fealty to him as 'superior lord', as he did on 20 November 1292, if he claimed
a fuller title, yet 'superior' alone is quoted here not only in the minute but
also in Caen's Great Roll.[16] This evidence seems to me incontrovertible:
during 1291 and 1292 Edward called himself 'superior lord' of the kingdom,
and nothing else.

When Scotland acquired her own king again, Edward I set about
demolishing the limitations on his authority which he had accepted in
June 1291, notably the promise that cases relating to Scotland would not be
heard outside that kingdom. In the critical appeal of Roger Bartholomew
(7 December 1292), he referred to the king's appointment of auditors of
causes in Scotland (in 1291) in terms which surely cried out for some such

---

[14] There are exceptions in Scotland in 1291, where he is called 'chief lord', which I discuss
later. They do not affect the argument here.

[15] Stones and Simpson, ii, 148, 230, 231, 232, 233, 234, 240, 243, 244, 247, 252, 254.

[16] Stones and Simpson, ii, A.113–A.116.

phrase as 'when he was direct lord', and we read of 'while the kingdom was in his hands by reason of his superior lordship of the same kingdom'; Edward was not bound by promises made *nuper vacante regno Scocie*.[17] 'Superior lord' continued in use in the king's style in letters to Scotland during the reign of King John, and is last found on 6 March 1296; on 15 April, ten days after John's renunciation of homage, it had disappeared, and thereafter in letters, even to Scotland, no reference was made in the royal style to overlordship.[18]

The task of explaining Balliol's fate was committed to the notary John of Caen, and his draft instrument, the first known essay for the Great Roll, survives. It covers 17 November 1292–96 and in it Edward I is still only *superior dominus*, but in a later addition, he has become 'superior and direct lord'. The date of Caen's work drafting this instrument was after the appointment of a Guardian, a treasurer and other officials, but not a chancellor, that is between 8 September and 2 October 1296; the 'and direct' paragraph was added thereafter, probably before the end of 1296.[19] Yet the Great Roll with its copies of short instruments is replete with references to Edward in 1291–92 as 'superior and direct lord', almost invariably the style given there to the king. The exception is texts quoted *in extenso*, for example the Award of Norham and the only two letters of Edward I quoted, both of 19 November 1292,[20] which retain 'superior lord(ship)'. Otherwise, as early as 10 May 1291, and regularly until January 1293, he is said to act by virtue of 'superior and direct lordship'. The introduction of this style must be ascribed to October 1296 or later,[21] when the short instruments and the Great Roll were compiled.

The editors rightly suggested that 'direct lord' showed the influence of Roman law upon Edward's notaries and that 'direct lordship' is used in the records in the sense evolved by thirteenth-century glossators of Roman law, of whom the greatest, Accursius, had acted for Edward I before the parlement of Paris. *Dominium directum* expresses the rights of the lord of a fief, contrasted with *dominium utile*, the rights enjoyed by the possessor of the

[17] *dominus rex, superior dominus regni Scotie, dum idem regnum in manum suum ratione superioritatis dominii sui eiusdem regni extitisset*; Stevenson, *Documents*, i, 377. *Nuper* ... Stones and Simpson, ii, 266. For the current style, *et soverein seignur de Escoce*, interlined on a draft of 4 January 1293, PRO, C47/22/12 (18), which, the editors note, was possibly written by Caen; Stones and Simpson, ii, 274.

[18] *Rot. Scot.*, i, 1–22. These are letters sent from the English chancery. After 1296 there was a separate Scottish administration, which used the same style as that used in England, Stevenson, *Documents*, ii, 244, no. 484, of 23 November 1296 (not 1297). Since the *regnum Scotie* was still referred to until 1303–4, *Dominus Hibernie et Scotie* was not an option; see Edward I's 1298 seal, Birch, *History of Scottish Seals*, i, 39.

[19] Palgrave, *Docs. Hist. Scot.*, no. 43, the addition on p. 151; *Cal. Pat. Rolls, 1292–1301*, 196; *Rot. Scot.*, i, 29–30, (chancellor) 35.

[20] Stones and Simpson, ii, A.111.

[21] The matter is discussed in Stones and Simpson, i, 120–22, but the editors, pursuing Sir James Ramsay, miss its significance, assuming that the usage was haphazard from 1291.

fief; 'the distinction in these terms [the editors say] is alien to English law'.[22] In the 1301 French draft of a letter from Edward I to Boniface VIII, the king's right in Scotland was asserted to be *par droit de seigneurie de tres anciens temps*; when his notaries wrote the Latin version, this became 'the right of superior and direct lordship', an indication of the duty of a notary to use Latin familiar to the recipient reader.[23] But in the parallel letter of the English barons to Boniface, English kings had had superior and direct lordship and had been 'in possession or quasi-superiority and direct lordship of [it] at successive times'.[24] Here possession, effectively Roman *dominium utile*, is equated with 'direct lordship', which is used in the English sense of 'immediate authority', not in its Roman sense. 'Direct rule' (to use a familiar modern parallel) after 1296, when King John resigned to Edward I 'the land of Scotland with all the people and all their homages',[25] may have been another reason for retrospectively stressing its existence in 1291–92, for Edward's direct authority then could seem to justify his exercising it again after 1296.

There is, however, one non-notarial text of mid-1292 which used the style 'superior and direct lord': the stated case submitted in 1292 to Paris lawyers. Although this survives only in manuscripts of the fourteenth century, some descend from a text preserved in Scotland, probably since 1292, and are unlikely to have tinkered with the wording about 'a king who holds his kingdom of another king for homage in feu as of a superior and direct lord'. Although the lawyers' responses use only 'superior', without 'direct' (three times),[26] 'superior and direct' was original to the text of the stated case. Its appearance here is understandable, for the notaries were sending from the Berwick environment of English law and its simpler relative, Scots law, to Paris, where civilian law-books were a frequently studied authority.[27]

'Direct lord' in civilian law schools expressed the same idea of over-lordship as 'superior lord' in English or Scots law,[28] and was therefore appropriate to describe the king's status in the case put to the lawyers of 1292. Otherwise it was inserted into Edward's style for 1291–92 retrospectively in 1296–97 and later. We cannot know whether Caen, who was evidently responsible for the expanded style, took his inspiration from the

---

[22] Stones and Simpson, i, 121; ii, 11n.; Reynolds, *Fiefs and Vasssals*, 255, 287, 392.

[23] *Anglo-Scottish Relations*, no. 30, p. 193.

[24] *Foedera*, i, 927.

[25] Stones, *Anglo-Scottish Relations*, no. 24.

[26] *a quodam alio rege ut superiori et directo domino eiusdem regni, pro homagio tenens in feodum.* Stones and Simpson, ii, 359, 362 line 11, 363 line 10 and bottom line; *Scotichronicon*, vi, 10, 22 (line 16). There is a brief discussion in Reynolds, *Fiefs and Vassals*, 392–93. The case sent to Paris was presumably intended for those skilled in the *Libri Feudorum.*

[27] Reynolds, *Fiefs and Vassals*, 321, citing Fournier, *Histoire de la science du droit*, which I have not seen.

[28] Feenstra, 'Les origines du *dominium utile* chez les glossateurs', *Fata Ivris Romani*, 226–59.

1292 stated case, which he certainly knew and might even have drafted, or took it from his stock of notarial rhetoric in 1296 as a relevant way of linking lordship in 1291–92 to that of 1296 and later.

There are inconsistent texts. In the fealties as recorded in the Great Roll, Edward is 'superior and direct lord' so this instrument was drawn up in 1296–97; but in the adminstrative memorandum about receiving fealties, made by the king at Stirling, probably on 12 July 1291, 'superior lord' in the heading fits the date, but the text itself requires fealty to the king, as 'superior and direct lord', surely an 'improvement' for the instrument.[29] There were two short instruments which were contemporary, not later confections, A.79 and D.123. The first, A.79, like A.48 (which it follows in the Great Roll), is contemporary with 1291–92, but as quoted in the Roll mentions both 'superior' and 'superior and direct' lordship. Under a heading, 'the tenor of a certain protest made by the king of England and superior lord', is the copy of a notarial instrument dated 3 July 1292 and therefore out of chronological place, the preamble describing Edward I as 'superior lord', followed by the sense (*sentencialiter intellectum*) of a protest made by him in French. In its course he reserves his rights of 'superior and direct lordship' and what pertained to him as 'superior lord', namely that once Scotland had a king he would not be bound by his [1291] promise to hear cases in Scotland, an outburst so important that Caen made it the subject of a short notarial instrument at the time.[30] The erratic single use of 'superior and direct' here was an 'improvement' on the original short instrument.

D.123, dated 27 December 1292, was handed over to the Exchequer on 16 January 1293,[31] and thus was certainly contemporaneous with the events it records. In it the Scots asked Edward I to keep his promise not to hear Scottish cases in England and Brabazon responded for Edward that this promise was for the time when the kingship was vacant and that [thereafter] he would exercise his superior lordship in appeals from Scotland. The right to hear appeals was supremely important to Edward I, and when D.123 was incorporated into the Great Roll, its date of 27 December in the docquet was ignored. It is likely that the Scottish plea took Edward's council by surprise and that Brabazon's response was less cogent than the instrument pretends, for the Roll has him renew it on 31 December (probably in the fully worked-out form), followed (as in A.79) by an outburst in French by Edward asserting his rights in no uncertain terms.[32] In D.123 there is mention only of 'superior lordship', and the Roll version of it, A.123, an exact copy, preserves this phrase. But Edward's speech, recorded only in the Roll,

[29] Stones and Simpson, ii, A.48, but I found it easier to see what Caen was doing by using here *Foedera*, i, 773–74.

[30] Stones and Simpson, ii, A.79. The original instrument does not survive.

[31] Stones and Simpson, i, 275–76

[32] Stones and Simpson, ii, A.123, A.124.

asserts his *superioritas et directum dominium*; whatever the 1292 record of this speech, it was updated in 1296–97, the usual practice of Caen in the Great Roll.

These two short instruments, A.79 and D.123, were the only notarial instruments known to have been drawn up by Caen in 1291–92, and both were concerned with the king's rights as overlord after the end of the Cause. Edward I knew exactly the significance of his protests recorded in these texts – that when the Cause was completed, these rights would be unfettered. Months before the Great Cause was terminated, and probably from 1289, this was his sole long-term interest in the affairs of Scotland, and the oral statement of his position, called forth by circumstances on 3 July 1292 (to which we shall come in their due place), and on 27 December 1292 had to be given public record of the most solemn kind available – a notarial instrument. After 1296 both A.79 and D.123 were copied in the Great Roll; to have omitted either would have weakened the force of Edward's denunciation, and Balliol's renunciation, of Edward's promises on 27, 31 December 1292 and 2 January 1293, with which the Great Roll ends.[33]

The other two short instruments by Caen, cited by the editors as suggesting a corpus of lost short instruments, belong together, but not with the two just discussed, for they are of later date. That of 20 November 1292 records the fealty of King John to Edward I, that of 26 December his homage.[34] They are not quoted as instruments in the Great Roll, but the transaction they record is there as letters of King John narrating the fealty or homage, from which short instruments and Roll would both be derived. Both instruments preserve the oath as to a 'superior lord' but the preamble to that of 26 December says it was an oath to a 'superior and direct' lord, so both, executed about the same time, belong, with the short instruments for 10 May – 13 June 1291, to 1296–98. They did not exist in 1291–92.

Why were the short instruments and the Great Roll compiled? Notaries public were a recent and exotic addition to means of recording in Britain. They came with papal legates and stayed on in the ecclesiastical courts, though even there they were used only rarely and particularly where contention might rise to the papal curia.[35] The 1287 treaty of Oloron with Aragon was denounced by the pope,[36] but when the two kings made terms in 1288 at Canfranc, their notaries, including John of Caen, recorded the agreement in instruments and Caen took it to Rome in 1289, when it was approved.[37] In October 1290 he notarised a royal speech protesting the intention to go timeously to the Holy Land as had been promised when the

---

[33] Stones and Simpson, ii, A.123–A.127.
[34] Stones and Simpson, ii, D.113.i; D.119.i; preserved in transcripts of 1298.
[35] Cheney, *Notaries Public*, chs 1–3.
[36] *Foedera*, i, 677–78, discussed in Prestwich, *Edward I*, 324.
[37] *Foedera*, i, 685, 687–92, 695; *Rôles Gascons*, ed. Bemont, ii, nos 1158, 1160.

pope granted a tenth for six years.[38] John of Caen was a royal notary, called upon when Edward presented his acts in a favourable light at the papal curia.[39]

In the 1301 arguments prepared by the Scots for the curia, Edward I, they said, had become *de facto* overlord with help from part of the Scottish nobles:

> and although, as a support to the kingdom, the Roman church had been named as lady (*domina*) of the kingdom in his presence, nevertheless he did not admit a claim of this kind, but rather is reported to have said before many (so he may never go back on his words) that 'if that Roman priest wished to say anything to him on behalf of the freedom of Scotland so far as it concerned him, he would have to come to London and put it forward before him there'.[40]

This was a remarkable contrast to the dossier of chronicle extracts and document-citations prepared in 1291, which happily summarised five papal bulls supporting English claims, and which may have suggested to the Scots invoking the authority of the Roman church in a desperate attempt to stave off that of the English crown. For when Edward's concessions to the Scots were engrossed in an inspeximus by two Scottish bishops on 14 June 1291,[41] it was surely with the intention of obtaining a papal confirmation to make them binding under ecclesiastical penalties. No such confirmation is known, and the Scots may have received the same brush-off from the pope as did Edward when he sent the submission of the Claimants (the Award of Norham) to the curia for papal confirmation. Nicholas IV would not derogate from the rights 'of anyone and especially the right which the Roman church has in that kingdom', a forewarning of the argument which the Scots came to use forcefully, though it had even less historical justification than King Edward's claim.[42]

The death on 4 April 1292 of Nicholas IV and the ensuing vacancy until the election of the hermit Celestine V (pope for only five months) on 5 July 1294 removed the threat of papal interest for that interim. But in July 1294 Edward I had just renounced his homage to the French king and expected the Scots to contribute men to his war. He alienated the quiescent Scots and identified a possible ally for them – France – at the very time when a Scottish

---

[38] *Foedera*, i, 741.

[39] The best account of John of Caen is in Cheney, *Notaries Public*, Appendix I, but see also Chaplais, *Essays in Medieval Diplomacy and Administration*, XXII, 170–71.

[40] *Scotichronicon*, vi, 159–61, 177; *Chron. Picts-Scots*, 261–62; from the *processus* and *instructiones* used by the Scots at the curia; they are placed in context by Goldstein, 'The Scottish Mission to Boniface VIII in 1301 …', *SHR*, lxx (1991), 1–15.

[41] Stones and Simpson, ii, D.40.

[42] Stones and Simpson, ii, D.70. It is not known whether Edward sent the text in a notarial instrument.

appeal to the papacy became possible. King John, 'by advice of his mad baronage', urged the pope (who never left the kingdom of Naples) that the kingdom should be held of the Holy See, and that his homage to the English king, done against his will, should be annulled; Celestine V, a political innocent, granted the annulment,[43] a critical step which destroyed the moral force of the oaths given by the Scots to the English king. The papal bull was probably received in Scotland early in 1295, whereupon the Scots made a formal alliance with Philip IV, not revealed to the English king. Only about March 1296 did the Scots (not King John) at last tell him that they owed him no obedience because Celestine V had absolved them from the fealty and homage extorted by his power.[44]

Without coming to London, the Roman priest had unravelled the complex concessions of Norham in June 1291, and in 1296 Edward, enforcing his rights by keeping the kingdom of his rebellious liege-man John Balliol, must not merely ignore that papal act, but also ensure that the new pope, Boniface VIII, did not renew it if importuned.[45] Between 1292 and 1296 there was no English need and no occasion for notarial instruments of the procedings of 1291–92, but in 1296 that situation changed drastically. The Scots may have been in no position to raise their case with Boniface, but their ally, Philip IV, was not constrained in the same way, and was well served by lawyer-advisers who would exploit any weakness of Edward I.[46] John of Caen's job was to prepare against papal interest a notarial record of the evidence for the subordination of the Scots and of King John, 'proving' that Edward became overlord rightfully, without fear, by acceptance, followed by 'facts' showing the overlord's careful treatment of relevant competing claims, and his judgement in favour of Balliol as *fidelis* with appropriate obligations to his lord. Hence the Great Roll, truly the Great Illusion, inflated with rhetoric, riddled with suppressions, misstatements and chronological absurdities.[47]

So what of the Norham instrument, that record of the tussle over overlordship, 10 May – 13 June 1291, derived from the short instruments? When

---

[43] No text of the bull of Celestine V is extant, but there is every reason to trust the hostile account of the episode in *Chron. Langtoft*, ii, 220–23; *Chron. Guisborough*, 270; *Eulogium Historiarum*, iii, 158–59.

[44] *Chron. Guisborough*, 270.

[45] Celestine V was a simple hermit, under whom papal business became disordered; he resigned the papacy. His successor, Boniface VIII, revoked his acts relating to benefices, the religious and other ecclesiastical matters, but not acts like the absolution of the Scottish king. *Chron. Cotton*, 265–71; *Registres de Boniface VIII*, eds Thomas and others, i, no. 770 (8 April 1295). Celestine was canonised under Clement V.

[46] The *différand* between Philip IV and Boniface VIII in 1302–3 has obscured the fact that they were allies from early 1297, and that during their dispute in 1296, Edward I was a much stronger opponent of Boniface. Bautier, 'Le jubilé romain de 1300 et l'alliance franco-pontificale', *Le Moyen Age*, lxxxvi (1980), 189–216, also as no. IX in his *Études sur la France capétienne*.

[47] See the comment in Clanchy, *From Memory to Written Record*, 305.

Caen chose to transcribe these for his Great Roll and not their derivative, the Norham instrument, the latter almost certainly did not then exist; it was a later edition of the short instruments. This editing was not haphazard, but removed or greatly diminished the role of one group: the Claimants, especially Edward the Claimant. In both versions they were interrogated on 2 June equally fully, but for 3 June and thereafter material relating to them in the Norham instrument was significantly reduced: the text of the Award of Norham by the Claimants, the appointment of auditors and all that related to the forthcoming Cause were omitted. The result is an instrument which records the acceptance of Edward's overlordship from the first claim on 10 May to the fealties of 13 June and largely ignores the kingship of the Scots. The omission of all dates from the narrative might suggest the holes in it, but the diary of dates and places at the end masks the lacunae.

For the most part it is no more seriously misleading than the Great Roll. And it has two notable additions, the admission that in June the Scots' community did produce a response to Edward's claim, and, near the end, a full, if edited ('and direct'), version of the 13 June oath of fealty given by the Scots,[48] to show their treachery. This oath is clumsily introduced by *sub hac forma ... videlicet*, a fair indication that its text is an addition.[49] The mention of an invalid response having been received from the Scots (i.e. on 1 June) is so curt as to seem pointless – unless it was introduced to dismiss a Scottish allegation that their community had indeed responded, an allegation perhaps made to Boniface VIII in 1297–98, before the bull *Scimus fili*, when Edward's right to judge, not the substance of his judgement, was under attack. The Norham instrument, which uses 'superior and direct lord' consistently, was later, not earlier, than the Great Roll. For that reason it figures but little in what follows.

Some notarial compression is understandable. But it bears repetition that the Roll is mostly, the short instruments and Norham instrument are wholly, about Edward's overlordship, in a tendentious narrative in which events of June 1291 were subjected to drastic revision to remove the resistance of the Scots and the ambiguous formula by which Edward obtained custody of the kingdom. Instead, in the short instruments speeches asserting his lordship were tediously repeated, and Scottish acceptance of it implied by bringing forward the setting up of the court. If there was interest in the pleadings or the Cause on the part of those who commissioned the Roll, that interest was limited to the justice of Edward's judgement for Balliol – and Balliol's acceptance of subordination. These were documents for the later 1290s, distantly, if at all, related to what went on in 1291–92. I now turn to the detail of May–June 1291.

Save in the two instances where the Norham instrument preserves some-

---

[48] Stones and Simpson, ii, C.10, C.35. I discuss the oath of 13 June below, pp. 251–52.
[49] Stones and Simpson, ii, C.35.

thing additional, the Great Roll's short instruments are our only guide when the Glasgow MS fails us. Thus the Roll has adjournment on 10 May to the next day, with a further adjournment then of three weeks from 10 May, when the Scots should produce written evidence against overlordship; the Norham instrument ignores the day's adjournment. On 2 June the short instrument states that nothing was produced against Edward's claim by the prelates and magnates which might delay or prevent the exercise of his overlordship – which does not deny a response but insists that there was nothing measuring up to the criteria set by Edward.[50]

The three weeks from Thursday, 10 May would expire on Thursday, 31 May, the day when Edward I issued to the Scots letters of safe conduct (to last until 10 June) and 'no prejudice';[51] both adjournment and these letters show that he expected the Scots to return on 1 June. The discrepancy is only one day, but that is not negligible; there is reason to believe that the Scots did indeed return to Upsetlington on 1 June, having spent the intervening period probably at Berwick but possibly at Edinburgh. For despite the safe conduct of 31 May to enter England, the business of 2 and (partly) 3 June, according to the Great Roll, was done at Upsetlington in Scotland.[52] The Scots must have refused to cross the Tweed, when, by implication, they expected the English to come to them; the notary did not report the frustration of his master on 1 June.

But that was not all that he suppressed. The response by the Scots to Edward's claim is preserved only in the Glasgow MS where the rubric says it was 'made and given to the king of England by the *hauts hommes descoce*', a contemporary English description of the Scottish political community also used in the rubric to Brabazon's address and in Edward's letters of 'no prejudice' on 10 and 31 May. But Brabazon had addressed the Scots at Norham on 10 May as *bone gent* and the text of their response uses the same term for them and for the Scots 'who have sent us here' and who 'answer you'; *bone gent* was a Scottish usage, was well understood by the English and was equivalent to, or comprehended, *hauts hommes*. Caen in his Norham instrument addition to the short instrument acknowledged that a response was 'made and given in writing in name of the community of the realm', but that there was no reply from the prelates and magnates – a dishonest evasion, for English clerks wrote of *les hauts homes ... et une partie de la communauté* as two contrasting social groups, knew that *hauts homes* were the magnates, and could see that the reply does not mention 'community'.[53]

[50] Stones and Simpson, ii, A.13, p. 36.

[51] *Foedera*, i. 774; Stones and Simpson, ii, D.8; *Cal. Pat. Rolls, 1281–1292*, 429. The text of the letters of 'no prejudice' enrolled and in the Glasgow MS (fo. 5v) was the French text of 10 May, with new date.

[52] Stones and Simpson, ii, A.2.ii–A.18; C.2.ii–C.14. Tang's instruments do give the meeting as 2 June, at Upsetlington.

[53] Stones and Simpson, ii, D.10, *Anglo-Scottish Relations*, no. 16, for the response; D.3.i,

But the Norham instrument places acknowledgment of the Scottish response not at the meeting with the Scots on 2 June, but *before* it: 'when the term [end of three weeks] came, a written response having been made and given ... the prelates [etc.] meeting again in the meadow...'[54] The answer would be 'made and given' on 1 June, at Upsetlington, when the Scots refused to cross the Tweed. That fits with the response itself, cast in the same form and language (French) as Brabazon's speech of 10 May, to which it refers with variations from Brabazon's written text, which was apparently not available to the Scots. Perhaps because of that, they sought to employ the same tactic, an oral message on the deliberations and decisions of the *bone gent*, 'made' to 'you' who had claimed overlordship – to Edward I. The text must have been what the Scots intended to say orally to the king, having brought him as guest, not overlord, into Scotland; it was probably read to the agent who took his place. Edward could not accept that status, just as the Scots could not enter England at his bidding. Their script was 'given' (because the Glasgow MS has it), to the same unknown agent, and brought Burnell to Upsetlington the next day, 2 June.

That there was not a more violent reaction may be attributed to the moderation of the text which summarised the message of Brabazon delivered at Norham on 10 May (I give the essentials): 'you say you are overlord and asked the good folk at Norham to adhere to you as such; you will maintain them in peace according to the laws and customs of Scotland; nobody should be disinherited, therefore the Claimants should show the right of each in your presence, and you will show your right; you will give justice to each by your advice and that of the good folk of the kingdom'.[55] At no point was that claim rebutted or rejected, which, it was admitted, had the strength of Edward's conviction. Caen was misleading but not lying when the Great Roll claimed that nothing was shown to impede the exercise of Edward's overlordship.

It makes no mention of Brabazon's insistence on the dangers of civil war since 1286, but does introduce new points not mentioned by Brabazon: the laws and customs of Scotland, and the king's own claim. The former was probably slipped in by the Scots to recall the promises at Northampton in 1290 in which the phrase figures, and later the Northampton treaty was explicitly invoked in the response. Edward's own claim does not figure in Burnell's supposed speeches of 2 June, but in those of 3 June, one by Burnell, the other by the king, Edward's right to prosecute his 'hereditary right' to the *proprietas* of the kingdom, 'as one among other' Claimants is

Anglo-Scottish Relations, no. 15 for Brabazon's speech; Stones and Simpson, ii, C.10 for the Norham instrument.

[54] Stones and Simpson, ii, 30, 32. My English summary omits much verbiage in order to show the tenses.

[55] Stones and Simpson, ii, D.10; *Anglo-Scottish Relations*, no. 16.

reserved at the end of each rigmarole.[56] The mention in their response shows that the Scots must have heard of this claim on 10–11 May; the 2–3 June speeches were Caen's invention, but confirm that Edward I intimated an intention to claim the Scottish throne for himself.

Having stated their understanding of Edward's claim of 10 May, the Scots' response went on to evade it. They denied knowledge of his right and any power to respond to his statement of it for lack of a lord to whom it should be made. If they were to accept it, that would neither help Edward nor damage their liege lord. 'He who shall be king' should do what reason and justice demanded in the matter, for he alone has power to act in it. They then emphasised their oath of 1286 as an obstacle to any other answer and mentioned also 'your deed and theirs', the recognition of a free and separate kingdom, sworn to by Edward at Northampton on 28 August 1290, as another obstacle. This emphasis upon oaths is particularly striking and suggests that the Scots imagined that Edward, bound by a Crusader's vow, would recognise the force in all oaths, his and theirs.

It has been remarked that the Scottish claim to have 'no knowledge of your right, nor did they ever see it claimed and used by you and your ancestors' ignores the 1278 episode when homage was undoubtedly claimed. It is likely that the Scots were being disingenuous here. The homage of 1278 is found in both English and Scottish chronicles, but they are few and make no mention of the claim to homage for Scotland. Only one Scot certainly accompanied the king then, Robert Bruce earl of Carrick, who was not sympathetic to the Scottish position in 1291.[57] The Scottish disclaimer in 1291 may well have been honest, but a slanted account of the homage was given to the pope in 1298–99, suggesting that it was known and that the key defence in 1291 was 'claimed *and used*'.[58]

From the weakness of their response it is evident that the Scots still hoped to draw on the *bone voluntee* which, they admitted, Edward had shown to the kingdom, for they ended by begging Edward to 'act' in a way which did not throw them into disgrace; they confessed a willingness to accommodate him, as always. These studiously vague words, taken with the intended context, that they were to be delivered to the king himself, in Scotland, surely meant that the Scots still wanted him to act as arbiter between their two claimants. By sending only messengers (in whatever numbers and of whatever standing is unknown) to Upsetlington they hoped to escape negotiations on the claim to overlordship and to conduct him to their

---

[56] *Proprietas* was a term in civil law; according to the glossators, with usufruct it made up *dominium*. It may here be used with the same meaning as *dominium directum*. Willoweit, 'Dominium und Proprietas', *Historische Jahrbuch*, xciv (1974), 131–56, esp. 141–44.

[57] Alexander took a harper and trumpeters to the English court, however; *Cal. Docs. Scot.*, ii, no. 131.

[58] The point made in *Anglo-Scottish Relations*, 109 and n. 4; for 1299, 164–65.

assembly. Their desperation was not ignoble, but it surely clouded their judgement.

In fact Edward I set about achieving overlordship and possession of Scotland, which he did some ten days later on 13 June 1291. His own claim was by heritable right,[59] by descent from Maelcoluim III. Manifestly there were better claims, so that the hope of gaining the Scottish throne can scarcely have been Edward's motive. Until 10 May there was a well-known schedule of Claimants with but two names, Bruce and Balliol, for there is no hint of another until that moment, and how he could pursue his claim in front of himself as judge was never put to the test, but his position as Claimant was bowdlerised in the instruments with their tally of thirteen Claimants; there were fourteen and the master among them was Edward I. He had already taken steps to enliven other Claimants, so that in June some nine names could be mustered without the king. Arbitration, which was possible only between two parties, thereby ceased to be an option. Edward's claim gave him a place at this stage among the Claimants; he managed them, perhaps not by plan in May, but once it became clear in June that the Scots could be required to submit if, collectively, the Claimants submitted.

That the Scots met Burnell at Upsetlington on 2 and 3 June is likely, but the matter of their discourse is not conveyed by his rhetoric in the instruments, where on 2 June Burnell lectured on Edward's position, then by question and answer (Bruce, Florence and Hastings in direct speech) eight Claimants accepted his overlordship; thereupon Sir Thomas Randolph rose and excused his lord, John Balliol, for failure to compear, asking that he be admitted the following day. In the next instrument, for 3 June at Upsetlington, Burnell's speech was repeated before he turned to question Balliol, quoted as direct speech. Balliol, after appropriate deliberation, accepted Edward as overlord before whom he would pursue his case; a notarial docquet gives place and date. Then in the third instrument, for on the same day but in Norham church (Plate 7), Burnell repeated his lecture on Edward's position, at the end of which Edward himself delivered a version of it; thereafter Balliol approached and accepted Edward's lordship, followed by John Comyn,[60] and the Claimants drew up and sealed the Award of Norham, which is quoted. Balliol, Bruce and Edward I agreed the make-up of the court (40:40:24 nominees), to be named on 5 June; the docquet follows. There is no instrument for 4 June (that is, the award of sasine on the day after the Award of Norham is ignored),[61] but, in two instruments, on

[59] Stones and Simpson, ii, A.18, A.110.

[60] *Scots Peerage*, i, 508. Stones and Simpson, ii, A.62 is the text of Comyn's claim, ending *et non vult quod istud cedat in prejudicium Johanni de Balliolo ullo modo*. A.21, and B.21, claim, surely falsely, that forty auditors were to be named by Balliol and Comyn, though B.24 has Balliol alone nominating. Comyn assisted Balliol in finding auditors.

[61] Tang, who compiled one daily instrument for each of these days, wrote two for 4 June,

5 June the three produced their 104 names and on 6 June the king asked the Claimants to name place and time for the hearing; they chose Berwick, but, disagreeing on time, left it to the king to fix 2 August 1291.[62]

Common sense must undermine a narrative devoted to wordy repetition of one position, lacking any suggestion that it was contested by the Scots. The submission of eight Claimants to Burnell, but Balliol to the king, is an unlikely distinction – all would surely submit to the king – which reflects the concerns of 1296 with Balliol's 'betrayal' of his oaths. The contemporary records include the Award of Norham which is self-dated 5 June and cannot possibly belong to 3 June. The composition of the court reflects the Scottish position that there were only two serious claimants, so is improbable on a day when nine Claimants were registered, and many of those named as auditors on '5 June' had not yet accepted Edward's lordship, surely an essential prerequisite for such service.

In fact there is no reason why the Scots should have crossed the Tweed to meet Edward on 3 June, for, even in Caen's narratives, they had not accepted overlordship and were nine days away from doing so. And if they had remained at Upsetlington, Caen would have invented an occupation for them; it seems that from a break on 3 June the two sides considered the situation apart, at Berwick and Norham, though Count Florence, Bruce, Hastings and four minor Claimants would be found at Norham, willing to accept Edward's lordship. With all the proceedings on 2 and 3 June, the instruments claim that the speeches and submissions were made in the presence of the prelates, magnates and community of Scotland, a claim not found in the awards, of overlordship on 5 June and of sasine on 6 June, while Edward's letter of 6 June, preserved only in the Glasgow MS, spoke of the Scots asking for his promise of their laws and customs but did not suggest that he was acceding in their presence. The awards and letter were contemporary, the notarial records were not. The Scottish presence in any numbers is fiction.

The short instrument's account that Randolph put in a plea for Balliol's later admission, and Balliol's compearance the following day, is, however, convincingly circumstantial. It has Randolph assert that Balliol had the stronger claim, which he may have done, as might all Claimants.[63] But the dating ascribed to these events is not convincing. Balliol's submission, a reluctant one the instrument suggests, probably correctly, completed a roll-call which allowed Edward to secure the awards, sealed on 5–6 June. That means that Balliol submitted not on 2 or 3 June, but no earlier than 5 June. The excuse assigned to Balliol, that he did not know the time appointed,

quoting the award of sasine. He clearly thought that Caen should have included this day, or that Caen had done so, but that his instrument was lost.

    [62] Stones and Simpson, ii, A.17–A.27. Probably they disagreed with Edward I.
    [63] Stones and Simpson, ii, A.15, C.17. The phrase used here, *pinguius ius*, is also used in the *Gest. Ann.* account of the establishment of the tribunal; *Chron. Fordun*, i, 313.

is disingenuous and probably fiction, for the record nowhere suggests that 2 June had been appointed as the day for submission, and we might also doubt that he and Comyn were the only Claimants whose submission was given to Edward in person, as the short instrument claims.

Recall that Caen's short instruments and his Great Roll were alike a justification compiled in 1296–97 of Edward I's treatment of the Scots and of their king, John Balliol. His generous act in 1291 in admitting Balliol after expiry of the due time, the report that Balliol had the best claim, and Balliol's acceptance of Edward's overlordship before the king in person, were highlighting by the notary against the grey background of the other Claimants and their claims, highlighting which prefigured the decision in Balliol's favour. As he alone claimed the best right, so he was chosen as having the best right; as a king who was to swear fealty to Edward I, he had as Claimant already accepted Edward's lordship in person; throughout Edward I had taken the correct decisions.

What had happened?[64] On Saturday, 2 and Sunday, 3 June the Scots refused to enter England, Edward to enter Scotland. Burnell came to Upsetlington and the claim and response would be debated fruitlessly. The Scots departed – for they surely did, they were, after all, only messengers – under unknown conditions, but Edward's court remained at Norham to plan the way forward through the Claimants. The Scots had placed responsibility for doing what reason and justice demanded upon 'him who shall be king', *celuy qui roy serra*, but without saying 'when he shall have become king'.[65] If Edward could secure the submission of the Claimants among whom the future king was to be found, he could require the community to bow to this acceptance by their 'lord' of his demand. He would also have been encouraged to think along these lines by Bruce, and later the Scots were to blame their submission upon a party of Scots who had no right to the throne – presumably Bruce and his supporters.[66] The problem for Edward was that the strongest Claimant in the eyes of many, John Balliol, was reluctant to join their number.

By 5 June, and perhaps long before, Bruce, Count Florence, Hastings and four minor figures were persuaded that they must accept Edward's over-lordship. Balliol (on whose whereabouts the sources are silent) would have foreseen this possibility and sent Randolph to protect his interests. For reasons at which the records do not even hint, but possibly a threat to proceed without Balliol, Randolph announced that his principal would

---

[64] In Duncan, 'Process of Norham', 219–20 I argued for redating Balliol's submission to 11 June; this drastic proposal ignores the testimony of the letter of 6 June, and is wrong.

[65] Stones and Simpson, ii, D.10; *Anglo-Scottish Relations*, no. 16. Elsewhere in the document the Scots refer to their king as 'liege lord' who might disinherit them if they gave any other answer.

[66] *Scotichronicon*, vi, 159, 177.

attend the following day and sent him word to do so. Clearly Balliol had not been at Upsetlington, whence he could have heard news and reached Norham church in a couple of hours. The delay implies a greater distance, while his appearance next day in company with John Comyn places them both as having been with the Scottish community, at Berwick.

Balliol's reluctance is hinted at, and he may have made a last plea for arbitration without overlordship, but, conscious of his solitary stance among the Claimants and perhaps threatened with exclusion from a judgement, he added his submission to that of the other Claimants, apparently at Upsetlington. Having secured this critical act, Burnell took Balliol and his group across the Tweed to Norham, where the submission was repeated to Edward I in person, and that of Comyn added.[67] If this desertion (if the term be not too strong) was venial, for Balliol had much to lose and knew Edward's masterful temper well, the loss of John Comyn, one of the Guardians, must have troubled the Scots greatly. We can only guess at his motives, but a belief in Balliol's right and a determination that the latter should not be displaced by Bruce were clearly important among them.

These nine Claimants (Pinkeny was not among them) executed the Award of Norham, dated 5 June, recognising that Edward should judge between them, as overlord, and the award of sasine, dated 6 June, recognising that Edward should have sasine of the kingdom,[68] with surety that he will return it to the successful Claimant within two months of judgement, saving Edward's right to homage. These two texts, each of which survives in two originals, were two stages of a single transaction, and were written and sealed at the same time.[69] There was a good reason why they should not be dated to the same day, for that would have left priority of execution unclear – an award of sasine which might have been executed before the award of lordship (the Award of Norham) would count for little. So the Award of Norham had to be dated on the day before the award of sasine, even though they were simultaneous acts. Both would be executed on 6 June, which, therefore, was probably the day of Balliol's and Comyn's submission.

This is confirmed by a letter of Edward of 6 June, which (it said) proceeded from the Claimants' awards of overlordship and of sasine, after which, at the request of the prelates, earls, barons and community of the realm of Scotland, he had granted that as long as the kingdom was in

[67] Stones and Simpson, ii, A.17, C.17, A.20, C.20.

[68] There has been debate about this point. The editors remarked that the Claimants did not *give* Edward sasine, for what they did not have they could not give; Professor Barrow pointed out that in his 6 June letter Edward I said that the Claimants 'have granted to us possession and sasine'. Stones and Simpson, i, 118–19; Barrow, *Bruce*, 334 n. 74. The verb here is *ottroiée*, in the *Anglo-Norman Dictionary*, 'grant, allow, permit, count upon, consent' – but not 'give'. I think that 'allowed' has the sense rather than 'granted', and that the words were chosen carefully because Edward's's'jurisdiction and his sasine did not come from the Claimants but from his overlordship.

[69] Duncan, 'Process of Norham', 230.

his hands, he would keep its rights, laws, franchises, usages and customs, both ecclesiastical and secular, heretofore kept. This recalls the assurances offered on 10 May,[70] but it is also a weak version of the general promise made at Northampton in 1290, that the rights, laws, franchises and customs of the kingdom should be kept, wholly and inviolably, in and through everything, in perpetuity.[71] The letter went on to reserve to the king the homage of 'him who will be king', and to reserve to the king and anyone else their future right to anything on the Border or elsewhere which was theirs heretofore;[72] this last is an exact quotation from the Northampton concessions and was probably common form with little specific significance in 1290 or 1291.

Nonetheless there can be little doubt that Edward was here responding to a Scottish request that the safeguards given at Northampton should be reaffirmed or confirmed in some way. The claim that this request was made after the Claimants' awards really does not bear examination, for the awards and the letter are clearly part of a single transaction at Norham on 6 June, and not one of these documents mentions the presence of Scottish magnates or community there. It seems likely therefore that between 2 and 5 June the Scots had asked for such a safeguard, and that a vaguer promise to maintain laws and customs so long as he held the kingdom was offered and tipped the balance in persuading Balliol and Comyn to travel up the Tweed and submit to Edward. Whether they were satisfied with the letter given must be an open question, but the Scots at Berwick certainly were not, for no castle, and therefore no sasine, was given to the king. On the other hand Edward had two problems: to persuade the Scots to let him have possession, and to establish who gave him that possession.

There was an unmistakeable logic in the Scottish position, that lordship was recognised by acts of a lord and his *fidelis*, and not by act of the men of that *fidelis*. What they probably had not anticipated was Edward's conjuring up the Claimants as a putative collective *fidelis* before the rightful individual had been identified. As such the Claimants had a role to play, and it was probably important that many were already subjects of the English king. In June 1291 only eleven Claimants were named; one, Edward I, presented himself as such on 10–11 May and again on 12 June. The rest were a motley group, five of wholly legitimate descent, five descended from (presumably) illegitimate royal daughters (Tables B and C, pp. 346–9).[73]

Of the legitimate Claimants there would certainly be no holding back Robert Bruce who, since early in 1291 had been urging Edward I to exercise

---

[70] Stones and Simpson, ii, 18, D.3.i: *Ne il ne entent rien pour prendre noun duement sur nulluy, ne nully droit delayer, ne nully fraunchise destourber ne amenuser, mes a touz faire droit come soverain.*

[71] Stevenson, *Documents*, i, 165.

[72] Stones and Simpson, ii, D.28

[73] For a fuller discussion of these Claimants, see my paper, 'Process of Norham'.

lordship and honour the Bruce claim;[74] he was now a very old man of about sixty-five or seventy. His seal urged 'Be fierce as a lion',[75] but his actions suggest that from 1286 he meant to be king, by hook or by crook, latterly by Edward I not by the Scottish community.

Florence count of Holland, descended from Ada, sister of King William and wife of Count Florence III, was son of Count William, king of the Romans in opposition to Frederick II from 1247, who was killed in 1256 by rebels when Florence was a year old.[76] From 1272 Florence wrestled with rebellions and difficult neighbours, and became familiar with arbitration by Edward I. Edward's daughter, Elizabeth, was affianced to his son, John, with a dowry of £12,500 sterling, owed by Edward when John arrived in England – which he had done in November 1290. In February 1291 Florence showed no sign of intending to visit England, but with a safe conduct dated 8 March he landed at Great Yarmouth in April–May with the Count of Cleves, going 'towards Scotland'.[77] He was at Norham by 16 May, when a writ of *liberate* ('pay') in his favour was issued (£1,000). Others followed on 26 September 1291 at Devizes (£2,500) and 20 June 1292 at Berwick (£1,250) – though getting payment on these was less easy.[78] Florence probably remained at Norham until mid-June 1291, to all intents and purposes Edward I's pensioner, willing to have his name used as Edward thought best.

John Balliol was probably about forty in 1291, fourth son of the late lord of Barnard Castle (his namesake) in county Durham (d. 1268), and of Dervorguilla, daughter and co-heiress of Alan lord of Galloway, but also of her mother, eldest daughter of David earl of Huntingdon. John was pretty certainly intended for the church and was literate, but must have returned to lay society when three older brothers died after their father. Two of these deaths (in 1272 and 1278) burdened the Balliol estates with widows' terces and reliefs, while his mother had her terce as well as her inherited lands until her death in January 1290. John had played some small part in Scottish affairs, for example sealing the *obligatorium* of 1284, but Galloway seems to have been his mother's business until 1290 and John 'remained an Englishman rather than a Scotsman'.[79]

---

[74] Stones and Simpson, ii, D.76(K).

[75] Macdonald, *Scottish Armorial Seals*, no. 270. For the career of Bruce V (the Claimant) before 1286, Duncan, 'Bruces of Annandale', *Transactions of Dumfriesshire and Galloway Natural History and Antiquarian Society*, lxix (1994), 94–99.

[76] *Krönungen*, i, 417–23 has a short well-illustrated account of William as king.

[77] *Oorkondenboek van Holland en Zeeland tot 1299*, iv, no. 2563; Stones and Simpson, i, 198–99; ii, 398.

[78] PRO C62/67 m.3, m.2; C62/68 m.4. In addition C62/67 m.4 shows a writ for £875 issued at Ashridge on 18 January 1291. Payments are in the issue rolls, PRO E403/66, E/403/70 and (for the £1,250) E403/74 and E403/1315. The editors used E403/70 (Stones and Simpson, ii, 399) but make no mention of these payments.

[79] Barrow, *Bruce*, 49 for the quotation; G. Stell, 'The Balliol family and the Great Cause of 1291–2', *Essays on the Nobility of Medieval Scotland*, ed. Stringer, 150–65 is invaluable. The relief on the death of the Lady Dervorguilla was assessed in 1293 at £3,290, which should have

He made no career in English royal administration, living as a country gentleman before seeking greatness as king of Scotland, then giving up the Scottish throne for some good hunting in 1296. On 5 and 9 May 1291 writs were issued to distrain all his goods and chattels in seven English counties for alleged debts of himself and his ancestors, amounting to £1,224. The timing of the demand, and the fact that it was suspended on 21 June 1291, after his acceptance of Edward's overlordship, speak volumes;[80] John Balliol behaved as a loyal subject of the English king.

John Comyn of Badenoch was descended from a presumably lawful daughter of Domnall III. His father had fought for Edward at Evesham in 1265 and been rewarded thereafter. John's age is unknown, but since he married the sister of John Balliol, and his son was active in 1298–99, he is likely to have been in his late forties in 1291. He had lands and castles in several sheriffdoms, including Dumfriesshire, as well as property in England, and was justiciar of Galloway, where his cousin and namesake, the earl of Buchan, was both sheriff and major landowner. John Comyn had been active politically under Alexander III and was dedicated now to the interests of John Balliol.[81]

Sir John Hastings, lord of Abergavenny, born in 1262, was descended from the youngest daughter of Earl David, and was the son of a supporter of Simon de Montfort, who had to redeem his lands after 1265 at heavy cost. He may have gone to Scotland in 1284, and served in Wales in 1287, but otherwise his career really begins with his appearance at Norham. His case surely stood a chance only if Edward were overlord.[82]

Of the five whose claim was tainted by illegitimacy, Vescy and Ros were northern English barons and Pinkeny held a barony in Northamptonshire;[83] Dunbar had recently succeeded his father and Nicholas de Soulis, claiming through his mother, had not yet succeeded to his father's heritage.[84] Thus by accepting Edward's lordship none of these broke the oath of 1286 (to preserve the royal dignity for the right heir), because none had taken it. They stood not the slightest chance of succeeding peaceably to the Scottish throne. True, the facts of descent over a century earlier, including illegitimacy, could be forgotten, and we have indeed little confirmation of the

---

been the annual value of her Scottish lands; *Cal. Docs. Scot.*, ii, nos 670–71. It is difficult to accept that she was so wealthy, especially after the endowment of a Cistercian abbey and an Oxford College.

[80] Stevenson, *Documents*, i, 225–27.

[81] Young, *Robert the Bruce's Rivals, The Comyns*, ch. 5.

[82] *CP*, vi, 346–49.

[83] For Vescy, *CP*, XII/2, 281–83 and below; for Ros, *CP*, XI, 96–97.

[84] Earl Patrick of Dunbar had died on 24 August 1289; his son was mature when he succeeded. *Scots Peerage*, iii, 258, 262. Thomas McMichael, 'The Feudal Family of de Soulis', *Trans. Dumfriesshire and Galloway Antiquarian and Natural History Soc.*, 3rd ser., xxvi (1947–48), 163–93, at pp. 173–74 for William de Soulis, who was an auditor named by Bruce and died by November 1293; at pp. 183–85 for his son and heir, Nicholas, who died in 1296.

descent claimed by some. Nonetheless the legitimate lines were well informed and unlikely to allow to others an unchallenged presumption of legitimacy. One group of Paris lawyers ruled out William de Ros because his royal ancestress had been legitimated, not born legitimate – without legitimation a weak claim became a hopeless one. And the lawyers did not bother with the representatives of the other illegitimate lines; they were no-hopers, and one might wonder why they submitted claims, unless King Edward had encouraged them.[85] That they did so lest in a future Great Cause non-participants in 1291 would be ruled out is a fairly remote possibility.

Pinkeny was not among the nine Claimants of the awards on 5–6 June, but was a Claimant before early August 1291.[86] When he died in 1296, he had demesne lands at Ballencrieff in East Lothian worth some £110 annually,[87] of which his brother and heir, Henry, was evidently his factor. Henry is twenty-third of the twenty-seven Scottish nobles who swore fealty to Edward I on 13 June 1291;[88] since that list includes the Claimants, Bruce, Balliol, Earl Patrick and John Comyn, the absence from it of Robert de Pinkeny confirms his absence from the Norham phase. He came to the Tweed after 12 June and was accepted as a Claimant later in June or, less probably, in July.

William de Vescy inherited his mother's lands in Ireland in 1290, was appointed justiciar there, landing on 11 November 1290 and did not return

[85] Stones and Simpson, ii, 362 at (v). Dr Paul Brand takes a less pessimistic view of the chances of illegitimate lines, particularly on the grounds that illegitimacy was easily forgotten and difficult to prove after the lapse of a century or more.

[86] Pinkeny's claim as recorded in the Great Roll (Stones and Simpson, ii, A.58) is confirmed back to 1249, when his grandmother, Alice, married Henry Pinkeny, their son being born probably in 1250 (CP, x, 521–25). Alice's mother in the claim, Margery, is documented as the wife of David de Lindsay, justiciar from c.1208 till his death before 1220; as a widow she founded the nunnery of Elcho, in this connection witnessing one of her son's charters (Dunfermline Registrum, no. 190). According to the claim Margery's father was Earl Henry (d. 1152), an impossibility which led Scots Peerage (iii, 6) to suggest instead one of two Henrys, illegitimate sons of Earl David (d. 1219). But these sons would be Margery's contemporaries, and it is much more likely that she was an illegitimate daughter of Earl David, in whose circle her husband moved (Stringer, Earl David, 157, 160, 170). Elcho lies in the Rhynd, at the confluence of Earn and Tay, where David I had land on which he sought unsuccessfully to establish a Cluniac cell; it is roughly equidistant between Earl David's known lands of Lindores (with Mugdrum island in the Tay) and the Inch of Perth. Elcho, I suggest, was also his, given to Margery as tocher on her marriage to David de Lindsay. The disappearance of Earl David from the pedigree in Pinkeny's claim could have been due to an omission in an early stage of the copying. There is a parallel in the loss of a generation from Count Florence's pedigree.

Sanders, English Baronies, 30, gives Eleanor as the mother of Alice de Pinkeny, but this is an error; Eleanor was her grandmother, mother of David de Lindsay. Dr Brand has given me confirmation in the pedigree enrolled in an eyre of 1285, PRO JUST 1/958, m.20d.

[87] Cal. Inquis. post mortem, iii, no. 366 for the full estate; Scottish details in Cal. Docs. Scot., ii, no. 857.

[88] Stones and Simpson, ii, 104.

to England till 1294.[89] He therefore appears in the awards as 'John de Vescy for his father'.[90] But the short instrument lists 'Walter de Huntercombe, procurator or attorney of William de Vescy for that William', as early as 2 June; in fact Huntercombe appeared on 25 June at Norham, not Berwick, seeking the parliament which had been adjourned; all the attendant circumstances suggest that the English government had a hand in de Vescy's submission and prompted the family to act in William's name. The lesson of Pinkney and Vescy is that Caen busied himself in 1296–97 tidying up events of 1291.

We not only have no contemporary documents from the days between 6 and 12 June but also no account from Caen's tidying pen of events until 11 June; even in their later exculpations the Scots offered only confused generalities about the events which led to Edward's obtaining possession of Scotland. The date 12 June saw the engrossment of new documents (the texts known from the Glasgow MS) which can only have been the outcome of negotiations, and a resolution accepted by the parties, though we do not know the whole truth of how this was achieved. We should neither rule out, nor blindly accept, that the parties negotiated on one side of, or across, the Tweed at Norham. The Claimants, or some of them, would be there, whence Balliol obtained a royal protection on 11 June for his men to buy provisions in England and Ireland.[91] The instruments claim that events occurred in the king's chamber of Norham Castle on 6 and 11 June, and we may take that as a hint that between those dates the English conducted a campaign from that room to overcome Scottish resistance. But we know only the outcome, in two 'obligatory letters' by Edward I with new promises, and in fourteen agreements with individual keepers of Scottish castles, all dated 12 June 1291.

In the first letter, because the Claimants, by assent of the Guardians and good folk of the realm, had allowed him overlordship and agreed to receive judgement before him, King Edward undertook to give 'them' judgement in Scotland and not elsewhere, until there was a king of Scotland. The assent of the Guardians and good folk is not mentioned in the Award of Norham and is fiction, but the wording here means that the 'them' of this promise extended to all Scottish cases coming before the king. Thus it recalled the promise at Northampton in July 1290 that no one of the Scottish kingdom would have to answer outside the realm in any action.[92] But it also recalls another promise of that document: that parliament touching the kingdom or its marches, or the standing of its inhabitants, be not held outside that

[89] *CP*, XII/2, 281–84; Stringer, 'Nobility and identity in medieval Britain and Ireland: the de Vescy family, *c.*1120–1314', *Britain and Ireland 900–1300*, ed. Smith, 199–239.

[90] On Vescy and Pinkeny and the sealing of the Awards, Duncan, 'Process of Norham', 216–17, 230.

[91] *CDS*, ii, no. 535, p. 130; *Cal. Pat. Rolls, 1281–1292*, 432; Stevenson, *Documents*, i, 236.

[92] Stones and Simpson, ii, D.33.i; Stevenson, *Documents*, i, 168–69.

kingdom.[93] The meeting summoned to Norham for 6 May was a parliament to deal with the Scottish kingdom and was adjourned to Berwick for the hearing of the Cause, which was certainly well within the Northampton definition of its business.

The second letter can be seen in two parts, the first half being the contents of the letter of 6 June, with additions from the award of sasine of the same day and hence a reaffirmation, but the rest is new and 'has many points of great interest'.[94] The promise in the first half to return kingdom and castles to the new king within two months of judgement would now carry sanctions of £100,000 for the crusade, and of papal excommunication and interdict, to all of which John de St John swore for the king. Save for this final oath, the text can be found with little difference as sanction at the end of the concessions promised by Edward at Northampton in July 1290.[95] Such sanctions were not uncommon in treaties, however, and by itself this borrowing would not establish a link with the earlier text. This was the nearest contemporaries could get to an international obligation, and may have impressed at the time, but precedents suggest that it was unlikely to be enforced.

There can be no doubt, however, that a clause from the Northampton concessions comes next, with additions italicised here: muniments touching the royal dignity of Scotland would be put in a secure place *agreed by the Claimants*, under the seals *of Edward's nominees and* of 'the greatest *and most loyal*' of the Scottish kingdom. There is no provision to return the muniments to the Scottish king, unlike Northampton which transferred them to the Maid and her husband. The amendments are all favourable to Edward, for 'most loyal' must mean 'loyal to the writer'. The king then acknowledged a request for a speedy decision 'from one (*aucun*) of the parties of the Claimants, that the hearing of their claim be continued from day to day and hastened so that the matter be not delayed'.[96] Although we cannot be certain, there is a high degree of probability that he who asked for no adjournments and for haste was Count Florence, anxious about his troublesome barons. Edward's accommodating response was bureaucrat-speak: 'our intention is appropriate speed ... as the nature of the business reasonably allows'. This does not seem to have arisen as a general request, and so owes nothing to the Northampton promises.

Finally the the king asserts (it is not a promise) that he and his heirs would not ask from future Scottish kings wardship, marriage or sasine of the kingdom during any future royal minority but only homage and what went

[93] Stevenson, *Documents*, i, 170.

[94] Stones and Simpson, ii, D.33.ii, English heading.

[95] Stevenson, *Documents*, i, 171–72.

[96] *daucun des parties des damaundantz que la conisance de lour demande feut continue de jour en jour et hastee si que la chose ne feust delaee.* A little later the letter has *Et si aucun ou aucuns autres* (for *aucun autre ou aucuns autres*).

with it and overlordship and what went with it; possession is limited but rights of overlordship carefully protected. Again this is probably rooted in the Northampton proviso that if the Maid or her husband died without heir, when the kingdom should be restored to the right heir, it would be restored to them if perchance it happened to come into Edward's hands. But on 12 June 1291 Edward also asserted that in any future claim on the kingdom the king and his heirs would have sasine and give justice as the right of an overlord,[97] a careful limitation which points unmistakeably to an overlord's right to hear judicial appeals.

Despite the claim of Edward's letter that the Claimants, Guardians and community asked for these assurances, it is likely that the only point made by a Claimant (probably Florence) was the need for a speedy resolution; the majority of Claimants would surely have preferred that the Cause be heard at Westminster. The promises were a price offered to the Scottish community, answering the concern or demand they conveyed to Norham castle: that the protection of their liberties, royal and private, promised at Northampton eleven months earlier should be renewed, presumably in a form appropriate to the new circumstances. If most of the clauses only hint at this demand, the provision for muniments about the royal dignity makes it explicit and, to my mind, certain.

There was another matter which had made the Northampton concessions a treaty: the Scots' promise to deliver the castles to the Maid and her husband. As we have seen, this issue had held up the conclusion of an agreement with Edward in 1290, and its resolution was less than what he wanted, immediate delivery of the castles into his hands to hold in the name of the young couple. And, sure enough, that is what he would have had if the award of sasine on 6 June had sufficed, for it allowed him possession and sasine *de tote la terre et des chasteaux* until a king was provided, not permanent, certainly, but a title to act as he did in 1296, requiring the handing over of three castles as surety that the king of Scots would jump at his lord's command. But from 6 June he had a parchment title to the castles without possession, until the resolution on 12 June which gave Edward the substance, possession, if the Scots kept a shadow in an agreed formula.

This agreement survives as fourteen versions of an agreement between the king and the Claimants (with agreement of the Guardians) on the one hand and each of fourteen keepers of twenty-two Scottish castles on the other, absolving the keeper for having surrendered his charge to Edward. They narrate that Edward had asked the keepers for the castles as overlord, and had been refused *after* the Claimants had accepted that lordship [on 5–6 June], but that on Thursday before St Barnabas [7 June] the castles were surrendered to Edward *as a Claimant on behalf of himself and his fellow Claimants*, as the rightful heritage of the Claimants and in accordance with

<hr />

[97] Stones and Simpson, ii, D.33.ii.

the oath taken [in 1286] 'to the nearest by blood who must inherit by law'. For this the keeper will suffer no distress in future, but the king and Claimants will warrant and defend him against any challenge. Each agreement was dated at Norham on 12 June, not by the saint's day.[98]

The emphasis upon the 1286 oath of the keepers shows that this warrandice was integral to the surrender, a condition without which they would not have given up their charges. The Scots had accepted the formula of concession to the Claimants, among whom was their king, as satisfying the demands of their oath, ignoring the poverty of Edward's claim compared with that of other Claimants. They also accepted another Edwardian pretence. There was no reason why, if the surrender took place on 7 June, execution of agreements would be delayed till 12 June. But there was a good reason why, when both took place on 12 June, the surrenders should be antedated to 7 June, for in this way they appeared to follow immediately upon the two awards dated 5 and 6 June – all three dates are given by saints' days; five days of refusal were consigned to oblivion and Edward's possession of the castles came smoothly, it seemed, after the awards of the Claimants. In a somewhat garbled passage in the Great Roll Caen claims that the keepers surrendered custody of their castles to Edward as superior and direct lord.[99] Gone without a trace from this untruth is Edward as one of the Claimants, the formula which had allowed this transaction to take place, and of which, indeed, we hear no more after 14 June. But it was the key to the settlement with the Scots.

The agreements about castles settled another piece of unfinished business from Northampton in 1290. The remaining promises from that agreement which do not reappear in the 12 June documents, other than those dealing with the succession to the Maid which were now irrelevant, were: that the kingdom should be separate, free, without subjection; that for ecclesiastical elections, for lay homages, fealties or reliefs, and for justice to widows and the poor there be no need to leave the kingdom; that the chancellor, chamberlain and others should be Scots resident in the kingdom; that the accustomed documents only be issued by chancery; that heirs be not disparaged; that taxes be only for the kingdom's business. Edward was insisting upon subjection, overlordship; if the overlord became direct ruler of Scotland, as guardian for the unidentified heir, these matters would be his business, but if he continued the Guardianship, they could continue to be handled as they had been since 1286. And on this too a deal was struck on 12 June 1291, a deal almost unrecorded, but manifest from actions of that day.

The Guardianship was to be continued, thus assuring that the kingdom would be clearly separate during the Cause; the Guardians, chancellor,

chamberlain and other officials would continue in office, but to each office
Edward would appoint an associate, to the chamberlain two associates, thus
meeting the Northampton promise that offices would be held by Scots in
Scotland, but giving the English king knowledge of what the Scottish
government was doing. The only office taken wholly into his patronage
was that of constable of a royal castle, an office not mentioned in the
Northampton treaty, but what he had sought from the beginning of
negotiations with the Scots in 1289 or earlier.

This settlement was made explicit only in the king's letter of 28 June 1291
recording that as 'had been unanimously agreed' between Edward I and the
the Guardians, Claimants and other Scots,[100] he appointed two clerks, for
north and south of Forth, to be associated with the chamberlain, Alexander
Balliol, who continued in office. The king's appointees, English clerks,
Roger Heron (north) and Robert Savage (south), swore their oath of office
before him on 14 June at Norham, and they were paid from that day.[101]
Caen's Great Roll tells us that the king appointed an associate to the
chancellor, and an additional Guardian, Brian fitz Alan, at this time, but, it
seems, with a difference. A royal letter of 23 August 1291 shows that the
king had made him and two other Englishmen auditors of complaints in
Scotland, to whom, as 'the king's justiciars and auditors of complaints', a
case heard 'before the Guardians' was later appealed.[102] Edward's appellate
rights were already in force, albeit exercised within Scotland. A further
office mentioned in 1290, that of clerk of the rolls, was not given an English
associate in 1291, and after promotion of the clerk to become chancellor on
23 February 1292, there is no trace of a replacement clerk.

The surrender of royal castles by their Scottish keepers, recorded on
12 June, was put into effect by royal orders on 13 and 14 June to surrender
twenty-two castles to fifteen English replacements, whose fees were then
fixed,[103] and who were of varying social standing, from the king's brother
to three valets and a clerk.[104] Seventeen of these castles were headquarters

---

[100] *Rot. Scot.*, i, 2b.

[101] For these appointments and their subsequent evolution into (the first Scottish)
escheators, *Rot. Scot.*, i, 2b; *Chron. Bury*, 99 (which mistakenly calls them 'keepers of the
peace'); Stevenson, *Documents*, i, 241, 253, 294, 300, 302. For Richard 'clerk of the escheator
of the royal dignity' south of Forth, Stevenson, *Documents*, i, 250–51, 277, 300–1.

[102] *Rot.Scot.*, i, 6; Stevenson, *Documents*, i, 377–78 (October 1291).

[103] *Rot. Scot.*, i, 1 of 13 June; the castles listed there are repeated in Stones and Simpson, ii,
D.40A, of 14 June. In addition a twenty-third, Kincardine, is listed, without old or new keeper.
Nine keepers were among the laymen who swore fealty to Edward on 13 June; five did not,
the keepers of Dingwall, Elgin, Forres, Nairn and Cromarty, all in the north. Nor are they
recorded as swearing fealty later, though two of them, Reginald Cheyne, father and son, were
named as auditors.

[104] Stones and Simpson, ii, 112–13. The new keeper of Jedburgh is to be Laurence of
St Maur *or his lieutenant*. The valets were Sweythorpe,Grey and Grant, the clerk Thomas
Braytoft. The account of Walter Langton, Keeper of the Wardrobe, shows that Roxburgh
castle, assigned to Edmund the king's brother, was given to William Grandison at the same

of their sheriffdom, and in thirteen cases the Scottish keeper had certainly been sheriff; in two, Aberdeen and Forfar, the sheriff was someone other than the keeper, but probably a sheriff depute, the keeper being sheriff principal.[105] The effect was to provide each Scottish sheriff with an English associate in charge of the seat and symbol of royal power, the castle. We have no letters of appointment for these or any others in June 1291 – Guardians, chancellor, chamberlain, auditors, sheriffs, keepers – nor even for the English associates. The chancellor of Scotland was told on 17 June that the king wished to keep the existing sheriffs holding office at the king's pleasure, and required to collect fealties from Scots,[106] and to issue commissions under the Scottish seal to that effect.[107]

Edward's letters of 13–14 June appointing new constables claim that the Guardians had handed over (*rendu*) the castles to him as Claimant acting for the Claimants, and that Claimants had delivered the castles to him as overlord until the Cause is tried before him. Of these acts the first conceded custody of the kingdom to Edward as Claimant, and the second, otherwise unrecorded, puts substance into the Claimants' recognition of 6 June, and shows how Edward metamorphosed from Claimant into overlord.[108] Since no castle was physically handed over by this date, we can only guess that one or both of these transactions took the form of statements before witnesses, with handover of a symbol.

This evidence makes impossible the narrative of the Great Roll, which, reopening events after 6 June, in substance claims that in Norham castle on 11 June the four Guardians gave up their custody of the kingdom to Edward as overlord, and the castellans similarly gave up the custody of the castles which had been entrusted to them, that Edward gave back custody of the kingdom to the same four (Guardians), who by his command chose Alan bishop of Caithness as chancellor, while he nominated Walter Amersham as the the chancellor's associate.[109] On the following day, 12 June, at Upset-

fee. The daily fee given was indeed for each castle (where a constable had more than one) and they were in possession from 18 June 1291 and paid by Langton till 27 July; PRO, E372/138, m.25. In 1292 only the castles of Berwick, Roxburgh, Jedburgh, Edinburgh, Stirling and Dumbarton were in the hands of English constables. PRO E101/631/3, fos 2r–3r; Stevenson, *Documents*, i, 206–8.

[105] I have used David Hunter-Marshall's lists of sheriffs, in Glasgow University Library. The keeper of Wigtown, Aberdeen, Kirkcudbright and Banff was the earl of Buchan, who was sheriff at Wigtown and Banff; William Meldrum was sheriff of Aberdeen; the keeper of Forfar and Dundee was the English magnate, the earl of Angus, whose agreement about his keeperships is uncollected in the PRO; David Beton was sheriff of Forfar.

[106] Stones and Simpson, ii, D.40A–D.42; *Rot. Scot.*, i, 2. It seems unlikely that the sheriffs were excluded from the castles, which were necessary for storing royal revenues.

[107] The only example of a royal writ under the seal of Guardianship is *Cal. Docs. Scot.*, ii, no. 620, now NAS, RH5/55, available as a postcard at NAS.

[108] Stones and Simpson, ii, D.40A; *Rot. Scot.*, i, 1a.

[109] Stones and Simpson, ii, A.30, part ii: the Norham instrument alters the Scots' choice of Bishop Alan in the Roll, to their consent to Edward's choice; *ibid.*, C.30 part (ii). Cf. *Chron.*

lington, Bishop Alan and Amersham took the oath of office to Edward, 'receiving the seal, carried to the place, before everyone', with no mention of Edward's presence, and the Guardians and Claimants crossed to Norham to be told by Edward to summon the Scots to meet him at Upsetlington on the morrow to swear fealty to him;[110] on 13 June, entering Scotland for the first time, he added Brian fitz Alan to the Guardians, from all five of whom he took the oath of office; oaths of fealty followed.[111]

The date and place of the chancellor's appointment is false; a royal letter of 28 June 1291 ordered payment of the chancellor's fee, because the seal of guardianship, given to the king on 12 June at Upsetlington, was committed by him on that day to Bishop Alan, the chancellor, and to Amersham.[112] The date and place are those recorded for appointment of the chamberlain's associates, and are borne out by payment to Mr Thomas Charteris, chancellor since at least 1284, of his fee to 11 June,[113] which would be his last full day in office; he would resign the seal to the Guardians, from whom he held office, on 12 June. We do not know why he lost office.[114]

Caen's version, appointing the Guardians and Chancellor on 11 June, yet waiting a day or two days before taking their oath of office, is most improbable. Why he spread the events of 12 June over 11–12 June is unclear; I can only suggest that something happened on 11 June which he did not wish to report, for example a message from the Scots demanding more of the Northampton concessions, to which Edward had to agree. But Caen also shifted the place of events on 12 June, for the chancellor's appointment took place at Upsetlington, not, as the Great Roll claims, at Norham. As earlier 'no-prejudice' letters show, both sides were well aware that were the Scots to cross the Tweed at Edward's behest, they would recognise his overlordship, a thing they had sternly resisted from 11 May on the consistent ground that it was not theirs to give. Caen has them crossing to Norham on the eleventh, but the contemporary evidence is that, on the contrary, on the twelfth Edward crossed into Scotland.

Only the appointment of chancellor is placed in Scotland by contemporary evidence, but the Great Roll is doubtless correct in its sequence: the Guardians gave Edward 'custody of the land' and of its castles, he appointed the Guardians, and they chose a new chancellor whom Edward appointed;

Bury, 99, the king 'stipulating that everything was to be done with [Amersham's] advice and consent'.

[110] Stones and Simpson, ii, A.32. The Norham instrument mentions Edward's presence, ibid., C.32.

[111] Stones and Simpson, ii, A.30–32, A.35.

[112] Stones and Simpson, ii, 94 n. 3; Rot. Scot., i, 2a.

[113] Stevenson, Documents, no. 156. For his career, Watt, Biographical Dictionary, 85–86.

[114] Unfortunately two cases can be made out, one that he had been too closely involved with English or Bruce interests, the other that Edward insisted upon a chancellor more favourable to English interests (Bishop Alan of St Edmund may have been an Englishman). Watt, Biographical Dictionary, 85–86, 477.

these events, however, happened at Upsetlington on 12 June, not, as the Roll claims, at Norham on the eleventh.[115] The Roll moreover has the Guardians and the keepers of castles 'give back and deliver' their charges to him as superior and direct lord, which he then 'committed and gave back' to them. If the keepers of castles (two of whom were Guardians) were to surrender their charges to the Claimants in the person of Edward I, if this was first agreed by the Guardians, and was according to their 1286 promise to observe their oath to 'the nearest by blood who of right should inherit', as the fourteen agreements say,[116] then that was surely how the Guardians agreed that he would have custody of the kingdom – as Claimant acting for all the Claimants until a king was provided, not as overlord. In the king's letters of 13–14 June, he became 'chief lord and keeper (*custos*) of the realm until a king is provided to rule there'. This purely Scottish transaction took place in Scotland.

It may be that the Great Roll is correct in implying a brief resignation of office by Guardians to king, but it does not use the verb *resignare*, but that they gave back and delivered the custody which they had from the community. When Edward appointed them Guardians on 12 June, he acted as one holding the custody of the kingdom for the Claimants, custody which the community had had, and from 1286 had delegated to Guardians. That change from community to Claimants was all that the Guardians had to recognise to receive a new appointment from him. They did not have to resign their charges, which it had clearly been agreed they would keep, and, despite the Great Roll, I suggest that they did not do so.[117]

In a society which saw the transfer of material symbols, crown and sceptre, ring and crozier, rod and staff, sod and stone, as essential in the conveyance of land and authority, there must have been a gesture, a *traditio*, a handing over of something to transfer to King Edward what the Scots could give him, the custody of the rule of the kingdom and the key and symbols thereof, its castles. After the Guardians chose Bishop Alan as chancellor later on 12 June, King Edward gave him 'the seal of Scotland deputed to the rule of the kingdom'.[118] How that came into the king's hands we are not told, but it had been used by the Guardians, and its surrender by them to Edward I, unrecorded but implied, on 12 June, would be their recognition of his and the other Claimants' authority in the realm until a king was provided.

Seventeen months later, on 19 November 1292, Edward I ordered that sasine of the kingdom and of its castles be delivered to John Balliol, the king provided. The same day, in the presence of John 'king of Scots' (the first time he was so called), but not, it seems, of King Edward, 'the seal deputed

---

[115] Stones and Simpson, ii, A.30.
[116] Stones and Simpson, ii, D.33.iii.
[117] Stones and Simpson, ii, A.30.
[118] A translation of the words on the seal in their Latin sequence.

for the rule of Scotland was broken in four parts, and the pieces put in a leather purse, placed to be kept in the king of England's treasury, as a sign and fuller evidence of the superior lordship of the king of England in the kingdom of Scotland, and to prove that lordship more plainly to posterity'; the retention of the parts showed the symbolism of the seal as rule of the realm here, in just the way that it had done on 12 June 1291, and surely not by coincidence.[119]

The Guardians and chancellor would swear their oath of office to the king, and the chancellor receive the seal at Upsetlington on the twelfth, as the Great Roll states, but in the presence of the king who gave the seal, on which the Roll says nothing. For this there was a reason, for the Roll then has the Scots cross to Norham to be told by the king that they should all assemble next day at Upsetlington to swear fealty. To justify the crossing, which established his overlordship, the king had to be at Norham; like the crossing attributed to 11 June, this is a falsification by Caen. Edward was at Upsetlington, where he could have commanded, and presumably did command, the assembly next day, and it was he, not the Scots, who crossed to Norham.

He did so not only to return to his quarters, but in order to secure from the Claimants that concession of the castles mentioned in his letters of 13–14 June, made to him as overlord of Scotland, king of England, and therefore in England. This was known to Caen, who clumsily altered the text of the instrument for 11 June when entering it on his Great Roll to say that the Guardians appointed by the community compeared before Edward and [handed over *omitted*] the custody of the kingdom, 'both they [the Guardians], and also the Claimants pursuing a right to the kingdom as above', and the castellans surrendered the custody of castles.[120]

But how the Claimants could confirm on 12 June what they had already given on 6 June, the awards of overlordship and sasine, is not apparent, and there may have been another and more significant reason for the delay to the thirteenth, namely that few Scots, perhaps only the Guardians and chancellor, were present at Upsetlington on the twelfth. The surrender on that day was so sudden that we must suspect deliberate obfuscation of a crucial circumstance, who took the decision to accept the assurances given by the English king and to yield to him as Claimant. If it was few, neither Edward nor the Scots would wish to admit to the fact.

Edward returned to Upsetlington on 13 June in a dual capacity, as overlord of the kingdom recognised by the Claimants, and as Claimant with custody of the land admitted by the Guardians. Royal letters of 15 June said that on 13 June the Scots had sworn fealty at Upsetlington to Edward as

---

[119] Stones and Simpson, ii, A.112, C.112.
[120] Stones and Simpson, ii, 90; the comma in *necnon tam illi, quam* should not be there. The insertion in the Great Roll makes no appearance in the Norham instrument.

'chief lord and guardian of the kingdom until a king is provided', which is a summary of, or gloss on, the oath appended to the letters. In this the magnate swore to bear good faith to Edward king of England and *soverein seignour* of the realm of Scotland, in life limb and earthly honour, to be attentive and obedient in keeping the peace 'and other things pertaining to the custody of the land, until the right of the heirs is tried before him as superior lord of the land'.[121]

There is an obvious shift in this text (which is ignored in Caen's Great Roll) from Edward as overlord of the kingdom, to his keeping of the land and trying the Cause as overlord of the land. Comparing this with yet another formula, that in the gloss, it would seem that at this time there was a compromise between, or an attempt to homologate, two positions: that Edward was superior lord of the kingdom, and that Edward was chief lord with guardianship of the land. 'Chief lord' was the position which the Scots, in their response of 1 June, had said that Edward claimed. Moreover, after the dust of 12–13 June had settled, of four mandates issued by the Guardians 'appointed by King Edward', two describe him as 'chief lord of the kingdom', and two as its 'superior lord' – perhaps the work of the chancellor and his English associate respectively.[122] Among the warrants and receipts issued by officials in Scotland in 1291–92, many speak of Edward, king of England, some thirty-two add 'superior lord' but only three add 'chief lord',[123] so there can be no doubt which usage won through, presumably through the insistence of Edward's officials, for this was the style on which he had fastened since at least 6 June. Nonetheless in the gloss his clerks admitted the sense of 'chief lord'.

In England both terms seem to have been used for the lord of whom a fief was held, and if *capitalis dominus* was used for that lord, then *superior dominus* might be used of *his* lord.[124] The Scots, it seems, saw their king's rights of lordship as 'chief lordship', of which Edward was now *custos*, having temporary keeping of these rights, subject to the promises he had made. This was all the Scots could grant in the absence of a king, as the limitation to the interim in both the gloss and the oath, 'until a king is provided', makes clear. It was a temporary lordship, conceded in defence of the rights of the kingdom as their king's inheritance, which should not have been affected. 'Chief lord' was used by the Scots; 'custody' was also their term since 1286, and fell far short of the overlordship and possession demanded by Edward.

---

[121] Stones and Simpson, ii, D.41; D.35.iii. Both of these come from the Glasgow MS fo. 10v; with slight and unimportant variants.

[122] Stevenson, *Documents*, i, 243 (18 August 1291), 279 (28 February 1292) (*capitalem*); 286 (24 March 1292), 323 (21 June 1292) (*superiorem*). In one case the Guardians call Edward simply king of England (*ibid.*, 278, 28 February 1292).

[123] The three are Stevenson, *Documents*, i, 250 (*bis*), 327. Few letters from Scots are found, but one (*ibid.*, 349) uses *superior dominus*.

[124] Reynolds, *Fiefs and Vassals*, 353, 358–60, 371.

These, then, were what the Scots thought, probably had insisted, that they were conceding on 12 June 1291.

While accepting them, the king did not compromise on *souverein seignur du reaume* in his title,[125] and very quickly showed his mastery of legal legerdemain by burying their *custos* formula in the pack and consistently dealing his own *souverein seignurie* as top card. In his 12 June 1291 letter of concessions, he had, after all, insisted that if in future anyone should claim right in the Scottish kingdom, the English king should have possession of the kingdom and the right to do justice to the claim 'as we have had right and as a sovereign lord must have of a kingdom held of him'.[126] Edward's superior lordship was for ever, despite temporary compromises over its exercise.[127]

His insistence thereupon owed at least something, probably much, to his Gascon experience. Edward had long been concerned with his own struggles with a superior lord, as duke of Aquitaine owing homage to the French king. By the treaty of Paris in 1259 Henry III had accepted that he also owed homage for Gascony, hitherto an allodial possession. But this treaty also provided that certain lands be surrendered to him by the French king, who in fact retained them, thus giving Edward, who bitterly opposed the treaty as early as 1260, grounds to argue that Gascony, unlike Aquitaine, was not part of the French kingdom.[128] These uncertainties were a fertile source of disputes between the kings of the two kingdoms, disputes which multiplied from the 1270s, when the French king would express his authority as *superioritas*. Thus in 1279, Philip III ceded the Agenais to Edward I as duke *salvis superioritate et ressorto ... regis Francie*. French lawyers such as the author of the Orléans customs in the *Établissements de S. Louis* knew the king as *souverain es choses temporeix*, in Latin (perhaps later than 1290) as having *summa superioritas in regno suo*.[129]

In practice this superiority was activated only when a subject of the duke appealed from him to the French king on grounds of denial or default of justice, appeals which grew in frequency in the last quarter of the thirteenth century. A modern author has commented that 'the notion of French royal sovereignty remained largely theoretical and judicial throughout this

[125] Stones and Simpson, ii, D.35.iii, D.41. But when he quoted this in the Norham instrument (C.35) Caen made Edward 'superior and direct lord' and transformed the 'land' into *regnum*.

[126] Stones and Simpson, ii, 99.

[127] The promises of 6 June, preserved in the Glasgow MS, begin *Edward etc.*, but in the text the king speaks of doing right *come soverein seignur de la terre*; if he had not then taken 'superior lord' into his title, he was clearly intent upon doing so; the awards speak of his being overlord but style him only *roy d'Engleterre*; Stones and Simpson, ii, A.20, B.23, D.28.

[128] Chaplais, 'Le Traité de Paris de 1259 et l'Inféodation de la Gascogne Allodiale' and 'Le Duché-Pairie de Guyenne: l'Hommage et les Services Féodaux de 1259 à 1303', nos II and III in his *Essays in Medieval Diplomacy and Administration*.

[129] Vale, *Origins of the Hundred Years War*, 17; *Établissements de S. Louis*, trans. Akehurst, 147; John of Paris, *On Royal and Papal Power*, ed. Watt, 18.

period',[130] but it so impinged upon Edward I that he spent three years, 1286–89, in Gascony and Aquitaine, seeking to establish his ducal authority. An ordinance of 1289 established or regularised a judge of first instance and a judge of appeals for the duchy, but there was already pressure for recourse to a higher tribunal, and judges of second appeals (to avoid recourse to the king in England) functioned in 1289–93 and from 1298; among the styles they used was *juge sovereyn*.[131] These efforts to discourage appeals to Paris had some success, but they show that Edward was well familiar with the meaning of *souverain* and its relationship to judicial supremacy.

He used 'superior/*souverain* lord' in and after 1291 only in Scottish business, and from July 1292 he showed a firm determination to limit the promise to hear cases in Scotland, asserting that after judgement on the Scottish throne they might be heard in England.[132] It seems likely that the style 'superior lord' was not just borrowed from conveyancing or pleading in English courts, but that it reflects the claims of Philip III and IV in France, and especially in the duchy of Aquitaine, and was adopted by Edward I in direct imitation of French overlordship and sovereignty over a subordinate provincial ruler. Essential to it was *ressort* to the *souverein*.

On 13 June three bishops, Bruce, Balliol, eight earls and seventeen barons swore fealty to Edward at Upsetlington, not a great company; Bruce and Balliol were placed before the earls, suggesting that the list was provided by the Scots, firm that there were only two serious Claimants, and showing the character of the Berwick assembly. The earls were preponderantly Bruce men, the barons preponderantly pro-Balliol, those of unknown allegiance few, though Henry Pinkeny presumably flew a lone pennon for his brother. Despite the order of 15 June that all freeholders were to swear fealty to him before a sheriff, further prelates and barons were slow to come forward.[133] The sheriffs were reluctant, for on 12 July commissions had to be appointed to facilitate the oath-taking. Only sixty-nine prelates and barons were listed as taking it, a total which must reflect great reluctance in the community at large.[134] The Scots indeed denied Edward 'recognition of his ... suzerainty from the community of the realm of Scotland in its fullest, most solemn, most representative character'.[135] The lordship they gave him was temporary, by dint of a formula, as Claimant on behalf of the Claimants, with interim custody. The lordship which he took was *souverein*, for ever.

---

[130] Vale, *Origins of Hundred Years War*, 17.

[131] Chaplais, 'Les appels Gascons au roi d'Angleterre sous la règne d'Édouard Ier', no. VI in his *Essays in Medieval Diplomacy and Administration*.

[132] Stones and Simpson, ii, A.79.

[133] Stones and Simpson, ii, A.35, D.41, A.43–A.47.

[134] Stones and Simpson, ii, A.48, Appendix F.

[135] Barrow, *Bruce*, 31.

CHAPTER 12

The Great Cause I:
August 1291 – July 1292

The narrative of the Great Cause given by Caen in his Great Roll is divided into five one-day sessions, on 3 August 1291, 2 June, 14 October, 6 November and 17 November 1292. Each of the first four of these was adjourned to the next date, so that all proceedings recorded seem to belong to that one day. This arrangement is 'implausible', and other evidence is 'decisively against' it,[1] though why Caen chose to present matters thus is unknown; charity might suggest that it was dictated by the materials at his disposal, but some of these survive and do not support the suggestion. Where other evidence gives us an event with its date which is mentioned by Caen under one of the above dates, generally I shall not comment on the discrepancy. The Great Roll is unreliable.

That must bear on an answer to the question: 'in what tribunal was the Great Cause heard?' The evidence that Edward I regarded the meeting of 6 May 1291, a fortnight after Easter, as in parliament is slight but sufficient.[2] Two Oxford clerks came 'to Norham, to our parliament' in May 1291 and the dean of York knew on 23 April that he was to go to the parliament of Norham.[3] Nonetheless the king's writs of safe conduct and 'no prejudice' for the Scots on 10 and 31 May make no mention of parliament, nor do his concessions on 6 and 12 June. Indeed the meeting of 2–12 June 1291 was nowhere called parliament, and the same is true of that of early August 1291 save that in November 1292 a royal writ said that Balliol had petitioned for the kingdom 'in our parliament at Berwick',[4] which must refer to the written petition of August 1291 and not to Balliol's admission as a Claimant in June 1291 at Norham.

The king adjourned the '3 August' session to a day 'in his next parliament', namely 2 June 1292 according to the Great Roll, but the contemporary minute for this adjournment on 12 August, to the same date, in simpler wording contains no reference to parliament. Moreover, the next

[1] Stones and Simpson, i, 106–10.
[2] This was discussed by Richardson and Sayles in 'The Scottish Parliaments of Edward I', *SHR*, xxv (1928), at 306–8, overtaken by the new edition of records of the Great Cause.
[3] Stones and Simpson, ii, 5–6.
[4] *Rot. Scot.*, i, 11, of 18 November 1292; *cf.* Stones and Simpson, i, 104.

parliament after August 1291 was held in January, not June, 1292.[5] Caen's phrase is an unjustified 'improvement'; he also replaced the description of procedure 'according to the form of previous proceedings (*retroactorum*) in the aforesaid business' by 'according to what is just and consonant with reason', thus suppressing an indication that procedure was unusual and perhaps peculiar to the case.[6]

But there were parliamentary proceedings in June 1292, in two cases. Eric II of Norway sought the arrears of his wife's tocher, an action heard 'before the king of England and his council of each realm, England and Scotland, at his parliament' held on 2 June 1292. After hearing the sworn evidence of councillors of Alexander III, judgement was given for Eric, probably on or soon before 14 July, when it was exemplified in letters patent.[7] Secondly, at Berwick on 7 July 1292 chiefs from the Western seaboard, complaining of each other, promised to keep peace until, and during, the parliament fixed by the king for 13 October, in which the complaints of the various parties would be dealt with by the king 'according to the laws and customs of the kingdom of Scotland'.[8] These complaints would have come in June or early July to the king, presumably in parliament, and were perhaps adjourned to make way for Eric's petition. Parliament had been summoned for, probably prorogued until, 13 October 1292 and Caen's Great Roll acknowledged this in the adjournment on '2 June' to 14 October, 'in his next parliament ... at which term and parliament ...' (on 14 October, proceedings follow). But apart from those introductory words the Roll does not mention parliament on 14 October, 6 or 17 November, and the contemporary record surviving from 14 October does not even have that one reference to parliament.

Thus it seems that Caen has inserted 'parliament' into two, but not all, prorogations. There were sessions in parliament at these times, but, apart from Caen's insertions, it occurs not in the context of the Great Cause but in that of other actions to which it was evidently relevant. It was King Edward's parliament in which he had the advice of the council of each realm, and in which he could give a remedy according to the laws and customs of Scotland, just as in later parliaments he dealt with petitions from England, Scotland, Ireland and Gascony, according to their several laws. The pattern of two parliaments yearly, at Easter and Michaelmas, established in 1275, had been suspended when the king was in Gascony (1286–89) and after his return parliaments were held in January, April and October (Easter and

---

[5] *Handbook of British Chronology*, 548.

[6] Stones and Simpson, ii, A.66; D.67.i.

[7] Stevenson, *Documents*, i, 313, the petition of Eric II heard at Berwick *coram ... rege ... et consilio suo utriusque regni ... ad parliamentum ... regis. Cal. Patent Rolls, 1281–92*, 501 calendars the same text and shows that the process was exemplified on 14 July. *Cf.* 'the parliaments of both realms', Stones and Simpson, ii, 196.

[8] *Foedera*, i, 761.

Michaelmas) 1290, in January and May [Easter] 1291 and January 1292.[9] If we add the proceedings at Berwick to this catalogue, then the adjourned session of 13 October 1292 was a return to Michaelmas parliaments, and indeed 1293 again shows Easter and Michaelmas parliaments. The year 1291 was exceptional with an adjournment from June to 3 August to give the king enough time to establish his position in Scotland, but not keeping him there, nor requiring his return for a Michaelmas session. The proceedings at Berwick had their own status and momentum.

The absence of any contemporary record or comment that right was done, or to be done, to the Claimants *in parliament*, is striking. Even before Brabazon spoke at Norham, King Edward had decided that a positive decision about the succession must be made by advice of the Scots, *par voz conseils*,[10] a conciliatory phrase which may conceal awareness of a Scottish programme and certainly demanded a formula for the hearing which gave a stronger voice to the Scots than to English counsellors. The chroniclers describe various combinations of appointees to form the tribunal (my neutral word), of which one category has an equal balance of Scots and English: twelve and twelve (Worcester annals, *Gest. Ann.* alternative); twenty of each (Malmesbury annals, Lanercost, Trivet, Knighton?); and a variant, fifty Scots, thirty English (Guisborough); and (uncertainly) eighty or forty or two twelves (*Gest. Ann.*).[11]

Equal numbers reflects well-established Marcher custom in cross-Border disputes, of empanelling an assize of six or twelve each, Scots and English. The establishment of March laws in 1249, and of the frontier-line in 1285, were carried out by such an assize of twenty-four, and a meeting at Norham in 1291 would not be ignorant of such precedents as a means of establishing law and custom relevant to both kingdoms.[12] The balanced tribunal represents one proposal, from the English king, perhaps beginning with two twelves, then suggesting twenties, and finally (it may be) conceding what Guisborough has, eighty made up of fifty and thirty. The progression can only be a suggestion, but *Gest. Ann.*, whose account is at first sight an epitome of ignorance, may record these stages.

A second category has higher figures: forty (each) of both kingdoms by Bruce and by Balliol, twenty by Edward I (Bury, St Benet); eighty Scots plus twenty-four English (Bartholomew Cotton of Norwich); these reflect the

[9] *Handbook of British Chronology*, 548–9.

[10] Stones and Simpson, ii, D.3.i, In their response the Scots took this to be the advice of the *bone gent du roiaume; ibid.*, D.10.

[11] *Ann. Monastici*, iv, 505; *Chron. Fordun*, i, 313; *Eulogium Historiarum*, iii, 155; *Chron. Lanercost*, 142; *Chron. Trivet*, 324; *Chron. Knighton*, i, 286 has 30 each, presumably a copying error (whence the ? in my text); *Chron. Guisborough*, 238; *Chron. Fordun*, i, 313.

[12] Neilson, 'The March Laws', *Stair Society, Miscellany One*, 15–16; Summerson, 'The early development of the laws of the Anglo-Scottish Marches, 1249–1448', *Legal History in the Making*, eds Fergus and Gordon, 29–42; Neville, *Violence, Custom and Law*, 1–14; *Cal. Docs. Scot.*, ii, no. 275; see also *ibid.*, i, nos 1676, 1699, appendix, no. 5.

actual make-up of the tribunal.[13] Only the Bury chronicle (and its derivative of St Benet of Hulme) is most nearly correct in naming Bruce and Balliol as nominators (the two Claimants whom the Scots agreed had the best right), and their nominees as ethnically mixed.[14] It errs in putting the royal group at twenty – totalling one hundred, a revealing error – where Cotton correctly has twenty-four. There are two statements about the appointment of the eighty which are independent of Caen's work. The first is the petition of Patrick Galightly, probably of July 1291, made 'before you lords auditors appointed by the king of England, superior lord ... and [by] the whole community', and the second a memorandum of 25 June 1292 saying that Bruce and Balliol had chosen their eighty 'by assent of the community of the realm of Scotland'.[15]

This feature of the composition is likely to stem from earlier consideration by those Scots who agreed to seek Edward's arbitration, intending that he should preside over a tribunal nominated equally by the only two Claimants then in contention. The list of auditors in the Glasgow MS, an early and unimpeachable source, is unambiguous in naming forty as chosen by Bruce and forty as chosen by Balliol,[16] so Caen and Tang are embellishing when they associate other Guardians with these two in the choice, and the embellishments confirm that Edward I is most unlikely to have suggested or favoured limiting *voz conseils* to nominees of two Claimants. In short, the strong Scottish element and its appointers are both likely to have been concessions made by Edward I, who would press for a tribunal appointed in equal numbers from each kingdom. He settled for naming twenty-four auditors, as a recognition of lordship, and possibly so that the claim of Florence would not be squeezed out.

The judgement of Professor Barrow, that Balliol's names are much more impressive than Bruce's, is certainly true, for only the first ten (or so) names in Bruce's list are prestigious, compared with at least twenty-eight in Balliol's.[17] Balliol's group included no fewer than ten men who were related to the Comyns, and some fifteen who had political connections with that family; it is clear that the Claimant John Comyn played a significant role in accumulating this influential cohort for Balliol.[18] Nonetheless, it is not clear

---

[13] *Chron. Bury*, 99; *Chron. Oxenedes*, 279; *Chron. Cotton*, 428; *cf.* 180.

[14] Bruce named Mr Adam Crokedayk, Mr William Gosford, Mr William Ireby and the two Conisbroughs, Balliol the earl of Angus who was a Northumberland baron. But contemporary documents do call the eighty 'of Scotland', for example Stones and Simpson, ii, D.77.

[15] Stones and Simpson, ii, A.60; D.77, p. 191, n. 2.

[16] Stones and Simpson, ii, A.21, B.21, D.24.ii.

[17] This is a very rough and ready judgement, which ignores the strong element of university clerks among Bruce's forty. Barrow, *Bruce*, 41.

[18] These figures are derived from Appendix 1 in the PhD Thesis (University of Edinburgh) of Dr Norman Reid. I am most grateful to Dr Reid for sending a copy of the appendix to me and allowing me to use it here.

that this tells us much about the capacity of the tribunal to deal with the legal issues raised by the Cause. Certainly the eighty would be familiar with the customs of succession to land in Scotland, with primogeniture, with partition among co-heiresses, with representation, for all these could occur in the family or among tenants, and were part of estate business. But the duration of the Cause showed that this familiarity was not enough, for these customs did not point unambiguously to the right heir to the throne. And beyond them, in a wider legal landscape, Bruce's university masters might take surer steps than Balliol's gentleman friends.

If Caen's '3 June 1291' seems an absurdly early agreement on the tribunal's composition, we can only suggest that an alternative date is unlikely to have been later than 12 June, when Edward's deal with the Scots was struck, and that it was most likely to have been part of that deal. A strong hint that the tribunal was agreed then is the king's undertaking on 12 June (ignored in the notarial instruments) 'that justice (*droit*) will be done within the kingdom of Scotland, and not anywhere else, until there is a king of Scotland', while the Glasgow MS places the list of 104 between that undertaking and the agreements with castellans of the same date – though nominations can scarcely have been made so early.[19]

Yet this leaves unexplained the very large size of the tribunal, whose balance would have been the same with a less unwieldy composition of 20:20:12. We must conclude that the model upon which the tribunal (though not its make-up) was based was the *iudicium centumvirale* of Roman law,[20] with 105 members charged to decide questions of heritage. This was first elucidated by George Neilson in 1918, when he showed how the composition of 40 + 40 + 24 + King Edward fitted this precedent, and cited an account which made the actual identification.[21] The editors are critical of this suggestion because of the late date at which, and inaccurate historical context in which, it first appeared, a draft anti-Valois narrative, probably of late 1339, in which Edward III recalled that John Balliol had been ajudged king *per centumvirale judicium*.[22]

Yet the *centumviri* explain the constitution of the tribunal as no other hypothesis does, and had the 1339 text never been penned, there would still

[19] Stones and Simpson, ii, D.33.i; Glasgow MS, fo. 8.

[20] There are a number of brief accounts of this court, for example in Berger, *Encyclopedic Dictionary of Roman Law* (with full bibliography); *Oxford Classical Dictionary*; Daremberg and Saglio, *Dictionnaire des antiquités grecques et romaines*. More recent literature I have not explored; it seems to be mainly in German and is admirably summarised in the first chapter of Kelly, *Studies in the Civil Judicature of the Roman Republic*, where the reader will find full references to the *iudicium* in classical sources. I have not seen Olivier-Martin, *Le tribunal des centumvirs* (1904).

[21] Neilson, 'Brus versus Balliol, 1291–1292: the Model for Edward I's Tribunal', *SHR*, xvi (1919), 1–14. For the editors' criticism see Stones and Simpson, ii, Appendix G, pp. 371–72.

[22] *Foedera*, ii, 1109–10. I know of no discussion of the date of this document, but it fits circumstances of 1339 described in Sumption, *The Hundred Years War*, i, ch. 8.

be good reason to believe that Edward I had been persuaded by Romanist advisers to follow this precedent.[23] It had one enormous advantage: not only was it the tribunal which ajudged on inheritance – and the Great Cause was an inheritance case and nothing else – but also actions before it were initiated by petition, *hereditatis petitio*, oral, certainly, in ancient Rome, but possibly also in the initial formalities at Berwick, though certainly submitted in writing. And of written petitions for this inheritance the king had a bag-full.

There was a further criticism by the editors of the suggested Roman origin of the tribunal: Edward I was to appoint twenty-four auditors 'or more or less',[24] and hence the total could have varied significantly from 105. But Edward did appoint only twenty-four; John of Caen added 'or more or less', found only in the Great Roll of 1296–97, to justify the abandonment of the *centumvirale*, in the October–November 1292 session, for a phase in which Edward's (much larger) council was decisive, replacing the twenty-four, while the Scottish eighty auditors were reduced to a consultative and consenting role.[25] Moreover, the Bury chronicler's account must be taken into account, for he alone shows accurate knowledge of the make-up of the eighty by Bruce and Balliol, and that Edward I appointed the rest. We may presume that he was also told the correct number of Edward I's nominees, but he nonetheless reduced that figure to twenty – because he had been told that the tribunal were *centumviri*, 'a hundred men'.

The *centumvirale iudicium* had flourished during the Roman republic, but to the thirteenth century Roman meant imperial, a universal authority, greater than that of kings, and, it may have been argued at Berwick, appropriate for a dispute which concerned kingship and kingly authority. Unlike the Castillian kings who had for a time used the title of 'emperor' to express their hegemony in Spain, Philip IV of France was to argue that his authority as king was already complete, 'imperial', within the kingdom.[26] Such political theorising is not found in England, but there were certainly those who would urge Edward I that he had authority over kings and princes in Ireland,

---

[23] Professor P. Stein, in a valuable short discussion of the Great Cause, states that 'this court was almost certainly a deliberate imitation of the Roman *centumviri*'; 'Roman Law in Scotland', *Ius Romanum Medii Aevi*, pars V, 3b, 28–31. Professor Barrow, too, seems disposed to accept Neilson and reject the editors' argument; *Robert Bruce*, 334 n. 2.

[24] Stones and Simpson, ii, A.21.

[25] This change occurs in *Gest. Ann.*, where the auditors, segregated in a private place, found against Balliol and for Bruce. Edward immediately took this opinion to his council, where Bek warned him of the dangers of the proud and independent Bruce. 'God's blood! said the king, you have sung a good [mass]', and he asked each in turn to hold the kingdom of him. Bruce refused but Balliol accepted and so Edward gave judgement for him. The dishonest questioning and belated overlordship are of course propaganda-serving myths, but the change to the council is correct. Stones and Simpson, i, 75–76 provides a convenient translation of this passage.

[26] *Rex est imperator in regno suo* was one of the arguments mustered for Philip IV over the status of Lyons in 1296–97; Kern, *Acta Imperii, Angliae et Franciae*, 199–200, no. 271; 201–6, no. 274 for *superioritas*. See also 54–55, no. 79 of 1292.

Scotland and Wales, which made him quasi 'emperor' in another view of that office, lord of several kingdoms. Therefore he should use the appropriate Roman tribunal.

Edward I never, so far as is known, experimented with either the procedure or the substantive law of the Roman system.[27] But that does not disprove the evidences that initially there was successful pressure to constitute the tribunal in the image of a Roman tribunal for hearing actions of inheritance; and since we have very few contemporary records, either notarial or non-notarial, for procedure in the first two sessions (August 1291, June 1292), it must remain possible that Roman influences were then greater than our evidence permits us to say.

The unusual character of the tribunal probably explains the apparently haphazard references to parliament during the hearing of the Cause. So long as it was argued before the auditors, the *centumviri*, it was not argued 'in parliament'; if asked 'was this an English court or a Scottish court?', the response of the records is a blank. The meetings are nowhere called a court;[28] the proceedings do not begin as those of a court might, *placitum coram rege et auditoribus*. Caen describes one session (3 August 1291) of those chosen 'to hear petitions and rights' of the Claimants, 'to understand and discuss them' and to 'refer their findings to the king', and in a much more reliable document of 21 June 1292, the 104 answered affirmitively the king's question, 'have the Claimants said enough to enable me to proceed to judgement?' Later, in the minute for October 1292, the king ordered his councillors to examine the *processus placiti* and report their findings to him.[29] The use of *jugement* on 17 November may tell us that we are in a court of Edward I.[30]

Between 6 June and 2 August the Great Roll has nothing about the Cause except an adjournment on 13 June to 2 August. But the last royal letters dated at Norham were of Sunday, 17 June,[31] and the more likely date for adjournment is 15 or 16 June, forty days before convening at Berwick on 2 August.[32] After 17 June the king was at Berwick till 4 July and then by Perth (20 July) and Edinburgh (29 July) back to Berwick for 2 August.[33]

[27] Stones and Simpson, i, 221 where the editors reject use of the Roman action of *sequestratio*, the deposit or temporary possession of something whose title was disputed in the Great Cause.

[28] There is an exception, the petition of John Comyn, Stones and Simpson, ii, A.62.

[29] Stones and Simpson, ii, A.53 (p. 130), D.77, C.81.

[30] Stones and Simpson, ii, C.109.

[31] *Rot. Scot.*, i, 2.

[32] Forty lawful days (i.e. without Sundays) from 16 June was Tuesday, 2 August. Stones and Simpson, ii, A.36. In 1292 parliament was adjourned to 13 October, but the Great Cause was adjourned to 14 October. The same thing probably happened 2–3 August 1291.

[33] *Itinerary of Edward I, part II, 1291–1307*, List and Index Society, vol. 132 (1976), under date. This work is the authority for other statements about Edward's whereabouts, and I have not cited it further.

A later claim, that Count Florence had had since 1 August 1291 to find a missing document, was his opponents' error for 12 August.[34] From 2 August we are largely reliant on the untrustworthy Great Roll, but fortunately the surviving minute, that for 12 August 1291, shows that the auditors (called that) were in active session on that day,[35] and had been so for some days; thus we can perhaps trust the Great Roll's claim under 3 August that they met on that day for consideration of the Claimants' petitions, whose texts it presents in series in Latin.

Most of the petitions are restricted to the relationship of the Claimant to Alexander III or the Maid of Norway, without any indication of the bar of illegitimacy (Table C, p. 348). There are marked differences in their fullness and relevance. Those of Count Florence, Earl Patrick, Vescy, Ros, Pinkeny, Soules, Galightly, Mandeville and Hastings are about, or less than, 200 words; in those of Florence, Galightly, Comyn, Balliol and Bruce, Edward is superior lord, but the rest (except Hastings) make no reference to the king. Hastings' petition to 'his lord the king of England', has only 100 words and differs from the others in claiming the lands of the late king for three co-heiresses as 'one heir', that is claiming partition among the co-heiresses' descendants.[36] In phrases describing the royal line from King William to the Maid of Norway there is a close correspondence between the petition of Vescy and that of Ros.

The fact that Balliol's and Ros's petitions explicitly assert that the kingdom is not partible may place them after that of Hastings, while the great length of Balliol's and Bruce's, with their detail on each generation, suggest that they were composed later than most others, for the hearing of August, perhaps replacing short statements like those of most other Claimants submitted in June. The original petition from Bruce survives, in French (showing that the Great Roll Latin version is accurate), but with a Latin heading giving a date, 3 August 1291, when it was [fa]cta (done), a word which, if correct, means only that it was submitted on that date.[37] It is likely that Balliol's was drawn up in July 1291 about the same time as Bruce's and Comyn's (Balliol and Comyn refer to the auditors as *electi* and *curia* respectively).[38] Comyn's petition ends by urging that he will not prejudice Balliol's case, and has many verbal similarities to the latter's petition; both reserve the right to add or remove points 'according to the laws and customs

[34] Stones and Simpson, ii, C.106.II (vi, 4) (p. 316).

[35] Stones and Simpson, ii, D.67.i.

[36] Stones and Simpson, ii, A.63.

[37] BL, Cotton Charter xii, 59. The editors remark (Stones and Simpson, ii, 142 n. *b*) that 'one cannot be sure if it was sealed'. When I called for it in March 2000, I was given a box with a magnificent detached large seal of Bruce in green wax, formerly appended by a string, which obviously was not given to the editors. The document was being repaired, without which circumstance I might never have known of the seal. I saw the document on a later occasion.

[38] Stones and Simpson, ii, A.54–64; Bruce's original petition is D.65.i (dated), and in the Great Roll version, A.65 (undated).

of Scotland'. They were pretty certainly the work of one (Scottish) hand, and they strengthen the evidence that Comyn was manager of Balliol's cause. These words also explain whence Caen derived his Great Roll claim that Balliol and Comyn acted together in choosing forty auditors.

Two new Claimants, Galightly and Mandeville, appear for the first time in Caen's account of 3 August. Patrick Galightly is almost unknown, save that his name occurs as last of the Perth burgesses to swear fealty on 24 July 1291.[39] There is no proof that the Claimant was the Perth burgess, but given the unusual name, later quite common in Perth, Dundee and Gowrie, it seems overwhelmingly likely that he was.[40] His petition, that his father Henry was a son of King William, is the only one to refer to *auditores* by that name, suggesting that it was submitted relatively late in the day; indeed it was probably compiled between 24 July and 3 August 1291.

Roger de Mandeville was a minor,[41] claiming through his mother, and telling the extraordinary story that King William had a son and two daughters whom before his death he handed over to his brother, Malcolm king of Scotland, who had the son killed.[42] Mandeville claimed to be fifth in descent from one of the daughters, Aufrica, who married an Ulsterman, William de Say, and had a son of the same name, father of another Aufrica. The generations would place King William in the early twelfth century, so his name may be an error for David. There is no other evidence of the existence of Henry Galightly or of Aufrica de Say.[43] The Roll's account of 3 August 1291 contains no reference to the claim of Edward I, of which nothing further is heard and he probably submitted no petition; nonetheless he seems to have raised some claim at this session, as we shall see.[44]

Few say whose inheritance they seek. Alexander III is mentioned by all except Count Florence, Mandeville and Comyn, but only Soules remarks that he died in sasine of the kingdom. The Maid of Norway is mentioned by

[39] Stones and Simpson, ii, 370.
[40] For the name, see Black, *Surnames of Scotland*, 286, under Galletly, where Patrick is wrongly said to be Henry's grandson. The usual form suggests that the second element was 'lightly' rather than 'lithely'. But Black says that the name has 'nothing to do with lightness of foot'. It was not place-name-derived. It is surely related to the saying 'Easy come, easy go' as found in *Three Prestis of Peblis*: 'Tharfor that lichtly cummis will lichtly ga', cited in *Dictionary of the Older Scottish Tongue* under 'ga' and 'lichtly'.
[41] Stones and Simpson, ii, 221, 229.
[42] Of course Malcolm (IV) preceded William as king. The story recalls the claim of Wyntoun that David I had a child, Malcolm, who was strangled by Domnall ban.
[43] On the Say family, *CP*, xi, 464–74. This, however, does not show the Ulster branch. The de Mandevilles were also prominent in Ulster, as were the Wardons; Roger de Mandeville claimed to be heir of Agatha (who must have married a de Mandeville). In 1189, on the death of William de Mandeville, earl of Essex, his heir was his aged aunt, Beatrice, whose husband William de Say had died in 1144. They had a son, William de Say, wife unknown, who died in 1177 leaving two daughters, Beatrice and Maud. The name Aufrica does not occur in connection with these two Williams; *CP*, v, 117–22.
[44] Below, pp. 266–67.

Count Florence, Vescy, Ros, Pinkeny, Balliol and Bruce as having died
without issue, but only Count Florence and Bruce give her more than a
silent and fruitless role. The former claims that she 'was seised *in dominico
suo* as of fee, of the kingdom, in time of peace, in the time of King Edward,
superior lord ... and recently died siesed ... without heir'. This farrago
about a lass who never saw Scotland came from an English lawyer, well
familiar with English forms of action, who may have been concerned
to 'prove' succession by a woman, and hence the right of Ada, Scottish
ancestress of Florence; there must be a strong supicion that he took his
instructions from those close to Edward I.

He was directly contradicted by Bruce: all three children of Alexander III
died before him and 'had (*expectauerunt*) no status of reigning in the
kingdom'. The king had his granddaughter recognised in writing by the
magnates as lady of the kingdom (in 1284) if he should die without an heir,
but she died without having (*expectando*) corporal possession of the kingdom and without an heir. This written recognition made more acceptable
Bruce's claim to have been acknowledged in writing as heir presumptive.

All seem to be agreed on the inheritance they seek: the kingdom, *regnum*,
real property, defined in 1284 as the whole kingdom and Isle of Man with
the other islands belonging to the kingdom with all other rights and liberties
belonging to the king of Scotland. The search was for the right heir to
wherein the king was king, to what supported his kingship. No Claimant
urged his inheritance as a dignity, an authority divinely sanctioned according to Old Testament precedents, save in a hint by Bruce at a dignity when
he referred to the children of Alexander III who had no standing (*status*) of
reigning in the kingdom. Yet even he made no reference in his petition to the
essential of his claim: a law by which king's reign, a law of *rex* rather than a
law of *regnum* by which a kingdom descends, the basis of every other claim.

'Thirteen Competitors' have jostled in the court room for seven centuries
since 1296; most of them were irrelevant to the real case; their number does
not include an important occasional claimant, Edward I himself; and as
Edward arrived and departed at different times, so too, did other claimants.
King Eric arrived late on the scene, when others had departed. The memorandum of 21 June 1292 lists the competitors on 16 June, and a pleading of
Comyn of that period has the same names; neither makes mention of Earl
Patrick, Soules, Galightly and Pinkeny, nor does the minute of 7 November
1292, listing the Claimants after the finding against Bruce.[45] Mandeville is
mentioned, with the explanation on 7 November that he was under age, and
next day he, with Comyn, was ruled out because they had not prosecuted
their petitions.[46] In Comyn's case this would be deliberate, as he wished

---

[45] Stones and Simpson, ii, 191, 170, 229. Thus the list of 21 June 1292 cannot have omitted
names by scribal error.
[46] Stones and Simpson, ii, 230.

Balliol to succeed, but Mandeville's case shows that heretofore simple failure to appear in person or by proxy had not led to elimination. The four who dropped out must have done so explicitly before 16 June 1292, though it is likely that Galightly, a supposed grandson of King William, was an old man who had simply died.

There is no list of Claimants between 12 June 1291 and 16 June 1292 except the petitions of twelve given on the Great Roll under 3 August 1291; but Caen, in the same Roll, lists all thirteen Claimants as active on the day of judgement, 17 November 1292,[47] claiming that the four who, we know, had withdrawn (or one possibly had died) by the previous June, withdrew in person (*retraxerunt se*) on that day. Like his false addition of Pinkeny to the Claimants of 5–6 June 1291, this detail matters little for our understanding of the Cause, but much for our trust in the Great Roll. Caen's placing of twelve petitions on 3 August, when only one of them is so dated, may be equally false, a tidying-up, and is not a firm reason for placing the withdrawal of three or four after that date. After they submitted petitions at uncertain dates, but perhaps as early as June 1291, they could have withdrawn at any time before June 1292.

When the Cause opened, effectively on 3 August 1291 in Berwick castle where much of the legal argument took place (Plate 8), considerable explanation and argument, written or oral, were required. The surviving minute of 12 August reveals a hearing in a predominantly, even overwhelmingly, Scottish context. Other Scottish prelates and nobles were present with the auditors on that day, when the claims, (written) answers of parties and arguments were sewn up and sealed in a bag by two bishops and two earls, all Scottish, to be kept in Berwick castle. The adjournment followed, to 2 June 1292, the date given in the Great Roll. There is only one hint as to the content of the arguments which had been before the court, and it is found in the minute, but not in the Roll. The king instructed a group (three Scots; three English, two of them Edward's nominees as auditors) to search the Scottish treasury, monasteries and other places for the document needed by Count Florence to found his 'exception' and to bring it, and anything else bearing on claims to the throne, to the June 1292 meeting.[48]

Count Florence's petition had alleged that with the death of the Maid of Norway, right went by resort to Ada, sister of King William, and so to her descendant, Florence, that is it ignored Earl David and his descendants. In August he must have lodged his exception to the right of Earl David's descendants on the basis of a supposed document, and would have united Bruce and Balliol against him for the whole of that session. The search has generally been accepted as the due of Florence, and by implication as

[47] Stones and Simpson, ii, A.108–9.
[48] Stones and Simpson, ii, D.67.i.

evidence of the evenness of the whole proceedings. A fairer assessment might find the adjournment of nine and a half months a breach of the spirit of Edward's undertaking (on 12 June) of 'appropriate speed ... as the nature of the business allows', and particularly that 'no delay will be made by us'.[49]

The minute does not claim, nor is it likely, that the long adjournment was only for the search; all parties, having submitted claims and arguments, would need some time to prepare replies – perhaps two or three months. But the much longer adjournment suggests that Edward had other concerns, including the Mamluke threat to Acre, known in the west for over a year. His own crusading expedition, promised to depart on 24 June 1293, was a commitment with far-reaching financial implications, the most likely reason for the long adjournment.[50] But the date of reconvening, 2 June 1292, almost exactly one year after Edward had required the Scots to answer his claim to overlordship, was surely foresight, not coincidence. The time taken to hear the Cause thereafter would give Edward a full year and a day (from 13 June) of acknowledged overlordship of the kingdom, something which, despite his promise to hear the Cause with proper speed, he may have been determined to have. Perhaps he would have replied that this was the proper time to allow new parties to hear of the Cause and submit petitions.[51]

That the document of Florence was singled out in the instructions to the research team is significant. Despite Bruce's claim of a missing record in his memorandum of early 1291 and later in his pleading of June 1292,[52] he was given neither adjournment nor search. In August 1291, Edward was leaning heavily in favour of Count Florence, in whom he saw a complaisant future king, linked to Edward's family by the marriage of his son. Caen's Great Roll tells us nothing about this or any other subject of the August session, but chancery's Scotch Rolls do hint at something else.

On 13 August 1291, the day after the adjournment, the king granted £100 annually from wardships and reliefs to the bishop of Glasgow, in return for his labours before and after 1286, and in keeping peace for the people; land worth £100 was given to the Steward, Earl Patrick, and William de Soules, worth 100 merks to John de Soules, William de Sinclair and Patrick de Graham. These grants were made 'if it happens that the kingdom of Scotland remains to the king and his heirs', to be assigned to the donees 'when that kingdom thus remains to the king'. They were soon cancelled, probably on 18 August, on which day letters were to be sent to the keeper of Ettrick Forest to give deer to three bishops (St Andrews, Glasgow and the

    [49] Stones and Simpson, ii, D.33.ii.
    [50] Prestwich, *Edward I*, 329; Schein, *Fideles Crucis*, 72–74. Acre fell on 28 May 1291, but this was not known at Rome till early August, at Berwick weeks later.
    [51] A year and a day was allowed in English law for third parties to put in a claim when land was transferred by final concord. I owe this point to Dr Brand.
    [52] Stones and Simpson, ii, 186, 170; he could presumably have made the same claim in August 1291.

chancellor), and to the Steward, Earl Patrick, and nine others, including William de Soules.[53] The numbers of deer varied from twenty downwards, but the value of these gifts was clearly much less than the lands had they been given. Moreover five of the donees on 13 August were 'Bruce men', with two Balliol-appointed auditors, while on 18 August the balance was 5:5 with two uncertain, and after a further gift on 23 August it was 5 Bruce: 7 Balliol.

The grants of 13 August are much more selective and politically significant, for they show that the possibility that the kingdom would be Edward's and his heirs' had been canvassed. The verb used is *remanere*, remain, which suggests that the issue may have been not his heritable claim, but escheat of the kingdom to him as overlord for default of an heir in a male line. If, as seems likely, he was buying off opposition, it was to this possibility. Yet there are no other traces of such a hope or intention, whereas the long adjournment must have been a heavy blow to the main Claimants, Bruce and Balliol. If their supporters argued that Edward seemed to be taking the kingdom into his hands for good, then his 13 August grants may have been a reassurance to the discontented. Later he softened the blow of the adjournment by gifts distributed to a wider audience. But other speculations are certainly possible, and the royal letters tell us only one thing for sure: that matters were discussed at the August session which were ignored by Caen.

For the first twelve days of the session which began on 2 June 1292 the Great Roll is our only source, narrating that King Eric's procurators now submitted a claim, and that the king referred the 'petitions, reasons, responses and allegations' of the Claimants to the auditors, who considered them and found difficulties with them which they reported to the king. He then considered the same texts with his council and decided that, to avoid delays, the proceedings must be speeded up; by consent of his council and the auditors he decided that the tribunal should first consider who had the better right, Bruce or Balliol. This decision, we know, was made on 16 June. As for what went before, supposedly a discussion of all the claims and all the pleadings submitted in August 1291, the auditors must have faced impossible procedural dilemmas over the priority to be given to each case. Debate on this, rather than on the substantive issue, right to the succession, is suggested by 'difficulties', by referring the texts back to Edward, and by the outcome, prioritising Bruce *v.* Balliol.

The evidence for the true dates of these events is the invaluable original memorandum dated 21 June 1292 in which the auditors recorded that they had considered the claims of Bruce and Balliol since 16 June, when Edward

---

[53] *Rot. Scot.*, i, 3a, 5a. For Clenhull (Clennell) see Barrow, *Bruce*, 155. On 23 August deer were gifted to Reginald le Chen father and son, Balliol-nominated auditors.

had decided to hasten proceedings.[54] It is this memorandum which lists the Claimants as nine in number, including now King Eric; Earl Patrick, Soules, Pinkeny and (if not dead) Galightly had withdrawn by 16 June. By consent of Count Florence 'and of all the other Claimants aforesaid' the decision had been made to try the claims of Bruce and Balliol first. This ignoring of King Eric and naming of Count Florence alone was not a scribal whim,[55] for Florence had just taken a drastic step.

On 14 June he made an agreement with Bruce, brokered by mutual friends, whereby each would help the other in pursuit of his claim, the successful one to infeft the other in a third of all lands and tenements within the kingdom, and belonging to the kingdom, or, as it is also called, 'in the third part of the said kingdom'.[56] Should Bruce win, all his English lands would go to Count Florence, reducing by the same value the lands in the third part in Scotland.[57] There are also clauses against agreements by either with a third party, and against the tenant of the third part granting it to another without the king's permission; both seem directed against John Balliol. There was a fearsome sanction, £100,000 payable by the party who broke the agreement to each of: the other party, aid to the Holy Land, and Edward I; for this the two Claimants subjected themselves to the jurisdiction of the Roman see and the power of the English king. The witnesses were five Bruce supporters, including the earl of Gloucester, with two Dutchmen.[58] With such sanctions and such witnesses this agreement cannot have been secret.

It was intended to favour Bruce's chances and carried the understanding that Florence would retire till Balliol had been defeated, making possible Edward's decision of 16 June to turn to Bruce *v* Balliol. For so important a matter Count Florence must have been at Berwick, where on 20 June Edward I ordered payment of £1,250 towards the marriage of John of Holland, money collected on 1 July by two attorneys of the count.[59] I find it difficult to see this payment as other than Edward's reward to Florence for allowing the case of Bruce *v.* Balliol to proceed; it underlines Florence's position as a Claimant to be taken seriously, and also as Edward's client – for

[54] Stones and Simpson, ii, D.75, D.77. 'in the presence of ... Edward'; the Great Roll attributes the decision to him and final responsibility would be his.

[55] The first Claimant in a list was now King Eric, but in this list he and others are not named, presumably as a reflection of Florence's agreement, otherwise ignored in the Great Roll.

[56] Stones and Simpson, ii, 163n refers to Barrow, *Bruce*, 47 in a previous edition. He suggests that this was a third of royal demesne. But 'a third of all lands and tenements in the kingdom and belonging to the kingdom however and wherever' seems to me to mean an appanage of several sheriffdoms, and to include a third of Man.

[57] Bruce's lands in England were worth about £180 annually in 1304; *Cal. Docs. Scot.*, ii, nos 1073, 1074, 1078.

[58] Stones and Simpson, ii, D.74; *Nat. MSS Scotland*, ii, no. VI, probably filched by Cotton from the Bruce family archive in the Duchy of Lancaster archive in the Tower.

[59] He had probably left soon after 20 June, for the money would go to pay off creditors.

no further instalment of this debt was paid until 1295.[60] Although the agreement makes no mention of advice or consent by King Edward, he must surely have approved the transfer of Bruce's English lands, and the penalty clauses which would have involved him as policeman. The purport was one which he clearly welcomed, clearing the way for ajudication between two key Claimants, Bruce and Balliol, sought by the Scots, and undertaken by the tribunal whose composition particularly suited that task. When that issue had been decided then the next one could be the victor *v.* Florence;[61] meantime the auditors could get down to the job envisaged for them before May 1291.

The pleadings submitted in June 1292 survive in the originals, but sadly fragmented and for long passages unintelligible, particularly Balliol's pleadings. Fortunately the first pleading of Bruce is intact (D.76(A)) and argues his case as follows. (1) On the extinction of the line of King William, right reverted to Earl David, to whom the heir, by right and by the law by which kings reign, is Bruce, as the nearest heir in degree. (2) Balliol can only claim through his mother and can have no better right than her. If she had been alive on the extinction of William's line (she died not long before the Maid), she could claim no right, because she was of the same degree as Bruce, and male blood is more worthy to rule than female, especially as a kingdom cannot be partitioned. (3) No usage of Scotland is against Bruce's claim and since Balliol is further from the royal blood, his claim cannot bar that of Bruce.[62] (4) The Cause should be settled by the law which makes a kingdom impartible, namely natural law, by which kings reign, not by the custom used among subjects and tenants of the kingdom of Scotland. This law gives a better right to the nearest in collateral blood to the royal blood at the time the kingdom fell vacant. (5) Custom among the people and tenants cannot bind the sovereign, namely the king, so although in partible heritages the oldest sister may have a prerogative (*aînesse*), in an impartible kingdom, (*words lost*: ? this is irrelevant), so Bruce claims the whole kingdom. (6) Custom of royal succession in Scotland is for Bruce, because it has happened that where a king had two sons, the younger reigned before the son of the older, by nearness of blood, as chronicles can show; Scottish examples and others from England, Castille and Savoy are cited in D.76(E).

There are further substantial fragments of Bruce pleading but, so far as legible, they mainly reiterate the case already made in D.76(A).[63] There was strong argument against the relevance of *aînesse*, the right of the oldest sister, with a challenge to Balliol to show when in England or Scotland, issue

---

[60] PRO C62/68 m.4; E403/1262 (liberate rolls); E403/74, E403/1315 (issue rolls).
[61] Stones and Simpson, ii, D.75, D.77.
[62] The middle sentence of this paragraph has defeated me.
[63] I suggest that the gap in D.76(B)vi on p. 170 must read *selom ley [natura]le par quele* ...

of a woman excluded the nearest male in degree in royal succession, a challenge which averred that Balliol had appealed to the laws and usages of England and Scotland. Bruce again denied the relevance of 'common law', the law of subjects, and asked Edward, as his sovereign lord and his emperor, to have his right tried by the law by which kings reign. As evidence of this law he cited the precedent of Alexander II, who had recognised Bruce, as nearest of his blood, as his heir, should he die without an heir of his body; a document recorded this decision, but if not to be found, the decision should be confirmed by asking some who had participated.[64] Other arguments cited the exclusion of women from public office, including the remarkable claim that since a bad king of France had been deposed for his wickedness, therefore *a fortiori* a woman can neither receive nor transmit royal dignity.[65]

The case of Balliol is not so well preserved, but a helpful Latin summary of it was included by Caen in his Great Roll, wrongly under 14 October 1292.[66] It is scarcely an argument for Balliol, but urged that right descended through the eldest daughter of Earl David, supporting this by the example of Scottish earldoms and offices like steward, marischal or constable, where the whole heritage went to the eldest of co-heiresses (in this differing from English custom).[67] Otherwise the pleading was a series of answers to points raised by Bruce. Alexander II's recognition of Bruce as heir (presumptive), if it had happened, was invalidated by the succession of Alexander III, who died in sasine of the kingdom. Bruce's claims of female unfitness were met by pointing out that the Maid of Norway had been queen and lady of Scotland, the Empress Matilda queen and lady of England, so women were not excluded, but if they had been, then Bruce's claim though his mother would also be excluded. (In fact neither Maid nor Empress was queen.) Bruce's argument that a brother had a better right than a son is dismissed by calling Domnall ban a usurper, and by pointing out that Alexander II, not Earl David, succeeded William.[68]

Balliol asked that right be done according to the usages of the kingdoms of Scotland and England 'and not by imperial law, inasmuch as the kingdom of Scotland is held of the crown of England and of no empire, for it would be in prejudice of the king's crown if lay fee was judged in his court by imperial law'.[69] Let Edward judge 'according to rules of his crown and land of England and also according to the laws and usages of Scotland of the time of Alexander [III]'.[70] And in a closing paragraph he asserted strongly that

---

[64] Stones and Simpson, ii, D.76(B)(iii–vii); D.76(C)(ii).

[65] Stones and Simpson, ii, D.76(C)(iii).

[66] Stones and Simpson, ii, A.84.

[67] Stones and Simpson, ii, D.76(F)(ii–iii). Professor Barrow reminds me that the Steward's office descended in uninterrupted male succession from 1150 to 1542.

[68] Stones and Simpson, ii, D.76(F)(v), D.76(G)(vii), D76(G)(iv–v).

[69] Stones and Simpson, ii, 179.

[70] Stones and Simpson, ii, D.76(G)(v).

Edward is sovereign lord, has sasine of Scotland which is held of him; in England he does not deprive a tenant of purprestures (illegal seizures) taken from the king's ancestors, but proceeds against them at law, just as earls, barons or lesser folk do. Balliol has made a claim for the kingdom by resort and by descent as these folk make claims in the kingdom of Scotland and in that of England to which Scotland is subject, and so the kingdom of Scotland should be given to him as any heritage claimed in Scotland or England would be. Let judgement be rightful, according to the laws and usages of the kingdoms of England and Scotland; in Caen's Great Roll version this is 'according to common law and custom of his kingdom', a not insignificant change.[71]

Balliol's rejection of 'imperial law' implies that Bruce had had recourse to it, though the latter's pleadings do not use the phrase. If it was part of his argument, the precise reference may have been to *Libri Feudorum*, II, tit. xi, where transfer to a new line of descendants (i.e. Earl David's) should heed the first and highest person in degree. The *Libri*, although a twelfth-century Lombard compilation, had become attached to the *Corpus* of Roman law, and purported to explain the regulation of the hereditary descent of fiefs by the Emperor Conrad II. This may explain Bruce's invitation to Edward to be emperor and Balliol's rejection of the applicability of imperial law. But in his surviving pleadings Bruce claimed by a law of kingship which is natural law, and (though his case does not say this) since natural law is inherent in every man, it must be part of the laws and customs of Scotland. Very relevant to his case would have been precedents from other kingships; the few cited show a limited acquaintance with the rest of Europe. The kingdom of Jerusalem is never mentioned despite the participation of Bruce and Edward I in a crusade in 1270; there the Haute Cour had ruled in 1264 that 'among collateral heirs, the throne should pass to the oldest living male relative in the nearest degree of relationship to the person last in seisin of the kingship'.[72] It would be difficult to find a more relevant dictum.

Bruce concentrated on two quite distinct issues – though neither he nor modern commentators seems to have made the distinction. The first argument was that succession went by nearness of blood, the sons of a king following him before succession went to the next generation; among the descendants of Earl David, Bruce was the only survivor of his generation, and this argument excluded John Hastings, if he was not excluded by Bruce's seniority of line. The argument occurs only at the end of his pleading, and he must have been aware of how weak it was, since it was contradicted by the succession of Alexander II in 1214, by three centuries of

---

[71] Stones and Simpson, ii, D.76(G)(ix), A.84 (p. 205); 'common' is used here in the sense that the relevant law and custom was ordinary and was used in all his lands, Scotland included. Note that p.183, line 12 should end not *genz c* but *conts e[t]*.

[72] Lamonte, *Feudal Monarchy in the Latin Kingdom of Jerusalem*, 49–51; see also 76–79.

French history and by recent English history. John's succession (against the claim of his nephew, Arthur of Brittany) in 1199 had given it life in England, where the *casus regis* caused the judges to hesitate briefly. But in the Scottish case it was not shown which, if any, daughter of Earl David predeceased him; and representation gave John Balliol his mother's right. And so far as I am aware, there was no argument in England that King John's right arose from a natural law by which kings reign.[73] Bruce's argument, the argument of degree, paid no regard to gender and could have been used against John Balliol even if he had claimed through a deceased father.

Quite separate was the argument that among descendants of the same degree a male had a better claim than a female. This principle of male primogeniture did operate among children of the same father, but Bruce wished to apply it not to siblings but to cousins, where the female was of a senior line. In effect this denied representation, for while the right of Earl David's eldest daughter descended to her daughter (in default of sons), of the second daughter to her son, Bruce, the right of Earl David would wander from line to line, to the nearest male descendant. Spattered through these arguments is one reiterated word, *saunk*, blood.[74] It finds almost no place in the records drawn up for Edward I.[75]

When Bruce claimed a law by which kings reigned, he meant a law of kingship, more specifically of royal blood, a genetic inheritance which conferred a right of succession, first to a dignity which was *sui generis*, divinely approved and of the same character throughout Christendom, and which brought the kingdom with it. Balliol made reference to 'blood' only in answering Bruce. His positive case was simple: succession to real property was customarily to and in the senior line, which he represented, and Scotland was real property held of the English king; that would appeal greatly to Edward I.

Some of this the auditors heard and considered after 16 June 1292 when Bruce and Balliol were to pursue their rights, day on day. 'Which (*les queux*) Robert [Bruce] and John [Balliol] before the eighty of Scotland, namely ...' and there follow the names of 104 auditors but no verb, a copyist's error.[76] The two probably agreed to produce their arguments (*resons*), for the next passage says that these were examined before the 104, until 21 June, when Bruce and Balliol, asked if they had anything more to say or submit in writing, replied in the negative, save that they reserved the right to make further *resons* before judgement, 'by which they might influence their

---

    [73] Holt, 'The *Casus Regis*', *Colonial England*, 307–26.

    [74] We talk commonly about 'blood' rather than 'genes', and 'blood relations' can still have a powerful public impact.

    [75] In the Great Roll I have noted it only twice in Stones and Simpson, ii, 201–9.

    [76] The original PRO E39/99/58 is largely illegible (Palgrave, *Docs. Hist. Scot.*, 52–55) and the text has been preserved in the Glasgow MS which presumably dropped something in the copying.

judge'. King Edward immediately asked the 104 if they had enough to enable him to proceed to judgement between these two, and received a positive reply. He could now 'go forward to make judgement'. To this narrative and commitment the 104 put their seals. It must have seemed a vital point and document in the whole Great Cause, firstly because it was sealed thus, secondly because, apart from the pleadings of the two Claimants, no other original document from the Cause has survived in the royal archives and none was listed there by Stapledon in 1323, and thirdly because it was copied into Liber A probably within the year, again uniquely.[77]

But what followed? There seems to have been a recess (perhaps for the feast of St John, 24 June) till, on Wednesday, 25 June, the 'Claims, answers, pleadings (*resons*) and the whole process' were read yet again, and the two Claimants, asked if they wished to add anything before judgement, replied 'certainly not unless the king had questions to ask of them, because they had been advised that enough had been said for the king to proceed to judge-ment'.[78] After so many assertions of full and final argument the reader can expect only one thing, a judgement. But that the reader is not given, because what the king heard was apparently just what has survived in fragments, what the auditors had heard and had passed to him on 21 June, two sides of the argument in raw undigested form, and with no conclusions, unless, perhaps, they expressed themselves for the laws and customs of Scotland.

This would perhaps explain why the Great Roll, having brought us to the decision to hear Bruce *v.* Balliol, moving the pleadings which we know took place before 21 June to the October session, launches into a quite different matter: the king ordered the (eighty) auditors of Scotland to advise him, after taking an oath, 'by what laws and customs [the case] should proceed to judgement'.[79] The reply of the eighty as recorded in the Roll was that 'they were in such disagreement about the laws and customs of Scotland in relation to so difficult and unheard-of a case, that they dared not advise the king without greater counsel and fuller deliberation'.[80] Although not strictly an answer to the question, this did identify a stumbling block in their deliberations and may be an approximate record of proceedings at some point after 25 June, for the obstacle immediately reappeared.

At the request of the eighty, Edward then added his twenty-four to their number. The 104 consulted and the twenty-four reported that whereas the king would have proceeded by the advice of the eighty if they had been agreed, they were in great discord on their (Scottish) laws and customs. The twenty-four were few, they said, and not the most authoritative in Edward's

---

[77] The protest of 3 July 1292 meets these criteria, but it deals with overlordship and not the Scottish succession. Stones and Simpson, ii, D.79.i.

[78] Stones and Simpson, ii, D.78.

[79] Stones and Simpson, ii, A.71, 72.

[80] Stones and Simpson, ii, A.71, 72.

kingdom, so he should seek the counsel of the prelates, magnates and wise men of his kingdom. Edward then adjourned the Cause to 14 October 1292, to which day he summoned weightier advisers, ordering those present to think carefully about the business until then. He would also send to wise men of various *regiones*, to obtain their advice.[81]

The date was probably Wednesday, 3 July 1292, when Edward protested that he was bound by his promise of 12 June 1291 to hear Scottish cases in Scotland for this time only, and not for any future such occasion. This was twice recorded, in the only short instrument known to have been drawn up before 20 November 1292, and in letters quoting also the 1291 promise, by English and Scottish bishops, and four Scottish magnates, in a balance of the two Scottish factions.[82] This protest was clearly critical for the English king and for the Scots, and, although it related to some future hypothetical situation, and had no immediate impact in July 1292, it must have been provoked by a challenge to Edward's rights. Given the obvious intention of the Great Roll to justify Edward taking the Cause to his council, the immediate issue would be a proposal to adjourn the Cause to an English venue, probably a Michaelmas parliament at, say, Westminster. This breach of the 1291 promise would meet immediate resistance by the Scots, for, if the court sat in England, then Scotland was under the lordship of the English king; if it did not, then that issue was postponed till a king of Scotland faced it.[83] Why the Scots were successful in their resistance is unknown, but it is not hard to see why the king's protest was taken out of its context by Caen and copied into the Great Roll before August 1291; he had no wish to explain the circumstances in which it was made.

The week 26 June – 3 July had been spent in seeking a judgement based on the process of 16–21 June, unsuccessfully because the heart of the matter, the applicable law, was undecided. The issue had probably been debated in this or that forum for a full month, so unproductively that there was nothing but argument to record. Edward, so far as we can tell, was fully justified in losing patience with the Scots and even with his own twenty-four, and should be given credit for allowing the Scots every opportunity to act as judges in their own Cause in August 1291 and June 1292. But there must be a suspicion that, having heard at length about the disagreements over Scots law, which promised to be interminable, Edward wished to move to a place and a tribunal which would admit the relevance of English law. He was frustrated over the move, but changed the tribunal. The adjournment to

---

[81] Stones and Simpson, ii, A.72.

[82] Stones and Simpson, ii, A.79, D.79.i.

[83] Balliol urged using the law of England and Scotland, and so some, objecting to 'law of England', may have argued that since the court must sit in Scotland, it must judge by Scots law and custom; if it could not sit in England, the law of England was not relevant. This was perhaps more than Edward and his lawyers would swallow.

October marked a significant break in the Cause, for after the resumption we hear no more of Edward I's twenty-four auditors.

A much larger group of councillors now advised the king, playing a critical role, while the eighty were marginalised, generally to answering questions or agreeing to propositions, devised by the council. This was clearly the court of Edward king of England, lord superior of Scotland, which strengthened the case of Balliol (urging the law of inferior tenures) and weakened that of Bruce, but that was probably not intentional; on the contrary, perhaps as quid pro quo for taking the issue to his council, the king consented to overseas consultations which must have seemed likely to favour Bruce. The Cause was probably adjourned on 3 July, after which the council continued to sit in parliament in the first half of July to hear complaints by Macdougalls and Macdonalds on 7 July, and Eric II's claim for funds, hearings which detained the king till the middle of the month. He must have been glad to leave Berwick and its intransigent and disputatious Scots.

Note

The lists of auditors

There are four lists of auditors' names of which only the two latest are dated, no. 3 to 21 June 1292 and no. 4 to 6 November 1292.[84] The earliest, no. 1, is given in the Great Roll under 5 June 1291 and contains 104 names, but one name of Bruce's forty (22) was a later substitute (*postea*) for another (21), so that he had filled only thirty-nine places – unless the list copied by Caen and Tang omitted a name, as I am inclined to think it did.[85]

The editors have unfortunately accepted Tang's list rather than Caen's, and show Bruce 22a as 'deputy' for 22. However, 22a was not a 'deputy', but is found in all lists; 22 is noted in list 1 as replacement for 21. Of five names added in lists 2 or 3 of Bruce, those replaced (29 by Ireby, 32 by Mr William Lamberton, 11 by 'Letheny') can be identified by the placing of the new name. Given the difficulty of identifying list 1, 32, Mr William de Anandia, convincingly,[86] I wonder if his name is not a version of Mr William de Lamberton who replaced him in lists 2 and 3. Two names do not replace another name, of which one might have been omitted by oversight from list 1: either Mr William (Wishart) archdeacon of Teviotdale, between 27 and 28 in list 2, or John of Conveth, between nos 34 and 35, possibly identifiable with the later John Wishart archdeacon of Glasgow.[87] Conveth may have replaced 39. The editors consign to n. 6 on p. 82, Mr Neil Campbell, who occurs in list 4, between Conveth and Rette (Rattray), and was probably

[84] Stones and Simpson, ii, D.77, C.94.

[85] Stones and Simpson, ii, 80–85 shows the four lists of 104 in tabular form.

[86] Watt, *Biographical Dictionary*, 10

[87] Watt, *Biographical Dictionary*, 584, *Note*.

replacement for 24 Colin Campbell, who should not be shown as listed under 4. Neil and Colin might both be Latinised as *Nicholas*, but Mr Neil was clearly not Colin, found among knights. In Balliol's list the bishop of Galloway had two deputies, the abbot of Holywood and the prior of Dryburgh. Whithorn, Holywood and Dryburgh were all Premonstratensian houses.

The substitutes shows that the first list had already been updated, evidently before the second undated list, no. 2, from the Glasgow MS (which has (22) but not (21) in the same place), unfortunately not printed as in the manuscript. It shows 104 names, among whom we can identify three replacements of names in list 1, plus one additional name in Bruce's forty but only one replacement among Balliol's forty.[88]

The editors, accepting 5 June 1291 for list 1, suggest August 1291 for list 2.[89] The evidence suggests otherwise. The August date for list 2 presents difficulties because there are five new names in list 2, four for Bruce, one for Balliol, all of whom are present in list 3, but only one of them in list 4, suggesting that list 2 was closer to June 1292 than to August 1291. The invincible obstacle to so late a date as June 1292 for list 2 is the occurrence among the king's appointees of the bishop of Carlisle who died on 1 March 1292. There is no reason to think that the different sections (king, Bruce, Balliol) in a list were of different dates, so lists 1 and 2 must be earlier than March 1292.

One of Bruce's nominees appearing in list 1 and disappearing by list 2 is William de Soules, father of Nicholas the Claimant; he had served Alexander III as justiciar of Lothian, and was sheriff of Roxburgh after 1286 and in June 1291. On 13 and 18 August 1291, however, he with others, mainly Bruce-appointed auditors, was rewarded by Edward I for his good service in Scotland, grants which show that he was then alive[90] and with the others must surely have been present at the 2–12 August 1291 session. List 1 could thus be of August 1291, and given the delays likely in gathering names and persons after 12 June, probably was of that date. List 2 must be later than August 1291 but earlier than 1 March 1292. Unfortunately there are few references to William de Soules' replacement in 2, 'Norman de Letheny', who, given the relative rarity of his first name in Scotland, can be identified with some confidence as Norman de Leslie ('Lescelyn', perhaps 'Lechelyn'), an important knightly tenant from the Garioch, who was probably replaced by Adam de Rattray in list 4. I can find no evidence to date list 2 more closely than August 1291 x February 1292.

---

[88] Frendraught for 37; it will be noted that in list 4 the reverse happens.

[89] Stones and Simpson, ii, 80. Note that the king's auditor, John de Lethegreyns, who disappears between lists 2 and 3, was appointed on 12 August 1291, as J. de Lodegreyns, to the commission to search the Scottish records; Stones and Simpson, ii, D.67.i. Indexed in Stones and Simpson under Lithegreynes.

[90] *Rot. Scot.*, i, 3b, 5a.

CHAPTER 13

The Great Cause II:
the final phase

We have seen some of the issues raised by the pleadings in the Great Cause, and how their success depended upon the answer to a prior question: what law is relevant? In this chapter I turn to how the learned in Paris were consulted, examine their responses to show their preference for a custom of the Scottish succession, failing which, by a majority, for the right of the nearer by degree. Some opinions referred to a court of peers, or to the advice of peers, and the early minute of proceedings at Berwick, that found in the *Annales*, shows that this concept was under discussion – that is that the opinions, ignored in the Great Roll, were debated seriously by the Claimants and the king's council. Nonetheless opinion in the council was evidently hostile to the Paris opinions' preferred fall-back, Roman law, which did favour Bruce, and sought a means of applying to an indivisible kingdom representation of the senior line, which, if Scotland were a barony, would have given Balliol the chief place, and Balliol, Bruce and Hastings each a third of the property. How a decision for Balliol, but keeping indivisibility, was achieved is only hinted at by a series of questions and answers recorded in the *Annales* minute; the debate behind them is not recorded, and understanding them is not made easier by the totally different version concocted by Caen for his Great Roll.

The final decision, against the impartibility of the Scottish kingdom, was rushed through with scarcely a debate. But that may not have been justice.

The pleadings which had been collected together about 25 June lay in waiting for the court which reassembled on 14 October 1292, more akin to a *coram rege* forum at Westminster than to the *centumviri*. Perhaps the most significant person now present was Gilbert de Rothbury, clerk of the council with responsibility for parliamentary business. He had been present at Norham in June 1291,[1] but not, it seems, in August 1291 or June 1292.[2] He

---

[1] *Cal. Close Rolls, 1288–1296*, 200.
[2] However, absence of evidence that he was there is not at all conclusive. For Gilbert see Richardson and Sayles 'The King's Ministers in Parliament, 1272–1307', *EHR*, xlvi (1931), 529–50, at 537–42. To which add the references in Stones and Simpson, ii, Index, under Rothbury, Gilbert de., showing that he was at Berwick in October–November 1292.

may have been responsible for the minute of the autumn 1292 session preserved in *Annales*, which is selective; if we are fortunate that written pleadings and even some notes by a reporter also survive, these pleadings cover business only after 7 November, when judgement had been given against Bruce in Bruce *v.* Balliol. The transfer by Caen of earlier pleadings to this October session, and what other sources report of that session, strongly suggests that no pleading from the thirty days of 25 June – 3 July and 14 October – 6 November has been lost. That time was devoted to debate, the context of which is unreported and may have been unrecorded. *Annales* minutes give a series of seven royal questions and the responses thereto, the first asked on 24 October after ten days of debate in Edward's council, the others asked over almost two weeks.

The king's decision in July 1292 to consult 'by solemn messengers from his council, wise men of divers *regiones*', has sent ghostly enquirers over Europe, not least to Bologna. But these words were the rhetoric of the Great Roll, ignoring the shortage of time and other factors. The responses from Paris were preserved both in England and in Scotland, to be included, in the fifteenth century, in Wyntoun's *Chronicle* and in Bower's *Scotichronicon*; almost certainly their text was at St Andrews cathedral, borne there by Bishop William Fraser or by the prior (both auditors at Berwick). The heading to Bower's text describes consultations of the learned of the French king's court, and of Paris University, while Wyntoun is more specific, naming the presidents and lords of the *parlement*, the wise men of that court and Paris University. Probably only Paris was, and was meant to be, consulted.[3] The Paris opinions were the reason why the court in October made such heavy weather of a matter on which it had been 'well-informed' by 21 June. Their role in the October deliberations is ignored in the records, but not wholly concealed there.

I shall refer to the sections of the text as they are numbered in the Stones and Simpson edition.[4] The stated case, numbered (i), seems to have been influenced by Edward I and by the Scottish auditors. A king, not crowned but inaugurated in a royal seat, and holding his kingdom of another king,

Biography under Gilbert de Rothbury in *Dictionary of National Biography, Missing Persons* (1993), 251.

[3] The heading to the opinions in the English text says that consultation was *peritorum de consilio regis Francie et discretorum studii Parisius et aliorum justic' et peritorum Anglie.* Thomas Weyland was the lone *justicia et peritus Anglie* (Stones and Simpson, ii, 359, 364). The *Scotichronicon* version has a different heading in the correct place: *Consultaciones peritorum de consilio curie regis Francie et discreciorum de studio Parisiasensi* [sic] *super causa de successione regni Scotorum* (*Scotichronicon*, vi, 12). The latter (but *Parisius*) was probably the original heading, altered by omitting *curie*, in the transmission of the English text. For Wyntoun, who may have known that the judges were called *president, Chron. Wyntoun*, vi, 174, 176.

[4] Stones and Simpson, ii, Appendix E, pp. 359–65. I have ignored the names of the respondents; (ii) and (iii) are each three individuals. There is an alternative modern edition with translation in *Scotichronicon*, vi, 10–27. Hand, 'Opinions of the Paris Lawyers', *Irish Jurist*, new series, v (1970), 145–51, numbers the opinions 1–10.

his superior and direct lord, for homage, as a fief, died without children or heirs. Many claimed to be heir, and the king who is superior lord, took the kingdom into his hands until the question of who had better right could be discussed before him. The strongest claimants (*potissime*) were two, Titius and Seius (the usual names in a case-report in Roman law), descended from the late king's grand-uncle: his *pronepos* by the elder daughter, and his *nepos* by the second daughter, both collateral relatives of the king, one with right of primogeniture, the other with nearness. 'Supposing that this kingdom is impartible, which of them ought to be preferred in succession to the kingdom?'[5]

The heavy emphasis upon the superior lord and his tenant-king (this is the only use of 'fief' in the Great Cause) not only justified Edward I's jurisdiction, but may also have suggested that his court should apply the law used there for his other tenants. It stated the grounds for Balliol's claim, but most of the respondent lawyers ignored the king's subordinate status unless it was raised with them in questioning. The question in Roman law format may have invited attention to the grounds in 'imperial law' for Bruce's claim, but what followed was a neutral statement of facts about the two lines, Balliol and Bruce. The invitation to answer did not ask for identification of a relevant law, but the the French respondents all made that attempt. The opinions, from six groups and four individuals, were mostly delivered orally (*dicit* or *dicunt*), but were not restricted to answering the question. All except (vi) and (xi) identified the kingdom as Scotland, but only (v) and (ix) named Bruce and Balliol.

The response of (iii) was followed by an interrogation, possibly also addressed to (ii), in which they were invited to agree that Scottish custom for earldoms and baronies was applicable; they rejected this, but accepted (iiib) the custom of the court of the English king relating to the peers of that court. When (iv) had responded in favour of proximity, (iiib) was put to him, and in (ivb) he distinguished procedural custom which should be English, and custom on the substantive issue which should be Scottish, but must be custom on the succession of Scottish kings, not of barons. Only if that fails is there recourse to custom of the English court in which the Cause is heard. Subsequently his response was put to (viii) who agreed with it, but added (viiib) that if there is no custom in the English court regarding the peers of that court, then there can be recourse to *ius scriptum*, Roman law, or, with advice of peers and others, the English king can make a new law. This respondent admits recourse to Roman law as a fall-back position, but the interrogator in all three is pressing for quite another response, one grounded in the law of succession to fiefs as known in England and Scotland.

In addition to these three respondents (or four, with (ii)), (v) and (ix) were also further interrogated. Eight respondents gave explicit priority to a

---

[5] Stones and Simpson, ii, 359.

custom of succession in Scotland: (ii), (iii), (iv), (v), (vi), (viii), (ix), (x); failing such a custom, six or seven came down in favour of nearness of degree: (ii), (iii), (iv), (vi), (x), (xi) and by implication (viii). Five regarded Roman law as a, or the, residuary system to be followed: (ii), (iii), (vi), (vii), (viii), but (iv), citing Roman-derived custom in the French royal court, might be added. The weight of five (out of ten) in favour of Roman law is greater than first appears, since two opinions of the six or seven were given by religious, who sought biblical authority for nearness of degree, the Franciscans (x) in God's judgement in Numbers, 27.1–11, with which the Dominicans (xi) agreed, confessing ignorance of custom in Scotland and England and of imperial laws.

Scottish custom was clearly the first recourse, but thereafter the preponderance of opinion in favour of nearness of degree is striking; the three who think differently ((v), (vii), (ix)) do not agree with each other in any of their idiosyncratic views. Respondent (vii), a canon lawyer, made no mention of Scottish custom and gave priority to any daughter of Earl David who survived Alexander III. If none did, then the first-born of the two Claimants, because he was the first to become a relative, had the better right. An authority, the Authentic, is added in a very oblique way: 'this is what the Authentic implies when speaking of the succession of collateral relatives', which can only refer to Nov. 118.3, on succession in intestacy of collaterals, the chapter on which the Romanist case for nearness of degree rests: where the direct line does not exist, succession goes to 'all collateral relatives according to the privilege of each degree, so that the nearer in degree shall be preferred; but where there are several in the same degree, the inheritance shall be divided among them according to the number of persons'. From this (vii) has, not unreasonably, deduced succession of the nearest in degree, should she have survived. But the Novel gives no preference to a first-born among cousins, but rather insists upon equal shares for those in the same degree. The source of this part of the opinion remains an enigma. Respondent (vii) may be accounted partially in favour of nearness of degree and Roman law; he adds no weight to the Balliol case for seniority of line.

The disgraced Chief Justice of Common Pleas, Thomas Weyland, (ix), would know the law of freehold in England better than most, and might have been sought out for that reason. On the other hand Weyland had fled the king's justice in 1289, choosing exile as a Franciscan in Paris rather than to stand trial. How he lived thereafter is unknown, but a place in chapter and at board with his order in Paris is not unlikely; there he would be found by the auditor Gainsborough, who, I suggest, came as a royal representative.[6] He delivered a wholly different view from the Frenchmen: '... unless the

---

[6] On Weyland see Brand, 'Chief Justice and Felon: the Career of Thomas Weyland', *The Political Context of Law*, eds Eales and Sullivan, 27–47, reprinted in Brand, *The Making of the Common Law*, 113–33.

law and custom ... was clear in the kingdom of Scots with regard to the succession to that kingdom ..., this case ... since the kingdom is held in fee ... for homage ... [is] altogether similar to a case of like nature which might arise with regard to an earldom or barony in the kingdom of England ...'. So close is this to the leading questions put to earlier respondents that it is difficult to believe that it had not been suggested to him, too; he went on to state the obvious conclusion, that the kingdom was partible, Balliol receiving the royal dignity and, with Bruce and Hastings, his purparty, a third of the kingdom. Weyland was clearly responding to the stated case ('in fee ... for homage' is a quotation from it), but could not accept its proviso of impartibility, which logically excluded the English law of tenures.

But he was taken up on this and asked: 'if Bruce received an unfavourable judgement on his petition in which he claims the whole kingdom ... could he go back afterwards and claim his purparty?' and answered in the affirmative. Since Weyland had already given Bruce his purparty, the point of this question must have been the fear that Bruce's claim for the whole would rule out a claim for part; the questioner would surely be Bruce's agent, who had found most other opinions in favour of his master and had no need to question them. Someone else 'led' respondents ((iii), (iv), (viii)) in search of agreement that an English or Scottish law of inferior tenures should apply to the kingdom; in the October proceedings at Berwick it became quite clear that Edward I saw this as the resolution to otherwise interminable wrangling, but Balliol had already advanced this argument in June 1292,[7] and these cross-examinations at Paris probably came from his agent.

One group of three respondents, (v), differs from the others in various respects. Out of pity for the reader I have discussed in a note at the end of this chapter the means of interrogation and the answers. They are interesting, but they were not critical in the Great Cause. The response of the three would have allowed Edward to apply the custom of England (where succession to the throne was not helpful) or to escheat Scotland to the overlord for default of a male line of heirs, otherwise to fall back on Roman law with nearness of degree. They seem to have dithered, while remaining robustly against the law of inferior tenures – Balliol's case. They were familiar with the *ius scriptum*, used in southern France and beyond the Alps, and they did not merely send a written response but were interviewed about it; the agents from Berwick may have found them in the law-school of Orleans. But the response of the Franciscans of Paris, (ix), was clearly given in writing also, with authorities, so those who needed to consult authorities, could do so and could present the result in writing.[8]

---

[7] Stones and Simpson, ii, 167 at (v); 169 at (iii).

[8] The respondents are often very difficult to identify, but a valiant effort is made in Stones and Simpson, ii, 400–1. For (v) Dr Brand has suggested to me that the three were Italian and were consulted in Italy or southern France, the land of *ius scriptum*. I would accept that

The efforts by the agents, and their failure, to secure opinions in favour of a law of inferior tenures explains why the notarial record of the Cause showed no further interest in the opinions; they were regarded as the Claimants' material, and were indeed used by them, as the questions and answers at Berwick were to show. There is almost no direct borrowing, because the opinions would be mediated through argument by supporters of Bruce (but perhaps not of Balliol). Their content was known to the king's council, though the direct evidence for this is a parchment completely illegible on the face, but endorsed 'Contains those things which must be demanded by E. king of England and his council from the eighty chosen from Scotland, concerning a certain advice on judgement to be made about the right of succession and of other [matters] touching John Balliol and Robert Bruce'.[9] Though we cannot know what this advice (*avisamentum*) said, the only external opinion known to have been sought on the sucession question was that of the learned men of Paris.

The insistence of all the respondents, including Weyland, that a custom of Scotland, if such there be, must prevail, is as striking as the evident need to find a fall-back if it did not exist. In fact, it is difficult to be sure what would have been regarded as establishing a relevant custom. The failure by each of the three kings who ruled between 1165 and 1286 to have more than one legitimate son surviving to puberty meant that by 1280 precedents about, and options for, the succession were very few. The exact circumstances of 1290 were most unlikely to have occurred before; indeed the simplest form of the problem, shown in France in 1316, 1322 and 1328 when a king's only issue was a daughter, and when a brother, or, in 1328, a cousin, established himself as king, had been raised in Scotland only in 1195, when the later French aversion to female right prevailed;[10] it had diminished almost to disappearance by 1280. But the Scots had considered issues which might have been thought relevant in 1292, as we have seen, no fewer than three times in 1281–84.

Let us recall that in the 1281 treaty with Norway, the rights of heirs general, with male primogeniture, to succession to the throne was said to be in accord with law and custom, though the right of the king's daughter to succeed in default of male heirs was carefully emphasised, as though it were a dubious idea.[11] An attempt was made to clarify the respective rights of king's granddaughter and king's daughter in the complex settlement made

---

the first two could well have been Italian, but time weighs against consultation beyond the Languedoil. Italians may have taught at Orleans.

[9] PRO E39/99/98; Stones and Simpson, ii, 237n; *Cal. Docs. Scot.*, v, no. 112; begins *Continet ea que exigi …*

[10] But the succession in 1328 greatly weakened the authority of Philip VI; it is arguable that if Isabella, queen of Edward II, had had a French husband, then their child would have succeeded – as Edward III did not.

[11] For a full account of the documents discussed here see above, pp. 165–71.

in December 1281 for the marriage of Alexander III's surviving son to Marguerite of Flanders – succession by heirs general with male primogeniture, but with qualifications which gave a second son of the king a better right than the daughter of his elder son, and then restored that daughter's right if her uncle had no child. This document in effect applied the custom of heritage in freehold to succession to the throne but with extempore modifications for which there was no justification in custom. The modifications might have supported the claim of Bruce, but the settlement seems to have been unknown in Scotland a decade after it was made.[12] Both treaties of 1281 emphasised that the king made them with advice (of his council, of barons), but in both the king, to meet the needs of the moment and placate the other party, interpreted the law of heritage; he was making custom of succession to the kingdom on the hoof.

In February 1284 the secular magnates undertook that if the king should die, or if his son should have died, leaving no son or daughter, they would receive the Maid and her lawful issue as their lady and rightful heir of the king. They also promised to secure payment of debts due on his death – a provision which underlined the nature of the document.[13] It made no claim to be custom or law, but was a warrandice of a property settlement, including that of the 1281 treaty on the Maid of Scotland, issued by those who might have disturbed it. Unlike the treaties of 1281, this 1284 text was cited later, correctly summarised in Bruce's petition, and in Balliol's version of that petition. Balliol himself argued that Bruce was wrong to claim that a woman could not reign, because the baronage 'received and held and did fealty to [the Maid] who lately was queen and lady of Scotland',[14] the 1284 deed distorted, so that the oath to receive the Maid as lady and heir, becomes fealty to a queen.

Neither Bruce nor Balliol used the exact terms of the text to argue for nearness of degree or representation, on both of which it had a bearing. The Maid of Norway would not inherit if Alexander III had another daughter, justifiable on grounds of nearness of degree; nor if the lord Alexander had a posthumous daughter, justifiable on grounds of representation. This document differed from the Flemish treaty in that its conditions did come about, though its provisions were not completed by the Maid taking possession of her inheritance. To a modern commentator it is extraordinary that reliance was placed upon recognition of Bruce in a document of the 1240s, if only it could be found, while the relevance of the Norwegian treaty

---

[12] The inventory of Scottish records on 29 September 1282 lists fully the documents of the 1281 Norwegian marriage, but has no heading for Flanders, naming only 'the business of Flanders, namely four pairs of letters'; *APS*, i, 108–9. The later inventories do not mention Flanders.

[13] *APS*, i, 424. This document was among the English public records; *ibid.*, 286.

[14] Stones and Simpson, ii, 142, 203, 182 para. vii.

and the 1284 undertaking, still extant, was almost ignored.[15] Arguably these were law, definitions of inadequate custom, the 'certain law of Scotland' of the Great Cause process, 'specialties' which might have been cited by either Bruce or Balliol. Their internal contradictions would have produced long debate but at least they had a bearing on the law and custom of Scotland to which the parties and their lawyers expressed such firm adherence.

The Cause resumed on 14 October 1292, when, according to the *Annales* minutes, the Claimants and the eighty were present and were warned to be ready from day to day to come when the king summoned them. Of what followed we are told only that the petitions and arguments were examined until on 25 October, ten days later, the king's council, forty-five in number, was asked to choose between judgement by imperial laws or by the laws and customs of the realms of England or Scotland. I call this question (1); it was designed to show that there was no conciliar support for imperial laws as against 'the laws of England or Scotland', offered not as alternatives to each other but as a body of generally similar laws. The Great Roll claims that it was also put to the Scottish auditors,[16] but the *Annales* minutes of this phase show that it was not, and therefore that the Scots had not so easily dismissed Bruce's case. Bruce's varying appeals to 'the law by which kings reign', natural law, and imperial laws, however, had been reduced by Edward and defined as the last of these. In their responses, one group of councillors rejected *iura scripta*, another *leges imperiales*; these designations of the Roman alternative are most likely to have come from the *leges imperiales* or *ius (pre)scriptum* offered in the Paris opinions. The bishop of Byblos, interpreting opinion (ii) in favour of imperial laws with ingenuity, had suggested that the king proceed by 'the laws by which he judges his subjects … because here he is held as emperor'.[17]

Antony Bek gave a more subtle response: 'in this case the laws and customs of the kingdoms of Scotland and England are to be used and not imperial laws, unless they say something "specially" for the case put forward'.[18] Since Roman law certainly had relevant things to say about succession, but was unlikely to make 'special' mention of Scotland, or even of kingdoms, Bek was seeking not to admit imperial laws, but to turn inside out the opinion of respondent (iii) that the nearer in degree was to be preferred according to Roman law and French custom, but that, if in Scottish custom primogeniture 'gave prerogative in the succession', then

---

[15] The editors remark on this: Stones and Simpson, ii, 190 n. 3. In fact, on 3 July 1292, the same day as his statement about not hearing a future Great Cause in Scotland, Edward told the chancellor of Scotland to issue letters enforcing payment to Alexander III's executors of debts due to that king; *Rot. Scot.*, i, 9a. This reflected the terms of the *obligatorium* of 1284, but it made no reference to that document.

[16] Stones and Simpson, ii, A.81.

[17] Stones and Simpson, ii, C.87.

[18] Stones and Simpson, ii, C.87. I have translated *nisi facerent specialiter pro casu proposito* as 'unless they say something specially…'

that custom was to be kept 'specially' above all other laws, written or customary.[19] It is significant that Bek gave priority to the laws and customs of the two kingdoms, and not of Scotland. It was agreed that no relevant Scottish custom about royal succession existed, but the question and Bek's words show that the search was on to establish English custom, too, as relevant.

The other early Paris opinion (ii) had also demanded a 'certain [i.e. definite, unambiguous] and approved custom' of royal succession in Scotland in favour of primogeniture, otherwise imperial laws were applicable. The agents, like Bek, knew that no such custom was acknowledged or 'certain', for they went on to ask respondent (iii) and possibly (ii): if there is no Scottish custom about succession to the kingdom, but there is one for earldoms, baronies and other tenures, should that be applied to the kingdom (as Balliol had urged)?[20] The respondents (iii) were firmly against, arguing that as the kingdom was a fief of the English king, it should be judged by the custom of his court, which had standing for the peers of that court.[21]

In the questions put to his council and the eighty Edward was clearly influenced by these arguments. The Parisian respondents had thrown out the law of Scottish tenures; in question (2) Edward sought to adjust to Anglo-Scottish conditions the French notion of a court and jurisdiction of peers (the most exalted nobles of the French realm), asking the council about exceptionality: is the kingdom of Scotland so excellent and honourable (*dignum*) that it ought to be adjudged differently from, or the same as, other tenures of the kingdoms of England and Scotland? He was asking, is there a law of exalted tenures, the tenures of peers?[22]

That this was directed at Bek is suggested by the fact that only his response was recorded, all other councillors simply agreeing. In the matter of succession he said, 'no other judgement should be made about the kingdom of Scotland by reason of any dignity or prerogative than [would be made] about other tenures of his [*or* their] peers; but the [*or* a] kingdom has, or can have, many other prerogatives in itself'.[23] Bek had picked up from respondent (iii) the notion of peerage and of a prerogative in succession and

---

[19] Stones and Simpson, ii, 360, end of first paragraph of (iii).

[20] Stones and Simpson, ii, D.76(G)(ii).

[21] In France the court of peers consisted of the king and twelve other peers, one of whom was the English king as duke of Aquitaine; neither in England nor in Scotland did the notion of a group of magnates who were exceptional for some purposes find favour, though one chronicler represented the ruling council of twelve appointed by the Scots in 1295 as peers. The notion would be anathema to the king of England.

[22] The 'court of peers of France' is discussed in Keeney, *Judgment by Peers*, ch. 1 and appendix B; and by Sautel-Boulet, 'Le rôle juridictionnel de la cour des pairs aux XIIIe et XIVe siècles', *Recueil ... Clovis Brunel*, ii, 507–20. She argues (p. 515) that the *ius parie* has the fundamental meaning of mastery given to the peer for the fief which he holds of the king, in virtue of the contract of vassalage between them.

[23] Stones and Simpson, ii, C.87.

rejected the latter, while admitting that a kingdom had other prerogatives. Unfortunately the identity of *suus* in *parium suorum*, 'his/their peers', is unclear; it should be the speaker, Bek, but it could be the Claimants, whose petitions were referred to, or just possibly a king of Scotland, implied by mention of the kingdom. In any case, Bek's reference to 'tenure of peers' leaves little doubt that a Paris opinion was under discussion.

Maitland explains prerogative as the exceptional rights enjoyed by the king within the law, such as the right to wardship of the lands of a tenant-in-chief, both those held of the king and those held of other lords. '"Prerogativity" is exceptionality.'[24] Bek rejected exceptionality for the royal succession to Scotland; whatever other prerogatives (for example, its own judicial system) it might have, succession to it was as to a tenure of unidentified, but presumably English, peers of the Scottish king. He was surely singled out to speak here because his position and his tenure came closest to being those of a peer, in the French sense, in England, and to matching the English view of the proper position of the Scottish king. As bishop of Durham he was lord of a liberty or franchise of hitherto unparalleled scope; between Tyne and Tees the bishop's peace was protected by the bishop's courts and the bishop's writ excluded that of the king; his rights included prerogative wardship and the prerogative of forest law. So great was his independence that at a later date John Balliol might have cited the precedent of Durham to stop appeals from his court to Westminster. But, unlike Balliol, Bek enjoyed the friendship of Edward I, whose secretary he was, and his liberty was supported by the king and his judges on many occasions; it was to escape unscathed from *Quo Warranto* enquiries in 1293, for example, and in 1300 a knight of the bishop even dared to claim that 'the bishop was king within his regality as the king was outside the waters of Tyne and Tees'.

Others, however, fretted at its use, particularly, after 1286, Bek's ecclesiastical superior, the archbishop of York. Friction culminated in the archbishop's clerks serving a summons on Bek on 23 August 1292, in the king's presence and without his prior consent. Arrested, the clerks had been brought to trial before king and council on 1 September, and ultimately the archbishop himself was charged in parliament (February 1293), where the king's attorney stood up for the secular rights of the bishop of Durham: '[he] has a double status, namely the status of bishop as to his spiritualities, and the status of earl palatine as to his temporal holdings', the earliest use of 'palatine' for such a franchise.[25]

[24] Pollock and Maitland, *History of English Law*, i, 512.

[25] Fraser, *History of Antony Bek*, ch. V. The quotations are on pp. 98, 95. For Bek's ambitions and the definition of the 'palatinate', Scammell, 'The Origins and Limitations of the Liberty of Durham', *English Historical Review*, lxxxi (1966), 449–73; for the definition of 'palatine' under Edward I, Alexander, 'The English Palatinates and Edward I', *Journal of British Studies*, xxii, part 2 (1983), 2–22. Bek was influenced in making a claim to palatine

This case must have been in the minds of the king, Bek and the council in October 1292, when the tenure of Scotland was in debate; it gives an exact context and meaning to the response of Bek, who had succeeded to his bishopric by royal nomination and canonical appointment, as to any other bishopric – no prerogative there. But his tenure was regalian and palatine for he enjoyed many of the prerogatives of a king, and surely spoke of himself when he spoke of the peers of the king of Scotland. The kingdom could have the 'many prerogatives' of the palatinate of Durham;[26] but in the matter of succession, it was not prerogative, did not escape the laws and customs of England and Scotland. Bek sought to show that among the tenures of England there were some like the kingdom of Scotland, and it would therefore be right to judge the kingdom in that way; at the same time he went some way to meet the Paris opinions in favour of a court of peers.

On 25 October Burnell died, and there was probably a short recess. On 29 October 1292 Edward spoke to his court: he was superior lord of Scotland by reason of the kingdom of England, and he had to give judgements between his subjects according to the laws of England and Scotland, where they were in agreement. This too stemmed from the Paris responses. Respondent (iv) gave an opinion on the stated case in favour of nearness in degree if there was no custom for the Scottish throne, and was then asked: 'other masters [this can only be (iii)] think that in the case of succession to the kingdom of Scotland, the custom of that kingdom is not to be followed but rather the custom of the court of England, which has standing for the peers of that court'. This entirely misrepresented (iii) who had come down explicitly in favour of Scottish custom on succession to the kingdom and against that to lesser dignities and tenures only. Nonetheless it raised a valid question: was Scottish custom overridden by English feudal law because Scotland was a fief held of the English king? Respondent (iv) distinguished between procedure, which should be English, and substantive law, which should be Scottish custom. Further interrogated, he insisted that this be the custom of the succession of kings, not of earls etc.; if there were no such custom for kings, then the custom of the superior court, the court of England, was to be followed, the position of respondent (iii), and the position which Edward developed in his statement of 29 October.

His question (3), however, addressed to Balliol, Bruce and the eighty, made no reference to the custom of the realms but was essentially a rewording of question (2) and again sought to establish the nature of the kingdom. He asked 'if you know any argument or have any specialty'

status by the use of the title 'count palatine' by Edmund, brother of Edward I, who was count (palatine) of Champagne by marriage, and a peer of France – which may also have been Bek's ambition in England. Cf. Matthew Paris under 1257; Chron. Majora, v, 606.

[26] Others might be the earl of Chester, an earldom now held inalienably by the king (James W. Alexander, 'New Evidence on the Palatinate of Chester', English Historical Review, lxxxv (1970), 715–29), and the extensive franchises of the Anglo-Irish lords.

whereby he should not decide 'on this kingdom as on earldoms, baronies and other tenures'.[27] Balliol and Bruce were given two days in which to produce anything relevant. The word 'specialty' was used in the question with its usual late thirteenth-century meaning of a deed, and was so understood by Bruce in his reply: 'for he has no specialty of the royalty of the kingdom in his possession, but if the kingdom comes into his hands he will show all the specialties and other things which can be found to the king'. He had already committed himself to the existence of one such specialty, Alexander II's recognition of Bruce as heir to the throne, sworn to, and sealed by, king, bishops and barons, and preserved (unfindably!) in the royal treasury of Scotland.[28]

Balliol replied apologetically that it was not for him to limit the power of the king as overlord as to the way he should proceed in this business, but that, as his petition made clear, there was indeed a 'specialty and prerogative' whereby judgement could not proceed as for partible earldoms and baronies: the kingdom was impartible, as Bruce too had earlier recognised. This response equated 'specialty' with Bek's 'prerogative' with the sense of 'exceptionality', 'governed by rules other than those of common law', a use which probably antedated and explains its other meaning of 'a deed'. 'Specialty' as exceptionality might be found in quite lowly tenures, so that while succession to a barony would follow common (ordinary) law in the custom and law of both kingdoms, there could be a local custom of succession (e.g. gavelkind) which, within the law and custom of England, was governed by rules other than those of the common law, exceptional rules; such was Balliol's use of the words 'specialty and prerogative' and his view of the kingdom of Scotland.[29] Balliol recognised the decisive shift in the court's proceedings towards accepting his argument that the law of inferior tenures applied, and was now anxiously protecting himself against the logic of that argument, seen by Weyland, that the kingdom would be partible.

No response to question (3) by the eighty is recorded in *Annales*.[30] Despite the terms of the treaties of 1281 and of the undertaking of 1284, they were untroubled (unlike Bruce and Balliol) by Edward's request for any 'specialty'. Yet the very fact of questions (4) and (5) shows that someone –

---

[27] Stones and Simpson, ii, C.88.

[28] Stones and Simpson, ii, D.76(B)(vii), D.76(J).

[29] Thus in a case quoted to me by Dr Brand, an eldest sister claimed to exercise an advowson at the first vacancy since the death of her father, against a younger sister who claimed that in the soke where the church was situated the youngest sister had 'benefit and prerogative' of the eldest (i.e. which the eldest would enjoy in common law). The judgement was that since it was the custom of the realm that the eldest is entitled, and the younger 'showed nothing of specialty', the plaintiff (the eldest) should recover. 'Prerogative' is used here for exceptionality, something outside the rules of common law; 'specialty' is used here for evidence proving the defendant's case. Chaddeworth *v.* Charneles, PRO CP40/60, m. 3.

[30] Stones and Simpson, ii, C.89.

and the eighty are the only candidates – must have taken up the other part
of his question (3), asking 'if you know any argument' whereby he should
not decide on the kingdom as for lesser tenures. There was an argument in
the Paris opinions, which were unsuspect; they were hostile to this proposal
and provided an alternative, imperial laws. Unfortunately they had little by
way of detailed reasoning. The arguments which took place are unrecorded,
and that in itself suggests that they were conducted among the eighty rather
than between them and the council. Nonetheless, the nature of the difficulty
would be known to the court, which pressed on, putting further questions
to the eighty.

Question (4) asked 'if a special case arises in England and an exactly
similar case in Scotland, and the laws of the two kingdoms on the matter
differ and disagree, by which laws, English or Scottish, should it be
judged?'[31] Probably the questioner meant that the English case ('special
case' implied something on which precedents were few and uncertain) had
been decided, when subsequently a similar Scottish case arose, where Scots
law suggested a different decision – so should that be overridden by the
English precedent?[32] The answer of the eighty was surely disingenuous: in
Scotland, if an express law existed on the matter, it should be applied. Since
it was common ground that there was no appropriate express law or custom
in Scotland for the case in hand, this was unhelpful, though at least the
eighty could agree on it.

But the king, by his statement before question (3) and by question (4), was
anxious to establish congruent laws, or, in their absence, an overriding law
for both kingdoms, because the eighty had been arguing about different laws
relevant to the succession. That argument is unreported in the record, but
the choice put to Paris respondent (iv) shows what it must have been: the
custom of Scotland, failing which imperial laws; or on the other hand, the
custom of Scotland, failing which the custom of England. Bruce would
argue that the law of Scotland in this case would fall back on imperial laws
in default of Scottish custom; Balliol that the law of England would accept
Scottish custom but would fall back not on Roman law but on succession
to lesser tenures; the laws of the kingdoms differed in a special case. It may
be significant that question and answer both speak of *lex* and *leges*, without
mention of custom.

Question (5) departed from disagreement of laws to investigate insufficient laws, asking: if the customary laws (*leges consuete*) of neither of the

---

[31] The text seems to be corrupt: *responsum est … quod si in casu subscripto in regno Scocie et
in eodem regno lex habeatur expressa sufficit et debet sufficere lex eadem.* The editors suggest *casu
suprascripto* which is indeed necessary. However, I am not persuaded that the omission of the
first *et* makes better sense, and suggest emending *et* to *emerso* or *emergente. Cf.* the question: *si
casus … emergat.* Stones and Simpson, ii, 215 and n. 3.

[32] This interpretation of the hypothesis was suggested to me by Dr Brand, and has the great
merit of making the answer apposite.

kingdoms sufficed in this case,[33] what then? In Paris respondent (viii) had agreed with respondent (iv) that the law of succession by earls, barons and other subjects was not to be followed, but an established custom of succession for kings in Scotland. If no such custom on this could be found, then he gave three further possibilities. Recourse should be had to the custom of the 'court of England, which is superior' and in which the action about Scotland occurs; but if in that court no custom could be found relevant to the peers of that court, the king might (indifferently, it seems) have recourse to *ius scriptum*, or make a new law on this and similar cases 'by advice of the peers of his court and the magnates of his land'.[34]

According to *Annales*, when the eighty were asked question (5) it was answered 'as before', that the king as overlord could and should make a new law sufficient upon the matter. This unreferenced earlier answer (which was not explicitly said to have come from the eighty but was now adopted by them) was, or was related to, the opinion of respondent (viii) at Paris, which had anticipated the grounds of question (5) ('custom does not cover the case'), and influenced the wording of the eighty's reply thereto. The king was interested not in making a new law, but in the opinion of the eighty on the fall-back authority, if Scottish custom failed to cover the case. Whereas (viii) had given an order of priority (the court (and custom) of England, *ius scriptum* or a new law), the response to question (5) in favour of a new law was a decisive rejection of *ius scriptum* (and therefore of Bruce's case). We do not know why this answer was agreed – perhaps Bruce hoped that Edward would make a new law in his favour. But it was a breakthrough and gave Edward what he sought, a way of avoiding the *ius scriptum* favoured by the Paris consultants; he had the answers to questions (4) and (5) (and possibly to earlier questions) read back to the eighty 'who changed them in no respect'.[35]

The *Annales* minute represents a prolonged argument in which the council declared for the law for lesser tenures (question (2)) but could not secure the same acceptance from the eighty with question (3). What had reopened the whole issue of the legal basis for judgement was the Paris responses, with their frequent and, to Edward, unfortunate, opinions in favour of imperial laws or nearness of degree. The terms of this prolonged argument are now recoverable only from the king's questions, but they, or the answers to them, seem to reflect Paris opinions (ii), (iii), (iv) and (viii) in that order. The agenda for this discussion was, it seems, the Paris dossier, or those parts of it supportive of the Bruce case, put forward as an alternative

---

[33] The Latin here is curiously phrased: *requisiti ... quod si nec regnorum Scocie et Anglie leges consuete sufficiant in hoc casu ...* One would expect, for example, *si regni nec Scocie nec Anglie leges ...*

[34] Stones and Simpson, ii, 364.

[35] Stones and Simpson, ii, C.90.

to what Edward now wanted, the law of lesser tenures as observed in both kingdoms. In the end he got his way.

To pursue the rearranged and edited version of these events presented in the Great Roll would help our understanding of the Great Cause not at all. Questions (4) and (5), put first, were altered to establish that in each kingdom custom must be followed, and that in its absence the king might make a new law. There follows a version of questions (2) and (3): should judgement be given on the kingdom otherwise than on earldoms, baronies and other tenures? The negative answer was presented as a critical decision, the way for which had been cleared by the questions which the Roll put earlier. *Annales* will have given the order of events in 1292; the Roll tidied these up to present the logical step before judgement ('follow the law for lesser tenures') into what it had not been, the last step in time.

On 3 November the king returned to his council with a long question, whose two parts descended from the general to the particular issue; I number the two parts as separate questions. Question (6) asked: having heard the pleadings of Bruce and Balliol, 'which is nearer to the kingdom according to the pleading as pled?' And (7): must the remoter in one degree of succession of the blood of an older daughter exclude the nearer in blood descending from a second daughter 'according to the laws and customs of both kingdoms, England and Scotland', or must the contrary apply?[36] 'Nearness' in (6) suggests Bruce's pleadings in which the laws and customs of both kingdoms were not appropriate. Question (7), on the other hand, made seniority of line *v.* nearness the simple issue, but within the laws and customs of both realms, which were the grounds in Balliol's pleading. The council, answering, not only agreed that the nearer in one degree of the second daughter's line did not exclude the remoter in one degree of the first daughter's line, but went on to assert that succession remained in the line of the first daughter until its issue should fail; thus degree, first, second or whatever, was irrelevant.[37] This answer sufficed for judgement on this part of the Cause, Bruce *v.* Balliol, a judgement drawn up by the council on 5 November, carefully if bleakly worded. It told Bruce that he had no case in terms of his petition, and Balliol that his petition could be answered only when those of the other Claimants had been heard.[38]

Nothing was recorded here about nearness of degree or seniority of line, tenures or the laws of both kingdoms, yet on the following day the Scottish auditors were polled individually, and the bishop of Glasgow, a Bruce nominee, said that whereas he had previously held by Bruce, now, having heard the judgement *and the reasons on which that judgement is founded*, he agreed with it. Thirty-eight from the Balliol camp accepted it; of Bruce's

[36] Stones and Simpson, ii, C.91. Question 6 is omitted from the English summary on p. 216.
[37] Stones and Simpson, ii, C.92.
[38] Stones and Simpson, ii, C.93.

twenty-nine present, some thirteen gave simple acceptance and sixteen the qualified acceptance of the bishop of Glasgow.[39] The rest, we may assume, would not go so far and absented themselves. A cosmetic had been applied to the role of the king's council, important, even necessary, in that it made the judgement acceptable to the Scottish community. But the judgement was that of the council of the English king. And, although no judgement had been given for Balliol, in fact he was treated from this point on as defender in an action in which other Claimants had to prove a better right.

Had the reasons given to the auditors survived, what might they have said? Not that the overlord had made a new law. The nearest we are likely to come is the repeated insistence, in questioning at Paris and Berwick, upon the custom of succession to earldoms, baronies and other tenures. Caen, who had avoided recording in his Great Roll the judgement on 6 November between Bruce and Balliol, evidently found material about it which he used in his final judgement of 17 November. Here he asserts that because all had accepted impartibility 'and because [King Edward], according to the laws and customs of the kingdoms in which he is head (*preest*) has jurisdiction on the right of subjects, and [found?] by the same laws and customs of both kingdoms agreeing in the present case, the remoter in degree descended in the first line is to be preferred to the nearer in degree in the second line in impartible hereditary succession'.[40]

The Latin is not elegant, and there are traces of Paris respondent (iii) even here,[41] but relevance to the 6 November decision is obvious, showing its reliance upon homolgating law and custom of both realms and then applying to the Scottish kingship a law of subjects, earls and barons. It does not mention *aînesse*, but that must have been the principle applied, as found in the pleadings of Balliol, where there was a relatively simple appeal to the 'privilege' of *aînesse* according to the laws and customs of both realms.[42] Found in succession to baronies, and, in England, earldoms, *aînesse* meant that in the event of the death of the tenant-in-chief of an honour leaving no son but daughters, or no issue but sisters, all real property would be divided equally among the women (or their descendants, if they had died), but the

[39] Stones and Simpson, ii, C.94. In the responses by Bruce's auditors some are said to agree with *eidem*, which I have taken to mean the preceding person. But some merely agreed, and there must be some doubt as to where they should be counted.

[40] Stones and Simpson, ii, A.110. At this point Caen was tinkering with his text, *ibid.*, p. 246 n. *a*.

[41] A participle is needed after *et per leges ... concordantes*, perhaps *optentum* (found in response (iii)). Compare the words of respondent (iii) *quo ad subditos ejusdem regni, puta comites, barones et alios ... ideo secundum consuetudinem curie regis Anglie, que in paribus illius curie locum haberet, judicari debet in hoc casu* with the Great Roll judgement, *secundum leges et consuetudines regnorum quibus preest, de jure subditorum habet judicare* (for *locum habet judicare?*). Stones and Simpson, ii, 360, 246.

[42] Balliol's only surviving pleadings against Bruce at this stage are Stones and Simpson, ii, D.76(F) and (G). However, important clues are given in Bruce's arguments, especially Stones and Simpson, ii, 169(iii), (v), 171(ii), 172(vi).

eldest woman had the right to what was indivisible as part of her share, what in Scotland came to be called the *praecipuum*: the castle and chief place of the honour. The judgement must have been limited to a decision that the rights of *aînesse*, to incorporeal and indivisible things attached to an honour or barony in either realm, could not be defeated by the representative of a younger line nearer in degree to the common ancestor.

But why should this apply to the Scottish succession? In his question (3), Edward had asked the eighty not that question, but its negative form: give reasons why it should not apply. This recalled his first demand that the Scots might show, if they could, that he was not their overlord. As then, it showed that he had now determined his course and would deal as necessary with any obstacles. In October the obstacles came from Paris, where the notion of custom ascending from barony to kingdom had been firmly rejected, ruling out what might have been the neatest solution – to apply the custom in Scottish earldoms that *aînesse* gave the whole heritage undivided to the eldest daughter. Such custom could not ascend.

The introduction by Edward of the notion of congruent laws suggests progress in the search for agreement on a principle, on parameters within which a judgement based on custom, or some other system of law, could be delivered. The replies to question (1) seemed to exclude imperial law, but the question also revealed an ambiguity in the alternative – English or Scottish law; that this was not a copyist's slip is shown by the councillors' responses in favour of English law.[43] Yet this law, almost wholly custom, had never been the custom of the realm of Scotland, and could not now be made so, for that would have been a contradiction of the very nature of custom. There was one important flaw in the enquiries at Paris: respondent (iv) was not corrected when he spoke in favour of procedure according to the custom of the English court, in which 'the kingdom of Scotland is sought'.[44] The insistence of the Scots on the Cause being heard in Scotland was an important barrier to what the Paris respondents favoured after (or, in the case of (viii), before) imperial laws – judgement according to the law of England. Neither law by itself was appropriate. For that reason Edward tried to set the parameters more widely, to search for a common law applicable to both realms, a British customary law we might call it, with the same authority in both realms as written (imperial) law had in non-customary lands.

The Paris opinions gave less support to any opponents of this line of progress, in that they allowed recourse to the court of Edward as overlord, and, by implication, to its law. To the council this meant treating the kingdom as held of the English king and applying the law of his other

[43] Stones and Simpson, ii, C.87.

[44] Stones and Simpson, ii, 361, 6 lines from bottom of text. *Cf.* 362, end of para. (iv) and 363, para. (viii), bottom line: *recurrendum erit ad consuetudinem curie Anglie que superior est et in qua de illo regno agitur.*

tenants' holdings, which was also the law for royal tenants in Scotland, of whom Edward was, for the time, lord. Thus Edward followed the law for lesser tenures in England and Scotland. He had long sought to do so. But it is not easy to say why the law of England should become the law of both realms, which is doubtless why no such argument was reported and perhaps none was offered. It was easier to ask why it should not be so. Whether that was right is another question; the lawyers of Paris certainly did not think so.

Judgement against Bruce was given on Thursday, 6 November 1292. On Saturday, 8 November Ros withdrew from the Cause, with Balliol submitting (what, is not explained) to the ordinance of two bishops and two English earls; on 10 November Vescy's attorney made a similar announcement, placing the ordinance in the next parliament of Edward I. These two were being bought off, ostensibly by Balliol, but parliament suggests that the magnates were persuaded into the task of 'ordaining' by the English king who now found the multiplicity of Claimants an obstacle to the conclusion of the Cause. And the deal with Balliol alone suggests that he was already seen as the next king of Scots, able to grant a feu in land or money.

Bruce and Balliol had been agreed on the impartibility of the kingdom, and the court still had to explore the contrast or conflict of that principle with *aînesse*, for, if Scotland were like an honour or barony, custom in both realms declared it partible. But Bruce was no longer a Claimant, and was not there when the other Claimants were summoned on 7 November.[45] On the following day the previous petitions and arguments of Florence and Balliol were read and they were given until 10 November to submit written 'responses and reasons', evidently against each other. In their submission Balliol and Hastings together referred to written 'answers and arguments' previously submitted by Balliol, Bruce and Hastings. Thus the reading of 8 November must have revived documents submitted in or by early June 1292, when Florence had last been active and when Bruce was still a Claimant.[46] On 10 November Bruce re-entered the Cause, protesting his intention to claim the whole kingdom, or part thereof, and his purparty of the English lands of the Scottish kings.[47] This was probably extemporised by his lawyers, for Bruce never did submit a new claim to the whole kingdom, and indeed did not have his new claim to a purparty ready till 14 November. But he moved on 10 November because on that day it became obvious that King Eric's claim (it was never recorded) was unlikely to defeat that of Balliol.

When Eric II's men came to Berwick for the session which began on 2 June 1292, they pursued the unpaid tocher of his late wife as *attornati*;[48]

---

[45] Stones and Simpson, ii, C.100.
[46] Stones and Simpson, ii, C.106 (II)(i).
[47] Stones and Simpson, ii, C.102, p. 233.
[48] Stevenson, *Documents*, i, 312–17.

but as his *nuncii et procuratores* they also submitted a petition claiming the Scottish throne, demanding that Edward must not adjudge the realm to anyone in prejudice of Eric.[49] The exact date is unknown, but this wording suggests that pleading was well advanced (between Bruce and Balliol after 16 June 1292), which would mean that the claim and the letters of attorney could not be examined meantime. The differing descriptions of the ambassadors mark the absence from their procuratory of any mention of claiming the throne, and hence, on 8 November, as soon as other claims were revived, Balliol challenged their powers.[50]

On 10 November these attorneys produced new powers issued on 8 September and listing Eric's claims in Scotland, to the kingdom 'lawfully devolved to us by full hereditary right',[51] to its revenues for 1286–89, to a penalty because the Scots had not received the Maid as queen, and to arrears of his late wife's tocher.[52] Eric's petition for the throne, of the previous June or July, with its standard clauses about making any necessary additions or alterations (no full text survives), was read to the attorneys who were asked for any such amendments. But, according to the *Annales* minute, they refused to comply before having a discussion 'with the said English king' (*cum dicto domino rege Anglie*).[53]

When these minutes were written up from notes, the words of the attorneys must have been misunderstood. The '*said* king of England' is erroneous, because Edward had not been recently mentioned; and the conclusion, that they were told to come back in two days to hear his will, does not fit with the request to talk to him, nor with the petition's quoted

---

[49] Stones and Simpson, ii, A.71.pt.1; the fact that this was a petition emerges in A.71.pt.2. Eric's claims are discussed by Helle, 'Norwegian Foreign Policy', *SHR*, lxix, 142–56, especially pp. 152–53; and by Johnsen, 'Kong Eirik Magnussons krav paa Skottland, 1292', *Historisk Tidsskrift (Norsk)*, xxxvii (1955), 145–75, which I have not read.

[50] Stones and Simpson, ii, C.101. The challenge was to a single attorney compearing 'who did not have power of petitioning without the attorneys of the same king jointly constituted by letters of the same king'. Thus the objection was not to the absence of a specific power, but it was a technical challenge, because Balliol probably wanted to see the exact terms of Eric's letters – which explains why they were recorded *in extenso* in the minute.

[51] *ad nos pleno iure hereditario devolutum legitime.*

[52] Stones and Simpson, ii, C.102, pp. 232–33; *Chron. Rishanger*, 270.

[53] Stones and Simpson, ii, C.101–2. This text reads: *Requisitum fuit ... quid volunt addere, minuere ... et quid in peticione sua danda declarent, qui dicunt quod nolunt declarare antequam habuerint colloquium cum ... dicto domino rege Anglie ... Et hec requisitio fuit facta quia alias in peticione sua ... reservavit sibi beneficium addendi, minuendi ...* The passage *quid volunt – declarent* does not make sense (and the editors saw the difficulty of the subjunctive *declarent*), and on the strength of the later *reservavit*, the following emendation is suggested (added words printed in roman type): *Requisitum fuit ...* quod *quid volunt addere, minuere ... et quid in peticione sua danda* reservant *declarent ...* (I owe this to Dr Brand). The passage seems to say that the council asked the attorneys if they wished to add anything and if they might show what was in Eric's petition still to be handed over (*danda*). This request was made 'because elsewhere in his petition, which has been read before them [the council]', he (Eric) reserved the right to add to it, as the tenor of the petition shows.

In the printed text; read: *que coram ipsis lecta fuit ibidem, reservavit sibi ...*

words *reservavit sibi beneficium*, where *sibi*, gramatically Edward I, must have meant Eric II. The whole passage would make sense if the request was to talk to 'the said king', Eric II, their principal, the request which they repeated when, two days later, seeking 'discussion with their aforesaid lord king of Norway'.[54] Although they had new powers, they had no new instructions, and like Maitland six hundred years later, they may have been unaware of any basis for the claim.[55] Their latest request meant further delays of months, were it to be granted.

Eric, having sent no instructions, relied on the expertise of his lawyers, and there does seem to be a respectable case in Roman law for 'ascendants' under the Justinianic rules of succession,[56] suggesting that civil lawyers had urged his attorneys in June 1292 to submit a claim, civil lawyers acting at Berwick for another Claimant. The identity of that Claimant emerges in September when the new letters of attorney had arrived: on 28 September an English safeconduct to visit Norway was issued to the earl of Carrick (Bruce VI) and his daughter Isabel,[57] who, within the year, had married Eric II,[58] evidently the arranged purpose of the trip to Norway, not its chance result. It had been part of a deal between Bruce V (the Claimant) and Eric's attorneys that they submit a claim, thus internationalising the Cause further, and bringing in a Claimant with an unimpeachable title to argue for a 'law by which kings reign'. The attorneys and King Eric would cooperate with Bruce if a promise had been included to pay all monies claimed by Eric should Bruce became king.

For Eric wanted one thing – the money he claimed from Scotland in addition to the unpaid tocher already adjudged to him in July 1292;[59] the attorneys would know this, but did not have power to make an agreement, like that of Florence, with Bruce, whence the need to consult their principal again. They obtained a favourable judgement at Berwick over the revenues for 1286–90, but the Scots were not of a paying disposition – Eric later argued that their failure to pay the annual 100 merks due for the Western Isles had escheated these isles to him.[60] He showed no such interest in the Scottish throne; he would never defeat the claim of Balliol.

The submission of Count Florence shows knowledge (for the first time)

---

[54] *quod voluerunt prius habere colloquium cum predicto domino suo rege Norwagie.* I am grateful to Dr Paul Brand for the correction suggested in this paragraph.

[55] Pollock and Maitland, *Hist. of Eng. Law*, ii, 300.

[56] Buckland, *Textbook of Roman Law*, 3rd edn, 375.

[57] *Cal. Docs. Scot.*, ii, no. 635, p. 148; *CPR 1281–92*, 508.

[58] *Cal. Docs. Scot.*, ii, no. 675. An important agent in this marriage was Mr Weland of Stiklaw, discussed by Crawford in 'Weland of Stiklaw', *Historisk Tidsskrift (Norsk)*, lii (1973). 329–39, and in 'North Sea Kingdoms, North Sea Bureaucrat', *SHR*, lxix (1990), 175–84; also by Watt, *Biographical Dictionary*, 516–17.

[59] Stevenson, *Documents*, i, 315–16.

[60] Stevenson, *Documents*, ii, 359.

of the wording of what may have been his missing 'exception': [61] Earl David's supposed resignation to his brother King William and his heirs 'whomsoever', of all his right in the kingdom of Scotland, in return for the Garioch. [62] On 14 June 1292, as we have seen, Bruce had entered into an agreement with Count Florence, whereby each would help the other in claiming the Scottish kingship, the winner to compensate the other with a third of the kingdom; neither, without consent of the other, would make a 'peace' with a third party on the kingship. The Garioch was not mentioned, and if Earl David's resignation was remembered, it was the last thing to be shown to Florence at this time, because it annulled the claim of Bruce, to whom Florence's claim was a means to defeat that of Balliol, should he, Bruce, fail to do so. Balliol had defeated Bruce, so the claim of Florence, committed to giving the kingdom to Bruce, was a vicarious second chance for the latter. Now was the time for Florence's evidence.

On 10 November also, Florence submitted his written case, basing it upon alleged events of the reign of King William, when Earl David both lost his rights as a consequence of felony against Henry II (in 1173–74), and resigned his right to the throne in return for the lordship of Garioch, a passage clearly based upon David's resignation forged in April 1290 to secure the Garioch for Bruce. Its text survives now, in the register of Count Florence, as two inspections issued by the prior of Pluscarden at Pluscarden on 8 November 1291, and by the bishop of Moray at Spynie on 10 November 1291. The narratives given to Bek by Bruce in early 1291 relating to the history of Moray and the claims of the earl of Mar there, and relating to the exclusion of Florence's ancestor from his wife's portion, the earldom of Ross, are now joined by a document seen only in Moray, relating to the district Bruce had sought, the Garioch, and to the succession to the throne. Its appearance now, when it could do Bruce no harm, was no coincidence. The evidence that it had been in Bruce's files and that the inspections of it were handed over by him soon after 6 November 1292 (when judgement went against him) may be circumstantial, but is surely compelling. But Florence never had the original resignation of David and admitted he could not produce it. [63]

The inspections are dated 8 and 10 November 1291, exactly a year before Florence's revivified pursuit of the Scottish throne at Berwick on 8 and 10 November 1292. Examination of the 1291 texts shows that the sealing and dating clauses of the bishop's and prior's letters are exercises in florid rhetoric, quite unlike their pedestrian openings and the text of Earl David's supposed resignation. [64] They raise a strong suspicion that they have been

[61] Stones and Simpson, ii, D.67.i.
[62] Stones and Simpson, ii, D.69 and p. 312, discussed above pp. 184–85.
[63] Stones and Simpson, ii, C.106 (V), p. 325.
[64] Stones and Simpson, ii, D.69, but for the prior's final clauses, *SHR*, xxxvi, 124.

added by one clerk, not when copying David's text, but when completing inspections which had been written for Bruce some time before November 1292, and then filed until 10 November 1292, when the 1291 dates were added. We shall meet another example of Bruce's cavalier way with dates later.

Earl David's resignation, if genuine, destroyed the claims of Bruce, Balliol and Hastings, but did nothing else for Florence. On 10 November he therefore went on to claim that King William had his prelates and magnates recognise his sister Ada as his heir presumptive and swear an oath to that effect, a far more important support of his claim, were it true. Unable to produce David's resignation or the names of those who swore the 'Ada' oath, Florence was reduced to arguing that the facts as to both should be established by a solemn inquest, because the resignation, a papal bull of confirmation and a roll of those who swore to accept Ada as heir presumptive had recently been stolen from the royal treasury and taken to the priory of Pluscarden, where the prior had them.[65] This 'history' was no novelty, for it bears an uncanny resemblance to the alleged recognition of Bruce's right to the throne at Alexander II's command[66] – as Balliol was quick to point out.[67]

The ascription of blame to the prior of Pluscarden sugggests that Florence possessed that prior's inspection of the forged resignation, for his last pleading ends piteously by returning to the priory, claiming that 'the charter which they have of the land of Garioch proves what the count says about exchanges [Garioch for the right of succession] and asks that they will show this charter' – a statement which would gain force if there were any hint as to who 'they' were.[68] Balliol's critique of documents which the tribunal could not see, reduced Florence's jerry-built edifice to rubble.

Bruce's lawyers were certainly 'helping' Florence, giving him some text of the resignation, probably the Pluscarden inspection of it, suggesting the assembly which recognised Ada as heir presumptive, and providing the elaborate cover story of other records and a theft from the treasury. Yet they were evidently reluctant to provide the resignation itself, perhaps because it was a forgery, but more probably because, if genuine, it would destroy Bruce's claim to both the throne and to a purparty of Scotland. He had to decide if he should give these claims up and throw his whole weight behind

---

[65] Stones and Simpson, ii, C.106.I–III, V, VI; the important passages are on pp. 312, 325.

[66] Stones and Simpson, ii, D.76(B)vii.

[67] Stones and Simpson, ii, C.106.III, p. 319. Compare, in Bruce's pleading in June 1292, the request that the king order an enquiry by the baronage if his document cannot be found (*ibid.*, p. 170) with Count Florence's plea that the king enquire into the truth of this 'matter' (*ibid.*, p. 325) where the matter is either the content of the detained document or the fact of its detention.

[68] Stones and Simpson, ii, 325, but *taken away to the priory of Pluscaden* in the summary. For a translation, *Chron. Rishanger*, 307–8.

Count Florence, hoping for the latter's success and willingness to stand by their agreement of 14 June 1292; that was a step too far to take. Distrust of Florence? Fear that Edward would reject the June agreement? Fear that the community would reject rule won in such a way? Advice that his claim for a purparty stood a better chance? We cannot know, for he left so many false trails at this juncture.

A reading of the claims submitted belatedly in 1291 by Mandeville and Galightly suggests that they too had links to Bruce. Mandeville from Ulster, where the earl of Carrick (Bruce VI) had lands, uncertainly 'begs that there shall be enquiry about the right he has to the kingdom of Scotland, by folk of England, Ireland and Scotland, inasmuch as' – and there follows a tale of twelfth-century skulduggery entirely worthy of the inaccurate recollections by Bruce's 'old folk'. Patrick Galightly, a Perth burgess who claimed that his father Henry (of whom nothing is known) was a son of William the Lion, twice alleged that he was nearest by degree to Alexander III, and then urged that he should have the throne 'since it was sworn by everyone after the death of [Alexander III] that in default of the Maid, they should assume as king the nearer (*propinquior*) of the royal blood.' This distortion of the oath of 1286 might serve to strengthen Bruce's claim by nearness of degree; Galightly can scarcely have expected anything from it.[69]

Reluctance to recognise Bruce's role in the claims of Florence and Eric is understandable, for, if either succeeded, Bruce, who wanted the throne, appeared to be the loser. But only by the amount he would have to pay to buy them off – and that was an acceptable sacrifice if he gained a throne. The other result of these claims, however, King Edward would not accept – delay. Had Edward listened to Florence's piteous pleas or the Jarndycean claims for more time from Eric's attorneys,[70] the Cause would have dragged on into the summer of 1293 or later. The Cause was moving slowly; there was no sitting on 11 November 1292, and on 12 November, Balliol was there to hear any plea of Hastings, the first hint of what becomes increasingly clear, that Balliol was defender of a right recognised by the court, while the others were all pursuers; thus Balliol on his own now opposed Florence. Hastings wished to submit a new petition, but his arguments were not ready, even on the following day. In his first petition of August 1291 he had sought a purparty of the heritage 'since the realm of Scotland recently fell vacant by the death of King Alexander';[71] on Friday, 14 November he submitted his claim for purparty under English common law, arguing that Scotland was a

[69] The claims are Stones and Simpson, ii, A.61 and 60. For Galightly the burgess, *ibid.*, 370, no. 225.

[70] Stones and Simpson, ii, C.106,VI(v), p. 325: Florence was a foreigner and Balliol had 'many agents and supporters against him'; 'if the truth be not enquired into now, it will never be better enquired into, nor will the truth of his claim be known, but he will be excluded from his right for ever'. *Ibid.*, ii, C.103 for Eric.

[71] Stones and Simpson, ii, A.63.

lordship, not a kingdom, seeking to exploit in this way the success of Balliol against Bruce.[72] It is possible, even probable, that Hastings did this by agreement with Bruce, who, however, having claimed the throne, could scarcely adopt Hastings' line.

Documents suggest that Bruce had prepared for this shift of ground as soon as judgement was given for Balliol against him on 6 November. On 'Friday [7 November] 1292',[73] he had resigned to his son, Bruce VI and his heirs, all right to seek the kingdom of Scotland.[74] In fact neither Bruce V nor his son followed up such a claim. On 'Sunday [9 November]', Bruce VI executed a letter to John king of Scotland, asking that, as he had resigned his earldom of Carrick to his son, Bruce VII, the king should receive the latter's homage.[75] The resignation of the earldom existed as a document,[76] and would have been dated 'Saturday 8 November', to complete a daily sequence (like the awards of 5–7 June 1291), and to mislead equally by sleight of calendar. For on 9 November John Balliol was not yet king, and was not to be so until the end of the month; and no one – particularly not the Bruces – could have anticipated that accession by conferring the royal title.

Despite their dates, these documents were executed when John had become king, after November 1292, probably in the first half of 1293, when King John's relationship with Edward I had been defined; their purpose was to preserve intact the Bruce heritage – lands and claim. By resigning his claim to the throne, Bruce V made it difficult for King John to refuse his homage for Annandale. Bruce VI, now Claimant in the wings, by resigning Carrick and his other Scottish lands to his son, had no Scottish possessions and could not be required to do homage to (and so recognise) the new king.[77] And the dating had to appear to be before Bruce V had entered his new claim for a purparty (and not the whole) of the kingdom, so that Bruce VI was not compromised by that climb-down. Devious was the path, and deviousness the guiding light, of the Bruce party.

On 14 November Bruce the Claimant, therefore, had resigned nothing to his son, and submitted a claim for purparty which recognised what Hastings denied, the right of John to be king. The pleadings of Hastings survive in some quantity; those of Bruce are fewer but, a bonus, include the terms of

[72] Stones and Simpson, ii, Appendix B, nos VII and X.

[73] The date is given as Friday after St Leonard.

[74] Stones and Simpson, ii, D.99, from the original resignation. It is noteworthy that the document follows the resignation with a purport clause: 'so that I have no claim'. There is a similar clause using the same phrases in Earl David's forged resignation.

[75] APS, i, 449 from a parliament roll of King John.

[76] Bruce VII promised in August 1293 to produce it for the king; APS, i, 449.

[77] Carrick (Bruce VI) was summoned to the parliament which met at Scone on 9 February 1293 and failed to compear; he was then summoned to compear before the king on 5 April. There is no evidence that he did so, but Bruce VII compeared in the parliament of August 1293; APS, i, 447b–49.

his new petition.[78] The first third of this text claimed a third of 'all the lands of Scotland' as Bruce's purparty, descended from one of the daughters of Earl David; let the king do justice according to the common law of England. The second third argued that, as a fief, Scotland, though a realm, was partible like an earldom or barony. The last third argued that in their previous litigation Balliol had made Scotland partible when he demanded justice 'according to the common law and the usages of Scotland [no 'realm'] and of the realm of England'; the king should therefore judge according to that common law for earldoms and baronies, 'as Scotland is member of the crown of England, unless Balliol can show specialty from the king or his ancestors'.[79] The 'member' theme was perhaps a topos, but it had occurred in Bruce's letter of early 1291 to Bek,[80] suggesting fairly long continuity in his legal advisers. More striking, however, is the use of Thomas Weyland's opinion in the earlier two thirds of the petition. Weyland was recorded in Latin and the petition was in French, but several clauses were borrowed with minor adaptation, and the general theme is identical; in particular both allowed to Balliol the dignity of king and the *caput* (*praecipuum*) as well as his purparty. The claim of 'common law of England and Scotland in default of specialty' in Weyland reappears in Bruce's pleadings.[81]

Hastings allowed no kingship to Balliol, but, applying the English law of partition of baronies, he sought his third of the whole 'or a certain allowance';[82] but he also had a secondary claim to a third of the purchases, acquisitions and escheats of what he found it convenient to call 'the gross' because he would not call it 'the realm'.[83] Scotland, no kingdom, was a 'member' of the realm of England, and 'an express common law' of all such members was partibility of tenancies in chief. The head (the English crown) may have specialty (presumably impartibility), but the members cannot be equal to the head, and so must follow common law. And in the 'law of England and Scotland' sisters have parity of right, unlike brothers.[84]

To Bruce and Hastings it probably mattered little which of their argu-

---

[78] Stones and Simpson, ii, C.106, VII, X.

[79] Stones and Simpson, ii, C.106 VIII. In this text the sense is obscured by the editorial comma in the phrase *solom la commune lei, e les usages* on p. 336, fourth line from the bottom of the text. The treatment of inheritance of English earldoms under Edward I is discussed in McFarlane, 'Had Edward I a Policy towards the Earls?' in *History*, 1 (1965), 145–59, and in his *The Nobility of Later Medieval England*, ch. 7. In *Henry III and the Lord Edward*, Appendix G, p. 789, Powicke claims that 'the right of aînesse on which [Balliol] relied made him admit, even urge, that the kingdom was partible'!

[80] Stones and Simpson, ii, D.76(K).

[81] Stones and Simpson, ii, C.106 XI(v).

[82] Stones and Simpson, ii, 331, line 9.

[83] Stones and Simpson, ii, 330, 334–35, 338–39.

[84] Stones and Simpson, ii, C.106 VII (i)–(iii). For modern comment see Milsom, *Studies in the History of the Common Law*, ch. 12, 'Inheritance by Women …' and Holt, *Colonial England*, 245–70; and for Scotland, Macqueen, *Common Law and Feudal Society in Medieval Scotland*, 173–74.

ments succeeded, so long as they were awarded their thirds. The English precedents were favourable, for partibility even for an exceptional earldom had been established by representatives of these litigants in a very similar case fifty-five years earlier, on the death of John earl of Chester and Huntingdon in 1237. Of his co-heiresses (married to Forz, Balliol, Bruce, Hastings), Forz, representing the elder daughter of John's oldest sister,[85] claimed impartibility and the whole earldom of Chester, on the grounds that it was *comitatus paleys*, an earldom with regal franchises. On the death of Earl Ranulph in 1232, his extensive property had been divided among his sisters or their representatives, but John, son of the eldest sister, had received Chester undivided. Was this because Chester was impartible, as Forz now claimed, suggesting, but not naming, prerogative or specialty? Or was Chester John's share by *aînesse*? The Bench in 1239 gave judgement against Forz: 'it has always been used up to now in England that if any inheritance descends to sisters, then that inheritance is divided equally between them, and the contrary has never been seen'.[86] The king subsequently bought Forz out from his right of *aînesse* to the dignity of earl 'with castle, seal and liberty of the sword'; he also bought out the other co-heirs.[87] Thus the law of England.

For the law of Scotland, Balliol had earlier argued, in his pleading against Bruce, that in Scotland earldoms were impartible (citing Atholl and Carrick) and that, like offices held heritably (e.g. the Stewartry and Constableship), they passed to the eldest daughter.[88] But Bruce, when he changed his plea, claiming a portioner's right, took a different view, arguing that the Cause should be judged by the law and peers of the English crown, but that 'if the king wishes to help himself by the usage of the earls, barons and subjects of

---

[85] The second daughter of the oldest sister was Dervorguilla, married to John Balliol; by the subsequent death of Christina, wife of Forz, without heirs, Balliol inherited her portion of the inheritance of Earl John, both from his father David earl of Huntingdon, and from his mother, the oldest co-heiress of Earl Ranulph. At one point in the pleading of 1239, it was argued by Bruce and Hastings that their wives were nearer in degree (sisters to the deceased earl), than was Christina (niece), and that 'they attained [i.e. survived] the death of each earl [Ranulph and John]'. The similarity to the last stage of pleading in 1292 is striking, save that in 1239 Balliol claimed with Bruce and Hastings, and Forz in 1239 stood in the position of Balliol in 1292. For the earldom of Huntingdon see Stringer, *Earl David*, 182–89.

[86] *Bracton's Note Book*, ed. Maitland, iii, no. 1273, p. 283.

[87] The most recent discussion of this case is by Eales, 'Henry III and the End of the Norman Earldom of Chester', *Thirteenth Century England*, i (1985), 100–12. It is also discussed by Alexander, 'The English Palatinates and Edward I', *Journal of British Studies*, xxii, part 2 (1983), 1–22, at 5–6, where the author claims that 'the earldom of Chester case [after 1237] ... was decided without reference to an alleged palatine position'.

[88] Stones and Simpson, ii, D.76(F)(iii), citing the earldoms of Atholl and Carrick. The constableship had passed from the de Morvilles by the marriage of Elena de Morville to Roland of Galloway, but she had no sisters. It passed from their son Alan of Galloway to his eldest daughter and her husband, Roger de Quincy, and so to their eldest daughter who sold her right to her sister's husband, Alexander Comyn, earl of Buchan. But the landed inheritance was divided among the daughters of Alan.

Scotland, Robert is ready to show and prove to the king that earldoms, baronies and other tenures in Scotland are partible'.[89] The earliest evidence for partition of an earldom among heirs portioners was in Buchan, whose earl, Robert I's mortal enemy, fled Scotland with his brother and heir in 1309; both died, the brother leaving two daughters, the younger of whom obtained her half.[90] Scots law apparently approximated to English in this matter, under English influence after 1296. But for the thirteenth century as a whole there seems no doubt that Balliol was correct, for the eighty auditors were to say the same thing; *aînesse* in Scots law gave a more complete right to an earldom than in English law.[91]

Reading the little of his pleading against Hastings and Bruce which survives, Balliol's position seems weak, except in arguing that the kingdom of Scotland was a historical fact.[92] Stung by Hastings' argument that services owed by the king to the English overlord deny the existence of kingship, 'John Balliol says that the royal dignity is in its nature so high that it draws to itself the things which are in the less, and therefore he says that neither by the homage nor by the service which it does, can the royal dignity perish'.[93] Having denied the relevance of Bruce's foreign precedents, he cited his own to show that crowning was symbolic only, not an essential of kingly dignity, and that other uncrowned kings had impartible realms.[94] He acknowledged a distinction between royal dignity, which must be impartible, and the resources of the royal dignity, arguing that 'they are annexed to it; without them it cannot be sustained; as the principal is impartible, things appendant to it must be impartible'.[95] Partition would bring 'inconveniences':[96] with emendation one passage reads 'many dis-advantages would ensue if the realm were partible, which would amount to this: that a realm so divided would come to nothing, if it was so'.[97]

This derives from a passage in Bracton: 'if the chief place were divided

---

[89] Stones and Simpson, ii, C.106 XI(iii).

[90] *RRS*, v, 691. In 1312 Robert I gave the earldom of Moray to his nephew with limitation to heirs male; in 1313 he gave the earldom of Carrick to his brother Edward with a strict male tailzie; *RRS*, v, no. 389; *RMS*, i, no. 45.

[91] In a much damaged passage of Stones and Simpson, ii, D.76(B)iii, Bruce stated that 'Balliol says that earldoms ... [*illegible*] ... are the highest tenures of the kingdom after the kingdom itself, ... are not partible ...'. The editors propose 'says that earldoms [and baronies which] are the highest tenures ...', but this cannot be correct for baronies were partible in both realms. Later in the passage Bruce rebuts some argument about '[*illegible*] of sergeanty' suggesting that the earlier text read 'says that earldoms [and sergeanties which] are the highest tenures'; these highest sergeanties would be heritable offices of state like the Stewartry and Constableship.

[92] Stones and Simpson, ii, 320.

[93] Stones and Simpson, ii, 332 at (xiv).

[94] Stones and Simpson, ii, 320 at (ii), 332 at (xiv), 182.

[95] Stones and Simpson, ii, 320.

[96] Stones and Simpson, ii, 329, at (ix) and n. 6; 330, line 6.

[97] Stones and Simpson, ii, 331, at (xi) and n. 5.

into several portions, and several times, the rights of earldoms and baronies
would be brought to nothing, to the destruction of the realm, since it is of
earldoms and baronies that it is said to be constituted'.[98] 'Disadvantage' had
then a stronger connotation, tantamount to destruction, than it has now, but
the contrast with Bracton reveals the weakness of the claim – baronies and
earldoms were partitioned among heiresses in common law, but Bracton
ignored the destructive effect of impoverishment (well shown by the heirs
to the earldom of Chester) in this context. Why should an exception be
made for the kingdom?

In his argument of the previous June, Balliol had claimed that 'in the
[laws] of Scotland earldoms were impartible', passing to the eldest sister, as
did offices; in a fragmentary passage he spoke of prerogative: 'Dervorguilla
his mother had [as eldest sister] the castle of Dundee which [was] of the
heritage of [Earl] David in Scotland ... since Margaret [mother of
Dervorguilla] and her heirs, by the prerogative of the eldest, have for all time
advantage in all [*decayed*]'.[99] Thus in June the laws of Scotland were invoked
as the context for his rights by *aînesse* and to impartibility as to an earldom.
But in November, arguing for impartibility for the realm, he appealed to
no laws, cited no prerogative or specialty. They were of the armoury of
his opponents, who challenged: let him produce specialty to show the
impartibility which he claimed. Otherwise let him abide by the common law
upon which he had insisted in his earlier pleading.[100] A specialty would have
had to come either from the overlord or from some council of a Scottish
king, but, despite the arrangements made between 1281 and 1284, Balliol
could produce no such document.

Instead he had a new argument, the nature of kingship: possessions
and resources 'do not make the king, nor confer the royal dignity, but it is
the royal dignity which makes the king ... this dignity is a whole and the
highest lordship where kings reign'.[101] Resources of the royal dignity do not
establish its nature; they take their impartible nature from its impartibility.
These are noble sentiments, but sentiments they remain, lacking any context
in law – unless perhaps they are given a context in a law of kingship, a
'natural law by which kings reign, and not a custom used between subjects
and tenants of the kingdom of Scotland'.[102] Other tenures are partible 'but
this is not so of a realm, for by law (*dreit*) each realm is impartible; and
neither king nor realm is bound by law (*ley*) of the same realm, but they are
beyond the law (*outre la ley*)'.[103] Balliol's case? Indeed, yes, but the words of

[98] Bracton, fo. 76; *Bracton on the Laws and Customs of England*, ed. Woodbine, trans.
Thorne, ii, 222.
[99] Stones and Simpson, ii, D.76(F)(iii).
[100] Stones and Simpson, ii, 331, at (xii).
[101] Stones and Simpson, ii, 320.
[102] Stones and Simpson, ii, D.76(A)(iv).
[103] Stones and Simpson, ii, D.76(B)(iii).

Robert Bruce in June, words which had failed against Balliol's then appeal to the common law of both kingdoms. It is extraordinary to find Bruce's argument, scarcely disguised, in the argument which won Balliol the undivided kingdom as well as the throne. If in June 1292 the court had addressed not Bruce *v.* Balliol, but Hastings' claim to purparty *v.* Bruce and Balliol claiming impartibility, a decision favouring the latter, grounded on a law of royal dignity as urged by both Bruce and Balliol, might well – should – have made a difference to the outcome of the case between those two.

Written pleadings were still being submitted on 14 November, and Bruce was given permission to hand in more on the morrow. On that day the council took no great interest in Balliol's claims for royal dignity, perhaps because they were so evidently right. Only the arguments of Bruce and Hastings were read out when the council asked four questions of the Scottish eighty.[104] The first of these was crucial and put the claim of Bruce and Hastings, not that of Balliol: (1) is the kingdom of Scotland partible? The response was a plain negative, a statement of fact without any explanation; had there been any, as the other responses show, it would probably have been reported.

Question (2) asked whether, if the kingdom were impartible, the lands of acquisitions and escheats were partible. This plainly arose from the complex secondary claim by Hastings, who had twice proposed a search of the Scottish chancery to identify these acquisitions,[105] but the Scots' answer to question (2) rendered that unnecessary: acquisitions and escheats in the kingdom are not partible from the moment that they come into the king's hands, but those outside the kingdom follow the law of the land (England) in which they lie. Hastings does not seem to have had his eye on the English possessions of Alexander III, acquired in 1157 and 1242, but Bruce did on 10 November;[106] no pleadings on the issue survive and probably there were none, but the final judgement in the Cause took the same view of these English lands as did the eighty.[107] Despite this, John king of Scotland was found heir to the whole Honour of Penrith in March 1293, perhaps because he had given a liferent of it to the bishop of Durham in 1290 – and was 'persuaded' in 1294 to leave it there.[108] Bruce and Hastings got no purparty.

The last two questions were intended to provide answers to claims of

---

[104] Stones and Simpson, ii, C.107.

[105] Stones and Simpson, ii, 334–35 at (xviii); 338–39 at (i). Hastings' proposal to search 'la chapele de Escoce' must have been independent from Bruce's and Florence's request to search for documents in the treasury, where indeed any chancery rolls of Alexander III (and they were few) would be found.

[106] Stones and Simpson, ii, C.102, p. 233. There should be a full stop after *que non sunt de regalitate Scocie.* The attorneys were appointed to pursue all Bruce's claims.

[107] Stones and Simpson, ii, 243, 399.

[108] *Cal. Docs. Scot.*, ii, no. 692; Fraser, *History of Antony Bek*, 57, 61–62, 204 for Bek's dealings over Penrith.

Bruce and Hastings. Question (3) asked: 'whether earldoms or baronies of the aforesaid kingdom are partible or not?' The only possible reason for asking this question was Bruce's assertion in his final pleading for his purparty that if the king wished to have recourse to the usage of these and other tenures in Scotland, Bruce could show partibility for them.[109] It is possible that the council was so minded, but difficult to see why in that case they should place this question third after impartibility had been decided. In fact the council already knew the substance of the eighty's answer, that in the kingdom of Scotland an earldom was not partible, as was found by a judgement in the court of the king of Scotland on the earldom of Atholl, but that baronies were partible. This brings out the way that Balliol was treated as defender, for it repeats his argument in June 1292, that earldoms were impartible, citing the elder daughter's right to the earldom of Atholl, adjudged before Alexander II and his council *en pleyn parlament*.[110] The fact that question (3) asked also about baronies suggests that the council was concerned about the contradiction between Balliol's and Bruce's evidence, and sought a definitive ruling from the eighty to tidy up a loose end which might have given Bruce a rather stronger case for a share of acquisitions if not of the kingdom.

The form of question (4), beginning 'assuming that the kingdom is impartible', represents a common procedure in the English courts of asking a series of questions, some of which had to be answered only if a particular answer had been given to earlier questions.[111] This question asked: 'if the right devolves to daughters, should any regard be had to the younger ones because of the equality of right which descends to all, as recompense or allowance for their right?' This was unanswerable (for lack of precedent), as the eighty pointed out. But they went on to say that in Scotland the eldest daughter of an earl took the whole but that the eldest owed something, of grace, to the younger as portioners. Probably this refers to Hastings' argument that he should have his third 'or a certain allowance', an argument which Balliol seems to have conceded by offering to do 'right and reason', on King Edward's advice, to it.[112]

Thus were the claims of Bruce and Hastings to a share in the property of the Scottish king disposed of. There remained the other claims to the kingship. Not one single moment was spent upon them.

From 15 November King Edward and his council took two days to formulate their judgement, which made no reference to the questions and answers of 15 November. Pronounced on 17 November 1292, it was a final reassertion of Edward's will that a kingdom, Scottish or English, should

[109] Stones and Simpson, ii, C.106 XI(ii).
[110] Stones and Simpson, ii, D.76(F)(iii).
[111] I owe this point about a series of questions to Dr Paul Brand.
[112] Stones and Simpson, ii, C.106 VII(x); C.106 IX(ii).

pass undivided to the eldest daughter of a king without male issue.[113] He had
said so for England in 1290,[114] and in June–July 1292, in his stated case about
Scotland to foreign scholars, had stated impartibility as a 'supposition'.[115]
Now the king, reviving the names of thirteen Claimants, gave judgement
against seven Claimants, including Count Florence, because they had withdrawn their claims (as four of them had done before 21 June 1292);[116] against
King Eric, Comyn and Mandeville because they had not pursued their
claims; against Bruce's claim to the whole heritage; against Bruce's and
Hastings' claims to thirds of the whole or of the acquisitions.

The final judgement was in form a series of judgements, that those who
had withdrawn should 'take' nothing by their petitions, the same for those
who had failed to pursue; it recalled that Bruce and Balliol had claimed the
whole kingdom and that 'it was said' to Bruce that he had no right in his
petition. Hastings and Bruce had claimed partibility and the king, having
examined their petitions, 'says that by law and by judgement the kingdom of
Scotland is not partible, nor are [its] acquisition or escheats ... partible;
therefore ... he says by judgement that you shall take nothing of the pur-
parties which you sought'.[117] Therefore the king gives to Balliol as the nearer
heir to the Maid of Norway, 'lady of Scotland', granddaughter of the last
king, by right of succession to hold the kingdom, the kingdom with its
pertinents, and sasine thereof, which had come to him as superior lord after
the death of the Maid, saving the right of the king and his heirs when they
wish to speak of it.' This is the *Annales* minute, contemporary, for its last
section is in substance identical with the precept of sasine issued for Balliol
on 19 November 1292. Already it contains a revision of history: the status
of the kingdom after the death of the 'last king' is ignored, the Maid introduced to cover the awkward fact that Edward obtained possession of it as
superior lord only after her death. But the pretence that she had been queen
is not revived.[118]

The version concocted for the Great Roll in 1296–97 changes the
structure considerably, for having narrated the withdrawals and failures
to pursue, it jumps to rule out Bruce's claim to a purparty, because he
had previously claimed impartibility, and because all had found that the
kingdom should remain to one heir, being by its nature impartible as other
kingdoms are; Hastings' claim is then ruled out on this last ground and Caen

---

[113] Stones and Simpson, ii, C.109–10.

[114] *Foedera*, i, 742.

[115] Stones and Simpson, ii, 359: *Unde, supposito quod regnum istud sit impartibile, queritur quis istorum preferri debeat in successione dicti regni.*

[116] Stones and Simpson, ii, C.108. These seven are given in the order Pinkeny, Dunbar, Soules, Galightly (the four who had withdrawn by June 1292), Ros (withdrew 8 November 1292), Vescy (withdrew 10 November 1292), Count Florence.

[117] Stones and Simpson, ii, C.109.

[118] Stones and Simpson, ii, C.110; the precept of sasine is A.111 = C.111.

turns to that of Balliol. He repeats the unanimous finding of impartibility
so that there can be only one heir, then, in a passage discussed above,[119]
expatiates on the laws of kingdoms in which King Edward is master, on the
unanimous advice that he may judge on the right of subjects, so that all
agreed that the laws of both kingdoms provided that the remoter in degree
of the senior line was to be preferred to the nearer in degree of the second
line. It was considered that Balliol therefore should have sasine of the
kingdom which had been in Edward's hand by reason of his superiority,
saving the king's right when he wishes to speak of it; the precept of sasine
follows. Caen has effectively suppressed Bruce's first petition and transferred to the final decision the issue between Bruce and Balliol put to
the council and auditors on 3–6 November, producing the judgement of
6 November against Bruce. This was not relevant to the debate of the
following ten days nor to the final decision.[120]

There is great emphasis on the decision for impartibility and on the
inconsistency of Bruce's claims, which latter is not touched upon in the
Annales minute. But the Roll having brought forward the pleadings of June
1292 to October and downplayed the finding of 6 November for Balliol, it
brings those forward to the final judgement of 17 November to give Balliol
a positive right as the nearer heir. The *Annales* minute of 17 November gives
sasine of the kingdom to Balliol perfunctorily, 'according to what has been
found before the lord king' by default, as it were, of all the other claims.
There is an enhanced emphasis in the Roll upon the rights of Edward
as overlord and upon the rightness of the finding for Balliol. But where is
Bruce?

The originals of Bruce's June 1292 pleadings survive, some in legible
condition, which is as well, because they are summarised in the Roll in some
twenty-seven lines of print, of which nine sketch the Scottish succession
before 1097. The essential (but not all) points are there, but so heavily
abbreviated as to amount only to perfunctory headings. We discover why in
Balliol's case, which takes some 164 lines of print, six times the length given
to Bruce, and mostly a well-argued counter to the points listed for Bruce.[121]
As a summing-up of Balliol's case this is masterly, but as a summing up
of the Cause, it is distinctly unjudicial. The distortion of the judgement in
the Great Roll was part of a larger distortion in that source, to play down the
case of Robert Bruce in favour of that of John Balliol.

This may have been simply because Balliol won, so that there seemed no
point in wasting space upon a case which was found to have no merit. But
the Great Roll was compiled after Balliol resigned the Scottish throne and
became a prisoner, his case unlikely to be revived. The Roll was a justifi-

[119] See p. 291.
[120] Stones and Simpson, ii, A.110.
[121] Stones and Simpson, ii, C.83–84.

cation of the overlord, anxious to show that his overlordship had been
exercised to give justice to the Claimant with the best right, who had proved
a false liege-man. There must also be a suspicion that the claim of Bruce was
downgraded at this point because it had once more become relevant. Bruce
the Claimant had died in 1295, but his son, Bruce VI, having supported
Edward in the invasion of Scotland, had asked for the kingdom soon after
the battle of Dunbar in 1296.[122] He retired to his lands in England and never
returned to Scotland, dying in 1304, but his son, earl of Carrick, did not
abandon the family's right and in 1302 Edward I was prepared at least to
make a show of re-examining it.[123] It is possible that as early as 1296–97 the
English king wished to remove the Bruce claim from the record because, not
having forfeited the kingdom of Scotland, he wished to avoid pressure to
give sasine to the next heir.

The hearings of the Great Cause had been devoted overwhelmingly to the
case of Bruce v. Balliol. Of the nine weeks spent on the Cause in 1292,
perhaps two days were devoted to the fancy tales of Florence, another two
to Hastings and his Johnny-come-lately ally, Bruce; along with the dithering
of King Eric's envoys, and two other still-unheard Claims, all were cast aside
by Edward I on 15 November 1292 for what they had always been, a
necessary indulgence to vindicate his judging the Cause as overlord.

So why did the Cause take so long? And why was it concluded so rapidly
in November 1292? Part of the answer to the first question lies in the ten-
month adjournment from August 1291. This adjournment was not to give
Florence time to search for missing evidences, but to give Edward I one full
year (June–June) of direct lordship of Scotland – despite his promise to hear
the Cause with proper speed. His intention to complete the Cause in June
1292 was thwarted by the intransigence of the Scots refusing to move the
Cause to Westminster, while the Paris opinions protracted matters for a
month in October–November, when the king's council was seeking to found
judgement upon the laws and customs of England and Scotland. The long
adjournment was Edward's responsibility; but he gave Balliol and Bruce
their full day in court, and capitulated to understandable impatience only in
the last days.

It is a tribute to Edward and his court that, in two formats, the *centumviri*
and the council, they gave such prolonged (at least two months) and careful
attention to the case of Bruce v. Balliol, always the only serious issue – the
rest was shadow-play. Whatever the majority view among the community,
and clearly it favoured Balliol, the legal issues were without precedent in
Scotland. The Scots gained enormously, in the next twelve years, from the
substance of the judgement for Balliol, for it left them as united as they had

[122] *Chron. Fordun*, i, 326.
[123] *Anglo-Scottish Relations*, no. 32.

any hope of being. Not once in their war of words with Edward I did they suggest that his judgement for John, or John's right to be king, was flawed.[124]

But a consensus among historians that the consensus among Scots in the 1290s proves an impartial trial and a just judgement is only sustainable if it is based upon the record and takes account of its difficulties. We should be nearer the truth if there were more reliable contemporary accounts of the sessions of August 1291 and June 1292, for which we rely upon the unsafe Great Roll of John of Caen. But for the last session we are close to the terms of debate with the misunderstood Paris opinions, the *Annales* minutes and the pleadings of the last few days. They reveal a fine balance in the choices before the court, in which the shift to the king's council influenced the final decision. They suggest that the case of Bruce was more appropriate than that of Balliol, even if it was more outlandish to Scottish and English ears. Perhaps Edward was determined to find in favour of primogeniture among daughters because he feared for trouble over the succession in England after his own death? Or did he seek to establish the inferiority of the Scottish king as no better than an English earl? Did he fear to lose the right to escheat and forfeiture of Scotland if he used imperial laws? There are no certain answers, and it really does not matter greatly, because the court was unable to show why the custom of English tenures should apply to the kingdom of Scotland. They willed it so, politics in the whited sepulchre of law, not for the first, and certainly not for the last, time.

Throughout the years 1291–92 Edward had other concerns, more important than the squabbles of the Scots and of the Claimants. He had taken a new Crusading vow in 1287, and was deeply committed to the recovery of the Holy Land, not only by inclination, but also by the financial assistance promised by, and received from, the church. Master of Wales and of domestic concerns, he was willing to discharge a reponsibility of leadership which Christendom seemed anxious to place on his shoulders, and in return for promises of payment of crusading monies, Edward committed himself to depart at midsummer 1293. If he did not do so, the financial penalties would be fierce.

Then the fall of Acre in May 1291 shocked Western Christendom, but it also removed the sense of urgent endeavour engendered by the fall of Tripoli in 1289, which had led Edward to send a contingent to Acre, while the prolonged vacancy in the papal throne after the death of Nicholas IV in April 1292 removed the immediate threat of penalties for failure to sail on time. Yet Edward was still anxious to play his part and needed more money to do so. The Italian bankers, holding funds collected by taxing the English church from 1276, and commanded by the Pope to transfer these to him (he was hoping for 100,000 marks in June 1292), simply could not meet

[124] But see the questions raised in Goldstein, 'The Scottish Mission ... in 1301', *SHR*, lxx (1991), 11–12.

this unexpected demand. His best hope was the further tenth of clerical revenues for six years granted by Nicholas IV in 1291, but this was slow to come in, and, if he was to go, the project would need far more attention than he was able to give it at Berwick.[125] He certainly could not waste another six months on Florence and Eric.[126] If he was to complete unfinished business before sailing, the Great Cause must be brought to an end. And so it was.

Two Notes

1. The enquirers sent to Paris

The editors suggested that the opinions, 'presumably were noted by an agent of Edward in France. He may have been [Mr] John de Lacy, whose return from France is recorded [on 3 November 1292]'.[127] It is possible that de Lacy, who had been much involved in the question of the succession to the county of Savoy, did play a part in obtaining the Paris opinions, but his protection on going abroad had been issued only on 28 August, too late for him to play a leading role, and he was not back by 24 October.[128] Gilbert de Rothbury, clerk of the council, would be an obvious agent on the council's business, although no protection for him is enrolled. Active agents at Paris can, I believe, be identified among the auditors.

Of the five royally appointed auditors in lists 1 and 2 who were replaced by 21 June 1292 (list 3), two, and only two, had returned to Berwick as royal councillors by 24 October 1292.[129] They were William Hotham, provincial of the Dominicans in England, and William Gainsborough, minister of the Franciscans in England. Hotham had taught at Paris c.1275–80, where, according to Guisborough, he became familiar with the French king and magnates, and presumably stayed at the Paris house of the order; in 1282–87 he was provincial prior in England, refusing to return to Paris to teach in 1287 as he refused the see of Llandaff in 1290. From 1289 he had played an increasingly important part in public affairs, headed the mission to Rome to facilitate the marriage of the Maid of Norway to Edward of England, and had drafted the king's claim for recognition of overlordship on 10 May

---

[125] These paragraphs are based on Powicke, *Thirteenth Century*, 265–67; Prestwich, *Edward I*, 326–32; Lloyd, *English Society and the Crusade*, 232–39; Stein, *Fideles Crucis*, chapters 2–4.

[126] He ordered Scottish officials to pay considerable sums to Eric II on 28 December 1292; *Rot. Scot.*, i, 14–15.

[127] Stones and Simpson, ii, 358, 216.

[128] *Cal. Pat. Rolls, 1281–1292*, 506. For Lacy see Emden, *Biographical Register of the University of Cambridge to 1500*, 346.

[129] For the lists see Stones and Simpson, ii, 80–85. The king's twenty-four does not have a list 4, but the councillors present were named on 24 October (Stones and Simpson, ii, C.87) and 3 November (Stones and Simpson, ii, C.92), where they included Hotham and Gainsborough.

1291.[130] He was no newcomer to the business of Scotland, nor to Paris.[131]

The Franciscan Gainsborough, another theologian, had been involved in the affairs of his order rather than those of the king, but between November 1291 and October 1292 he lost the office of minister (head of the order in England), which he had held since c.1285, probably because he had gone abroad; in 1294 he was sent to Paris with an ex-provincial of the Dominicans to protest to Philip IV against the seizure of Gascony, possibly a sign of previous experience there. He served the king within his order even after going to the papal curia in 1300 to lecture on theology and in 1301 researched the papal registers for the king's Scottish business.[132]

Their efforts at Paris are attested by the presence among the Paris opinions of responses by Raymond Gaufridi, minister general of the Franciscans (who had been in England in 1291),[133] with the convent at Paris, and by 'the greater and wiser' of the Dominicans of Paris. The latter, despite their wisdom, disclaimed any knowledge of the customs of kingdoms, and of imperial laws, and both cited a marginally-relevant Old Testament chapter in favour of female succession; such improbable, not to say extraordinary, consultants on law and politics would have been quizzed when Hotham and Gainsborough lodged in the houses at Paris when pursuing the learned of that city with the stated case; that lodging may also explain the opinion of Weyland.

Bruce too was represented in Paris; his agent must have rejoiced in the spontaneous opinions which favoured his case, but the one respondent who spoke otherwise was cross-examined to extract an admission that, if the court found for Balliol, it would be competent for Bruce to lodge a new claim for a purparty. That questioner-agent was, I suggest, Geoffrey de Caldecote, one of Bruce's thirty-nine auditors in the earliest list (1). He had been replaced in list 2 by John of Conveth, and in a document of 2–14 June 1292, Bruce appointed a new attorney, probably to replace Caldecote in that position. On 10 November 1292, however, Bruce appointed three new

---

[130] *Chron. Guisborough*, 235; Little and Pelster (see next note) identified this *oratio* with a sermon before cardinals in 1295 (*Chron. Guisborough*, 256), but this is expressly said to have been in Latin.

[131] For Hotham, who went on to become archbishop of Dublin (misunderstood by Guisborough as Dunblane), see the biographies: Palmer, 'Fasti Ordinis Fratrum Predicatorum', *Archaeological Journal*, xxxv (1878), 140–43; *Dictionary of National Biography*, 'Hothum'; Little and Pelster, *Oxford Theology and Theologians*, 83–87; Douie, *Archbishop Pecham*; and M. H. MacInerny, *History of the Irish Dominicans*, i (1916). The last I have not seen, but according to Powicke (*Thirteenth Century*, 265n.) MacInerny saw Edward I as a 'rude, greedy and treacherous humbug'.

[132] There is a short biography of Gainsborough in Little, *Franciscan Papers, Lists and Documents*, 193–94, a fuller one in Little and Pelster, *Oxford Theology*, 185–86. For 1301, *Cal. Docs. Scot.*, v, no. 255. Gainsborough was bishop of Worcester, 1302–7.

[133] Little and Pelster, *Oxford Theology*, 189–90, where it is pointed out that Raymond seems to have been related to Eleanor of Provence, queen of Henry III.

attorneys, the first of whom was Geoffrey de Caldecote, familiar with the claim to purparty which Bruce lodged on that day.[134]

The representation of Balliol in Paris is less clear. His attorneys are nowhere named; the only two auditors who were on lists 1 or 2, absent from list 3 and present again in list 4, were the abbot of Holywood and a layman, William Moray of Tullibardine; neither seems a likely agent. His forty also included the elderly Mr Nicholas (Balmyle) on 6 November 1292,[135] and Mr John Nepos (nephew of the archdeacon of Galloway), a Doctor of Civil Law, probably of Bologna, who was present on 21 June and 6 November 1292 (lists 3 and 4);[136] neither seems as likely a candidate as Mr Alpin de Strathearn. He had certainly studied at Bologna, had acted among the auditors as depute for the abbot of Coupar at some time before 6 November 1292, when, with the abbot, he was one of Balliol's thirty-eight surviving auditors.[137] He is named in a document issued in Scotland about 1 August 1292, when he was a sub-collector of the papal tenth – as was the abbot of Coupar; but there is reason to think he was not then in the country.[138] He must have served Balliol well, for in 1293 he became the king's treasurer, a new office in Scotland, but of considerable importance. Since he had had no earlier obvious connection with Balliol, his promotion is likely to have been earned by political services during the Great Cause, and I suggest that he, too, had gone to Paris.

2. The reply of respondents (v) at Paris

The opening words of this reply present a different picture from the others, for the three respondents consulted the *Libri Feudorum*, where they 'found many appropriate answers to the questions put to them'. Unlike all the other respondents except the English lawyer, Weyland, for them the key to the 'business' lay in one phrase of the stated case: the king (of Scotland) holds

---

[134] Stones and Simpson, ii, 170 and n., 83, 233, 222. The other two attorneys seem to have French names. On 24 June 1292 Bruce nominated John de Burley (on whom I can find nothing) and Mr Adam de Crokedayk as his attorneys in England for two years; *Cal. Pat. Rolls, 1281–1292*, 494. Crokedayk was appointed Bruce's auditor in list 1. On him see Watt, *Biographical Dictionary*, 127–29.

[135] Watt, *Biographical Dictionary*, 23–24.

[136] Watt, *Biographical Dictionary*, 425–26.

[137] Stones and Simpson, ii, 220: *qui ante loco ipsius abbatis positus fuerat.*

[138] Stones and Simpson, ii, 84; Watt, *Biographical Dictionary*, 521–22. The document of *c.*1 August 1292 is a letter by Mr Alpin and the Vicar of Garvock, commanding the clergy of a deanery to hold an assembly in connection with the papal tenth. It is dated at Garvock about (a word is missing) that day. In the letter they say they do this as the result of a letter from Mr Alpin. I owe this information to Professor Watt. It seems to me that the Vicar used Alpin's name to bolster the authority of his letter, and that he was probably acting so because Alpin had gone abroad.

in feodo pro homagio. Homage they ignore, but 'fief' sends them to the Lombardic *Libri Feodorum*; indeed they were probably chosen as experts in that text.[139] The report which follows does suggest that the respondents were given a sequence of selected claims, on which they gave written findings (*invenerunt*) from the *Libri*; they were then questioned (*dicunt*).

I number the clauses of this opinion for ease of reference. (1) They found a title of the *Libri* (II, tit. 50) excluding right by ascent, King Eric's. Afterwards they found against claims through an illegitimate line, even if subsequently legitimated (II, tit. 26), Ros's claim. Then after that they found that right could not descend to a woman or her issue, hence excluding Count Florence, Bruce and Balliol (II, tit. 11). Next they cited a 'particular case' (*casus expressus*), according to which the fief of the deceased (Alexander III) could not pass to his great-uncle (David earl of Huntingdon) or his issue but reverts to the superior lord of that fief. This is a quotation from II, tit. 11, with the addition of 'superior', taken from the stated case, though as Dr Hand has shown, the citation omits an important qualification in the source – fiefs in which the grandfather (of Alexander III, i.e. King William) is *newly invested* could not pass (to David and issue).

There follow two general findings, first (2) that when there is no custom, the final recourse for fiefs is *leges communes* (II, tit. 1), clarified later as *imperiales*, so a legist's name for Roman law. This derives from II, tit. 1, in which the authority of Roman law, the Lombard laws and the custom of a kingdom is mentioned, and it is concluded that in a case 'which is not comprehended in the custom of a fief, without challenge written law may be used'.[140] The second general finding is (3), that a custom of fiefs observed for greater (vassals) must be observed for lesser, for the lesser cannot bind the greater, according to the *Libri* (I, tit. 7). The applicability of the law of lesser fiefs to a kingdom, was a question which dogged the final stages of the Cause.[141]

The whole of (1) – (3) gives a reference in the *Libri* for each statement,

---

[139] I cite this text by book and title of the vulgate text of the *Libri Feudorum*, which is printed with the *Corpus Iuris Civilis* in pre-Mommsen editions; I have used that of Edward Osenbrüggen, the fourteenth impression, Leipzig, 1872. I have also used the scholarly edition of *LF* edited by (Karl) Carolus Lehmann, whose two volumes were reprinted together in *Bibliotheca Rerum Historicarum, Neudrucke 1, Consuetudines Feudorum*, ed. Eckhardt. There is an English translation by Lord Clyde, *Craig's Jus Feudale*, 1081–1183. The indispensible work in English on the *Libri Feudorum* is Reynolds, *Fiefs and Vassals*.

[140] As Miss Reynolds has pointed out, the writer has here neatly reversed the sense of a remark in the *Corpus Iuris Civilis* about the authority of custom, in order to leave Roman law ('written law') with merely auxiliary authority; Reynolds, *Fiefs and Vassals*, 217.

[141] Dr Hand claims that in this sentence 'the principle that custom does not ascend was reiterated', p. 148. 'Reiterate' implies that he identifies this as Eric's claim by ascent – but Eric's right ascended to him, not a custom. (3) says that 'custom observed among greater men must also be observed among lesser ... but the custom of lesser men does not bind greater'. This has nothing to do with Eric. On the context of I, tit. 7, see Reynolds, *Fiefs and Vassals*, 218.

clear evidence of a written finding, not an oral response, yet here the past tense is used in contrast to the present tense for oral cross-examination. The whole corpus of ten opinions suggests that these respondents were given first a version of selected claims on which they commented (1), and then the record of an earlier response, (iiib), (ivb) or (viii), delivering their opinion of it in (2) and (3).

Thus far this opinion has been solicited by a party anxious to stress the feudal status of the disputed *res*, asking experts in the *Libri Feudorum* to look at claims to a fief and at the applicable law. In what follows he sought the application of these opinions to a kingdom, and the respondents answer questions, giving no authorities. (4) If there is a custom of succession to the Scottish kingdom, it prevails over any law, a much stronger reworking of (2); if there is not, (5) then recourse can be had to the custom of neighbouring kingdoms. If this fails, recourse is to (6) the *leges de usibus feodorum* which exclude all the Claimants so that the kingdom devolves to the superior lord, or (7) to *leges communes imperiales*, whereby succession to collaterals more remote than brothers and nephews must go to the nearest in degree, notwithstanding primogeniture (a reference to Nov. 118).

Thus for a kingdom they gave only third place, (6), to the *Libri Feudorum*, calling for escheat to the lord,[142] and fourth place to Roman law, which favoured the nearer in degree notwithstanding the other claim by primogeniture – though the alternatives, (6) and (7), probably represent a division of opinion among the respondents. The findings here are very different from those in other interrogations, (iiib), (ivb) and (viii), but they also differed from the findings about fiefs in (1) – (3), notably in inserting (5), the custom of neighbouring kingdoms, between custom and Roman law as given in (2). The most likely pattern before them here was another response which offered a sequence of authorities, (iii), (iv) or (viii).

---

[142] Dr Hand interprets these *leges* as 'general feudal law' (p. 148), but the conclusion, escheat to the superior lord, shows that the *LF* is again meant.

CHAPTER 14

Epilogue and conclusion

Among the unfinished business which could not be allowed to wait was the relationship of the Scottish king to the English. From 13 June 1291 till November 1292 Edward I had been direct lord of Scotland, yet constrained by the promises he had made for the time of the Cause. He did not (as he had in 1290) appoint the pushy Antony Bek to supervise, nor even to be a colleague of, the Guardians, and it has been said of his conduct that routine was little affected, Edward's interference confined to occasional orders and appointments.[1] He moved softly and may even have given the Scots renewed hope that the amiable relations between the kingdoms could continue. Yet in the hearing of the Cause there was a warning of the king's outlook and intentions when he sought to move the court to England and insisted that his promise on hearing causes in Scotland was for this occasion only.

This holding operation was conducted on the principle (suggested by the Scots) that the nature of the permanent relationship, overlordship, could only be established with the rightful king of Scots. The very judgement of 17 November 1292 ended with a peremptory 'and the lord king assigns to you [John] next Thursday [20 November] to do your fealty to him for the kingdom of Scotland and Christmas day to do homage to him for the kingdom of Scotland'.[2] On 19 November the precept to give sasine of the kingdom and its castles to Balliol was issued, the matrix of the seal of Guardianship, handed over not to the new king but to his overlord, was broken but stored in the English treasury as evidence of superior lordship, this at Berwick.[3]

The following day a largely Scottish group had moved to Norham castle, to be in the kingdom of England, where 'John de Balliol king of Scotland' spoke the words of fealty in French to Edward:

> You hear this, my lord Edward King of England, *soverein seigneur du reaume de Escoce*, that I, John de Balliol, king of Scotland, do fealty to you for the kingdom of Scotland which I hold and claim to hold of you, that I will be

[1] Marshall, 'Two Early English Occupations in Scotland', *SHR*, xxv (1928), 20–40, at pp. 26, 33.
[2] Stones and Simpson, ii, C.110, p. 249.
[3] Stones and Simpson, ii, C.110–12.

faithful and loyal to you and will bear faith and loyalty to you of life, of limb and of earthly honour, against all folk who can live and die, and will loyally acknowledge and loyally do to you the services due to you from the aforesaid realm of Scotland, as God helps me and these holy Gospels.[4]

Edward obtained from John a letter engrossing the fact and the words of this fealty, under his baronial seal and those of witnesses; on 24 December 1292 he secured another engrossment (which survives) under John's seal as king. This was liege homage, an oath of exclusive personal loyalty which undoubtedly 'derogated from the majesty' of a king, such as was owed by Edward I and his son, duke-peers of France, for their French possessions, but always refused.[5]

In John's oath the professions of loyalty were conventional and performing of services had been specified in the 1278 oath.[6] The novelty was the specification of the lands held of the English king – Scotland – for neither precedent nor agreement defined services from that realm.[7] A startling novelty too, were the circumstances of the oath, spoken by King John himself, and not, as befitted a king, by a magnate on his behalf.[8] The withdrawal to Norham in England made another point – that the Scottish king would have to go to his overlord in his overlord's kingdom to do fealty and homage. And so did styling John as king – that in awarding the kingdom, Edward had conferred the kingship.

Only ten days elapsed to the new king's inauguration at Scone, on St Andrew's day, 30 November, the last possible day before Advent. On 21 November John de St John was nominated by Edward to discharge the function of the infant earl of Fife in enthroning the new king, and Antony Bek, bishop of Durham, was also present at the inauguration.[9] On 24 December at Newcastle the new-made king reissued his letters of fealty under his royal seal, and on 26 December there he did homage to Edward I for the kingdom and its appurtenances. No fewer than twenty-three Scottish notables were present, of whom four[10] were Bruce adherents, the rest Balliol's.[11]

But for Edward I there was still much outstanding business: the validity of his promises made at Northampton in August 1290 and at Norham in

---

[4] Stones and Simpson, ii, p. 257; A.115–16, C.115–16, D.118 (= PRO E39/21).

[5] Vale, *Origins of Hundred Years War*, 51–59, the 'derogated' quotation on 51.

[6] *Anglo-Scottish Relations*, 81.

[7] 'Claim to hold', was probably not unusual and is found again in 1296; *Anglo-Scottish Relations*, 139.

[8] *Cf.* 1278, dicussed above pp. 160–64.

[9] *Rot. Scot.*, i, 12a; Palgrave, *Docs. Hist. Scot.*, 141. Fraser, *History of Antony Bek*, 61 makes his presence only 'probable', but the Caen instrument is of 1296 and unlikely to be inaccurate here.

[10] The bishop of Glasgow, the abbot of Jedburgh, the earl of Atholl and John de Stirling.

[11] Stones and Simpson, ii, D.119.i, A.122. Those present also sealed the king's letter. There is a claim that King John was rejected by the Scots, *Chron. Rishanger*, 371, written after 1296.

June 1291, and the parameters of the 'homage and what pertains to homage' to which alone Edward was entitled. The issue of the overlord's rights must be brought to crisis and resolution. The case of Roger Bartholomew, which revealed the iron fist without glove, had reached the highest court, that of the Guardians, in October 1291, and was appealed to Edward I at Berwick on 7 December 1292. From Berwick it was adjourned to Newcastle to 22 December, a move which can only have been a deliberate signal that Edward would hear appeals and that he would hear them in England; the unwonted brevity of the adjournment, excused as 'to do swifter justice', was surely to make the point immediately, perhaps before King John's homage.

On the day after that homage, 27 December, a group from his council appeared before Edward's councillors and 'asked', in relation to the appeal, that he would keep his promise to observe the laws and customs of the kingdom, and specifically that actions over things Scottish would not be taken outside the realm. We do not know King John's attitude to what was undoubtedly a protest – in his pleadings he had admitted that overlordship included a right to hear appeals – but there is no doubt that his advisers took their stand upon the promises sworn to at Northampton in 1290, before overlordship had been heard of, promises which they had understood to be definitive. Brabazon delivered Edward's rejection on 30 December and on 2 January 1293 King John acknowledged that, castles and sasine of the kingdom having been restored to him as rightful king as promised, he acquitted Edward of obligations and penalties arising from Edward's promises made as overlord on 12 June 1291.[12] This was a day *before* the kingdom came into Edward's hands, but John accepted Edward's version that they were made by virtue of overlordship. Otherwise the text is a correct statement of an obligation discharged, and the verb used, 'quit', is appropriate.

But King John's letter of 2 January 1293 goes on to deal with the Northampton concessions by Edward to the Guardians and community concerning a marriage between his son and the Maid of Norway 'lady and queen of Scotland, whose heir we are, containing articles, concessions, promises ... touching the estate, laws, franchises ... and quittance of subjection of the kingdom and its inhabitants'. These are to be 'quashed, void, of no strength or force, but from henceforth completely annulled and held for nothing ... and of all these ...we acquit [the English king]'.[13] Absent here is 'free in itself' in the Northampton text while the promise of 'without subjection as heretofore' is distorted into 'quittance of subjection' with its implication that Scotland had previously been subject. Whether the

[12] King John abandoned the promises made by Edward for himself, his heirs, kings of Scotland, and 'for all those who will hold the kingdom after us, whoever they may be' (Stones and Simpson, ii, A.127). This last phrase implies that the kingdom might be held by those who were not King John's heirs, and may represent the threat which caused him to submit.

[13] Stones and Simpson, ii, A.127, D.127.

promises of 1290 would have come within the reach of canon law for enforcement or annulment is unclear to me. But it is clear that Edward I realised that, although made for a purpose, the proposed marriage, they had not been made conditionally nor for a limited period, and that they were a contradiction of his overlordship. By this time, it seems, neither the twelve senior Scots who sealed John's letter, nor John himself, had the wit, wisdom or courage to preserve what they were signing away.[14]

There remained one promise of 12 June 1291 which was not limited to the period of the Great Cause, to make no demand for the wardship, marriage or possession of Scotland or other rights, 'apart from homage and over-lordship and what belongs to overlordship', should a minor ascend the Scottish throne. The hearing of appeals belonged to overlordship, so this reservation benefited the English king. On 4 January 1293 he therefore issued a new exemplification of this promise and its saving clause from the 1291 letter, not confirming it, but merely 'witnessing by this letter that it was thus'.[15] Whether the promise was still valid, or had been cancelled by King John's acquittance, is – and was – unclear. Nonetheless the way was clear for Edward to hear appeals from King John's court; of the eight known,[16] the most important was lodged by Macduff, a cadet of the family of the earls of Fife, claiming that after a judgement of the Guardians restoring certain Fife lands to him, he had been disseised and refused a remedy by King John. The latter was cited before Edward I on 25 May 1293 for his failure to give justice, and when he failed to turn up, the King's Bench set itself to the congenial task of drawing up rules for cases brought against the Scottish king.

If he failed to compear at the due term he lost jurisdiction over the case; the English court could order an inquest in Scotland or England into a trespass; if the court found that John had disseised anyone (e.g. Macduff) the English king could order that he be reseised, with costs, could amerce King John, and the appellant would then do homage to the English king and would hold all his Scottish lands of him, the Scottish king having no rights or jurisdiction there for the lifetime of the king and the appellant. Similar rules were laid down for other actions and finally the court provided for the appointment in each case of a protector of the appellant's family lands and goods.[17]

Thus the king of Scots must trot to Westminster at the beck of any

---

[14] Bryson, 'Papal Releases from Royal Oaths', *Journal of Ecclesiastical History*, xxii (1971), 19–33.

[15] Stones and Simpson, ii, A.127; *Rot. Scot.*, i, 15–16.

[16] For a survey of the appellants, Barrow, *Bruce*, 57–58.

[17] *Rot. Scot.*, i, 18a; *Rot. Parliamentorum*, i, 110–11 from PRO SC9/7. On p. 110 column b, the sentence *Et hoc idem fiet si non venerit...* has been added partly by interlineation. Compare the treatment of Llywelyn of Wales in Davies, *Age of Conquest*, 340–47, and the judgement in Davies, *History of Wales*, 158–60.

disgruntled subject, bearing the record of his court to be inspected for faults. He must allow the empanelling of an assize anywhere in his realm to make a retour to Westminster. He faced the prospect of unlimited fines and costs, while his kingdom would become a patchwork of English peculiars, each with its protector waiting to pounce upon any Scottish intromission there. For this King John, on 2 January 1293, had freed Edward from his solemn promises.

He tried to escape the consequences. In November 1293, answering a second summons, he compeared before the English council in parliament, where Macduff claimed that he was in contempt of Edward I to the tune of 10,000 marks and owed the appellant damages of 700 marks. After some shilly-shallying, the king, told to answer Macduff, said with some dignity:

> I am king of the kingdom of Scotland, and I dare not answer the plea of Macduff nor anything concerning my kingdom without the advice of responsible men of my kingdom.

How he came to be there without that advice we do not know, but the judges offered him an adjournment for consultation if he would recognise the court by asking for one. The king refused, was found in contempt for denying the overlordship he had accepted, and ordered to hand over three chief castles and towns.[18]

This was but the beginning of a series of measures taken against him between 16 and 22 November. Macduff was awarded damages for his imprisonment, and an inquest was to look into his disseisin. The lands of the earldom of Fife where he had been disseised were committed to an English agent, and presumably became a peculiar, for Edward behaved as direct lord of lands in Fife, even granting a market in the 'manor' of Crail to its lady.[19] A new appeal by Simon de Restalrig led to another summons of the king, the taking of Simon's lands into King Edward's protection, with William Hay of Lochwharret as protector. King John was ordered to release rents towards the 7,000 marks claimed by King Eric as his first wife's tocher. A further action was raised by Macduff, of spoliation of goods worth 200 marks, with another summons of the king.[20] This harrying, in which Robert Bruce was probably not entirely innocent,[21] was completely successful: John appeared

---

[18] *Anglo-Scottish Relations*, no. 21 gives the progress of the Macduff case from November 1293 to May 1295.

[19] *Cal. Docs. Scot.*, ii, nos 701, 704, 708. The market at the 'manor' of Crail is an enigma, for Crail had apparently been a royal burgh since 1178, and the position of its lady, Isabel de Beaumont, is unexplained. She was widow of John de Vescy, grandson of Eustace de Vescy and Margaret, illegitimate daughter of King William, and her husband would have been a Claimant had he not died in 1290 without children. Isabel was related to Eleanor of Castille, queen of Edward I. If the manor was not held of the earl of Fife, Edward's intromission is even more remarkable. Stevenson, *Documents*, i, no. 331.

[20] *Rot. Scot.*, i, 19–20.

[21] The MacDonald appellant, and Hay of Lochwharret, had supported Bruce.

before the English king and his council, not as king but as 'your man of the realm Scotland', promised obedience and asked an adjournment (thus recognising the court), which was granted until June 1294, later postponed to 1295.

The wonder is not that the Scots cried 'enough' at the destruction of their kingship and all that had seemed to protect it, but that they waited two years (from June 1293) before doing so. One reason was King Edward's preoccupation with the French confiscation of Gascony, to defend which he summoned an army for 1 September 1294, including in those called to London twenty-six Scots and their king.[22] But the muster never took place, nor was the summons given in 1296 as a reason for King John's renunciation of homage. By May 1295 the Scots were being wooed by Philip IV of France and in July they deprived their king of his authority, appointing a group of twelve to be his council, three of them Bruce supporters.[23] At the due date in 1295 King John did not compear, and Edward asked for judgement against him, for which a hearing was fixed for 12 October 1295. When he again failed to compear, orders were sent to two English prelates to take possession of the castles and towns of Berwick, Roxburgh and Jedburgh, as sureties, from 'our dear and faithful John, King of Scotland'.

Edward promised that the places would be returned at the end of the war with France, a device to secure trouble-free surrender in a matter to which he could not attend until then. Nonetheless to increase the pressure, and to inhibit Scottish sympathy for France, in noticeably harsher terms he ordered the seizure of the English possessions of King John and of all Scots not remaining in England.[24] On 3 November Edward still assumed that John would submit and had a writ served on him thereafter at Buittle to appear as defender in an appeal on 8 April 1296. Even the writs of 16 December 1295, summoning a muster at Newcastle on 1 March 1296, spoke of journeying to Scotland to obtain a remedy from 'King John'.[25] Only a show of force would be needed.

There is absolutely no trace in these English records of any knowledge of the treaty which four ambassadors from the Scottish council had made with Philip IV at Paris on 23 October 1295, a treaty which we know was to infuriate Edward.[26] Three ambassadors remained in France and the fourth,

[22] Foedera, i, 804. Parliamentary Writs, i, 261–63. Writs cancelling the expedition do not survive (compare the summons to Norham for June 1291), but a Welsh revolt turned Edward's attention from Gascony. Armies went to both. Prestwich, Edward I, 406.

[23] Barrow, Bruce, 63 and refs. on 338 n. 47. The Bruce supporters were the bishop of Glasgow, earl of Mar and James Stewart.

[24] Rot. Scot., i, 21b, 22b; Stevenson, Documents, ii, no. 342 = Cal. Docs. Scot., ii, no. 718; Cal. Close Rolls, 1288–1296, 435, forbidding exports of supplies and arms to Scotland, 16 October 1295.

[25] Rot. Scot., i, 22b–23a; Parliamentary Writs, i, 275.

[26] APS, i, 451–53; Foedera, i, 830–31 (not vol. ii as in Stones and Simpson, ii, 286); Barrow, Bruce, 64–65. On 22 October 1295 the French made a treaty with Eric of Norway which was

Sir Ingram de Umfraville, was stranded there until he begged a lift in a German ship.[27] The year 1296 came with no word, and the abbot and prior of Arbroath were sent to the English court to excuse their king's non-compearance and to protest at injuries done to Scots on land and sea; they left to return to Scotland about 23 January, informed that Edward would be at Newcastle on 1 March when he would give remedy on their complaints.[28] On the same 23 January he ordered that £5,000–£15,000 be sent to Newcastle to pay 1,000 men at arms and 60,000 infantry there for up to four weeks;[29] clearly the abbot had shown him that the Scots were likely to prove stiff-necked, but Edward also gave King John a further adjournment to 1 March, a date to which the abbot was to forewarn John to attend at Newcastle.

Soon after January, Umfraville and the treaty must have reached Scotland, where it was confirmed at an assembly on 23 February 1296, and the Scots, knowing of Edward's muster, and made bold by French promises, summoned their host. Edward had expected to have troops at Newcastle for up to four weeks but for two weeks did nothing, hoping that the three castles and towns would be surrendered. The Scots came to Wark on Tweed castle (near Carham) on 17 March, expecting its surrender, but Edward forced their withdrawal. There, on 25 March, the Bruces and the earl of Dunbar took an oath of service to him under pain of loss of life and property, and renewed their homage and fealty to him. The king received their homages for all the lands which they hold, except those given by 'John de Balliol formerly king of Scotland', a telling phrase except that it comes from a roll of homages drawn up in 1298 by two notaries, one of them John of Caen, and from some manuscripts of Guisborough's chronicle where it figures after the homages of August 1296.[30] It belongs to later days, when Edward's notaries were determined that John had forfeited the throne by his alliance with France, before Edward invaded Scotland, and when the notary inserted 'formerly' into 'John king of Scotland'.

On 23 March the Scots attacked Carham, on 26 March Carlisle. Two days later Edward at last crossed the Tweed at Coldstream, but we cannot be sure

linked to the Scottish treaty, as Nicholson showed, 'Treaties of 1295', *SHR*, xxxviii (1959), 114–32.

[27] Barrow, *Bruce*, 341 n. 70, citing *Chron. Lanercost*, 168–69.

[28] *Cal. Pat. Rolls, 1292–1301*, 183; Palgrave, *Docs. Hist. Scot.*, 144–47; Stones and Simpson, ii, 285–86, and esp. n. 5 on 286. This is a draft notarial instrument by Caen, drawn up soon after 3 September 1296 (it mentions the appointment of Warenne, of that day), and already distorting events. It denounces Scottish agreements with the king's enemies, Palgrave, pp. 146–47.

[29] PRO E 159/69, m.11d, Stevenson, *Documents*, ii, no. 346, but read £5,000 weekly for £1,000; Prestwich, *Edward I*, 469–70. The same source, m.12r, shows the earl of Carrick planning to go to Scotland on 11 February.

[30] *Chron. Guisborough*, 283; for the notarial roll, *Anglo-Scottish Relations*, no. 22, Stones and Simpson, i, 92 (no. 4).

that he was even now intent upon conquest rather than seizing the sureties.[31] He aimed first at the richest surety, Berwick, offering peace to the burgesses. When they did not submit, Edward's general attack took the town easily on 30 March and was followed by a dreadful massacre.[32] That gave the Scots justification for King John's defiance to the English king, cataloguing the injuries inflicted by Edward, against which the king was bound by oath to defend himself and his kingdom. He could not bear these, nor remain in homage and fealty, 'although [they were] extorted by your violent pressure', and therefore renounced those homages done by himself and by any of his subjects with lands in England.[33] The rhetoric is strong, and isolated incidents have been blown out of all proportion, so that alleged violent oppression outweighs what the text first alleges, summonses to compear before Edward, the real *gravamen*, but which alone scarcely justified breaking an oath. And the claim that fealty had been extorted by force may have been necessary for ecclesiastical eyes and ears, but was so manifestly false that it could only be noted parenthetically. If oaths meant anything, this was a rebellion.

From the delivery of this document on 5 April, Edward's armies advanced in and beyond the Tweed valley, determined on suppression of that rebellion. The battle of Dunbar on 27 April 1296, a disaster for the Scots, achieved this because King John had no stomach for retreat to the mountains to reclaim his kingdom when Edward and his army should withdraw; indeed he was later to claim that he thought the Scots a miserable lot who had tried to poison him.[34] King Edward advanced inexorably to Edinburgh castle, Perth and then for a week, 26 June–2 July, Clunie.[35] King John entered into negotiations late in June with his representative, Anthony Bek, and their agreement assured John an English earldom and some good hunting country in return for his 'grant and quit-claim' of the kingdom to Edward, to be handed over on 8 July.

But that must have been rapidly overtaken by discovery at Edinburgh of the treaty made in John's name with Philip IV, a discovery which caused Edward to set aside the recent settlement.[36] John, taking blame for the treaty, executed his first written resignation, at Kincardine in Mearns, on 2 July. He

---

[31] Nicholson, 'Treaties of 1295', *SHR*, xxxviii (1959), 114 follows the story as told by Edward's notaries. There is a full discussion in Prestwich, *Edward I*, 372–75, giving alternative interpretations.

[32] Prestwich, *Edward I*, 470–71. Again this massacre has been cited as punishment for the French alliance, though no source says it was. The laws of war permitted such action for failure to submit when peace was offered.

[33] *Anglo-Scottish Relations*, no. 23.

[34] *Anglo-Scottish Relations*, no. 27.

[35] Stevenson, *Documents*, ii, 27–28.

[36] This sentence is my reconstruction – we know only that the first settlement made no mention of an alliance with France and that the second was a humiliating surrender attributed to it.

seems to have agreed to surrender his person to Edward, presumably on a promise of life and limb, and was then required to renounce the French treaty at Stracathro on 7 July and undergo at Montrose on 8 July a dishonourable act of personal submission to King Edward, in which his tabard was in some way degraded and his kingship demitted by the symbol of a white wand.

John issued a letter 'giving back' (*avons rendu*) the kingdom on 2 July at Kincardine and 10 July at Brechin, both before and after the act of resignation at Montrose (8 July), a deliberate reflection of his fealty (20 November 1292), inauguration (30 November) and homage (26 December).[37] From Brechin he was taken into captivity in England, and, although to most Scots he remained their king, his failure to come back, notably in 1302, must have weakened his hold on their allegiance. Edward moved gradually toward denying the existence of a Scottish kingdom, a position he finally took up when the leading magnates submitted to him in 1303–4, deserted by their French ally. Edward had possession; with the death of Boniface VIII in 1303 the papacy lost interest, and the overlordship which justified possession was uncontested. In 1304–5 Edward was able to soften his punishment of those who had opposed him, and in his ordinance for the government of Scotland showed a realisation that control would come only with the cooperation of Scots in their traditional spheres of interest.[38]

The revolt of Robert Bruce (VII), earl of Carrick, in 1306 was not planned; after the slaying of John Comyn he was persuaded, apparently by Robert Wishart bishop of Glasgow, to abandon hopes that Edward I would acknowledge his right and to take the throne. Edward had his revenge in the execution of three of Robert I's brothers and imprisonment of his wife and daughter, Marjory. The Bruce line survived only in that daughter, one surviving brother, Edward, married but childless, and four or five sisters, one of whom was queen of Norway.[39] With the release of his wife and daughter early in 1315, the question of the succession had to be faced again. The form of settlement followed then and for the rest of the fourteenth century was that used in 1284, an *obligatorium*, sealed by prelates and nobles assembled to give assent and the force of law to a tailzie (entail) of the throne.

There were five of these, in 1315, 1318, 1326, 1371 and 1373, and a proposal for another in 1363–64, all laying down succession to the reigning

---

[37] Stones, 'Surrender', *Bulletin of the Institute of Historical Research*, xlviii (1975), 94–106, at 104–5; M. Prestwich, 'English Campaign', *ibid.*, xlix (1976), 135–38; *Anglo-Scottish Relations*, no. 24. There are difficulties about the sources for the abortive resignation, derived from a newsletter, as Stones and Prestwich agree.

[38] Watson, *Under the Hammer*, chapters 6 and 7 are a very good assessment of this period.

[39] Dunbar, *Scottish Kings*, 67, 141–42; *Scots Peerage*, ii, 433–35. I think his 'sister' Margaret was illegitimate. Robert I later had two daughters: one married a squire and had two daughters, the other married the earl of Sutherland and had a son who died a prisoner in England, without issue.

king, with the king's great seal appended in 1315 and 1371, when the assemblies were not parliaments. The first, known in a later copy, is worth some attention, for it is not a straightforward text. It narrates that the April 1315 meeting at Ayr was 'gathered to treat, deliberate and ordain about the status, defence and perpetual security of the kingdom', as well as to muster for the expedition of Edward Bruce to seek the kingship of Ireland.

Those participating agreed first that they would all be obedient to, and stand by, King Robert and the legitimate male heirs of his body as their king and liege lord. Then by consent of the king, and of Marjory 'on the day of this ordinance his heir apparent', they ordained that if the king should die without a male heir, then his brother Edward, 'as a vigorous man, most highly skilled in warlike deeds for the defence of the right and freedom of the kingdom'[40] and his heirs male should succeed, and they would be obedient to him. Failing Edward and his heirs male, succession should revert to Marjory, whom failing to the nearest heir lineally descended from King Robert (presumably Marjory's child), provided that Marjory should be married by consent of King Robert, or, failing him, by consent of the greater part of the community. The king's half-nephew, Thomas Randolph earl of Moray,[41] would be guardian if the king or his brother Edward was succeeded by a boy or if Marjory were to die as a widow leaving an heir (presumably her husband would be guardian if he was widower). Finally came provision for the situation where heirs failed.[42]

This was clearly meant to obviate the uncertainty which had arisen after the death of Alexander III and the disastrous involvement of the English king, but is nonetheless a puzzling document. Opening with a promise to hold Robert *and heirs male of his body* as king,[43] and recognising Marjory as then heir apparent (heir, that is, unless the king had a son, which would now be called heir presumptive), the text proceeds to alter that line of succession. The placing of a collateral, Edward Bruce and his male issue, next in line of succession to Robert's male issue, ousts Marjory, an overt intrusion into the lawful succession for which no reason in law was offered. The rhetoric – 'spin' – about the military virtues of Edward Bruce was inappropriate in a document which is otherwise about lawful – not the most expedient – heirs to the throne. That the marriage of Marjory should be by Robert's consent seems an otiose statement, but the alternative, failing the king (i.e. if he had died), by consent of the community, makes it clear that Edward Bruce is not there to approve of her husband. Then the provision that King Robert's boy is to have the earl of Moray and not his uncle, Edward Bruce, as guardian,

---

[40] *tanquam vir strenuus et in actibus bellicis pro defensione iuris et libertatis regni Scocie quam plurimum expertus*

[41] Moray's mother was Robert's half-sister, daughter of Marjory countess of Carrick by her first husband. Moray had no Bruce blood and no claim to the throne.

[42] *APS*, i, 464–65, 290 (for the seals); *RRS*, v, no. 58; *Scotichronicon*, vi, 378–81.

[43] Shortened versions in translation tend to omit the opening promise.

though Edward would be next in line to the throne, is another striking omission.

But finally the document provides that 'if Marjory dies leaving no surviving heir of her body and no surviving heir of King Robert's body' Moray should be Guardian until the community could meet to decide on the lawful succession and government of the kingdom. The 'surviving heir' here, at least of King Robert, must include both male and female, so the rights of females, Marjory or her sister, as yet unborn, were admitted in default of heirs male. But we seem to be again in the impossible world where King Robert may be succeeded by King Edward, whose only daughter, it seemed, could not succeed, for right returned to King Robert's daughter. The alternative explanation is that this final provision was drafted for a document which assumed that Edward Bruce and his issue could not become kings of Scots.

All these considerations suggest that the document we have was not the first intention of the king as he went to Ayr to oversee the departure of his brother who, until this year, had been his only possible successor, who was to acquire his own kingdom and to lose his right to the Scottish throne – for there is a contrast between the tailzie's encomium of Edward and the consensus of commentators, associated with the Irish adventure, that Edward was too big for his boots, unable to share Scotland with Robert.[44] Robert (aged forty) hoped for a son and heir – he was to have four more children – who might well succeed as a child, so there was need to provide for a minority, the more so if succession passed to a child of his 'heir apparent', Marjory. The obvious Guardian, Edward, the king's own brother, was now ruling himself out and the community was to be persuaded to settle the office on Moray. But there was a war to be won, and if the king had no son the community wanted Edward Bruce as his successor. Probably Edward wanted that too, and King Robert conceded the point, provided that Marjory's residual right and Moray's contingent Guardianship were acknowledged. It was a rerun of the issue of 1195 with the same outcome: a daughter might succeed, but her uncle had a better right.

Twice Moray is called upon to act as Guardian, first for a boy king, then in assembling the community to find an heir, but in both cases 'if he is prepared to agree', an odd proviso since he was present and swore to fulfil the tailzie. But if an earlier version had made no mention of Edward Bruce, but dealt with Robert's issue and named Moray as Guardian in these contingencies, then a claim by Edward Bruce for the office could well influence Moray to decline it. In short, the place of Edward Bruce in this tailzie was not the king's original intention but the result of pressure from the community.

[44] Barbour, *The Bruce*, bk 14, lines 3–5; Duncan, 'Scots' Invasion of Ireland', *The British Isles, 1100–1500*, ed. Davies, 113–15.

Edward Bruce was killed at Dundalk on 14 October 1318, leaving no legitimate issue. By then Marjory had married Walter Stewart, borne him a son, Robert, and died, perhaps in childbirth. A hastily summoned parliament at Scone on 3 December agreed a new tailzie,[45] apparently sealed by a larger group than that of 1315.[46] Its first provision was a variant version of that of 1315: all would stand by King Robert and his heirs (no 'male'), but adding that anyone who failed to do so would be a traitor, guilty of *lèse majesté*. Then the succession was laid down as reversion from the king, failing an heir male, to Robert Stewart. Guardianship of a minor king until the community or the greater and wiser part decided he was able to govern was to be given to Moray, whom failing to Sir James Douglas, and the two men swore they would discharge the office well.

The king and his advisors must have known how slight the royal line had become, yet nothing was said explicitly about the succession should Robert Stewart die. Instead of the 1315 provision for an assembly to consider the succession if Robert had no descendants, there was a definition:

> Formerly doubt had been cast (though inadequately) by some on by what law succession to the kingdom should be decided, if perchance it was not obvious; now it was defined and declared by clergy and people that succession to the kingdom should not be decided in future by the custom observed in the kingdom in inferior feus or heritages, since any such custom had not heretofore been introduced in succession to the kingdom, but that the nearer male descended from a right line at the time of the death of the king, or, failing a male, the nearer female from a right line, or failing that line, the nearer male from a collateral line (having regard to the right of blood by which the right of reigning belonged to the deceased king),[47] ought to succeed, without any gainsaying or impediment, in the kingdom to the king of whose succession perchance there happened to be discussion.[48] This is determined to be sufficiently in accordance with imperial law.

These tailzies are first and foremost loyalty pledges, not against the English, but against the Balliol right to the throne. King John was dead, but his sons

---

[45] *APS*, i, 465–66; *RRS*, v, 560–61; *Scotichronicon*, vii, 38–43 (with translation). If forty days' (excluding Sundays) notice was given, the summons must have gone out on 18 October, or if six weeks' notice, Sundays included, then about 21 October. A parliament can scarcely have been planned for a Scottish December in the king's probable absence in Ireland. Such haste would be possible because Edward Bruce's wife (in Scotland) could not be pregnant.

[46] *APS*, i, 290, showing 11 bishops, 9 religious, 3 earls and 7 barons, with many others. The short list of barons suggests that the cataloguer lost interest in his work.

[47] The point of this parenthesis is that right must pass to a collateral descended from the line by which Bruce had title to the throne (his father, father's father, father's father's mother, Earl David, etc.) and not to a collateral of, for example, his mother or her ancestors, his father's mother or her ancestors (which would have given a right to Thomas Randolph), etc.

[48] *Cf.* the translation of these last words, *regi de cuius successione agi forsan contigerit*, in *Scotichronicon*, vii, 41. I have taken *censetur* as present tense, 'is determined'.

lived and, as the conspiracy in 1320 showed, had no small following among Robert's fair-weather subjects. Hence the opening commitment to his line in both tailzies, and the fierce penalty for adherence to any other line in the 1318 text. For if the Bruce line should seem, or be alleged, to have died out, men might cry that the next heir was Edward Balliol. Hence, too, the final declaration against the law of feus which had given the throne to King John in 1292, and the attempt to put in its place in 1318 a rule based on the Bruce claim of 1291–92 to be the *nearer* heir to the throne, at a specific time, the death of the king, as Bruce the Claimant was in 1290 when the Maid died.

The rule makes no appeal to 'the law by which kings reign', but asserts compatibility with 'imperial law', to which Bruce the Claimant probably appealed, though we have only Balliol's word for it. It does seem to accord with the relevant title (II, tit. xi) of the *Libri Feudorum*, but the point is not given great importance, suggesting that whoever drafted these words knew how little help imperial law was likely to be in any succession crisis. This clause was at last a response to Edward I's judgement in the Great Cause, a response which good fortune in the birth and survival of kings' sons made otiose. It made secure the title of Robert Stewart, which was good also under the law of inferior feus. The gender issue of 1195 was at last faced , the king's daughter acknowledged to have a better right than his brother. It does, however, ignore representation, and so would apparently have made (for example) John of Gaunt king of England in 1377, not Richard II; but that may have been bad drafting, not the intended meaning.

On 5 March 1324, at Dunfermline, Robert's queen at last gave him male heirs, not one but two boys, David, who seems to have been the older, and John, who died young at Restenneth.[49] The date of his death is not known, but on 15 July 1326 in a parliament at Cambuskenneth, the king secured a further tailzie of the throne. According to accounts of this, clergy, nobles and people gathered at the parliament swore fealty to David, and to his nephew Robert Stewart should David die childless.[50] This renewed version of the tailzie, and the fealty which enacted what the tailzie said, was made when war was a distant threat, during a thirteen-year truce with England. The point of it would not be the succession of David, whose right was unquestionable, but the heir apparent; probably John, heir after David, had recently died, leaving David, aged two, still heir of the king but a precarious life, so that Robert Stewart, aged ten, was once again recognised as the heir presumptive.

These tailzies were not the only documents in this form under Robert I,

---

[49] *Scotichronicon*, vii, 14: *proles est data bina*. Since this poem was written not long after the event and celebrates David as heir, he was the elder. His twin would be the John who was buried at Restenneth Priory; *APS*, i, 514, no. 12*. The choice of the name John is decidedly odd, but it had also been given to the child born into the French crown in 1316, when kings had been Louis or Philippe since 1060. John I of France died after a few days.

[50] *RRS*, v, no. 301; *Chron Fordun*, i, 351; *Scotichronicon*, vii, 34–35.

for four others were sealed by prelates and magnates as well as the king: the sentence of forfeiture on the king's opponents (1314), the restoration of the earl of Fife (1315), a confirmation of Moray's possessions (1316) and the grant of a tenth of rents (1326), the last a deal between king and community, each party having a text sealed by the other.[51] The first three reflect the uncertainties of title during and after a period of shifting allegiances, but there is no escaping the overall impression that Robert I was attentive to the wishes of the community, like Philip VI of France debtor to those who had supported his taking kingship; the tailzies of 1315 and 1318 were above all requirements of loyalty to him when such loyalty could not be taken for granted.

When Robert I died on 7 June 1329 David II was only five, but was treated at once as king. It seems that the government knew that Pope John XXII was to grant crowning and anointing to the king of Scots, and that they put inauguration ceremonies on hold until the papal bull (it had been issued on 13 June 1329, a week after Robert died) became available after its cost, 12,000 florins, had been paid. David II was crowned and anointed king in November 1331, having waited till the monies due to Edward III as part of the peace settlement of 1328 (£20,000) had been paid in full. His regnal year is thought to have begun on 8 June 1329.

Although David had enjoyed a more elaborate sacring than any previous king of Scots, his reign showed that the logic of tailzies of the crown, that the succession was laid down by assemblies of the political elite, was as well understood by the laity as coronation and unction was by the clergy. In this Scotland was not alone, for in 1327 Edward II was first deposed for a list of offences by an assembly of prelates and magnates summoned as a parliament in Edward's name, and then cajoled into abdicating under the threat that if he did not do so 'the people' would choose as king someone not of his blood. A year later Charles IV of France died, leaving a pregnant wife. The nobility met and chose as regent his cousin Philip of Valois descended in the male line from Philip III, overlooking the claims of Edward III of England, whose mother was Charles IV's sister. In making this choice they must have known that if the child born was a girl, Philip would become king, as indeed did happen.

There were precedents in the recent past for rejecting succession by a king's daughter to the French throne,[52] but at this juncture the nobles were influenced not by a Salic law, unknown at the time and discovered later to justify the exclusion of females, but by the fact that Edward was English.[53]

---

[51] The last was enacted twice, one sealed by the king, the other by the community. *RRS*, v, 117–18, and nos 41, 58, 72, 101, 300, 301.

[52] Louis X (d. 1316) left a daughter who was passed over in favour of Louis' brother, Philip V. But she resigned her rights – i.e. had had rights – in 1318.

[53] The French royal line had acquired other kingships by a claim through a female – Hungary, Sicily, Navarre. On the discovery of the Salic law in the reign of Charles V and

Philip VI paid dearly for the circumstances of his accession in gifts to those to whom he owed it, and although Edward made no protest in 1328, his claim to the French throne disturbed Europe for over a century.[54] In a peaceful interval Charles V regulated the age of majority and regency arrangements by royal *ordonnance*. From the fifteenth century the Salic law was accepted as a fundamental law of the kingdom which might not be changed; it is arguable that this was the foundation of the monarch's authority upon which the *ancien régime* first flourished and then mouldered, unchallenged.[55]

Edward III, seeking to re-establish overlordship in Scotland, revived the claims of Edward Balliol, despite the acknowledgment of Scottish independence and marriage of his sister to David (II) in 1328. Edward Balliol was crowned king of a truncated Scotland while David fled to France, and though he recovered the kingdom by 1341, he was captured and imprisoned in 1346, while Balliol lost all save the title of king. Edward had a choice of Scottish kings, and restored recognition of David when he hoped to secure from the latter, in return for release without ransom, an acknowledgment that, failing David's male heirs, the throne would pass to Edward III or his younger son. The proposition was rejected by the Scots in 1352, but revived in 1363 and again rejected forcibly in 1364, by which time Edward had secured from the childless Balliol resignation of his claim to the Scottish throne.[56]

The 1363 negotiations produced two interesting documents, the first, heads of agreement to be put to a Scottish parliament. These are detailed and cover matters not touched upon in 1290, but they were clearly drafted on the basis of the Northampton treaty, whose promises were thought to appeal still to the Scots. The second is a scholar's argument about the proposed change in the succession, a debate which uncertainly approved accepting Edward's younger son as David's heir. Written by a Scot, it rehearses a multiplicity of arguments both for and against the 1363 proposal, arguments which at no point suggest that the succession could be neither negotiated nor altered, as part of the law and custom of Scotland. On the contrary, there are comments that 'the people' ought, or ought not, to consent to a change, on the balance of advantage, a balance which was the author's main concern, and evidently also that of David II.[57] There had been

its gradual application to the monarchy in the fifteenth century, Beaune, *Birth of an Ideology*, ch. 9.

[54] Sumption, *Hundred Years War*, i, 103–10.

[55] Autrand, 'La succession à la couronne de France et les ordonnances de 1374', *Représentation, pouvoir et royauté à la fin du moyen âge*, ed. Blanchard, 25–32; Giesey, 'The Juristic Basis of Dynastic Right to the French Throne', *Transactions of the American Philosophical Society*, new series, 51, 5 (1961), 3–47.

[56] Duncan, '*Honi soit* ... David II and Edward III, 1346–52', *SHR*, lxvii (1988), 113–41.

[57] 'A Question about the Succession, 1364', ed. Duncan, *Miscellany of the Scottish History Society*, xii, 1–57.

some advantage in the *obligatorium* of 1284 and in the tailzies of Robert I's reign but in essence they were a clarification, if also an extension, of the established custom of succession. In David II's hands kingship was a negotiable commodity held in the bank of 'the people' – in effect, of a council general or parliament, anticipating the realpolitik of 1688–89. David died on 22 February 1371 without having had children from any of his liaisons, the 1363 proposals decisively rejected.

His heir, Robert Stewart, was at first opposed by the earl of Douglas on unknown grounds,[58] and the opposition faded, but at his coronation Robert II secured another sealed declaration from prelates and magnates that his oldest son John was heir to the throne. Two years later, in 1373, a more elaborate tailzie gave the succession to his five sons and their heirs male, successively; only failing these should 'the lawful heirs of the royal blood and lineage *ex tunc in antea*, succeed'.[59] Thus female descendants were excluded until all legitimate descendants in the male line of Robert II had failed, a recipe for disastrous contention had the elder sons left only daughters, and the younger male line died out after some generations of kings; fortunately the senior line retained the kingship, but the 1373 tailzie provided the rules against which the heir to the throne could be murdered in 1402, executed in 1425, the king murdered in 1437 and the new king's heir executed in the same year.[60] It is scarcely necessary to list the parallels from England between 1399 and 1485 to show that kingship had become a different game, with new rules.[61]

On 1 March 1328 Edward III had sealed the second explicit recognition by an English king of the independence of Scotland.[62] Considerably shorter than the Northampton recognition of 1290, it was also part of a larger deal, the Anglo-Scottish peace made at Edinburgh on 17 March, when it would be handed to the Scots. A year later the papacy gave coronation and unction, recognition delayed for two centuries, of the status of the Scottish king as ruler of an independent kingdom. The English recognition was rejected by Edward III when he escaped from tutelage and sought once more to create an English empire in Britain. Intermittently revived as a military effort by Henry IV in 1400, Edward IV in 1482 and Henry VIII after 1542, this aspiration offered few rewards, for it met articulate and determined

---

[58] Boardman, *The Early Stewart Kings: Robert II and Robert III*, 39–44.

[59] *APS*, i, 546 (1371), 549 (1373).

[60] David duke of Rothesay, Murdoch duke of Albany, James I, Walter earl of Atholl, respectively; add the use of James (IV) to give respectability to a revolt against James III in 1488.

[61] Nenner, *Right to be King*, Introduction, is an interesting account of the English establishment of parliamentary title in the guise of strict inheritance.

[62] *Anglo-Scottish Relations*, no. 41. The first such recognition was the treaty of Northampton; the Canterbury quittance of 1189 was not explicit.

resistence from the Scottish communities, supported fairly consistently by the Valois kings of France – another sign of international acceptance of the status of Scotland's kings. The peace of 1328 was a brief interval in a long struggle, but nonetheless a definitive defeat for the imperial aim bequeathed by Edward I to his successors.[63]

The claim to overlordship did not disappear completely; there is an extensive and scarcely legible (hence unpublished) vindication of it apparently drawn up for Henry IV,[64] and in 1482 James III's brother, styling himself 'king of Scotland', promised homage to Edward IV when he had obtained the kingdom of Scotland; it could still be argued in the sixteenth century. On the other hand no attempt was made by Henry IV or V to extort homage from their prisoner, James I, nor was the topic mentioned in the treaty for his release in 1424, and while Anglo-Scottish war revived spasmodically over Berwick, Roxburgh and truce infringements, no serious intention attempted conquest of Scotland between 1337 and 1543, save perhaps in 1400. A well-known rhetoric of 'freedom' flourished under Robert I and was brilliantly revived by his biographer, John Barbour, in the 1370s. That work continued to be read for a century or more, but 'freedom' faded towards the end of that century and had little or no place in the occasional rhetoric of enmity to England in the fifteenth century. It is markedly absent from the (fictional) biography of Wallace, written in the 1470s.

Despite the existence of a formal state of war between English and Scottish kings for a century and a half from 1333, then, there was little active conflict and no political achievement. The war sank into the exhaustion of stalemate, partly because the fruits of war promised to be considerably less than its costs, both to the chivalry which participated and for the king whose rights were to be asserted. These rights, so central to the efforts of Edward I, were increasingly seen as legal antiquities, useful but in a very minor way. It would scarcely be a consolation to Edward I to suggest that his aims were achieved only in the second English empire, that constructed by Oliver Cromwell.

The two themes of this book, the Scottish custom of succession and the English claim to overlordship, meet at two points: in the 1090s and in 1291. The custom of succession develops from circulation within the royal kin, the descendants of Fergus and of Cinaed mac Alpin, with an apparent rejection of Pictish custom, to a struggle between branches of that kin from which one, that represented by Maelcoluim II, emerged as victor. Whether we should make anything of the absence of reference to a king or kings as *Ua/Ui Feargusa* or *Ua/Ui Cinaedha*, 'descendant(s) of Feargus' or 'of

---

[63] Davies, *First English Empire*, ch. 7.
[64] BL, MS Cotton Vespasian C XVI.4.

Cinaed', is doubtful, given the exiguous nature of the sources, but if there is a significance to this absence, it is likely to lie in the limited number of segments, the narrowness of the range of cousins, playing for kingship.

Whatever the level of internecine conflict within the ruling kindred, the command they exercised does suggest that before succeeding these kings had a territorial power-base, a share of the kingdom. But no source suggests that they were 'kings'; this was no longer, if it ever had been, a land of petty kings of fractured provinces, in ranks graded for Irish law-books, nor of 'kings' of war-bands preying on neighbours or lands overseas. Kings of the kindred of Alpin doubtless built followings by successful raids and battles, but they also survived disasters and yet retained a monopoly of kingship, apparently unchallenged until the accession of Macbeth. The role of provincial leaders, which Macbeth clearly was, is almost unknown, for the only account, the death of Cinaed II at the hands of a *comes* of Angus because of his daughter, smacks of literary invention.

The extraordinary success of Macbeth, who could visit Rome and survive a heavy defeat by Earl Siward in 1054, suggests secure control through provincial rulers committed to his kingship, men who put his stepson Lulach on the throne even after Macbeth's defeat and death. They would submit or be cleared out on Lulach's death and the accession of Maelcoluim III. Yet Macbeth was unlike all other kings between 1005 and 1093, a ruler who launched no raids into England, even in the uncertain years after Cnut's death, a king, it would seem, with no need of the spoils of war to reward his supporters, a king of peace two of whose known battles ended in heavy losses (1054) and death (1057). The contrast with Maelcoluim III's five invasions of England is not wholly explained by assuming Maelcoluim's hostility to Norman kings; some of the invasions (1061 and 1093) were reactions to perceived dishonesty by the English king, but the others were futile and costly, possibly because lacking support. The capitulations of Maelcoluim in 1072, 1081 and 1091 would fit with that suggestion.

His succession, as his father's son, was a move towards acceptance of primogeniture, but the choice of his brother in 1093 showed that it was not a conclusive shift in that direction. The 'Scots' who weakened and destroyed Duncan II were clearly unconvinced, but their hostility was explicitly directed against the 'English and French' he had introduced, and the imposition of Edgar as king by English forces in 1097 must have been open to the same hostility. We may see the twelfth century as a time of tension between a native tradition and the expectations of incomers, including those resented in 1094.

The native tradition may be seen in the rebellions of 1130–34 and 1153–56, when illegitimate descendants of Alexander I were involved; the risings in 1179–87 and 1211 had a parallel involvment of Donald mac William and his line. These risings are not to be seen as exclusively or mainly prompted by claims to the throne against David I and his grandsons, for in the Mac William risings there was clearly hostility to King William's subservience to the English king, while those of 1130–56 represented the particularism of Moray, but also hostility to royal support of incomers. The most revealing manifestation of the native tradition occurred in 1160–61, when Malcolm IV was besieged in Perth by six earls, for here the key figures are identified, one, Earl Ferteth of Strathearn, by name. Five years later, when William went to France to claim his Northumbrian earldom and for tournaments, Scotland was untroubled, suggesting that the objective in 1160–61 had been to make the king forswear his association with Angevin kingship and chivalry, a rejection of the dominance of Henry II over Malcolm IV.

In Jordan's account of 1173 Earl Duncan opposed the king's going to war with Henry II, but in the campaign of 1174, William ravaged Northumberland, then withdrew to Berwick, sending for his 'knights, the earls of his land, all his best warriors' for a further assault; and later, in marching on Carlisle, 'the earls of Scotland lead the detestable people' – a view of Scots akin to the 'brute Scots' of *Gest. Ann.*[65] The traditional leaders of *Scotia* took a traditional attitude to war in England. But tension within the kingdom was heightened by William's failure in 1173–74, when his kingship collapsed into subordination.

The incomers, with their dependents, offered the king a contingent of knights and preponderated at the royal court according to the witness lists of royal charters. Often younger sons with little prospect at home, when given land in Scotland they followed the custom of male primogeniture in inheritance known in Henry I's England, to protect the service due by their dependents; lay documents are rare before 1153, but such few as survive show that the custom was then well established in Scotland. The reliance of David I upon incomers was rhetorically described by Ailred's account of 1138, but the Barnwell chronicler was anachronistic in claiming of 1212 that 'the more recent kings of Scots profess themselves to be rather Frenchmen in race, manners, language and culture; and after reducing Scots to utter servitude they admit only Frenchmen to their friendship and service'.[66]

In 1188, when landed men were threatened with a tax whose proceeds were to be given to Henry II, they were not to be divided into Scots and incomers. The financial demand made apparent a unity which may have grown steadily as a result of the humiliation at York in 1175 and the compliant conduct of King William (however unavoidable) which followed. Traditional leaders and those of immigrant origin found a common response in a common allegiance; it was surely no coincidence that in the last years of William's reign a marriage brought a man of immigrant origin to

[65] *Jordan Fantosme's Chronicle*, ed. Johnston, lines 1185–86, 1342; see also 471–76.
[66] *Memoriale Fratis Walteri de Coventreia*, ii, 206; *SAEC*, 33 n.

the rank of earl of Buchan; by 1250 there were four such earls, a third of the total number of earldoms.

Thirteenth-century Scotland was still a divided society. In the Gaelic west, with a largely pastoral economy, territorial lords maintained an uncertain peace through the responsible heads of kindreds. Agents of royal government were imposed on Galloway in 1235 but a different culture persisted on the western seaboard, uncertainly accepting royal lordship after the termination of Norwegian sovereignty in 1266. In 1284 three heads of kindred from that zone were at last counted among the barons of the kingdom, an uncertain recruitment to complete the community, which overwhelmingly was identified with the Anglicised lowland east, prosperous with agrarian activity and sheep-farming for wool. Judicial brieves were brought from the king's chancellor to the sheriff or justice, the sheriff went to render his accounts at the king's exchequer, and the king's justices made their ayres around the sheriffdoms.

The latter sounds not at all unlike the English society and government documented in hundreds of rolls at Kew. But no such documentation exists in Scotland, and though we know something has been lost, it is pretty clear that no comparable documentation ever existed. The brieves available to the wronged, dispossessed or disinherited were few and not always required to bring an action; much of the justice's time seems to have been taken up with resolving boundary disputes by perambulation and with trying serious crimes. The courts of lowland Scotland, including the courts of private lords, the lowest tier, functioned adequately following customary pro-cedures to implement lawful custom; they needed little royal prompting, though royal action made use of the assize (jury) general. Royal supervision seems to have been irregular, there was no professional bench with the king, none for ordinary pleas, and the justices who went on ayre had no pro-fessional training but were drawn from those with landed wealth; for much of the thirteenth century the justiciarship of *Scocia* was held by the earls of Buchan.[67]

Nor was society plagued by scutages, tallages or aids, save when, as in 1189 and 1209, debts to the king of England were incurred, debts to keep the peace between two kings, not to wage war. Nothing costs quite as war costs, as Alexander II found when, in 1216, he took money in lieu of army service for his expedition to Dover. But war against a neighbour, requiring mobilisation of wide resources, had been rare in the twelfth century (1138–41, 1173–74, 1215–17), and in no way compared with the demands made by the English crown for war overseas. The absence of stone castles on the scale of Dover, Norwich or Norham is as striking as the evident lack of artillery to assault those built south of Tweed. Despite the obligation to

---

[67] MacQueen, *Common Law and Feudal Society*, especially 33–50.

'common army', this was a kingdom without a capacity for war against a more professional enemy; it also lacked the machinery to raise resources for such a war, and lacked the stresses of financial exactions and the bureaucracy enabling them. In an uncertain world, it was a kingdom accustomed to peace.

The tradition of consultation and shared decision-making, of cooperation between king and community, upon which this equable society depended was not recorded, even by chroniclers, with any regularity, so that we cannot see the division between traditional and new elites disappear as a single regnal community was formed. One factor in its formation had been the acceptance of the custom of male primogeniture in inheritance. Those who lived by it would enforce it on their tenants and expect it of their lords, including the king. And from 1097 that is how kingship descended, to a brother in the absence of sons, to the oldest grandson representing the deceased son in 1153. The divisions which emerged over a proposed female transmission in 1195 certify agreement on male primogeniture in kingship and landed heritage irrespective of family origins. The exogamy arranged for the king's son and daughter and for the king himself in the 1280s may have been progenitively unwise, but undoubtedly had communal approval. So far as he could, Alexander III remedied the lack of heirs, and secured overt acceptance of the right of a female heir to the throne in default of males; but, recognising that his granddaughter might inherit the throne as a child, he sought to bring Edward I on side by suggesting that there could be advantage to England in her marriage. That suggestion was unlikely to be a royal whim unknown to those around the king. Consultation explains not only the efficient moves made after the king's death to set up a Guardianship but also the frequent *colloquia* – parliaments – held by the Guardians in the following three years, sharing responsibility for their acts and decisions with a wider community. To community they made appeal now as the source of their authority to defend the royal dignity.

English overlordship was not effective in the century 1189–1291, though it was aired then before various popes, and threatened ineffectually to Scottish kings in 1251 and 1278; it was probably seen by Scots as an unrealistic aspiration in 1286, for they had long eschewed all hint of collusion or friendship with the French, which alone had aroused the hostility of English kings. Now, lacking a king who could speak to Edward I as an equal, the Scots rightly sought to reassure him, to keep him a friendly neighbour, until, in 1289, they found that control of their future was passing into the hands of colluding English and Norwegian kings. They could not frustrate the proposed marriage of the Scottish heiress to Edward I's son, and some may not have wanted to, but were able to extract a price for their acceptence of it: recognition of the kingdom as separate, free and without subjection. That text was explicit, as the 1189 quittance was not, but more than a recognition of independence such as was given in 1328, for it assumed that the marriage would take place and laid down post-marriage arrangements. The marriage was not a condition for the recognition that the kingdom was free, but the reason why freedom 'as heretofore' was promised to continue. This recognition, clearly extracted by the Scots, diminished or destroyed the claims made in 1251 and 1278. The treaty of Northampton became the sheet-anchor for Scottish hopes and claims throughout the 1290s.

All that followed was Edward's betrayal of those words, for they did not purchase Scotland for him, but Scotland he determined to have, not by conquest, as Wales, but by persistence, persuasion and wiles. Seeing the dissociation of the king of Scotland from the king of France as weakness (which it was) and restraint, imposed by formal subordination to England (which it had long ceased to be), the English king rightly judged that he could push the friendless and acephalous Scots back into that subordination. His cagey negotiations at Norham in June 1291 showed an awareness that Scotland was a kingdom, its kings sharing with England and other Christian realms a status licensed and empowered by Old Testament prophets and the contemporary church. Kings must beware when diminishing the status of other kings, but Edward showed little awareness that the 'kingdom' whose descent he was to ajudge had a political class and a political life which would persist under his overlordship, expecting the freedom without subjection which the kingdom had long enjoyed.

By this time the Scots had significant experience of collective rule, and, if they began new dealings with Edward to find the rightful king with some naivety, they very quickly chose their ground and refused to budge from it. We can speculate on alternative courses of action, but thanking Edward and departing to resolve the succession themselves threatened both civil war and Edward's military intervention on behalf of a Claimant or of his own overlordship. So they stayed at Berwick and eventually were persuaded into a temporary submission, not to the king of England, but to the Claimants, for whom the English king acted. It was a fudge, because when Edward accepted this he did not drop his title, nor one iota of his right, as 'superior lord of the kingdom of Scotland'; the Scots must have perceived the deceit in this relationship but averted their eyes.

In fact Edward gave them more time and attention than they had wanted when they sought arbitration between Bruce and Balliol. External circumstances led to long adjournments, and the tribunal as set up proved an unweildy replication of the two contentious Scottish factions. We have been misled in many ways by the post-1296 version of the Cause by Edward's notary, for it ignored Edward's initial attempt to make Count Florence a serious contender. When that was deferred in favour of argument as to who represented the right of Earl David, Balliol or Bruce, the intransigent division of the Scots was a demonstration of the fragility of 'community' when 'royal majesty' was the the thing in dispute. It is not surprising that Edward gave a controlling say to his council at this stage, but questionable

whether they were willing or able to look positively on the opinions obtained
from Paris jurists.

The inadequate reports of their debates at this juncture show that, like
the Claimants, they concerned themselves not with kingship but with the
kingdom, whose descent by a law of freehold fitted with its being held of
the king of England. The only Claimant to benefit from this approach was
Balliol, but the reason for adopting it was to secure Edward I's future
position, not Balliol's. The decision in favour of the latter, representing the
eldest line, gave Bruce no right in terms of his petition for the whole
kingdom, with no finding, as yet, on partibility. And so far as we can tell
(for reasons do not survive), the subsequent rejection of partibility was both
acceptable and inconsistent; Balliol won kingship by claiming a special
status for it, after he had defeated Bruce by stressing that his right was that
of the heir to a kingdom held of the king of England.

The historian, privy to the early search of Robert Bruce (V) for Edward
I's support and to his subsequent dodging and weaving, may find little
sympathy for him when he received his come-uppance. He may have been
badly advised and acted inconsistently, deserving the reproof of the court in
a modern trial. But his case was by no means weak, and although his son was
prepared to accept the defeat, his grandson plainly was not, and was moved
by an identification with the independence of the kingdom, with nationality,
wholly unknown to his grandfather. In nationality, which was more important, the custom of succession to the throne, or the security of the kingdom
and community? The struggle in Edward's court and with English armies
shifted the weight of opinion from the former to the latter. Community
counted for more than the king when survival depended upon an armed
struggle.

And that is the tragedy of the events of 1290–96: a relentless drift to war
between two neighbours, one ruled by an ineffectual with no stomach for his
responsibilities, the other by a driven master whose ambitions outstripped
his resources. War was provoked by the French alliance which gave the Scots
courage to rebel, but the Scots were provoked to the French alliance by the
betrayal of Edward I's promises of 1290 and by the unprecedented rights
which he claimed over their kingdom. Some would say that he felt a duty to
his ancestors and successors to insist on what he believed was rightfully
theirs; the evidence suggests that the decision to insist came first, grounds
for its rectitude a hasty second, and belief, if at all, only when it justified
terminating the kingship of the Scots.

The long-term prospects of that termination we can only judge by its
rapid collapse and the manifest impossibility of a military occupation like
that inflicted upon Wales. The reasons for this failure include geography,
finance and domestic English politics, but by themselves these were not
decisive, since English successes in 1306–37 were each followed by a
Scottish revival. The rock on which English empire-building in Scotland

foundered was the resurgent community whose identity was defined by loyalty to the kingship; as we see that identity about 1300, it was a growth of some two centuries, but now invested with and justified by a mythical antiquity. The Scots defined their leader, the king of Scots. This identification had been advertised by neither learned 'history' nor vernacular literature, which may explain why it had been so misread and misunderstood by those English who came into contact with it. But Edward I's challenge to it with claims of 'super-overlordship',[68] whether a duty inherited or a chance seized, was on all counts a political failure.

[68] Davies, *First English Empire*, 200.

Concessions proposed by Edward I,
20 June 1290

Sources

A: PRO C47/22/13(12), partly summarised in *Cal. Docs. Scot.*, v, no. 83.
This draft or file copy has been cancelled and is badly stained on the right,
especially at the top, where much is illegible.

B: PRO C66/109 m.19 printed in Stevenson, *Docs. Hist. Scot.*, i, no. CVI, a
transcript on the patent roll of the same text as far as *in portibus maris et
aque dulcis* in [d]. This is marked in the margin *vacat quia restituta fuit
littera ista per dominum Antonium Dunolmensem episcopum.*

C: Stevenson, *Docs. Hist. Scot.*, i, no. 108, the text of the concessions offered
by English proctors at Birgham on 18 July 1290.

The text of A has been reconstructed with help from B and C, and passages
not legible in A are given in [square brackets]. Minor variants of B are not
noted. Passages unique to A (and as far as d to B) are given in **bold type**.
Line breaks in A are shown by /.

Each provision is distinguished by a new line and a reference letter,
[a] – [t].

**Edwardus Dei gracia rex Anglie dominus Hibernie et Dux
Aquitanie dilectis** [... custodibus, prelatis, nobilibus et vniuersitati
regni]/ **Scocie salutem et dileccionem scinceram. Justis desideriis**
[vestris cum vberioris gracie et fauoris amplitudine jugiter
prosequendis eo pronius]/ **et facilius inclinamur, quo circa nos
et eorum qui nos con**[tingunt expedicionem vota vestra versari
nouimus cum grata promptitudine et stu-]/**dio complacendi vt ex
ipsius facti experiencia comper**[imus euidenter. Cupientes igitur
propensius iura liberatates et consuetudines]/ **predicti regni Scocie
ad vtilitatem et honorem karissime consanguinee** [nostre domine
Margarete regine et domine vestre regni eiusdem et vestram
solidam]/ **tranquillitatem et pacem integras et illes**[as conseruare
pro] **viribus** [et tueri quibusdam peticionibus vestris quas nobis
nuper London']/ **per vestros solempnes nuncios pro statu vestro et
tocius** [regni predicti direxistis, in forma que sequitur singillatim et

articulatim, gra-]/tanter et expresse tenore presencium duximus annuendum.

[a] In primis videlicet [ad peticionem dotis ipsius domine regine taliter respondemus quod quando ipsa]/ Margareta domina et regina vestra maritabitur karissimo nato et heredi nostro Edwardo, dota[bitur vel habebit in donatione propter nup-]/tias de certis terris in regno Anglie prout decet congrue statum suum vnde ipsa regina [et amici sui contenti racionabiliter esse po-]/terunt et debebunt.

[b] Ad articulum vero continentem quod regnum Scocie remaneat separatum et diuisum [et liberum in se, sine subieccione]/ a regno Anglie per suas rectas diuisas et marchias sicut a retro hactenus [extitit] obserua[tum et quod nulla castra et for-]/talicia fiant de nouo in marchii[s, volu]mus et concedimus [quod regna Anglie et Scocie sint separata et diuisa per suas rectas diuisas]/ et marchias sicut f[uerunt a temporibus] retroactis. [Saluo iure nostro et alterius cuiuscunque quod nobis vel alii cuicunque super hiis que]/ consistunt in marchiis ante presentis concessionis tempora comp[eciit vel iusto modo competere poterit in futurum.

[c] Sed quod castra et]/ fortalicia de nouo in marchiis non [firmentur] non sumus in hoc consult[i quod nos talem imponeremus seruitutem vbi antecessores]/ nos[tri nos et] homines nostri vsi simus hactenus firmare castra fortalicia [et domos in terris nostris sicut fecerunt nostri progenitores, quia]/ alias maiori subiiceremur seruituti quam vos de regno Scocie [vel aliqui antecessorum vestrorum ante fuerunt.

[d] Ceterum vobis concedimus per presentes]/ quod leges, consuetudines et libertates ipsius regni et marchie [hactenus racionabiliter vsitate in burgis, foris, ponderibus,]/ mensuris, in portibus maris et aque dulcis et quod moneta sit in recta cude et illius ponderis quod [tempore regis] Scocie et antecessorum suorum integre conseruetur sine noua et inconsueta exaccione vel demanda in preiudicium [regalis dignita-]/tis eiusdem saluo iure nostro et alterius cuiuslibet quod nobis vel alii ante presentem concessionem super hiis [que consistunt in]/ marchiis competiit vel competit sicut superius est expressum.

[e] Et quod libertates consuetudines et iurisdiccion[es] …/-dem secundum instituta canonica et obseruancie cleri a retroactis temporibus vsitate in iuribus possessionibus et liber[tatibus …]/ et illese seruentur absque noua et inconsueta demanda in preiudicium ecclesie siue cleri.

[f] Concedentes expresse quod ca[pitula ecclesiarum ca-]/thedralium collegiatarum [et conuentualium] que proprias habent elecciones non compell[antur exire regnum ipsum Scocie ad petendum licen-]/ciam

eligendi vel prestandi suos electos vel fidelitatem rego Scocie facere [seu sacramentum].

[g] Et quod [nullus tenens in capite de]/ predicto rege Scocie ex**eat** regnum pro homagio fidelitate seu fine pro releuio faciendo.

[h] [Illud idem] viduis [et miserabilibus personis in]/ petendis et habendis dotibus [et queren]da iusticia concedentes.

[j] **Super eo siquidem quod** [**nullus** de regno Scocie pro contracto inito vel delicto]/ commisso in eodem regno t[eneatur] respondere extra regnum contra iura et consuetudines [eiusdem] reg[ni, **concedimus**]/ **quod nunc fiat** sicut hactenus extitit racionabiliter obseruatum.

[k] **Volentes** [quod] sigillum regni quod **nunc vtitur**[et quod currit post]/ mortem regis custodiatur et currat quousque predicta domina regina venerit in regnum suum et fecerit Deo [et ecclesie et commun-]/itati ipsius regni in loco specialiter ad hoc **prouiso** quod faciendum fuerit secundum leges et consuetudines dicti regni./

[l] **De custodia ipsius sigilli per vestrum et dictorum procuratorum et nunciorum nostrorum consilium aliter quam hactenus extitit ordinatu**[r. Et quod tunc]/ fiat nouum sigillum de armis regis Scocie **pro negociis regni et** remaneat penes cancellarium eiusdem regni [qui pro tempore fuerit.

[m] Reliquie vero et]/ carte priuilegia et alia munimenta que tangunt regalem dignitatem et regnum Scocie in tuto loco ponantur sub firma/ custodia infra regnum Scocie, sub sigillis maiorum de regno et per visum eorum donec predicta domina venerit in regnum suum/ dicta munimenta [et] priuilegia in suis viribus integraliter custodiantur. Nulla **preter hec** fiat alienacio vel obligacio [rerum perti-]/nencium ad regalem dignitatem regni Scocie donec in regnum suum venerit domina supradicta.

[n] **Promittimus etiam fideliter et s..d..-/mus quod si matrimonium seu sponsalia inter predictum Edwardum et ipsam Margaretam** [aliquo] **modo infirmentur vel tenere non**/ **possent ipsa regina in Anglia existente, quod libera et quieta ab omnimodo contractu matri**[monii seu] **sponsalium ad regnum suum**/ **Scocie remittatur** secundum ordinacionem **inter nos et vos** factam apud S.

[o] **Et si** [dictus] **Edwardus premoriatur, quod absit, pre sponsalia vel matrimonium factum sine herede de corpore suo, predicta Margareta** [in] **Anglia ex**[istente], **prefatum regnum Scocie integraliter**/ **cum castris fortaliciis et omnibus aliis bonis ad idem regnum pertinentibus libere pacifice et in** [eodem] **statu quo pre mortem dicti Edwardi** / **fuerint, sine aliqua diminucione et omnimoda subieccione liberentur predicte Margaret et suis** [heredibus] **secundum predictam ordinacionem** ita quod/ **nobis** vel alii nichil inde accrescat vel decrescat racione presentis facti.

[p] **Quod si predicta Margareta moriatur sine herede de corpore**/ **suo, quod absit, viuente predicto Edwardo, prefatum regnum Scocie**

in statu quo illud in e ... retinuit cum castris fortaliciis et aliis/ suis pertinenciis libere et quiete sine aliqua subieccione integraliter restituantur seu redduntur recto heredi supradicti ita quod [nobis]/ vel alii nichil inde accrescat vel decrescat racione presentis facti vt superius est expressum.

[q] Et si vterque moriatur sine herede de corporibus/ suis, quod absit, antedictum regnum sub eisdem modo et forma in proximo articulo iam preteratis recto restituatur heredi.

[r] Con/cedimus eciam et promittimus bona fidequod nati et heredes comitum baronum et nobilium predicte terre decedencium qui pro tempore erint/ in custodiam et maritagium nostrum post mortem antecessorum suorum per nos nullatenus disparagentur.

[s] Nec parleamentum teneatur ex[tra reg-]/num et marchias Scocie super hiis que contingunt ipsum regnum vel marchias seu statum inhabitancium ipsum regnum.

[t] Nec/ tallagia vel auxilia exigantur a predicto regno aut imponantur gentibus eiusdem regni nisi pro communibus regni negociis [expe-]/diendis et maxime in casibus in quibus reges talia petere consueuerunt.

In quorum omnium et singulorum premissorum [testimonium]/ et euidenciam pleniorem sigillum nostrum presentibus duximus apponendum. Dat' ... vicesimo die mensis Junii anno [regni]/ nostri octauo decimo.

Textual notes

[a] *B has* ipsa regina Margareta *and omits the last twelve words,* vnde ipsa ... et debebunt

[c] B *omits* sicut a retro ... de nouo in marchiis *by haplography*
A *omits* et *before* homines nostri

[d] B *gives the reading* forestis *which I have emended to* foris (*markets*); A *is illegible here.*
[tempore regis] Scocie *is my suggestion. For unnamed Alexander III see also* [k], post mortem regis
Conseruetur *should perhaps read* conseruebatur
A *omits* in *before* preiudicium
Regalis dignitatis *is supplied by analogy with* [m]

[f] *The use of* expresse *here, logical after* [e], *explains its illogical appearance in* C, *which lacks* [e]

[n] *Perhaps* fideliter et concedimus
The final S represents Sarisburiam (*Salisbury*)

[o] A *omits* in *before* Anglia

[q] preteratis (*sic*, A)

Obligation by William earl of Sutherland, 1290–91

Omnibus hoc scriptum visuris vel audituris Willelmus comes Suthern-landye salutem in Domino. Nouerit vniuersitas vestra nos teneri et per presens scriptum et per fidem nostram prestitam firmiter obligari nobili viro domino Roberto de Brus domino Vallis Anandye in consilio et auxilio cum tota potencia nostra eidem prestando et succurendo ad prosequendum perquirendum et optinendum totum ius suum et honorem quod [habe]t in regimine regni Scocie. Et ho[c] eidem domino de Brus per legitimam stipulacionem et fidelem promissionem fideliter promittimus. In cuius rei testimonium et maiorem securitatem presenti scripto sigillum nostrum [app]osuimus.

Source: PRO, DL 25/82. Size: 165 × 45 mm (l.h.), × 35 mm (r.h.). Formerly sealed on a narrow (10 mm) tongue, approx. 100 mm long, now missing from the root.

Comment

The document was preserved in the Bruce archives.

The first three known earls of Sutherland were all called William, and there is no reliable evidence as to the date of creation or death of the first earl; a seventeenth-century genealogy gives his obit in 1248. There is a gap until Earl William, attested from 1263, usually identified as the one who died in 1306–7 (therefore aged at least 65, even if 1248 be ignored), leaving a son William who was a minor. Perhaps the three earls should be four. *Scots Peerage*, viii, 321–23; *CP*, xii/1, 538–40.

The descent of the throne of Alba and the kindred of Moray

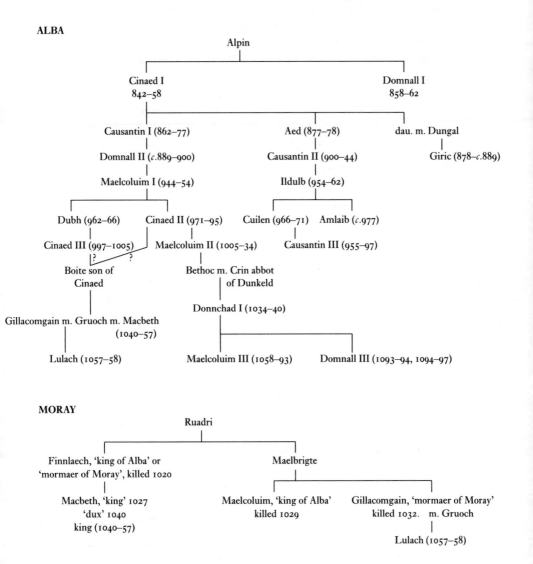

ALBA

Alpin

Cinaed I 842–58

Domnall I 858–62

Causantin I (862–77)

Aed (877–78)

dau. m. Dungal

Domnall II (c.889–900)

Causantin II (900–44)

Giric (878–c.889)

Maelcoluim I (944–54)

Ildulb (954–62)

Dubh (962–66)

Cinaed II (971–95)

Cuilen (966–71)

Amlaib (c.977)

Cinaed III (997–1005)

Maelcoluim II (1005–34)

Causantin III (955–97)

Boite son of Cinaed

Bethoc m. Crin abbot of Dunkeld

Donnchad I (1034–40)

Gillacomgain m. Gruoch m. Macbeth (1040–57)

Lulach (1057–58)

Maelcoluim III (1058–93)

Domnall III (1093–94, 1094–97)

MORAY

Ruadri

Finnlaech, 'king of Alba' or 'mormaer of Moray', killed 1020

Maelbrigte

Macbeth, 'king' 1027 'dux' 1040 king (1040–57)

Maelcoluim, 'king of Alba' killed 1029

Gillacomgain, 'mormaer of Moray' killed 1032. m. Gruoch

Lulach (1057–58)

The royal line in Scotland

Kings of Scots in CAPITALS
A line under a name denotes no surviving issue.
A dotted line denotes illegitimate issue.
The descent indicated by an arrow is shown on Table C.

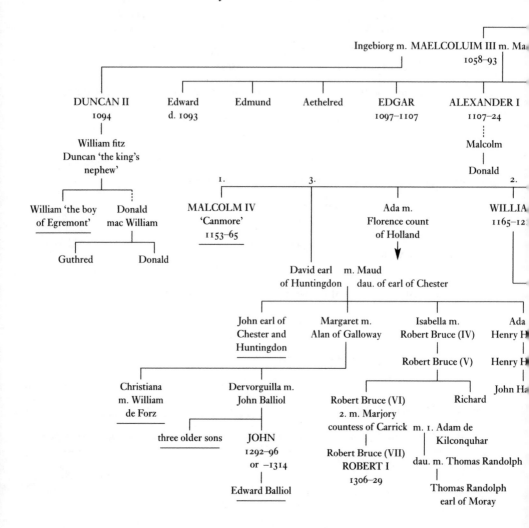

Ingebiorg m. MAELCOLUIM III m. Ma[...]
1058–93

DUNCAN II
1094

Edward
d. 1093

Edmund

Aethelred

EDGAR
1097–1107

ALEXANDER I
1107–24

William fitz
Duncan 'the king's
nephew'

Malcolm

Donald

William 'the boy
of Egremont'

Donald
mac William

MALCOLM IV
'Canmore'
1153–65

Ada m.
Florence count
of Holland

WILLIA[...]
1165–12[...]

Guthred

Donald

David earl   m. Maud
of Huntingdon   dau. of earl of Chester

Christiana
m. William
de Forz

John earl of
Chester and
Huntingdon

Margaret m.
Alan of Galloway

Isabella m.
Robert Bruce (IV)

Ada
Henry H[...]

Robert Bruce (V)

Henry H[...]

Dervorguilla m.
John Balliol

Robert Bruce (VI)
2. m. Marjory
countess of Carrick

Richard

John Ha[...]

three older sons

JOHN
1292–96
or –1314

Robert Bruce (VII)
ROBERT I
1306–29

m. 1. Adam de
Kilconquhar

Edward Balliol

dau. m. Thomas Randolph

Thomas Randolph
earl of Moray

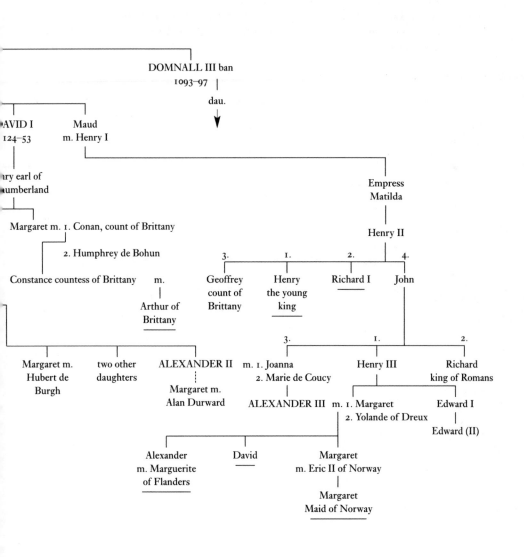

DOMNALL III ban
1093–97

dau.

DAVID I   Maud
124–53   m. Henry I

Empress
Matilda

ary earl of
umberland

Henry II

Margaret m. 1. Conan, count of Brittany

2. Humphrey de Bohun

Constance countess of Brittany   m.

Arthur of
Brittany

3.   1.   2.   4.

Geoffrey   Henry   Richard I   John
count of   the young
Brittany   king

3.   1.   2.

Margaret m.   two other   ALEXANDER II   m. 1. Joanna   Henry III   Richard
Hubert de   daughters   2. Marie de Coucy   king of Romans
Burgh   Margaret m.
Alan Durward   ALEXANDER III   m. 1. Margaret   Edward I
2. Yolande of Dreux
Edward (II)

Alexander   David   Margaret
m. Marguerite   m. Eric II of Norway
of Flanders   Margaret
Maid of Norway

TABLE C

The fourteen Claimants 1291–92

The Claimants are given in CAPITALS. The descents are as claimed but a possible correction of the Pinkeny claim and a certain correction of Count Florence's are indicated. For abbreviated descents, indicated by an arrow, see Table B. The illegitimate birth indicated by a dotted line was not mentioned by the Claimant, and is presumed for Aufrica, Henry Galightly and Marjory.

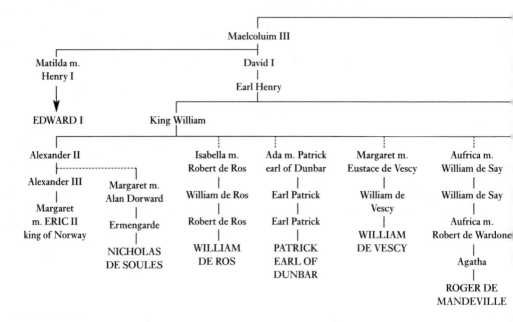

TABLE C   349

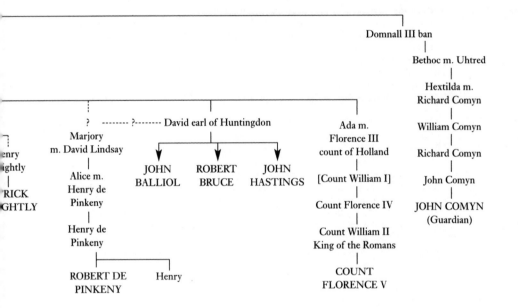

Domnall III ban
|
Bethoc m. Uhtred
|
Hextilda m.
Richard Comyn
|
William Comyn
|
Richard Comyn
|
John Comyn
|
JOHN COMYN
(Guardian)

? -------- ?-------- David earl of Huntingdon   Ada m.
                                                     Florence III
Marjory   count of Holland
m. David Lindsay   JOHN   ROBERT   JOHN
                      BALLIOL   BRUCE   HASTINGS   [Count William I]
Alice m.
Henry de   Count Florence IV
Pinkeny
| Count William II
Henry de   King of the Romans
Pinkeny
| COUNT
ROBERT DE   Henry   FLORENCE V
PINKENY

enry
ightly

RICK
GHTLY

Bibliography

Aberdeen-Banff Collections: Collections for a History of the Shires of Aberdeen and Banff (Spalding Club, 1843).

Acts of the Parliaments of Scotland, i, ed. C. Innes (Edinburgh, 1844).

Adomnán's Life of Columba, eds A. O. and M. O. Anderson, 2nd edn (Oxford, 1991).

Aitchison, N., *Macbeth, Man and Myth* (Stroud, 1999).

Alcock, L., Alcock, E. A. and Driscoll, S. T., 'Reconnaissance excavations on Early Historic fortifications and other royal sites ..., 3: Dundurn', *PSAS*, vol. 119 (1989), 189–226.

Alcock, L. and Alcock, E. A., 'Reconnaissance excavations on Early Historic fortifications and other royal sites...', *PSAS*, vol. 122 (1992), 215–42.

Alexander, J. W., 'New Evidence on the Palatinate of Chester', *English Historical Review*, lxxxv (1970), 715–29.

——, 'The English Palatinates and Edward I', *Journal of British Studies*, xxii, part 2 (1983), 2–22.

Allen, J. R. and Anderson, J., *The Early Christian Monuments of Scotland* (Edinburgh, 1903).

Althoff, G., *Verwandte, Freunde und Getreue* (Darmstadt, 1990).

Anderson, A. O., *Scottish Annals from English Chroniclers, A.D. 500 to 1286* (London, 1908).

——, 'Wimund, Bishop and Pretender', *SHR*, vii (1910), 29–36.

——, *Early Sources of Scottish History, A.D. 500–1286* (Edinburgh, 1922).

Anderson, J., 'Notes on some Entries in the Icelandic Annals regarding the Death of the Princess Margaret', *PSAS*, xi (1873–74), 403–18.

Anderson, M. O., 'Lothian and the early Scottish kings', *SHR*, xxxix (1960), 98–112.

——, *Kings and Kingship in Early Scotland*, 2nd edn (Edinburgh, 1980).

——, 'Dalriada and the creation of the kingdom of the Scots', *Ireland in Early Medieval Europe*, eds D. Whitelock, R. McKitterick and D. Dumville (Cambridge, 1982).

Anglo-Norman Dictionary, eds W. Rothwell and others (London, 1992).

Anglo-Scottish Relations, 1174–1328, Some Selected Documents, ed. E. L. G. Stones (Oxford, 1970).

Annales Cambriae, ed. J. Williams ab Ithel (Rolls Series, 1860).

Annales Monastici, ed. H. R. Luard (Rolls Series, 1864–69).

Annals of Clonmacnoise, ed. D. Murphy (Dublin, 1896).

The Annals of Tigernach, ed. Whitley Stokes (Felinfach, 1993).

The Annals of Ulster (to A.D. 1131), i, eds Seán mac Airt and Gearóid mac Niocaill (Dublin, 1983).

Annals of Ulster, ii, ed. B. Mac Carthy (Dublin, 1893).

Arbroath Liber, i: *Liber S. Thome de Aberbrothoc, Registrum Vetus* (Bannatine Club, 1848).

Armstrong, C. A. J., 'Inauguration Ceremonies of the Yorkist Kings', *Transactions of the Royal Historical Society*, fourth series, xxx (1948), 51–73.

Autrand, F., 'La succession à la couronne de France et les ordonnances de 1374', *Représentation, pouvoir et royauté à la fin du moyen âge*, ed. J. Blanchard (Paris, 1995).

Aylmer, G. E. and R. Cant (eds), *History of York Minster* (Oxford, 1977).

Bannerman, J., 'The King's Poet and the Inauguration of Alexander III', *SHR*, lxviii (1989), 120–49.

——, 'Macduff of Fife', *Medieval Scotland, Crown, Lordship and Community*, eds A. Grant and K. J. Stringer (Edinburgh, 1993), 20–38.

——, 'The Scottish takeover of Pictland', *Spes Scotorum; Hope of Scots*, eds D. Broun and T. O. Clancy (Edinburgh, 1999), 71–94.

Barbour, J., *The Bruce*, ed. A. A. M. Duncan (Edinburgh, 1997) [references are by book and line and can be found in other editions].

Barlow, F., 'The King's Evil', *English Historical Review*, xcv (1980), 3–27.

——, *Thomas Becket* (London, 1987).

——, *Edward the Confessor*, 2nd edn (London, 1997).

——, *William Rufus*, 2nd edn (London, 2000).

Barrow, G. W. S., 'The Reign of William the Lion, King of Scotland', *Historical Studies*, vii (1969), 21–44; also in his *Scotland and its Neighbours in the Middle Ages* (London, 1992), 67–90.

——, *The Kingdom of the Scots* (London, 1973).

——, 'Some Problems in Twelfth- and Thirteenth-Century Scottish History; a Genealogical Approach', *Scottish Genealogist*, xxv (1978), 97–112.

——, *Robert Bruce and the Community of the Realm of Scotland*, 3rd edn (Edinburgh, 1988).

——, 'A Kingdom in Crisis: Scotland and the Maid of Norway', *SHR*, lxix (1990), 120–41.

——, 'French after the Style of Petithachengon', *Church, Chronicle and Learning in Medieval and Early Renaissance Scotland*, ed. B. E. Crawford (Edinburgh, 1999), 187–94.

Bautier, R.-H., 'Le jubilé romain de 1300 et l'alliance franco-pontificale au temps de Philippe le Bel et de Boniface VIII', *Le Moyen Age*, lxxxvi (1980), 186–216; also as no. IX in his *Études sur la France capétienne* (*Variorum*, Hampshire, 1992).

——, *Chartes, Sceaux et Chancelleries: Études de diplomatique et de sigillographie médiévales*, Mémoires et documents de l'École des Chartes, 34 (Paris, 1990).

Beaune, C., *The Birth of an Ideology: Myths and Symbols of Nation in Late-Medieval France* (Oxford, 1991).

Bede's Ecclesiastical History of the English People, eds B. Colgrave and R. A. B. Mynors (Oxford, 1969).

Bedos-Rezak, B., 'The King enthroned, a new theme in Anglo-Saxon royal iconography: the seal of Edward the Confessor and its political implications', *Kings and Kingship*, ed. J. Rosenthal (Binghampton, 1986), 53–88; also no. IV in B. Bedos-Rezak, *Form and Order in Medieval France* (Aldershot, 1993).

Benedict Peterb.: Gesta Henrici Secundi Benedicti Abbatis, ed. W. Stubbs (Rolls Series, 1867).

Berger, A., *Encyclopedic Dictionary of Roman Law*, Transactions of the American Philosophical Society, new series, vol. 43, part 2 (Philadelphia, 1953).

Bethell, D., 'Two Letters of Paschal II to Scotland', *SHR*, xlix (1970).

Binski, P., *Westminster Abbey and the Plantagenets: Kingship and the Representation of Power, 1200–1400* (London, 1995).

Birch, W. de G., *History of Scottish Seals* (Stirling, 1907).

Black, G. F., *The Surnames of Scotland* (New York, 1946).

Bloch, M., 'An unknown testimony on the history of coronation in Scotland', *SHR*, xxiii (1926), 105–6.

Boardman, S. I., *The Early Stewart Kings: Robert II and Robert III, 1371–1406* (East Linton, 1996).

Bouman, C. A., *Sacring and Crowning* (Groningen, 1957).

Bracton on the Laws and Customs of England, ed. G. Woodbine, trans. S. E. Thorne, ii (Cambridge, MA, 1968).

Bracton's Note Book, ed. F. W. Maitland (London, 1887).

Brand, P., 'Chief Justice and Felon: the Career of Thomas Weyland', *The Political Context of Law*, eds R. Eales and D. Sullivan (London, 1987, 27–47); also in P. Brand, *The Making of the Common Law* (London 1992), 113–33.

Breeze, D. and Munro, G., *The Stone of Destiny: Symbol of Nationhood* (Edinburgh, 1997).

Brett, M., 'John of Worcester and his contemporaries', *The Writing of History in the Middle Ages*, eds R. H. C. Davies and J. M. Wallace-Hadrill (Oxford, 1981), 101–26.

Broun, D., 'The Origin of Scottish Identity', *Nations, Nationalism and Patriotism in the*

European Past, eds C. Bjørn, A. Grant and K. J. Stringer (Copenhagen, 1994), 35–55.

——, 'Dunkeld and the origin of Scottish identity', *Spes Scotorum; Hope of Scots*, eds D. Broun and T. O. Clancy (Edinburgh, 1999), 95–114.

——, *The Irish Identity of the Kings of Scots* (Woodbridge, 1999).

——, 'A New Look at *Gesta Annalia* attributed to John of Fordun', *Church Chronicle and Learning in Medieval and Early Renaissance Scotland*, ed. B. E. Crawford (Edinburgh, 1999), 9–30.

——, 'The church of St Andrews and its foundation legend in the early twelfth century: recovering the full text of Version A of the foundation legend', *Kings, Clerics and Chronicles in Scotland, 500–1297*, ed. S. Taylor (Dublin, 2000), 108–14.

——, 'The Seven Kingdoms in the *De Situ Albanie* ...', *Alba; Celtic Scotland in the Middle Ages*, eds E. J. Cowan and R. Andrew McDonald (East Linton, 2000), 24–42.

Bruford, A., 'What happened to the Caledonians?' *Alba: Celtic Scotland in the Middle Ages*, eds E. J. Cowan and R. Andrew McDonald (East Linton, 2000), 43–68.

Bryson, W. H., 'Papal Releases from Royal Oaths', *Journal of Ecclesiastical History*, xxii (1971), 19–33.

Buckland, W. W., *Textbook of Roman Law from Augustus to Justinian*, 3rd edn, revised P. Stein (Cambridge, 1963).

Burns, R. I., *Society and Documentation in Crusader Valencia* (Princeton, NJ, 1985).

Byock and Skia, J. L., 'Disease and Archaeology in *Egil's Saga*: A First Look', *Haskins Society Journal*, iv (1992), 11–22.

Byrne, F. J., *Irish Kings and High Kings* (London, 1973).

Calendar of the Close Rolls (London, 1892–1954).

Calendar of Documents Relating to Scotland, ed. J. Bain and (vol. 5) G. G. Simpson and J. D. Galbraith (Edinburgh, 1881–1986).

Calendar of Entries in the Papal Registers relating to Great Britain and Ireland: Papal Letters, i, ed. W. H. Bliss (1893).

Calendar of Patent Rolls (London, 1891–).

Calendar of Scottish Supplications to Rome, i, eds E. R. Lindsay and A. I. Cameron (Edinburgh, 1934); ii, ed. A. I. Dunlop (Edinburgh, 1956); iii, eds A. I. Dunlop and I. B. Cowan (Edinburgh, 1970); iv, eds A. I. Dunlop and D. MacLauchlan (Glasgow, 1983); v, eds J. Kirk, R. Tanner and A. I. Dunlop (Edinburgh, 1997).

Cameron, K., *English Place Names* (London, 1996).

Carpenter, D., *The Minority of Henry III* (London, 1990).

Chadwick, N. K., 'The Story of Macbeth', *Scottish Gaelic Studies*, vi (1947–49), 189–211; vii (1951–53), 1–25.

Chaplais, P., *Essays in Medieval Diplomacy and Administration* (London, 1981).

Charles-Edwards, T. M., *Early Irish and Welsh Kinship* (Oxford, 1993).

——, *Early Christian Ireland* (Cambridge, 2000).

Cheney, C. R., *Notaries Public in England in the Thirteenth and Fourteenth Centuries* (Oxford, 1972).

Chron. Abingdon: *Chronicon Monasterii de Abingdon*, ed. J. Stevenson (Rolls Series, 1858).

Chron. Bury: *The Chronicle of Bury St Edmunds 1212–1301*, ed. A. Gransden (Edinburgh, 1964).

Chron. Cotton: Bartholomew Cotton, *Historia Anglicana*, ed. H. R. Luard (Rolls Series, 1859).

Chron. Fordun: *Johannis de Fordun Chronica Gentis Scotorum*, ed. W. F. Skene (Edinburgh, 1871–72).

Chron. Guisborough: *The Chronicle of Walter of Guisborough*, ed. H. Rothwell (Camden Third Series, 1957).

Chron. Holyrood: *A Scottish Chronicle known as the Chronicle of Holyrood*, ed. M. O. Anderson (Scottish History Society, 1938).

Chron. Howden: *Chronica Rogeri de Houedene*, ed. W. Stubbs (Rolls Series, 1868–71).

Chron. John of Worcester, *The Chronicle of John of Worcester*, eds R. R. Darlington and P. McGurk (Oxford, 1995–).

Chron. Knighton: *Chronicon Henrici Knighton vel Cnihtton Monachi Leycestrensis*, ed. J. R.

Lumby (Rolls Series, 1889–95).

Chron. Lanercost: Chronicon de Lanercost, 1201–1346, ed. J. Stevenson (Bannatyne Club, 1839).

Chron. Langtoft: The Chronicle of Pierre de Langtoft, ed. T. Wright (Rolls Series, 1866–68).

Chron. Melrose: The Chronicle of Melrose, A.D. 735–1270, facsimile edition, eds A. O. and M. O. Anderson (London, 1936) [references are generally to a year and can be checked in other editions].

Chron. Melsa: Chronica Monasterii de Melsa, ed. E. A. Bond (Rolls Series, 1866–68).

Chron. Oxenedes: Chronica Johannis de Oxenedes, ed. H. Ellis (Rolls Series, 1859).

Chron. Picts-Scots: Chronicles of the Picts: Chronicles of the Scots, ed. W. F. Skene (Edinburgh, 1867).

Chron. Rishanger: Willelmi Rishanger quondam monachi S. Albani ... Chronica et Annales, ed. H. T. Riley (Rolls Series, 1865).

Chron. Trivet: Nicholai Triveti Annales, ed. T. Hog (English Historical Society, 1845).

Chron. Wyntoun: The Original Chronicle of Andrew of Wyntoun, ed. F. J. Amours (Scottish Text Society, 1903–14).

Chronicles of the Reigns of Stephen, Henry II and Richard I, ed. R. Howlett (Rolls Series, 1884–89).

Chronicon Scottorum: a chronicle of Irish affairs ..., ed. W. M. Hennessy (Rolls Series, 1866).

Clanchy, M. T., *From Memory to Written Record*, 2nd edn (Oxford, 1993).

Clancy, T. O., 'Columba, Adomnan and the Cult of Saints in Scotland', *Innes Review*, xlviii (1997), 1–26.

——, 'King-making and images of kingship in medieval Gaelic literature', forthcoming.

The Claudius Pontificals, ed. D. H. Turner (Henry Bradshaw Society, 1971).

Clayton, M., *Cult of the Virgin Mary in Anglo-Saxon England* (Cambridge, 1990).

Clyde, Lord, *Craig's Jus Feudale* (Edinburgh and London, 1934).

Cogadh Gaedhel re Gallaibh, ed. J. H. Todd (Rolls Series, 1867).

The Complete Peerage, by G. E. C. [Cokayne], 2nd edn (London, 1910–59).

Concilia Scotiae: Ecclesiae Scoticanae Statuta tam Provincialia quam Synodalia quae supersunt, 1225–1559, ed. J. Robertson (Bannatyne Club, 1866) [often cited elsewhere as *Statuta Ecclesiae Scoticanae*].

Corpus Genealogiarum Hiberniae, i, ed. M. A. O'Brien (Dublin, 1962).

Correspondence of Thomas Becket, ed. A. J. Duggan, i (Oxford, 2000).

Councils and Ecclesiastical Documents relating to Great Britain and Ireland, eds A. W. Haddan and W. Stubbs, ii (Oxford, 1873).

Coupar Angus Rental: Rental Book of the Cistercian Abbey of Cupar Angus, ed. C. Rogers (Grampian Club, 1879–80).

Cowan, E. J., 'The Scottish Chronicle in the Poppleton Manuscript', *Innes Review*, xxxii (1982), 3–21.

——, 'The Historical MacBeth', *Moray: Province and People*, ed. W. D. H. Sellar (Edinburgh, 1993), 117–42.

Cowan, I. B. and Easson, D. E., *Medieval Religious Houses, Scotland* (London, 1976).

Cowdrey, H. E. J., *Pope Gregory VII, 1073–1085* (Oxford, 1998).

——, *Popes and Church Reform in the Eleventh Century* (Aldershot, 2000).

Crawford, B. E., 'Weland of Stiklaw: a Scottish Royal Servant at the Norwegian Court', *Historisk Tidsskrift (Norsk)*, lii (1973), 329–39.

——, *Scandinavian Scotland* (London, 1987).

——, 'North Sea Kingdoms, North Sea Beaurocrat', *SHR*, lxix (1990), 175–84.

Crouch, D., *The Image of Aristocracy in Britain, 1000–1300* (London, 1992).

——, *The Reign of King Stephen, 1135–54* (Harlow, 2000).

Cuttino, G. P., *English Diplomatic Administration, 1259–1339*, 2nd edn (Oxford, 1971).

Dalton, P., *Conquest, Anarchy and Lordship: Yorkshire, 1066–1154* (Cambridge, 1994).

Daremberg, C. and E. Saglio, *Dictionnaire des antiquités grecques et romaines* (Paris, 1877–1919).

Darlington, R. R. and McGurk, P., 'The *Chronicon ex Chronicis* of Florence of Worcester', *Anglo-Norman Studies*, v (1982), 185–96.

David I Charters: The Charters of David I, ed. G. W. S. Barrow (Woodbridge, 1999).

Davidson, M. R., 'The (non)submission of the northern kings in 920', *Edward the Elder*, eds N. J. Higham and D. H. Hill (London, 2001), 200–11.

Davies, J., *A History of Wales* (London, 1993).

Davies, R. R., *The Age of Conquest: Wales 1063–1415* (Oxford, 1987).

——, *The First English Empire: Power and Identities in the British Isles 1093–1343* (Oxford, 2000).

Diceto: Diceto, Ralph de, *Opera Historica*, ed. W. Stubbs (Rolls Series, 1876).

Dictionary of National Biography, eds L. Stephen and S. Lee (London, 1885–1900).

——, *Missing Persons*, ed. C. S. Nichols (London, 1993).

Dictionary of the Older Scottish Tongue, ed. W. L. Craigie and others (Chicago, Aberdeen, Oxford, 1931–).

Dictionnaire d'archéologie et de liturgie, iii (Paris, 1914), article 'Chaire épiscopale'.

Dictionnaire de droit canonique (Paris, 1935–65).

Dillon, M., 'The consecration of Irish kings', *Celtica*, x (1973), 5–8.

Douie, D. L., *Archbishop Pecham* (Oxford, 1952).

Driscoll, S., 'Political Discourse and the Growth of Christian Ceremonialism in Pictland', in *The St Andrews Sarcophagus*, ed. S. M. Foster (Dunblin, 1998).

Dumville, D., 'Kingship, Genealogies and Regnal Lists', *Early Medieval Kingship*, eds P. H. Sawyer and I. N. Wood (Leeds, 1977), 72–104.

——, 'The Chronicle of the Kings of Alba', *Kings, Clerics and Chronicles in Scotland 500–1297*, ed. S. Taylor (Dublin, 2000), 73–86.

Dunbar, A. H., *Scottish Kings: a Revised Chronology of Scottish History, 1005–1625*, 2nd edn (Edinburgh, 1906).

Duncan, A. A. M. 'The Community of the Realm and Robert Bruce', *SHR*, xlv (1966), 184–201.

——, *Scotland: The Making of the Kingdom* (Edinburgh, 1975).

——, 'The Battle of Carham, 1018', *SHR*, l (1976), 20–28.

——, 'The Kingdom of the Scots', *The Making of Britain: The Dark Ages*, ed. L. M. Smith (London, 1984), 131–44.

——, '*Honi soit qui mal y pense*: David II and Edward III, 1346–52', *SHR*, lxvii (1988), 113–41.

——, 'The Scots' Invasion of Ireland, 1315', *The British Isles, 1100–1500*, ed. R. R. Davies (East Linton, 1988), 100–17.

——, 'The "Laws of Malcolm MacKenneth"', *Medieval Scotland: Crown, Lordship and Community*, eds A. Grant and K. J. Stringer (Edinburgh, 1993), 239–73.

——, 'A Question about the Succession, 1364', ed. A. A. M. Duncan, *Miscellany of the Scottish History Society*, xii (1994), 1–57.

——, 'The Process of Norham, 1291', *Thirteenth Century England*, v (Woodbridge, 1995), 207–30.

——, 'The Bruces of Annandale, 1100–1304', *Transactions of the Dumfriesshire and Galloway Natural History and Antiquarian Society*, lxix (1994, pub. 1996), 89–102.

——, 'John King of England and the Kings of Scots', *King John: New Interpretations*, ed. S. D. Church (Woodbridge, 1999), 247–71.

——, 'Roger of Howden and Scotland', *Church, Chronicle and Learning in Medieval and Early Renaissance Scotland*, ed. B. E. Crawford (Edinburgh, 1999), 135–60.

——, 'Yes, the Earliest Scottish Charters', *SHR*, lxxviii (1999), 1–35.

——, 'Sources and Uses of the Chronicle of Melrose, 1165–1297', *Kings, Clerics and Chronicles in Scotland 500–1297*, ed. S. Taylor (Dublin, 2000), 146–86.

Dunfermline Registrum: *Registrum de Dunfermelyn* (Bannatyne Club, 1842).

Eales, R., 'Henry III and the End of the Norman Earldom of Chester', *Thirteenth Century England*, i (Woodbridge, 1985), 100–12.

Early Yorkshire Charters, eds W. Farrer and C. T. Clay (1914–65).

Eckhardt, K. A. – see Lehmann, K.

Eickels, K. van, '*Homagium* and *Amicitia*: Rituals of Peace and their Significance in the Anglo-French Negotiations of the Twelfth Century', *Francia*, xxiv, part 1 (1997), 133–40.

Emden, A. B., *Biographical Register of the University of Cambridge to 1500* (Cambridge, 1963).

Engel, P., *The Realm of St Stephen: A History of Medieval Hungary, 895–1526* (London, 2001).
Établissements de S. Louis, trans. F. R. P. Akehurst (Philadelphia, 1996).
Eterovich, F. H. and Spalatin, C., *Croatia, Land, People, Culture*, i (Toronto, 1964).
Eulogium Historiarum sive Temporis, ed. F. S. Haydon (Rolls Series, 1858–63).
Exchequer Rolls, i, ed. J. Stuart (Edinburgh, 1878).
Farrow, K. D., 'The Historiographical Evolution of the Macbeth Narrative', *Scottish Literary Journal*, vol. 21, no. 1 (May 1994), 5–23.
Feenstra, R., *Fata Ivris Romani* (Leyden, 1974).
Flanagan, M. T., *Irish Society, Anglo-Norman Settlers, Angevin Kingship: Interactions in Ireland in the Late Twelfth Century* (Oxford, 1989).
Flores Historiarum, ed. H. R. Luard (Rolls Series, 1890).
Foedera, Conventiones, Litterae ... (London, 1816–69).
Folz, R., *Concept of Empire in Western Europe* (London, 1969).
Fortey, N. J., Phillips, E. R. and others, 'A geological perspective on the Stone of Destiny', *Scottish Journal of Geology*, vol. 34(2) (1998), 145–52, and see also same journal, vol. 35(2) (1990), 187–88.
Fraser, C. M., *A History of Antony Bek, bishop of Durham, 1283–1311* (Oxford, 1957).
Freemen, E. A., *The Norman Conquest*, iii (Oxford, 1869).
Gaimar, *L'estoire des Engleis*, ed. A. Bell (Oxford, 1960).
Garnett, G., 'Coronation and Propaganda: Some Implications of the Norman Claim to the Throne of England in 1066', *Transactions of the Royal Historical Society*, fifth series, xxxvi (1986), 91–116.
Gervase of Canterbury – see *Historical Works of.*
Giesey, R. E., 'The Juristic Basis of Dynastic Right to the French Throne', *Transactions of the American Philosophical Society*, new series, vol. 51, 5 (1961), 3–47.
Giraldi Cambrensis Opera, eds J. S. Brewer, J. F. Dimock and G. F. Warner (Rolls Series, 1861–91).
Gjerset, K., *History of the Norwegian People* (New York, 1915).
Glaber Opera: Rodvlfi Glabri Historiarvm Libri Qvinqve; Rodulfus Glaber, The Five Books of the Histories, ed. J. France (Oxford, 1989).
Glasgow Registrum: Registrum Episcopatus Glasguensis, ed. C. Innes (Bannatyne Club, 1843).
Goldstein, R. J., 'The Scottish Mission to Boniface VIII in 1301', *SHR*, lxx (1991), 1–15.
GRA – see William of Malmesbury.
Graham-Campbell, J., *Viking Age Gold and Silver of Scotland, A.D. 850–1100* (Edinburgh, 1995).
Gransden, A., *Historical Writing in England, c. 500 to c. 1307* (London, 1974).
——, 'John de Northwold, Abbot of Bury', *Thirteenth Century England*, iii (1991), 91–112.
Green, J. A., *The Government of England under Henry I* (Cambridge, 1986).
——, 'David I and Henry I', *SHR*, lxxv (1996), 1–19.
Guenée, B., 'L'enquête historique ordonnée par Édouard Ier ... en 1291', *Comptes rendus de l'Académie des Inscriptions et Belles-Lettres, 1975* (n.d.), 572–84.
Hand, G. J., 'The Opinions of the Paris Lawyers upon the Scottish Succession c.1292', *The Irish Jurist*, new series, v (1970), 142–54.
Handbook of British Chronology, eds E. B. Fryde, D. E. Greenway, S. Porter and I. Roy, 3rd edn (London, 1986).
Handlist of the Acts of Alexander II, 1214–49, compiled by J. M. Scoular (Edinburgh, 1959).
Handlist of the Acts of Alexander III, the Guardians, John, 1249–96, compiled by G. G. Simpson (Edinburgh, 1960).
Helle, K., 'Norwegian Foreign Policy and the Maid of Norway', *SHR*, lxix (1990), 142–56.
Herbert, M., '*Rí Éirenn, Rí Alban*: kingship and identity in the ninth and tenth centuries', *Kings, Clerics and Chronicles in Scotland, 500–1297*, ed. S. Taylor (Dublin, 2000), 62–72.
Highland Papers, i, ed. J. R. N. Macphail (Scottish History Society, 1914).
Historical Manuscripts Commission, Fourth Report (1873).
The Historical Works of Gervase of Ganterbury, ed. W. Stubbs (Rolls Series, 1879–80).
Hollister, C. W., 'Normandy, France and the Anglo-Norman *Regnum*', *Speculum*, li (1976),

202–42.

Holt, J. C., *Colonial England, 1066–1215* (London, 1997).

Holyrood Liber: Liber Cartarum Sancte Crucis (Bannatyne Club, 1840).

Howarth, H. H., 'The Chronicle of John of Worcester previously assigned to Florence of Worcester', *Archaeological Journal*, lxxiii (1916), 1–170.

Howell, M., *Eleanor of Provence* (Oxford, 1998).

Howlett, D., 'The Structure of *De Situ Albanie*', *Kings, Clerics and Chronicles in Scotland 500–1297*, ed. S. Taylor (Dublin, 2000), 124–45.

Huber, A., *Der Kärntner Fürstenstein im Europäischen Vergleich* (Gmünd, 1996).

Hudson, B. T., 'Cnut and the Scottish Kings', *English Historical Review*, cvii (1992), 350–60.

——, *Kings of Celtic Scotland* (Westport, CT, 1994).

——, *The Prophecy of Berchan: Irish and Scottish High-Kings of the Early Middle Ages* (Westport, CT, 1996).

——, 'The Scottish Chronicle', *SHR*, lxxvii (1998), 129–61.

Hudson, J., *Land, Law and Lordship in Anglo-Norman England* (Oxford, 1994).

Hughes, K., *The Church in Early Irish Society* (London, 1966).

Inchaffray Lib.: Liber Insule Missarum (Bannatyne Club, 1847).

Inchcolm Charters: Charters of the Abbey of Inchcolm, eds D. E. Easson and A. Macdonald (Edinburgh, 1938).

Inventory of Argyll, vol. 5 (Islay, Jura, Colonsay and Oransay), Royal Commission on the Ancient and Historical Monuments of Scotland (Edinburgh, 1984).

Itinerary of Edward I, part II, 1291–1307, List and Index Society, vol. 132 (London, 1976).

Jackson, K. H., 'The Duan Albanach', *SHR*, xxxvi (1957), 125–37.

Jaffé, P., *Regesta Pontificum Romanorum, 882–1198*, ed. S. Löwenfeld (Leipzig, 1885–88).

Jaski, B., *Early Irish Kingship and Succession* (Dublin, 2000).

Jenkins, D, 'Kings, Lords and Princes. The Nomenclature of Authority in Thirteenth-Century Wales', *Bulletin of the Board of Celtic Studies*, xxvi (1974–76), 451–62.

Jochens, J. M., 'The Politics of Reproduction: Medieval Norwegian Kingship', *American Historical Review*, xcii (1987), 327–49.

John of Paris, *On Royal and Papal Power*, ed. J. A. Watt (Toronto, 1971).

John of Salisbury, *Historia Pontificalis*, ed. M. Chibnall (Edinburgh, 1956).

Jordan Fantosme's Chronicle, ed. R. C. Johnston (Oxford, 1981).

Kapelle, W. E., *The Norman Conquest of the North* (Chapel Hill, NC, 1979).

Keeney, B. C., *Judgment by Peers* (Cambridge, MA, 1949).

Kehr, P., *Italia Pontificia*, viii (Berlin, 1935).

Kelly, J. M., *Studies in the Civil Judicature of the Roman Republic* (Oxford, 1976).

Kenney, J. F., *Sources for the Early History of Ireland, Ecclesiastical* (1929; revised Shannon, 1966).

Kern, F., *Acta Imperii, Angliae et Franciae, 1267–1313* (Tübingen, 1911).

Kirby, D., 'Strathclyde and Cumbria', *Transactions of the Cumberland and Westmorland Antiquarian and Archaeological Society*, lxii (1962), 84–94.

Körner, S, *The Battle of Hastings and Europe, 1035–66* (Lund, 1964).

Kossmann-Putto, J. A., 'Florence V, Count of Holland, Claimant to the Scottish Throne in 1291–2: his Personal and Political Background', *Scotland and the Low Countries, 1124–1994*, ed. G. G. Simpson (East Linton, 1996).

Krönungen: Könige in Aachen – Geschichte und Mythos, ed. M. Kramp (Mainz, 2000).

Lamonte, J. L., *Feudal Monarchy in the Latin Kingdom of Jerusalem, 1100 to 1291* (Cambridge, MA, 1932).

Lapidge, M., 'Some Latin poems as evidence for the reign of Athelstan', *Anglo-Saxon England*, ix (1981), 61–98.

Lawrie, *ESC*: Lawrie, A. C., *Early Scottish Charters, Prior to A.D. 1153* (Glasgow, 1905).

Lawrie, A. C., *Annals of the Reigns of Malcolm and William, Kings of Scotland, A.D. 1153–1214* (Glasgow, 1910).

Lawson, M. K., *Cnut* (London, 1993).

Legg, L. G. W., *English Coronation Records* (London, 1901).

Lehmann, K., *Consuetudines Feudorum, I, Compilatio Antiqua* (Göttingen, 1892; also his *Das Langobardische Lehnrecht* (Göttingen, 1896); republished in one volume as *Bibliotheca Rerum Historicarum, Neudrucke 1, Consuetudines Feudorum*, ed. K. A. Eckhardt (Aalen, 1971).

Levison, W., 'Die *"Annales Lindisfarnenses ac Dunelmenses"'*, *Deutsches Archiv*, xvii (1961), 447–506.

Lewis, A. W., 'Anticipatory Association of the Heir in Early Capetian France', *American Historical Review*, lxxxiii (1978), 906–27.

——, *Royal Succession in Capetian France: Studies on Familial Order and the State* (London, 1981).

Liber Vitae Ecclesiae Dunelmensis (Surtees Society, 1841).

Libri Feudorum – see Lehmann, K.

Life of Malachy: Bernard of Clairvaux, *The Life and Death of Saint Malachy the Irishman*, trans. and annotated R. E. Meyer (Kalamazoo, MI, 1978).

Linehan, P. A., 'A Fourteenth-Century History of Anglo-Scottish Relations in a Spanish Manuscript', *Bulletin of the Institute of Historical Research*, xlviii (1975), 106–22.

——, 'The posthumous reputation of King William the Lion of Scotland', *SHR*, lvii (1978), 182–86.

——, *History and Historians of Medieval Spain* (Oxford, 1993).

Little, A. G., *Franciscan Papers, Lists and Documents* (Manchester, 1943).

Little, A. G. and Pelster, F., *Oxford Theology and Theologians* (Oxford Historical Society, 1934).

Lloyd, S., *English Society and the Crusade* (Oxford, 1988).

Lunt, W. E., *Financial Relations of the Papacy with England, to 1327* (Cambridge, MA, 1939).

McCormick, M., *Eternal Victory* (Cambridge, 1986).

McDonald, R. A., 'Kings and Princes in Scotland; Aristocratioc Interactions in the Anglo-Norman era', University of Guelph PhD thesis, 1993.

McDonald W. R., Scottish Armorial Seals (Edinburgh, 1904).

McFarlane, K. B., 'Had Edward I a Policy towards the Earls?', *History*, l (1965), 145–59; also in his *Nobility of Later Medieval England* (Oxford, 1973).

McMichael, T., 'The Feudal Family of de Soulis', *Transactions of the Dumfriesshire and Galloway Antiquarian and Natural History Society*, third series, xxvi (1947–48), 163–93.

Macquarrie, A., *Scotland and the Crusades, 1095–1560* (Edinburgh, 1985).

——, 'The Kings of Strathclyde, *c.*400–1018', *Medieval Scotland; Crown, Lordship and Community*, eds A. Grant and K. J. Stringer (Edinburgh, 1993), 1–19.

Macqueen, H. L., *Common Law and Feudal Society in Medieval Scotland* (Edinburgh, 1993).

Mann, H. K., *Lives of the Popes of the Middle Ages*, ix (London, 1925).

Marshall, D. W. Hunter, 'Two Early English Occupations in Scotland – Their Administrative Organisation', *SHR*, xxv (1928), 20–40.

The Martyrology of Oengus the Culdee, ed. Whitley Stokes (Henry Bradshaw Society, 1905).

Materials for the History of Thomas Becket, ed. J. C. Robertson (Rolls Series, 1875–85).

Matthew, D., *The Norman Kingdom of Sicily* (Cambridge, 1992).

Memoriale Fratris Walteri de Coventria, ed. W. Stubbs (Rolls Series, 1872–73).

Ménager, L.-R., 'L'institution monarchique dans les États normands d'Italie', *Cahiers de civilisation médiévale*, ii (1959), 445–68.

Milsom, S. F. C., *Studies in the History of the Common Law* (London, 1985).

Monroe, N. H., 'Two Medieval Genealogical Roll-Chronicles in the Bodleian Library', *Bodleian Library Record*, x (1981), 115–21.

Monumenta Germaniae Historica, Scriptores, xix (Hannover, 1866).

Moore, M., 'The King's New Clothes: royal and episcopal regalia in the Frankish empire', *Robes and Honor: The Medieval World of Investiture*, ed. S. Gordon (New York, 2001), 95–136.

Morris, C. J., *Marriage and Murder in Eleventh-Century Northumbria: A Study of the 'De Obsessione Dunelmi'* (York, 1992).

Munz, P., *Frederick Barbarossa* (Ithaca, NY, 1969).

National Manuscripts of Scotland, ed. C. Innes (Southampton, 1867–71).

Neilson, G., 'Brus versus Balliol, 1291–1292: The Model for Edward I's Tribunal', *SHR*, xvi (1919), 1–14.

——, 'The March Laws', *Stair Society, Miscellany One* (Edinburgh, 1971).

Nelson, J. L., 'The Problem of King Alfred's Royal Anointing', Nelson, *Politics and Ritual*, 309–27; also in *Journal of Ecclesiastical History*, xviii (1967), 145–63.

——, 'Symbols in Context, Rulers' Inauguration Rituals in Byzantium and the West ...', *Studies in Church History*, xiii (1976), ed. D. Baker, 97–119; also no. 11 in Nelson, *Politics and Ritual*.

——, 'Inauguration Rituals', *Early Medieval Kingship*, eds P. H. Sawyer and I. N. Wood (Leeds, 1977), 50–71; also no. 12 in Nelson, *Politics and Ritual*.

——, 'The Rites of the Conqueror', in Nelson, *Politics and Ritual*, 375–401; also in *Proceedings of the Fourth Battle Conference on Anglo-Norman Studies* (Woodbridge, 1982), 117–32, 210–21.

——, *Politics and Ritual in Early Medieval Europe* (London, 1986).

Nenner, H., *The Right to be King. The Succession to the Crown of England, 1603–1714* (London, 1995).

Neville, C. J., *Violence, Custom and Law: The Anglo-Scottish Border Lands in the Later Middle Ages* (Edinburgh, 1998).

Nicholson, R. G., 'The Franco-Scottish and Franco-Norwegian Treaties of 1295', *SHR*, xxxviii (1959), 114–32.

Ó Corráin, D., *Ireland before the Normans* (Dublin, 1972).

——, 'Irish Regnal Succession, a Reappraisal', *Studia Hibernica*, xi (1971), 7–39.

Olaus Magnus, *Historia de Gentibus Septentrionalibus*, trans. P. Fisher and H. Higgins, ed. P. Foote, ii (Hakluyt Society, 1998).

Oliveira Marques, A. H. de, *History of Portugal*, i (London, 1972).

Oorkondenboek van Holland en Zeeland tot 1299, iv (1278–91), ed. J. G. Kruisheer (Assen, 1997).

Orderic Vitalis, *The Ecclesiastical History of Orderic Vitalis*, ed. M. Chibnall (Oxford, 1969–80).

Orkneyinga Saga, eds H. Pálsson and P. Edwards (London, 1978) [references are by chapter number and can be found in other editions].

Owen, D. D. R., *William the Lion, 1143–1214: Kingship and Culture* (East Linton, 1997).

The Oxford Classical Dictionary, 3rd edn, eds S. Hornblower and A. Spawforth (Oxford, 1996).

The Oxford Textbook of Medicine, eds D. J. Weatherall, J. G. G. Ledingham and D. A. Warrell 3rd edn (Oxford, 1996).

Palgrave, F., *Documents and Records illustrating the History of Scotland*, i (all published London, 1837).

Palmer, C. F. R., 'Fasti Ordinis Fratrum Predicatorum', *Archaeological Journal*, xxxv (1878), 134–65.

Paris, M., *Historia Anglorum sive historia minor*, ed. F. Madden (Rolls Series, 1866–69).

——, *Chronica Majora*, ed. H. R. Luard (Rolls Series, 1872–83).

Parliamentary Writs and Writs of Military Summons, ed. F. Palgrave, i (London, 1827).

Patrologia Latina, ed. J.-P. Migne, vol. 195 (Paris, 1844–64).

Phythian-Adams, C., *Land of the Cumbrians* (Aldershot, 1996).

Pollock, F. and Maitland, F. W., *The History of English Law before the time of Edward I* (Cambridge, 1898).

Powicke, F. M., *Henry III and the Lord Edward* (Oxford, 1947).

——, *The Thirteenth Century, 1216–1307*, 2nd edn (Oxford, 1962).

Prestwich, M., 'The English Campaign in Scotland in 1296 and the surrender of John Balliol: some supporting evidence', *Bulletin of the Institute of Historical Research*, xlix (1976), 135–38.

——, *Edward I* (London, 1988).

——, 'Edward I and the Maid of Norway', *SHR*, lxix (1990), 157–73.

Regesta Regum Anglo-Normannorum, ii (1100–35), eds C. Johnson and H. A. Cronne (Oxford,

1956).

Regesta Regum Scottorum, i, Acts of Malcolm IV, ed. G. W. S. Barrow (Edinburgh, 1960); ii, Acts of William I, eds G. W. S. Barrow and W. W. Scott (Edinburgh, 1971); v, Acts of Robert I, ed. A. A. M. Duncan (Edinburgh, 1988); vi, Acts of David II, ed. A. B. Webster (Edinburgh, 1982).

Regis Magni Legum Reformatoris Leges Gula-Thingenses, sive Jus Commune Norvegicum (Havniae [Copenhagen], 1817).

Les Registres de Boniface VIII, eds A. Thomas, M. Faucon and G. Digard, i (Paris, 1907).

Les Registres de Gregoire IX, ed. L. Auvray (Paris, 1896–1910).

Les Registres de Nicholas IV, ed. E. Langlois (Paris, 1886–1905).

Registrum Magni Sigilli Regum Scotorum (Edinburgh, 1882–1914).

Reid, N., 'The Kingless Kingdom; the Scottish Guardianships of 1286–1306', *SHR*, lxi (1982), 105–29.

Reynolds, S., *Kingdoms and Communities in Western Europe, 900–1300* (Oxford, 1984).

——, *Fiefs and Vassals: The Medieval Evidence Reinterpreted* (Oxford, 1994).

Richardson, H. G., 'The Coronation of Edward I', *Bulletin of the Institute of Historical Research*, xv (1937–38), 94–99.

——, 'The Coronation in Medieval England', *Traditio*, xvi (1960), 111–202.

Richardson, H. G. and Sayles, G. O., 'The Scottish Parliaments of Edward I', *SHR*, xxv (1928), 300–17; also in their *The English Parliament in the Middle Ages* (London, 1981).

——, 'The King's Ministers in Parliament, 1272–1307', *English Historical Review*, xlvi (1931), 529–50, also in their *English Parliament in the Middle Ages* (London, 1981).

Rôles Gascons, ii, ed. C. Bémont (Paris, 1900).

Rotuli Litterarum Patentium in Turri Londinensi asservati, i (1835), ed. T. D. Hardy.

Rotuli Parliamentorum (no date).

Rotuli Scotiae in Turri Londinensi et in domo Westmonasteriensi asservati, 1291–1516 (1814–19).

Ruiz, T. F., 'Unsacred Monarchy: The Kings of Castille in the Late Middle Ages', *Rites of Power*, ed. S. Wilentz (Philadelphia, 1985), 109–44.

St Andrews Liber: Liber Cartarum Prioratus Sancti Andree in Scotia (Bannatyne Club, 1841).

Sandler, L. F., *Gothic Manuscripts, 1285–1385* (Oxford and London, 1986).

Saunders, I. J., *English Baronies* (Oxford, 1960).

Sautel-Boulet, M, 'Le rôle juridictionnel de la cour des pairs aux XIIIe et XIVe siècles', *Recueil des travaux offert à M. Clovis Brunel*, Mémoires et documents publiés par la Société de l'École des Chartes, vol. 12 (Paris, 1955), ii, 507–20.

Sawyer, P. H., 'The last Scandinavian kings of York', *Northern History*, xxxi (1995), 39–44.

Sayles, G. O., 'A reputed royal charter of 1218', *SHR*, xxxi (1952), 137–39.

Scammell, J., 'The Origins and Limitations of the Liberty of Durham', *English Historical Review*, lxxxi (1966), 449–73.

Schein, S., *Fidelis Crucis: The Papacy the West and the Recovery of the Holy Land, 1274–1314* (Oxford, 1991).

Schneider, R., *Königswahl und Königserhebung im Frühmittelalter* (Stuttgart, 1972).

Schramm, P. E., 'Der König von Navarra, 1035–1512', *Zeitschrift der Savigny-Stiftung für Rechtsgeschichte, Germanistische Abteilung*, lxxxi (1951).

——, *Kaiser, Könige und Päpste*, ii (Stuttgart, 1968).

Scone Liber: Liber Ecclesie de Scon (Bannatyne Club, 1843).

Scotichronicon by Walter Bower, ed. D. E. R. Watt, 9 vols (Aberdeen and Edinburgh, 1987–98).

Scots Peerage, ed. J. Balfour Paul (Edinburgh, 1904–14).

Scott, W. W., 'Fordun's description of the inauguration of Alexander II', *SHR*, l (1971), 198–200.

Scottish Supplications to Rome, Calendar of, i, eds E. R. Lindsay and A. I. Cameron (1934); ii, ed. A. I. Dunlop (1956); iii, eds A. I. Dunlop and I. B. Cowan (1970); iv, eds A. I. Dunlop and D. MacLauchlan (1983); v, eds J. Kirk, R. Tanner and A. I. Dunlop (1997).

Sellar, D., 'Sueno's Stone and its Interpreters', *Moray: Province and People*, ed. W. D. H. Sellar (Edinburgh, 1993), 97–116.

Sharpe, R., 'The thriving of Dalriada', *Kings Clerics and Chronicles in Scotland 500–1297*, ed.

S. Taylor (Dublin, 2000), 47–61.

Simms, K., *From Kings to Warlords* (Woodbridge, 1987).

Simpson, G. G., 'Why was John Balliol called Toom Tabard?', *SHR*, xlvii (1968), 196–99.

——, 'Kingship in Miniature', *Medieval Scotland; Crown, Lordship and Community*, eds A. Grant and K. J. Stringer (Edinburgh, 1993), 131–39.

Smyth, A. P., *Scandinavian Kings and the British Isles, 850–880* (Oxford, 1977).

——, *Warlords and Holy Men* (London, 1984).

Somerville, R., *Scotia Pontificaia* (Oxford, 1982).

Stein, P., 'Roman Law in Scotland', *Ius Romanum Medii Aevi*, Pars V, 13b (Milan, 1968).

Stell, G., 'The Balliol family and the Great Cause of 1291–92', *Essays on the Nobility of Medieval Scotland*, ed. K. J. Stringer (Edinburgh, 1985).

Stenton, F. M., *Anglo-Saxon England*, 3rd edn (Oxford, 1971).

Stevenson, J., *Documents illustrative of the History of Scotland … 1286–1306* (Edinburgh, 1870).

Stevenson, J. H. and Wood, M., *Scottish Heraldic Seals* (Glasgow, 1940).

Stones, E. L. G., 'The Appeal to History in Anglo-Scottish Relations between 1291 and 1401, Part 1', *Archives*, ix (1969–70), 11–21.

Stones, E. L. G. and Blount, M. N., 'The Surrender of King John of Scotland to Edward I in 1296: Some New Evidence', *Bulletin of the Institute of Historical Research*, xlviii (1975), 94–106.

Stones, E. L. G. and Simpson, G. G., *Edward I and the Throne of Scotland, 1290–1296* (Oxford, 1978).

Stringer, K. J., *Earl David of Huntingdon* (Edinburgh, 1985).

——, *The Reign of Stephen* (London, 1993).

——, 'Nobility and Identity in medieval Britain and Ireland: the de Vescy family, c.1120–1314', *Britain and Ireland 900–1300*, ed. B. Smith (Cambridge, 1999), 199–239.

Stubbs, W., *Select Charters and other Illustrations of English Constitutional History…*, 9th edn by H. W. C. Davis (Oxford, 1913).

Summerson, H., 'The Early development of the laws of the Anglo-Scottish Marches, 1249–1448', *Legal History in the Making*, eds T. D. Fergus and W. M. Gordon (London, 1991).

——, *Medieval Carlisle: The City and the Borders from the late eleventh to the mid-sixteenth century* (Kendal, 1993).

Sumption, J., *The Hundred Years War*, i (London, 1990).

Symeon of Durham, Historian of Durham and the North, ed. D. Rollason (Stamford, 1998).

Symeon of Durham, *Libellvs de Exordio atqve procursu istivs, hoc est Dvnhelmensis, Ecclesie*, ed. D. Rollason (Oxford, 2000).

Symeonis Monachi Opera Omnia, eds T. Arnold (Rolls Series, 1882–85).

Szovák, K., 'The Image of the Ideal King in Twelfth-Century Hungary', *Kings and Kingship in Medieval Europe*, ed. A. J. Duggan (London, 1993), 241–64.

Taylor, S., 'The coming of the Augustinians to St Andrews and version B of the St Andrews foundation legend', *Kings, Clerics and Chronicles in Scotland, 500–1297*, ed. S. Taylor (Dublin, 2000), 115–23.

Temperley, H. W. V., *History of Serbia* (London, 1919).

Twining, Lord, *European Regalia* (London, 1967).

Vale, M., *The Origins of the Hundred Years War* (Oxford, 1996).

Vita Ædwardi Regis, ed. F. Barlow, 2nd edn (London, 1992).

Vita Edwardi Secundi, ed. N. Denholm-Young (Edinburgh, 1957).

Walter, C., 'Raising on a shield in Byzantine Iconography', *Revue des Études Byzantines*, xxxi (1975), 157–66.

Watson, F., *Under the Hammer: Edward I and Scotland, 1286–1307* (East Linton, 1998).

Watt, D. E. R., 'The Minority of Alexander III of Scotland', *Transactions of the Royal Historical Society*, fifth series, xxi (1971), 1–23.

——, *A Biographical Dictionary of Scottish Graduates to A.D. 1410* (Oxford, 1977).

——, *Series Episcoporum Ecclesiae Catholicae Occidentalis*, Series VI, tom. I (*Ecclesia Scoticana*)

(Stuttgart, 1991).

——, *Medieval Church Councils in Scotland* (Edinburgh, 2000).

Wendover, Roger of, *Flores Historiarum*, ed. H. G. Hewlett (Rolls Series, 1886–89).

Widukind von Corvey, *Die Sachsengeschichte des Widukind von Korvey*, eds H.-E. Lohmann and P. Hirsch (Hannover, 1935).

William of Malmesbury, *Gesta Regvm Anglorvm: The History of the English Kings [GRA]*, eds R. A. B. Mynors, R. M. Thomson and M. Winterbottom (Oxford, 1998–99).

Willoweit, D., '*Dominium* und *Proprietas*', *Historische Jahrbuch*, xciv (1974), 131–56.

Wilson, J., 'Foundation of the Austin Priories of Nostell and Scone', *SHR*, vii (1910), 141–59.

Woolf, A., 'The Moray Question and Kingship of Alba in the Tenth and Eleventh Centuries', *SHR*, lxxix (2000), 145–64.

Wyon, A. B. and Wyon, A., *The Great Seals of England from the Earliest Period to the Present Time* (London, 1887).

Young, A., *Robert the Bruce's Rivals: The Comyns, 1212–1314* (East Linton, 1997).

Index

In the following index, names of persons without date are almost entirely those active in 1291–92. The following abbreviations are used: abp. archbishop (of); bp. bishop (of); ct. count (of); d. died; dau. daughter of; e. earl (of); Ed. I, Edward I; k. king (of); m. married; s. son of; Sc. Scotland, Scots. The tables are not indexed.

UNIVERSITY
OF
GLASGOW
LIBRARY

WITHDRAWN